Lecture Notes in Computer Science 12794

More information about this subseries at http://www.springer.com/series/7409

Matthias Rauterberg (Ed.)

Culture and Computing

Interactive Cultural Heritage and Arts

9th International Conference, C&C 2021
Held as Part of the 23rd HCI International Conference, HCII 2021
Virtual Event, July 24–29, 2021
Proceedings, Part I

 Springer

Editor
Matthias Rauterberg
Eindhoven University of Technology
Eindhoven, The Netherlands

ISSN 0302-9743   ISSN 1611-3349 (electronic)
Lecture Notes in Computer Science
ISBN 978-3-030-77410-3   ISBN 978-3-030-77411-0 (eBook)
https://doi.org/10.1007/978-3-030-77411-0

LNCS Sublibrary: SL3 – Information Systems and Applications, incl. Internet/Web, and HCI

This Springer imprint is published by the registered company Springer Nature Switzerland AG
The registered company address is: Gewerbestrasse 11, 6330 Cham, Switzerland

Foreword

Human-Computer Interaction (HCI) is acquiring an ever-increasing scientific and industrial importance, and having more impact on people's everyday life, as an ever-growing number of human activities are progressively moving from the physical to the digital world. This process, which has been ongoing for some time now, has been dramatically accelerated by the COVID-19 pandemic. The HCI International (HCII) conference series, held yearly, aims to respond to the compelling need to advance the exchange of knowledge and research and development efforts on the human aspects of design and use of computing systems.

The 23rd International Conference on Human-Computer Interaction, HCI International 2021 (HCII 2021), was planned to be held at the Washington Hilton Hotel, Washington DC, USA, during July 24–29, 2021. Due to the COVID-19 pandemic and with everyone's health and safety in mind, HCII 2021 was organized and run as a virtual conference. It incorporated the 21 thematic areas and affiliated conferences listed on the following page.

A total of 5222 individuals from academia, research institutes, industry, and governmental agencies from 81 countries submitted contributions, and 1276 papers and 241 posters were included in the proceedings to appear just before the start of the conference. The contributions thoroughly cover the entire field of HCI, addressing major advances in knowledge and effective use of computers in a variety of application areas. These papers provide academics, researchers, engineers, scientists, practitioners, and students with state-of-the-art information on the most recent advances in HCI. The volumes constituting the set of proceedings to appear before the start of the conference are listed in the following pages.

The HCI International (HCII) conference also offers the option of 'Late Breaking Work' which applies both for papers and posters, and the corresponding volume(s) of the proceedings will appear after the conference. Full papers will be included in the 'HCII 2021 - Late Breaking Papers' volumes of the proceedings to be published in the Springer LNCS series, while 'Poster Extended Abstracts' will be included as short research papers in the 'HCII 2021 - Late Breaking Posters' volumes to be published in the Springer CCIS series.

The present volume contains papers submitted and presented in the context of the 9th International Conference on Culture and Computing (C&C 2021) affiliated conference to HCII 2021. I would like to thank the Chair, Matthias Rauterberg, for his invaluable contribution in its organization and the preparation of the Proceedings, as well as the members of the program board for their contributions and support. This year, the C&C affiliated conference has focused on topics related to ICT for cultural heritage and art, visitors' experiences in digital culture, Design Thinking in cultural contexts, and applications in Cultural Computing in Digital Humanities and New Media.

I would also like to thank the Program Board Chairs and the members of the Program Boards of all thematic areas and affiliated conferences for their contribution towards the highest scientific quality and overall success of the HCI International 2021 conference.

This conference would not have been possible without the continuous and unwavering support and advice of Gavriel Salvendy, founder, General Chair Emeritus, and Scientific Advisor. For his outstanding efforts, I would like to express my appreciation to Abbas Moallem, Communications Chair and Editor of HCI International News.

July 2021   Constantine Stephanidis

HCI International 2021 Thematic Areas and Affiliated Conferences

Thematic Areas

- HCI: Human-Computer Interaction
- HIMI: Human Interface and the Management of Information

Affiliated Conferences

- EPCE: 18th International Conference on Engineering Psychology and Cognitive Ergonomics
- UAHCI: 15th International Conference on Universal Access in Human-Computer Interaction
- VAMR: 13th International Conference on Virtual, Augmented and Mixed Reality
- CCD: 13th International Conference on Cross-Cultural Design
- SCSM: 13th International Conference on Social Computing and Social Media
- AC: 15th International Conference on Augmented Cognition
- DHM: 12th International Conference on Digital Human Modeling and Applications in Health, Safety, Ergonomics and Risk Management
- DUXU: 10th International Conference on Design, User Experience, and Usability
- DAPI: 9th International Conference on Distributed, Ambient and Pervasive Interactions
- HCIBGO: 8th International Conference on HCI in Business, Government and Organizations
- LCT: 8th International Conference on Learning and Collaboration Technologies
- ITAP: 7th International Conference on Human Aspects of IT for the Aged Population
- HCI-CPT: 3rd International Conference on HCI for Cybersecurity, Privacy and Trust
- HCI-Games: 3rd International Conference on HCI in Games
- MobiTAS: 3rd International Conference on HCI in Mobility, Transport and Automotive Systems
- AIS: 3rd International Conference on Adaptive Instructional Systems
- C&C: 9th International Conference on Culture and Computing
- MOBILE: 2nd International Conference on Design, Operation and Evaluation of Mobile Communications
- AI-HCI: 2nd International Conference on Artificial Intelligence in HCI

List of Conference Proceedings Volumes Appearing
Before the Conference

1. LNCS 12762, Human-Computer Interaction: Theory, Methods and Tools (Part I), edited by Masaaki Kurosu
2. LNCS 12763, Human-Computer Interaction: Interaction Techniques and Novel Applications (Part II), edited by Masaaki Kurosu
3. LNCS 12764, Human-Computer Interaction: Design and User Experience Case Studies (Part III), edited by Masaaki Kurosu
4. LNCS 12765, Human Interface and the Management of Information: Information Presentation and Visualization (Part I), edited by Sakae Yamamoto and Hirohiko Mori
5. LNCS 12766, Human Interface and the Management of Information: Information-rich and Intelligent Environments (Part II), edited by Sakae Yamamoto and Hirohiko Mori
6. LNAI 12767, Engineering Psychology and Cognitive Ergonomics, edited by Don Harris and Wen-Chin Li
7. LNCS 12768, Universal Access in Human-Computer Interaction: Design Methods and User Experience (Part I), edited by Margherita Antona and Constantine Stephanidis
8. LNCS 12769, Universal Access in Human-Computer Interaction: Access to Media, Learning and Assistive Environments (Part II), edited by Margherita Antona and Constantine Stephanidis
9. LNCS 12770, Virtual, Augmented and Mixed Reality, edited by Jessie Y. C. Chen and Gino Fragomeni
10. LNCS 12771, Cross-Cultural Design: Experience and Product Design Across Cultures (Part I), edited by P. L. Patrick Rau
11. LNCS 12772, Cross-Cultural Design: Applications in Arts, Learning, Well-being, and Social Development (Part II), edited by P. L. Patrick Rau
12. LNCS 12773, Cross-Cultural Design: Applications in Cultural Heritage, Tourism, Autonomous Vehicles, and Intelligent Agents (Part III), edited by P. L. Patrick Rau
13. LNCS 12774, Social Computing and Social Media: Experience Design and Social Network Analysis (Part I), edited by Gabriele Meiselwitz
14. LNCS 12775, Social Computing and Social Media: Applications in Marketing, Learning, and Health (Part II), edited by Gabriele Meiselwitz
15. LNAI 12776, Augmented Cognition, edited by Dylan D. Schmorrow and Cali M. Fidopiastis
16. LNCS 12777, Digital Human Modeling and Applications in Health, Safety, Ergonomics and Risk Management: Human Body, Motion and Behavior (Part I), edited by Vincent G. Duffy
17. LNCS 12778, Digital Human Modeling and Applications in Health, Safety, Ergonomics and Risk Management: AI, Product and Service (Part II), edited by Vincent G. Duffy

http://2021.hci.international/proceedings

9th International Conference on Culture and Computing (C&C 2021)

Program Board Chair: **Matthias Rauterberg,** *Eindhoven University of Technology, Netherlands*

- Juan Barcelo, Spain
- Melodee Beals, UK
- Emmanuel G. Blanchard, Canada
- Jean-Pierre Briot, France
- Erik Champion, Australia
- Torkil Clemmensen, Denmark
- Fabiana Lopes Da Cunha, Brazil
- Jean-Gabriel Ganascia, France
- Halina Gottlieb, Sweden
- D. Fox Harrell, USA
- Susan Hazan, Israel
- Rüdiger Heimgärtner, Germany
- Yiyuan Huang, China
- Isto Huvila, Sweden
- Toru Ishida, Japan
- Katerina Kabassi, Greece
- Sagini Keengwe, USA
- Gertraud Koch, Germany
- Marcia Langton, Australia
- Susan Liggett, UK
- Donghui Lin, Japan
- Lev Manovich, USA
- Yohei Murakami, Japan
- Ryohei Nakatsu, Japan
- Jong-Il Park, Korea
- Robert Parthesius, UAE
- Dilip A. Patel, India
- Claus Pias, Germany
- Antonio Rodà, Italy
- Kasper Rodil, Denmark
- Pertti Saariluoma, Finland
- Hooman Samani, UK
- Vibeke Sorensen, Singapore
- William Swartout, USA
- Daniel Thalmann, Switzerland
- Claudia Trillo, UK
- Frans Vogelaar, Germany
- Michael Walsh, Singapore
- Jianjiang Wang, China
- Lin Zhang, China

The full list with the Program Board Chairs and the members of the Program Boards of all thematic areas and affiliated conferences is available online at:

http://www.hci.international/board-members-2021.php

HCI International 2022

The 24th International Conference on Human-Computer Interaction, HCI International 2022, will be held jointly with the affiliated conferences at the Gothia Towers Hotel and Swedish Exhibition & Congress Centre, Gothenburg, Sweden, June 26 – July 1, 2022. It will cover a broad spectrum of themes related to Human-Computer Interaction, including theoretical issues, methods, tools, processes, and case studies in HCI design, as well as novel interaction techniques, interfaces, and applications. The proceedings will be published by Springer. More information will be available on the conference website: http://2022.hci.international/:

General Chair
Prof. Constantine Stephanidis
University of Crete and ICS-FORTH
Heraklion, Crete, Greece
Email: general_chair@hcii2022.org

http://2022.hci.international/

Contents – Part I

Technology and Art

Contents – Part II

Digital Humanities, New Media and Culture

Perspectives on Cultural Computing

ICT for Cultural Heritage

Heritage Building Information Modelling (HBIM) as a Tool for Heritage Conservation: Observations and Reflections on Data Collection, Management and Use in Research in a Middle Eastern Context

Rania Aburamadan[1], Athena Moustaka[2], Claudia Trillo[2],
Busisiwe Chikomborero Ncube Makore[2](✉), Chika Udeaja[3],
and Kwasi Gyau Baffour Awuah[2]

[1] School of Architectural Engineering, Middle East University, Amman, Jordan
[2] School of Science, Engineering and Environment, Salford University, Salford M5 4WT, UK
A.Moustaka@salford.ac.uk, b.c.ncube@edu.salford.ac.uk
[3] School of Construction and Project Management,
London South Bank University, London 10AA, UK

Abstract. The rich architectural and urban heritage of Jordan is under continuing threat not only through means of physical attack but also physical disaster, increasing urbanization and a diminishing value from multiple stakeholders such as owners and users. This research study explores the potential of digital technologies in documenting and preserving urban architectural heritage in Jordan. Data was collected from diverse stackholders on heritage conservation in Jordan. The findings evidence that Building Information Modelling (BIM) has the potential to create a classification system for heritage buildings under threat and set forth the application of legislation and regulations about heritage . The study demonstrated that the collection of data information needs to be understood through the context of cultural sensitivity. Lack of awareness in the value of cultural heritage from local communities exacerbates the diminishing efforts in preserving cultural assets. In collecting information for the documentation of this heritage, this study categorizes the challenges of preserving urban heritage as either hierarchical or cultural. The collection, management and storing of data for digital heritage requires an awareness of the issues of time and the power structures that are involved in their collection and upon which they have a profound effect.

Keywords: Cultural heritage · BIM · HBIM · Point cloud · Middle East · Data collection · Culturally sensitive data

1 Introduction

Jordan is well known for its diverse and valuable cultural heritage assets. It is an urbanized country with the northern part historically more urbanized than the southern part, largely a

© Springer Nature Switzerland AG 2021
M. Rauterberg (Ed.): HCII 2021, LNCS 12794, pp. 3–14, 2021.
https://doi.org/10.1007/978-3-030-77411-0_1

desert (The World Bank 2007). This includes archaeological sites and the crusader castles to more recent urban fabric and traditional community public spaces that represent the Ottoman and post Ottoman architectural heritage and urban tissue. In a country like Jordan, cultural heritage resources require delicate treatment and conservation works, as these archaeological sites are continuously exposed to natural and human dangers that accelerate their deterioration.

Urban heritage of the Middle Eastern and North African region is vulnerable to growing threats, including growth in population in urban areas, industrial development and looting and illicit trafficking (Bewley and Kennedy 2013; Zerbini 2018). The pressures represent a particular threat to the traditional historic cores of Jordan (Ministry of Tourism and Antiquities & Bank 2005). Therefore, recording and documenting of cultural heritage remains a high priority with the aim to assist heritage professionals and decision makers to protect those sites and evaluate their condition on the ground, specifically to the sites which cannot be visited. Digital technologies such as Building Information Modelling (BIM) are becoming increasingly popular in their application to support heritage conversation planning and management (Trillo et al. 2020; Udeaja et al. 2020). BIM is an information platform that is capable of holding heterogeneous data to enable access for multiple stakeholders for specific heritage assets.

For this purpose, our research group has made a systematic effort to preserve some of the local urban heritage in Jordan through documentation. Funded by the British Royal Academy of Engineering, the project IT conservation of traditional architecture and heritage aims at filling a gap in Jordan, by applying digital technologies to support heritage conservation plans. The research has included collaboration with a heritage city as a testbed to develop a set of virtual models (3D models and BIM objects) suitable to document tangible heritage and support the construction sector on urban architectural conservation. Furthermore, developing BIM objects for heritage buildings has the potential to pave the road for communication between all parts and stakeholders (governmental body, private sector, and owners). The project combined technical data collection (scanning and architectural surveys) with interviews and focus groups with multiple identified stakeholders to uncover possible ways of collecting, managing and governance of data collection. During its course, the research has uncovered the intricacies in managing this data in the Middle Eastern context.

For the purpose of this paper, the definition of *heritage* (and its distinction from what is characterized as "*antiquities*") in the Jordanian context is used. According to Jordanian law: any structure constructed after 1750 falls under the "*Heritage*" umbrella. While a strict regulatory and legislator framework is in place for "*antiquities*", "*Heritage*" is not as strictly and clearly protected (Ministry of Tourism 2005). As a result, these buildings are often neglected by their owners, either because of complicated inheritance that surround their ownership, financial constraints that prevent them from renovation, or simply lack of knowledge for their potential. The only mechanism currently in place available to preserve post-1750 "*Heritage*" buildings is the Urban Heritage Law, which at the time of writing this paper provides a limited assistance through clear provisions on heritage protection. Therefore, the preservation of architectural elements through technology is important and essential in the absence of clear criteria for the classification of heritage buildings in this period.

2 Methodology

Achieving a positive outcome in Urban Architectural Heritage in Jordan involves a complete series of interactions with high profile and influential stakeholders taking part in governance decisions at a local and national level. As part of our data collection, a series of interviews and focus groups took place in February 2020 and included 6 interviews with key stakeholders and experts complemented with 3 focus groups with 24 additional stakeholders. All participants were from one of the following three sectors: (1) academia, (2) government, and (3) private companies, with the aim to capture different views and perspectives on heritage conservation and digital technologies in Jordan. Senior officials from all three types of institutions were involved in these interviews. The discussions were held mainly in English; however, some limited Arabic translation was provided to ensure full and in-depth understanding of complex concepts. The discussions were open-ended and, in the case of the focus groups, facilitated by the research members with the goal to gather opinion stemming from the group discussion rather than recording individual viewpoints (Table 1).

Table 1. Focus group participants

Participant	Expert group	Role in the organization
1	Private University	Academic & Architect
2	Private University	Senior Academic
3	Public Organisation	Manager & Architect
4	Private University	Academic & Engineer
5	Local Government	Architect Assistant
6	Local Government	Architect Assistant
7	Local Government	Senior Government Officer & Engineer
8	Public Organisation	Senior Architect
9	Private Organisation	Senior Architect
10	Private Organisation	Senior Academic
11	Local Government	Senior Government Officer
12	Local Government	Senior Government Officer
13	Private Organisation	Industry Engineer
14	Public Organisation	Senior Architect
15	Local Government	Senior Government Officer
16	Private Organisation	Heritage Expert
17	Private Organisation	Industry Architect
18	Private Industry Organisation	Industry Surveying Engineer
19	Private Industry Organisation	Industry Architect

(*continued*)

Table 1. (*continued*)

Participant	Expert group	Role in the organization
20	Private Industry Organisation	Industry Surveying Engineer
21	Local Government	Senior Government Officer & Architect
22	Public Organisation	Architect
23	Private University	Academic & Engineer
24	Public Organisation	Tourism Officer

Throughout the data collection it has become evident that stakeholders are generally aware of the importance of activating a law of heritage, and the potential it has to preserve heritage sites and buildings. However, they were also aware that such activation requires significant effort and collaboration from stakeholders, experts, and local community. Many of the participants agreed that more clarity was needed on the mechanisms of data collection and the governance of the information collected.

With the data collected from our project, we are proposing that developing BIM objects can help in this direction and can form part of the efforts to set in motion heritage related regulations and legislation. Furthermore, BIM objects can help introduce to heritage buildings, classifications that relate to the importance of heritage construction, structure, materials, and other features. The findings of the paper are also drawn from general participant observations made during the course of the research in an ethnographic tradition. During data collection, the researchers have observed from the "*inside*" (Fine 1993), the practices of data generation, collection and management related to urban heritage in Jordan. Furthermore, some members of the team have their own experience of working in this context, making them "*indigenous ethnographers*" (Clifford 1986). The observations are therefore the result of a deep understanding and embeddedness in the local context, cultural practices and social limitations that impact on data collection and management.

Being sensitive towards culture within a context of heritage research is particularly important, because culture is embedded in the very object of investigation. When researching within a particular environment about heritage, the cultural nuances that one can pick up, can reveal to the study information about its characteristics. Becoming attuned to the cultural context within which these nuances are positioned, is in itself illuminating and informative about the heritage which they represent. It is impossible to isolate the culture of the interviewee, and the context within which the research is taking place from the object that is being studied. Instead, the socioeconomic, ethnic and political background, inadvertently inform the research in every instance the researcher comes into contact with subjects rooted in the cultural context of the heritage under review. This approach, of embeddedness is extensively appreciated in ethnographical and anthropological studies (e.g. Lewis and Russel 2011), but not as much in urban (Duneier et al. 2014) and cultural heritage studies (Butler 2007; Hollowell and Nicholas 2009; Silva and Santos 2012).

3 Cultural and Social Aspects of Data Collection

3.1 Cultural Hierarchy and Access to Data

A first observation made during the course of the data collection is that cultural hierarchical practices when contacting and attempting to speak to officials, need to be carefully observed. There are instances, where the data required for analysis have not been collected by the officials themselves. For example, during our research, we came across a case where a junior planning officers had responsibility for all the data collection and analysis relating to heritage buildings. The junior members of the office were possibly more aware of all the technicalities involved in the data collection and how working with a software enabled them to store and manage such information. They had been creating a photographic documentation of all local heritage building, a process that took months. They had then organized the photographs collected and presented them in a report under the name of the local planning office.

Within that particular team, whenever there is international interest in their data, the local planning officer meets with the interested researchers. This was no different in our case. In our meeting they were indeed very knowledgeable and aware of the local context as well as having a deep knowledge about heritage buildings of their area. The officer was also very willing to inform us of the local buildings and offer to guide us in some. However, the junior members of the team did not participate in the discussion. In the course of our interview, it became clear that a large amount of the photographic documentation was conducted by the two junior members of staff, which had taken an initiative in some cases about how to organize and present the material in a report. Furthermore, only the junior staff were aware of some strictly technical information (i.e. File type, size, storage etc.).

Lack of awareness of a senior officer of the practicalities of collecting and organizing data, and the technicalities of assembling them can create a gap in communication between the team of researchers. While ensuring contact with a senior official allows more information to be accessed, the role which local junior staff have should not be underestimated. The cultural practice of meetings with only senior officials can lead to hierarchical collection of data, where the technical aspects of information are set aside, in favor for a more general, high-level overview of the project. Accessibility to junior staff who conduct large amounts of technical work should not come as secondary, as it risks rendering some of the technical expertise inaccessible, thus potentially creating a gap in the knowledge transfer.

3.2 Arab Hospitality and Data Collection

It is customary within the Arab culture for the host to provide an exceptional level of care for a visitor (Sobh et al. 2013). Within this practice, as international researchers we were overwhelmed with the offering of beverages and food from hosts when visiting for an interview. These practices, however enjoyable, made it sometimes difficult to discern where the informal discussions ended and when the formal interview practice begun. The importance of non-verbal clues and ethnographical observations in interviews is well documented in methodology literature (McGovern and Tinsley 1978; Heyl 2001;

Wimpenny 2000). Including a cultural practice in the interview process, can pose both an opportunity and a threat. An opportunity because it breaks the ice very early on in the interview and lets the interviewer discuss in a more relaxed manner. It can be however also a threat in that it may create in the interviewer a stronger sense of obligation towards the interviewee, adjusting the usual balance of interviewer/interviewee non-verbal interaction.

On occasions, the discussions extended beyond the formal office setting to a meal provided following the interview. This leads inevitably to collecting ethnographical observations outside a formally defined research context raising the question of whether this type of information is admissible in the research. Discussions on heritage aspects that continue beyond the formal part of the interview, can leave out more technical information and specialized knowledge as the discussion takes on a more informal character. On one occasion, the discussion over such a meal turned to the relationship between Revit (BIM software) and laser scanning. The technicalities of how these two software (limitedly) communicate are difficult to be analyzed to the interviewer when the discussion is firstly taking place over a meal, and secondly happening with a senior member of staff that has little or no experience in how these software communicate. This would normally have been the topic of a formal interview taking place in an office with junior staff being interviewed, that are experienced in articulating the transfer of information between these software. The latter, however, are not participating in the discussion outside of the office, and the setting creates to both parties, researchers and interviewees alike, the sense of vagueness, of a territory that is in between a formal interview setting.

3.3 Respecting Sensitive Cultural Power and Knowledge Relationships

Within the Arab culture, the family name has a crucial role. There is a kinship within extended families, and names of high societal and hierarchical status. In the efforts of our project to make information available for the private and public sector it is important to respectfully notify and advise prominent individuals and families that may have interests in specific heritage projects or greater interests in the development of heritage areas. Information on what data will be publicly available should be disseminated among families which are prominent socially and financially. This approach needs to be done respectfully, educating them about the benefits of heritage. Trying to enforce a planned conservation may be hindered if local influential people are not convinced of the necessity and greater purpose of the project. By ensuring they are informed and aware of the type of information that will be included in the repository we can ensure that information to be included will not be viewed as disrespectful. Furthermore, having informed influential families and taken them onboard the project, can help to further inform the greater public of the purposes of the project. It is our intention to keep the project aligned with the culture of the area.

3.4 Outsiders of Local Arab Culture

As international researchers, we were aware of our position as "outsiders" to the local culture. However, it became apparent within fieldwork that some suggestions and comments made were met by local interviewees with disbelief. Although members of the team are well established in their respective heritage areas, the local interviewees were not intent to directing the research in the directions we suggested and comments were not accepted due to the "outsider effect". Indeed, local expertise was valued within our research team, and the perspectives of local stakeholders were sought and amplified throughout the project so as to align with the project aims of co-production. Despite this, there was a sense that our team were unable to meaningfully contribute to the outputs and potential, because our thoughts about the project were those of outsiders. Their low expectation of international researchers may be due to previous adverse experiences with international projects. In several interviews, previous work with other international teams was mentioned, ranging from areas like the European Union, to the United States of America, to Japan. When these research projects were over, the researchers in some cases left, taking the bulk of the data collected, leaving little to the local teams. The issue of collected data leaving the country has led the local authorities to doubt the results that may come from some projects and considering that spending time on these projects is of little potential value. These experiences raise critical questions of ownership and accessibility of data within internationally funded research projects in local areas. If the collected raw data and findings are not shared, then consequently this will cause delay in developing and implementing interventions for heritage conservation. Considering the time sensitive nature of heritage, it can have a detrimental effect on efforts for architectural urban heritage conservation.

4 Collecting and Managing Digital Data

4.1 Accessibility of Digital Information Collected

The example of research data leaving the country to follow the origin of the researchers as explained in the section above, brings to light the issue of access to information collected. According to Jordanian Legislation and the Heritage Law (N.5), the governmental body has the authority to collect, maintain, manage and utilize information that relates to its built urban heritage. But as Law N.5 has not been officially activated and the information of buildings is not available to the public, data from international research conducted in the country frequently leaves abroad upon conclusion of the project. We came across instances where authorities that have contributed to the compilation of research work, are unable to use the information and access the raw data for processing. One such instance was the case of a Heritage city, in which a Japan funded project had taken place. Upon departure of the research team, the local planning office were left with a hard copy of information collected during the research. Although they had significantly contributed to its compilation, they did not have access to digital files.

In the absence of a legislation providing explicit guidance on how data collected need to be shared, accessibility to information is compromised and therefore hindering the efforts to preserve tangible and intangible heritage. This could be rectified with the inclusion of a relevant clause in legislation: for information to be passed on by local authorities to research groups interested in the country's heritage, it could become mandatory to leave a physical and digital record of information collected. Alternatively, such data may be passed on to a common online repository or a governmental body.

Finally, the importance of these buildings to the heritage of Jordan, seems secondary to the context of its users. There is the intention to preserve and maintain information by legislation, but targets for what this maintenance should involve is more fluid. This is not only a result of the legislation, but more importantly of the absence of local awareness as to what constitutes heritage and which values it should encompass. The heritage sites are often affected by owners because they are unclear what its importance is for the greater urban assemblage. Heritage buildings are left to collapse because the measurable individual importance in terms of ownership is more substantial than its public importance. The existing body of the National Committee, under governmental guidance, is trying hard to establish the heritage law to protect heritage period structures (post 1750), but while relevant legislation remains inactivated, initiating action remains difficult. Furthermore, the number of stakeholders involved in its activation remains vast, and frequently with competing public and individual benefits. While it is being processed, with all agreements of acceptance for activation still pending, unfortunately many parts who are related to finalizing this activation, do not proceed for fear of triggering conflict with other stakeholders or individual benefits whether social, economically or politically.

4.2 Software Accuracy in Data Collected

In order to create a database of BIM objects, one must go through the process of data collection (manually or by using point clouds) depending on the building situation. The former one involves a manual survey and onsite observations. The latter involves the use of a scanning equipment onsite and inserting data on a computer. The difficulty that it presents is the absence of communication between the point cloud and BIM: There is no direct communication and instead, a manual process and coding on Autodesk families is necessary to include the various levels of information. The advantage, however, is that there are various options offered for data to be included: technical aspects of construction and structures and even social and cultural layers of information. This holistic approach to data included is beneficial when documenting buildings for preservation and conservation.

Think for example of the case of a window in a heritage building. The BIM model, would include layers of information about its heritage and methods of construction behind the visible components, but it would lack the imperfections a heritage component typically has. Although BIM can achieve a standardized object for heritage, using it exclusively to focus on the object of a window is devoid of the inconsistencies that make it characteristically part of heritage. Point cloud can come in at this moment to include the layers of charming irregularities heritage objects have.

Using technology helps in obtaining accuracy by reading the details for a building. However, using technology in heritage building might be useful in terms of timesaving but not cost saving. To create highly accurate models, it is essential to go through the entire process of creating 3D model for each part of the building. In this sense, the team members must have expertise in each step of processing of collecting measurement data.

Collecting data in this instance refers to the holistic practice of gathering information from the very early parts of the measurements to managing the site to maintain the heritage building after creating 3D objects.

4.3 Suggestions in Practice

Both the role of culture in the way data is collected and managed, and the limitations to the access and management of data, highlight the necessity of establishing and maintaining a digital repository of publicly available information on details of architectural urban heritage in Jordan, something our project is suggesting to create. The fragmented nature of currently available information remains at risk and is jeopardized when there are inconsistencies in the way data is collected, stored and managed. The opportunities afforded by technologies such as point clouds, 3D scanning, and BIM objects can be maximized when information on the remains of heritage sights is consistently handled.

In our case, we are suggesting that BIM for heritage is a way of establishing a data base of heritage sites. The information included can help the project in meeting several diverse information requirements that consider the buildings performance socially, environmentally and technically for supporting and protecting heritage buildings and sites from disappeared or ignoring the significance of their contents.

4.4 Time Is Precious When Dealing with Urban Heritage

Reflection upon cultural practices has already revealed that it can make data collection feel more informal to researchers interviewing in the Arab context. Furthermore, in data accessibility and public availability of digital information of heritage buildings in Jordan is limited. In creating a repository of information, we need to be considerate as researchers of the time-sensitive nature of preserving urban architectural heritage and respectful to the sensitive power/knowledge relationships dealing with such information entails.

Unfortunately, the condition of many of these structures do not allow them to stand for much longer and in the absence of data sharing, is hindering their renovation and delaying development efforts further. On one occasion, when we were shown around an internationally important heritage sight, we came across a collapsed wall of a heritage building. The host was as surprised as we were to see the damage and mentioned that this had probably happened during a storm that had happened a few days ago. Such events are common when dealing with heritage buildings, because of the structural sensitivity many buildings have due to their age. While they have lasted a long period of time, they can be vulnerable for collapse at the next storm. While remaining unoccupied and without maintenance, it is only a matter of time for them to become irreparable. A solution to preserving the knowledge and information concerning a heritage asset is their digital documentation. By introducing a protocol of data sharing on a digital platform, such buildings have a better chance at preserving their knowledge of construction techniques, features and ornamentation, and can be more easily restored later (Fig. 1).

Fig. 1. A recently collapsed wall discovered by chance while walking in the heritage site

Alongside the damage and loss of knowledge that takes place while these buildings remain undocumented, there are also economic implications to consider. In recent years, tourism development has been rapid in certain areas of the country. While as there is no publicly available digital repository for architectural urban heritage, there is a risk of either hindering the development of such buildings (which have a large potential to be turned into tourism and hospitality attractions) or allowing local tourism development to occur rapidly without any consideration for heritage, thus irreparably damaging the potential of such buildings in the future. Both effects can be devastating for the tourism and economic development potential of heritage areas.

5   Conclusion

The findings suggest that digital technologies, and in particular BIM (Building Information Modelling), are instrumental to update the traditional approach of urban heritage conservation in Jordan. The application of BIM to heritage can contribute to the revitalization of the country's traditional heritage and also the promotion of its heritage tourism. BIM is a well-established process to optimize the building process with many benefits such as avoiding issues of conflict, reworking and duplication whether in offices or on a construction site. However, using BIM in heritage conservation is a still a novel opportunity of using BIM in terms of documentation, urban reservation and socio-cultural criteria. Another opportunity is creating concrete connection between components of building design, environment, construction site, social elements, and economical issues. In order to achieve accuracy, data is captured and inserted concerning the morphology of the house and the surrounding and the contexts have to be surveyed using high-definition technologies (point clouds) which are state of the art for preservation of elements, complemented by fieldwork and direct observation. It is expected that as a result of such a study, engagement with local planners and residents will raise awareness on the importance of valuing conservation. The main aim of this project is to apply IT to support conservation of traditional architecture and heritage promotion in Jordan.

Using BIM objects to support heritage sites in Jordan is paving the road for preservation tangible and intangible culture heritage (TICH). Utilizing all techniques available (point clouds and BIM objects alongside typical photographic surveys and 2D drawings) will allow to simulate these buildings effectively in digital form. Moreover, they can allow activities that had taken place inside these buildings at the point of their original construction to be visualized in the way they had originally existed. Thus, digitalization of heritage elements whether tangible or intangible is a crucial step forward to preserving and maintaining the relation between heritage sites, researchers, private sector and governmental body.

The questions that remain unanswered and need to be addressed before proceeding further with a database of Heritage Building Information Modelling (HBIM) objects are the issues of public data sharing with relevant stakeholders, and the engagement of people and members of the public in its use. Publicly sharing the information available will be beneficial for positive outcomes in the field of cultural urban heritage, and is a unique approach, currently not available in the country. We suggest that a protocol for its use needs to be created, that outlines the methods of engagement (ie who maintains rights, how are authors attributed etc.) Finally, necessary disclaimers need to be in place for implications arising from its use.

In sum, creating HBIM is a step forward to establish obvious process in countries rich in heritage sites and that could be a prototype for other countries in the same region. Jordan has a rich history and as a result numerous heritage sites and buildings from north to south and east to west, so it is necessary to consider the importance of conservation and preservation. Creating a process in terms of data and urban management are required. In this regard, stakeholders, private and public sectors must be involved with the whole process by creating this platform or management plan strategy; however that must be done by using technology and documentation for sites in general, by using HBIM as a systematic approach for any heritage sites in Jordan. The paper recommends using two levels of awareness to present the importance of achieving the benefit of utilising technology in heritage sites. At the first level, the paper encourages spreading the awareness among governmental bodies to give access to information by experts, professionals, planners, architects, and industrial partners. At the second level of awareness it recommends using accessible data by the governmental sector and local municipalities.

Acknowledgments. This work was supported by the Royal Academy of Engineering and Industrial Research Development Fund with the Industry Academia Partnership Programme - 18/19 (project: IT and Conservation of traditional architecture and heritage, IAPP18-19\244). The authors thank all the stakeholders and experts who generously offered their time and expertise to support the data collection, including industrial partners.

References

1. Bewley, R., Kennedy, D.: Historical aerial imagery in Jordan and the Wider Middle East. In: Hanson, W.S., Oltean, I.A. (eds.) Archaeology from Historical Aerial and Satellite Archives, pp. 221–242. Springer New York, New York (2013). https://doi.org/10.1007/978-1-4614-4505-0_13
2. Butler, B.: Return to Alexandria: An Ethnography of Cultural Heritage Revivalism and Museum Memory, vol. 1. Left Coast Press, Walnut Creek (2007)

3. Clifford, J., Marcus, G.E. (eds.): Writing Culture: The Poetics and Politics of Ethnography: A School of American Research Advanced Seminar. University of California Press, Berkeley (1986)
4. Duneier, M., Kasinitz, P., Murphy, A. (eds.): The Urban Ethnography Reader. Oxford University Press, Oxford (2014)
5. Fine, G.A.: Ten lies of ethnography: moral dilemmas of field research. J. Contemp. Ethnogr. **22**(3), 267–294 (1993)
6. Heyl, B.S.: Ethnographic Interviewing, pp. 369–383. Sage, London (2001)
7. Hollowell, J., Nicholas, G.: Using ethnographic methods to articulate community-based conceptions of cultural heritage management. Pub. Archaeol. **8**(2–3), 141–160 (2009)
8. Lewis, S.J., Russell, A.J.: Being embedded: a way forward for ethnographic research. Ethnography **12**(3), 398–416 (2011)
9. Ministry of Tourism and Antiquities, Law N.5 of 2005 on the protection of immovable heritage (2005). https://www.uaipit.com/en/documents-record?/5054/law-no-5-of-2005-on-the-protection-of-architectural-and-urban-heritage
10. Ministry of Tourism and Antiquities, & The World Bank, Salt, Detailed description of the city revitalisation program, Salt, Jordan (2005). https://www.mota.gov.jo/Documents/Salt/Main_Report.pdf
11. McGovern, T.V., Tinsley, H.E.: Interviewer evaluations of interviewee nonverbal behavior. J. Vocat. Behav. **13**(2), 163–171 (1978)
12. Silva, L., Santos, P.M.: Ethnographies of heritage and power. Int. J. Heritage Stud. **18**(5), 437–443 (2012)
13. Sobh, R., Belk, R.W., Wilson, J.A.: Islamic Arab hospitality and multiculturalism. Mark. Theory **13**(4), 443–463 (2013)
14. The World Bank: Project appraisal document on a proposed loan in the amount of US$56 million to the Hashemite Kingdom of Jordan for a Cultural Heritage Tourism and Urban Development Project, Jordan (2007). http://documents1.worldbank.org/curated/en/655381468088745132/text/381620JO0R20071000511.txt
15. Trillo, C., Aburamadan, R., Udeaja, C., Moustaka, A., Baffour, K.G., Makore, B.C.N.: Enhancing heritage and traditional architecture conservation through digital technologies. Developing a digital conservation handbook for As-Salt, Jordan. In: International Symposium: New Metropolitan Perspectives, pp. 211–219. Springer, Cham (2020)
16. Udeaja, C., Trillo, C., Awuah, K.G., Makore, B.C., Patel, D.A., Mansuri, L.E., Jha, K.N.: Urban heritage conservation and rapid urbanization: insights from Surat, India. Sustainability **12**(6), 2172 (2020)
17. Wimpenny, P., Gass, J.: Interviewing in phenomenology and grounded theory: is there a difference? J. Adv. Nurs. **31**(6), 1485–1492 (2000)
18. Zerbini, A.: Developing a heritage database for the Middle East and North Africa. J. Field Archaeol. **43**(sup1), S9–S18 (2018)

The MaDiH (مديح): Mapping Digital Cultural Heritage in Jordan, Opportunities and Limitations

Fadi Bala'awi[1]([⊠]), Shatha Mubaideen[2], James Smithies[3], Pascal Flohr[4], Alessandra Esposito[3], Carol Palmer[2], and Sahar Idwan[1]

[1] The Hashemite University, Zarqa, Jordan
fadi.balaawi@hu.edu.jo
[2] The Council for British Research in the Levant, Amman, Jordan
[3] King's Digital Lab, King's College London, London, UK
[4] EAMENA Project, School of Archaeology, University of Oxford, Oxford, UK

Abstract. MaDiH (مديح): Mapping Digital Cultural Heritage in Jordan is an AHRC/Newton funded collaborative project between King's Digital Lab (KDL), the Hashemite University, the Council for British Research in the Levant (CBRL), the Department of Antiquities of Jordan, the Jordanian Open Source Association, and the Endangered Archaeology in the Middle East and North Africa (EAMENA) project. The project aims to contribute to the development of Jordan's digital cultural heritage by identifying systems, datasets, standards, and policies, and aligning them to government digital infrastructure capabilities and strategies. The MaDiH data catalogue or, in future, repository includes datasets that have been created over the past 50 years by archaeological teams, official institutions, museums, research institutions, or individuals from Jordan and other countries such as the United Kingdom, United States, Germany, France, Japan, and Canada.

In total 325 datasets on Jordanian cultural heritage were recorded in the MaDiH CKAN repository. This representative sample is designed to be the core of the prototype for a national data catalogue using CKAN (ckan.org), an open-source data publishing tool for data collection. The project represented stage one of a larger three stage vision to 'Map', 'Build' and 'Deliver' enhanced Digital Cultural Heritage (DCH) capability for Jordan. MaDiH (مديح) sits at the intersection of numerous currents in contemporary DCH activity. It engages in long-standing practices such as software engineering, information management, data curation, open knowledge, and archive management informed by more recent initiatives such as Critical Infrastructure Studies, Postcolonial Digital Humanities (DH), Indigenous DH, and Global DH.

Keywords: Digital Cultural Heritage · MaDiH CKAN repository · Jordan · Documentation · Communication strategy · Datasets · Infrastructure and digital tools

© Springer Nature Switzerland AG 2021
M. Rauterberg (Ed.): HCII 2021, LNCS 12794, pp. 15–26, 2021.
https://doi.org/10.1007/978-3-030-77411-0_2

1 Introduction

Jordan is a MENA (Middle East and North Africa) country rich with cultural heritage assets. The diverse heritage of the country has attracted the attention of the research community to explore, study, interpret, protect, and present its heritage. Many international, regional, and local organizations and individuals have produced meta(data) as part of these projects and made it available online or offline -whether for pure scientific analysis, tourism promotion purposes, or other reasons. The originators and maintainers of the data are scattered around the world. MaDiH (مديح): Mapping Digital Cultural heritage in Jordan project is an AHRC/Newton funded collaborative project between King's Digital Lab (KDL), the Hashemite University, the Council for British Research in the Levant (CBRL), the Department of Antiquities of Jordan, the Jordanian Open Source Association, and the Endangered Archaeology in the Middle East and North Africa (EAMENA) project. The high-level mapping and analysis aim described at a high level in this paper informs a technical white paper that describes the current state of standards, datasets, data repositories and other assets and defines technical requirements for future activity (Smithies et al. 2021a), as well as a policy white paper that focuses on the alignment to national and international policies and standards and makes recommendations for future action (Smithies et al. 2021b).

To facilitate production of its primary white paper outputs, MaDiH (مديح) has identified essential systems, datasets, and standards, and described them in a prototype data repository (built using the CKAN open source system) that introduces, links, and classifies the data collected by the project, that managed, in its first mapping stage (2019–2021), to sit at the intersection of numerous currents in contemporary Digital Cultural Heritage research. The project represented stage one of a larger three stage vision to 'Map', 'Build' and 'Deliver' enhanced Digital Cultural Heritage (DCH) capability for Jordan. The Mapping stage reflected the opportunities and limitations of using and developing similar digital tools to enhance and sustain cultural heritage in Jordan. This paper will discuss the issues, challenges and opportunities related to building a national heritage data repository for Jordan, to identify lessons and learn from the MaDiH model so it can be applied to similar initiatives in other countries.

2 Overview of the MaDiH Project Dimensions

2.1 The MaDiH Content

Jordan is a country rich in archeological content, with over 100,000 identified archaeological sites. Except for internationally recognized sites, like Petra and Jerash, there are many more sites so far unknown to the general public. These sites can represent anything from prehistoric hunter-gatherers, the first farmers, to towns and cities of former kingdoms and empires.

UNESCO defines cultural heritage as a product and a process that manifests the past and should be transferred to future generations, including tangible and intangible heritage. The MaDiH project team has made a conscious decision to accept this wider international definition. This multidimensional understanding of heritage resulted in diverse content being identified. In total 325 datasets related to Jordanian cultural heritage were recorded in the MaDiH CKAN repository. The diversity and richness of cultural heritage in Jordan are reflected in the collected sample, with 82% relating to tangible heritage and 41% covering intangible heritage (one dataset can contain both tangible and intangible heritage). The datasets (and the projects that produced them) vary in their focus, from maintenance and restoration, documentation, archaeological excavations and the interpretation and presentation of cultural heritage assets. Multiple international and local institutions have partnered to produce heritage data for different purposes, (fig. 1).

Projects include the Documentation of the Objects in Jordanian Archaeological Museums (DOJAM) Amman Citadel Museum by the German Protestant Institute of Archaeology in the Holy Land (GPIA), and the Department of Antiquities of Jordan (DoA), which aims to create a national archaeological database for Jordanian museum-management and scientific research (GPIA Amman 2017). Another project is the 'Our Past, Our Future, All Together in Faynan' (OPOF), which is a collaboration between the University of Reading, the Council for British Research in the Levant (CBRL), the Department of Antiquities of Jordan (DoA) and other partners to utilize the cultural heritage of Faynan to support the local community sustainable growth through ecotourism, archaeological research and educational development (Faynan Heritage 2018).

The University of Cape Town in cooperation with the Petra Development & Tourism Region Authority (PDTRA), the UNESCO Amman office, and the DoA created a GIS platform for data relevant for the Petra Archaeological Park area as part of the Siq Stability project. The online platform offers a virtual tour of Petra with maps, videos, images, and a 3D computer model of the structures and landscape of the site. In contrast, as reflected in the research sample, there appears to be more interest in intangible heritage at the local level. For instance, the Royal Hashemite Documentation Center is responsible for restoring historical archives, from the period of the Emirates of Transjordan in 1921, that was central to the development of contemporary Jordan. The Jordanian Ministry of Culture worked on several intangible heritage documentation projects with regional and local partners, too. Analogue collections of photographs, books and papers that belong to individual historians, artists or photographers are also present in the MaDiH CKAN repository.

The context may vary according to each project purpose, funding, or expected outcome. Other factors might be the dataset content, the teams, as well as the specialty of the projects' partners.

59% of the datasets are 'local', i.e. mainly focused on archaeological sites or heritage in Jordan or are datasets that were created as part of local documentation projects by Jordanian institutions. An example of this is the Petra Great Temple Excavation Database, https://opencontext.org/projects/A5DDBEA2-B3C8-43F9-8151-33343CBDC857. 19% relate to Jordan's wider regional context which stretches from the Middle East, the Islamic world, the Mediterranean region, to the 'Ancient World' and the 'Holy Land'. For example, the Endangered Archaeology in the Middle East and North Africa (EAMENA) project aims at creating a database of archaeological sites for the whole Middle East and North Africa region, including Jordan (Sheldrick and Zerbini 2017). In another example, the Manar Al-Athar project is a photographic online archive covering the Levant, Arabia, Egypt, North Africa, and Spain (McKenzie 2013).

It is important to note that Jordan is also represented in many international datasets, which resemble 22% of the datasets documented by the project. The Endangered Archaeology in the Middle East and North Africa (EAMENA) project is an example of a major international project with important Jordanian DCH content. The project aims to create a database of threatened sites for the Middle East and North Africa, including Jordan. Another image-based repository, Manar Al-Athar, focuses on content related to the Levant, Arabia, Egypt, North Africa, and Spain, dating between the Roman and the Islamic periods. A wide variety of factors influence dataset content from the nationality of the teams involved, as well to the research and professional specialities of project partners. International online museum collections that include objects from the region, including Jordan, are also presented in the MaDiH datasets, such as the British Museum, https://www.britishmuseum.org/collection, which displays the two-headed Neolithic statue from Ain Ghazal, and the Museum of Ancient Near East in Berlin, http://www.smb-digital.de/eMuseumPlus, which holds the Palace of Mshatta façade. Some datasets feature stories of historical excavations or exploration projects such as the Petra 1929 website, https://www.petra1929.co.uk/diary, which is an online transcription of a diary with photographs, contextual essays, and indexes from the first intensive excavations at the Petra World Heritage Site in 1929.

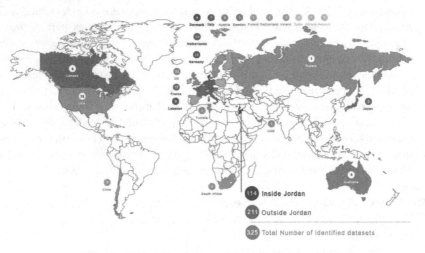

Fig. 1. Global distribution of the recorded datasets.

2.2 Technical Dimension and Digital Transformation

The MaDiH team chose CKAN (Comprehensive Knowledge Archive Network), an open-source data portal designed to facilitate the storage and distribution of open data, to create the data repository. The system easily supported the project's basic requirements, and could be enhanced through plugins or further development with additional funding. It is also suitable to become a data repository in a future phase of the project (see Smithies et al. 2021a).

The basic MaDiH CKAN template was customized and updated during the initial phases of the project, with the guidance of the project partners and in light of requirements elicited in a series of workshops, which helped develop a very good understanding of the project from the outset. The MaDiH CKAN catalogue, https://madih-data.kdl.kcl. ac.uk/, is currently in its most rudimentary form, where each dataset record in CKAN is structured on three levels that include the organization, the dataset (links to) the resources. The user can search the repository to view essential information about datasets but need to visit the external links to view the content of each dataset. Figure 2 and 3.

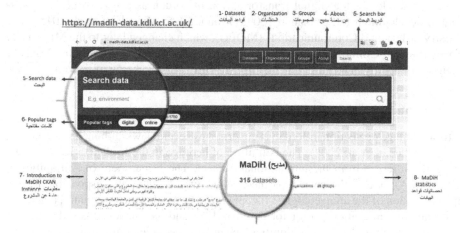

Fig. 2. The MaDiH CKAN interface.

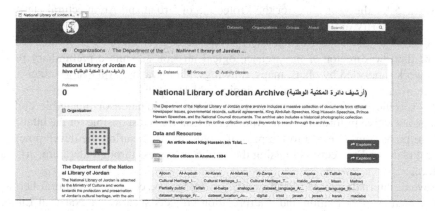

Fig. 3. An example of a record in the MaDiH CKAN catalogue.

The team also developed and published a dataset identification and publication protocol (Esposito et al. 2020), and a data vocabulary (MaDiH 2020), which determined and controlled the range of data and the data quality, to avoid bias in the data entry and communicate the process to the audience. The outputs have been made publicly available to allow other teams to build on them. More than 100 records were manually identified and cross-checked by multiple team members to resolve inconsistencies, focusing on quality and accuracy over quantity. The goal was to develop a representative rather than a comprehensive dataset, to inform high level analysis and production of the white papers.

The MaDiH project demonstrates how digital can technologies can support documentation and planning for the protection of heritage sites and findings at various levels (Ioannides et al. 2018). It is well integrated into wider Jordanian efforts to enhance national digital strategy across all sectors of culture, government, and society. The Jordanian government launched several initiatives in the early decades of the twentieth century to accelerate the digital transformation of Jordan as a way to promote sustainable development (Abu Shanab 2009; Ottoum 2015; Majdalawi et al. 2015). The Ministry of Post and Communications (MOPC), which changed later to the Ministry of Information and Communications Technology (MOICT) and is currently the Ministry of Digital Economy and Entrepreneurship (MODEE) was in charge of these initiatives.

2.3 Operational and Legal Dimensions

Cultural heritage protection in Jordan is governed by several laws, although some are not activated (Hassan et al. 2008). The definition of heritage in the Jordanian legal context is slightly different from the international context. The Department of Antiquities of Jordan (DoA), one of the project partners, is the official authority responsible for the implementation of the archaeological (i.e. pre-1750 CE) policy in the country, mandated by the law of Antiquities No. 21 for the year 1988 and its amendments (Al-Qatarneh 2013). According to that law, 'antiquities' mean 'any movable or immovable object that was made, written, inscribed, built, discovered or modified by a human being before the year AD 1750' (DoA 2004). While more recent heritage, i.e., after AD 1750, is protected by law no.5 for the year 2005 for the Protection of Urban and Architectural Heritage, under the authority of the Ministry of Tourism and Antiquities.

In terms of data, the Regulations for Archaeological Projects in Jordan (2016), require that the director of the archaeological mission submits a preliminary report of his work supported by plans, maps, drawings, photographs, explanatory notes and a special inventory list of all the archaeological objects found.

No specific regulations on the conservation or digitization of intangible cultural heritage are active in Jordan, but the Ministry of Culture is responsible for the intangible heritage protection assigned to the passing civilizations, ensuring the development of cultural plans and projects and raising the public awareness through literature, arts and folklore.

Several international and local entities in Jordan are conducting cultural heritage documentation, preservation and interpretation projects such as the National Library of Jordan, the Ministry of Culture, the Royal Hashemite Documentation Centre, the Department of Antiquities and Royal Jordanian Geographic Centre as well as non-governmental organizations, international research institutions and individuals.

2.4   Human and Socio-cultural Dimensions

Human capital in Jordan is considered a highly valuable asset as Jordanians are highly educated in engineering, science and other technical fields (Rabadi et al. 2010). As a collaborative project between Jordanian and UK partners from different backgrounds (digital humanities, architecture, archaeology, computer science), MaDiH was a diverse project that reflected multiple interdisciplinary dimensions, across the education, government, cultural heritage and technology sectors. On a broader level, project workshops and online surveys engaged the national and international cultural heritage research and institutional communities and identified the specific facilities needed by system stakeholders.

To mitigate any risks during the data collection process, a clear communication strategy was established. Dataset information was mainly collected from published resources, speeding up the process, and supported collecting dataset information from the owners within the project timeframe of two years. The team also set up a social media strategy soon after project initiation to ensure a consistent approach with the heritage community and support the data collection channels.

A collaboration agreement (an administrative document that sets out the modalities of the relations among the partners to the requirements of the UK funders), was also prepared by the team. Differences between the UK and Jordanian legal contexts delayed the process of signing this agreement, suggesting the need for policy development and improved communication between UK and Jordanian funding agencies. The project itself contributed to this process by building a strong transnational team culture, and (although the MaDiH repository functions in English at this stage), ensuring that all project communications and publications were bilingual to reach a Jordanian audience.

3   Discussion: Issues, Challenges and Opportunities

The MaDiH project has provided a general view of the landscape of cultural heritage protection projects in Jordan. The preliminary analysis provides researchers with a firm foundation for future development initiatives and identifies possible limitations of similar or complementary initiatives in DCH in the Jordanian context.

In doing so the project has enabled (through an increased understanding of digital infrastructure and DCH assets) increased use of digital technologies, such as laser scanning, photogrammetry, and satellite imagery to answer archaeological research questions, support conservation work, and reduce the time spent in extracting documents using traditional methods of document management. Many of the identified datasets also support the production of more engaging experiences for the site presentation purposes to the visitors.

In comparison to other countries in the region, Jordan has the longest experience of digital cultural heritage (Drzewiecki and Arinat 2017). Despite this, and Jordanian government IT policies having a positive impact on attitudes towards sharing of data, cultural heritage is still not a priority in terms of the wider national digital transformation process. Despite this, the MaDiH project has demonstrated that, Jordanian institutions are willing to develop their technical capacities and learn from international best practice in the use of modern technology in cultural heritage protection projects (Sheldrick and Zerbini 2017).

Jordanian regulators can play a role in encouraging the development and adoption of IT and open data, including DCH content. The Jordanian government considers the development of its open data platform a national priority that contributes to supporting all aspects of the development process and counts access to information as a fundamental right for citizens (The Ministry of Planning and International Cooperation 2018). Technical requirements such as machine readability, accessibility, etc., are clearly defined to decrease complexity, resources usage, risk, and expenses (Jordanian Open Government Data Policy). Initiatives that raise the awareness of DCH best practice to heritage professionals and decision makers, with a view to promoting open data policies and best practices (and collaborations between cultural heritage institutions and IT professionals) are therefore encouraged - to build upon the MaDiH initiative and other similar DCH projects.

According to Kurniawan (2011), unintegrated databases, incomprehensive inventories, and limited public access are just some of the issues that face the management of cultural heritage around the world. Downtime or systems failure due to inadequate infrastructure, information technology, or lack of systems, and any failure or malfunction in those systems are threats that undermine the deployment of digital technologies in any field, including cultural heritage. Driving global partnerships and bridges with international digital hubs will support the creation of strong governance structures to effectively and dynamically manage digital transformations in cultural heritage.

On the technical level, the diversity of datasets recorded in the MaDiH repository allows for multidisciplinary cooperation between the dataset's owners. Moreover, the adaption of archaeological databases such as DOJAM and EAMENA to include the more recent heritage of Jordan, i.e., post-1750, can support the documentation of tangible and intangible heritage that falls under the 2005-year law, since basic requirements for databases are developed through long-term global collaborations, which can prompt the establishment of post 1750 documentation projects.

According to a UNESCO report (2014), some Jordanian institutions working in cultural heritage require training to cover indexing, conservation and digitization of their archives. The experience of the MaDiH project, and in particular feedback from its community workshops, supports this perception. Otoum (2015) claims that social and administrative regimes are delaying Jordan's digital transformation through resistance of governmental agencies and institutions to engage in digital transformation. While this is an important issue, the MaDiH project found that this situation is changing, as several institutions and individuals were interested in getting assistance in the digitization of their analogue archives.

The team has recorded issues and challenges that emerged at each phase in the project, across all project dimensions. Table 1 summarises those issues and explains how they were mitigated.

Table 1. Issues and Challenges

Category	Title	Description	Impact	Mitigation	Status
The MaDiH Content	Data quality	Data quality and/or consistency in the resulting repository is low	High	Data collection protocol & data dictionary approved before data collection started and reviewed throughout the project	Resolved
	Research Bias	The data collection is biased by the knowledge areas of the Research Team member	High	Track the typologies of datasets entered via tags over a 1-month period. The potential research bias is taken into account in the white papers and journal papers	Resolved
Technical Dimension and Digital Transformation	CKAN	CKAN repository not implemented in time and with appropriate fields	High	Close contact with KDL development team, requirements elicitation workshops and online surveys to involve the heritage professionals in the continuous evaluation of the repository	Resolved
	Usefulness/searchability of data	The data is not searchable well enough to deliver results for researchers	Medium	Discussions of the right terms to use and test entries were done during summer 2019 Controlled vocabularies were used and published. While the search is not user-friendly, the datasets can be searched, and increasing the user-friendliness of the search has been taken onboard as a recommendation for phase 2	Resolved

(continued)

Table 1. (*continued*)

Category	Title	Description	Impact	Mitigation	Status
Operational and Legal Dimensions	Licenses	Appropriate licenses are not assigned, or cannot be defined	Medium	Approval at weekly meeting before publication as part of normal data publishing protocol. Add a disclaimer to the 'About' page on CKAN All datasets were given appropriate citation information. They were derived from published datasets, or permission was given by the dataset owner	Resolved
Human and Socio-cultural Dimensions	Translation	The project outcomes need Arabic - Jordan translation	Low	Bilingual content on social media platforms for wider communications. Adequate peer review before publication. Translation of the project white papers	Resolved
	Project Audience	Unclear understanding of the project audience(s) leads to an amorphous repository	Medium	Workshops and other feedback gave a clear understanding of the audiences. A research paper on the user experience is also being prepared	Resolved

4   Conclusion

MaDiH is conceived as a pilot project, so at the end of its initial funding period (2019–2021), will still be 'incomplete'. The project is designed to provide foundations that can be scaled in the future, to include content related to natural heritage and digital social sciences and potentially (with significant additional funding and effort) even further towards a cross-sector national data repository such as https://www.data.gov/ or https://data.gov.uk/.Having said that, another option presents itself: with a total 325 datasets on Jordanian cultural heritage and significant policy, technical, and data analyses completed, the project succeeded in laying the foundation stone for a future national laboratory for digital heritage studies. The current project blends long-standing practices such as software engineering, information management, data curation, open knowledge, and archive management with more recent initiatives such as Critical Infrastructure Studies, Postcolonial DH, Indigenous DH, and Global DH.

In essence, MaDiH was a practical DCH project that aimed to use digital tools to enhance and sustain the cultural heritage of a significant region. The wider intention is to start designing a digital infrastructure worthy to sit atop the millennia of physical (and intellectual) infrastructure it describes. The hope is that the project provides a model that can be adapted to other countries that need to integrate information across their cultural heritage sector, establishing significant preliminary engineering and design processes for future national cultural heritage data portals.

To be sure, the project faced a number of challenges on both technical and administrative levels. But considering it was a pilot study, and taking into consideration the relatively short duration of the project, its limited budget, and the impact of the COVID-19 pandemic, what was achieved is remarkable. The outcomes of the project (phase 1), data collection and migration to Jordan, will be used as a strong base to develop phase 2 of the project with more data collection and analysis, ultimately reaching the major goal of the project in its third phase by establishing a national Jordanian digital cultural heritage lab.

References

1. Abu Shanab, E., Al-Radaideh, Q.: Jordan's e-government program: a user centered approach (2009). http://repository.yu.edu.jo/bitstream/123456789/1734/1/476100.pdf
2. Al-Qaatarneh, M.: Conserving the archaeological heritage in Jordan is the mission of the department of antiquities. In: Paper presented at the JOCHERA Final Conference (2013)
3. Department of Antiquities, The law of Antiquities No. 21 for the year 1988 and its amendments in 2004 (2004). http://publication.doa.gov.jo/uploads/publications/203/Law%20of%20Antiquities-Jordan.pdf
4. Drzewiecki, M., Arinat, M.: The impact of online archaeological databases on research and heritage protection in Jordan. Levant **49** https://doi.org/10.1080/00758914.2017.1308117 (2017)
5. Esposito, A., et al.: MaDiH (مديح) Mapping the Digital Cultural Heritage in Jordan Project, p. 4. Datasets Identification and Publication Protocol, Zenodo (2020). https://doi.org/10.5281/zenodo.4146756
6. Faynan Heritage (إرث فينان): http://faynanheritage.org/ (2018). Accessed 23 Mar 2020
7. GPIA Amman: Documentation of Objects in Jordanian Archaeological Museums (DOJAM). https://www.zitadelle-amman.de/projekt/ (2017). Accessed 20 Nov 2020
8. Hassan, F., de Trafford, A., Youssef, M., Serageldin, I.: Cultural Heritage and Development in the Arab World. Bibliotheca Alexandrina, Alexandria (2008)
9. Kurniawan, H., Salim, A., Suhartanto, H., Hasibuan, Z.A.: E-cultural heritage and natural history framework: an integrated approach to digital preservation. In: International Conference on Telecommunication Technology and Applications (IACSIT), pp. 177–182 (2011)
10. Ioannides, M., Fink, E., Brumana, R., Patias, P., Doulamis, A., Martins, J., Wallace, M. (eds.) Digital Heritage. Progress in Cultural Heritage: Documentation, Preservation, and Protection: 7th International Conference, EuroMed 2018, Nicosia, Cyprus, October 29–November 3, 2018, Proceedings, Part I. Vol. 11196. Springer, Cham (2018)
11. MaDiH - Mapping Digital Heritage in Jordan: Madih Vocabulary English and Arabic_sep 2020.xlsx. figshare, 14 Sept 2020. https://doi.org/10.6084/m9.figshare.12950879.v1
12. Manar Al-Athar: https://www.classics.ox.ac.uk/manar-al-athar-photo-archive (2013). Accessed 12 May 2021

13. Majdalawi, Y., Almarabeh, T., Mohammad, H., Quteshate, W.: E-government strategy and plans in Jordan. J. Softw. Eng. Appl. **8**(04), 211 (2015)
14. Ministry of Planning and International Cooperation: The Fourth National Action Plan 2018 - 2020 under the Open Government Partnership Initiative (OGP), pp. 27 (2018)
15. Ottoum, I.: Launching E-Government in Jordan. World Comput. Sci. Inf. Technol. J. **5**(4), 61–68 (2015)
16. Rabadi, G., Kaylani, H.: Towards a centre for modelling and simulation: the case for Jordan. In: Proceedings of the 6th International Workshop on Enterprise & Organizational Modeling and Simulation, pp. 99–112. CEUR-WS.org. (2011)
17. Sheldrick, N., Zerbini, A.: A heritage inventory for documenting endangered archaeology in the Middle East and North Africa. ISPRS Ann. Photogram. Remote Sens. Spat. Inf. Sci. **IV-2/W2**, 237–241 (2017). https://doi.org/10.5194/isprs-annals-IV-2-W2-237-2017
18. Smithies, et al.: Mapping Digital Heritage in Jordan (MaDiH): Policy White Paper, in preparation (2021a)
19. Smithies, et al.: Mapping Digital Heritage in Jordan (MaDiH): Technical White Paper, in preparation (2021b)
20. UNESCO, "Jordanian Documentary Heritage", UNESCO (2014). http://www.unesco.org/new/fileadmin/MULTIMEDIA/FIELD/Amman/pdf/Jordan_Documentary_Heritage.pdf

A SLAM Integrated Approach for Digital Heritage Documentation

Salvatore Barba(✉) , Carla Ferreyra , Victoria Andrea Cotella ,
Andrea di Filippo , and Secondo Amalfitano

Dipartimento di Ingegneria Civile, Università degli Studi di Salerno, Fisciano, Italy
sbarba@unisa.it

Abstract. The digital acquisition of Cultural Heritage is a complex process, highly depending on the nature of the object as well as the purpose of its detection. Even if there are different survey techniques and sensors that allow the generation of realistic 3D models, defined by a good metric quality and a detail consistent with the geometric characteristics of the object, an interesting goal could be to develop a unified treatment of the methodologies. Villa Rufolo, with its intricate articulation, becomes the benchmark to test an integrated protocol between photogrammetry, Terrestrial Laser Scanning (TLS) and a Wearable Mobile Laser System (WMLS) based on a SLAM approach. To quantify the accuracy of the latter solution, a comparison is proposed. For the case study the ZEB1, produced and marketed by GeoSLAM, is tested. Computations of cloud-to-cloud (C2C) absolute distances is performed, using stationary laser scanner (Faro Focus^{3D} X130) as a reference. Finally, the obtained results are reported, allowing us to assert that the quality of the WMLS measurements is compatible with the data provided by the manufacturer, thus making the instrumentation suitable for certain specific applications.

Keywords: Indoor mapping · Laser scanning · Photogrammetry

1 Introduction

Cultural Heritage can be defined as a living memory of our society, an irreplaceable testimony of a particular moment in human history. The guidelines for its conservation and enhancement, codified in the Athens Charter and repeatedly reiterated by subsequent documents up to the most recent UNESCO Recommendations, underline the importance of multidisciplinary and scientific approaches for the management of interventions in cultural heritage sites.

The digital survey plays a key role in their documentation; it provides an interesting and innovative scientific basis for study and research, as well as ensuring an effective dissemination approach even for a non-technical audience.

Currently, the use of new technologies for data acquisition in the architectural field has reached a wide diffusion, mainly due to the ability to digitize artifacts with great accuracy and the possibility to generate information models useful for the phases of analysis, simulation, and interpretation [1, 2]. The most widespread techniques, which have

© Springer Nature Switzerland AG 2021
M. Rauterberg (Ed.): HCII 2021, LNCS 12794, pp. 27–39, 2021.
https://doi.org/10.1007/978-3-030-77411-0_3

now become a reference standard, are modern photogrammetry and laser scanning. Photogrammetry acquires two-dimensional images that require mathematical processing to derive 3D information. Through precise formulations based on projective or perspective geometry, it transforms the data extracted from the images into three-dimensional metric coordinates with colour information [3]. For its part, laser scanning can directly obtain the spatial position of the 3D point [4, 5] with high accuracy and without need of illumination conditions, especially useful for homogeneous surfaces where photogrammetry cannot provide reliable results. Integration is then a result that overcomes the limitations of each technique.

The main products obtained from both 3D point cloud and 2D orthoimage techniques have been used for the virtual reconstruction of cultural heritage sites, as the analysis of cave paintings [6], the creation of accurate numerical simulations, or the analysis of pathological processes [7], among others.

In addition to the wide range of advantages that these solutions can offer, the digitization of large and complex areas, especially indoor scenarios, generally involves the use of many images (in the case of photogrammetry) or scanning stations (in the case of laser scanning), resulting in time-consuming fieldwork and moreover in an important propagation of errors [8]. Hybrid solutions, such as mobile mapping systems (MMS), have emerged with great capabilities and possibilities in recent years, allowing the management of multiple sensors and the ability to operate in complex outdoor and indoor scenarios [9–13].

The main purpose of this paper is to highlight the advantages of an integrated approach to digital heritage documentation, resulting from the combination of techniques and technologies that stand out for their strengths but also for their criticalities [14]. Villa Rufolo (Fig. 1), a cultural symbol of the city of Ravello on the Amalfi coast, represents the test case of the experience conducted. It was built between the twelfth and thirteenth centuries as a family residence and a material representation of social status. It has almost unique architectural features, which blend Arab-Byzantine typologies and ornaments with elements of local culture. In the period of maximum splendour, it is said that the Villa had "more rooms than days of the year", although today it is possible to appreciate only some parts of the original construction, such as the Moorish cloister, the entrance tower, and the main tower whose 30 m in height represented the family's prestige.

In detail, this paper evaluates the suitability of a wearable mobile laser system (WMLS) for the digitalization of a complex indoor environment belonging to a cultural heritage building, as well as for the generation of cartographic products required for its conservation and restoration. This wearable system combines laser scanning technology and an inertial measurement unit (IMU) in portable equipment that can be handled by an operator while walking through the cultural heritage site. This sensor acquires point clouds on the move, thanks to the Simultaneous Localization and Mapping algorithms (SLAM) [10, 14], without needing the support of a global navigation satellite system (GNSS).

During this evaluation, possible integration strategies are examined and tested to guarantee a result that is compatible with the levels of accuracy and definition required by the survey, trying to optimise the procedure and make it applicable in other contexts

Fig. 1. Villa Rufolo, general view of the Palace with southern gardens.

as well. The most innovative aspect of the proposed application is the integration of data from diachronic surveys, differentiated not only by the technique used but also by a different time of detection. The joining element that makes their fusion possible is, however, the presence of a GNSS support network that also makes it possible to control the quality of the output model.

2 Materials and Methods

2.1 Equipment

GeoSLAM ZEB1. The ZEB1 consists of a 2D time-of-flight laser range scanner rigidly coupled to an inertial measurement unit (IMU) mounted on a spring. The motion of the scanning head on the spring provides the third dimension required to generate 3D information. A simultaneous localization and mapping (SLAM) algorithm combines the 2D laser scan data with the IMU data to generate accurate 3D point clouds, employing a full SLAM approach [15, 16]. Regarding accuracy, the manufacturer declares a value of 0.1% in relative accuracy for a 10-min scan, with a single loop closing. Special thanks are due to engineer Mariella Danzi, who kindly provided us with the instrumentation. It is worth mentioning that the acquisitions were performed in May 2019, when more advanced versions of the instrument, able to offer greater control over error propagation, were not yet available.

DJI Phantom 4. The UAV has an approximate weight of 1.4 kg. Its camera is equipped with a 12 MP Sony Exmor sensor (size 6.3×4.7 mm, pixel size 1.56 µm), and a wide-angle lens with a 4 mm focal length and FOV (Field of View) of 94°. The camera is integrated in a gimbal to maximize the stability of the images during the movements.

Faro Focus³ᴰX130. The X130 is a stationary laser scanner of the Continuous Wave - Frequency Modulation (CW-FM) type. The system can measure with great precision the direction of pointing, in addition to a distance meter that emits continuous light radiation. This one, thanks to a coding of the frequency modulated light signal that allows the identification of a phase shift between the emitted wave and the recorded one, guarantees the indirect calculation of the time of flight and therefore of the distance. In terms of error, this solution guarantees a systematic component of ±2 mm and an accidental component of ±0.5 mm.

2.2 Survey Design and Detection

WMLS. Systems that use SLAM algorithms to generate final models require special attention when planning acquisitions. More than any other solution, in fact, the quality of the produced data is highly dependent on how the acquisition campaign is conducted. It is important to inspect the site of interest to identify critical areas not detected during planning and remove any obstacles along the way. In addition to the focus on poorly referenced environments, transition areas and forward speeds, it should be remembered that full SLAM systems, such as the one employed, require the self-intersection of paths to ensure an appropriate redistribution of the accumulated errors. At least one loop must be closed, although it is advisable to plan routes with several self-intersections. Geometric features extracted by the algorithm are significant if the ratio of their size and their range is approximately 1:10 (e.g., a feature must be textgreater 0.5 m in size for a distance of 5 m). In addition, if there are not sufficient features along the direction of travel, the SLAM algorithm cannot correctly determine forward motion. In general, it is better to do circular loops rather than "there and back" loops where the path simply doubles back on itself. It is important to scan the closed loop regions carefully to ensure that the key features are scanned from a similar perspective. It may be necessary to turn around to return to a region from another direction. This is a crucial feature in poor environments. With these concepts in mind, the acquisition campaign is organised in this way (Fig. 2):

- *First path*, which includes the management offices on level 0 and the auditorium on level 1.
- *Second path*, covering the entrance at level 0, the west garden, the central courtyard and the east garden.
- *Third path*, which covers storage areas and rooms closed to the public located on level 1, as well as part of the east garden.
- *Fourth path*, which takes place on the underground level, going through the lower part of the Moorish cloister up to the exhibition rooms in the current "theatre".
- *Fifth path*, that covers all the "museum" rooms and the auditorium on level 1.

Digitizing the entire scene has taken 2 h, about 1/2 of the time needed to complete the TLS campaign, but covering a larger area.

Aerial Photogrammetry. To control the metric error, 14 GCP are detected on the arena floor by a Geomax Zenith 25 used in nRTK mode. The accuracy of planimetry is below

1 cm and 2.5 cm for altimetry. For the acquisition of the frames, two flight are prepared, both automatic and with double grid: a first one for the acquisition of nadir photogrammetric images and a second one, with the optical axis tilted about 45°, to survey the vertical walls and any shadow cones.

The flight lines are designed using the DJI Ground- Station software package. For all the grids, the UAV is set to a target altitude of 16 m above take off point - Torre Maggiore - (46 m from Duomo Square) and horizontal ground speed of $4.0 \text{ m} \cdot \text{s}^{-1}$. The height is calculated in the DJI Ground- Station software using elevation data derived from Google Earth. Parallel flights lines are programmed to have an image overlap of 60% as well as sidelap of 60%, setting the proper camera parameters (dimensions of the sensor, focal length, and flight height). In the nadir flights, 93 and 94 images are acquired for the first (from North to South) and second (from West to East) grid, respectively. Two other flights, with the camera tilted at 45° on the horizontal plan, are carried out acquiring, respectively, other 92 and 163 photos. The image acquisition is planned bearing in mind the project requirements - a Ground Sampling Distance (GSD) of about 1 cm - and, at the same time, with the aim of guaranteeing a high level of automation in the following phases.

Fig. 2. Registered SLAM paths, highlighted with different colors: the first in purple, the second in pink, the third in red, the fourth in grey and the fifth in green. (Color figure online).

TLS. A survey design should be first defining the positions of TLS stations, so that the whole object coverage at requested spatial resolution could be guaranteed. The instrument has been set to have a resolution of 6 mm–10 m. As far as the quality of the acquisition is concerned, for each point of the cloud three measurements are made to define the distance from the station as the average of the above measurements. Great attention has also paid to the problem of environmental occlusions, due to the presence of vegetation. In the first instance, 5 scans are acquired in the west garden, 4 at the level of the central courtyard, and 5 in the east garden. The need to connect these three parts has required additional stations to ensure the completeness of the model: 3 of them are placed between the west garden and the courtyard and 3 between the latter and the east garden. With the features listed above, the TLS acquisition campaign has taken almost 5 h, with a single-scan time of approximately 12 min.

2.3 Processing: The Generation of the 3D Point Cloud

High-level, point-based approach to data fusion has been opted for, where all raw data streams are kept separate and processed independently. Only at the end the resulting point clouds are merged to obtain a complete 3D model. The processing of the raw data, coming from the acquisition phase, starts from the registration of the point clouds [17, 18] (Fig. 3).

WMLS Data Registration. Due to the low overlap between the five acquisition paths, a progressive registration approach based on an ICP pairwise algorithm is employed, each time choosing the reference scan. All preceded by a manual raw alignment. The maximum value of the RMSE on all the registration pairs, defined above, is about 1.74 cm. The idea of defining a pipeline for the registration of WMLS data that does not resort to TLS scans arises from the observation that it is not always possible to have homologous models deriving from different systems to perform accuracy checks. For this reason, the workflows for the two systems are kept separate until comparison. The individual paths are maintained disjoined (but rigidly bound to each other) for a comparison with the final TLS model, after mutual registration with ICP algorithm.

Photogrammetric Process. Data treatment is performed by Agisoft Metashape, 1.5.3 build 8469 version. Its workflow is based on four steps: Align Photos, Build Dense Cloud, Build Mesh and Build Texture. At the first step an algorithm evaluates the camera internal parameters (Focal Length, position of the principal point, radial and tangential distortions), the camera positions for each photo and the Sparse Cloud. In the next phase, a greater pixel number is re-projected for each aligned camera, creating the Dense Cloud. In the Build Mesh step, it is possible to generate a polygonal mesh model based on the dense cloud data. Finally, the polygon model is textured in the Build Texture step. The outputs of the photogrammetric model, necessary for further documentation studies and data integration with active sensors, are a nadir orthophoto of the entire villa and the dense point cloud. The extracted point cloud has more than 48 million points, with average errors of about 2.8 cm (Fig. 4).

TLS Scan Registration. These data are used to create a reference network (our ground truth), indispensable for performing a quality assessment on the WMLS. The clouds are characterized by a high degree of overlap and for this reason are registered employing a global bundle adjustment procedure, accomplished after a top view-based pre-registration. Given the set of scans, the algorithm searches for all the possible connections between the pairs of point clouds with overlap. For each connection, a pairwise ICP is performed and the best matching point pairs between the two scans are saved.

Fig. 3. High-level integrated point cloud from different sources: SLAM in grey, photogrammetry in pink and TLS in yellow. (Color figure online).

Fig. 4. Orthophoto showing the homogeneous distribution of the 14 GCPs, with an elevation difference between P4 and P9 of about 19 meters (by Marco Limongiello).

A final non-linear minimization is run only among these matching point pairs of all the connections. The global registration error of these point pairs is minimized, having as unknown variables the scan poses [19]. To define a common reference system for all the items produced, the coordinates of the 14 GCPs used for photogrammetric orientation are imported as external references into the TLS station registration process. The RMSE on the registration is about 3.4 mm and the maximum value is 32.4 mm.

2.4   Accuracy Assessment

The comparison between homologous models, produced with the TLS technique and the SLAM approach, is performed according to different modalities. Before proceeding, it may be useful to identify the error components when comparing point clouds:

- The component of position of the cloud, depending on the technology used in the acquisition phase.
- The component of registration among the point clouds, depending on the technique used to define a common reference system.
- The errors depending on occlusions and on the process of discretization of the survey.

Once the error components have been defined, some algorithms are selected to perform the comparison. The main ones are presented below.

Direct C2C Comparison with Closest Point Technique. This method is the simplest and fastest direct 3D comparison method of point clouds, as it does not require gridding or meshing of the data, nor calculation of surface normal vectors. For each point of the analysed cloud, a closest point can be defined in the reference. In its simplest version, the surface change is estimated as the distance between the two points [20]. An improvement may consist of local modelling of the reference mesh. This technique is also used in cloud matching techniques such as the ICP. The difference lies in the fact that the computation of the closest point for the ICP is performed only on sample used to construct the matching pairs. In the case of a comparison, instead, all the points of the analysed cloud are considered. This type of distance is sensitive to the cloud roughness, outliers and point spacing. For this reason, the technique is developed for rapid change detection on very dense point clouds (like out TLS model) rather than accurate distance measurement.

3   Results

3.1   C2C Absolute Distance Computation

This analysis involves the selection of the SLAM path that shows the greatest overlap with the fused TLS cloud, used as a reference for the subsequent C2C comparison. For the case study, no local modelling is used due to the high surface density of the TLS model, but simply the absolute C2C distance is calculated. The designated route is number two, which runs from the west garden to the east garden via the central courtyard.

The purpose of this operation is to verify whether, along the acquisition path, drifts from the reference cloud had occurred, typical of solutions based on SLAM approach. To this end, three portions are extracted from route two (Fig. 5): A - east garden, starting and ending point of the path; B - central courtyard; C - east garden. A registration of the whole route on the TLS model, with ICP, would produce a partial compensation of possible drifts. It was therefore decided to limit the registration to portion A, which is rich in geometric elements easily recognisable by the SLAM algorithm and therefore less subject to deformations. The path selection itself is not random. The designated path is in fact characterised by a very limited number of loops, with a prevalence of "round trips" on the same path, a possible cause of drift (Fig. 6).

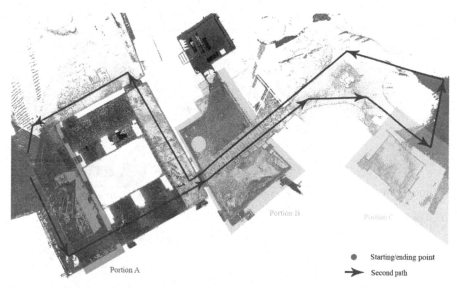

Fig. 5. Identification of portions extracted from the second path to perform the comparison. To avoid the partial compensation of path deformations, produced by a global registration on the TLS model, it was preferred to perform the alignment using only the portion A.

A mean distance value of 2.67 cm is obtained for portion A (corresponding to the mean absolute error - MAE - value). The value of the MAE, which defines the accuracy in terms of magnitude, it progressively increases to 14.81 cm for portion B and finally 32.73 cm for portion C. This shows a progressive accumulation of drift, which can be attributed to various causes. Some of the scanned environments are repetitive and characterised by architectural elements with very similar dimensions (such as the gallery that connects the west garden to the central courtyard) and this factor can greatly condition the performance of the SLAM algorithm.

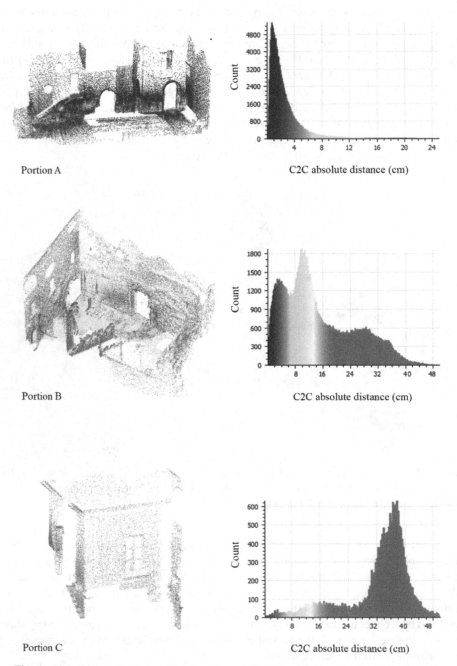

Portion A

C2C absolute distance (cm)

Portion B

C2C absolute distance (cm)

Portion C

C2C absolute distance (cm)

Fig. 6. C2C distance for the analysed portions, with accumulation of error along the path.

4 Conclusions

In this paper, the quality of point clouds acquired by a wearable mobile mapping system, the handheld GeoSLAM ZEB1, is tested in a controlled environment. Quantitative and qualitative analysis of the point clouds are performed using the point cloud of a Faro Focus^{3D} X130 as reference. The main purpose of the study is not, in fact, to define a general integration methodology, but to understand how SLAM fits into a process that includes established techniques such as photogrammetry and TLS. To do so, it is necessary to go through the evaluation of errors, in this case the drift that the mobile system may manifest along the acquisition path.

To further corroborate the proposed analysis, for this case study, data from a first version of the instrument were used, which can only be processed with a raw algorithm that cannot make use of external control points to check the results (Fig. 7).

Fig. 7. Cloud section integrated with optimized SLAM, TLS, and photogrammetric data.

The computed MAE, which defines the accuracy in terms of magnitude, is compatible with the limits of accuracy declared by the manufacturer for a 10-min path with a single loop closure, equal to 30 cm. Numerical calculations are always accompanied by a visual inspection to prove the results.

The main novelty of the proposed experiment is found precisely in the methodology of checking and quantifying, through the comparison of point clouds, the limitations that afflict the SLAM algorithms if they are not controlled by external elements, which may be coordinates of points detected by other techniques. For this aspect in particular, the paper is addressed to technicians working in the field of surveying and the AEC (Architectural, Engineering and Construction) industry. The integration of techniques and technologies characterised by different accuracies is in fact a very topical issue. It is worth remembering that rigorous data acquisition and processing produce a strong impact also on the activity of the other stakeholders involved in heritage documentation, constituting the basis for future decision making in the process of managing the building's life cycle.

Currently, digital innovations, and in particular SLAM, provide greater agility in the process and make it possible to generate 3D restitutions that are more accurate, faster, interoperable, and combinable between different methods. With this application it was possible to systematise the results produced through the application of three different digital survey techniques (WMLS, photogrammetry, TLS), applied at different times and by different operators.

The applications of SLAM are not only limited to heritage documentation in combination with other techniques but, considering the distinctive features of the methodology, can range from expeditious mapping in emergency conditions to the production of models for the dissemination of content to a non-technical audience, for example the generation of a digital environment through the application of VR/ and A/R where the user is fully immersed.

Therefore, future work will focus on improving the statistical analysis of errors and on the creation of a structured database from the fusion of different sensor data by performing an analytical review of the latest advances and potentialities in this field.

References

1. Garcia-Gago, J., Gomez-Lahoz, J., Rodríguez-Méndez, J., González-Aguilera, D.: Historical single image-based modeling: the case of gobierna tower, Zamora (Spain). Remote Sens. **6**(2), 1085–1101 (2014)
2. Allegra, V., Di Paola, F., Lo , M., Vinci, C.: Scan-to-BIM for the management of heritage buildings: the case study of the castle of maredolce (Palermo, Italy). ISPRS - Int. Arch. Photogram. Remote Sens. Spatial Inform. Sci. **XLIII-**, 1355–1362 (2020). https://doi.org/10.5194/isprs-archives-XLIII-B2-2020-1355-2020
3. Remondino, F., El-Hakim, S.: Image-based 3D modelling: a review: image-based 3D modelling: a review. Photogram. Rec. **21**(115), 269–291 (2006). https://doi.org/10.1111/j.1477-9730.2006.00383.x
4. Francois, B.: Review of 20 years of range sensor development. J. Electron. Imaging **13**(1), 231–243 (2004). https://doi.org/10.1117/1.1631921
5. Guidi, G., Beraldin, J.A.: Acquisizione 3D e modellazione poligonale: dall'oggetto fisico al suo calco digitale. Poli. Design **2004**, 189 (2004)
6. Torres-Martínez, J.A., Sánchez-Aparicio, L.J., Hernández-López, D., González-Aguilera, D.: Combining geometrical and radiometrical features in the evaluation of rock art paintings. Digital Appl. Archaeol. Cul. Heritage **5**, 10–20 (2017). https://doi.org/10.1016/j.daach.2017.04.001
7. Sánchez-Aparicio, L.J., Del Pozo, S., Ramos, L.F., Arce, A., Fernandes, F.M.: Heritage site preservation with combined radiometric and geometric analysis of TLS data. Autom. Constr. **85**, 24–39 (2018). https://doi.org/10.1016/j.autcon.2017.09.023

8. Guidi, G., Beraldin, J.-A., Ciofi, S., Atzeni, C.: Fusion of range camera and photogrammetry: a systematic procedure for improving 3-D models metric accuracy. IEEE Trans. Syst. Man Cybern. Part B (Cybernetics) **33**(4), 667–676 (2003). https://doi.org/10.1109/TSMCB.2003.814282
9. Al-Hamad, A., El-Sheimy, N.: Smartphones based mobile mapping systems. Int. Arch. Photogram. Remote Sens. Spatial Inform. Sci. **XL–5**, 29–34 (2014). https://doi.org/10.5194/isprsarchives-XL-5-29-2014
10. Limongiello, M., Ronchi, D., Albano, V.: BLK2GO for DTM generation in highly vegetated area for detecting and documenting archaeological earthwork anomalies. In: Proceeding of Metroarchaeo - Metrology for Archaeology and Cultural Heritag (2020)
11. di Filippo, A., Sánchez-Aparicio, L.J., Barba, S., Martín-Jiménez, J.A., Mora, R., González-Aguilera, D.: Use of a wearable mobile laser system in seamless indoor 3D mapping of a complex historical site. Remote Sens. **10**(12), 1897 (2018). https://doi.org/10.3390/rs1012 1897
12. Ortiz-Coder, P., Sánchez-Ríos, A.: An integrated solution for 3D heritage modeling based on videogrammetry and V-SLAM technology. Remote Sens. **12**(9), 1529 (2020). https://doi.org/10.3390/rs12091529
13. Di Stefano, F., Gorreja, A., Malinverni, E.S., Mariotti, C.: Knowledge modeling for heritage conservation process: from survey to HBIM implementation. Int. Arch. Photogram. Remote Sens. Spatial Inform. Sci. **XLIV-4/W1-2020**, 19–26 (2020). https://doi.org/10.5194/isprs-arc hives-XLIV-4-W1-2020-19-2020
14. Mandelli, A., Achille, C., Tommasi, C., Fassi, F.: Integration of 3D models and diagnostic analyses through a conservation-oriented information system. Int. Arch. Photogram. Remote Sens. Spatial Inform. Sci. **XLII-2/W1-2017**, 497–504 (2017). https://doi.org/10.5194/isprs-archives-XLII-2-W5-497-2017
15. Bosse, M., Zlot, R., Flick, P.: Zebedee: design of a spring-mounted 3-D range sensor with application to mobile mapping. IEEE Trans. Rob. **28**(5), 1104–1119 (2012). https://doi.org/10.1109/TRO.2012.2200990
16. Grisetti, G., Kümmerle, R., Stachniss, C., Burgard, W.: A tutorial on graph-based SLAM. IEEE Intell. Transp. Syst. Mag. **2**(4), 31–43 (2010). https://doi.org/10.1109/MITS.2010.939925
17. Besl, P., McKay, N.: Method for registration of 3-D shapes, vol. 1611. Robotics '91. SPIE, (1992)
18. Chen, Y., Medioni, G.: Object modelling by registration of multiple range images. Image Vis. Comput. **10**(3), 145–155 (1992). https://doi.org/10.1016/0262-8856(92)90066-C
19. Santamaría, J., Cordón, O., Damas, S.: A comparative study of state-of-the-art evolutionary image registration methods for 3D modeling. Comput. Vis. Image Underst. **115**(9), 1340–1354 (2011). https://doi.org/10.1016/j.cviu.2011.05.006
20. Lague, D., Brodu, N., Leroux, J.: Accurate 3D comparison of complex topography with terrestrial laser scanner: application to the Rangitikei canyon (N-Z). ISPRS J. Photogramm. Remote. Sens. **82**, 10–26 (2013). https://doi.org/10.1016/j.isprsjprs.2013.04.009

The Circular City Implementation: Cultural Heritage and Digital Technology

Martina Bosone[1]([envelope]) [iD], Francesca Nocca[2] [iD], and Luigi Fusco Girard[2] [iD]

[1] Institute for Research on Innovation and Services for Development (IRISS) – National Research Council (CNR), Guglielmo Sanfelice Street, 8, Naples, Italy
m.bosone@iriss.cnr.it
[2] University of Naples "Federico II", Forno Vecchio Street, 36, 80134 Naples, Italy
{francesca.nocca,girard}@unina.it

Abstract. In a word that is increasingly facing issues related to climate change, environmental degradation, economic crisis and social inequalities, rethinking the urban development models is becoming an "imperative". Furthermore, the COVID-19 is accelerating this necessity. In fact, the health emergency has affected almost all sectors, determining radical change in economic and social systems. Tourism and culture are among those most affected and therefore they require strategies to support their recovery and to strengthen their resilience for the future. The closure of cultural venues has highlighted the importance of finding alternative ways to join cultural heritage and to allow it continuing to develop its productive potential. In this context, the importance of the opportunities offered by digital technologies for conservation, valorization and enjoyment of cultural heritage has emerged. This study proposes the circular city as a new urban development model to achieve a more sustainable future, focusing in particular on cultural heritage as an entry point to implement this model. Furthermore, the role of technology is investigated as "enabler" of inclusive and sustainable culture-based development processes for supporting the implementation of the circular city model.

Keywords: Circular city · Cultural-led urban development · Digital technology

1 Introduction

In a word that is increasingly facing issues related to climate change, environmental degradation, economic crisis and social inequalities, rethinking the urban development models is becoming an "imperative". Urban activities (construction, energy production, industrial production, etc.) are increasingly degrading urban space and producing negative impacts on ecosystems and quality of life.

Cities represent 85% of global GDP production and are collectors of materials and nutrients, accounting for 75% of natural resource consumption. Cities are also responsible of 60–80% of greenhouse gas emissions and produce 50% of global waste. These are signs of its organization, of its linear "take, make, waste" economy.

© Springer Nature Switzerland AG 2021
M. Rauterberg (Ed.): HCII 2021, LNCS 12794, pp. 40–62, 2021.
https://doi.org/10.1007/978-3-030-77411-0_4

Considering their high concentration of resources, materials, data and talent, they are among the "best candidates" to lead the transition to new development models, such as the circular economy model[1].

Today, urban development models are even more investigated because of the pandemic due to COVID-19. The health emergency has changed the way all populations live and work and is having impacts on all sectors. It is also forcing a reformulation of urban studies. In fact, the spatial organization of the city, as well as specific aspects related for example to mobility and production systems, have to be reformulated to meet the changes due to the health crisis.

The crisis due to the COVID-19 pandemic has affected almost all sectors. Tourism and culture are among those most affected and therefore they require strategies to support their recovery and to strengthen their resilience for the future.

Today it is the pandemic crisis, but in the future, other phenomena can "put cities in crisis". Therefore, urban development models capable of making cities resilient and ready to manage their own fragilities are needed.

In this perspective, the United Nations has drafted in recent years the 2030 Agenda [1] and the New Urban Agenda [2], two important strategic documents to guide the achievement of sustainable urban development. The 2030 Agenda includes 17 Sustainable Development Goals (SDGs), for a total of 169 targets. Among the various goals, closely interconnected, there is one that refers explicitly to cities, Goal 11: "Make cities and human settlements inclusive, safe, resilient and sustainable".

Furthermore, the New Urban Agenda, adopted in 2016 during the Habitat III Conference, represents a "translation" of the principles of the 2030 Agenda in space, that is in the city and the territory, representing an interesting opportunity to address the role of cities in sustainable development.

Here the circular city is proposed as a new urban development model to achieve a more sustainable future. In this model, the importance of assuming the organization of natural systems (in which "nothing is waste") as a paradigm to organize the city's systems is highlighted. The circular city model is characterized by the principles of the circular economy making an urban system more regenerative and accessible [3, 4]. However, the circular city cannot be considered as a simple sum of urban circular economy projects [5], but it is linked to a systemic vision of the city as a "complex system" [6].

In particular, the attention is focused on cultural heritage, as an entry point to implement the circular city model [7]. The role of technology is investigated as "enabler" of inclusive and sustainable culture-based development processes able to implement the circular city model.

Today, that is in this moment of crisis due to the health emergency, the green and digital transition (which represent our generational challenges) become even more important than before [8]. In fact, there are many investments foreseen in the European recovery plan in this perspective that guarantees an acceleration in this direction, always ensuring that people are at the heart of the recovery [8].

Also in one of the two recent documents of the European Commission on the human-centred city, digitization is presented as one of the "three issues that cut across and shape the overall dynamic landscape of cities and their potential futures" (p. 25) [9].

---

[1] https://www.ellenmacarthurfoundation.org/explore/cities-and-the-circular-economy.

Indeed, digitization is a phenomenon that is already showing its impacts at different levels and in different sectors [10, 11]. It is therefore necessary to fully understand and exploit its potential to facilitate the transition to a circular city model capable of "make cities and human settlements inclusive, safe, resilient and sustainable" [1].

The use of digital technologies for the implementation of the circular model requires a paradigm shift in which all economic values co-exist and co-evolve with ecological values and with social/human ones, thus allowing the implementation of a human-centred strategy [12, 13].

After an analysis of international documents about the use of digital tools in cultural field (Sect. 2), the circular city model and the cultural heritage as the entrance point for its implementation are proposed (Sect. 3). The attention is then focused on the role of digitalization in cultural heritage conservation and valorization (Sect. 4) and on the experience of urban regeneration held in the cultural site of Catacombe di San Gennaro (Naples, Italy) (Sect. 5) in which digital technologies have played a key role for the success of the conservation and valorization strategies. Thus, the importance of value-centred approach in urban circular strategies is highlighted to emphasize the multidimensional productivity of the conservation and valorization of cultural heritage through digital technologies (Sect. 6).

2 Digital Technologies for Cultural Heritage

Cities are particularly rich and diverse in terms of culture. This aspect has influenced the elaboration of development strategies which, over time, have increasingly emphasized the central role of cultural heritage as a driver of development [14–17].

Furthermore, cities change and evolve over time. So, it is necessary to develop strategies capable of adapting over time to the dynamics of change, adopting approaches and tools able to meet community's need [18, 19]. Digital technologies can play a central role in supporting the culture-led development strategies and thus, in conservation, valorization and enjoyment of cultural heritage.

In recent times, the European Commission has supported the culture-based development policies of the Member States with strategies aimed to favor the use of digital technologies both for virtual enjoyment and conservation and valorization cultural heritage activities [11]. Underlying the many projects undertaken is the view that the use of digital technologies can play an essential role not only in fostering cultural experiences, knowledge creation, conservation, valorization and enjoyment of cultural heritage across borders, but also in producing wider social and economic benefits, positively influencing other sectors such as tourism, education and the creative industries[2].

The European Year of Cultural Heritage 2018 and the recent European Framework for Action on Cultural Heritage [9] have highlighted the importance of digital solutions to make cultural heritage more accessible to all, putting this goal at the centre of policy initiatives and legislations [20, 21].

In order to monitor progress in the implementation of policies established at European level, the European Commission has set up an Expert Group on Digital Cultural Heritage

---

[2] https://ec.europa.eu/digital-single-market/en/news/eu-member-states-sign-cooperate-digiti sing-cultural-heritage.

and Europeana (DCHE) which, continuing the work of the Member States' Expert Group on Digitisation and Digital Preservation, reviews and discusses the choices made in the area of digitization, online accessibility of cultural material and digital preservation. Indeed, the creation of the Europeana platform (https://www.europeana.eu/it) aims to strengthen the "cultural heritage community" [22] through a renewed cultural supply favored by digital technologies and by partnerships with key players in the cultural sector.

Through the DCHE, following the clear need to widen online access to cultural heritage highlighted also by COVID-19, the Commission has defined "Basic Principles" [11] to enable all actors in the cultural sector in 3D digitization processes. The Principles emphasize that the digital technologies have the advantage that they can be implemented at several levels and for different purposes. Particularly for cultural heritage, their use opens up new horizons both from the point of view of conservation, use, valorization and transmission for future generations.

Considering the advantages of the use of digital technologies, they should be incorporated into future strategies for the conservation and valorization of cultural heritage, fostering 3D digitization processes, strengthening cross-sectoral cooperation, developing new skills, improving citizen engagement and supporting spillovers in other sectors [9].

New technologies can offer an opportunity to creatively regenerate tangible and intangible values of cultural heritage, also stimulating the emergence of new organizational forms for the management, conservation and valorization of cultural heritage[3]. Indeed, digital technologies have the advantage of both enabling institutions to renew their approaches and tools for the preservation, knowledge, use and management of cultural heritage, and of increasing people's interest by fostering greater cultural accessibility [23].

The creation of heritage communities [24], which until now has been experimented in the spatial dimension of cities, during the pandemic has found in the virtual dimension a new space in which to stimulate the sharing of values and facilitate cultural exchange and enjoyment [25, 26]. The heritage community is linked to the concept of "culture as a common good" [27–29], that is emerging as the product of a group of people or a community sharing this resource on the basis of common interests and values [30]. The "cultural commons" [29] - unlike the common resources described by Elinor Ostrom [31] - consist mainly of and therefore have the advantage of being an unlimited resource as they are mostly information content and therefore their use by one person does not affect the possibility of others using it as well (non-rivalry). However, for cultural goods the problem arises of their management and protection [32] to ensure their transmission to future generations.

The definition of "cultural commons" [29] highlights the close relationship between culture, space and community. Indeed, community members are directly involved in the cultural process as, through the relationships they establish among themselves in the environment in which they live, they produce and manage the cultural resource in a shared way, contributing to strengthening the identity and symbolic dimension [27, 33] of the community.

---

[3] http://www.rinascimentodigitale.it/new-technologies-for-culture-and-heritage.html.

The recognition of the interaction between the tangible and intangible components of cultural heritage and the increasing role of communities in co-production processes [34–36] are elements underlying the definition of "cultural commons". In "cultural commons" the constitutive elements of a community would be identified in the common cultural orientation, in the identity based on shared interests or common projects [37], in the sense of mutual dependence and in the active involvement of at least a minority of members who indirectly conduct the activities of the community [29].

Besides cultural commons rooted in physical space, new spatial conditions are emerging [38] for which spatial proximity or direct interaction are no longer necessary conditions for a community to develop a common culture [22, 26]. In some cases, space loses its physical dimension and communities are born whose identity is based simply on sharing interests and points of view rather than on physical proximity (e.g. platforms such as Wikipedia, open source software or social networks, where users express cultural interests and points of view). The analysis of this kind of links between community members thus becomes a tool to understand what the common cultural dynamics are.

Consequently, even the concept of community no longer indicates a static structure but is an expression of relational dynamics that are built up over time.

In this perspective the concept of "digital commons" is emerging[4] to indicate a category of open resources, freely used and democratically shared by people which have also the opportunity to further develop them and to intervene in their management. The binomial between producer and consumer is progressively diminishing and users are becoming active participants in the production, consumption and management of cultural content [34, 39], assuming the role of so-called "prosumers" [40, 41].

In this way digital technologies allow people to be easily connected with their cultural roots and thus increase their awareness of the value of their cultural heritage.

It is evident that the use of digital technologies also concerns areas that do not originate in this field, as in the case of cultural heritage, but which are nevertheless increasingly based on digital infrastructures [42] for the achievement of the goals of sharing, participation and inclusiveness [39, 43]. They are therefore only one aspect of a vision of human-centred development for a participatory, democratic and ecological society in which the objective of the common good is capable of rebalancing the relationship between individual and collective rights.

In order to take full advantage of the great opportunity offered by the use of digital technologies, it is necessary to take a systemic view, as it does not in itself replace physical conservation and does not imply digital preservation in the long term (European Commission 2020).

3   The Circular City Model Implementation: Cultural Heritage as Entrance Point

The circular economy represents a great opportunity for increasing urban productivity. To date, there are some good practices of circular processes implementation at different

---

[4] https://www.igi-global.com/dictionary/social-technologies-digital-commons/7581; https://whatis.techtarget.com/definition/digital-commons.

scales in which some benefits are achieved (i.e. reduction of materials and energy costs, reduction of carbon emissions) [44].

Today there are many cities that are defining themselves as a "circular city", but today a clear definition does not exist. Cities are implementing this new urban development model in different ways [45].

The circular city is a metaphor for a new way of looking at the city and of organizing it, transforming city linear processes in circular processes establishing long-term connections and flows (of people, food, waste, etc.) [45–47].

The circular city is a model of urban development that allows to face together, in a systemic perspective, the social inequalities and the ecological crisis that represent two fundamental nodes of today's city. It aims to manage in a systemic way the dichotomy between environmental issues (goal of ecological sustainability) and social issues (goal of social justice), to ensure the social well-being and quality of life of all its inhabitants.

In the circular approach, resources are re-used, recycled, recovered, regenerated and shared. The construction sector is one of the most involved in the circular transition of cities. Cultural heritage represents a part or the built environment characterized by particular values and attributes that, to date, is almost lacking in the circular strategies of the city (both in literature and in concrete experiences).

Cultural heritage conservation|valorization and circular economy are intertwined, in fact both of them aim to prolong the values of a resource over time, decoupling "growth from resources consumption" [3]. The conservation and valorization of cultural heritage can be achieved through circular economy processes, and vice versa, the circular economy model can be implemented through the conservation and valorization of cultural heritage.

In particular, the conservation and valorization of cultural heritage allow conserving its use values, but also the other values as for example the intrinsic one. Conserving and valorizing cultural heritage allows to adapt the heritage to the changing needs of the community (within a threshold that does not compromise its "complex value"), guaranteeing also to future generations to join it [48].

There are many experiences related to circularization of the processes in cultural heritage field (such as in Dublin, Liverpool, Hamburg, Rijeka, Salerno, etc.), demonstrating that circular economic processes can contribute to reduce costs (i.e. management and operating costs) and that the underused or not-used cultural heritage is a "cost".

Conservation and valorization of cultural heritage can produce multidimensional benefits: economic benefits (i.e. in terms of productivity), social benefits (i.e. in terms of employment and generation|regeneration of relationships), environmental benefits (i.e. in terms of reduction of energy consumption, waste reduction), cultural benefits (i.e. conserving "alive" a symbol of community identity) [49].

4   The Role of Digitalization in Cultural Heritage Conservation and Valorization

The role of technology in the circular city implementation is highlighted in all the definitions of "circular city", both in literature [3, 49] and in the reports of concrete experiences [50–54]. As recognized in many scientific contributions, it can be considered an "enabler" of that city [45]. The use of digital technologies a vital process enabler in the circular city [4]. Technology can create opportunities for innovation and the development of new products and production techniques [50].

However, the technologies, although they play a fundamental role in the implementation of circular city, they are a mean and not the aim and thus they necessarily require a strong cultural base [45].

The transition towards a more sustainable city also "passes through" the protection and valorization of cultural heritage, that are intrinsically ecological policies [8].

In fact, these activities contribute to the limitation of land consumption, the minimization of the use of natural resources and energy and they can be carried out with low environmental impacts. Both physical and cognitive accessibility to cultural heritage has to be improved.

To date, digital access to public information about cultural heritage is limited, thus reducing the opportunities for a wide use by a large number of users.

New digital platforms and strategies for accessing cultural heritage are needed to enable new experiences for citizens and operators and to improve service supply.

The development of digital technologies (increasingly rapid) also requires specific skills and new professional profiles. Therefore, investments in the training of such profiles are necessary.

As above mentioned, digital technologies have the advantage of being inter-scalar and cross-cutting across different application domains [11, 55].

From a social point of view - especially in times of pandemic - it has shown the great advantage of being able to overcome distances, ensuring continuity in both formal and informal relationships. Especially in cities, virtual relations have favored the increase of networks of active citizens on urban regeneration issues (i.e. Digital Social Innovation, Smart Citizens, Digital Commons, ecc.), leading to the authorities' awareness about the importance of the opinion expressed by these increasingly influential social groups. In this perspective, digitization has also opened the horizons to new models of governance based on inclusion and collaboration of different stakeholders categories in decision-making. At the social level, digitization has also had another aspect relating to employment. In fact, if on the one hand it entails the 'substitution' of certain jobs with robot, determining unemployment, on the other it also offers the opportunity to create new jobs characterized by new skills and professional profiles [55–57].

In the economic field, digitization, thanks to the possibility of reducing the costs of shared information and managing information over large distances, has made it possible to reorganize the global economic value chain, relocating advanced economic activities to low-cost locations [58, 59].

From an environmental point of view, digital technologies are creating more and more opportunities for the improvement of the quality of environment (and consequently of quality of life), through solutions that allow a better management of resources and control of waste production and energy consumption.

At cultural level, the increasing use of digital technologies as a tool to join and share knowledge has favored the start of processes of democratization of culture, through an opening towards an increasing number of users and the involvement of the same in processes of co-production of cultural contents [34]. These new forms of interaction and cultural experience have fostered an increase in people's awareness of the value of their cultural heritage, reinforcing the perception that it is a common and shared resource. But, in spite of these positive aspects, digitalization can be considered also as a "social divide" [60–62]. In fact, digital tools are not accessible to all: some age groups (children and elderly) and some countries (the poorest) often do not have equal access to digital goods and services and this makes social differences more distinct [63, 64].

Thus, based on the above considerations, the implementation of digital technologies represents an opportunity to improve the quality of life of citizens and increase economic prosperity while respecting European values of sustainability, prosperity and inclusion. While on the one hand this is a phenomenon that should be managed with caution in order to avoid potential risks (e.g. mismanagement of data, lack of privacy, etc.), on the other hand it is certainly a tool to address and manage the current dynamics of change at both global and local level, facilitating a fair, democratic and inclusive society, ensuring the protection of fundamental freedoms and rights, ensuring the common good through fair and transparent public institutions.

In this perspective, the goal of "circular cities" is not only to use digital technologies for waste reduction [3, 47], but it is above all to achieve human-centred development, ensuring and expanding access and use of both services and digital tools to as many people as possible, towards a more inclusive city in which citizens are "not just a resident but an actor, a stakeholder to be empowered" (p. 38) [9].

5 Cultural Heritage and Digitalization: The Italian Experience of the Catacombs of San Gennaro (Naples, Italy)

There is an increasing number of researches focused on practices that use digital technologies as a tool for valorization, conservation and innovative enjoyment of cultural heritage [26, 38, 65–77].

In this research, the case of the Catacombs of San Gennaro in Naples (Italy) was identified as a good experience.

The Catacombs of San Gennaro are ancient cemetery areas that are located underground in Naples and date back to the 2nd and 3rd centuries AD. They represent one of the oldest monuments of Christianity in Naples. The Catacombs of San Gennaro cover approximately 5600 m^2 excavated in the tufa of the Capodimonte hillside. They are the largest in southern Italy, are located under one of the most densely populated and characteristic neighborhoods of Naples, the Sanità District, and are an important part of the city's history, strongly intertwined with that of its patron saint, San Gennaro, whose remains were moved to the existing catacombs in the 5th century. Since then, these cemetery burial places became a place of pilgrimage until the end of the 9th century. Forgotten over the centuries, they have been rediscovered in recent times.

The recovering process of the Catacombs had to face cultural barriers that affected the entire Sanità District. Within the Ward there was maximum support because the community of the neighborhood has seen this project as an opportunity, a positive alternative for their future. It was difficult to work on the bad "reputation" of the Sanità District and the negative image that the Ward had and that blocked tourism.

Residents have increased their awareness of the value of their heritage, of the favorable strategic position of Sanità District with respect to the centre of Naples (re-establishing a connection rather than feeling isolated). The Catacombs have entered in a symbiotic relationship with the neighborhood, entering into dialogue and supporting initiatives and encouraging the creation of other activities and, at the same time, the neighborhood has reacted well by connecting with the city. This double circular process between the archaeological site and the neighborhood and between the neighborhood and the city is one of the main success factors of this experience.

This experience has had positive impacts not only on the asset itself but also on the context.

In this case of urban regeneration, digital technologies were used to respond to several needs:

– make the "visit" accessible to an increasing number of users through 3D digitization processes,
– encourage a more correct analysis of the spaces that can be used by archaeologists working on the site,
– to ensure better conservation and valorization of the site;
– reduce environmental impact by controlling energy consumption;
– enhance the values of the asset;
– foster the creation of a "heritage community" through user involvement and inclusion initiatives.

Regarding the first two aspects, in 2019 an international team elaborated the 3D model of the Catacombs of San Gennaro and the Capodimonte Observatory for the development of a virtual digital tour. This was an opportunity to experience a fruitful collaboration between different entities: Global Digital Heritage (GDH), a US-based NGO, coordinated and funded the project, establishing as its mission to democratize science and make data freely available to the world in support of cultural heritage, heritage management, education, public access and scientific research. The team also included a working group from the 'Zamani Project' - a non-profit organization that aims to acquire spatial information on tangible cultural heritage sites in Africa and other parts of the world for the creation of permanent digital records for future generations - and the Interdepartmental Centre for Archaeological Services of the University of Naples 'L'Orientale'. The acquisition work, carried out in ten days, enabled the elaboration of a 3D model that served a dual purpose: it was put at the service of the archaeologists working at the site as a tool for greater knowledge of the spaces and also formed the basis for allowing virtual navigation of the site. The latter is now possible through the Google Arts & Culture app.

As mentioned before, in this practice digital technologies were also used as a tool to ensure better conservation and protection of the property and to reduce the environmental impact through the control of energy consumption. In particular, a lighting system has been elaborated through a collaboration between different bodies and professionals for enhancing the historical/artistic value of the frescoes and mosaics on the site, ensuring the conservation of the different surfaces. The system was entirely made with LED technology both for the considerable energy saving and for the ability to protect the frescoes and mosaics from the microclimate and light, or rather the associated radiation, mainly ultraviolet and infrared. As well as being determined by the choice of LEDs, the focus on reduced environmental impact is also reflected in other measures such as the management of the on/off system via an app. During the tour, the guides turn on the lights, progressively revealing the rooms while at the same time making visitors aware of the importance of using electricity correctly and sparingly. All the rooms are also equipped with radon and humidity detection systems.

Although this project is already remarkable for its attention to reduced environmental impact and the perfect integration of the modern high-tech installation in the particular spatial setting of the early Christian Catacombs, a further important benefit is in social terms. In fact, the installation was carried out by exploiting the potential of the neighborhood, entrusting the work to "Officina dei Talenti", a cooperative of young electricians from the Sanità District, formed thanks to the support of the Association. In this aspect, the great potential of digital technologies to offer new job opportunities through the creation of new skills emerges.

The installation of a lighting system specifically designed for the spatial peculiarities of the Catacombs, characterized by irregular shapes and strong contrasts between light and shadow, has also encouraged the organization of attractive initiatives, capable of attracting tourists and generating more income for the site. For example, in the winter of 2014–2015, the show "Le luci di dentro" was organized, part of a wider project called "Sanità A.ppI.L." supported by MIUR (Italian Ministry of Education, University and Research), in which multimedia and new technologies play a fundamental role in enhancing the historical and artistic resources of the Sanità District in an innovative way, putting culture, beauty and humanity at the centre of development.

Finally, the recent "Global Remarkable Venue Awards 2020", awarded by the online booking platform Tiqets, recognized that the experience of the Catacombs goes beyond the "guided tour" in that it is based on a process of development born of the local community and which, thanks to its authenticity, is able to involve users as an active part of an ongoing project of conservation, valorization and enjoyment. In this case, the Tiqets platform was recognized by the project leaders themselves as a useful tool to reach broader categories of users, but above all more predisposed to a more authentic enjoyment of the asset.

Between November 2018 and October 2019, the Departments of Economics of the University of Campania Vanvitelli and of Social Sciences of the University of Naples Federico II conducted a study to assess the social and economic impact generated on the city of Naples by the activities carried out by the cooperative "La Paranza" (which has managed the property since 2006) for the enhancement of the Catacombs of Naples.

The survey conducted on 765 visitors interviewed in 2019 shows that the degree of satisfaction of visitors is particularly high for the relationship established with the guides, whose courtesy and competence they appreciate. In addition, those interviewed say that the Catacombs represent a memorable experience, to be shared and recounted above all because of the involvement of the community and the inhabitants of the entire neighborhood who, through a process of cultural empowerment, have improved their services and skills to guarantee the visitor a complete experience. In this way, not only is the sense of identity strengthened among the local inhabitants, but a virtuous mechanism of involvement of the tourist is created, nourishing his sense of belonging to the heritage even if it does not belong to his cultural identity.

Indeed, some positive trends [78] confirm the above: in 2006, the cooperative managing the site was composed of 5 volunteers and welcomed 6,000 visitors. Today, direct employees of the cooperative "La Paranza" increased from 5 to 40, while 217 people were indirectly employed. 43 cultural sites were regenerated, with a further 260 employees and contractors involved [79]. In 2019, 150,000 visitors were welcomed [78]. These activities have allowed the development of a social economy that has created a network of small cooperatives and artisans. The visibility of the Catacombs and the reputation of the Paranza have led in a few years to a profound change in the safety perception in the neighborhood, with the direct effect of a multiplication of commercial and tourist activities (pizzerias, bars, b&b's, pastry shops, etc.).

In the 10 years of operation, thanks to private donations, 13,000 m^2 of frescoes, mosaics and places of art have been brought back to light.

The perception of Sanità District in the mass and social media, analyzed through a survey media, analyzed through a survey conducted in the main Italian newspapers (1,450 articles) and on Google Trends [79], thanks to the reopening of the Catacombs and the activities of the cooperative in the neighborhood, has profoundly changed, giving the neighborhood an image and reputation strongly characterized in a negative sense by the presence of the Camorra phenomenon. More and more space is given to "good news" and to stories of social rehabilitation.

The perception of Sanità District by inhabitants and traders, analyzed through interviews in the field, has significantly changed, recording a clear and indisputable improvement in the sense of belonging, community identity and general climate. These factors are fundamental, as shown by many studies, to foster processes of entrepreneurial genesis in difficult areas and 'hostile' environmental contexts.

The success and media visibility acquired by the Catacombs has rapidly enabled the site to become one of the must-see tourist destinations in Naples, as demonstrated by the survey conducted on TripAdvisor, benefiting from the large flow of international tourism that has affected the city in recent years (visitors come from about 40 different countries) that the city has experienced in recent years. In particular, an analysis of travelers' comments and reviews, in both English and Italian, shows that visitors are extremely appreciative of the immersive experience in the district. Satisfaction with the experience led to an increase in tourist spending and encouraged positive word of mouth, amplified by the spread of social networks, with a very high impact on attracting new tourist flows. The annual variations in the number of visitors to the Catacombs of San Gennaro between 2006 and 2018 have always been in double figures, ranging from a low of 16% to a high of 54% [78].

The success and visibility achieved by the Catacombs is reflected in the increasing attention that tourist guides, specialized magazines, social media and mass media devote to the site and to the Sanità District, with numerous other related effects (e.g. by urging the CitySightSeeing bus line to include the Catacombs as a stop on the route, thus encouraging the influx of other tourists).

This case is the demonstration that digital technologies at the service of innovative and creative solutions can offer great development opportunities in facilitating the participation of communities [39] in cultural and heritage-related activities, fostering community digital heritage initiatives [69, 80].

The activities mentioned above, together with other initiatives disseminated through social and other communication channels, have had the capacity to stimulate the regeneration not only of the site but of the entire neighborhood, increasing the number of tourists and thus increasing the economic attractiveness of the place for the birth of new activities, improving the quality of life of the local community through the physical regeneration of the context and the creation of new job opportunities, gradually reducing the condition of marginalization that existed until about ten years ago.

The case of the Catacombs, like many other recent experiences, shows that, in order to implement culture-based valorization and development processes with truly significant and long-lasting impacts, it is necessary to develop strategies based on the needs of users [18, 19], including them in the co-production processes of cultural contents [34] assuring, at the same time, the respect of local cultural identity. Digital technologies can be used as enablers of new organization, management, training, information and financing model in which participation, innovation, cooperation have represented the major success factors [81] contributing also to create community life.

The capacity of digital processes to influence socio-spatial dynamics in urban planning strategies, has highlighted the importance of adopting an approach aimed at making culture increasingly democratic and inclusive, capable of stimulating collaborative partnerships between different stakeholders (e.g. among bodies responsible for managing assets, companies, districts, business networks, local institutions and social organizations, universities and research bodies) [82].

In many of these cases it is possible to speak of a "Digital Cultural Heritage Community". Many projects (i.e. Digital Cultural Heritage Community Project (DCHC)[5], Open-Heritage.eu[6]) and courses (such as the one organized by Leuven University MOOC "Creating a Digital Cultural Heritage Community"[7]) have been set up on this topic, aiming at developing theoretical approaches and practical solutions to understand how digital technologies can play a fundamental role in contributing to the interaction between different actors and to the creation of collaborative relationships between them for the initiation of valorization processes of tangible and intangible cultural heritage.

Some apps, created with the aim of fostering community participation in heritage knowledge sharing and contribution [83, 84] have shown that digital technologies offer not only the opportunity to be used as a knowledge tool, but they become a real means to reconstruct a collective cultural identity and memory [33, 85] through the sharing of values, contents and visions.

---

[5] The Digital Cultural Heritage Community Project (DCHC) was one of the first grants awarded by the Institute of Museum and Library Services (IMLS) under its Model Programs of Cooperation program. The primary goal of the DCHC project was to develop a model framework for collaboration on digitization projects between museums, libraries, and K–12 schools. The DCHC project was set among a group of central Illinois museums, libraries, and elementary schools. (https://firstmonday.org/ojs/index.php/fm/article/view/872/781).

[6] https://www.open-heritage.eu/.

[7] https://www.edx.org/course/creating-a-digital-cultural-heritage-community.

An example in this perspective is the platform "MUSEIDE", founded to "give voice" to a community made up of "lovers" of cultural heritage. Born in 2017 from the idea of an Italian architect, today it is a digital platform funded by Mibact (Ministry for Cultural Heritage and Activities and Tourism) for the valorization of cultural heritage.

This community, whose name comes from the union of "Muse" and "Eneide", aims to support the sharing of knowledge and the improvement of cognitive accessibility to cultural heritage.

Therefore, a micro-community of people who are passionate about cultural heritage is being built around Museide. Actors who play a fundamental active role in the community are the "Storytellers", those who "tell" the cultural heritage contributing to the sharing of knowledge.

Museide makes use of a website, a specific app, an Instagram page and a Facebook page as platforms for sharing content and discussion among users.

Storytellers can "tell the story" of a cultural asset, tangible or intangible, by sharing a significant photo and description of the asset itself. After sharing, on the Museide social page, a "dialogue" is activated among the members of the community who comment on the "post" with their opinions, questions and curiosities.

There are different skills, and therefore professional figures, involved in the development and operation of this platform: programmers, translators, graphic designers, art historians and tour guides.

Considering data referring to the Instagram app, analyzing the gender of users who shared cultural content, it emerges that 55.4% of them are female.

Regarding the age of the users, the statistics show that the app is mostly used by young people, especially in the age group between 25 and 44. Most of the reviewed heritage is located in Italy (52.7%). However there are also reviews referring to international heritage: United States (4.3%), Spain (3.7%), France (3.6%), Brazil (3.5%). Surely these data depend on the fact that Museide was born in Italy, but probably they will change with the evolution and the spreading of the platform.

Analyzing the type of cultural heritage, it emerges that most of the assets reviewed are physical cultural assets and very few are related to intangible heritage, as traditions, customs, etc. This clearly reflects a cultural aspect related to the lack of awareness of users with regard to the recognition of the intangible component of cultural heritage.

6   A Value-Centred Approach for the Conservation and Valorization of Cultural Heritage Through Digital Technologies

As emerges also from the aforementioned Italian experience of the Catacombs, the success of the practices of conservation and valorization of cultural heritage depends also on the ability to adopt a systemic perspective that respects the "intrinsic value" of the asset. In other words, it is necessary to analyze and interpret its values, the characteristics of the impacts determined by culture-based development strategies, in a perspective that is as inclusive as possible and based on the expressed needs of the local community [18, 19].

The use of technology makes it possible to implement the principle of 'integrated conservation' expressed by the Historic Urban Landscape (HUL) approach [86], combining conservation and valorization and overcoming the dichotomy between 'heritage to be conserved' - as only historical evidence without significance in the present time - and 'resources to be enhanced'. This approach, stressing the importance of innovation in conservation strategies, allows to interpret it in a dynamic and creative perspective that, going beyond the prescriptive approach of the various conservation charters [87], stimulates new productive synergies between different sectors and actors. In this perspective, cultural heritage conservation becomes a "productive activity" [6] not only of contents but above all of values, both material and immaterial, preserving the existing ones and producing "new" ones in multiple dimensions.

In fact, the HUL approach, assuming a multidimensional point of view, recognizes the links, relationships and connections (even latent) within the same system, interpreting reality in a global/holistic perspective that integrates different values.

This approach aims to promote the complementarity of heterogeneous elements/components (e.g. between a site and its general urban/territorial context, etc.), enhancing those particular conditions that determine a positive interaction between them that leads to a mutual valorization [88] and to an improvement of productivity also at an economic, social and environmental level.

In this perspective, it becomes crucial to assess the multidimensional impacts of the implementation of the circular economy model in cultural heritage conservation and valorization processes.

The circular economy model and the HUL approach offer a perspective to orient cultural heritage strategies towards an increase in productivity at a multidimensional level through the use of digital technologies, while seeking both the "maximization" of intrinsic value and the maximum congruity between it and possible other values [89].

The complexity of this approach has repercussions on the evaluation level. Indeed, considering all the values of a resource, implies the adoption of value-centred valuation methods able to "capture" the value produced thanks to the circular model.

In particular, we refer to the "Complex Social Value" (VSC) [90, 91] to emphasize the multidimensionality in the evaluation process through the combination of use and non-use values. Complex Social Value, recognizing the relationship of continuous co-evolution between these two categories of values, is congruent with the multidimensional idea of sustainable development [90] in which man is at the centre of a system of relationships both with the ecological context in which he lives and with the other members of the community to which he belongs.

Embedded in the Complex Social Value there is the "intrinsic value" [91], i.e. a value in itself that a resource possesses regardless of the presence of man. Therefore, the challenge of heritage conservation and valorization strategies is to preserve the "intrinsic value" over time through the regeneration of "instrumental values" for local communities (ecosystem services - provisioning, regulation and maintenance, cultural services [92].

The importance of recognizing this intrinsic value and granting it continuity lies in the fact that it represents the link that over time has bound man to his context, giving physical-spatial form to cultural heritage [12, 93]. It is therefore a relational value that binds the cultural asset to the context in which it arose and to the community that recognizes it as such. This relationship in the digital environment becomes interactivity [94] and expresses the capacity of digital technologies to strengthen the role of cultural heritage as a driver for human-centred development processes, preventing it from becoming a mere consumer good.

This interdependence, i.e. this conscious mutual interaction between the asset, the tool and the user, is capable of generating a value that goes beyond mere fruition and is based on relational and circular dynamics. Indeed, digitization applied to cultural heritage contributes to the preservation and regeneration of values.

If on the one hand digital technologies are able to guarantee the preservation of the "use value" of the heritage asset, prolonging its life cycle, on the other hand they contribute to generating and regenerating its social value, fostering relationships and nurturing the construction of micro-communities based on shared values and visions [37, 69]. The ease and speed with which digital technologies enable cultural exchange, increases people's knowledge of their cultural heritage and strengthens their awareness of the importance of passing it on to future generations, the so-called "bequest value" [95]. In this case, digital technologies are increasingly used as tools not only for transmission but also for collection to build permanent archives.

Digitization applied to cultural heritage, by increasing the opportunities for its conservation, valorization and enjoyment, increases the "option value" [96] for those who, although not having direct access to the resource, see the advantage of its possible future use and are therefore willing to pay to ensure its preservation over time. This aspect is linked to the importance that people attach to the existence of the good, regardless of whether they enjoy it directly or not. This "existence value" [97] exists especially for cultural goods, as their contribution to the formation of the cultural identity of a community [33] or country enhances the well-being of even those who would not attribute any use, option or legacy value to that good.

It is evident that the richness of the value-centred approach implies a notion of value that is not limited to the economic aspect but is able to consider also other values that include cultural, social and environmental components. This is why it is preferable to speak of Total Economic Value (VET) [98–101], expressing an economic value in which non-economic values are integrated. The integration of use value, indirect use value, option value and existence value determine the general VET equation in which option value and existence value represent the rates of the so-called "independent of use value".

Based on these considerations, it is necessary to operationalize this value-centred approach to guide and support decision-making processes for the conservation, valorization and enjoyment of cultural heritage through the circular economy model, considering the specific attributes of digitization in these processes.

Indeed, as demonstrated by the Catacombs experience, digital technologies can contribute to the achievement of the objectives of the circular economy model and its implementation in the physical space of cities for conservation and valorization of cultural heritage.

In fact they are able to:

– activate symbiotic relationships between cultural heritage and its context through complementary systemic interdependencies, both economic, social and environmental;

- increase the capacity to make more regenerative the implemented activities (autopoietic capacity), improving their ability to self-sustain themselves through virtuous circular processes able to generate plus value at economic and social level;
- favor the establishment of a network of direct and indirect relationships with other activities;
- stimulate the activation of cooperative and collaborative processes among different stakeholders involved in a dynamic and adaptive perspective;
- implement actions for the reduction of energy and resources consumption for conservation and valorization of cultural heritage.

These attributes correspond to some of the objectives of the circular city to which the use of digital technologies [10] is able to contribute. Therefore, it is important to integrate the value-centred approach with specific evaluation methods capable of analyzing the multidimensional impacts of digitization in heritage conservation and valorization processes. In the transition towards the circular city and in its implementation, tools (i.e. evaluation, governance, financial, business tools) play a fundamental role.

The evaluation tools are important to assess and monitor the impacts of the circular projects|strategies, that is to evaluate the efficiency of this new urban development model.

To date, an officially recognized evaluative framework for assessing the circular city still does not exist. However, there are several studies that are moving in this direction[8] [45]. A set of indicators capable of capturing the multidimensionality of the impacts that this model of urban development is able to produce is needed, while at the same time considering all the actors and stakeholders involved in the process.

In fact, these evaluation methods must be able to incorporate both quantifiable benefits (more related to economic and financial aspects) and non-quantifiable qualitative impacts that concern subjectively perceived impacts related to the well-being of inhabitants, improved quality of life and increased social capital.

In this framework, evaluation methods should be people-oriented [45] to ensure the sustainability of development processes in the medium to long term.

7 Conclusions

The crisis caused by COVID-19 showed the weakness of a world based on hyperconnection but totally disconnected with the ecosystem networks of life, ecology, biology. The ever-increasing development of digital technologies and their application in different sectors has on the one hand improved and fostered development processes, but on the other hand it has created an ever-increasing gap between humans and the ecosystem, turning the dream of a desirable future into an unsustainable world.

The current generations are strongly feeling the problem of not being able to guarantee a sustainable world for future generations and, for this reason, the need to protect the current cultural heritage to ensure its transmission is increasingly emerging.

In this perspective, the importance of the role of digital technologies in the conservation, valorization and enjoyment of cultural heritage emerges. Indeed, the usefulness

---

[8] https://www.clicproject.eu.

of digital technologies in the service of cultural heritage, already widely acknowledged in the field of conservation and valorization (3D modelling, virtual tours, cataloguing of assets, diagnosis of pathology problems, etc.), has been enriched by a new vision in which they, rather than replacing traditional methods of conservation, valorization and enjoyment of cultural heritage, complement, support and improve them in order to make "cities and human settlements inclusive, safe, resilient and sustainable".

Finally, a future perspective is attempted, in order to foresee the path that the implementation of these technological advances will take to the worldwide effort to document and preserve our cultural heritage.

For this reason, it has been internationally recognized that a digital transformation is needed to support the ecological transition, exploiting the potential of digital technologies to achieve the sustainability goals of the Green Deal in many different sectors [102].

In the perspective proposed by the New Green Deal, digital technologies (i.e. artificial intelligence, G5, cloud, edge computing and the Internet of Things) are fundamental to implement the circular city model, establishing a new relationship between city and periphery, city and nature.

On this basis, it is clear that there is a need to go beyond the interpretation of digital technologies as a tool for maximizing use and to re-interpret them considering their potential for implementing the ecological and circular economy model, assuming the human being at the centre of this new development model. To operationalize this vision is necessary to recover all forms of interconnection with the ecosystem, establishing a new human-earth symbiosis.

In this perspective, the interpretation of cultural heritage as part of the wider "dynamic complex adaptive system" [6] of the city, implies to consider that its evolution is closely linked to society's one, reflecting its changes and responding to the new needs of the inhabitants, in an adaptive and circular way.

The assumption of a systemic logic and the ability to "read" complex systems, through the recognition of the interdependencies that occur within it, reflects a cultural point of view based on the principle of relationality that represents the conceptual foundation of the integrated conservation approach.

In this perspective, the role of digital technologies becomes fundamental in the realization of this principle and in the enhancement of complementarities, underlining the need to use digital tools following a broader vision than their use only for the purpose of fruition and communication.

It is therefore necessary to consider digital technologies as an opportunity to make concrete the principle of relationality that is the essence of both the HUL approach and the circular economy model. They are fundamental for circularizing the traditional economic model, promoting new forms of economy based on technology, creativity, human capital, and the capacity to innovate [103], fostering interaction and inter-institutional cooperation and stimulating forms of public-private partnership.

On this basis, it is clear that there is a need to go beyond the interpretation of digital technologies as a tool for maximizing use and to re-interpret them considering their potential for implementing the ecological and circular economy model. In fact, if on the one hand digital technologies have increased the expectations and possibilities of public use of cultural heritage, in many cases facilitating and contributing to the valorization of intangible heritage, on the other hand it is also true that they have promoted new organization, management, training, information and financing model based on innovation and inclusion as their major success factors. The creative integration between conservation and development, from a dynamic and proactive point of view [88], contributes to the elaboration of innovative conservation strategies that, in addition to increasing the attractiveness of cultural heritage, prefigure new perspectives of rights and responsibilities of users, who from "consumers" of the good become "prosumers", which means producers as well as users, contributing to actions of co-creation of values and meanings.

In general, digital technologies open very interesting perspective for joining and sharing knowledge, but live cultural experience is not assimilable to digital fruition because it is not capable of reproduce the multisensory perception of cultural heritage. The additional possibilities offered by such tools represent a great opportunity to implement the circular city model without abandoning the importance of putting people at the centre of development strategies.

References

1. United Nations Transforming our World: the 2030 Agenda for Sustainable Development (2015)
2. United Nations (Habitat III) Habitat III New Urban Agenda: Quito Declaration on Sustainable Cities and Human Settlements for All. Habitat III Conf. (2016)
3. Ellen MacArthur Foundation: Growth within: a circular economy vision for a competitive Europe (2015). www.ellenmacarthurfoundation.org
4. Forum World Economic White Paper. Circular Economy in Cities. Evolving the model for a sustainable urban future (2018)
5. Marin, J., De Meulder, B.: Interpreting circularity. circular city representations concealing transition drivers. Sustain **10**, 1–24 (2018)
6. Fusco Girard, L., De Rosa, F., Nocca, F.: Verso il piano strategico di una città storica: viterbo. BDC. Boll. Del Cent. Calza Bini **14**, 11–38 (2014)
7. Girard, L.F.: Implementing the circular economy: the role of cultural heritage as the entry point. Which evaluation approaches? BDC. Boll. Del Cent. Calza Bini **19**, 245–277 (2019)
8. European Commission Communication from the Commission to the European Parliament, the European Council, the Council, the European Economic and Social Committee and the Committee of the Regions. Europess moment: Repair and Prepare for the Next Generation.; Brussels, 27.5.2020 COM(2020) 456 final (2020)
9. European Commission: European Framework for Action on Cultural Heritage (2019). ISBN 9789276034407
10. OECD Measuring the Digital Transformation: A Roadmap For The Future. Meas. Digit. Transform. (2019)
11. European Commission: A New Industrial Strategy for Europe (2020)
12. Fusco Girard, L., Nocca, F.: La rigenerazione del "Sistema Matera" nella prospettiva dell'economia circolare. In: Fusco Girard, L., Trillo, C., Bosone, M. (eds.) Matera, Città Del Sistema Ecologico Uomo/Società/Natura Il Ruolo Della Cultura Per La Rigenerazione Del Sistema Urbano/Territoriale, pp. 69–100. Giannini Publisher, Naples (2019)

13. Bosone, M., Fusco Girard, L.: Nuovo umanesimo e rigenerazione urbana: l'economia civile tra l'economia della scuola francescana e l'economia circolare per la città prospera ed inclusiva. In: Fusco Girard, L., Trillo, C., Bosone, M. (eds.) Matera, Città Del Sistema Ecologico Uomo/Società/Natura Il Ruolo Della Cultura Per La Rigenerazione Del Sistema Urbano/Territoriale, pp. 101–109. Giannini Publisher, Naples (2019). ISBN 9788869061202
14. Unesco Culture: A driver and an enabler of sustainable development Thematic Think Piece, 10 (2012)
15. Coben, L.S.: Sustainability and cultural heritage. In: Smith, C. (ed.) Encyclopedia of Global Archaeology. Springer, New York (2014). https://doi.org/10.1007/978-1-4419-0465-2_1935. ISBN 978-1-4419-0465-2
16. United Nations: Transforming Our World: The 2030 Agenda For Sustainable Development (2015)
17. United Nations (Habitat III): New Urban Agenda (2017). ISBN 9789211327311
18. Blake, J.: UNESCO's 2003 convention on intangible cultural heritage: the implications of community involvement in "safeguarding". In: Intangible Heritage (2008). ISBN 0203884973
19. Fischer, G.: End-user development: from creating technologies to transforming cultures. In: Dittrich, Y., Burnett, M., Mørch, A., Redmiles, D. (eds.) IS-EUD 2013. LNCS, vol. 7897, pp. 217–222. Springer, Heidelberg (2013). https://doi.org/10.1007/978-3-642-38706-7_16
20. European Commission: Commission recommendation of 27 October 2011 on the digitisation and online accessibility of cultural material and digital preservation, pp. 39–45 (2011). https://eur-lex.europa.eu/LexUriServ/LexUriServ.do?uri=OJ:L:2011:283:0039:0045:EN:PDF
21. European Commission: A monitoring framework for the circular economy. COM(2018) 29 final. 16.1.2018, Strasbourg, France (2018)
22. Ciolfi, L., Damala, A., Hornecker, E., Lechner, M., Maye, L.: Cultural Heritage Communities: Technologies and Challenges. Routledge, Abingdon (2017)
23. UNESCO: The UNESCO convention on the protection and promotion of the diversity of cultural expressions (2005)
24. Council of Europe FARO Convention (2005)
25. Giaccardi, E.: Heritage and social media: Understanding heritage in a participatory culture (2012). ISBN 9780203112984
26. Affleck, J., Kvan, T.: A virtual community as the context for discursive interpretation: a role in cultural heritage engagement. Int. J. Herit. Stud. (2008). https://doi.org/10.1080/13527250801953751
27. Boyd, R., Richerson, P.J.: Why culture is common, but cultural evolution is rare. Proc. Br. Acad. (1995). citeulike-article-id:1339814
28. Zou, X., Tam, K.P., Morris, M.W., Lee, S.-L., Lau, I.Y.M., Chiu, C.-Y.: Culture as common sense: perccived consensus versus personal beliefs as mechanisms of cultural influence. J. Pers. Soc. Psychol. (2009). https://doi.org/10.1037/a0016399
29. Santagata, W., Bertacchini, E., Bravo, G., Marrelli, M.: Cultural commons and cultural communities. In Proceedings of the Proceedings del convegno "Sustaining Commons: Sustaining Our Future, the Thirteenth Biennial Conference of the International Association for the Study of the Commons", pp. 10–14 (2011)
30. Radhakrishnan, R.: Culture as common ground: ethnicity and beyond. MELUS **14**, 5–19 (1987). https://doi.org/10.2307/467349
31. Ostrom, E.: Governing the Commons (1990)
32. Hess, C.: Mapping the new commons. SSRN Electron. J. (2008). https://doi.org/10.2139/ssrn.1356835
33. Stephens, J., Tiwari, R.: Symbolic estates: community identity and empowerment through heritage. Int. J. Herit. Stud. (2015)

34. Sacco, P.L., Teti, E.: Cultura 3.0: un nuovo paradigma di creazione del valore. E&M, **1**, 79–96 (2017)
35. Bovaird, T., Loeffler, E.: From engagement to co-production: the contribution of users and communities to outcomes and public value. Voluntas (2012). https://doi.org/10.1007/s11 266-012-9309-6
36. Bovaird, T., Van Ryzin, G.G., Loeffler, E., Parrado, S.: Activating citizens to participate in collective co-production of public services. J. Soc. Policy (2015)
37. Winschiers-Theophilus, H., Bidwell, N.J., Blake, E.: Community consensus: design beyond participation. Des. Issues (2012). https://doi.org/10.1162/DESI_a_00164
38. Kalay, Y.E., Kvan, T., Affleck, J.: New Heritage: New Media and Cultural Heritage. Routledge, Milton Park (2007). ISBN 0203937880
39. Simonsen, J., Robertson, T.: Routledge International Handbook of Participatory Design. Routledge, Milton Park (2012). ISBN 9781136266263
40. Boeri, A., Gaspari, J., Gianfrate, V., Longo, D., Pussetti, C.: The adaptive reuse of historic city centres. Bologna and Lisbon: solutions for urban regeneration. TECHNE (2016). https://doi.org/10.13128/techne-19357
41. Izvercianu, M., Şeran, S.A., Branea, A.-M.: Prosumer-oriented value co-creation strategies for tomorrow's urban management. Procedia Soc. Behav. Sci. (2014). https://doi.org/10.1016/j.sbspro.2014.02.471
42. de Rosnay, M.D., Stalder, F.: Digital commons. Int. Policy Rev. (2020). https://doi.org/10.14763/2020.4.1530
43. Liu, J.S., Tseng, M.H., Huang, T.K.: Building digital heritage with teamwork empowerment. Inf. Technol. Libr. (2005). https://doi.org/10.6017/ital.v24i3.3374
44. Fujita, T., Ohnishi, S., Liang, D., Fujii, M.: Eco-industrial development as a circularization policy framework toward sustainable industrial cities. Lesson and suggestions from the eco town program in Japan. BDC. Boll. Del Cent. Calza Bini **13**, 35–52 (2013). https://doi.org/10.6092/2284 4732/2449
45. Fusco Girard, L., Nocca, F.: Moving towards the circular economy/city model: which tools for operationalizing this model? Sustainability **11**, 6253 (2019). https://doi.org/10.3390/su1 1226253
46. Agenda Stad: The perspective of the circular city. Agenda Stad, Amsterdam, The Netherlands (2015)
47. Sukhdev, A., Vol, J., Brandt, K., Yeoman, R.: Cities in the circular economy: the role of digital technology (2018)
48. World Commission on Environment and Development Brundtland Report - Our common future. Our Common Futur. (2017)
49. Nocca, F.: The role of cultural heritage in sustainable development: Multidimensional indicators as decision-making tool. Sustain **9** (2017). https://doi.org/10.3390/su9101882
50. Circle Economy Circular Glasgow: A vision and action plan for the city of Glasgow (2016). https://circularglasgow.com/wp-content/uploads/2019/01/Glasgow-City-Scan.pdf. Accessed 12 July 2020
51. Circle Economy: Circular Amsterdam: A vision and action agenda for the city and metropolitan area, Amsterdam (2016)
52. Gemeente Rotterdam: Roadmap Circular Economy Rotterdam. Gemeente Rotterdam, Rotterdam, The Netherlands (2016)
53. LWARB: London's circular economy route map – Circular London. LWARB, London, UK (2017)
54. Mairie de Paris: White paper on the circular economy of greater Paris. Mairie de Paris, Paris, France (2017)
55. Kuusisto, M.: Organizational effects of digitalization: a literature review. Int. J. Organ. Theory Behav. (2017)

56. Dachs, B.: The Impact of New Technologies on the Labour Market and the Social Economy (2018). ISBN 9789284625864

57. Aksoy, C.G., Giesing, Y., Laurentsyeva, N., Wirsching, E.: Skills, employment and automation. In: Transition Report 2018-19. Work in transition (2018)

58. Henriette, E., Feki, M., Boughzala, I.: The shape of digital transformation: a systematic literature review. Mediterr. Conf. Inf. Syst. Proc. **10**, 431-443 (2015)

59. Freddi, D.: Digitalisation and employment in manufacturing. AI Soc. (2018). https://doi. org/10.1007/s00146-017-0740-5

60. Warschauer, M.: Technology and Social Inclusion: Rethinking the Digital Divide. MIT Press, London (2004)

61. Alam, K., Imran, S.: The digital divide and social inclusion among refugee migrants: a case in regional Australia. Inf. Technol. People (2015). https://doi.org/10.1108/ITP-04-2014-0083

62. Andrade, A.D., Doolin, B.: Information and communication technology and the social inclusion of refugees. MIS Q. Manag. Inf. Syst. (2016)

63. Helsper, E.: Digital Inclusion: An Analysis of Social Disadvantage and the Information Society, London, UK (2008)

64. Sourbati, M.: Disabling communications? A capabilities perspective on media access, social inclusion and communication policy. Media Cult. Soc. (2012). https://doi.org/10.1177/016 3443712442702

65. Rialti, R., Zollo, L., Ciappei, C., Laudano, M.: Digital cultural heritage marketing: the role of digital technologies in cultural heritage valorization (2016)

66. Georgopoulos, A.: Contemporary digital technologies at the service of cultural heritage. In: Chanda, B., Chaudhuri, S., Chaudhury, S. (eds.) Heritage Preservation, pp. 1–20. Springer, Singapore (2018). https://doi.org/10.1007/978-981-10-7221-5_1

67. Ciasullo, M.V., Gaeta, A., Gaeta, M., Monetta, G.: New modalities for enhancing cultural heritage experience. The enabling role of digital technologies. Sinergie Ital. J. Manag. (2018). https://doi.org/10.7433/s99.2016.08

68. Bekele, M.K., Pierdicca, R., Frontoni, E., Malinverni, E.S., Gain, J.: A survey of augmented, virtual, and mixed reality for cultural heritage. J. Comput. Cult. Herit. **11**, 1–36 (2018)

69. Giglitto, D., Claisse, C., Ciolfi, L., Lockley, E.: Bridging cultural heritage and communities through digital technologies: understanding perspectives and challenges. In: Proceedings of the ACM International Conference Proceeding Series (2019)

70. McGettigan, F., Burns, K., Candon, F.: Community empowerment through voluntary input: a case study of Kiltimagh Integrated Resource Development (IRD). In: Cultural Tourism in a Changing World: Politics, Participation and (Re)Presentation (2006). ISBN 9781845410452

71. Mudge, M., Ashley, M., Schroer, C.: A digital future for cultural heritage. In: Proceedings of the International Archives of the Photogrammetry, Remote Sensing and Spatial Information Sciences - ISPRS Archives (2007)

72. Ardito, C., Costabile, M.F., Lanzilotti, R., Simeone, A.L.: Combining multimedia resources for an engaging experience of cultural heritage. In: Proceedings of the SAPMIA'10 - Proceedings of the 2010 ACM Workshop on Social, Adaptive and Personalized Multimedia Interaction and Access, Co-located with ACM Multimedia 2010 (2010)

73. Styliaras, G., Koukopoulos, D., Lazarinis, F.: Handbook of Research on Technologies and Cultural Heritage: Applications and Environments (2010). ISBN 9781609600440

74. Nitzky, W.: Community empowerment at the periphery? Participatory approaches to heritage protection in Guizhou, China. In: Blumenfield, T., Silverman, H. (eds.) Cultural Heritage Politics in China, pp. 205–232. Springer, New York (2013). https://doi.org/10.1007/978-1-4614-6874-5_11

75. Beel, D.E., Webster, G., Taylor, S., Jekjantuk, N., Mellish, C., Wallace, C.: CURIOS: connecting community heritage through linked data. In: Proceedings of the DE2013: Open Digital – The Fourth Annual Digital Economy All Hands Meeting, Salford, United Kingdom (2013)

76. Beltrán, M.E., et al.: Engaging people with cultural heritage: users' perspective. In: Stephanidis, C., Antona, M. (eds.) UAHCI 2014. LNCS, vol. 8514, pp. 639–649. Springer, Cham (2014). https://doi.org/10.1007/978-3-319-07440-5_58

77. Mancini, F.: Incorporating user participation in heritage institutions: approaching institutional strategies in relation to new social media and audience needs. J. New Media Mass Commun. **2**, 1–15 (2015)

78. Izzo, F.: Catacombe di Napoli L'impatto economico. In: Proceedings of the Cultura e Sociale muovono il Sud. Il modello Catacombe di Napoli: 50 anni dopo l'apertura, 10 dalla loro rinascita; Naples (2019)

79. Sannino, C.: La Repubblica - Napoli. Naples (2019). p. 9

80. Tait, E., Macleod, M., Beel, D., Wallace, C., Mellish, C., Taylor, S.: Linking to the past: an analysis of community digital heritage initiatives. Aslib Proc. New Inf. Perspect. (2013). https://doi.org/10.1108/AP-05-2013-0039

81. Re, A.: Patrimonio culturale – Processi di valorizzazione e governance del patrimonio culturale. https://www.symbola.net/approfondimento/patrimonio-culturale-processi-di-valorizzazione-e-governance-del-patrimonio-culturale-2/

82. Nuccio, M.R.: Tecnologie "in soccorso" dei beni culturali. IDIBE - Inst. Derecho Iberoam (2020)

83. Noor, N.L.M., Razali, S., Adnan, W.A.W.: Digital cultural heritage: community empowerment via community-based e-museum. In: Proceedings of the 2010 International Conference on Information Society, i-Society 2010 (2010)

84. Ott, M., Dagnino, F.M., Pozzi, F., Tavella, M.: Widening access to intangible cultural heritage: towards the development of an innovative platform. In: Stephanidis, C., Antona, M. (eds.) UAHCI 2014. LNCS, vol. 8514, pp. 705–713. Springer, Cham (2014). https://doi.org/10.1007/978-3-319-07440-5_64

85. Burkey, B.: Total recall: how cultural heritage communities use digital initiatives and platforms for collective remembering. J. Creat. Commun. (2019). https://doi.org/10.1177/0973258619868045

86. UNESCO Recommendation on Historic Urban Landscape (2011)

87. Bandarin, F., van Oers, R.: The Historic Urban Landscape: Managing Heritage in an Urban Century (2012). ISBN 9780470655740

88. Fusco Girard, L.: Creative cities: the challenge of "humanization" in the city development. BDC Boll. del Cent. Calza Bini **13**, 9–33 (2013). https://doi.org/10.6092/2284-4732/2448

89. Girard, L.F., Nocca, F., Gravagnuolo, A.: Matera: city of nature, city of culture, city of regeneration. towards a landscape-based and culture-based urban circular economy. Aestimum (2019). https://doi.org/10.13128/aestim-7007

90. Fusco Girard, L.: Risorse architettoniche e culturali: valutazioni e strategie di conservazione. Franco Angeli, Milano (1987)

91. Fusco Girard, L., Nijkamp, P.: Le valutazioni per lo sviluppo sostenibile della città e del territorio. Franco Angeli, Milano (1997). ISBN 978-88-464-0182-3

92. TEEB (The Economics of Ecosystems & Biodiversity) Mainstreaming the economics of nature : A synthesis of the approach, conclusions and recommendations of TEEB (2010). ISBN 9783981341034

93. Fusco Girard, L., Gravagnuolo, A.: Il riuso del patrimonio culturale religioso: criteri e strumenti di valutazione. BDC Boll. del Cent. Calza Bini **18**, 237–246 (2018)

94. Marcato, L.: Culturally digital, digitally cultural. towards a digital cultural heritage? In: Pinton, S., Zagato, L. (eds.) Cultural Heritage Scenarios 2015–2017. Edizioni Cà Foscari, Venezia, pp. 507–520 (2017). ISBN 2611-0040
95. Lichfield, N.: La conservazione dell'ambiente costruito e lo sviluppo: verso un valore culturale totale. In: Fusco Girard, L. (ed.) Estimo ed economia ambientale: le nuove frontiere nel campo della valutazione. FrancoAngeli, Milano (1993)
96. Weisbrod, B.A.: Collective-consumption services of individual-consumption goods. Q. J. Econ. (1964). https://doi.org/10.2307/1879478
97. Kling, R.: Determinazione del valore economico dei beni culturali. In: Fusco Girard, L. (ed.) Estimo ed economia ambientale: le nuove frontiere nel campo della valutazione. FrancoAngeli, Milano (1993)
98. Krutilla, J.V.: Conservation reconsidered. Am. Econ. Rev. **57**, 777–786 (1967)
99. Turner, R.K., Pearce, D.W.: Sustainable economic development: economic and ethical principles. In: Economics and Ecology (1993)
100. Pearce, D., Atkinson, G., Mourato, S.: Total economic value. In: Cost-Benefit Analysis and the Environment: Recent Developments (2006). ISBN 9789264010055
101. Randall, A., Stoll, J.R.: Existence value in a total value framework. In: Rowe, R.D., Chestnut, L.G. (eds.) Managing Air Quality and Scenic Resources at National Parks and Wilderness Areas. Westview Press, Boulder (1983)
102. European Commission: The European Green Deal. Eur. Comm. (2019). https://doi.org/10.1017/CBO9781107415324.004
103. Mercer, C.: Towards Cultural Citizenship: Tools for Cultural Policy and Development (2012). ISBN 9178446228

Research on Digital Dissemination of Chinese Classical Garden Culture

Tianhong Fang$^{(\boxtimes)}$ and Fanfan Zhao

School of Art Design and Media, East China University of Science and Technology,
Shanghai, China
thfang@ecust.edu.cn

Abstract. Chinese classical garden is one of the three major garden systems in the world. It is recognized as the mother of the world garden. It carries the profound Chinese traditional spiritual and cultural heritage, and has important protection, inheritance and dissemination value. In recent years, the rapid development of digital technology has promoted the reform of all walks of life, and also provided new ideas and carriers for the protection and dissemination of cultural heritage. Through research, the current application of digital technology in classical gardens is mainly reflected in three aspects: construction and protection, scenic area management and three-dimensional display. However, the application of digital technology in the cultural communication of classical gardens has not yet been realized, and the communication effect of digital media has not been fully demonstrated. Therefore, how to give full play to the advantages of digital technology, build a systematic communication system of classical garden culture, and expand the influence of classical garden culture is of great significance. In order to further clarify the ideas of digital dissemination of Chinese classical gardens, this paper discusses the problems, basic principles and objectives of digital dissemination of Chinese classical gardens from multiple perspectives. In addition, on the basis of Laswell's "5W" communication theory, this paper puts forward the "TC5W" communication mode based on digital technology, and puts forward the basic mode and system architecture of Chinese classical garden digital dissemination, so as to provide some ideas and reference for the current digital dissemination of classical garden cultural heritage.

Keywords: Digital technology · Chinese classical garden · Cultural heritage · Digital dissemination · TC5W mode

1 Introduction

Chinese classical gardens have a long history and distinct personality, especially the northern royal gardens with rough style, the small and elegant private gardens in the south of the Yangtze River, and the Lingnan gardens with unique tropical scenery. Chinese classical gardens cover mountains, water, architecture, plaques, couplets, stone carvings, animals and plants. They are deeply influenced by traditional naturalism, metaphysics, Confucianism, Taoism and Zen. They also widely use borrowing, framing, leaking,

© Springer Nature Switzerland AG 2021
M. Rauterberg (Ed.): HCII 2021, LNCS 12794, pp. 63–73, 2021.
https://doi.org/10.1007/978-3-030-77411-0_5

blocking, contrast and foil gardening techniques. They are the artistic representation of natural garden images.

With the development of modern technology, using digital technology to spread excellent traditional culture has become a trend. The so-called digital dissemination is a new form of communication, which takes the computer as the main body, multimedia as the auxiliary, integrates multiple exchange functions of language, text, sound, image and other information, and combines all kinds of data, text, language, image, graphics, animation, music, film and video information through the network. As early as the 1990s, developed countries in Europe and the United States took the lead in exploring the digital protection of cultural heritage [1]. In addition, in 2003, the "Charter for the Preservation of Digital Heritage" issued by UNESCO included cultural works and information products that were "digitally generated or converted from existing resources into digital form" [2]. How to use modern digital technology to show the classical garden culture, enrich the communication form of classical garden culture, fully show the essence of Chinese classical garden culture with stronger interaction and sense of experience, and expand the world influence of garden culture has become an urgent problem to be solved.

2   Digital Status of Chinese Classical Gardens

Compared with newspapers, magazines, word of mouth and other traditional means of communication, digital technology has created a new era of cultural heritage communication. With the support of various media, the content of cultural communication is more abundant and the audience is more extensive. At present, the combination of digital technology and Chinese classical garden is increasingly close. Digital technology plays a vital role in the construction and protection of classical garden, scenic spot management, real scene presentation and so on, which promotes the spread of garden culture to a great extent.

2.1   Digital Application of Garden Architecture Protection

Compared with traditional gardening technology, digital technology has incomparable advantages, so it has been widely used in the design and planning of contemporary gardens and the repair and protection of classical gardens. The application of digital technology in garden construction and protection is mainly reflected in three-dimensional mapping, three-dimensional simulation and the establishment of database [3]. Using 3S technology, Internet of things, cloud computing and other technical means, combined with smart3d capture, pix4d and other software, build a three-dimensional real model, and with the help of a large number of precision instruments, carry out data collection and analysis, scheme simulation and digital construction, so as to expand the feasibility space of garden design and development, and improve the accuracy and efficiency of garden construction. In addition, classical garden resources are non-renewable precious natural and cultural heritage, a considerable part of the garden has been included in the world natural and cultural heritage list. The digital resources of classical garden contribute to the long-term preservation and dissemination of cultural heritage.

2.2 Digital Management of Scenic Spots

The digital management of garden scenic spots can also be understood as intelligent garden service and management. The management of gardens is becoming more and more complex. The use of modern technology such as digital technology and information technology can improve the level of scientific management and service of gardens. The digital management of garden mainly includes the construction of basic database, the construction of digital information system platform, the dynamic monitoring in the process of garden maintenance, the monitoring and management of garden passenger flow, and the formulation of relevant specifications [4]. Through the establishment and improvement of large database, promote the integration of digital technology and garden management services, so as to achieve scientific management decision-making and management mode innovation. Zhuozheng garden, Liu garden and other representative classical gardens have carried out the construction of relevant monitoring and early warning system platform, focusing on building intelligent management information platform to realize the wisdom of garden management.

2.3 Digital Display of Garden Scenery

The realization of real scene digitization mainly relies on the rapid development of 3D simulation technology, computer graphics, VR and MR and other modern technical means to realize the digital presentation of real scenes [5]. The current digitalization of gardens is mainly reflected in two aspects: three-dimensional panoramic virtual tourist maps and digital museums. Through 3D modeling, virtual scenes and other technologies, the classical garden culture is presented with a sense of time and innovation in terms of content, form and means, focusing on the interactive and interesting user experience. In 2016, the "720° panoramic tour" launched after the upgrading of Suzhou Zhuozheng garden official website has two options: "panoramic" and "navigation". The "panoramic" mode can overlook Zhuozheng garden, while the "navigation" mode starts from the entrance and takes tourists to shuttle through various scenic spots step by step. Through the virtual tourism map, tourists can not only understand the history and culture of classical gardens, but also intuitively appreciate the garden architecture. Different from virtual tourism map, digital museum mainly analyzes the construction process, characteristics and cultural connotation of classical gardens from multiple perspectives and dimensions through scene simulation, interactive special effects, immersive experience, image and video display, etc.

3 Problems Faced by Digital Dissemination of Chinese Classical Gardens

3.1 The Intrinsic Value of Classical Gardens Needs to Be Further Reflected

Chinese classical gardens carry the Chinese wisdom of learning from nature, repose the lofty and elegant life interest, endow the flowers, trees, bamboo and stone with personality significance, and achieve the artistic realm of virtual reality, which has rich and profound cultural deposits [6]. Although the combination of digital technology and

Chinese classical gardens is becoming more and more close, it still stays at the surface, and the promotion of classical garden culture is insufficient. Digital garden and digital garden culture reflect different levels of significance. Digital garden focuses on the presentation of garden, while digital garden culture carries a deeper cultural heritage and communication value. As far as the digital dissemination of classical gardens is concerned, the key is not only the digital presentation of the external appearance of gardens, but also the effective dissemination and display of their internal value and quality through digital technology [7]. The digital presentation of Chinese classical garden should go hand in hand with the spread of garden culture.

3.2 The Digital Promotion of Classical Gardens Lacks Systematic and Integrated Strategy

There are a large number of Chinese classical gardens. In addition to the four most famous classical gardens in China-Beijing Summer Palace, Chengde Mountain Resort, Suzhou Zhuozheng Garden, Liu Garden, there are many other classical gardens worth stopping and watching, such as the Ge Garden in Yangzhou, Zhan Garden in Nanjing, Yu Garden in Shanghai, Huanxiu Villa in Suzhou, etc., are all important cultural heritages of China. However, in the actual publicity and promotion, due to the lack of a systematic and integrated promotion strategy, the integrity of classical gardens is obviously fragmented, and the promotion and attention gaps of different gardens are too wide. With the use of digital technology, the exposure and publicity of famous gardens have been increasing, and some niche gardens have gradually faded out of public view because they are not taken seriously. This is not conducive to the inheritance of the excellent cultural heritage of Chinese classical gardens.

3.3 The Digital Dissemination Channels of Classical Gardens Need to Be Further Expanded and Integrated

The current digital dissemination of classical gardens is mainly reflected in three points. One is to establish a digital resource library of classical gardens through 3D surveying and mapping, 3D simulation, panoramic photography and other technologies, and to realize the true reproduction of landscapes through digital museums and 3D virtual tourist maps; Second, combine VR, MR and other virtual scene technologies to realize the dynamic display of landscapes and enhance the interactive and interesting user experience; third, in the context of online social networks based on user relationships, social media platforms such as WeChat, Weibo, TikTok, and Kuaishou, as well as official websites, utilize the community effect and fan attention effect to promote classical garden culture. However, the above channels have not been fully utilized in the dissemination of classical garden culture, and the value of the community effect has not been effectively used. The multi-channel dissemination model of classical gardens lacks systematic ideological guidance. Digital dissemination channels need to be further expanded and integrated.

4 Analysis on Digital Dissemination Mode of Chinese Classical Gardens

In the digital era, media communication is developing towards multi-dimensional. At this stage, although the Chinese classical garden has been in the process of digital dissemination, due to the lack of systematic communication strategy, its communication effect is not ideal. Therefore, it is necessary to further explore the digital dissemination mode of classical garden with a holistic approach, so as to help the Chinese classical garden culture break through the limitation of physical space and enter thousands of households.

4.1 Basic Principles of Digital Dissemination

The Content of Communication Must be Authentic and Rich. Chinese classical gardens are constantly evolving with the change of history, with distinctive characteristics of the times and profound cultural connotations. Classical gardens cover private gardens, royal gardens, academies gardens, temple gardens and other different types, and garden gardens in different regions also have their own characteristics [8]. In the process of digital dissemination of gardens, it is necessary to be able to truly and as comprehensively reflect the historical culture and structural characteristics of major classical gardens, and respect the inherent value of traditional culture.

Communication Channels Should be Convenient and Diverse. On the basis of combining the two basic modes of offline and online communication, we should clarify the source of information dissemination, audience groups, and basic goals of dissemination, and actively explore the possibility of achieving multiple cultural dissemination channels. In addition, the operability and convenience of communication channels should be fully considered, targeted information should be released, and the framework for the transmission of classical garden culture should be built to deepen the influence of classical garden culture.

The Audience Should be Diverse and Broad. Chinese classical garden culture must be able to break through the constraints of time, space, and regional culture, and face a wider public group. In the process of cultural dissemination, the audience's personal preferences, behavior habits, acceptance of modern new technologies, usage tendencies, and usage frequency should be considered, and targeted information should be delivered. In addition, we must be aware of the international influence of classical garden culture, let classical garden culture go abroad, and let people all over the world have the opportunity to appreciate the beautiful art of Chinese classical gardens.

Cultural Dissemination Must be Contemporary and Extensive. Chinese classical gardens have historical values for their existence, as well as times values that follow the trend of the times. The report of the 19th National Congress of China pointed out that "culture is the soul of a country and a nation. Culture rejuvenates the country and prosperity, and culture is strong and nation is strong." Chinese classical garden culture is an important part of Chinese culture. The inheritance of classical garden culture should always represent the direction of Chinese culture and the development requirements of China's advanced productivity. With the support of modern technology, we will enhance the depth and breadth of cultural communication, and innovate and develop through inheritance.

4.2   Basic Objectives of Digital Dissemination

To Achieve the Balance Between Protection and Dissemination of Classical Gardens. Chinese classical garden culture is an artistic treasure of China and the world. In the process of promoting the digital dissemination of classical garden culture, we must first handle the relationship between the protection of classical gardens and cultural dissemination. Protection is fundamental, followed by the exploration of cultural inheritance. It is necessary to find the highest point of balance between protection and cultural inheritance and dissemination.

Maintain the Sustainable Inheritance of Classical Garden Culture. The Chinese classical garden culture is the outstanding traditional culture of the Chinese nation, the crystallization of the labor and wisdom of the Chinese people, and has the value of sustainable inheritance. On the basis of the existing communication model, we must actively use modern technology to build a platform for telling the story of classical gardens, so that the inheritance of Chinese classical garden culture can be endless.

Enhance the Depth and Breadth of Classical Garden Culture Spread. Chinese classical garden culture should be fully integrated with digital technology, so as to break the barriers of cultural transmission, broaden the channels of cultural transmission, promote classical garden culture to a deeper level, and enhance the depth and breadth of classical garden culture. Fully demonstrate the historical and cultural heritage of Chinese classical gardens and the inheritance and development of contemporary garden culture in the digital environment. Facing China and the world, let the Chinese classical garden culture take root and sprout everywhere, and let many people realize the profound connotation of Chinese classical garden culture.

5   The Basic Frame of the Digital Dissemination Mode of Chinese Classical Gardens

Based on Laswell's "5W" theory, this part adds 1T (Technology) and 1C (Circumstance), and combines the characteristics of the data media era to propose a new TC5W communication model. Based on this, it discusses and analyzes the constituent elements of the digital dissemination mode of Chinese classical gardens, and finally integrates the basic framework of the digital dissemination mode of classical gardens on this basis.

The TC5W mode is as follows (Fig. 1):

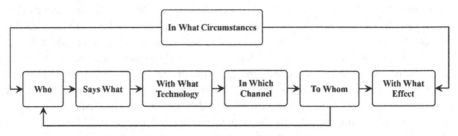

Fig. 1. TC5W propagation mode diagram

5.1 Analysis of the Elements

① In What Circumstances

Stable social environment and healthy network environment are the basis and premise of cultural communication in the digital era. Establishing and improving laws and regulations, ensuring long-term political stability and sustained economic growth, improving the training mechanism of digital technology talents, clarifying the cultural needs of the audience, increasing support for cultural communication, and maintaining international exchanges and cooperation are the necessary conditions for promoting the construction and communication of digital culture.

② Who

Communicators are the starting point of communication activities, and control the communication content. Communicators who can output high-quality content are in the leading position in the whole cultural communication chain. In the past, garden culture communication was mostly based on books, newspapers, competitions, exhibitions, academic forums, works of art and other forms. With the advent of the data age, the main body of cultural communication has been greatly expanded. Cultural communicators are no longer limited to a small range of experts, but extend to all classical garden workers and lovers. Anyone can reasonably share their attitudes and opinions on classical garden culture through the network media. In order to give consideration to the quality and breadth of cultural communication, cultural communicators can be divided into three categories: the first is the relevant government agencies, classical garden cultural heritage research institutions, museums, expert forums, garden associations and other professional institutions or organizations; the second is the designers, builders and park managers who use digital technology to design, build, repair and virtual display the classical garden heritage; the third is the Garden Tourism enthusiasts and researchers who are willing to share on the network platform.

③ Says What

Chinese classical garden is an excellent cultural heritage in the world. The content of cultural communication can be considered from both horizontal and vertical aspects.

From the horizontal perspective, it mainly includes the overall presentation of garden scenic spots, the classified presentation of garden characteristic elements and structures. For example, the "720° panoramic tour" of Zhuozheng garden and the immersive experience based on VR and MR in some pavilions are intuitively showing the park garden and layout to tourists. Vertically, the spread of classical garden culture should not only focus on the construction of digital garden, but also fully explore and show the historical and cultural heritage of classical garden. In the process of digital dissemination, it is necessary to sort out and inherit the history and culture, establish and improve the garden resource database. Taking the unique window culture of classical gardens as an example, we should not only let the audience intuitively appreciate all kinds of leaky windows, but also let them understand the symbolism, difference, role in garden construction, development and evolution of all kinds of leaky windows in the process of appreciation. For example, more contacts can be added in the process of virtual experience, and tourists can click on the corresponding position to have relevant introduction or voice explanation, or directly cut into the relevant scene. From the horizontal and vertical aspects of comprehensive analysis, it is possible to comprehensively and truly show the cultural heritage of classical gardens.

④ With What Technology

Different digital technologies are involved in different stages of digital dissemination.

In the early stage of information resources collection, we can use 3S technology, three-dimensional mapping, aerial photography, computer simulation technology, sound driven technology to build the garden resources database; in the middle stage of data processing and scene production, we can rely on VR, AR, 3D modeling, virtual repair, multi touch and other technical means to process data resources; in the later stage of digital dissemination, the digital garden culture can be promoted and spread through the classical garden digital museum, three-dimensional virtual reality map, holographic projection, three-dimensional animation and video display, artificial intelligence, voice interaction, APP application, etc. Artificial intelligence is used to select, organize and automatically obtain relevant cultural resources, and these data are combined with the narrative characteristics of digital display environment through the way of digital cultural history expression, supplemented by efficient search and retrieval functions, supporting visitor interpretation, augmented reality and robot technology, so as to realize the personalized output of intangible cultural heritage display effect [9].

⑤ In Which Channel

The development of digital technology expands the channels of cultural communication. The digital dissemination channels of classical garden culture can be considered from offline and online levels. We can build a digital museum or a characteristic exhibition hall offline, and enhance the audience's cultural identity of the classical garden by means of image display, holographic projection, virtual interaction, game scene design, immersive experience, voice guidance, etc. The construction of Jiangsu ancient garden digital museum is a good start. There are a wider range of online channels, such as official websites, official accounts, data resource libraries, documentaries, cloud live broadcasts, and some social media platforms such as WeChat and Weibo, and short video platforms such as TikTok and Kuaishou, or cooperate with bilibili to launch a series of high-quality tourism Vlog or garden culture propaganda films, telling the past and present of classical gardens and gardening wisdom. In addition, we can also consider cooperating with network companies to integrate the elements of classical garden into the scene design of the game, so that players can unconsciously be influenced by the classical garden culture in the process of playing the game.

⑥ To Whom
Classical garden culture is aimed at a wide range of garden lovers or potential people. Traditional media are mostly spread in a net-like manner, and the user positioning is not clear. With the establishment of a big data information platform, user portraits based on user behavior patterns and preferences are accurately constructed, so that targeted communication strategies can be formulated to provide personalized services to target audiences [10]. In addition, the application of digital technology has enriched the scenes and experiences of cultural dissemination, allowing the audience to enjoy the real-time beauty of the garden even when travel time is limited. During the COVID-19 pandemic, the Suzhou Municipal Administration of Gardens and Greening promoted the "720° Panoramic Tour" in a timely manner. Tourists only need to log on to the official website or official account to "cloud" tour Suzhou gardens and scenic spots without leaving home. In the era of digital media, the role of the audience has also undergone a fundamental change. These audiences are no longer just passive recipients of culture, but also participants and disseminators of cultural communication. It is necessary to give full play to the influence of the audience in the process of cultural communication.

⑦ With What Effect
The innovative use of digital technology in the dissemination of Chinese classical garden culture, on the one hand, carries the historical mission of protecting and promoting the excellent Chinese classical garden culture; on the other hand, it also deepens the connotation of classical garden culture, maintains the sustainable inheritance of classical garden culture, enhances the depth and breadth of cultural dissemination, and meets the development requirements of building socialist culture in the new era. With the deepening of the spread of excellent classical garden culture, the general public who keeps up with the trend of the times have increasingly strengthened their tendency and sense of identity with classical garden culture, and their cultural self-confidence has increased significantly.

5.2 Basic Framework

Based on the above analysis of the constituent elements of the digital dissemination mode of Chinese classical gardens, the following structural diagrams are integrated in order to provide a more intuitive reference for the digital dissemination of classical gardens. In this framework, digital technical support is the foundation, and the other components of each part progressively step by step, interact with each other, and dominate cultural output in all directions (Fig. 2).

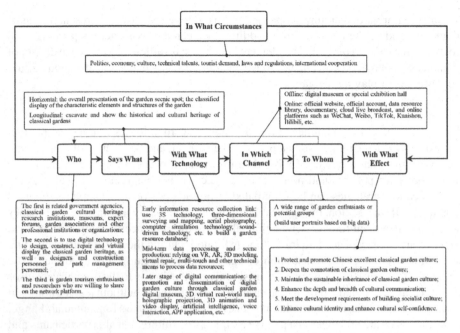

Fig. 2. Digital dissemination mode of Chinese classical garden culture

6 Summary

Chinese classical garden is not only the art treasure of the Chinese nation, but also the unique cultural heritage in the world. At present, with the continuous development of various digital technologies, the maturity and application of information media technology, virtual simulation, artificial intelligence, 5 g technology, etc., enrich the ways of cultural communication, broaden the channels of cultural communication, and become a powerful booster for building socialist culture and enhancing national cultural confidence in the new era. With innovative thinking, the combination of digital technology and classical garden culture can make more people understand Chinese classical garden culture, and make the cultural inheritance endless. At the same time, the construction of digital dissemination mode of classical gardens is a process of development and dynamic change. Digital technology has more potential value, which is worthy of further exploration and application. The application of digital technology in cultural communication will continue to expand and extend with the development of the times.

References

1. Ma, X., Tula, Xu, Y.: The development of intangible cultural heritage digitization. Chin. Sci. Inf. Sci. **49**(02), 121–142 2019
2. Charter for the preservation of Digital Heritage. Arch. China (02), 51–52 (2004)
3. Qin, R.: Digital research of garden architecture. J. Inf. (01), 31–33 (2005)

4. Shi, W., Ji, J., Zhang, Y., Zhao, M.: Discussion on intelligent management system and platform construction of urban landscaping. Chin. Gard. **35**(08), 134–138 (2019)
5. Liu, P.: Prospect and direction of online virtual tourism from the perspective of new residential life. Geogr. Sci. **40**(09), 1403–1411 (2020)
6. Zhao, G.: Deep cultural implication of Chinese classical gardens. Jianghuai Forum (03), 113–117 (2003)
7. Jia, J.: The advanced way of intangible cultural heritage digital dissemination under the background of artificial intelligence. Contemp. Commun. (01), 98–101 (2020)
8. Xu, T.: Discussion on the establishment of "Chinese garden architecture" special heritage system – taking garden architecture heritage as an example. Chin. Gard. Archit. **36**(07), 58–63 (2020)
9. Bordoni, L., Mele, F., Sorgente, A.: Artificial Intelligence for Cultural Heritage, p. 20. Cambridge Scholars Publishing, Cambridge (2016)
10. Nie, W.: Application and reflection of intelligent technology in traditional culture communication – based on Laswell's 5W model. Sichuan Drama (01), 168–172 (2019)

The Method of Mining the Relationship Between the Use of Architectural Elements in Buildings and Cultural Connotation It Reflects: Case of Beijing's Representative Buildings

Wen-jun Hou, Qi-ying He$^{(\boxtimes)}$, Tong Li, and Bing Bai

School of Digital Media and Design Arts, Beijing University of Posts and Telecommunications, Beijing 100876, China

Abstract. Aiming at representative buildings in Beijing, to dig out the cultural factors reflected behind the use of architectural elements in buildings, a set of cultural calculation processes for data collection, quantitative modeling, and analysis have been completed. Firstly, organize and analyze Beijing buildings' entities and relationships and the architectural elements they use and obtain related corpora. Secondly, use natural language processing methods to complete the structuring and vectorization of the corpus. Finally, combine the clustering algorithm results with the prior knowledge in the humanities field to produce conclusions. It concludes that the word vector cluster clustered by semantics can significantly represent the cultural source of the architectural elements in the corresponding category, so the application of the architectural elements to the elements can reflect the cultural connotations behind them.

Keywords: Architectural elements · Cultural connotation · Word vector · Clustering · Natural language processing

1 Introduction

Chinese architecture has a long history and culture. Different buildings have not only different architectural styles and significance but also have traceable similar elements and characteristics. Beijing, as the capital, is incredibly real for its urban architecture. However, the relationship between Beijing architecture and architectural elements needs to be further explored. In the current research of architectural culture, most researchers [1, 2] lack an objective analysis of the architectural elements used in buildings. In Natural Language Processing (NLP), most studies [3, 4] have not proposed a set of suitable methods for analyzing data with an inherent structure, such as the use of architectural elements in buildings. Therefore, this paper takes Beijing's representative buildings as the research object, and innovatively proposes a set of methods to excavate the culture of architectural elements, and finally excavates the use of architectural elements in buildings and the cultural connotation it reflects.

M. Rauterberg (Ed.): HCII 2021, LNCS 12794, pp. 74–87, 2021.
https://doi.org/10.1007/978-3-030-77411-0_6

2   Related Research

2.1   Related Research in the Cultural Field

As China's cultural center [5] and a historical and cultural city, Beijing's architectural culture is an essential part of the ancient capital's cultural resources. The diversity of Beijing's architectural design concepts stems from the richness of traditional architectural culture, and the strong regional characteristics and cultural flavor of modern architecture come from the inheritance of architectural culture, which is of great significance to the study of traditional architectural culture [1]. It can be seen that a large part of the creative inspiration and cultural connotation in modern architectural design is related to traditional architectural culture, and modern architectural design will still fully and reasonably apply the advantages of traditional architectural culture. Among them, traditional cultural elements are the most prominent place in modern architectural design [6], and the design method of using traditional elements in modern buildings in Beijing has a history of many years [2]. The builders have adopted reasonable design and integration so that the scattered initially and relatively isolated elements can be reasonably presented in the new building as a whole, thereby strengthening its historical characteristics [7]. Compared with the building itself as the entity presentation result of architectural culture, the architectural elements it uses are the concrete manifestation and important carrier of cultural inheritance, and also an essential medium for the public to recognize and understand the architectural culture.

2.2   Related Research in the NLP Field

Against the background of today's very hot artificial intelligence, NLP, as a critical part of AI, has played an enormous role in many important scenarios such as machine translation, dialogue question and answer systems, and text mining. In 2013, Tomas Mikolov [3] et al.'s word embedding model CBOW and skip-gram Expressing words into the vector space. The performance of RNN on sequence data had attracted people's attention and then introduced Hochreiter [8] and others into the NLP field, which is improved by adding gated units-LSTM. Sutskever [9] et al. proposed a sequence-to-sequence learning model Seq2seq, and the Transformer model structure [4] proposed by Google in 2017 is also widely used, until the BERT model proposed by Jacob Devlin [10] in 2019 is used in major NLP tasks, A breakthrough has been made. The process of the Chinese NLP task can be roughly divided into five steps: the first step is to obtain the corpus, the second step is to segment the corpus, part-of-speech tagging, to remove the preprocessing of stop words, etc., and the third step is the characterization, which is the training word vector, The fourth step is to train the model, and the last step is to evaluate the model, including indicators such as accuracy and recall [11]. However, there is not much work in applying NLP technology to the field of cultural computing. At this stage, the mainstream cultural computing method is cultural quantification and cultural omics-based on metadata. This article attempts to apply NLP text preprocessing methods and text mining algorithms to research in the cultural field.

3   Methodology

3.1   Overview of Our Approach

The research process mainly includes the following six steps, as shown in Fig. 1.

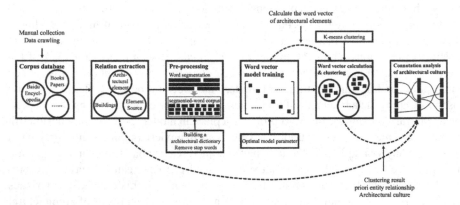

Fig. 1. Research flow chart

Step 1: Establish a professional corpus database as data support. Use manual collection and data crawling to construct a corpus through relevant books, papers, and Baidu Encyclopedia in the architectural field.

Step 2: Extract a priori entity relationship. According to the corpus, analyze the entities and relationships that appear frequently and then obtain the three entities of architecture, architectural element, element source, and the relationship between them.

Step 3: Pre-processing, which includes cleaning the data, using regular matching to remove useless information. Establish A dictionary in the architecture field to ensure the word segmentation's granularity and make the entity vocabulary in step 2 be correctly segmented. The current mainstream Hanlp Chinese Tokenizer is used to obtain the segmented-word corpus.

Step 4: Word vector training. Use the Word2Vec [12] model to train the segmented-word corpus to obtain the word vector model. In model tuning, the word vector latitude is 128 when the effect is best, and the training algorithm chooses skip-gram, which is more accurate.

Step 5: Word vector calculation and clustering. Calculate the word vector of every building element extracted in Step 2. Cluster them by k-means, and use the elbow method to evaluate the sum of the squared errors (SSE) to determine the optimal number of clusters, and correspond the prior relationship between architectural elements and element sources with the clustering results.

Step 6: Analyze the connotation of architectural culture. According to the clustering results and the relationship between the architectural elements and element source extracted in step 2, combined with the relevant cultural background in the architectural field, It is concluded that the clustering results for the word vectors of architectural elements have a high degree of matching with the corresponding relationship between architectural elements and their sources in the prior relationship.

Next, the related work of each step will be elaborated on in detail.

3.2 Data Gathering

At present, most researches on natural language processing tend to use only corpora to train models. This paper considers that based on constructing a corpus, extracted the entity relationship data in architecture from the existing corpus, as the prior knowledge of the research, and the knowledge support of mutual verification for the subsequent analysis process.

Corpus Construction. Wang Ning [13] analyzed the training optimization effect of Word2Vec and found that the stronger the domain of the corpus and the purer the corpus, the higher the accuracy of the trained word vector model. Therefore, when constructing the corpus, the corpus used in this study Composed of data from four sources:
1. Baidu encyclopedia introduction text of architectural names and architectural elements; 2. Articles on open journal websites related to architectural culture; 3. Documents in the field of architectural elements and culture in Beijing; 4. Publications by famous scholars in the field of architectural culture Things. The first and second parts are obtained by web crawler based on the selenium automated web framework, including Guoxue.com, Architectural Culture.com, Yanjing-style Beijing Ancient Architecture Section, and the "Architecture and Culture" magazine, Artisan Ancient Architecture website, etc. The third part contains papers such as "Inheritance and Development of Traditional Chinese Architectural Culture by Traditional Architectural Elements" and "Research on Traditional Elements in Contemporary Beijing Architecture" by Wang Qinglan [2]. The fourth part is the collection of publications through the advice of experts in the field of ancient architecture and history, including Liang Sicheng's "History of Chinese Architecture," Mr. Hou Renzhi's "The Imprint of Beijing City," and "The Weiwei Imperial Capital."

Extraction of Architectural Entities and Relationships. From the perspective of humanistic understanding of the field of architectural culture, there is a certain relationship between architecture, architectural elements, and the source of architectural elements. First of all, for the actual architecture carrier and the local application of architectural elements, there is a one-to-many relationship between applying certain architectural elements in a building. Secondly, for architectural elements and their sources, there is a many-to-one relationship in which certain architectural elements originate from one architectural element source. These relationships exist objectively. Therefore, there is a priori relationship between architecture, architectural elements, and the source of architectural elements. Consequently, they are used as the basis for judging the clustering results of the algorithm model in this experiment. To maximize this relationship's characteristics and make the prior relationship representative, we use the landmark buildings in Beijing as the starting point to search for the relationships between these buildings and many architectural elements, and then categorize the sources of the architectural elements involved. The extraction of these relationships is mainly based on the relevant information mentioned in the current literature and related scholars, confirmed or recognized by professional scholars. Then the prior relationship collection of architecture-building elements is obtained through manual collation.

3.3 Preprocessing

The word vector model training trains the vocabulary according to the context, so it is necessary to segment the corpus. Before the word segmentation, the experiment preprocessed the data to make the segmentation corpus more professional and pure.

Data Cleaning. After the acquired data converted into a plain text format, the text data will have varying degrees of format confusion. To meet the subsequent analysis, we need to clean the corpus data. The methods used include but are not limited to removing the chart information and garbled parts based on regular matching items, removing the page number information, and removing blank lines and spaces. Finally, the original corpus is converted into a plain text file corpus without format.

Stop Word Removal. In the processing of any natural language data, stop words will have a great impact on the training results. There are two types of stop words: one is the functional vocabularies in human language, which are extremely common and have no actual meaning, and the other includes lexical words. The presence or absence of such words has little effect on the semantics of the entire sentence. To ensure that the data after removing the stop words is ideal, we use the Chinese stop word list provided by official platforms such as Harbin Institute of Technology and Baidu. And remove some vocabularies that appear more frequently and affect the word vector model's training.

Domain Dictionary Establishment to Ensure Word Segmentation Granularity. The built-in dictionary of the existing word segmentation model is incomplete for the proper nouns or data in most specific fields, which will cause the word segmentation model to segment these unique professional nouns incorrectly. Based on commonly used word segmentation dictionaries, this experiment refers to the researcher's [14] domain dictionary solution for semantic retrieval of academic resources. We directly introduce the original data of buildings, architectural elements, and other entities as professional vocabulary in the field. Secondly, we use word frequency as a statistical standard to extract domain words from the constructed corpus and construct a domain dictionary in the format of "word," "part of speech," and "word frequency." Finally, this experiment will process the word segmentation's granularity, which means the vocabulary in the domain dictionary can be recognized and cut into one word correctly. For example, avoid the word "Yenjing University" in the domain dictionary from being cut into two words "Yanjing" and "University" in common dictionaries. For the convenience of explanation, words such as "Yanjing University" are called "father words," and words such as "Yanjing" and "University" are called "child words." The experiment reduces the frequency of "child words" in common dictionaries or deletes those common "child words" in common dictionaries and exists in the word segmentation model's built-in dictionary to avoid the above-mentioned wrong segmentation.

Word Segmentation. We selected the Hanlp Chinese word segmenter, which is currently more mainstream. When a custom dictionary is added, Hanlp has a good word segmentation effect. Because this experiment involves professional vocabulary in architecture and requires a custom dictionary, the Hanlp tokenizer is finally selected for word segmentation and output the word segmentation database.

3.4 Word Vector Modeling

In natural language processing, we need to hand over natural language vectorization to a machine for processing and use word vector tools to convert natural language symbols into digital information in vector form. At present, there are two ways of word vector representation: the first is the one-hot representation, which uses a very long zero-one vector to represent a word. This representation method's shortcomings will cause the matrix to be too sparse and can't describe the relationship between words well; the second is word embedding, which maps words in the language to a low-dimensional real number vector through training meaning to words.

The Word2Vec method is a word vector expression model, which is the word vector expression method of the second word embedding mentioned above. The output word vector can be used for many natural language processing related tasks. Scholars [15, 16] have fully introduced the relevant principles and applications of Word2Vec. Word2Vec mainly has two training models, one is skip-gram, which uses the current word to predict the context, and the other is CBOW, which predicts the current word based on the context. The two model networks are shown in Fig. 2.

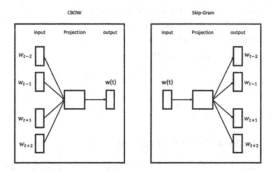

Fig. 2. Word2Vec training network.

We uses the Word2Vec model for word vector training, and the choice of model parameters has a significant impact on the final training effect. Wang Ning [13] conducted a multi-factor comparative experiment on the various parameters of the model in the study of the factors affecting Word2Vec training optimization, and finally obtained:

1. The word vector's training effect is directly proportional to the capacity of the corpus (sentences).
2. The training effect is the best when the word vector latitude (size) is 128, which takes considerable time.
3. In the training algorithm, skip-gram is more effective than CBOW.

Therefore, these parameters are used as the optimal choice for training in this experiment. Other parameters are determined as default values. The core training parameter values of the Word2Vec model in this experiment are shown in Table 1.

Table 1. Word2Vec model parameters.

Training parameters	Parameter meaning	Value
Sentences	Corpus	A large-scale architectural corpus constructed with word segmentation and lineSentence
Size	Latitude of word vector after training	128
Window	The size of the training window, which represents the maximum distance between the current training word and the predicted word in a sentence	5
sg	Word vector training algorithm: sg = 0 uses CBOW algorithm; sg = 1 uses skip-gram algorithm	sg = 1
hs	Selection of training techniques. Training techniques are used to reduce complexity and accelerate training. The essence is to optimize softmax, hs = 0 uses Negative Sampling; hs = 1 uses Hierarchical Softmax	hs = 0 (default)

3.5 Word Vector Calculation and Clustering

This experiment attempts to explore the cultural connotation behind the architectural elements used in the building. In the data construction part, we have obtained the data sets of the three entities and their relationships: architecture, architectural elements, and architectural element sources. Therefore, we can cluster all the established building element data sets to explore each type of building element's meaning in the clustering results and whether there is a certain connection with other entities.

Calculation of Word Vectors of Architectural Elements. After the word vector model training is completed, we can use the building element as the research center to calculate the word vector of each building element in the data set through the model, as the clustering data source.

Word Vector Clustering. The K-Means algorithm is the most commonly used clustering algorithm. It can aggregate the sample data set $S = \{s_1, s_2, s_3, \ldots, s_n\}$ (s_i is a d-dimensional vector) into k clusters $C = \{c_1, c_2, c_3, \ldots, c_k\}$. The core principle of K-Means is to first randomly find k data points from S as the initial center, calculate the Euclidean distance from each data point s_i to the k data centers. Then, assign each data point to the cluster closest to them, calculate the center points of each type of cluster separately, and finally set these center points as the next iteration cluster centers until the maximum number of iterations is reached. This experiment uses the K-Means method to aggregate the word vectors of architectural elements with similar semantics, and the final clustering result represents k clusters with similar semantics. The experiment uses the elbow method SSE (sum of the squared errors) to evaluate the K-Means clustering results. The main principle of SSE is to select different K values and calculate the squared errors of the distance from the point to the center point in the cluster corresponding to each K value. As the value of K increases, the degree of aggregation of each cluster will gradually increase, and the sum of the squared errors will gradually become smaller. When the K value reaches the true number of clusters, the return on the degree of aggregation will decrease rapidly, while the magnitude of SSE Will quickly decreases. The relationship between K value and SSE will form an elbow shape, and the elbow is the best cluster number.

4   Results and Analysis

4.1   Experimental Environment

This experiment is based on the Python language in the macOS environment. The core algorithm model includes word segmentation, word vector training, vector clustering, and data association. We use but are not limited to word segmentation module like Hanlp, NPL module like Gensim, clustering algorithm module, and table reading data calculation module.

4.2   Database

Corpus. We used Baidu Encyclopedia, the official website, and journals related to architectural culture, papers, and publications as corpus sources, using the manual collection and automated web framework crawlers to construct the original corpus.

Prior Data. We use the manual collection to extract the three entities of architecture, architectural elements, source of architectural elements, and the relationships between them from documents related to Beijing architecture or related materials that have been confirmed by researchers. At this stage, we collected 51 landmark buildings, 60 traditional architectural elements, four architectural element sources, and 228 prior relationships.

We visualized these prior relationships to validate better and analyze the clustering results. First of all, the experiment imported the collected entities and the corresponding entity relationships as data sources into the neo4j graph database. We can initially see the connections between the entities (see Fig. 3).

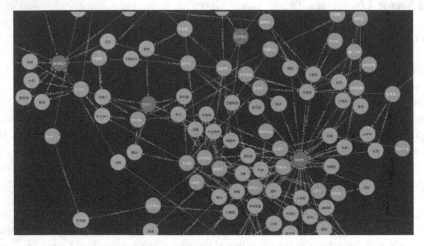

Fig. 3. Priori architectural entity relationship diagram

Besides, we also use a visual Sankey diagram to represent the relationship between entities, which can intuitively see which architectural elements are used in a building and where these architectural elements come from (see Fig. 4).

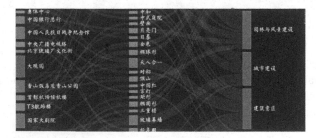

Fig. 4. Priori architectural sankey diagram

4.3 Preprocessing

Before training the word vector model, we need to perform preprocessing, including data cleaning and corpus word segmentation. We use regular matching to remove blank lines and some useless vocabulary for data cleaning, such as chart text in the paper. The corpus word segmentation preprocessing includes establishing a stop vocabulary list and a domain dictionary (see Fig. 5). The final word segmentation database obtained by the Hanlp tokenizer is shown in Fig. 6.

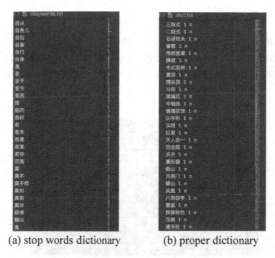

(a) stop words dictionary (b) proper dictionary

Fig. 5. Stop words and proper dictionary

Fig. 6. Word segmentation database

4.4 Word Vector Modeling

After adjusting the training model according to the parameter settings in Table 1 in the experimental design, we import the corpus and train the Word2Vec model to obtain the model dictionary (see Fig. 7).

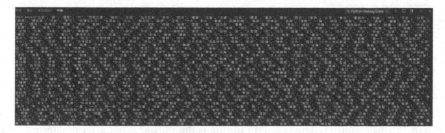

Fig. 7. Word2Vec model dictionary

4.5 Word Vector Calculation and Clustering

After the word vector model training is completed, we use model ['(word name)'] to sequentially calculate the word vector expressions corresponding to all architectural element entities. For example, the word vector of the architectural element "Dougong" is shown in Fig. 8.

Fig. 8. "Dougong" word vector

After getting the word vectors of all building element entities, we cluster these word vectors by K-means. According to the related description of the SSE elbow method in 3.5, when K's value is 4, the error sum of squares drops sharply, so we set the K to 4. Finally, to facilitate subsequent analysis, we match the relationship between a priori architectural element and the architectural element source to correspond one by one the relationship between the architectural element and its category after clustering and the relationship between the architectural element and its source. The clustering results and the corresponding building element source results are shown in Fig. 9.

word	label	source	word	label	source	word	label	source
Hanging tower	0	Urban Construction	yin and yang	1	Architecture artistic conception	Phoenix	3	Architecture artistic conception
lantern	0	Urban Construction	Ice crack	1	Traditional architectural features and fragments	National characteristics	3	Architecture artistic conception
Combination of Chinese and Western	0	Urban Construction	pavilion	1	Garden and landscape construction	rockery	3	Garden and landscape construction
Traditional pattern	0	Traditional architectural features and fragments	marble	1	Traditional architectural features and fragments	yellow	3	Architecture artistic conception
people oriented	0	Urban Construction	Piyong	1	Traditional architectural features and fragments	Universe	3	Architecture artistic conception
Chinese courtyard	0	Urban Construction	Hall of Prayer for Good Harvest	1	Garden and landscape construction	Palace lantern	3	Architecture artistic conception
steeple	0	Garden and landscape construction	Color painting	1	Traditional architectural features and fragments	Ancient capital	3	Architecture artistic conception
Zanjianding	1	Traditional architectural features and fragments	Folding fan	1	Garden and landscape construction	arc	3	Urban Construction
Dou Gong	1	Traditional architectural features and fragments	symmetry	2	Urban Construction	Moon gate	3	Architecture artistic conception
decorated archway	1	Traditional architectural features and fragments	Glass curtain wall	2	Urban Construction	bamboo	3	Architecture artistic conception
Glazed tiles	1	Traditional architectural features and fragments	mural	2	Garden and landscape construction	Hard mountain	3	Garden and landscape construction
Siheyuan	1	Urban Construction	Gray brick	2	Garden and landscape construction	Chinese garden	3	Garden and landscape construction
Three-stage	1	Traditional architectural features and fragments	Hall of Supreme Harmony	2	Garden and landscape construction	China red	3	Architecture artistic conception
Kuding	1	Traditional architectural features and fragments	Cornice	2	Garden and landscape construction	Oval	3	Urban Construction
Harmony of Man and Nature	1	Architecture artistic conception	rectangle	2	Urban Construction	Queti	3	Garden and landscape construction
Central axis	1	Traditional architectural features and fragments	Minority style	2	Garden and landscape construction	Golden	3	Architecture artistic conception
Big roof	1	Traditional architectural features and fragments	Tibetan	2	Garden and landscape construction	Round sky and Square ground	3	Architecture artistic conception
Relief	1	Traditional architectural features and fragments	Framework	2	Garden and landscape construction	sustainable development	3	Architecture artistic conception
tower	1	Garden and landscape construction	Covered bridge	2	Garden and landscape construction	Bell tower	3	Architecture artistic conception
Terracotta Warriors	1	Traditional architectural features and fragments	Diamond window	2	Garden and landscape construction	Sundial	3	Architecture artistic conception

Fig. 9. Clustering result graph

The first column in Fig. 9 is architectural elements, and we use the word vectors of these words for clustering. The second column is the cluster label after clustering. The third column is the source of architectural elements corresponding to prior knowledge.

4.6 Cultural Connotation of Architectural Elements

The analysis results show that the clustering results for the word vectors of architectural elements have a high degree of matching with the corresponding clusters of architectural elements and their sources in the prior relationship. The data shows that the word vectors in the first cluster have a matching degree of (5/7) * 100% = 71.43% with the architectural elements derived from "urban construction" in the prior relationship; Table 2 shows the remaining clusters. The average percentage of these four clusters is 70.77%; from this, the experiment, which has an accuracy of 70.77%, shows that these word vector clusters based on semantics represent the source of architectural elements. Combined with relevant knowledge in the architectural field, we can conclude that the application of architectural elements in buildings is deeply related to the source of architectural elements, which means the source of architectural elements is an essential driving factor influencing architects to choose architectural elements.

Table 2. Matching degree of clustering results.

Cluster	Catching degree	Mean
0	(5/7) * 100% = 71.43% is from "Urban Construction"	m = (71.43% + 66.66% + 75% + 70%)/4 = 70.77%
1	(14/21) * 100% = 66.66% is from "Traditional architectural features and fragments"	
2	(9/12) * 100% = 75% is from "Garden and landscape construction"	
3	(14/20) * 100% = 70% is from "Architecture artistic conception"	

Taking Xiangshan Park as an example, Table 3 shows the clustering results and related relationships. When extracting the a priori entity-relationship, we found the application relationship between "Xiangshan Park" and the architectural elements "central axis," "diamond windows," "moon gate," "harmony of nature and man" and "rockery" and the corresponding relationship between these architectural elements and their sources. According to the cluster labels obtained by the calculation model proposed in this paper, we compare these architectural elements with their sources in the prior relationship. The results are shown in Table 3.

We can conclude that the sources of the various architectural elements used in Xiangshan Park match the clustering results obtained by the experimental calculation model. Xiangshan Park is a royal garden with a rich cultural heritage and mountain forest characteristics from a humanistic perspective. Therefore, at the beginning of the design, the builders considered the landscape garden's characteristics and the expression of traditional cultural fragments and Chinese artisans' output. The same clustering results can also significantly explain other buildings.

Table 3. Relationship related to Xiangshan Park.

Building	Applied architectural elements	Cluster	Architectural elements source
Xiangshan Park	Central axis	1	Traditional architectural features and fragments
	Diamond window	2	Garden and landscape construction
	Moon gate	3	Architecture artistic conception
	Harmony of Man and Nature	1	Traditional architectural features and fragments
	Rockery	3	Architecture artistic conception

Finally, the method of mining the architectural element culture proposed in this paper can also be applied to the analysis of more architectural elements. Scholars can judge the possible sources of input architectural elements and their affiliation with other architectural element clusters based on the clustering results. This information is of great significance to the research and inheritance of traditional architectural culture and the development of modern architectural culture.

5   Summary and Future Work

This article focuses on the in-depth exploration of the cultural connotations behind the use of architectural elements. First, we extract the prior relationships in the architectural field, build a professional corpus of architecture, and then train the Word2Vec word vector model on the corpus after segmentation. Then calculate the word vectors of the building elements according to the model and use the K-means algorithm to cluster the word vectors. Finally, combining the architectural-culture background and prior knowledge for verification and analysis, we conclude that the use of architectural elements is the use of the source behind the architectural elements.

Besides, we propose the following prospects for the current research in this experiment. First, we will further improve the relevant model in the follow-up experiment to optimize the training effect. Second, this paper's research uses the more traditional Word2Vec word cmbedding notation, and then we will try to use better pre-training models such as BERT.

References

1. Wang, H.: The development and inheritance of traditional architectural culture in modern architecture. Dev. Guide Build. Mat. (Part 1) **17**(9), 135 (2019). https://doi.org/10.3969/j.issn.1672-1675.2019.09.119
2. Wang, Q.: Study on Traditional Elements in Contemporary Architectures in Beijing. North China University of Technology (2011)
3. Mikolov, T., Chen, K., Corrado, G., et al.: Efficient estimation of word representations in vector space. Comput. Sci. (2013)

4. Vaswani, A., et al.: Attention is all you need. In: Advances in Neural Information Processing Systems (2017)
5. Beijing city construction master plan.Beijing: Ministry of Housing and Urban-Rural Development of the People's Republic of China (2001)
6. Ma, S.: Analysis on the Inheritance and application of traditional architecture culture in modern architecture design. Archit. Eng. Technol. Des. (33), 862 (2019). https://doi.org/10.12159/j.issn.2095-6630.2019.33.0823
7. Miao, Y.: Research on assessments and inheritance method of chinese traditional urban contextual constitutions. Urban Plan. Forum (04), 40–44 + 27 (2005)
8. Hochreiter, S., Schmidhuber, J.: Long short-term memory. Neural Comput. **9**(8), 1735–1780 (1997)
9. Sutskever, I., Vinyals, O., Le, Q.V.: Sequence to sequence learning with neural networks. In: Advances in Neural Information Processing Systems (2014)
10. Devlin, J., Chang, M.W., Lee, K., et al.: BERT: pre-training of deep bidirectional transformers for language understanding (2018)
11. Zhao, J., Song, M., Gao, X.: Summary of the development and application of natural language processing. Inf. Technol. Inf. **000**(007), 142–145 (2019)
12. Goldberg, Y., Levy, O.: Word2Vec explained: deriving Mikolov et al.'s negative-sampling word-embedding method. Eprint Arxiv, 3–5 (2014)
13. Wang, N.: Research on Affecting Factors of Word2vec Training Optimization. SoochowUniversity (2018)
14. Wang, R., Chen, C., Meng, X.: Semantic retrieval technology of academic resources based on word embedding extension. Libr. Inf. Ser. **62**(19), 111–119 (2018)
15. Wang, F., Tan, X.: Research On optimization strategy of training performance based on Word2Vec. Comp. Appl. Softw. **35**(01), 97–102+174 (2018)
16. Goldberg, Y., Levy, O.: Word2Vec Explained:deriving Mikolov et al.'s negative-sampling word-embedding method. Eprint Arxiv, 3–5 (2014)

IkebanaGAN: New GANs Technique for Digital Ikebana Art

Mai Cong Hung[1(✉)], Mai Xuan Trang[2], Naoko Tosa[1], and Ryohei Nakatsu[1]

[1] Kyoto University, Kyoto, Japan
tosa.naoko.5c@kyoto-u.ac.jp, ryohei.nakatsu@design.kyoto-u.ac.jp
[2] Faculty of Computer Science, Phenikaa University, Hanoi, Vietnam
trang.maixuan@phenikaa-uni.edu.vn

Abstract. In this research, we have carried out various experiments to perform mutual transformation between a domain of Ikebana (Japanese traditional flower arrangement) photos and other domains of images (landscapes, animals, portraits) to create new artworks via a variation of CycleGAN - a GANs technique based on cycle-consistency loss. A pre-trained process on object detection was added to improve the efficiency by avoiding over-transformation.

Keywords: GANs · Cycle GAN · Ikebana · Image transformation

1 Introduction

The rapid advance of Deep Learning in recent years raises an interesting question for both computer scientists and artists: "What is the role of AI/Machine Learning/Deep Learning in the future art scene?". For instance, the machine learning technique was used in artwork clustering tasks [1] as well as art evaluation [2]. On the other side, the application of AI, especially Deep Learning in art creation is of interest.

One basic approach of AI toward art is to use the style transfer technique to transform normal photos or sketches into artworks of specific styles. On Deep Learning, style transfer tasks can be performed by applying generative models in GANs (Generative Adversarial Networks [3]). In the training of GANs, generator network G learns to generate new data while discriminator network D tries to identify the generated data whether it is real or fake. The training process can be interpreted as a zero-sum game between G and D: G tries to maximize the probability of the generated data to lie on the distribution of target sets while D tries to minimize it. GANs training can converge even with a relatively small number of learning data.

A large number of GANs variation has been developed by modifying the basic configuration and performs impressive results on style transfer tasks. Among the variations of GANs, CycleGAN is an elegant method to study the mutual transformation between two sets of data [4]. In comparison to traditional GANs, in CycleGAN an inverse transformation of the generator network has been added to transform data on the target domain back to the input domain. Also, two discriminators are used for the two domains. The training process on CycleGAN tries to minimize the error caused by applying a cycle of

© Springer Nature Switzerland AG 2021
M. Rauterberg (Ed.): HCII 2021, LNCS 12794, pp. 88–99, 2021.
https://doi.org/10.1007/978-3-030-77411-0_7

forwarding and backward transformation. CycleGAN is flexible and useful for art style transfer because it uses unpaired training sets and set-to-set level transformation to learn the distribution of the target sets, which we could consider as an art style.

Classic examples of CycleGAN and other style transfer techniques were developed by taking the transformation between two sets of data of relatively similar size, with themes or categories such as the transformation between artworks by Monet and landscapes photos, winter and summer landscapes, or horse and zebra photos. So, what would happen if one performs a transfer between two sets of relatively different domains of objects. The authors proposed the idea of "unusual transformation [5]," which achieves a mutual transformation between two sets of different sizes and themes. Several examples were given by transforming portraits and animal photos into Ikebana, the Japanese art of flower arrangement, via CycleGAN. It is impressive that portraits and horse photos turn into Ikebana while one can still recognize the original shape of human faces and horses (Fig. 1). This "unusual transformation" concept would open a new way to create an original art style.

Fig. 1. Transformation of portraits and horse photos into Ikebana by CycleGAN

However, there are some limitations of traditional GANs techniques to perform this unusual transformation task. The experiments with Ikebana in [5] show some failures of CycleGAN to transform photos of complex backgrounds into abstract Ikebana (Fig. 2). In some cases, some photos were over-transformed so that we could not recognize the original shape of the main object. The structure of classic GANs techniques was not designed to learn specific high abstract representation and was difficult to learn an object with various sizes in a collection of photos. In our research, we would improve this limitation by mixing GANs with classic Computer Vision techniques. This idea appeared on CartoonGAN [6] when the authors used edge detection to emphasize the weight of edges to fit with the task of the anime-style transfer. Another interesting example is the Attentive Adversarial Network [7] which uses face recognition to improve the performance of art style transfer for selfie images.

Fig. 2. Several failed transformation in [5]

In our research, we would use pre-trained object recognition and edge detection to overcome the limitation of CycleGAN to improve the transformation of portraits, landscape, and animal photos into Ikebana. The object recognition technique would remove complex background while edge detection would be used to keep the original shape of the main object to avoid over-transformed problems. The adversarial loss function of our proposed method would add an "object edge-promoting loss" to the CycleGAN's adversarial loss so that the training process would also minimize the loss of the original shape of the main object in input photos.

Our paper is organized as follows: in Sect. 2, we would introduce the basic concept of Ikebana and its connection to modern art. In Sect. 3, we would describe the concept of the "unusual transformation" and the architecture of our IkebanaGAN would be proposed in Sect. 4. The experiment results would be shown in Sect. 5 and we would discuss further the obtained research in Sect. 6.

2   Ikebana

Ikebana is one of the most important art forms in Japanese culture. The word "Ikebana" comes from the Japanese words "Ikeru" (means "be living" or "to have a life") and "Hana" (means "flower"). Ikebana is the art of flower arrangement where the flowers are given life under the conceptual arrangements of the artists [8].

Ikebana has a deep root in the Japanese philosophy of art under the strong influence of Zen Buddhism. The tradition of arranging flowers on Buddha from China was brought to Japan in the Heian period (794–1185) by Zen Buddhist monks. In the early stage, Ikebana was just placing flowers in vases under the philosophy of Zen. But Ikebana then grew to be an important art form along with the development of Zen, it is not just beautifully arranging flowers, but it gives the path to be harmony with nature.

Ikebana has a long history of development and has continued to be a great source of inspiration in modern art. For instance, we note a series of artwork named "Sound of Ikebana" created by one of the authors, Naoko Tosa (Fig. 3) [9]. In this work, she used fluid dynamics to create Ikebana-like forms from different types of water-based solutions. The idea of connecting Ikebana and modern technology inspired the study of developing Ikebana as a digital painting tool in [5]. In this work, the authors use the Deep Learning technique to transfer portrait and animal photos into Ikebana paintings. Our present research continues the work in [5] to improve the quality of Deep Learning-based Ikebana.

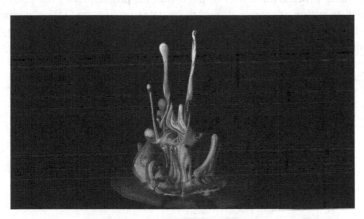

Fig. 3. Sound of Ikebana by Naoko Tosa

We emphasize two important elements in Ikebana influenced by Oriental philosophy which would support our idea of the "unusual transformation" - the mutual transfer of relatively different domains of objects. They are the "minimality" and the "flexibility". Under the influence of Zen, "emptiness" plays an essential role in Ikebana. The emptiness appearing in an Ikebana artwork is believed to provide meaning and be harmonic to the whole scene. Moreover, we call Ikebana flexible as the materials can be placed in various shapes and arrangements. We would explain how important these two properties are in our experiment in the next section.

3   Unusual Transformation

3.1   GANs and CycleGAN

As mentioned above, this research is conducted to improve the work in [5]. The fundamental approach of the method is to use the generative models in Deep Learning to transfer photos into Ikebana paintings. Generative models and discriminative models are two kinds of neural networks in Deep Learning. Informally, the goal of generative models is to generate new data instances while discriminative models would discriminate between different categories of data. Mathematically, the generative model learns the joint probability $p(X, Y)$ of data instances set X and label set Y while the discriminative model learns the conditional probability $p(Y|X)$.

In recent years, GANs (Generative Adversarial Networks) [3] has become a big topic in Deep Learning as their generative model provides a powerful performance on the task of art style transfer with just a relatively small number of training data. The structure of GANs could be described as in Fig. 4 with the basic configuration of two networks, a generator network (G) and a discriminator network (D). The training of GANs is based on a minimax mechanism where network G learns to generate data from random noise while D tries to identify the generated data whether it is real or fake. In mathematics terms, the training process on G tries to maximize the probability of the generated data to lie on the distribution of target sets and the training process on D tries to minimize it. Recently, a large number of GANs variation has been developed by modifying the basic configuration of this minimax mechanism.

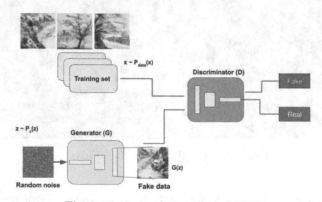

Fig. 4. The basic configuration of GANs

Among the variations of GAN, CycleGAN [4] is an elegant method to study the set-to-set level of mutual transformation between two categories of objects. Its architecture consists of two generators and two discriminators as shown in Fig. 5. Given two image sets A and B, the core goal of CycleGAN is to learn two mappings $G_{AB} : A \rightarrow B$ and $G_{BA} : B \rightarrow A$ given the training samples: $\{a_i\}_{i=1}^{N} \in A$ and $\{b_j\}_{j=1}^{M} \in B$ with the data distributions $a \sim p_A(a)$ and $b \sim p_B(b)$. The two discriminators are D_A and D_B where D_A aims to distinguish between images $\{a\}$ and translated images $\{G_{BA}(b)\}$ and the same analogy applies to D_B. The objective function of CycleGAN contains two types of loss: adversarial losses for matching the generated images to the target images; and cycle consistency loss for preventing the mappings G_{AB} and G_{BA} from contradicting each other.

Adversarial Loss: The adversarial loss applies to both mapping functions.

- For the mapping function $G_{AB} : A \rightarrow B$ and its discriminator D_B:

$$\mathcal{L}_{GAN}(G_{AB}, D_B, A, B)$$
$$= \mathbb{E}_{b \sim p_B(b)}\big[\log D_B(b)\big]$$
$$+ \mathbb{E}_{a \sim p_A(a)}[\log(1 - D_B(G_{AB}(a)))] \tag{1}$$

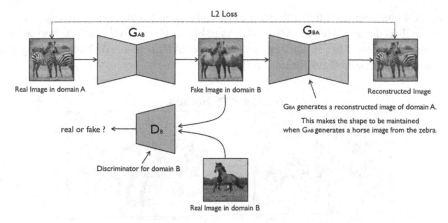

Fig. 5. The basic configuration of CycleGAN [4]

- For the mapping function $G_{BA} : B \rightarrow A$ and its discriminator D_A:

$$\mathcal{L}_{GAN}(G_{BA}, D_A, B, A)$$
$$= \mathbb{E}_{a \sim p_A(a)}\big[\log D_A(a)\big]$$
$$+ \mathbb{E}_{b \sim p_B(b)}[\log(1 - D_A(G_{BA}(b)))] \qquad (2)$$

Cycle Consistency Loss: For each image, a from domain A, the generated image $\hat{}$ after applying two transformation G_{AB} and G_{BA} should be similar to a: $a \rightarrow G_{AB}(a) \rightarrow G_{BA}(G_{AB}(a)) \approx a$. This is called forward cycle consistency. Similarly, for the backward path, we have backward cycle consistency: $b \rightarrow G_{BA}(b) \rightarrow G_{AB}(G_{BA}(b)) \approx b$. The cycle consistency loss is a combination of forwarding and backward cycle consistency losses:

$$\mathcal{L}_{cyc}(G_{AB}, G_{BA}) = \mathbb{E}_{a \sim p_A(a)}\big[\|G_{BA}(G_{AB}(a)) - a\|_1\big]$$
$$+ \mathbb{E}_{b \sim p_B(b)}\big[\|G_{AB}(G_{BA}(b)) - b\|_1\big] \qquad (3)$$

The full objective function of CycleGAN is a combination of the adversarial losses and the cycle consistency loss:

$$\mathcal{L}(G_{AB}, G_{BA}, D_A, D_B) = \mathcal{L}_{GAN}(G_{AB}, D_B, A, B)$$
$$+ \mathcal{L}_{GAN}(G_{BA}, D_A, B, A)$$
$$+ \lambda \mathcal{L}_{cyc}(G_{AB}, G_{BA}) \qquad (4)$$

where λ is the weight of the cycle consistency loss. In the training phase, the parameters of the networks (G_{AB}, G_{BA}, D_A, and D_B) are estimated by optimizing the full objective function:

$$G_{AB}^*, G_{BA}^* = \arg \min_{G_{AB}, G_{BA}} \max_{D_A, D_B} \mathcal{L}(G_{AB}, G_{BA}, D_A, D_B). \qquad (5)$$

In general, generative models in CycleGAN learn the set-to-set level of transformation while the original GANs learn to generate data to fit in a target set. Therefore,

CycleGAN could be used to establish mutual conversion between these two groups of images such as the art styles of two artists. As in Fig. 4, CycleGAN converts horses into zebras and vice versa. In [5], the authors use CycleGAN to create Ikebana painting via the concept of Unusual Transformation (Fig. 6).

Zebras ⟲ Horses

Fig. 6. Horses-Zebras transfer (Image source [3])

3.2   Concept of Unusual Transformation

In classic examples of CycleGAN in [4], the generative models were used to make a mutual transformation between landscape photos and Monet paintings, horses and zebras, winter landscapes, and summer landscapes. The transformation was made between images of relatively similar size, theme, and category. In [5], the authors give the idea of *unusual transformation*, a high-abstracted transformation where CycleGAN was applied to relatively different domains of objects which are difficult to imagine the mutual transformation such as macro and micro-size worlds or between plants and animals.

This concept of unusual transformation is believed to be a key point to create new art. For example in [5], portraits and animals were *unusually transformed* into Ikebana paintings. Another example was made by us in Fig. 7 where portraits are transformed into Sansui paintings.

The unusual transformation is a naturally difficult task with a very low rate of a successful transfer. We suggest a good transformation would include a *painting tool*set of data. The painting toolset would overcome some limitations of Deep Learning transfer including local-based transformation and noise vulnerability. Therefore, we use Ikebana as a good example of a painting toolset because of its minimality and flexibility. Sansui paintings would be another good painting tool as well because emptiness plays an important role in Sansui and natural elements such as rock, stream, mountain would be put in flexible positions.

Fig. 7. Example of unusual transformation: Portrait and Sansui Paintings

4 IkebanaGAN

CycleGAN works well on performing transformation between two sets of data of relatively similar size, themes, or categories such as transformation between artworks by Monet and landscape photos, winter and summer landscapes. In [5], the authors used CycleGAN to perform the usual transformation task between photos with complex backgrounds and abstract Ikebana (Fig. 1, 2). The experiments showed that the original CycleGAN suffers the over-transformation problem, i.e., we could not recognize the original shape of the main object in a photo after transforming.

To circumvent this problem, we try to combine CycleGAN with several computer vision techniques. To keep the original shape of the main objects, we first apply object recognition techniques to remove complex background, then edge detection is used to strengthen the shape of the objects. We define an object edge-promoting loss to enforce the model to keep the original shapes of main objects.

To include object edge-promoting loss to the adversarial loss, from the training images A, we automatically generate a set of images $E = \{e_i\}_{i=1}^{N}$ Z by removing clear edges of the main object in $\{a_i\}_{i=1}^{N}$. In more detail, for each image $a_i \in A$, we apply the following steps: (1) recognize objects in the image by using a pre-trained object detector (e.g., Mobile_Net_SSD), (2) detect edge pixels of objects using Canny edge detector [10], (3) dilate the edge regions, and (4) apply Gaussian smoothing in the dilated edge regions.

In our proposed IkebanaGAN, the goal of discriminator D_A is to maximize the probability of assigning the correct label to $G_{BA}(b)$, the real photos without clear edges of the photos' main objects (i.e., $e_j \in E$) and the real photos (i.e., $a_i \in A$). Therefore, we include object edge-promoting loss to the adversarial loss as follows:

$$\mathcal{L}_{GAN}(G_{BA}, D_A, B, A) = \mathbb{E}_{a \sim p_A(a)}\big[\log D_A(a)\big]$$
$$+ \mathbb{E}_{b \sim p_B(b)}[\log(1 - D_A(G_{BA}(b)))]$$
$$+ \gamma \mathbb{E}_{e \sim p_E(e)}[\log(1 - D_A(G_{BA}(e)))] \tag{6}$$

where γ controls the relative importance of the object edge-promoting loss.

5 Experiment

We performed the unusual transformation via IkebanaGAN with the style set A and the object sets B1 and B2 as follows:

- Dataset A: Ikebana photos in Google Image Search
- Dataset B1: Portrait photos in Flickr
- Dataset B2: Kaggle Animal-10 dataset.
  (https://www.kaggle.com/alessiocorrado99/animals10, partially)

Figures 8a and 8b show several results of A to B1 transformation and Figs. 9a and 9b show several results of A to B2 transformation.

Fig. 8a. Experiment result A-B1: IkebanaGAN and CycleGAN both generate acceptable transformation (the first row is the original photo, the second row is the transformation by CycleGAN, the last row is the transformation by IkebanaGAN)

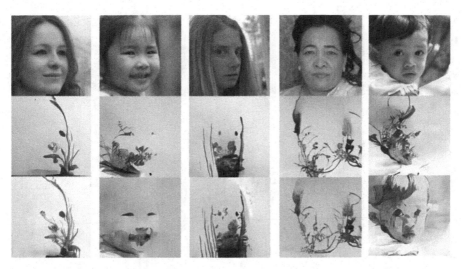

Fig. 8b. Experiment result A-B1: IkebanaGAN performs better than CycleGAN (the first row is the original photo, the second row is the transformation by CycleGAN, the last row is the transformation by IkebanaGAN)

Fig. 9a. Experiment result A-B2: IkebanaGAN and CycleGAN both generate acceptable transformation (the first row is the original photo, the second row is the transformation by CycleGAN, the last row is the transformation by IkebanaGAN)

Fig. 9b. Experiment result A-B2: IkebanaGAN performs better than CycleGAN (the first row is the original photo, the second row is the transformation by CycleGAN, the last row is the transformation by IkebanaGAN)

6 Discussion and Conclusion

In the examples which IkebanaGAN performs better than CycleGAN, we found that the original shape were well-preserved as in our assumption. IkebanaGAN would improve the successful rate as well as the performance of the unusual transformation of Ikebana and portraits more than animal photos. We consider the reason as the structures of objects in animal photos are more complex than human faces.

As we mentioned before, the unusual transformation is a challenging task because of the different structures of the two data sets. We hope to improve that difficulty by providing some techniques that mixed Deep Learning-based style transfer and classic Computer Vision's object detection. We remark that because of the natural difficulty, the success rate of the transformation is still low.

In the future, we would use another approach by mixing two GANs networks. We would provide a transformation between photos and sketches as well as sketches and Ikebana with the assumption that the sketch structure would remove the difficulty of over-transformation.

References

1. Gultepe, E., Conturo, T.E., Makrehchi, M.: Predicting and grouping digitized paintings by style using unsupervised feature learning. J Cult. Herit. **31**, 13–23 (2018). https://doi.org/10.1016/j.culher.2017.11.008. Epub 2017 Dec 20. PMID: 30034259; PMCID: PMC6051702
2. Mai, C.H., Nakatsu, R., Tosa, N., Kusumi, T., Koyamada, K.: Learning of art style using AI and its evaluation based on psychological experiments. In: Nunes, N.J., Ma, L., Wang, M., Correia, N., Pan, Z. (eds.) ICEC 2020. LNCS, vol. 12523, pp. 308–316. Springer, Cham (2020). https://doi.org/10.1007/978-3-030-65736-9_28

3. Creswell, A., et al.: Generative adversarial networks: an overview. IEEE Sig. Process. Mag. **35**(1), 53–65 (2018)
4. Zhu, J., Park, T., Isola, P., Efros, A.A.: Unpaired image-to-image translation using cycle-consistent adversarial networks. In: 2017 IEEE International Conference on Computer Vision (ICCV), pp. 2242–2251 (2017)
5. Mai, C.H., Nakatsu, R., Tosa, N.: Developing Japanese Ikebana as a digital painting tool via AI. In: Nunes, N.J., Ma, L., Wang, M., Correia, N., Pan, Z. (eds.) ICEC 2020. LNCS, vol. 12523, pp. 297–307. Springer, Cham (2020). https://doi.org/10.1007/978-3-030-65736-9_27
6. Chen, Y., Lai, Y., Liu, Y.: CartoonGAN: generative adversarial networks for photo cartoonization. In: 2018 IEEE/CVF Conference on Computer Vision and Pattern Recognition, pp. 9465–9474 (2018)
7. Li, X., Zhang, W., Shen, T.: Mei, everyone is a cartoonist: selfie cartoonization with attentive adversarial networks. In: 2019 IEEE International Conference on Multimedia and Expo (ICME), pp. 652–657 (2019)
8. Sato, S.: The Art of Arranging Flowers: A Complete Guide to Japanese Culture. Harry N. Abrams (1965)
9. Tosa, N., Pang, Y., Yang, Q., Nakatsu, R.: Pursuit and expression of Japanese beauty using technology. In: Fol Leymarie, F., Bessette, J., Smith, G.W. (eds.) The Machine as Art/The Machine as Artist, MDPI, pp. 267–280 (2020)
10. Canny, J.: A computational approach to edge detection. IEEE Trans. Pattern Anal. Mach. Intell. **6**, 679–698 (1986)

Interactive Tools for the Visualization of Tangible and Intangible Silk Heritage Emerging from an Interdisciplinary Work

Cristina Portalés[1]([⊠]) [iD], Jorge Sebastián[1] [iD], Javier Sevilla[1] [iD], Ester Alba[1] [iD], Marcos Fernández[1] [iD], Mar Gaitán[1] [iD], Pablo Casanova-Salas[1] [iD], Arabella León[2] [iD], Manolo Pérez[1] [iD], Eliseo Martínez Roig[1], and Jesús Gimeno[1] [iD]

[1] Universitat de València, 46010 València, Spain
cristina.portales@uv.es
[2] Garín 1820 S.A., 46113 Montcada, València, Spain

Abstract. Silk is a unique example of heritage where memory, identity, creativity and knowledge can be found in just one piece. It is a multifaceted, living heritage, as it consists of more than the fabrics themselves, but also the techniques associated with them, historical buildings, trades, festivities, etc. Therefore, designers, weavers, painters, sellers and users are involved in it. However, it is also a fragile heritage, alive in the few industries that still weave with historical looms. Additionally, the COVID19 pandemic has put the entire artisanal and small industrial sector of European silk in risk of disappearing. In this, paper we show some results of the SILKNOW project, whose main objective is to improves the understanding, conservation, and dissemination of European silk heritage. To that aim, we provide a variety of interactive tools and computational technologies, which have been designed and developed in close collaboration among experts in ICT (Information and Communication Technologies) and SSH (Social Sciences and Humanities). We focus the paper in addressing the interdisciplinary work carried out in the project to produce two interactive tools: Virtual Loom and STMaps. Results show that this way of working has been essential to produce such outcomes.

Keywords: Silk fabrics · Cultural heritage · 3D representation · Weaving techniques · Spatio-temporal maps · Ontologies · Interdisciplinarity

1 Introduction

The conservation, documentation, dissemination, and enhancement of tangible and intangible Cultural Heritage (CH) is of great relevance, as CH is a fundamental expression of the richness and diversity of our culture. Silk is a unique example of heritage where memory, identity, creativity and knowledge can be found in just one piece. Few materials have had such an outstanding impact: economic, technical, functional, cultural and symbolic. From flags to canopies, tapestries to furniture, fans to sword sheaths, wedding gowns to traditional costumes, we can find silk in countless contexts over the last millennia. It is usually linked to the Silk Road that for many centuries connected Asia and

M. Rauterberg (Ed.): HCII 2021, LNCS 12794, pp. 100–118, 2021.
https://doi.org/10.1007/978-3-030-77411-0_8

Europe, permitting the exchange of precious goods—not just silk—as well as various techniques, knowledge and religions. Within Europe, that route was later expanded by a network of regions and cities that served as creative, productive and commercial hubs for the textile industry, reaching its peak development in the 18th century. However, it is also a multifaceted, living heritage, as it consists of more than the textile itself. Designers, weavers, painters, sellers and users are involved in it. Moreover, its conservation relies not only on heritage professionals, but also on local communities and different stakeholders who are still connected through many life stories and collective narratives. Hence, this heritage represents not only fabrics themselves but also, the techniques associated with them (intangible heritage conserved by current weavers), historical buildings or even hoods such as La Lonja de Valencia (Valencia, Spain), or the Quartier des Canuts (Lyon, France), trades, festivities and so many other representations that connects this heritage from to the past to the present and marks the future thanks to creativity of modern designers.

This unique heritage, still alive in the few industries that still weave with historical looms, is stored in important and big museums such as the Victoria and Albert Museum (England) or the Musée des Arts Decoratifs (France), but it is also stored in smaller and medium-size museums and industries that are still weaving using Jacquard looms. The result is a multitude of data dispersed in a multitude of cultural institutions, who usually don't have the means (human and technological) to properly conserve and show this fragile heritage, the result is poorly tagged, variously formatted, in different languages, of random quality data that is inaccessible to professionals and the public in general and the information is presented partially and disconnected. To this end, it is necessary to protect and disseminate this fragile heritage which, by its nature, has been linked to the development of European culture, and to develop strategies that allow for regional interconnection, which must not only be historical, but from a heritage perspective as a sustainable development of economic, social and cultural realities.

Now more than ever, the fragility of this heritage is an evidence, and its subsistence is in danger. The small creative industries that live off silk weaving in Europe have survived the transformations of the global economy of the 20th and 21st centuries in a precarious way. In many European spaces, silk as a material linked to the cultural history and identity of a multitude of European regions, is revealed as a European transregional heritage. For this reason, its survival has largely depended on traditional and historical festivals and its contemporary maintenance, from a broad dimension: design, use of Jacquard looms, use of traditional techniques, or historical visual repertoires, has been possible thanks to its link with the intangible heritage of festive traditions [1, 2]. Furthermore, the current crisis of COVID19 has put the entire artisanal and small industrial sector of European silk in risk, unable to cope with almost a year and a half of paralysis of festive and, therefore, massive activities. The lack of specific protection programs, national plans or European dimension puts this cultural creative sector, which can be considered cultural heritage in itself because of the know-how it holds and its rich collections of historical designs and models, in its latest rales before disappearing forever. On the other hand, the non-existence of training programs in this craft and the lack of generational renewal pose an added risk to the preservation of such an important heritage in the historical construction of Europe. From our project, we put a variety of technologies at the service of cultural heritage, seek to preserve and document a heritage that is material, but also the techniques that keep it alive today, with the desire that it is not lost forever.

In this regard, SILKNOW is an EU funded research project that improves the understanding, conservation, and dissemination of European silk heritage from the 15th to the 19th century [3]. It applies advanced computing research to the needs of diverse users (museums, education, tourism, creative industries, media, etc.), and preserves the tangible and intangible heritage associated with silk. SILKNOW involves experts in the fields of ICT (Information and Communication Technologies) and SSH (Social Sciences and Humanities), that work together in an interdisciplinary way, in order to achieve project's objectives.

Thanks to the collaboration of ICT and SSH experts, among other results, we have developed two interactive tools which are here addressed: "Virtual Loom", an application that deals with the 3D virtual representation of historical silk fabrics at the yarn level, and "STMaps" (spatio-temporal maps), an interactive tool to visualize silk-related objects in both temporal and spatial scales, also depicting the relationship among their properties. In this paper, we show these tools and how they can be used to explore silk heritage. We further explain how these tools have been developed, from a tight interdisciplinary work.

The paper is organized as follows: in the first place, we bring a section on the related work. Then, we explain the key points that make SILKNOW an interdisciplinary project. In the results section, we detail how we have collaborated to achieve Virtual Loom and STMaps. Finally, we bring some conclusions, summarizing the actions taken and the lessons learned, before and during the project lifetime, to succeed in the co-creation process.

2   Related Work

The process of globalization we are going through makes technology essential for accessing cultural heritage. Technologies are relevant for the CH field from two aspects [4]. On one side, they provide professionals with tools that make heritage accessible such as 3D representation, big databases, AI technologies. On the other side, they provide access to the general audience such as virtual and augmented realities, semantic webs, geolocation. In this sense, technology can be used as cultural mediator that can be used to transmit knowledge, but also to attract different categories of the public to museums [5]. CH must be understood as tangible and intangible cultural manifestations inherited to society who interpret it, enjoy it and transmit it. CH institutions should integrate and understand these new technologies to guarantee management, conservation and dissemination of the heritage they are safeguarding.

Within this, there can be found a lot of works where researchers from different areas of knowledge have collaborated. For instance, [6] describes a framework for computer-based visualizations of CH sites. The project focuses on a workflow for a visualization illustrated on a specific solution for the site of Çukuriçi Höyük, in Turkey. In [7] Geographic Information Technologies are applied to the field of CH, aiming to analyze patrimonial valuation through digital representations. And [8] aims to propose a value co-creation framework through examining the opportunities of implementing augmented reality, virtual reality and 3D printing into the visitor experience at cultural heritage places. However, most of the works found in the literature focus on describing the methodology to derive the desired solution, but do not usually give details of how the collaboration took place. For instance, it is not clear if the work is multidisciplinary or interdisciplinary, or if it has transcended to other areas of knowledge. In fact, as pointed in [9], the terms multidisciplinary, interdisciplinary and transdisciplinary sometimes are ambiguously defined and interchangeably used by some authors, what should not be done. In this sense, it is worth to clarify that multidisciplinarity draws on knowledge from different disciplines but stays within their boundaries. On the other hand, interdisciplinarity analyzes, synthesizes and harmonizes links between disciplines into a coordinated and coherent whole. Finally, transdisciplinarity connotes a research strategy that crosses different disciplinary boundaries to create a holistic approach, crossing the boundaries of two or more disciplines.

The work carried out in SILKNOW is interdisciplinary, and we also expect to transcend to other disciplines. In this paper we describe the key collaboration issues that have led to produce the interactive tools derived in the project, focusing on two of them, which are reported in the results section.

3   Interdisciplinary Work in SILKNOW

SILKNOW has only been possible with the close cooperation of partners with different expertise, including text analytics, image processing, semantics, big data, 3D printing, visualization, art history, terminology, textile fabrication and conservation. The way we have cooperated, results in an interdisciplinary work. We have also stablished new synergies among other projects and institutions outside our consortium, with the aim that the results transcend to other disciplines. In the following sub-sections, we give details on the key points leading to the interdisciplinary work.

3.1   The Dual ICT-SSH Coordination Team

The SILKNOW project is coordinated by the Universitat de València. Two research teams are involved: on the one hand, the Institute of Robotics and Information and Communication Technologies (from now on, the ICT coordination team) and, on the other hand, the Faculty of Arts History (from now on, the SSH coordination team). Since before the idea of the project was born, we have collaborated very closely. It is worth mentioning, that both teams are at different locations within the area of Valencia (Spain), and therefore, we have used remote collaboration tools (email, WhatsApp, etc.) quite often.

The first time our teams met was in Sep-16. We decided to collaborate in writing a proposal for the call SC6 CULT-COOP-09 of the Horizon 2020 Framework Programme, with the deadlines Feb-17 (first stage) and Sep-17 (second stage). We stablished a calendar with regular online meetings, usually one per week or per two weeks, that lasted about one hour each one. At the beginning, we talked about why silk fabrics were so much fragile, and why it was an endangered heritage. In this way, the SSH coordination team transferred knowledge about this heritage to the ICT coordination team.

The conversations evolved to how we could do to protect this heritage, and also ensure knowledge transfer to future generations. Then, the ICT coordination team proposed different technological solutions, and the SSH coordination team selected one of them. That was only the starting point to better elaborate the "idea" of the proposal. We wrote a first draft of the proposal (only 3 pages) with the key points and identified the roles we needed in the project. Afterwards, we proposed different institutions that could met the criteria, and started contacting them. Once the partners accepted to join the proposal, we finalized writing it for the first stage and submit on time. After a period of three months, we were notified that the proposal was accepted, so we continued writing an extended proposal for the second stage. As before, the two coordination teams had weekly meetings, usually online, until the proposal was submitted.

The project began on the Apr-18 and will last until the Aug-21 (41 months). During the project life, the two teams have kept a continuous communication through different channels, including: email (daily), WhatsApp (daily), telephone calls (weekly), videoconferences (daily/weekly) and face to face meetings (monthly, until the pandemic began). In Fig. 1, we show the number of emails sent between the two teams, since the beginning of the preparation of the proposal (Sep-16) until today (Jan-21). Some milestones are also depicted. This graph exemplifies how much the two teams are collaborating, and it is only one of the communication channels we are using. The low values in the graph correspond to summer vacation periods (mainly in August) and after the first stage deadline. The high values are related to the project milestones and plenary meetings.

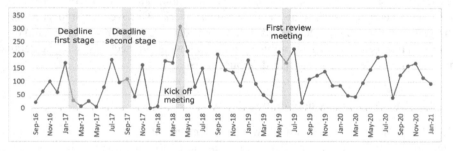

Fig. 1. Number of emails between the two coordination teams, directly related to SILKNOW. Some milestones are also depicted.

3.2 The Multidisciplinary Consortium

SILKNOW involves partners of different disciplines, and that is why we state that our consortium is multidisciplinary. Although we have different expertise among our partners, we can classify our partners in two big areas: ICT and SSH. This fact is summarized in Table 1, also showing the main role that each partner is taken in the project.

Table 1. Classification of partners in either ICT, SSH or SSH&ICT, according to their main role in the project.

Partner	Area (main role in the project)
Universitat de València	ICT&SSH (coordination, interactive tools, thesaurus, dissemination)
Gottfried Wilhelm Leibniz Universitaet Hannover	ICT (image analysis)
Institut Jozef Stefan	ICT (text analytics)
Universita degli Studio di Palermo	SSH (data provider, evaluations)
Instituto Cervantes	SSH (educational materials, communication)
Garín 1820 S.A.	SSH (data provider, expert in silk fabrics)
EURECOM	ICT (exploratory search engine, integrator)
Centre National de la Recherche Scientifique	SSH (data provider, ontology)
MonkeyFab S.C.	ICT (3D printing)

The grant amount and efforts dedicated to the project are around 60% for ICT and 40% for SSH, as schematized in Fig. 2. Taking into account that the outcomes of the project involve a variety of technological solutions (see Sect. 3.3), this shows a quite good balance between the two disciplines.

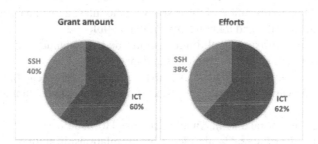

Fig. 2. Graphical representation of the project costs and efforts per area.

The interaction among partners is also quite intense through different channels. We have monthly online meetings, and every 5–6 months, plenary meetings. All partners participate in these meetings. Plenary meetings are face to face and have been organized by different partners at different countries. However, since the COVID19 pandemic, we have moved plenary meetings online. In parallel, we schedule other online meetings to solve technical problems or to discuss specific issues, with the partners involved in that. In a daily basis, we are communicated through a dedicated mailing list for the project (starting in Sep-18), and also through Slack. In Fig. 3, the number of emails from the mailing list are shown, and the plenary meetings are also depicted. Similar to Fig. 1, the low values in the graph correspond to summer vacation periods (mainly in August), whereas the high values are related to the project milestones and plenary meetings.

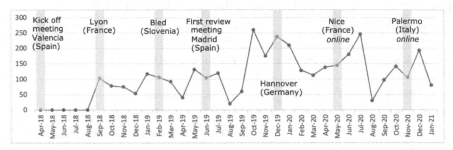

Fig. 3. Number of emails among the consortium, from the SILKNOW mailing list. Plenary meetings are also depicted.

3.3 Designing the Tools in an Interdisciplinary Way

A number of tools are being developed under the SILKNOW project [10]:

- *ADASilk* (Advanced Data Analysis for Silk heritage): An exploratory search engine built on top of the SILKNOW's knowledge graph that contains nearly 40,000 fabric entries with images and other relevant information describing them. This information is enriched by the combination of three software modules: a text analytic module, an image retrieval module, and a knowledge graph module.
- *Multilingual Thesaurus*: A multilingual controlled vocabulary for silk heritage, describing mainly production techniques and materials.
- *Virtual Loom*: An application that deals with the 3D virtual representation of historical silk fabrics at the yarn level. It is provided as an standalone application and integrated in ADASilk.
- *STMaps* (spatio-temporal maps): An interactive tool to visualize silk-related objects in both temporal and spatial scales, also depicting the relationship among their properties. It is integrated in ADASilk.
- *Educational Material*: La Ruta de la Seda (The Silk Road) educational material has been specially designed for learning Spanish through different aspects related to silk in Europe.

All these tools have been developed in an interdisciplinary way, involving ICT and SSH experts from the different partners. In the result section, we explain in detail the way we have worked to achieve two of these tools: Virtual Loom and STMaps.

3.4 Validation and Evaluation

The validation of the project results is carried out by partners belonging to both ICT and SSH areas. For instance, ICT partners use techniques such as cross validation for a scientific evaluation of the classification software that combines training, classification and evaluation in a specific way. On the other hand, validation by SSH partners is aimed at providing feedback on the processing software modules that feed ADASilk, to guarantee quality and alignment with the SILKNOW project objectives. These modules are:

- *The text analytic module*: a tool for the textual analysis of data from museum collections.
- *The image retrieval module*: a deep learning-based module aiming at predicting the properties of silk fabric by processing images.
- *The knowledge graph module*: a tool used for browsing the SILKNOW ontology. It is populated with text and images extracted from records, originally created for documenting the collections of museums.

Testing of these modules has been done during the development phase by the responsible partners, belonging to the ICT field. Validation by SSH partners focuses on the semantic annotation of the text analysis module, the verification of the correct mapping within the ontology of the elements coming from the collections, the correctness of the value assigned to the "production location" field and the similarity of retrieved images.

On the other hand, the interactive tools (ADASilk, Multilingual Thesaurus, Virtual Loom, STMaps and Educational Materials) have also been evaluated by both ICT and SSH partners. Internal testing of these tools has been done during the development phase by the responsible partners, that have corrected any possible bug. Other partners, not directly related to the implementation of these tools, have also participated in the internal evaluations. Currently, our tools are being evaluated by the general public. The material for the evaluation (manual, training and questionnaires) has been mainly developed by SSH partners, with the support of ICT partners, and is available at [11].

3.5 Dissemination of Project Results in Different Channels

We have disseminated the project results in different channels related to ICT and SSH. In Fig. 4, we show the number of papers published in journals and conferences so far which are related to only ICT, only SSH, or both ICT and SSH. On the one hand, the graph shows the number of papers whose authors belong to these areas in blue color. On the other hand, the scope of the journals and conferences belonging to these areas are shown in orange color. As it can be seen, there is a majority of papers where authors of ICT and SSH have collaborated. Regarding to the scope, the difference is not so evident, but still there are more papers published in interdisciplinary (ICT & SSH) journals and conferences.

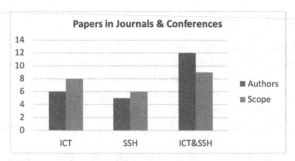

Fig. 4. Number of papers published in journals and conferences in SILKNOW so far, for the areas related to ICT, SSH and ICT&SSH, taking into account the authors of the publications, and the scope of the journals and conferences.

3.6 Towards Transdisciplinarity

We are establishing synergies with other actors, aiming at crossing the borders of the disciplines directly involved in the project. In this regard, we have stablished collaboration with other projects, networks, fashion designers and institutions at different levels. A summary is given in Table 2, of the most relevant collaborations we have carried out so far. We expect to keep opening new collaboration channels, until the end of the project, and also that some of these collaborations transcend the project itself.

Table 2. Summary of collaborations with other actors outside the consortium, and/or reaching audiences outside the consortium.

Actors	Type of collaboration
Lucerne University of Applied Science and Arts/Silk Memory project	We have carried out two workshops, one in Valencia (Spain) and the other in Lucerne (Switzerland), where we have discussed about the common links between the two projects. The coordinators of Silk Memory participated in Weaving Europe, a conference organized by SILKNOW
FORTH/Mingei project	We have carried out two online meetings, discussing about the possible links between the two projects. We have shared information related to accurate documentation of silk fabrics (Mingei) and their 3D representation (SILKNOW). We expect to collaborate in a joint paper. The coordinators of Mingei participated in Weaving Europe, a conference organized by SILKNOW

(*continued*)

Table 2. (*continued*)

Actors	Type of collaboration
Escola d'Art Superior de Disseny de València (EASD)	We have intensively collaborated with this institution in different ways. Firstly, sharing the contents & results of SILKNOW project which serve as inspiration to young creative professionals in the field of fashion design, mainly. But we also worked together with other creatives, as product designers, digital designers, interior designers, etc. For those tasks, we visited the school several times and we presented our tools as the Thesaurus, Virtual Loom and our prospective website where all the collections we have worked with would be available. During their creative process and during the academic year, they would use and work on the basis of our tools. Furthermore, we encouraged the students to take a look at the tools, to, use them, and to evaluate them in order to improve the user's experience. As we consider silk as alive heritage, we started a very interesting conversation on how all the compiled knowledge, methods, processes, etc. could motivate and inspire new creative professionals with the aim of valuing the silk tradition and importance and on how to spread the word into society
Europeana Fashion Association	The director of Europeana Fashion Association is a member of SILKNOW's external advisory board, and he has participated in Weaving Europe, a conference organized by SILKNOW
Fashion designer: Patrik Wojciechowski	Mr. Wojciechowski is a well-known fashion designer in Poland where he was part of the TV show "Project Runway". We invited him to make a collection making use of 3D printing technology based on SILKNOW's database, where he selected Garin's designs. He visited Garin's industry where he had the chance to talk with weavers and art historians who are experts in silk weaving. In collaboration with our partner MonkeyFab, he has produced a collection that will be shown in Poland in February 2021. Some preliminary results are shown in Fig. 5

(*continued*)

Table 2. (*continued*)

Actors	Type of collaboration
ICCROM	We have signed an MoU with this intergovernmental organization that will disseminate SILKNOW's results among their latest programme called "Our Collections Matter"
EuroWeb: pan-European COST Action "Europe Through Textiles"	The director of this COST-Action Agatha Ulanowska has participated in Weaving Europe, a conference organized by SILKNOW. We had two-day workshop with the whole consortium where E. Alba represents Spain
Fashion designer: Francis Montesinos	We visited Francis Montesinos' atelier and showed him our Virtual Loom. Mr. Montesinos participated at the SILKNOW Conference
Instituto Cervantes/Events	We are preparing 5 events in different EU countries: Italy, France, England, Belgium and Poland. These activities will go from exhibitions to fashion catwalks or academic conferences, reaching different targeted audiences
Universitat de València/SeMap project	SeMap "advanced access to cultural assets through the Semantic web and spatio-temporal Maps" is a project coordinated by C. Portalés. The lessons learned in STMaps, will have a direct impact in SeMap

Fig. 5. Some preliminary results of the collaboration with the fashion designer Patrik Wojciechowski. The image shows 3D printouts on top of fabrics.

4 Results

In this section, we show two of the tools developed under the SILKNOW project. On the one hand, Virtual Loom, an application that deals with the 3D virtual representation of historical silk fabrics at the yarn level. On the other hand, STMaps, an interactive tool to visualize silk-related objects in both temporal and spatial scales, also depicting the relationship among their properties. Both tools have been developed by Universitat de València.

4.1 Virtual Loom

Virtual Loom is an application that deals with the 3D virtual representation of historical silk fabrics at the yarn level. Silk fabrics have specific characteristics, as they are nearly flat objects and very fragile. The documentation of their visual appearance has been traditionally done by means of imaging devices (e.g., RGB cameras, digital microscopes, etc.). However, within these devices, only the surface of the objects is documented, so the complex internal structure composed of a variety of yarns and their interlaces, remains undiscovered. To deal with this, in Virtual Loom we produce 3D models of silk fabrics at the yarn level, with the minimum information of an image as input data.

The implementation of Virtual Loom has been deeply described in [12], its relationship with 3D printing is described in [13], and some case studies are presented in [14]. In this paper, we focus on describing the interdisciplinary work that has led to the current version of the tool.

The design and implementation of such a tool involves a deep knowledge of the fabrics' geometry. This is not trivial, as it involves understanding important parts of the process of producing a fabric, such as:

- *Looming*: To understand how a real loom works and to know what the role of an artisan in the process of looming is.
- *Weaving techniques*: To know the different historical weaving techniques related to silk fabrics. To know how many layers of yarns are needed to compose a fabric, depending on the weaving technique. To understand what a weave is, and how yarns interlace each other. To know what weaves were used, depending on the weaving technique.
- *Yarns*: To know what the properties of silk yarns are (thickness, composition, colors, etc.), that were used in historical fabrics.

Therefore, the definition and computational modelling of historical weaving techniques has been possible thanks to a tight collaboration among experts in computer engineering (in this case, the ICT team of Universitat de València) and domain experts related to the production of silk textiles (in this case, the company Garín 1820 S.A., a partner of the project, recall Table 1).

We began our collaboration very early in the project. The ICT coordination team, visited Garín on several occasions, having access to the real looms and silk fabrics, and being able of asking specific questions to the artisans. Additionally, Garín produced some fabrics for the project making use of different techniques, that allowed us to inspect them in more detail. For instance, the SSH coordination team conducted an optical study of the fabrics [15], that was relevant for the ICT coordination team for the definition of the main characteristics of yarns and the production of their 3D models.

The ICT coordination team produced a first version of Virtual Loom, that consisted in a single window with two selection bars (Fig. 6): weave technique (only few of weaves were available), damask drawing (only some drawings were available, and only the damask weaving technique was considered). A slide that we called "level of detail" produced a 3D model with more/less yarns.

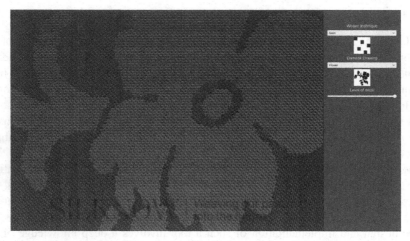

Fig. 6. A damask produced with the first release of Virtual Loom.

This first version of the tool was shown to Garín, the SSH coordination team, and the rest of partners. Their feedback was useful for the ICT coordination team to improve the tool from the point of view of the interface design and interaction. Additionally, with the continuous advice of Garín, we implemented more weaving techniques, weaves and 3D yarns.

In Fig. 7 an example is given showing how to produce a brocaded damask, the most complex technique that we have considered in Virtual Loom. In the first place, the user loads an image in Virtual Loom and selects the area that she/he wants to model (Fig. 7-a). Afterwards, she/he has to select the weaving technique (in this case, brocaded damask) and the number of clusters (in this case, four clusters) (Fig. 7-b). In the next step, the type of yarns and colors are selected, and user also needs to indicate what yarn corresponds to the background, and what yarn corresponds to the pictorial part of the background (Fig. 7-c). In the same window, she/he can also select a weave, otherwise, a default weave is applied (Fig. 7-d). With the settings applied so far, a 3D model is derived (Fig. 7-e), which can be rotated, translated, zoomed, and also the visualization of individual yarns can be activated/deactivated (Fig. 7-f). At any time, users can return to previous steps, to modify the settings of the 3D model, for instance, a different weave can be selected (Fig. 7-h). The "Visualization" window will show the 3D model with the new settings, which can also be inspected (Fig. 7-i-j).

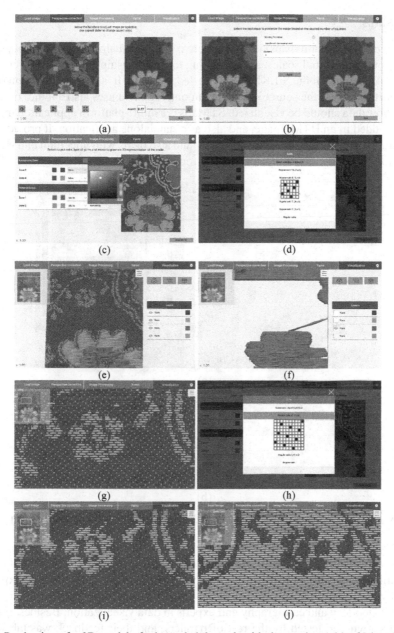

Fig. 7. Production of a 3D model of a brocaded damask with the version 1.00 of Virtual Loom, where: (a) area selection; (b) weaving technique selection and definition of the number of clusters; (c) selection of yarns and colors; (d) selection of the weave; (e) derived 3D model with the settings selected from (a) to (d); (f) inspection of one of the yanrs of the 3D model; (g) a close look to the 3D model; (h) change of the weave; (i) a close look to the new 3D model, with the weave selected in (h); (j) the same 3D model as in (i), seen from the backside.

4.2 STMaps

STMaps (spatio-temporal maps) is an interactive tool to visualize silk-related objects in both temporal and spatial scales, also depicting the relationship among their properties. STMaps take data from the SILKNOW Knowledge Graph. It is entirely based on ontology support, as it gets the source data from an ontology and uses also another ontology to define how data should be visualized. STMaps is a multi-platform application that can work embedded in an HTML page, and also as a standalone application. It provides different solutions to show spatio-temporal data, and also deals with uncertain and missing information. More details of this tool can be found in [16].

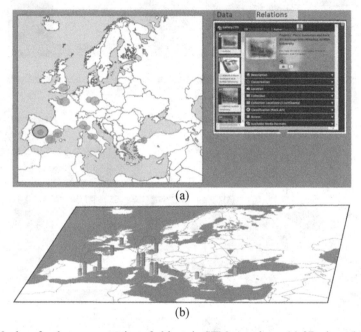

(a)

(b)

Fig. 8. Mockup for the representation of objects in STMaps, where: (a) 2D view; (b) 3D view.

In this case, the design and implementation of STMaps has been carried out by the coordination team. On the one hand, in the SSH coordination team, people expert in geography are involved. On the other hand, in the ICT coordination team, there is an engineer in geodesy and cartography and experts in data visualization. Besides, the tool has been shown and tested by the rest of partners, and their feedback was taken into account for the improvements of the tool.

In Fig. 8, mockup images are shown, both for the representation of data in a 2D view, and in a 3D view. This mockup was produced early in the project and shown to the rest of partners during one of the plenary meetings (Lyon, France).

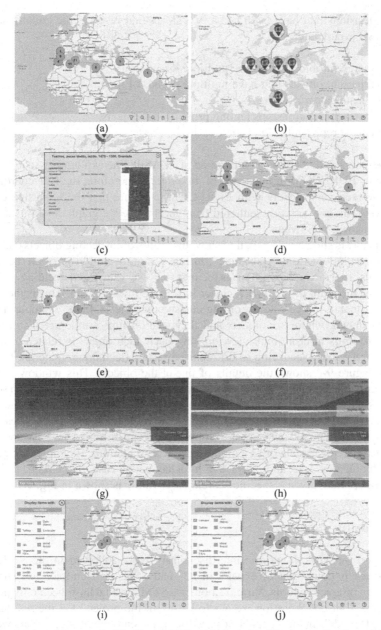

Fig. 9. Inspecting objects embedded in ADASilk with depiction "Arabesque", where: (a) an overall view, where all objects are shown in the map; (b) a zoom in a region in Spain, where six objects and they relationships are depicted in ring-like forms; (c) inspection of one of the objects and activating the relationships for the property "technique"; (d) visualization of the relationships for the property "technique" of the inspected object in (c), in linear forms; (e) showing the objects for the 15th century, in a linear scale; (f) showing the objects for the 18th century, in a linear scale; (g) showing the objects from the 12th to the 14th century, in a multilayer representation; (h) showing the objects from the 17th to the 18th century, in a multilayer representation; (i) filtering by the material "material thread"; (j) filtering by the technique "lampas".

Some decisions that have been taken in STMaps that involves the collaboration of ICT and SSH experts are:

- How to represent objects that have multiple locations.
- How to represent objects that have multiple periods of time.
- What the main categories are.
- How to represent relationships among properties of objects.
- What the most representative properties are.

On the other hand, STMaps is integrated in ADASilk, the exploratory search engine developed by EURECOM in the scope of the project. Therefore, the ICT coordination team has worked very closely with EURECOM to ensure that the requested data by users in ADASilk are correctly gathered from the knowledge graph, and thus they can be properly shown in STMaps.

An example is shown in Fig. 9, that show the results of inspecting objects embedded in ADASilk with depiction "Arabesque". In Fig. 9-a, an overall view of all the objects that meet this criterion is shown. This is the first view users see when deciding to display the results on the map. In Fig. 9-b, a closer look to the map is given. This is the type of visualization that users see when zooming into specific objects. In the example, a region in Spain is shown, where six objects and they relationships are depicted in ring-like forms. These rings offer a quick view on how much each object is related to the rest of objects in the map, according to different properties (technique, material, time and category). Figure 9-c shows the details of one of the objects. This window is shown when a user clicks on one of the objects. Additionally, in Fig. 9-c, we can also see that the user has activated the relationships for the property "technique", that will show lines between all the objects in the map that have the same value for this property. These linear visualizations are depicted in Fig. 9-d. Temporal maps can be derived in STMaps, in two ways: either in a linear scale or as a multilayers' representations. Examples are given in Fig. 9-e-f for the first case, and in Fig. 9-g-h for the second case. In STMaps, additional filers can be applied, given a specific search. An example is shown in Fig. 9-i-j.

5   Conclusion

In this paper, we have shown the interdisciplinary work followed in the SILKNOW project, which is composed of experts in ICT and SSH. As examples, we show the results of two interactive tools, Virtual Loom and STMaps, that have been only possible thanks to the tight collaboration we are following in the project. On the one hand, to derive the 3D models in the Virtual Loom, a deep understanding on weaves and weaving techniques is required, among others. For STMaps, it is important to identify which properties are relevant to the field, and how they can be visualized (e.g., timelines, relationships, etc.) in order to provide meaningful results for the study and preservation of this heritage.

A final step in the development of these tools, will be to take in consideration the feedback of the general public, considering different targeted audiences: cultural heritage, education related to SSH, ICT, textile or creative industries, tourism and media.

To that end, we are currently in the process of evaluating our tools with an open, online procedure, which can be accessed from [11]. Testers of our tools can fulfill an online questionnaire, to give us feedback on different aspects, such as the usability of the tools. In this regards, we also intend to measure how relevant are our outcomes to these audiences.

Our targeted audiences have already identified some potential uses of the tools. For instance, ADASilk and STMaps can be relevant for artists and designers as an inspiration tool for creating new designs, as they can explore the silk collection at different levels, including the visualization of the relationships among collections. Virtual Loom is relevant not only for learning purposes on weaving techniques, but also for traditional industries that want to make use of new ways of showing their products to their clients. Therefore, Virtual Loom can be used as a demonstrator, as it provides 3D models by combining different weaves, techniques, colors and yarns, without the need to use a real loom, what would increase costs.

After the project ends, the outcomes of the project will remain openly accessible through different platforms (e.g., GitHub, ADASilk), they will be maintained in the mid-term by the ICT coordination team and updated by the SSH coordination team.

Acknowledgement. The research leading to these results is in the frame of the "SILKNOW. Silk heritage in the Knowledge Society: from punched cards to big data, deep learning and visual/tangible simulations" project, which has received funding from the European Union's Horizon 2020 research and innovation program under grant agreement No. 769504. Cristina Portalés is supported by the Spanish government postdoctoral grant Ramón y Cajal, under grant No. RYC2018–025009-I.

References

1. Storm, H.J., Berger S, S.H.J.: The spatial turn and the history of nationalism: nationalism between regionalism and transnational approaches. In: Writing the History of Nationalism, pp. 215–238. Bloomsbury (2019)
2. Applegate, C.: A europe of regions: reflections on the historiography of sub-national places in modern times. Am. Hist. Rev. **104**, 1157–1182 (1999). https://doi.org/10.1086/ahr/104.4.1157
3. Portalés, C., et al.: Interactive tools for the preservation, dissemination and study of silk heritage—an introduction to the SILKNOW project. Multimodal Technol. Interact. **2**, 28 (2018). https://doi.org/10.3390/mti2020028
4. Silberman, N.A.: Beyond Theme Parks and Digitized Data: What Can Cultural Heritage Technologies Contribute to the Public Understanding of the Past? (2005)
5. Kéfi, H., Pallud, J.: The role of technologies in cultural mediation in museums: an Actor-Network Theory view applied in France. Museum Manage. Curatorship. **26**, 273–289 (2011). https://doi.org/10.1080/09647775.2011.585803
6. Lužnik-Jancsary, N., Horejs, B., Klein, M., Schwall, C.: Integration and workflow framework for virtual visualisation of cultural heritage. Revisiting the tell of Çukuriçi Höyük, Turkey. In: Virtual Archaeology Review, pp. 63–74. Universitat Politècnica de València (2020). https://doi.org/10.4995/var.2020.13086
7. Marques, L., et al.: Cultural heritage 3D modelling and visualisation within an augmented reality environment, based on geographic information technologies and mobile platforms. Arch. City Environ. **11**, 117–136 (2017). https://doi.org/10.5821/ace.11.33.4686

8. Jung, T.H., tom Dieck, M.C.: Augmented reality, virtual reality and 3D printing for the co-creation of value for the visitor experience at cultural heritage places. J. Place Manage. Dev. **10**, 140–151 (2017). https://doi.org/10.1108/JPMD-07-2016-0045

9. Choi, B.C.K., Pak, A.W.P.: Multidisciplinarity, interdisciplinarity and transdisciplinarity in health research, services, education and policy: 1. Definitions, objectives, and evidence of effectiveness. Clin. Invest. Med. **29**, 351–364 (2006)

10. SILKNOW. Our tools, https://silknow.eu/index.php/our-results/. Accessed on 31 Jan 2021

11. Virtual Loom & ADASilk Evaluation, https://silknow.eu/index.php/evaluation/test_en/. Accessed on 31 Jan 2021

12. Portalés, C., Pérez, M., Casanova-Salas, P., Gimeno, J.: Virtual Loom: a tool for the interactive 3D representation of historical fabrics. Multimed. Tools Appl. (2021). https://doi.org/10.1007/s11042-020-10294-w

13. Pérez, M., et al.: From historical silk fabrics to their interactive virtual representation and 3D printing. Sustainability. **12**, 7539 (2020). https://doi.org/10.3390/su12187539

14. Gaitán, M., Portalés, C., Sevilla, J., Alba, E.: Applying axial symmetries to historical silk fabrics: SILKNOW's virtual loom. Symmetry. **12**, 742 (2020). https://doi.org/10.3390/sym12050742

15. Vázquez de Ágredos Pascual, M.L., Rojo Iranzo, L.: Report. Study of historical silks by Scanning Electron Microscope (SEM) and Inverted Optical Microscope (LMi) (2020). http://silknow.eu/wp-content/uploads/Study-of-historical-silks-by-Scanning-Electron-Microscope-SEM-and-Inverted-Optical-Microscope-LMi_VA%CC%83%C2%A1zquez-de-A%CC%83%C2%81gredos-and-Rojo-Iranzo.pdf

16. Sevilla, J., Casanova-Salas, P., Casas-Yrurzum, S., Portalés, C.: Multi-purpose ontology-based visualization of spatio-temporal data: a case study on silk heritage. Appl. Sci. **11**, 1636 (2021). https://doi.org/10.3390/app11041636

Soundscape Singapore: Sound as Mediated Cultural Heritage

Marcus Cheng Chyc Tan$^{(\boxtimes)}$ (iD)

National Institute of Education, Nanyang Technological University, Singapore, Singapore
marcus.tan@nie.edu.sg

Abstract. This paper will examine the poetics of sound archiving as a means of documenting and evaluating Singapore's cultural and political economy. It is twofold in consideration: an inquiry into sound's significance for/in Singapore and the media/tion of archiving sound. This first concern involves an investigation of selected sound events and their relation to the cultural and political life-worlds (*Lebenswelt*) of Singapore/ans. The second section argues for an importance of archiving sounds in/of Singapore given the absence of any authoritative sound library or sound map. Many iconic, culturally defining sounds are now lost to time; this loss further underscores the importance of archiving for past sounds and the perception of these sounds by historical actors inform us about the changing character and identity of cities, people and cultural practices. Technology today provides the means to capture and contain sound, as ephemeral phenomena, in high fidelity and this paper will include a discussion of an ongoing research project in collaboration with the National Archives of Singapore (SoundscapeSG) which involves a web-based platform that contains Singapore soundscapes in ambisonic formats.

Keywords: Soundscapes · Singapore · SoundscapeSG · Cultural heritage · Sound archiving

1 Introduction: 'Cry Fowl'

In 2017, news of some 24 free-roaming chickens being culled by authorities at Sin Ming, a residential estate in Singapore, made the headlines in the local broadsheets. Wildlife in Singapore's primarily built-up, concrete landscape is not particularly common even as encounters with wild boars, otters and snakes have been increasing in frequency as more forests and green spaces are cleared for urban development. The culling sparked an outcry among nature lovers with much of the debate being centered around the value of nature, wildlife and what remains of Singapore's natural landscape, but more importantly there was particular attention to an ascertainment of the type of fowl these were. Naturalists believed these chickens were the endangered Red Junglefowl known to be rapidly disappearing due to the loss of habitat but authorities claimed they were simply "regular" chickens. What was perhaps most interesting were the reasons why

© Springer Nature Switzerland AG 2021
M. Rauterberg (Ed.): HCII 2021, LNCS 12794, pp. 119–132, 2021.
https://doi.org/10.1007/978-3-030-77411-0_9

the Agri-food and Veterinary Authority of Singapore (AVA)[1] took extreme measures to terminate the fowls and eradicate their presence. Then Minister of State of National Development Koh Poh Koon explained in Parliament that the chickens were culled because of concerns about avian flu and that there were over 20 complaints made by various residents about noise which included the morning crows and incessant cackling.

This curious incident of clucking chickens in the daytime prompt curious questions about sound, noise, aurality and listening as these become contextualized and contained in a particular habitus. Considered from a sonic perspective, the event underscores how the urban space of a first-world developed society shapes, determines and perhaps distorts our sense of aurality, of what "permissible" sound is and how "noise" is comprehended. In turn, aurality consequently reveals our lived experiences of what is 'natural' and 'unnatural'. Singapore is an archetype of a hyper-urban, megacity with a dense population (of 8358 people per km^2) residing, shuffling and colliding in skyscrapers and high-rise apartment blocks that continually infringe on natural space. The lived experience of urbanity has led to a desensitization of particular sounds and of sound as a means of knowing, also termed acoustemology; it has restructured our ossicular sensitivities of what is tolerable and intolerable. Living beside busy highways, roads, rail networks and shopping malls have led some Singaporeans to become accustomed to extremely loud sounds that even exceed the World Health Organization's acceptable recommendation of below 70 decibels for sounds levels (Ng and Tang 2017). The "fowls at Sin Ming" event further exemplifies how (urban) space impacts akoumenological reception – an acoustic phenomenology – and demonstrates how "many conflicts about sound [involve] issues of power and the right to dominate some environment with specific sounds or, conversely to free a setting from such sounds" (Bijsterveld 2013, 17). Sound frequently figures as a deeply contested phenomenon given its subjectivity of reception (Bijsterveld 2013, 14). In the context of a city, what some residents may consider as unwanted sound, and so deem it as noise, is "music" to others' ears. As Karin Bijsterveld posits, such disagreements over urban sound do not only touch on their individual meanings to those who hear them, but also express ideas about what the character of the city should be like, and what is allowed to be audible or not (Bijsterveld 2013, 14).

Sound does not only resonate with the cultural realities of a society, community or country but shapes its practices and policies. Historian Alain Corbin stresses how citizens' habitus condition their ways of listening (Corbin 1999, 16). Likewise, Jacques Attali, in *Noise: The Political Economy of Music* (2009), asserts that 'More than colors and forms, it is sounds and their arrangements that fashion societies' (Attali 2009/1985, 6). In an attempt to comprehend the acoustic ecologies of Singapore and their impact on lived experiences, this paper will examine the poetics of sound as a means of accessing and understanding the society's cultural and political realities. "Poetics" is understood to mean an objective and systematic inquiry into the mechanics of a work of art (Olsen 1976, 338). It is inevitably concerned with the hermeneutic and epistemological even as it engages primarily with the laws and principles of the work. Yet, "poetics" has increasingly and necessarily engaged with intermediality in the ways that technological media (inter)mediate experience and interpretation. The paper is thus twofold in its

---

[1] The AVA has been re-structured and renamed as the Animal and Veterinary Service (AVS) since 2019.

considerations: it is an inquiry into Singapore's sonicities and the media/tion of archiving these iconic sounds, or what R. Murray Shafer terms "soundmarks". In considering the poetics of sound, the paper will explore significant sound events in Singapore, in the recent years, to consider, hermeneutically, what they signify politically, socially, and culturally. It will explore some sounds in their dramatization and their relation to the cultural and political life-worlds (*Lebenswelt*) of Singapore/ans. As Jürgen Müller posits, nations "quite often make collective acoustic experiences which help to shape the national identity" (Müller 2012, 447). The studied events will reveal how the nation listens – to what it chooses to hear and what it remains deaf to. The second section argues for an importance of archiving sounds in/of Singapore given the absence of any authoritative sound library or sound map. Many iconic, culturally defining sounds are now lost to time; this loss further underscores the importance of archiving for past sounds and the perception of these sounds by historical actors inform us about the changing character and identity of cities, people and cultural practices (Bijsterveld 2013, 14). Technology today provides the means to capture and contain sound, as ephemeral phenomena, in high fidelity and this paper will consider the affordances of these technologies such as ambisonic sound recording and online digital sound maps. It will also include a discussion of an ongoing research project in collaboration with the National Archives of Singapore (SoundscapeSG) to record distinctive soundscapes in Singapore for a Singapore sound map. This will be followed by a critical investigation of the efficacies of sonic immersion and sonic cartography.

2   'Noise' and/as Cultural Heritage

The secondary title of this paper is made as an explicit acknowledgement and reference to Karin Bijsterveld's edited collection *Soundscapes of the Urban Past: Staged Sound as Mediated Cultural Heritage* (2013). Even as the essays in the book engage with various aspects of the sonic and acoustic in cityscapes, they converge on the argument that the dramatization of sounds reflects cultural meanings and, in turn, (urban) topography and spatiality shift modes of listening. These views are also posited in *Soundscapes of Modernity* (2002). Emily Thompson articulates the ways in which the soundscape of modernity reveals significant transformations in what people hear and the ways they listen to sounds, of how technology changes the nature of sounds and of listening such that the urban landscape leads to compulsions to control the behaviour of sound which in turn drives technological developments in architectural acoustics. With time, the elimination of noise and the retention of "good sound" became a preoccupation of urban landscape design.

In Singapore, this landscape design has primarily been constrained (and contained) by antithetical realties of limited land mass and desire for economic super-growth through the artificial insemination of new migrant populations. The highly built-up environment and omnipresence of skyscrapers and high-rise apartments are a consequence of the State's insatiable desire for material progress, further compounded by a conundrum of a densely packed population. This "growth-at-all-costs" mentality has come at the expense of natural sounds as natural spaces become transformed to spaces of concrete and steel; it has also turned urban noise into (acceptable) sound. Even as the government regulates and manages the volume of urban sounds (such as construction, traffic, and air-conditioning ventilators) with "permissible noise limits",[2] sound/noise pollution has increasingly become a concern for some as exemplified in a study done by the National University of Singapore in 2017. In the study, it was uncovered that many residential districts exceeded the World Health Organization's recommended threshold of 70 decibels and the National Environment Agency's limit of 67 decibels. The sounds of progress are deafening and in some cases literally so for even as the majority of Singaporeans who have grown accustomed to the incessant sound of construction, demolition and renovation, many, such as those that live beside shopping malls or train tracks, live with sound pollution, without option (Ng and Tang 2017).

In recent years, there has been discussion, both in Parliament and among the public on various media platforms, about the "loss" of Singapore's "kampung spirit" and a need to revitalize this. A "kampung" is the Malay word for "village" and in the context of Singapore kampungs were the prevalent form of residential organization in the days of pre-independence. These villages are composed of huts built in close proximity, and they formed a social and communal nucleus. Such modes of living led to a strong sense of neighborliness, camaraderie, and community, otherwise known as "kampung spirit". With rapid urbanization and the reallocation of land-use, all but one kampung remains in Singapore today as the government began relocating the resident population to high-rise flats, earlier mentioned, in the 1960s. While the earlier residential towns in Singapore, those built in the 60s and 70s, retained some sense of this "spirit" in spite of the enclosed designs of public housing, there are views that such neighborliness is dissipating particularly in the newer towns, and for which the architectural design of these spaces is to be partly responsible for (Au-Yong 2017). Yet this waning kampung spirit has an acoustic dimension. If one listens carefully, one hears Singapore's rapid material progress and economic competitiveness; the sounds of community are, arguably, becoming inaudible. In an interview with Singapore's main broadsheet *The Straits Times*, Kelvin Cham, a Singaporean who moved from an older residential estate of Bedok to the newer town Punggol, speaks of his new lived experience as a condition where "no one talks [...] Maybe it's because we're all at the same stage of life so there's either no small talk left to make, or an unspoken sense of competition makes us more prone to comparison, but you don't get the warmth you do at older estates" (Au-Yong 2017).

To add, even as some sounds become inaudible, others are amplified: For most Singaporeans living in public housing, the proximity of apartments and neighbors can breed sonic dissensions. Grievances about "noise disturbances" from neighboring residents are among the most common complaints attended to by Members of Parliament in charge of residential neighbourhoods (The Online Citizen 2021). Noise (and sound) knows few boundaries and heavy footsteps, grating sounds of furniture movement, screams of pleasure and pain, all permeate through the windows and walls of shoebox apartments stacked above and beside one another. According to the Community Disputes Resolution Tribunals at the State Court, 70% of neighbour disputes heard involve "excessive noise" (Lee 2016). These examples evidence Paul Hegarty's view of noise as a judgement of sound, "a social one, based on unacceptability, the breaking of norms and a fear of violence" (Hegarty 2008). "Noise is cultural" (Hegarty 2009, 3) and the sounds of

---

[2] See https://www.noisyneighboursingapore.com/articles/singapore-noise-regulations/.

other people "are the ones that are most complicit with power" (Hegarty 2009, 4). While these "background" sounds are, abiding by Schafer's delineations, keynotes of a residential neighborhood's soundscape, they are increasingly attaining a narrative iconicity – a sonic icon (Bijsterveld 2013, 15) that does not necessarily bear any relationship to the actual location and one that becomes associated with a narrative – that is arguably becoming a soundmark. The stories these "noises" of dense urban living reveal are ones of autonomy and control over what should be heard and what should not, of what sounds constitute harmonious living and which ones are intolerable. What is further posited here is the view that soundmarks are not necessarily 'harmonious' or pleasant, and perceived "noise" can be regarded as soundmarks that reveal as much a society's *Lebenswelt* – the realm of everyday being, a socially and culturally established sense and meaning[3] – as does its cultural, material and political location at a point in time.

2.1 The Politics of Sound/ing (and) Multicultural Heritage

As sound scholars, such as Steven Feld, would posit, sound is central to making sense, to knowing, to experiential truth (Feld 1996, 97). If so, what social and political truths are revealed when we devote an attentive listening to sonicities both audible and "inaudible" (or rather, silenced)? Sound (and aurality) are distinctly revelatory of a State's political lifeworld. In Singapore, multiculturalism is one of the city-state's core foundational (social-political) principles that further determines many of the government's policies from education to housing and the rule of law. It is the belief that the different ethnic groups (and for the government, race can be categorically determined to be "Chinese", "Malay", "Indian" and "Others") can (and will) live and work together as a united and cohesive people, and no particular cultural heritage or ethnic, religious identities will precede the national identity and the nation's shared values.[4] While the State advances the principle (which encompasses multireligiosity) primarily through visual signifiers such as ethnic costumes, religious festivals and, of course, skin color, multiculturalism has an acoustic dimension.

While a long discourse can be written about the acoustic dimensions of multicultural practice in Singapore, I will here examine a particular religious ceremony whose sacred sounds have been regulated and restricted. The Hindu Thaipusam festival is an annual ritual procession practiced by Singapore's Tamil Indian minority population and it commemorates the Hindu deity Lord Subramaniam who is also known as Lord Murugan, the god of youth, power, and virtue. The rite involves a procession of young devotees carrying a "kavadi", an elaborately decorated semi-circular frame made from steel and wood, and which, in some designs, has segments that are pierced into the flesh of the bearer who, supposedly, feels no pain for he is sustained by faith while being in a trancelike state; it

---

[3] Lifeworld is used here in the Husserlian sense. See Edumud Husserl, *Ideas Pertaining to a Pure Phenomenology and to a Phenomenological Philosophy—First Book: General Introduction to a Pure Phenomenology*, trans. F. Kersten, Nijhoff, The Hague (1982).

[4] For an overview of multiculturalism in Singapore, see Mathew Mathews, Introduction: Ethnic Diversity, Identity and Everyday Multiculturalism in Singapore, in Mathew Mathews (ed.), *The Singapore Ethnic Mosaic: Many Cultures, One People*, pp. xi-xxxix, Institute of Policy Studies, Singapore (2018).

is an act of penance and sacrifice. These kavadi bearers, along with other devotees, then proceed in colorful procession along public roads. The procession is accompanied by music and drumming, sacred sounds that are meant to sustain the devotees and create a soundscape of devotion and worship.

Broadly, religious foot processions in Singapore are not permitted by law; Thaipusam is an exception. The conditions for dispensing this exemption include a ban on music and drumming, a restriction that has been in place since 1973 after fights between rival groups of broke out, and music was used as a means of sonic competition thereby evidencing music's capacity to "inspire" disorderly behaviour. This restriction has eased in the recent years: in 2015, the government permitted specific spots where live music could be played; in 2019, traditional Indian drums such as the thavil, dhol, khol and urumi could make their rhythms heard, at (more) designated points and within specific hours but musicians needed to register themselves and their instruments prior with Singapore's Hindu Endowment Board.

Critically considered, the ban reflects how Hindu sacred sound is metonymic of danger and considered noise pollution by Singapore authorities. Yet sound participates at every level of the Hindu cosmos and is a key concept in Hindu theology, as Guy Beck argues. The Hindu world is permeated by sound and these sacred sounds are integral to the worship experience. Unlike other religious traditions that emphasize the ideal of silence and quietism, "Hinduism has sacred sound as its heart and soul. As such the ambiance of the traditional Hindu is consistently saturated with an astounding variety of different sounds" (Beck 1995, 6). In its practice, the religious (and its rites of sound) becomes confronted by the secular in public space where sound cannot be effectively contained as it saturates the immediate spaces with reverberations; the sounds dissipate the visual boundaries of public and private, religious and secular. Writing about the sonic politics of Thaipusam, Jim Sykes observes how "some heard (and continue to hear) Hindu processional drumming as crossing the chasm between public and private, and thus as being an unnecessary disruption of the public marketplace by communal culture" (Sykes 2015, 384). There is distinctly conflict between "governmental understandings of what sacred sounds can do and notions articulated by religious traditions that come to be defined in the public sphere as ethnic heritage" (Sykes 2015, 382).

Such distinctions are also true of sacred Islamic sounds. In all Islamic communities, the loudspeaker, radio, and television are integral to the traditional call to prayer, or *adhan/azan*. The adhan is a soundmark of the Muslim lifeworld. Broadcast technology became a means to amplify and transmit sacred sounds as Muslims responded physically and spiritually to the call. While older mosques in Singapore, those built before 1975, had loudspeakers that faced outwards of the mosque (for purposes of amplification to public spaces), those built after 1975 were compelled by law to have speakers face the interior of the building. With urbanization, and with multicultural practice in view, there was a need for new considerations of the soundscapes of shared spaces for sacred sonicities were regarded as "intrusive" to those outside that community (Lee 1999, 89). In another survey done in 2019 by the Institute of Policy Studies, an independent think-thank that studies and generates public policy ideas in Singapore, religious chanting or praying were among the loud events at void decks and common areas members of the public were put off by. The survey reveals how, as Lily Kong observes, "new urban social setup had caused sound production to sometimes be regarded as intrusive by those not involved in that religion or those particular events" (Kong 2005, 239).

This sonic politics has not escaped controversy or interrogation by some Singaporeans who have criticized the censuring of sacred sounds as possibly "racist" and discriminatory.[5] These netizens note how sounds of the cymbals and drums of lion dances, a characteristic feature of the Chinese New Year, singing of Christmas carols in public spaces, the loud rhythmic beats of from the *kompang*, a traditional Malay membranophone, heard during processional Malay weddings, and the piercing sounds of the *suona*, a Chinese double-reeded horn, played during Taoist funerals and some religious rites, are not prohibited. These events take place in public spaces but are permitted to continue despite the possible "noise" that can occur. The government, however, articulates its defence with a threadbare distinction between religious celebrations and social/community, non-religious celebrations. Social celebrations can involve music, song and drumming but (some) religious ceremonies, in particular those whose rites involve public processions, must manage (and silence) sonic output. The justification for this tenuous distinction between religious and social/cultural is founded on a belief that religious ceremonies carry a particular sensitivity with "the risks of incidents [...] considered to be higher" (Jalelah 2015).

Whether these risks can be distinctly attributed to sonicity remains unaddressed and undeliberated. Still, the regulation of sound is a distinct feature of contemporary urban societies. As sound does not recognise boundaries, borders, distinctions, categories, class, or classifications, its "management" and control become an inevitability in shared spaces. In Singapore, activities, most broadly defined, likely to create noise nuisance cannot be carried out after 10.30pm; there are also laws against making excessive noise on public transport and interestingly, in 2020, a member of the public contributed an opinion piece to the forum section of the broadsheet *The Straits Times*. This person requested that the Land Transport Authority of Singapore ban commuters from playing religious music out loud on trains and buses, even if these were played on their personal devices. This questionable opinion was rationalized on the basis that Singapore, being characteristically multi-religious, and public transport being a public good, must remain a secular space. Even as Singapore is regarded as a global exemplar of contemporary multicultural practice in which races and religious coexist harmoniously, such auditory events resound with a contrasting reality: complaints about religious/sacred sounds reverberate with frequencies of difference and absent aurality - a lack of active, sonorous understanding. As Sykes observes, 'A society's soundscape, then, may consist of multiple, overlapping soundscapes, containing contrasting definitions of sonic efficacy, of the characteristics and possibilities for sacred sounds in public space, and of personhood' (Sykes 2015, 382]. Lived multiculturalism, "multiculturalism as it is lived out as an everyday reality" (Nazry 2014), is, more accurately, "practiced tolerance through a fierce possession of a right to not be harassed and to keep a safe distance from the Other" (Tan 2020, 72).

---

[5] See for example, Crystal Ang, Thaipusam Drums Ban is so Racist We Can't Even, Mustsharenews, 5 February 2015, https://mustsharenews.com/thaipusam-saga/, last accessed 2021/02/02.

2.2 Sounding Local, Hearing Foreign

In the recent decade, Singapore's multicultural trademark has also become interrogated by many Singaporeans in the light of rapid growth in the immigrant population, with the nonresident population increasing at an unprecedented pace in the first decade of the 21st century (Yeoh and Lin 2012). This visible increase in the number of non-Singaporeans, delineated by some netizens are those not born in Singapore, which include foreigners here on various work passes and work permits, new citizens and permanent residents, have triggered concerns about a "Singaporean core"[6] being compromised and about what it is (or means) to be Singaporean. In virtual spaces and online places, at times with the aid of anonymity, there have been increasing vitriol against the foreign Other for occupying jobs, housing, and social spaces, and causing an erosion of a Singapore identity and culture. Equal contempt has been shown against the ruling People's Action Party for opening the immigration floodgates in the quest for greater material wealth, at the expense of cultural identity and Singaporean's social welfare and well-being. Many of these "foreigners" look like local Chinese or Indian, and visual signifiers such as the "color" of one's skin is no longer reliable in labelling Otherness. Evidently, in an increasingly interethnic, intercultural, and transcultural world, especially true in multiracial Singapore, Otherness is no longer just seen but heard. And xenophobia has a distinctly sonic quality.

In *Sonic Persuasion: Reading Sound in the Recorded Age* (2011), Greg Goodale expounds on the ways the use of dialect in early twentieth-century American sound recordings of dialogue signified urban immigrants, and played out elite pronunciation against lower-class dialect and immigrant slang (Goodale 2011, 16–26). Such discomforts of vocality and vocalism, or the sonicities of belonging and foreignness, have resounded in Singapore in the last forty years. Singlish, sometimes known as colloquial Singapore English, once a pidgin now a creole, is an amalgam of English, local additives from other languages and dialects spoken in Singapore, and Singapore slangs and colloquialisms. Singlish and its accompanying accent have always been the heart of controversy vis-à-vis a Singapore identity and self-fashioning. In the late 90s and early 2000s, the government viewed Singlish with caution and reservation as the sounds of the language came across as unrefined, crude and unsophisticated; it was regarded as the speech (patterns) of the "heartlanders" – a term that can be considered to carry nuances of caste and class since it refers to the common average (lower) middle-class Singaporean who lives in public housing. In 2000, the then Prime Minister Goh Chok Tong, at the 'Speak Good English' movement, reminded the population to "mind their language" for speaking Singlish would disadvantage Singaporeans on the global platform since no one else apart from Singaporeans would comprehend Singlish. Singaporeans, as such, would risk not being understood or taken seriously. Goh urged Singaporeans to speak good,

---

[6] This term was first introduced in a Parliamentary speech on 17 October 2011, by Dr Amy Khor, then Minister of State for Health and Chairman of REACH, the government unit for feedback. It was made in reference to keeping a core in the workforce made up of Singaporeans and imposing a quota of foreign workers. See the parliamentary proceedings here, https://sprs.parl.gov.sg/search/topic?reportid=009_20111017_S0010_T0001.

standard English so that they could compete on the global playing field.[7] On the other hand, some artists and linguists saw Singlish as distinctly unique and an audible marker of Singapore and Singaporeanness – it was evidence of a Singapore culture. Even as the debate about language and cultural identity ensued, speaking (and sounding) "Singapore Standard English" as opposed to Singlish or Singapore Colloquial English became entangled with issues of prestige and identity (Cavallaro et al. 2014). Given the mostly autocratic and directive attitudes adopted in governance, the media in Singapore hastily adhered to the government's linguistic position and subsequently disproved, discouraged or censored programmes that featured Singlish. Locally produced television series that ironically became popular because there were identifiable Singlish-touting characters were made to revise their positions on Singlish and have characters speak "better", standard English. An example of this would be the well-known television series entitled *Phua Chu Kang*. The weekly sitcom featured an average Singaporean, by the same name, who works as a building contractor and carelessly and carefreely uses Singlish in his daily interactions with other characters without inhibition. His authenticity and genuineness, evidenced from his willingness to spout Singlish ironically, was what made him an endearing character.

While the debate gradually waned and Singlish became an irrefutable reality for Singaporeans and their lived experiences, more recently, there has been a shift in attitudes toward Singlish particularly in the last decade given the rapidly changing population demographics in Singapore. In the last twenty-odd years, the country has seen a rapidly rising population of immigrants and foreigners, with the non-native population reaching 38 percent in 2020.[8] There has been a "reclamation" of Singlish as an identity marker; Singlish has become a means of identity-assertion to distinguish between the locals and the foreigners, a sonority of "sounding out" who is Singaporean and who is not, especially since many expatriates and foreign workers are from India and China (they physically resemble the native population). It is not simply the insertions of common discourse particles such as 'lah' or 'lor', or the inclusion of characteristic Singlish phrases such as 'wah lau' or 'tio' in daily discourse but the unique phonology – the accent, cadences, and 'melodies' – of Singlish which foreign speakers find difficult to replicate even if they were to master the grammar of Singlish. The resurgent interest in (speaking) Singlish and its more apparent adoption in the media and on the street can be regarded as a performativity of individual and national identity in the light of rising immigration due to the government's permissive labour laws on hiring 'foreign talent' and the country's addiction to cheap foreign labour; it is an acoustic assertion of being Singaporean, a sonic delineation of 'them' and 'us', 'I' and 'thou'. A sense of place is, as Feld reminds us, "also heard" (Feld 1996, 94). "Singaporeanness" is now a lived concept that is heard – in the Singapore accent, in Singlish, in the sonorities that the Other cannot produce.

---

[7] Goh Chok Tong, Speech by Prime Minister Goh Chok Tong at the Launch of the Speak Good English Movement 2000, 10.30am, Institute of Technical Education Headquarters Auditorium, https://www.languagecouncils.sg/goodenglish/-/media/sgem/document/pressroom/2000/sgem-launch-2000-goh-speech.pdf. Accessed 5 February 2021.

[8] See 'Population and Population Structure', Department of Statistics Singapore, https://www.singstat.gov.sg/find-data/search-by-theme/population/population-and-population-structure/latest-data.

3   Media/ting Sound: SoundscapeSG as Digital Archive

Recording sounds are an important alternative to ethnographic practice and the affordances of technology today in rendering and (re)producing sounds in high fidelity, in being able to offer an audio quality with audible detail of distinct tonal signatures, have enabled archives to document narratives in high-quality. Sound mapping has also become widespread because of the advent of internet technologies and user-friendly platforms such as Google Maps. This is in addition to low-cost digital audio recording devices abundant in the market today. Beginning with the World Soundscape Project in the 1972, with the numerous soundscape recordings that have been placed on tape and CD, there are now notable digital sound maps on the internet. Some of these include Radio Aporee (https://aporee.org/maps/), the "Cities and Memory" project (https://cit iesandmemory.com/), the Montréal Sound Map (https://www.montrealsoundmap.com/), the Nature Soundmap (http://www.naturesoundmap.com/about-the-project/), Sound of the Netherlands (http://geluidvannederland.nl/), The Soundscape of Istanbul (https://sou ndscapeofistanbul.ku.edu.tr/about) and the British Library's sound archive and sound map ((https://sounds.bl.uk/). These are but a small number, among several, of sonic cartographs one can find easily.

The race to record and archive sounds reveals its importance as a means of knowing and experience, its acoustemological significance as it were. Sound maps become tools of social memorialization as they reflect a culture's heritage and a society's "beingness". Sound maps serve to document cultural practices as means of comprehending community spaces; a concept of habitus and community must include a history of listening. Given the absence of any concerted attempt at archiving Singapore's acoustic ecologies, the National Archives in collaboration with "Aural Heritage: Developing a Singapore Sound Map as Cultural Archive" (RI 2/19 TCC), a research project funded by the Ministry of Education Singapore (Academic Research Fund Tier 1), developed SoundscapeSG (https://www.nas.gov.sg/citizenarchivist/SoundScape/des cribe). At present, SoundscapeSG is a user-contributed sound map that seeks to preserve the sounds of Singapore through community effort. Very much in its early stages of development and like many other sonic cartographs, the platform exploits existing map data and in the case of SoundscapeSG, it is 'OneMap", a digital mapping service developed by the Singapore Land Authority. With five categories of sounds at present, "Festivals and Celebrations", "Accents and Dialects", "Nature and Wildlife", "Sounds of the Heartlands", "Sounds at the Workplace", members of the public are able to upload sounds of up to 8Mb in m4a or mp3 formats. In addition to the crowdsourced sounds, the research project will facilitate the collection of specialized, third-order ambisonic recordings of specific soundscapes in Singapore and, along with a 360-degree image of that location, these will be subsequently imported into SoundscapeSG such that users can experience (a simulation of) the sounds in high fidelity. The intention is to create an immersive experience for the user. Ambisonics provide a complete spherical surround sound that pans with the source. Users will be able to listen clearly to the foreground/background sounds and the distinct components or layers in the soundscape, with this rendering a rich auditory experience. Ambisonics can also be adapted for stereo or multichannel formats and would benefit users of SoundscapeSG that may access the soundscapes on home computers accompanied by speakers or headphones, even as the experience remains fuller when using a VR headset as the level of immersion increases significantly.

While such forms of recent ambisonic and 3D, 360-degree technologies facilitate effective and novel ways of cartographizing and archiving, since they capture sonic events in even greater fidelity that arguably facilitate a deeper sense of immersion, of 'being there' in the space, sound mapping, more broadly, raises critical questions about the process of mediatization (and mediation). As Peter McMurray, tracing the evolution of what he terms "ephemeral cartographies" (the mapping of sound as ephemeral phenomenon) across history, writes, "With the advent of digital sound mapping practices, certain issues of aesthetics, ethics and storage came to fore [...] What is the relationship of sound to power? How can the temporality of sound be adequately represented in combination with static political and topographic cartography? How do sound recording technologies mediate geographic experience?" (McMurray 2018, 22). In relation to sound maps' capacities as archives to reflect (and possibly reify) heritage, history and culture of a society, to McMurray's list can be added: what sounds/soundscapes are sufficiently representative of a culture; who (should) determine(s) what these sonic archetypes or soundmarks are?; what is the politics of these otobiographies?[9]; "who is listening to whom right here?" (Derrida 1985, 35). Such purposeful sonic cartographising in many ways mediate authenticity through simulation even as they attempt to replicate authentic acoustemologies. Mediatization compels an inevitable mediation of experience which interpellates questions of what authenticities become depicted and what are excluded (or lost). These are pertinent issues to pose and ones that I have had to deliberate on in my course of archiving various Singapore soundscapes thus far.

A significant example of the politics of (digital) sonic cartographizing involves the acoustic representation of religious sounds in Singapore. Religion, under the State's definitional umbrella of multiculturalism, remains a delicate matter not only in its portrayal and narrativizing, but in daily discourse. Despite being among the world's most religiously diverse nation, Singaporeans remain uncomfortable speaking about religion for fear of causing offence. This culture of fear is propagated by frequent reminders from State officials about the need to be vigilant and cautious where issues of religion (and race) are concerned. In 2015, Prime Minister Lee Hsien Loong cautioned the populace that it is "quite unrealistic" to claim that religion is no long a sensitive no-go area (Lim 2015); in the 2020 Singapore General Elections, he once again reminded the public that issues of religion can cause "great umbrage" and so must be handled delicately (Ho 2020). In attempting to archive some religious soundscapes in Singapore, I have been posed questions about representation and iconicity, about why only the major religions are represented and archived, and not the rest?; Why is one denomination of a religion made audible and not others?; Should some religious ceremonial soundscapes be represented and publicly accessed since this could be regarded by some as a means of

---

[9] Otobiography is a portmanteau of autobiography and otology. Coined by Jacques Derrida, the term refers to the processes of an autobiography being constituted only by the 'ear' of the Other. Derrida is using the ear not as a metaphor but as a corporeal and physiological constant that listens and signs (or acknowledges) the identity of the autobiographer. It is also a call for the ear to listen for the noises in a text where the ear needs to listen to the unpredictable, the uncanny, the unheard, the heterogeneousness of *differance* of each utterance.

proselytizing, or misused by others as a means of encouraging radicalization? I have also been confronted with questions of linguistic representation and ones that border on the absence of translation and incomprehensibility: is there a need for re-presentation with surtitles, and if so, what is its effect on a sense of authenticity (and on immersiveness, given the 360-degree format of the accompanying image to the recorded soundscape).

Most of these are pertinent issues in mediatizing and archiving sound for there is intentional mediation in the ways that sounds are captured and represented. These questions also advent a politics of aurality – of hearing and of being heard. It evokes questions of who decides what should be heard and what is silenced or muted, of what and how these sounds be should heard. And while technology offers the ability to refine or attenuate soundscapes recorded, to shape and modulate frequencies to one's expectation and ideal, it also raises issues of what sonicities should be foregrounded and what should be placed in the background (such a quandary is absent in hearing soundscapes live for the ears attune accordingly in relation to the space). Questions of who determines what a soundmark is, as mentioned, arise as well. More significantly, mediating sound raises questions of authenticity and the immanence of experience – these are identical issues to the recomposition of digital images today, specifically of the ways in which they can be easily manipulated by various software and encoders. DeepFake, for example, has been a concern when it is employed for fake news or political gain. Questions of "authentic" aurality arise in the mediated re-composition of a soundscape for digital recording and editing can record and devise frequencies that the ear cannot hear. Even as the objective is one of "capturing" a soundscape in time, in its authentic, even "realistic", detail, mediatization will always already intervene in any attempt at re-presenting the real.

The questions above would surely extend beyond sound archiving and certainly holds true for all forms of documentation that involve digital media today. While one can never satisfactorily address these issues, cognizance of these challenges remains imperative and a persistent interrogation serves as a reminder than the endeavor to recreate experience in its authenticity must be considered critically and responsibly, and there must be an ethics of sound archiving; there must be an ethics of the sonic archivist as 'earwitnesses'.

4   Conclusion: Listening

In addition to the principle purpose of archiving what are distinct cultural sonicities, SoundscapeSG's equally important intention is to inspire users, particularly Singapore-ans who have arguably lost the art of listening, to listen again amidst the cacophony of sounds and noises, to locate meaning and meaningfulness in the soundscapes that surround them, and to encourage a culture of aurality.

In his TED talk, sound consultant Julian Treasure firmly asserts that "we are losing our listening [...] the premium on accurate and careful listening has simply disappeared" (Treasure 2011). Listening is intentional, conscious hearing and meaning making, or locating meaningfulness in the frequencies that envelop us. This loss is significant for, as Treasure postulates, sound places us in time and space; it is meaningful in the ways that sound reverberates not simply with physical or material characteristics of a space (and place) but also reveal signification - of social relations, cultural connections, and intersections of communal intentions (and community). To listen then, as Jean-Luc

Nancy reminds is, "is to enter that spatiality by which, at the same time, I am penetrated, for it opens up in me as well as around me, and from me as well as toward me: it opens me inside me as well as outside" (Nancy 2007, 14). Listening conjoins us with a space and in that constitution of sonority and space, identity is heard and identity is formed. "The ear opens into s sonorous cave that we then become" (Nancy 2007, 37).

References

Attali, J.: Noise: The political economy of music. Trans. Brian Massumi. Minneapolis/University of Minnesota Press, London (1985, 2009)

Au-Yong, R.: Less kampung spirit and vibrancy in newer towns?. The Straits Times. 28 September 2017. https://www.straitstimes.com/singapore/less-kampung-spirit-and-vibrancy-in-newer-towns. Accessed 18 Jan 2021

Beck, G.L.: Sonic Theology: Hinduism and Sacred Sound. Motilal Banarsidass Publishers Private Limited, Delhi (1995)

Bijsterveld, K. (ed.): Soundscapes of the urban past: staged sound as mediated cultural heritage. Transcript Verlag, Bielefeld (2013)

Cavallaro, F., Ng, B.C., Seilhamer, M.F.: Singapore colloquial English: issues of prestige and identity. World English. **33**(3), 378–397 (2014)

Corbin, A.: Village bells, sound and meaning in the nineteenth-century French countryside. London (1999). Originally published in 1994 as Les cloches de la terre Paysage sonore et culture sensible dans les cam pag nes au XIXe siècle, Paris

Derrida, J.: The Ear of the Other: Otobiography, Transference, Translation. Ed. Christie V. McDonald. Trans. Peggy Kamuf. Schocken Books, New York (1985)

Feld, S.: Waterfalls of song: an acoustemology of place resounding in Basavi, Papua New Guinea. In: Feld, S., Basso, K.H. (eds.) Senses of Place, pp. 91–135. School of American Research Press, New Mexico (1996)

Goh, C.T. Speech by Prime Minister Goh Chok Tong at the launch of the Speak Good English Movement 2000, 10.30am, Institute of Technical Education Headquarters Auditorium. https://www.languagecouncils.sg/goodenglish/-/media/sgem/document/press-room/2000/sgem-launch-2000-goh-speech.pdf. Accessed 05 Feb 2021

Goodale, G.: Sonic Persuasion: Reading Sound in the Recorded Age. University of Illinois Press, Urbana (2011)

Hegarty, P.: Come on, feel the noise. The Guardian, 11 November 2008. https://www.theguardian.com/music/2008/nov/10/squarepusher-paul-hegarty-noise. Accessed 07 Jan 2021

Hegarty, P.: Noise/Music: A History. Continuum, New York (2009)

Ho, G.: Singapore GE2020: race and religion a sensitive issue to be discussed with care, says PM Lee. The Straits Times. 9 July 2020. https://www.straitstimes.com/politics/race-and-religion-a-sensitive-issue-to-be-discussed-with-care-pm. Accessed 24 Jan 2021

Jalelah, A.B.: Shanmugam addresses questions over ban on playing music at Thaipusam. The Straits Times. 6 February 2015. https://www.straitstimes.com/singapore/shanmugam-addresses-questions-over-ban-on-playing-music-at-thaipusam. Accessed 02 Jan 2021

Kong, L.: Religious processions: urban politics and poetics. Temenos **41**(2), 225–249 (2005)

Lee, A.: Almost 70% of neighbour disputes heard by tribunals involve "excessive noise". Today. 23 September 2016. https://www.todayonline.com/singapore/70-neighbourly-spats-involve-excessive-noise-court. Accessed 17 Jan 2021

Lee, T.S.: Technology and the production of Islamic space: the Call to Prayer in Singapore. Ethnomusicology **43**(1), 86–100 (1999)

Lim, Y.L.: "Unrealistic" to say religion is no longer sensitive issue: PM Lee. The Straits Times. 12 May 2015. https://www.straitstimes.com/singapore/unrealistic-to-say-religion-is-no-longer-sensitive-issue-pm-lee. Accessed 24 Jan 2021

McMurray, P.: Ephemeral cartography: on mapping sound. Sound Stud.: Interdiscip. J. **4**(2), 110–142 (2018)

Müller, J.: The sound of history and acoustic memory: where psychology and history converge. Cult. Psychol. **18**(4), 443–464 (2012)

Nancy, J.-L.: Listening. Fordham University Press, Trans. By Charlotte Mandell. U.S. (2007)

Nazry, B.: Is Singapore truly multicultural?. Today. 14 February 2014. http://www.todayonline.com/singapore/singapore-truly-multicultural. Accessed 28 April 2017

Ng, J., Tang, F.X.: Living with noise pollution: Serangoon, Bukit Timah and Clementi among the noisiest neighbourhoods in Singapore. The Straits Times. 23 April 2017. https://www.straitstimes.com/singapore/housing/sounds-awful-cant-sleep-cant-talk-because-of-noise/. Accessed 15 Jan 2021

Olsen, S.H.: What is poetics? Philos. Q. **26**(105), 338–351 (1976)

Sykes, J.: Sound studies, religion and urban space: Tamil music and the rthical Life in Singapore. Ethnomusicol. Forum **24**(3), 380–413 (2015)

Tan, M.C.C.: "Pornography disguised as art": bare/d bodies, biopolitics and multicultural tolerance in Singapore. In: Tan, M.C.C., Rajendran, C. (eds.) Performing Southeast Asia: Performance, Politics and the Contemporary, pp. 61–84. Palgrave Macmillan, Cham (2020)

The Online Citizen.: WP's Jamus Lim highlights noise issue at Anchorvale; encourages residents to be mindful of noises they make at home. The Online Citizen. 15 January 2021. https://www.theonlinecitizen.com/2021/01/15/wps-jamus-lim-highlights-noise-issue-at-anchorvale-encourages-residents-to-be-mindful-of-noises-they-make-at-home/. Accessed 17 Jan 2021

Treasure, J.: Five Ways to listen better. TED. July 2011. https://www.ted.com/talks/julian_treasure_5_ways_to_listen_better?utm_source=whatsapp&utm_medium=social&utm_campaign=tedspread. Accessed 07 Feb 2021

Yeoh, B., Lin, W.: Rapid growth in Singapore's immigrant population brings policy changes. Migration Policy Institute. 3 April 2012. https://www.migrationpolicy.org/article/rapid-growth-singapores-immigrant-population-brings-policy-challenges. Accessed 19 Jan 2021

Towards Smart Planning Conservation of Heritage Cities: Digital Technologies and Heritage Conservation Planning

Claudia Trillo[1](✉) ⓘ, Rania Aburamadan[2],
Busisiwe Chikomborero Ncube Makore[1] ⓘ, Chika Udeaja[3] ⓘ, Athena Moustaka[1] ⓘ,
Kwasi Gyau Baffour Awuah[1] ⓘ, Dilip A. Patel[4] ⓘ, and Lukman E. Mansuri[4] ⓘ

[1] School of Science, Engineering and the Environment, University of Salford, Salford, UK
c.trillo2@salford.ac.uk
[2] School of Architectural Engineering, Middle East University, Amman, Jordan
[3] London South Bank University, London, UK
[4] Sardar Vallabhbahi National Institute of Technology, Surat 395007, India

Abstract. Consensus exists on the importance of local identity and diversity in the sustainability discourse, including community resilience. As result, cultural policies are essential to enable sustainability goals. In the construction industry, digital technologies are playing a significant role in flattening the richness and distinctiveness of local contexts and homogenizing languages and practices, under the pressure of the constant urge to reduce costs and the necessity to comply with a sometime overwhelming plethora of technical and legal requirements and standards. The ambition of this paper is to shed light to the interplay between digital technologies, planning practice and tangible heritage conservation in the city, by clarifying the dynamic among the three fields and their implications in the practice. In so doing, this paper aims at offering recommendations that can inform the smart heritage conservation planning practice worldwide, and can be used by experts working for heritage conservation authorities, local authorities, professional practices, charities and digital technologies companies.

Keywords: Smart heritage · Smart cities · Heritage conservation · Planning · Digital technologies · India · Jordan

1 Introduction

Interest in applying digital technologies in the two domains of urban planning and heritage conservation is growing, both in the scholarship, and in the applied practice. The application of digital technologies to the planning area relies on a widespread body of knowledge, included within the broader domain of "smart cities". Scholarship on smart cities unveiled benefits and threats deriving from the massive use of digital technologies on people's lives, by exploring the variety of issues and opportunities that big data, platforms and IT tools can offer. Examples of IT tools includes the uses of Geographic Information systems (GIS), Global Positioning System (GPS). Digital camera, laser

© Springer Nature Switzerland AG 2021
M. Rauterberg (Ed.): HCII 2021, LNCS 12794, pp. 133–151, 2021.
https://doi.org/10.1007/978-3-030-77411-0_10

scanners, virtual and augmented reality, Building Information Modelling (BIM) (Trillo et al. 2020; Udeaja et al. 2019), Artificial Intelligence (Mansuri et. al. 2019; Mansuri and Patel 2021). The various Communities Of Practices and stakeholders around the world, including chartered associations and global institutions such as the Royal Town of Planning Institution (RTPI) in the UK (RTPI 2021), American Planning Association (APA) in the United States (Barth 2019), the European Commission in the European member states (European Commission 2021a, b), nowadays converge on the belief that digital technologies are so pervasive, that they need to be operationalized within all levels of management and systems, thus setting the context for a new disciplinary approach to the planning practice, which requires critical understanding of the implications of such a massive use of digital technologies on issues such as democracy, diversity, cultural meanings.

For what concerns the impact of digital technologies on conservation of tangible heritage, the wider discourse that incorporates this domain is usually the application of digital technologies on the construction industry. This spans from the pervasive influence of digital design on architectural and engineering practice, to the use of digital instruments and tools, including digital platforms for data sharing and collaboration. Other examples include Building Information Modelling (BIM) objects, digital archives for materials and technical details, instruments and tools for digitalization of the different step of traditionally hand-made surveys, such as laser scanning, digital photogrammetry. The advantages offered by digital technologies to tangible heritage conservation often emphasize time and money saving in surveying and opportunities for storing and exchanging large amount of data, whilst detrimental impacts of such a use are associated with impoverishment and banalization of complex and articulated assets.

The interplay between the three domains, i.e. digital technologies, planning practice and heritage conservation, is still largely uncovered by both the international scholarship and international practice, one possible reason being the difficulty of cross-analysis three areas of increasing complexity and encompassing very different conceptual backgrounds, from cultural matters, identity, diversity, history (the domain of tangible heritage) to socio- political, legal and technical matters (the domain of planning) and technical, philosophical, ethical matters (the domain of digital technologies).

The ambition of this paper is to shed light to the interplay between digital technologies, planning practice and tangible heritage conservation, by clarifying the dynamic among the three fields and their implications in the practice. In so doing, this paper aims at offering recommendations that can inform the heritage conservation planning practice at a global level, and can be used by experts working for heritage conservation authorities, local authorities, local planning officials, professional practices, charities and digital technologies companies.

2 Smart Heritage in Urban Planning: A Literature Review

The discussion in this section covers the themes emerging from a literature review on smart heritage in urban planning. Keyword searches were used including "smart heritage" as the main term and secondary terms such as, "planning", "heritage conservation". Papers found in the keyword searches were checked manually against the selection criteria. Therefore, this section includes the conceptualization of smart heritage in urban planning (Sect. 2.1), the identified smart technologies for sustainable urban heritage management (Sect. 2.2) and the challenges emerged from the data analytics for the processes and practices of smart heritage planning (Sect. 2.3). Finally, the literature review has been complemented with more investigation in existing reports and guidelines, allowing to identify gaps and justify the necessity of this study in Sect. 2.4.

2.1 Conceptualizing Smart Heritage for Urban Heritage Conservation Planning and Management

The concept of the "smart city" has evolved in recent years shifting towards an intelligent infrastructure that harnesses the capabilities of technology to create an interactive dialogue between the citizens of a city and the city. New technologies (smart infrastructure) merges with the social capital of a city (users, innovation, learning, knowledge) to construct a smart and effective urban system that connects, protects and enhances the lives of a city's citizens. This dynamic interaction has been recognized as leading to a more efficient use of a city's resources and consequently, becoming an ideological vision for self-promotion. The new practices and services merging from smart cities have significant impacts on policy making and urban planning. More recently urban planning has increased engagement with the "smart cities" discourse and agendas of smart cities as a means to better understand the heightened role of technology in the management of collective urban services (Coletta et al. 2019; Karvonen et al. 2019). The conceptualization of the term "smart" in the context of heritage and planning showed relative variety in the selected literature. Traditional discourses have often viewed the matters of heritage conservation and planning and issues of sustainability and smart cities as antagonistic. Smart city agendas have traditionally been understood as promoting universal standardization and thereby reducing the nuances of the mode of planning. However, the selected literature suggests a clear shift from this discourse and towards a complementary relationship in creating smart heritage cities in a manner that respects cultural heritage and carefully endeavours to embed the diversity of data related to heritage (Dornelles et al. 2020). The new technologies applied to contemporary urban development create an interconnected information system through processes, measuring instruments, simulators, equipment, software systems and hardware. In this context the open, sustainable city can be created through real-time analysis of urban life and innovative modes of urban management (Kitchin 2014). In some cases, smart heritage cities remain at this "branding" and associative level often combining with terms such as "sustainable cities" and "inclusive cities" with no clear articulation of the use of smart technologies and how they are embedded into the planning system (Ji and Shao 2017; Badawi 2017). Liu (2018) acknowledges that themes such as cultural, touristic, creativity and innovation driven development, accessibility to services and quality of life are horizontally present throughout smart city strategies in China. However, cultural heritage promotion as an objective is not explicit in any of them. Although the evidence of publications from India in the search were low, it is clear that there is a continuing discourse in urban planning relevant to the implementation of smart heritage cities. In India, incredible investment has been made into the creation of smart cities. Cities are continuously identified for inclusion in smart city programs, often due to tourist and economic potential such as

Jaipur. In this regard, the heritage preservation of the city is embedded within the programs for creating smart cities (Jawaid et al. 2017). Specific aspects of the program such as master-planning are endorsed by the regional and local authorities and used for heritage and resource management and environment (Ghadei 2018).

A frequent conceptualization is the integration of historic preservation, heritage development, and tourism in local and regional smart cities and growth strategies and policies to stimulate the state and local economies (Facca and Aldrich 2011; Mar et al. 2018). The formulation of regional innovation policies and strategies currently implemented in regions of the European Union (2014–2020), assume an entrepreneurial approach to innovation, where local institutions play a central role through a smart specialization approach (Mc Cann and Ortega-Argiles 2011). This approach also stresses the crucial role of "enabling technologies" which is explained in the next section for the purposes of information and communication technologies as core strategic elements in the planning process and practice.

2.2 Smart Enabling Technologies for Sustainable Urban Heritage Management

In the context of smart cultural heritage, the "smartness" requirements of each are equally aligned to emerging intelligent and contextualized services. Across the literature, these services are generally made possible by a common set of key technologies that are becoming ubiquitous and inseparably identified with the realization of smart developments (Borda and Bowen 2017). Diverse smart technologies were suggested from the selected literature to effectively preserve and manage cultural heritage. Dutra et al. (2020) and Borda and Bowen (2017) conducted a literature search on smart tools used in heritage planning and identified that 3D scanning techniques, Building Information Modelling (BIM), mobile applications for integrated management of asset preservation and the sensors for acquisition and analysis of data from the collections in real time were some of the smart technologies used for planning the preservation of cultural heritage in the context of the smart cities. Other deployment of technologies includes the use of Internet of Things (IoT) technology for the digitalization of a database or museum information system (MIS) typically used as an electronic archive or catalog for cultural heritage (Korzun et al. 2017). Koukopoulos et al. (2018) proposes an intelligent system in South Korea designed using a combination of technologies from dedicated mobile applications to analyze collected data in real-time for the effective management of urban cultural heritage events such as carnivals. The potential of gathering real time data from smart mobiles for spatial mapping and tracking in urban planning was also suggested by Toha and Ismail (2015). Sun et al. (2016) and Navarro de Pablos et al. (2019) argue that IoT and big data analytics has the potential to provide a ubiquitous network of connected devices and smart sensors for smart heritage and enhance the services in the area of tourism and cultural heritage. In the study by Sun et al. (2016) on an Italian town, Sun et al. (2016) identify two opportunities of IoT in smart heritage cities: (1) mobile crowdsensing, (2) cyber-physical cloud computing. Mobile crowdsensing relies on data collected from mobile sensing devices. Cyber-physical cloud computing systems are smart networked systems with embedded sensors, processors and actuators that are designed to sense and interact with the physical world. Emerging technologies that provide a visualization to aid decision making such as augmented reality (AR), virtual reality (VR), and mixed reality (MR), are also recommended as valuable for urban regeneration project management (Pica et al. 2019).

Building Information Modelling (BIM) is described as a valuable tool for the effective communication and management of heritage information and within the area of urban planning. Characteristically, BIM uses three-dimensional building modelling software with smart parametric object features, combining tangible and intangible data to increase efficiency in building design and construction (Udeaja et al. 2020). The advantages of using BIM offer a platform with heterogeneous information that is available multiple stakeholders to enable better decision making at a local level. Geographic Information Systems (GIS) are mentioned as widely accepted and accessible for urban planners. Planners have adapted the GIS tools to meet their particular requirements for the purpose of decision making and often integrated existing analytical techniques with GIS packages to develop user friendly planning tools (Sabri et al. 2014). A possible limitation is the use of GIS with other technologies and software to provide a holistic data for strategic and local heritage conservation planning. Integrating GIS is described through the Historical Small Smart City Protocol, dataset framework based on GIS (geographic information system) software proposed by Pica et al. (2019). The framework is primarily implemented using open big data and local data. Its purpose is to assess future scenarios for developing integrated strategic planning that is oriented toward sustainable management, in order to develop and preserve minor historical centers.

2.3 Data Analytics for Smart Heritage

The literature search revealed significant opportunities for the use of smart data in urban heritage planning. The smart physical and computational processes will enable the accumulation of large amounts of data, which can be analyzed, interpreted, and appropriately leveraged to facilitate reasonably accurate decision-making and control in urban heritage planning and management (Sun et al. 2016). Several challenges with data analytics in the creation of smart heritage cities are identified in the literature include: Data standards and interoperability, Data architecture, Data heterogeneity, Data administration and management, Organizational capacity and lack of skills and awareness of smart technologies.

Inconsistency in the production and conceptualization of data and different standardizations reduces interoperability of data and tools (Petti et al. 2020; Mar et al. 2018). The incorporation of such standards aide in the creation of a generic system for heritage planning and management in diverse contexts and promote sharing and longevity of data regardless of inevitable technological advances. Sabri et al. (2014) suggests that monolithic systems are replaced by smart components designed to interoperate through compliance with industry-wide standards. Therefore, the existing challenge in many national contexts is how to improve intelligent data interpretation and semantic interoperability? Without a clear standardization, decision making is very uncertain. Interoperability and standardization of data platforms improves decision making under uncertainty by understanding assessment, representation and propagation of uncertainty, developing robust-optimization methods, and designing optimal sequential decision making (Sun et al. 2016). To enhance the comparability of heritage data across cities and countries, there is a crucial requirement for standardized methods for perceiving, valuing, measuring and monitoring heritage. Therefore, national and local capacity development is needed to ensure the sustainability of national and local processes. The harmonization of these processes using similar standards and conceptualization can allow for the comparison of data among countries toward the achievement of the Sustainable Development Goals.

A robust data architecture is crucial to successful implementation of smart technologies. Riganti (2017) proposes a smart heritage intelligent environment with an architecture dedicated to deliver elements such as crowdsourcing, e-governance, valuation and case-based reasoning. Open Data platforms with static data sources are useful. In this regard an example is the OpenData Trentino which combines data concerning tourist attractions/services, photos, videos, 3D content and special location data of specific businesses (Sun et al. 2016). Dynamic real-time data will often use the capabilities of real-time data sources and stations and more recently the use of crowdsourcing. Open geo data published freely online by municipal, regional, and national authorities is used to develop smart heritage frameworks (Pica et al. 2019; Pili 2018; Scorza et al. 2019).

The data relevant to urban heritage planning and management is typically heterogeneous and diverse. Smart data on a heritage building may including the tangible qualities such as building structure and materials and the state of the building components such as doors and windows. In addition to this data is the intangible qualities of the building such as occupancy, history, cultural values. The challenge therefore is how to unify data representation and processing models to accommodate heterogeneous or new types of data. The use of information management platforms such as HBIM are suggested in literature as playing a significant role in harmonising heterogeneous data in one system (Trillo et al. 2020; Udeaja et al. 2020).

Furthermore, the trends towards smart heritage management have influenced a shift in data administration and management. The roles of national government, state/local government and private sector are changing to accommodate how data is shared and managed and therefore localizing decision making (Sabri et al. 2014). The shifts are largely seen in developed countries that have upskilled and developed structures that support the integration of technologies. Smart heritage systems could significantly facilitate the management of public affairs by local administrations moving gradually towards widespread data distribution to the general public (citizens, professionals, public, and/or private bodies) (Pica et al. 2019).

However, in many countries, there exists a definite gap in skills, capacity and awareness of the integrating of new technologies in planning strategies and implementations. This suggests a resistance to shifting of traditional structures and ways of working that may limit the success of smart technologies and processes. Navarro de Pablos et al. (2019) describe the consequences of technological enclosures that may cause disconnection and fragility within a city infrastructure. In the example of Valdenebro and Gimena (2018), urban planners hesitated to engage with the proposed smart technologies due to the complexity of heritage such as in the case study of the city of Pamplona, Spain. Valdenebro and Gimena (2018) describe that there was knowledge of some previous experiences of technology executed in new urban developments but not in constrained spaces as the case of a medieval historic centre.

2.4   The Interplay Between Digital Technologies, Planning Practice and Heritage Conservation

The literature search revealed significant opportunities for the use of digital technologies in both the domain of planning (smart cities) and heritage (smart heritage), however, it also revealed paucity of reflection on the interconnections between smart cities and smart heritage, which is reflected in gaps at policy level. As an example, the European continent has been a pioneer in the acknowledgement of the necessity to cooperate towards digitalization of cultural heritage (2019 Declaration of Cooperation on advancing the digitization of cultural heritage) (Petti et al. 2019). In support of the principles expressed by this declaration, the Expert Group on Digital Cultural Heritage and Europeana has issued a document explaining the "Basic principles and tips for 3D digitisation of tangible cultural heritage for cultural heritage professionals and institutions and other custodians of cultural heritage" (European Commission 2021b). This document covers issues that are quite common in data management (costs, quality, storage, ownership), and offers valuable insights and guidance, but does not articulate the discussion with respect to the different strategies that enable heritage conservation and most importantly, does not differentiate among isolated heritage episodes and complex heritage environments.

Indeed, the concept that not only the individual tangible heritage objects deserve attention, but also their articulation through the materiality of the urban fabric, has been capturing the attention of planning theory and practice gradually, and this has happened systematically at international level only in recent times. Italy has pioneered the conceptualization of the so called "historic centre", which became popular following the Gubbio Charter, back in 1960. This latter was signed by a group of politicians, local administrators, experts and academic, and paved the way to a rich set of planning policies and tools enabling an effective conservation of major and minor historic centres (ANCSA 1960). One of the key-principles stated in the charter was based on the idea that conservation should be extended to the entirety of the physical urban fabric and therefore conservation policies should be pursued at neighborhood level, not at the level of the individual building. In fact, it was the neighbourhood and not the individual building that had to be identified for planning interventions, by including private and public assets, main and minor roads, exterior and interior of the buildings.

Moving forward, the ICOMOS Washington Charter (1987), by building on the UNESCO "Recommendation Concerning the Safeguarding and Contemporary Role of Historic Areas" (Warsaw - Nairobi 1976). This was reinforced at international level the concept that the entirety of the urban fabric needed attention from conservation policies, and should be included in the wider socio-economic policies and urban and regional planning (ICOMOS 1987). The Washington Charter was then revisited in 2011 by the 17th ICOMOS General Assembly, with the document "The Valletta Principles for the Safeguarding and Management of Historic Cities, Towns and Urban Areas". This was done by incorporating the concept of sustainable development in the notion of heritage conservation, and by emphasizing the interconnected nature of tangible and intangible values underpinned in the materiality of the urban fabric, as such, considering heritage as part of the urban ecosystem. In the same year (2011), the 36th session of the UNESCO's General Conference adopted the "Recommendation on the Historic Urban Landscape", popularizing internationally the acronym HUL (Historic Urban Landscape), as instrumental to vehicle the complexity of the societal, cultural and developmental values incorporated in the materiality of the urban shape.

The inextricability of the interconnection between heritage and urban shape challenges the idea that conservation policies can remain confined within the perspective of the individual building, and therefore digitalization of heritage for the purpose of heritage conservation requires re-casting it within the wider scope of planning for conservation, i.e., in the contemporary digital era, within the wider domain of smart cities. What mechanisms are the most appropriate to disentangle the complexity of this nexus and to make it manageable through the appropriate digital technologies? This is a question that as far as in our knowledge remains unresolved. It is the aim of this paper to push the body of knowledge forward, by drawing insights from two parallel research projects in India and in Jordan.

3 Methodology

The research study aims to shed light to the interplay between digital technologies, planning practice and tangible heritage conservation, by clarifying the dynamic among the three fields and their implications in the practice. The discussion offered in this paper is a body of knowledge accumulated in two research projects over a 3 years' time by a team of researchers located in three countries, United Kingdom, India and Jordan. Two case studies in Jordan and India have been conducted over the last 3 years on urban heritage conservation and digital technologies. The findings from these case studies have been analyzed and developed into a set of guidelines of general applicability. The guidelines suggested in this paper can inform the heritage conservation planning practice worldwide, and can be used by experts working for heritage conservation authorities, local authorities, professional practices, charities and digital technologies companies. The research methodology for both case studies consisted in producing 3D digital models of a range of different heritage assets, and by questioning the usability of the data produced through a discussion with local stakeholders. The two case studies are the two cities of Surat in Gujarat, India, and As Salt in Jordan (Fig. 1). Both case studies have required extensive data collection, both in terms of data acquisition (heritage assets) and in terms of stakeholders' engagement.

The qualitative set of data includes national laws on heritage conservation, local plans, regulations and guidelines on heritage conservation and planning, strategic documents on smart cities, any other document and report relevant to the topic. The team has engaged in numerous exploratory interviews with a wide range of experts, to make sure that the context was clear, by triangulating secondary data with primary data collected through non-structured interviews, with local city planners, architects and experts in the fields covered by this research, as broadly discussed in previous works (Udeaja et al. 2020; Trillo et al. 2020). Site visits to the heritage centres were conducted by the team, to accurately contextualize the 3D models. The data set for both cases included digital acquisition of 3D images of chosen buildings within the heritage centres, delivered through different technologies. Finally, both case studies were discussed through various real and virtual focus groups, involving a high number of local experts (in the order of 50 participants per case study).

The data set regarding the buildings has been built with different criteria in the two case studies. In the case of Surat, the team focused on the selection of a variety of monuments, with the aim to support promotion of heritage assets and raising awareness at local level on the importance of tangible and intangible heritage. The city of Surat is a mid-size Indian city in the Gujarat state, with a glorious past based on the diamonds industry and currently challenged by rapid urbanization, including the construction of a new metro line cross cutting the heritage core, and the demolition of private housing in the two historic areas of the city, i.e. Gopi Surat and Rander. Meetings with planning officials and local experts confirmed the challenges to local heritage and the potential of digital technologies, including a Surat Smart City programme led by the local authority. In this case study, digital technologies have been used to support the creation of a narrative, aimed at eliciting sense of proud and belonging in the community and hopefully contribute to the conservation of heritage through local regulations, focused on heritage monuments, e.g. the British Cemetery (Fig. 1).

In the case of As-Salt, the team focused on private houses. The City of As Salt is a small-size town close to the capital city of Amman in Jordan, rich in architectural heritage due to its importance in the Ottoman period. The local government is keen to build on this unique feature to foster local economic development, and as part of this strategy, the City has applied to be inscribed within the UNESCO heritage list. In this case study, digital technologies have been used to explore the potential of 3D models as a vehicle to support a management plan for heritage conservation, following the tradition of the "Handbook for conservation" (Trillo et al. 2020). The concept that lies at the core of this planning instrument, which was developed through some pioneering cases in both large and small Italian cities in the late 1970s (Pesaro, Rome, Citta' di Castello), is the assumption that heritage centres are made of the interconnection of different scales: urban fabric/buildings/architectural components. The physical shape of heritage cities rests on the structured articulation of technological details, which are rooted in local materials and in skills often developed through generations. Handbooks for conservation included a range of exemplar buildings, disassembled by components with the purpose to support architects and designers in their work of designing interventions on similar buildings. In the case of As Salt, where the uniqueness of the HUL rests on the golden limestone magnificent Ottoman houses, choosing two Ottoman houses (e.g. Qaqeesh house, Fig. 1) was instrumental to create a library of digital components for heritage houses.

Because of the nature of the two research projects, aimed at tailoring the digitalization of the chosen heritage to the local context by co-deciding and co-producing the project operational strategy in collaboration with local stakeholders, the two cases are not suitable to be discussed in a comparative perspective. However, both cases present commonalities that are worth discussing in the following section, as well as, they produced insights of general applicability.

Fig. 1. Location and Built Heritage of the City of Surat, India and the City of As Salt, Jordan

4 Towards Smart Urban Heritage Planning: Insights from Two Research Projects

Section 4 is articulated in 3 sub-sections, the first 2 sections illustrate the 2 research projects (Sects. 4.1 and 4.2), and Sect. 4.3 discusses common issues and differences. It has to be highlighted that the 2 research projects started at 1-year distance, therefore while the first case project started in 2018 and is now concluded, the second case project started in 2019 and is still ongoing. There is unbalance in terms of findings, which are still preliminary for the second case. As anticipated in the methodological section, it is not the goal of this discussion to attempt a comparative analysis of the two cases, nevertheless, some mechanisms are recurrent and it should also be noticed that all the tips and recommendation elaborated for the digitization of heritage, look perfectly pertinent to the two cases studies, located in Asia and the Middle East. Finally, the lessons learned from both cases reflect general issues arising from the implementation of digital technologies on planning heritage conservation, thus, they can be of interest for the wider international audience.

4.1 IT Indian Heritage Platform: Enhancing Cultural Resilience in India by Applying Digital Technologies to the Indian Tangible and Intangible Heritage

The "IT Indian Heritage Platform: Enhancing cultural resilience in India by applying digital technologies to the Indian tangible and intangible heritage" is a bi-national and 2 years project funded by the UK Arts and Humanities Research Council (AHRC) UK and Indian Council of Historical Research (ICHR) New Delhi. It aims at exploiting the potential of digital technologies in raising awareness on the extraordinary cultural value of the tangible and intangible Indian heritage, currently under threat because of a variety of challenges, including rapid urbanization and demographic changes associated with the flow of new population moving from different areas of the country.

The case study for this project is the city of Surat in Gujarat, a major metropolitan area experiencing dramatic migration flows. The research team has produced a sample of 10 exemplar heritage buildings, which will be made available to the wider public. It will be possible for the website users to navigate the buildings through 3D models, including information on constructive techniques and state of conservation. The data on the buildings will be complemented with further information reflecting intangible values connected to the tangible heritage. Although the website and associated dataset is the main outcome of this research, partner institutions from India and UK will continue working jointly beyond the project through a Center of Excellence. This will be internet based and will offer support to all those authorities, willing to implement the same approach (gtr.ukri.org). This project has been recently concluded and was conducted by an interdisciplinary team including experts on different fields, including engineering, architectural heritage conservation and planning. Key stakeholders in this project include the Archaeological Survey of India (ASI) and the city of Surat, with which the team has been engaging since the beginning of this project, by producing in 2018 recommendations for the city planners on how to implement the "Regulations for Heritage Buildings, Sites and Precincts in Surat". Following a stakeholder engagement workshop held in Surat in September 2018, the selection of the tangible heritage to digitalize has privileged paradigmatic examples of heritage buildings, expression of the unique identity of Surat. The process of acquisition of the formal authorization for capturing data in the chosen heritage areas has been extremely time consuming and has involved different levels (local, national and state authorities). It is paramount that researchers are aware about the difficulties and constraints in getting permissions to acquire the data, since they may have a significant impact on the project delivery. Following the data capture, the exploration of these heritage assets through digital technologies has been conducted by applying different techniques, with the aim to identify the most pertinent and achievable within the specific context of Surat. Isolated assets such as the Clock Tower or specific buildings within the wider archaeological areas of the Dutch and British cemeteries (Fig. 2) have been either laser scanned or captured through photogrammetry. Larger areas or heritage sites, such as the complex archaeological sites of the Dutch and British cemeteries and the breath-taking Khammavati Step well have been either laser scanner or captured through aerial photos taken by UAV (Unmanned Aerial Vehicle) technology (drones) (Fig. 3).

The digitalization conducted within this project has allowed to offer to both the authorities in charge of heritage conservation and to the wider public a variety of exemplar buildings, which will be made available through the Centre of Excellence, under construction, although challenged by issues of ownership and financial sustainability. Further considerations emerged from the application of different technologies allowed to confirm that: (1) Point clouds (raw data) from laser scanning technologies are the preferable option for the purpose of heritage documentation, although it is crucial to budget for sufficient data storage and to make sure that public authorities retain ownership on the raw data; (2) HBIM objects allow pulling together a variety of data, including costs, environmental performance, etc. and are therefore ideal to complement smart planning instruments and tools as well as smart heritage management plans for heritage cities, however, they require a simplification of the original point cloud and therefore should

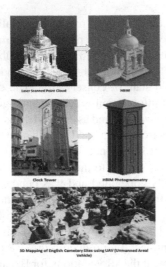

Fig. 2. Digitization of heritage

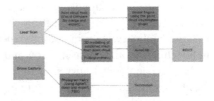

Fig. 3. Workflow

never be considered a replacement for raw data for the purpose of documentation; (3) For the purpose of tourist promotion and marketing, photogrammetry and aero photogrammetry remain the most viable options in financial terms, and lead to satisfactory outputs, however, they should not be considered a suitable replacement of raw data captured through laser scanning for the purpose of heritage documentation.

4.2 IT and Conservation of Traditional Architecture and Heritage in Jordan

The "IT and conservation of traditional architecture and heritage in Jordan" is a bi-national and 2 year project funded by the UK Royal Academy of Engineering. It aims at developing a set of virtual models (3D models and BIM objects) suitable to support the construction sector and traditional architecture and heritage in Jordan. By developing a new set of BIM (Building Information Modelling) objects related to the traditional architecture heritage in Jordan, engineers and architects will be supported in the development of interventions on the historic city. 3D models will also be used to promote Jordanian heritage through virtual tours. The team initially focused on the City of As Salt. As-Salt is a historic city in Jordan, located 28 km west of Amman and approximately 50 km north-east of Jerusalem and 240 km south of Damascus, situated within the region of Al-Balqa, between the Jordan Valley and the Eastern Desert. The city of As-Salt is considered a unique city in Jordan, and probably in the whole region (Trillo et al. 2020; Ministry of Tourism and Antiquities & Bank 2005; ASCOP 2016; Khirfan 2013; Khuraisat 2015; Khureisat and Farid 2015; Tarif 2015). The built characteristics of the city such as the use of golden stone for the houses and its geographical location and social landscape differentiate the city from other Jordanian cities. As-Salt is one of the most consolidated and oldest urban settlements in Jordan and today the old city centre maintains a very local original character. However, the city's heritage is threatened by lack of maintenance, neglect and encroachment and the traditional built heritage of the Ottoman period is not protected by an appropriate legal framework.

Fig. 4. Qaqeesh house point cloud and photos

The project approach is based on co-creation and is end-users centred. As such, the project implementation started with a Stakeholders' engagement and co-creation workshop hosted in Amman on 20th February 2020 by the Jordan Tourist Board. Researchers and experts worked collaboratively to identify challenges and opportunities for the application of Digital Technologies on Heritage Conservation in Jordan. The workshop also helped to refocus the mission for the Center of Excellence (COE), with an emphasis on documentation and knowledge sharing of international best practices on UAH conservation and a call for more clarity on the role that such a COE may play in the actual UAH Jordanian governance system. Two virtual local and international workshops were held in November 2020. The international stakeholder workshop was held to gauge suggestions and feedback on the Project from international experts, discuss transferability of international best practice with Jordan local stakeholders, and Knowledge transfer across international experts and local stakeholders. Over 100 participants from both workshops participated from government, industry, private sector and academia. The project has so far produced the point cloud and related virtual tour for a chosen exemplar house in the historic precinct of As Salt, the Qaqeesh house, with in the process to acquire data on a second exemplar building, Al-Jaghbeer house. HBIM objects are being derived from the raw data, or manually produced by resting on fieldwork with the aim to create a library of objects useful to be used by local architects and engineers. Figure 4 illustrates the characteristic features of Qaqeesh house based on laser scanned images and the development of a BIM object and a virtual tour. Through the use of digital technologies, the details of the unique features of the house can be interpreted. The walls of the house were built using local yellow stones and the cross vaults are the main roofing system with some barrel vaults. Wooden beams from tree trunks covered by reeds were used on a small area on the upper level. Further considerations emerged from the survey of Qaqeesh house and creation of BIM object process, which include: (1) Documentation of the house was necessary to start working on BIM objects. Many of the key documents related to As-Salt's built heritage were originally written in Arabic and therefore were translated for the purpose of this study. (2) Visualisations can be developed from 3D models such as the case with the laser scans for the Qaqeesh house which were further developed into a virtual 3D tour by the project's research partner. This 3D tour of the Qaqeesh house is made available on the Jordan Tourism website purposed to increase awareness of As-Salt's heritage and promote heritage tourism in Jordan.

The BIM process includes on several steps to get the full benefit from BIM technology, importing data manually remains essential to include extra data which can support architects and engineers. For example, materials characteristics is one requirement of using BOQ (Bill Of Quality) and BOM (Bill Of Materials), such data can be generated through specific studies and be added to the HBIM objects (Fig. 5). While geometry can be derived from the point cloud, further data including thermal characteristic of the materials, resistance, can be generated and added manually, as well as, further data can include (Fig. 6).

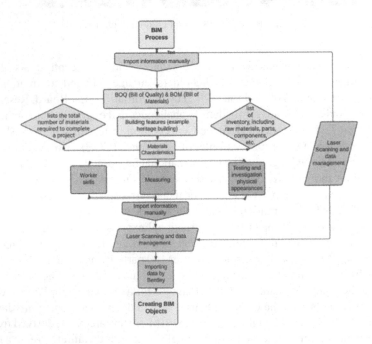

Fig. 5. Workflow process of BIM object creation

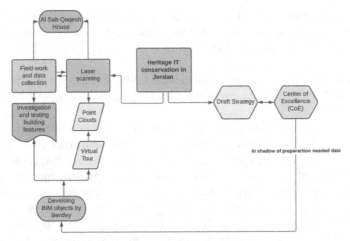

Fig. 6. Workflow process of Scan to BIM for Qaqeesh house

4.3 Lessons Learned for Smart-Planning Smart-Heritage Conservation.

Both cases have confirmed a variety of issues that the literature and scholarship on heritage digitalization had clearly stated, such as:

(1) Digitalizing heritage assets request as first stage a data capture process, which should be carefully thought through the project delivery and specification. Time consuming process may be required in order to get permission from a variety of authorities, wherever the heritage is listed or protected. On the other hand, non-listed heritage often coincides with the wealth of historic buildings, which constitute the elements of the urban fabric, i.e. privately owned residential and mixed-use buildings. Issues in getting access to such heritage can be sometime insurmountable, and therefore the only option remains articulating the description of the building to the mere external shell.

(2) Different technologies present pros and cons, however, achieving the goal of acquiring high quality point clouds and storing raw data, remains essential for the purpose of heritage documentation and most importantly, in case any missing elements needs replacement due to natural or man-made disasters.

(3) Point 2 leads to two further points, issues in data storage and data exchange and issues in data ownership, which will be considered jointly because of their interconnected nature. The issue of the lack of awareness of local and national authorities in charge of heritage conservation seems acute in all the context investigated either through secondary data, or in the specific cases investigated through these projects, despite the fact that both case studies are included in context in which heritage is highly valued and properly protected. As matter of facts, the lack of systematic practices in creating structured public archives collating all data related to heritage mirrors the lack of awareness on the relevance of the issue. Heritage is a different object than standardized building elements and the necessity to store raw data to keep trace of the complexity and "imperfection" of historic buildings is paramount. This leads to difficulties in cross-collaboration as far as in the current performance of the web and hardware commonly used, but most importantly there is very little consideration of the necessity to create large storage spaces to be able to keep

data in a systematic way. Finally, it is often unclear to the authorities in charge of managing heritage conservation that point clouds, i.e. raw data and not the final outcomes, are to be acquired to the public domain.

In addition to confirming aspects that the scholarship has flagged up, this study adds the planning and heritage management component to the discussion, with the following:

(4) For the purpose of planning heritage conservation, it would be extremely useful if architects and engineers could benefit from a systematic archive of HBIM object that, shadowing the rationale of the Handbooks for conservation, could offer guidance and support in deciding the best solutions. Those HBIM objects will present a simplified version of the original heritage elements, by readjusting the complexity of the geometry of the initial object through approximations, which are inevitable in the light of generating lighter 3D object, however, perfectly fit to the purpose of offering a living example rather than serving the aim to recreate them in case of destruction. Systematic archives of HBIM objects could feed into the management and conservation policies of heritage cities, in support to the work of engineers and architects and of the whole supply chain involved in the conservation process. In fact, HBIM can incorporate extra layers of information, usable in the construction industry, and suitable to enrich and make stronger any policy guidance and recommendation. The opportunity for architects and engineers to have available HBIM objects related to some exemplar buildings, would be un-valuable, since information retrieved for the exemplar buildings such as energy performance or structural resistance could be easily transposed thanks to the parametric nature of the BIM objects.
(5) Point 4 leads to another key aspect which makes HBIM models relevant to the planning process in heritage cities, i.e. the issue of transferring skills. In fact, HBIM include layers of information that go under the skin of the building and offer an opportunity to learn about the constructional techniques, which are the backbone of the materiality of the city. By circulating HBIM objects across the wider public of designers, architects, decision makers, builders, the culture and materiality of the heritage buildings could be preserved and transferred.

5   Conclusion

This paper was aimed at discussing the intersection between smart cities and smart heritage, with the aspiration to produce recommendations for planners, architects, local authorities and heritage conservation authorities. This goal has been achieved by discussing the findings of two research programmes, in the perspective of their applicability to the conservation planning process. In fact, it is through planning policies and plans that conservation is extended to the wider urban fabric, and this is an aspect that tends to be overlooked by both the scholarship and non-academic documents on heritage conservation because it is situated in a grey area between two distinct fields of specialism, i.e. heritage conservation on the one hand, planning on the other hand. As a result, while smart heritage and smart cities have been thoroughly scrutinized, and the correlation between digital technologies and planning and digital technologies and heritage widely investigated, the role of digital technologies on planning heritage conservation hasn't been covered.

Indeed, heritage is a very different object from other component of the urban fabric, this is because, the majority of heritage assets were produced before the system of industrial production of the built environment became pervasive. For this reason, concepts such as standardization of the architectural components or industrialization of the building elements are not applicable, and this tends to become a limitation in the application of technologies, that benefit from clustering information through similarities. On the one hand, heritage is not a standardized object and its beauty lies on "imperfections". On the other hand, a thoroughly precise representation of heritage is not necessarily functional to support planning instruments such as guidelines and regulations, while it can be un-valuable in case of post-disaster reconstruction.

It is therefore suggested that raw data based on high quality point clouds are always kept in the public ownership, to make sure that in case of forced reconstructions of missing elements or of the entire building, still it is possible to retrieve an accurate description of the physical details. Obviously, such data would require large amount of virtual infrastructure (data storage) and would result in limited opportunity for data sharing, and it is paramount that national and local authorities understand the importance of archiving properly all the raw data and to keep them in the public domain.

For what concerns the use of digital technologies for heritage representation, functional to support planning guidance and regulations, there is no need for such a detailed level of information regarding the physical details, while there might be the opportunity to upload layers of data, enriching the information attached to the architectural component such as availability, energy performance, etc. More agile files other than raw point cloud dataset may present a simplified version of the architectural component (e.g. revit files) and incorporate extra layers of information relevant to architects and planners. By making these components available in 3D objects open access libraries, the work of professionals will be hugely facilitated.

Acknowledgments. This work was supported by the Royal Academy of Engineering and Industrial Research Development Fund with the Industry Academia Partnership Programme - 18/19 (project: IT and Conservation of traditional architecture and heritage, IAPP18-19\244). The authors thank all the stakeholders and experts who generously offered their time and expertise to support the data collection, including industrial partners.

References

ANCSA: Carta di Gubbio, Gubbio Charter (1960). http://www.ancsa.org/in-sviluppo/wp-content/uploads/2020/01/Carta-di-Gubbio-1960.pdf

ASCOP: Architectural Heritage in As-Salt City, Jordan (2016)

Badawi, F., Nayer, A.: Jeddah city as a contemporary gateway: new vision for city smart growth management. Procedia Environ. Sci. **37**, 330–341 (2017). https://doi.org/10.1016/j.proenv.2017.03.063

Barth, B.: Smart Cities or Surveillance Cities? Planning Magazine, American Planning Association (2019). https://www.planning.org/planning/2019/mar/smartcities/. Accessed on 1 Dec 2020

Borda, A., Bowen, J.: Smart cities and cultural heritage - a review of developments and future opportunities. In: Bowen, J.P., Diprose, G., Lambert, N. (eds.) Electronic Visualisation and the Arts (EVA 2017), 11–13 July 2017. BCS, London, UK (2017).

Coletta, C., Evans, L., Heaphy, L., Kitchin, R. (eds.).: Creating Smart Cities, 1st edn. Routledge (2018). https://doi.org/10.4324/9781351182409

Dornelles, A., et al.: Towards a bridging concept for undesirable resilience in social-ecological systems. Global Sustain. **3**, E20 (2020). https://doi.org/10.1017/sus.2020.15

Dutra, L.F., Porto, R.: Smart alternatives for the preservation of cultural heritage in the context of smart cities. Ibero-Am. J. Inform. Sci. **13**(1), 372–390 (2020). https://doi.org/10.26512/rici.v13.n1.2020.26210

European Commission: Smart Cities (2021a). https://ec.europa.eu/info/eu-regional-and-urban-development/topics/cities-and-urban-development/city-initiatives/smart-cities_en. Accessed on 1 Jan 2021

European Commission: Expert Group on Digital Cultural Heritage and Europeana (DCHE), European Commission (2021b). https://ec.europa.eu/digital-single-market/en/expert-group-digital-cultural-heritage-and-europeana-dche. Accessed on 1 Feb 2021

Facca, A., Aldrich, J.: Putting the past to work for the future. Public Hist. **33**(3), 38–57 (2011). https://doi.org/10.1525/tph.2011.33.3.38

Ghadei, M.: Amaravati - A city reborn, journey towards a world-class smart city. In: Calautit, J., Rodrigues, F., Chaudhry, H., Altan, H. (eds.) GeoMEast. SCI, pp. 15–29. Springer, Cham (2018). https://doi.org/10.1007/978-3-319-61645-2_2

ICOMOS: Charter for the Conservation of Historic Towns and Urban Areas (Washington Charter 1987) (1987). https://5129c385-3847-464f-90f1-46e3571d8ee3.filesusr.com/ugd/57365b_012ee3b47bea4183b8a7d344d1bcd340.pdf

Jawaid, M.F., Sharma, M., Pipralia, S., Kumar, A.: City profile: Jaipur, Cities **68**, 63–81 (2017) https://doi.org/10.1016/j.cities.2017.05.006.

Ji, X., Shao, L.: The application of landscape infrastructure approaches in the planning of heritage corridor supporting system. Procedia Eng. **198**, 1123–1127 (2017). https://doi.org/10.1016/j.proeng.2017.07.154

Karvonen, A., Cugurullo, F., Caprotti, F. (eds.): Inside Smart Cities: Place, Politics and Urban Innovation. Routledge, London (2019)

Kitchin, R.: Big data, new epistemologies and paradigm shifts. Big Data Soc. (2014). https://doi.org/10.1177/2053951714528481

Koukopoulos, Z., Koukopoulos, D., Jung, J.J.: Real-time Crowd Management for Cultural Heritage Events: A Case Study on Carnival Parades, pp. 275–287 (2018)

Korzun, D., Varfolomeyev, A., Yalovitsyna, S., Volokhova, V.: Semantic infrastructure of a smart museum: toward making cultural heritage knowledge usable and creatable by visitors and professionals. Pers. Ubiquitous Comput. **21**, 345–354 (2017)

Khirfan, L.: Ornamented facades and panoramic views: the impact of tourism development on al-salt's historic urban landscape. In: Gharipour, M. (ed.), International Journal of Islamic Architecture. Vol. 2, pp. 307–324. Intellect., Bristol (2013)

Khuraisat, M.A.-Q.: Trades in Al-Salt from the second half of the Nineteenth Century to the first quarter of the Twentieth Century. Unpublished Report (2015)

Khureisat, M. A.-Q., Farid, G.: Social and Economic Changes in Al-Salt between 1850 and 1921. Unpublished Report (2015)

Liu, C.: Smart solution for protecting cultural heritage in China. In: 2018 3rd International Conference on Smart City and Systems Engineering (ICSCSE), pp. 788–791. Xiamen, China (2018). https://doi.org/10.1109/ICSCSE.2018.00170.

Mansuri, L., et al.: Scientometric analysis and mapping of digital technologies used in cultural heritage field. In: Gorse, C., Neilson, C.J. (eds.) Proceedings of the 35th Annual ARCOM Conference, pp. 255–264, 2–4 September 2019. Association of Researchers in Construction Management, Leeds, UK (2019)

Mansuri, L.E., Patel, D.A.: "Artificial Intelligence-based Automatic Visual Inspection System for Built Heritage" Smart and Sustainable Built Environment (2021). https://doi.org/10.1108/SASBE-09-2020-0139

Mar, A., Monteiro, F., Pereira, P., Martins, J.: An application to improve smart heritage city experience. In: Ioannides, M., Martins, J., Žarnić, R., Lim, V. (eds.) Advances in Digital Cultural Heritage. LNCS, vol. 10754, pp. 89–103. Springer, Cham (2018). https://doi.org/10.1007/978-3-319-75789-6_7

Mc, C.P., Ortega-Argiles, R.: Smart specialisation, regional growth and applications to EU cohesion policy. Reg. Stud. **49**(8), 1291–1302 (2011)

Ministry of Tourism and Antiquities, & Bank, W.: Salt, Detailed description of the city revitalisation program (2005)

Navarro De Pablos, F.J., Mosquera Pérez, C., Cubero Hernández, A.: Ancient cartographies as a basis for geolocation models in public space: the case of Giambattista Nolli and its heritage application. IOP Conf. Ser.: Mater. Sci. Eng. **471**, 1–9 (2019)

Petti L, Trillo C, Makore BCN.: Towards a shared understanding of the concept of heritage in the European context. Heritage **2**(3) 2531–2544 (2019) https://doi.org/10.3390/heritage2030155

Petti, L., Trillo, C., Makore, B.N.: Cultural heritage and sustainable development targets: a possible harmonisation? Insights from the European perspective. Sustainability **12**(3), 926 (2020). https://doi.org/10.3390/su12030926

Pica, V., Cecili, A., Annicchiarico, S., Volkova, E.: The historical small smart city protocol (HISMACITY): toward an intelligent tool using geo big data for the sustainable management of minor historical assets. Data **4**, 30 (2019). https://doi.org/10.3390/data4010030

Pili S.: Experimentation of a Smart-planning approach for the sustainable renewal of the building heritage of smaller sardinian historic centers. In: Bisello A., Vettorato D., Laconte P., Costa S. (eds.) Smart and Sustainable Planning for Cities and Regions. SSPCR 2017. Green Energy and Technology. Springer, Cham (2018). https://doi.org/10.1007/978-3-319-75774-2_5

Riganti, P.: Smart cities and heritage conservation: developing a smartheritage agenda for sustainable inclusive communities. Int. J. Arch. Res.: Archnet-IJAR **11**, 16–27 (2017)

Sabri, S., et al.: IOP Conf. Ser.: Earth Environ. Sci. **18** 012176 (2014)

Scorza, F., Pilogallo, A., Casas, G.: Investigating Tourism Attractiveness in Inland Areas: Ecosystem Services, Open Data and Smart Specializations, in New Metropolitan Perspectives (2019)

Sun, Y., Song, H., Jara, A., Bie, R.: Internet of things and big data analytics for smart and connected communities. IEEE Access **4**, 766–773 (2016). https://doi.org/10.1109/ACCESS.2016.2529723

RTPI: Smart City Regions (2021). https://www.rtpi.org.uk/policy-and-research/programmes/better-planning/smart-city-regions/. Accessed on 1 Feb 2021

Tarif, G.F.: Al-Salt and its relationship with its surroundings 1850–1921 AD. Unpublished Report (2015)

Toha, M., Ismail, H.: A heritage tourism and tourist flow pattern: a perspective on traditional versus modern technologies. Int. J. Built Environ. Sustain. **2**(2), 85–92 (2015). https://doi.org/10.11113/ijbes.v2.n2.61

Trillo, C., Aburamadan, R., Udeaja, C., Moustaka, A., Baffour, K.G., Makore, B.C.N.: Enhancing heritage and traditional architecture conservation through digital technologies. Developing a digital conservation handbook for As-Salt, Jordan. In: Bevilacqua, C., Calabrò, F., Della Spina, L. (eds.) NMP. SIST, vol. 177, pp. 211–219. Springer, Cham (2020). https://doi.org/10.1007/978-3-030-52869-0_18

Udeaja, C.: Urban heritage conservation and rapid urbanization: insights from Surat, India. Sustainability **12**(6), 2172 (2020). https://doi.org/10.3390/su12062172

Valdenebro, J.V., Gimena, F.N.: Urban utility tunnels as a long-term solution for the sustainable revitalization of historic centres: the case study of Pamplona-Spain. Tunn. Undergr. Space Technol. **81**, 228–236 (2018)

Digital Storytelling: The Integration of Intangible and Tangible Heritage in the City of Surat, India

Chika Udeaja[1] , Lukman E. Mansuri[2(✉)] ,
Busisiwe Chikomborero Ncube Makore[3] , Kwasi Gyau Baffour Awuah[3] ,
Dilip A. Patel[2] , Claudia Trillo[3] , and K. N. Jha[4]

[1] London South Bank University, 103 Borough Road, London SE1 0AA, UK
[2] Sardar Vallabhbahi National Institute of Technology, Surat 395007, India
erlukman@gmail.com
[3] University of Salford, Manchester M5 4WT, UK
[4] Indian Institute of Technology Delhi, New Delhi 110016, India

Abstract. The impact of digital technologies to the domain of cultural heritage has increased the speed and automation of the processes and practices that involve processing and presentation of digital heritage data. Heritage Building Information Modelling (HBIM) and Virtual Reality (VR) can play a key role towards the conservation, preservation, and management of architectural heritage. This includes the preservation of both tangible and intangible cultural heritage at multiple levels. The purpose of this study is to explore the potential of digital storytelling through digital technologies by integrating intangible data and information to the tangible heritage in the scan-to-BIM process. The paper builds on few works that have begun to investigate the classification of intangible qualitative heritage data within a BIM and VR context for heritage assets. This exploration demonstrates that the incorporation of both qualitative and quantitative information about a heritage-built asset has value in the (re)interpretation, documentation and preservation of cultural heritage. The development of HBIM and VR in this paper is to bring together heterogeneous data that has the potential to provide a model for future work in the field of heritage conservation and digital technologies. The city of Surat is used as a case study for exploring the potential of digital storytelling for the city's urban heritage. Indeed, this holistic integration can enhance the awareness of urban cultural heritage to support the processes of local urban heritage conservation for key stakeholders such as local Government, heritage conservation experts, urban planners and local communities.

Keywords: Digital storytelling · Digital technologies · Intangible heritage · Tangible heritage · HBIM · VR · India · Surat

1 Introduction

The extensive benefits of digital technologies for the Architectural, Engineering, Construction and Operation (AECO) industry are increasingly recognized in academic and

M. Rauterberg (Ed.): HCII 2021, LNCS 12794, pp. 152–168, 2021.
https://doi.org/10.1007/978-3-030-77411-0_11

professional practice [1–3]. To effectively assess and quantify the risk on cultural heritage, information needs to be accurately and comprehensively collected, easily available and managed. In particular, the spatial extent and location defined by co-ordinates of built heritage are essential for risk reduction and management. Digital technologies can be used as tools for achieving its potential benefits [4, 5]. As technology has advanced, heritage asset information and the development of new recording techniques have an increasingly important role to play in protecting heritage and especially in developing management tools for integrating heritage protection and land-use management [6]. The use of digital technologies for documenting tangible heritage assets allows for the ability to frequently track changes of heritage in terms of form, function and sometimes location. This may involve "subjective interpretations that may need to be qualified, adjusted, and improved over time" [4]. This is a compulsory part of nearly every cultural heritage conservation project as it was firstly mandated in the International Council on Monuments and Sites (ICOMOS) Venice Charter in 1964. The impact of digital technologies to the domain of cultural heritage has increased speed and automation of the processes and practices that involve processing and presentation of digital heritage data [7]. The purpose of this study is to explore the potential of digital storytelling through digital technologies such as HBIM and VR by integrating intangible data and information to the tangible heritage in the scan-to-BIM process.

2 Background

2.1 Digital Storytelling

Digital storytelling is an emerging field achieved by developing a narrative through the application of digital technologies. As a practice, digital storytelling within the heritage sector allows for a holistic narration to multiple stakeholders of the intangible and tangible qualities of a heritage asset. Digital tools, often used in visualisations such as Augmented Reality and Virtual Reality are selected for telling a story. In this study the story refers to the historical layers of Surat's tangible heritage. The digital storytelling is the modern extension of conventional storytelling with digital models, text, images and audio. It provides the platform to understand, promote and preserve the tangible and intangible heritage.

2.2 Digital Storytelling Using Heritage Building Information Modelling

Building Information Modelling (BIM) has warranted increasing attention over the past decade in the field of Architecture, Engineering and Construction (AEC) [3]. BIM in AEC industry has been extensively utilized to cope with the complexity and difficulty of managing multiple activities and contractors across the globe [8]. The benefits of using BIM have been progressively recognized as a potential digital technology in the heritage sector also known as HBIM (Heritage Building Information Modelling). In current conventional practice, non-availability of documentation, drawings, specifications of materials and other technical information of historic buildings results into time and cost overrun of their maintenance and rehabilitation projects [9]. BIM plays a critical role in the heritage sector in minimizing those challenges by efficiently support historic information management, design and build decisions resulting in the production of sustainable and inclusive heritage assets. By incorporating high-quality digital survey datasets, HBIM represents the appearance of the existing historic fabric and allows the exploration and complex analysis of several applications such as conservation planning, maintenance, heritage management, interpretation and tourist attraction [10]. Parallel to this interest in HBIM is a growing discourse recognising the crucial role of cultural heritage in achieving sustainable development goals [11]. BIM can also enhance the "storytelling experience" for multiple stakeholders by enabling them to understand and interpret the heritage asset early on in the HBIM process. The offer of diverse types of data such as geometric data and non-geometric and intangible data provides a holistic perspective of the heritage asset and can enable effective and sustainable decision making. Indeed, this type of decision making can allow for a sensitivity to the intangible socio-cultural associative aspects of heritage that can often be overlooked in urban heritage conservation planning and management. Geometric data for tangible heritage assets (Sect. 2.2) is a fundamental part of the HBIM process. However, the platform allows for successful integration of non-geometric data for intangible heritage associated with the heritage asset. This is a symbiotic relationship often overlooked in the narrative formation within the HBIM process. HBIM improves availability and accessibility of all the knowledge related to a historical/archaeological artefact, making easier to interpret its nature, monitor its changes and document each investigation and intervention activity. As a consequence, intervention decisions will be made by relying on the knowledge accurately formalized in the proposed model, supporting the identification of emergency situations, the scheduling of intervention activities and the planning of routine management and maintenance.

2.3 Geometric Data for Tangible Heritage Assets

BIM objects are parametric, defined using rules and automatically adjusting to changes in their context. Information is integrated within the model in a structured way, by adding the relevant pieces of information to the corresponding BIM objects. In this way, BIM constitutes a digital information resource for the built asset. HBIM should be based on accurate as-existing metric survey datasets (preferably 3D), which document the position, size and dimensions of all visible surfaces, components and context of the historic asset, referenced to a local or national coordinate system. Different heritage conservation projects utilize specific digital technologies in isolation or combined depending on the expected outcome [12]. Three-dimensional digital survey techniques are often used as they are fast, reliable, non-contact methods for obtaining metrically accurate 3D data, and have been used extensively to document historic buildings and sites. Such techniques include laser scanning, photogrammetry, lidar, closer range scanning, mobile mapping or a combination of methods can be used to produce 3D datasets of the historic asset [2].

2.4 Non-geometric Data for Intangible Heritage

A crucial benefit of BIM is its capability of incorporating both qualitative and quantitative information about a built asset to represent physical and functional characteristics. Scholars are increasingly recognizing the capability of BIM to provide simulations of the appearance, development and performance of an asset but also the representation of heterogeneous data including intangible non-geometric data [3, 12–14]. Very few case studies can be found that have explored how intangible data can be integrated in the HBIM and VR process and none of them illustrate full implementation. Intangible Cultural Heritage in general and likewise in India can be found difficult to explain or interpret, because of its complexity and variation [15]. Tangible heritage on the other hand, being more visible is much better understood by stakeholders and the public. The term "intangible" can sometimes add to this confusion and lack of usage because it is used as an antithesis to the term "tangible" defining the concept by what it is not than what it is. It can often be viewed as a technical term used by experts and not by artists and musicians. India's intangible heritage exists in a framework of interconnectedness [15] with diverse expressions in the ideas, practices, beliefs and values shared by communities across long stretches of time, and forming part of the collective memory of the nation. In India, the Ministry of Culture (MoC) deals with two UNESCO Conventions, which have been ratified by India. These are: the UNESCO "Convention for the Safeguarding of the Intangible Cultural Heritage" [16] to safeguard and promote intangible cultural heritage worldwide, and the "Convention for the Protection and Promotion of the Diversity of Cultural Expressions" (2005). The UNESCO 2003 Convention emphasizes the importance of the values of intangible cultural heritage. The definition of intangible cultural heritage is better defined in this convention as stated below:

Article 2 (Definitions) practices, representations, expressions, knowledge, skills, instruments, objects, artefacts and cultural spaces associated with communities, groups and individuals [16]. The 2003 convention proposes five broad domains (Fig. 2) in which intangible cultural heritage is manifested: Oral traditions and expressions, including language as a vehicle of the intangible cultural heritage; performing arts; social practices, rituals and festive events; knowledge and practices concerning nature and the universe and traditional craftsmanship. Historic England [17] defines intangible characteristics as such as cultural, historical and architectural values, and style, age and significance that can be integrated into the 3D model in a structured and consistent way, which allows easy information extraction and the production of deliverables. This intangible information can be included in the model, attached to individual building components such as a door or spaces such as a room [17]. Salam [18] also suggest that intangible data can be used in a legacy way to strengthen the heritage significance; such as cultural and historical memories, events occurred throughout the building lifecycle, famous characters' personal visits and observations [18]. One of the reasons for this limited investigation is the lack of a comprehensive solution specifically designed to model and manage semantically enhanced 3D models of historic buildings [19].

2.5 Literature Study of Digital Storytelling Through Tangible and Intangible Data in the HBIM Process

The following section of the paper provides example literature review studies that have explored the integration of intangible data in the HBIM process as a means to provide a holistic storytelling of heritage assets. Three examples were selected: (1) Documenting 19th century heritage assets of Batawa in the urban core of Toronto, Canada, (2) Integration of heterogeneous data in a BIM environment: the case study of the temple of Castor and Pollux, Italy and (3) A collaborative Heritage BIM (HBIM) of a 19th Century multibuilding industrial site in the UK. These case studies were selected as they illustrate a progression in the exploration of integrating intangible data in the HBIM environment. In literature study 1, Fai et al. [20] develop a model (Batawa model) that manages to include intangible data (such as archival photo, previous reports and historical layers) into a mixed-level BIM model. The selected intangible data was incorporated to provide a historical perspective of the heritage asset. However, the form of integration was limited to secondary data sources without full implementation of this intangible data [20]. This literature is an attempt of embedding both quantitative and intangible data for the purposes of developing a BIM that will serve as a digital archive to help in conserving the heritage buildings. The model also has the capacity for time-based representation—coordinating past, current, and possible futures of Batawa heritage assets. An extensive review of multi-scale Heterogeneous Datasets was undertaken. The archival material is both heterogeneous, comprised of architectural and planning documents (original drawings and paper copies of hand-drawn and computer-generated blueprints and black line documents), paper and digitized photographs (some as early as 1939), and both digital and paper-based texts. Fai et al. [20] demonstrate the potential of parametric relationships between all data types for heritage documentation. Thus, contributing to the field of heritage documentation by showcasing the ability to reveal time-based parametric relationships between tangible and intangible heritage assets.

In literature study 2, Simeone et al. [21] propose a model that has been conceived as the integration of a BIM environment with a knowledge base developed by means of ontologies. Thereby, presenting a more standardized approach of integrating intangible data [21]. This literature defines the intangible aspects of the artefact such as its evolution during time, its historical, social and technological context, its intended use, materials caves and sources. Additionally, they include any kind of data and documentation that can be useful for its interpretation such as external links, textual documents, images, modelled objects, bibliographic references. Specifically, the presented case study included paintings and pictures from the first excavation phase (1940–1950) representing the heritage site in different times and ancient texts about the temple and the city of Cori. The purpose of the integration was to demonstrate how knowledge representation and management play a key role in built heritage field, deeply influencing decisions and actions of the different specialists involved in investigation, intervention, conservation and fruition processes. Therefore, the authors aimed to justify how an accurate and complete representation and comprehension of an architectural heritage artefact requires a large amount of semantics related to its intangible aspects such as social and historical context.

The framework developed in literature 3 by Heesom et al. [22] goes beyond the other case studies by presenting a method for identifying and categorizing intangible heritage information through the developed Level of Intangible Cultural Heritage (LOICH) [22]. The different levels included:

- LOICH1 – Desk Study/Published information. This included written accounts of practices, photographs and documents related to the operation of the
- LOICH2 – First Person accounts. The collation of intangible heritage data was undertaken using unstructured interviews of small focus group.
- LOICH3 – Interactive Social Media. Social media interaction used to gather information and create awareness.

The authors suggest that this method can be reproduced by future researchers and practitioners. This data was integrated into a full HBIM database via a Common Data Environment. The data was audio and video recorded and thematically analysed and categorized based on which building or part of the site. Markers were used as place holders to link the intangible data to the 3D geometric elements.

3   Case Study of Surat

3.1   Background of the City of Surat

The city of Surat (Figs. 1 and 2) is currently urbanizing rapidly with demands of urban sprawl and development. According to the census taken in 2011, Surat's urban district had a population of 4,849,213 people but the actual population may exceed these figures due to rapid development in Surat's metropolitan region [23]. Surat's urban context includes social cohesion challenges, increasing rural to urban migration, rising housing demands, and considerable stress on city management and resource [24]. Yet, in the context of these urban pressures, there is an evolution of approaches recognizing tangible and intangible heritage as strategic assets in creating cities that are more resilient, inclusive, and sustainable [25, 26]. Surat has a diverse and vibrant heritage that has created and shaped the cultural identity of the city. Historic social practices and processes have remained interdependent and reciprocal with Surat's built fabric. However, urban heritage conservation is not perceived as a priority when considering other urban development objectives [27]. Cultural heritage continues to remain marginal in urban development agendas, often overlooked in the context of urban poverty, social inequalities, and a severe lack of basic infrastructure [28]. Although it is evident that effort is being made to improve sustainable planning and heritage conservation [23], there exist significant challenges that limit the impact and scope of these initiatives.

Having survived numerous historic invasions and power structures, Surat is presently in the top ten largest cities in India and recognized as one of the fastest growing cities. The strategic location of the city aided in forming historic overseas links with the rest of Asia, Europe, Africa, and the Middle East, which date back from 300 BC. These trading connections influenced the living patterns and built heritage in Surat, particularly in the historic precincts Gopipara Surat Central Zone and Rander Gamtal. Historically, Surat's heritage conservation was mostly concerned with safeguarding the remains of

Fig. 1. Location of Surat

Fig. 2. City of Surat and its heritage

architectural monuments. Key historic monuments include major development by Malek Gopi, a rich trader in 1496–1521 AD, the establishing of silk and cotton factories from the 1600s, the construction of the inner-city wall in 1664 AD, and the outer-city wall in 1715

AD. The city of Surat grew in the 17th and 18th centuries to become an established and formidable export and import center of India. Settlement in Surat continued to develop with custom houses and gardens along the River Tapi and Surat's fort. By 1901 AD, the diamond cutting industry was established and began exporting diamonds to the United States of America from the 1970s. Currently, 80% of diamonds of the world are cut in Surat and the jewelry and textile industry has allowed a steady flow of wealth into the city.

The Surat Municipal Corporation (SMC) is the main government body in Surat responsible for urban planning schemes, alongside the Surat Urban Development Authority (SUDA) (which includes the municipal corporation area) and the Hazira Development Authority, which governs the port and industrial hub located downriver from Surat city. SUDA is responsible for preparing the area development plan and for controlling unauthorized developments. The South Gujarat Chamber of Commerce and Industry (SGCCI) is influential in Surat's governance structure as it takes the lead on several critical regional and city development initiatives [29]. Achieving urban sustainability is of significance in Surat as it is particularly vulnerable to the effects of climate change. The city lies in a flood plain area and the southwest area of the city hosts a number of creeks. Natural disasters have been recurrent and devastating, such as a plague in 1994 and floods in 2006 and 2008. Surat's climate change predictions and risk profile all indicate an increase in rainfall, with monsoons dominated by heavy spells of rain combined with longer dry spells, leading to an increase of floods.

3.2 Surat's Intangible Heritage

The evolution of the concept of heritage preservation has developed in parallel with the evolution of Surat, becoming a practice that goes beyond tangible assets and possesses a human and socio-cultural element [29]. However, the practice of conservation in Surat still lags behind the actualization of this diverse concept. The city lacks an official holistic values-based approach that specifies the significance of Surat's historic areas whilst taking into account the existing built environment, intangible heritage, cultural diversity, socio-economic and environmental factors, and local community values [30]. Digital storytelling which includes Surat's intangible heritage can include the combination of diverse narratives: (1) the community narrative, (2) the craftsmanship narrative, (3) the narrative of social practices and plural forms of living. Figure 3 illustrates some of the examples of intangible heritage of Surat.

The Community Narrative

The Surat city was very populated and full of various merchants. Hindu, Muslim and Parsi were the main population of Surat. The richest were the Hindu Wanias. The Muslims were generally employed in the army instead of trading. The Parsi community were also a large and prosperous class, ship builders, and good carpenters, exquisite weavers and embroiderers in 17th century. Later the Parsi community were raise in wealth and power. Though, being good merchants, they were also reached to high positions in the East India Company. Thus, several parts of city (paras) were named after them like Rustumpara around in 1785. The Bohra community were migrated in Surat from Jamnagar and they were renowned merchants. The four most important European settlers includes the British, Dutch, French and the Portuguese.

Fig. 3. Some intangible heritage of Surat (upper left: Jari work; upper right and lower left: Farsan; lower right: street bazar)

Generational Craftsmanship Narrative

Suart is reputable for quality craftsmanship. The architecture of Surat and Rander express the diverse levels of craftsmanship in Surat. One example of this is the Jari work, which is the weaving of brocade by gold and silver thread. The Jari industry had received wide uplift and encouragement under the Mughal Emperors. The Jari industry has been a small scale craftsmanship. The Jari work skills and craftsmanship were firmly established in Surat by some families of skilled artists. The art of craftsmanship has been passed from one generation to another. The families involved in Jari work are mainly from Gola (rana) and Khatri community. The Jari work is still remain the conserved art skill in the Surat city with some limited families.

Narratives of Social Practices and Plural Forms of Living

The earlier neighborhood of Surat, Rander was the main trading hub with the trading links to Middle East, China and Sumatra. There was the main trading of silk, musk, porcelain and spices. The international trading connection of Rander had influenced the living pattern and its architecture. The prosperity of Rander was declined during 16th century when Portuguese raid on it. Then Surat became an important port and prosperous city. This history influenced the social practices of the citizens of Surat and consequently brought about multiple forms of living and understanding the city. As a modern city, Surat has evolved and these pluralistic forms of identifying with Surat have evolved with it.

4   Scan to BIM and VR Process with Integrating Intangible Data

The integration of intangible data with the tangible heritage is explored using the digital technologies such as BIM and VR. The digital storytelling was developed as the effective means to create awareness about the heritage and for its better conservation and preservation. The tangible heritage is converted into the digital format as BIM model. The laser scanning and photogrammetry were used as as-built modelling tools for creation of BIM and VR. The process of Scan to BIM and VR has been documented in detail and presented here as an important outcome of this study and experience. The complex process of scan to BIM and VR has been documented using IDEF0 modelling technique [30].

To understand the complexity and various requirements for the process of scan to BIM/VR, the integrated definition function (IDEF0) modelling technique has been used. IDEF0 is, in many ways, a very simple method that are used to describe the activities of complex processes and consists of a hierarchical series of diagrams, text, and glossary cross referenced to each other. IDEF0 has two main components for modelling: functions (represented on a diagram by boxes), and data and objects that interrelate those functions (represented by arrows). As shown in Fig. 4, the position at which the arrow attaches to a box conveys the specific role of the interface. The controls enter the top of the box and is used to capture various guidelines, regulations, constrains. The inputs, the data or objects acted upon by the operation, enter the box from the left. The outputs of the operation leave the right-hand side of the box and captures what the functions have generated. Mechanism arrows provides supporting means for performing the function join (point up to) the bottom of the box and are used to capture tools, assets and resources required to run the function. The process of IDEF0 starts with the identification of the prime function to be decomposed. This function is identified as "top level context diagram (TLCD)" that defines the scope of the particular IDEF0 analysis. In this case study, TLCD for the process of Scan to BIM and VR is shown in Fig. 4 and further lower-level diagrams are generated, which are "child" in IDEF0 terminology. In this case study, three levels of IDEF0 were modelled to capture the holistic procedure of the scan to BIM/VR that integrates the intangible as well (see Table 1). The created IDEF0 model can be useful for various purposes like understanding the complexity of the process, planning of all required resources and making the scan to BIM/VR process smooth and speedy.

To enable the aspect of digital storytelling within the scan to BIM approach, a classification of intangible heritage was undertaken as described in the figures below. The figures illustrate two categories of intangible data that can be integrated within the scan to BIM process as also listed in Table 2: (1) primary intangible data and (2) secondary intangible data. The different forms of data types can be collected according to the association with the heritage type. The table shows an example of a mapping of Surat's intangible heritage that can allow for the collection of this data and subsequently included within the HBIM model.

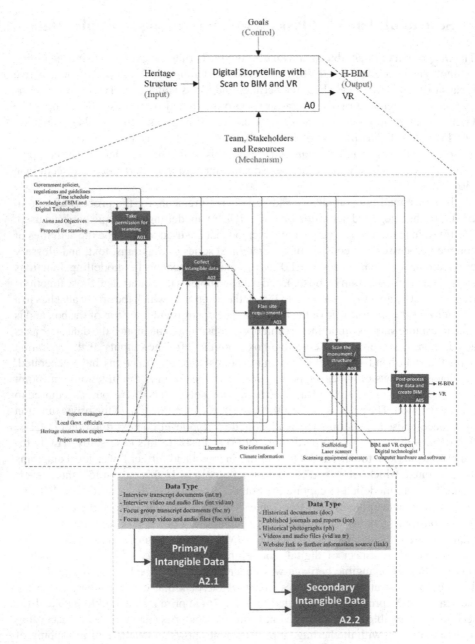

Fig. 4. IDEF0 for scan to BIM and VR

Table 1. Function information

Function ID	Function
Level 0	
A0	Digital storytelling with scan to BIM and VR
Level 1 (Decomposition of A0)	
A01	Take permission for scanning
A02	Collect intangible data
A03	Plan site requirements
A04	Scan the monument
A05	Post process the data and create BIM and or VR
Level 2 (Decomposition of A02)	
A2.1	Primary intangible data
A2.2	Secondary intangible data

4.1   Using Visualization Through Virtual Reality

Laser Scanning of two monuments of English cemetery as shown in the Fig. 5, in Surat was carried out to create storytelling through the application of Virtual Reality. The English Cemetery is a centrally protected heritage site by the Archeological Survey of India (ASI). As a heritage site, it is interesting as it consists of various monumental tombs and structures built during the seventeenth century (1649–1669 AD). This site has historical significance in Surat as it is home to attractive European tombs of the graves of President of English factory and Governor of Bombay of that time, their family members and other members of British community. The style and nature of these monuments gives insight into cultural interactions between the English merchants and Surat's local population. Furthermore, the heritage site indicates the political aspirations of the East India Company officials. The site it provides one of the most visible reminders of the early British presence in the subcontinent of India.

As a project team, we decided to use the English cemetery as a pilot study to begin articulating the integration of intangible heritage through Virtual Reality. This section gives insight into some of the work done in this regard.

The laser scanning of the monuments in the English cemetery was undertaken to develop a point cloud. It was then cleaned and imported into Unreal Engine as combined high resolution point clouds. As a first step to integrating the data, a basic environment was created to drop the scans into with plants, trees and a surrounding wall. Lighting and interactive cameras were added for navigation as shown in the Fig. 6.

The mapping and classification of intangible data was used in this process as detailed in Fig. 4 and Table 2. Secondary data was selected as the first data type to use within the virtual environment. Research into the English Cemetery was conducted and journal papers were collected describing the knowledge and social practices that existed during the time the English cemetery was built. We collected historical information concerning the site and thematically captured certain elements that reflected the different aspects

Table 2. Example of data types for Surat heritage

Intangible heritage	Examples of Surat Intangible Heritage Secondary data type (doc); (jor); (ph); (vid/au); (vid/au tr); (link) Primary data type (int.tr); (int.vid/au); (foc.tr); (foc.vid/au)
Oral traditions and expressions, language	• Diverse expressions from Hindus, Muslims, Sikhs, Christians, Bohras, Surti Gujarati • Diverse oral traditions from Surtis, Parsis, the western Chalukyas
Performing arts	• Dandiya raas dances • Garba dances • Gujarati plays
Social practices, rituals and festive events	• Navaratri • Diwali • Chandni Padvo • Ganesh Chaturthi • Kite-flying festival of Uttarayan • Moharram Julus
Knowledge and practices	• Jari work • Diamond polishing • Textile dying and printing
Traditional skills and craftsmanship	• Handcrafted doors and facades reflecting European and British influences • Art deco façade design on houses • Sadeli Art in the wooden furniture
Food	• Surati Ghari • Surati Farsan and Surati Khaja

of intangible data as referred to in Table 1. Two data types were chosen for the first phase of the digital storytelling of the English cemetery: (1) audio files (au) & (2) document textual information (doc). The audio of selected text that provides a historical layer to understanding the monuments. The audio was pre-recorded in three languages; English, Hindi and Gujarati. The audio and text were integrated with the digital model. Information text (history of monument) was added and positioned next to the digital model of the structure while the audio was placed as the cone near the structure. Blue prints were created to trigger the audio files when a user walked into an audio cone and turn the sound off when they left. This digital model then exported into the VR headset. Future phases will include additional primary and secondary data types as detailed in Table 2 to provide a comprehensive experience of digital storytelling for heritage assets.

Fig. 5. Laser scanned Structures

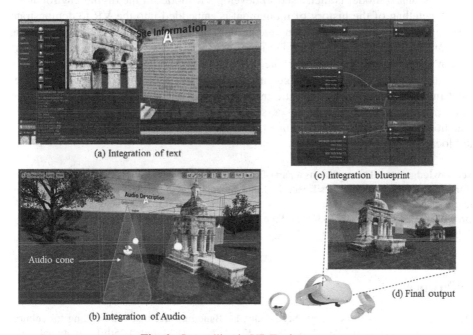

(a) Integration of text

(c) Integration blueprint

(b) Integration of Audio

(d) Final output

Fig. 6. Storytelling in VR Environment

5 Conclusion

The digital technologies in the field of cultural heritage has proven that there are remarkable benefits. Digital technologies such as BIM and VR can play vital role in storytelling and narration of the integration of intangible and tangible heritage with the aim of sustainable promotion, conservation, preservation and management of heritage. The data related to the physical heritage structure such as history, documents, traditions etc. considered as intangible data. The integration of intangible data with the tangible heritage expedites the process of conservation and management. Digital technologies provides the suitable platform to integrate the intangible and tangible heritage using various digital tools.

The case of Surat city is selected to explore digital technologies for integration of tangible and intangible heritage. Monuments of English cemetery has been converted into digital model using laser scanning and then used to create the BIM and VR. The process of scanning to BIM and VR consists of various functions and activities, which are generally overlooked. To understand the detailed process of scan to BIM and VR, the IDEF0 function modelling is presented. Every small requirement of resources, tools and persons have been carefully modeled using IDEF0. The proposed function of IDEF0 modeling is to understand the complexity of system, plan the requirements of various resources and manage the whole scan to BIM as well as the integration of intangible aspects effectively.

The scanned model is then used to develop VR model in the digital environment. The storytelling of the history of monument is embedded into the VR to demonstrate the integration of tangible and intangible heritage in the single virtual environment. This integration demonstrates the incorporation of both qualitative and quantitative information about heritage-built assets. The information about conditions assessment of the heritage structures can be embedded and the model can be prepared for asset management in further studies. The holistic integration will enhance the awareness of urban cultural heritage to support the processes of local urban heritage conservation for key stakeholders such as local government, heritage conservation experts, urban planners and local communities.

Acknowledgemnt. This work was a part of the research project 'IT INDIAN HERITAGE PLATFORM: Enhancing cultural resilience in India by applying digital technologies to the Indian tangible and intangible heritage' funded by Arts and Humanities Research Council (AHRC), UK [project reference: AH/R014183/1] and the Indian Council of Historical Research (ICHR), New Delhi, India.

References

1. Logothetis, S., Delinasiou, A., Stylianidis, E.: Building information modelling for cultural heritage: a review. In: Yen, Y.N., Weng, K.H., Cheng, H.M. (eds.) 25th International CIPA Symposium 2015. pp. 177–183. International Society for Photogrammetry Remote Sensing C/O School of Surveyin, University of New South Wales, Po Box 1, Kensington, 2033, Australia (2015). https://doi.org/10.5194/isprsannals-II-5-W3-177-2015
2. Manferdini, A.M., Galassi, M.: Assessments for 3D reconstructions of cultural heritage using digital technologies. In: Boehm, J., Remondino, F., Kersten, T., Fuse, T., GonzalezAguilera, D. (eds.) 3D-ARCH 2013 - 3D Virtual Reconstruction and Visualization of Complex Architectures, pp. 167–174. Copernicus Gesellschaft Mbh, Bahnhofsalle 1e, Gottingen, 37081, Germany (2013). https://doi.org/10.5194/isprsarchives-XL-5-W1-167-2013
3. Pocobelli, D.P., Boehm, J., Bryan, P., Still, J., Grau-Bové, J.: BIM for heritage science: a review. Herit. Sci. **6**, 30 (2018). https://doi.org/10.1186/s40494-018-0191-4

4. Myers, D.: Heritage inventories: promoting effectiveness as a vital tool for sustainable heritage management David. J. Cult. Herit. Manag. Sustain. Dev. **6**, 38–152 (2016). https://doi.org/10.1108/JCHMSD-02-2016-0009

5. Mansuri, L.E., Patel, D.A.: Artificial intelligence-based automatic visual inspection system for built heritage. In press, Smart Sustain. Built Environ (2021). https://doi.org/10.1108/SASBE-09-2020-0139

6. Pickard, R.: A comparative review of policy for the protection of the architectural heritage of Europe. Int. J. Herit. Stud. **8**, 349–363 (2002). https://doi.org/10.1080/135272502200003 7191e

7. Mansuri, L., et al.: Scientometric analysis and mapping of digital technologies used in cultural heritage field. In: Association of Researchers in Construction Management, ARCOM 2019 - Proceedings of the 35th Annual Conference, pp. 255–264 (2019)

8. Ahuja, R., Jain, M., Sawhney, A., Arif, M.: Adoption of BIM by architectural firms in India: technology–organization–environment perspective. Archit. Eng. Des. Manag. **12**, 311–330 (2016). https://doi.org/10.1080/17452007.2016.1186589

9. Gursel, I., Sariyildiz, S., Akin, Ö., Stouffs, R.: Modeling and visualization of lifecycle building performance assessment. Adv. Eng. Inform. **23**, 396–417 (2009). https://doi.org/10.1016/j.aei.2009.06.010

10. Oreni, D.: From 3D content models to HBIM for conservation and management of built heritage. In: Murgante, B., et al. (eds.) ICCSA. LNCS, vol. 7974, pp. 344–357. Springer, Heidelberg (2013). https://doi.org/10.1007/978-3-642-39649-6_25

11. Petti, L., Trillo, C., Makore, B.N.: Cultural heritage and sustainable development targets: a possible harmonisation? Insights from the European Perspective. Sustainability. **12**, 926 (2020). https://doi.org/10.3390/su12030926

12. Trillo, C., Aburamadan, R., Udeaja, C., Moustaka, A., Baffour, K.G., Makore, B.C.N.: Enhancing heritage and traditional architecture conservation through digital technologies. Developing a digital conservation handbook for As-Salt, Jordan. In: International Symposium: New Metropolitan Perspectives, pp. 211–219. Springer, Cham (2020). https://doi.org/10.1007/978-3-030-52869-0_18

13. Baik, A., Boehm, J.: Building information modelling for historical building historic Jeddah - Saudi Arabia. In: Guidi, G., et al. (eds.) 2015 Digital Heritage International Congress, Vol 2: Analysis and Interpretation Theory, Methodologies, Preservation and Standards Digital Heritage Projects and Applications, pp. 125–128. IEEE, 345 E 47th St, New York, NY 10017 USA (2015). https://doi.org/10.1109/DigitalHeritage.2015.7419468

14. Volk, R., Stengel, J., Schultmann, F.: Building Information Modeling (BIM) for existing buildings - literature review and future needs. Autom. Constr. **38**, 109–127 (2014). https://doi.org/10.1016/j.autcon.2013.10.023

15. Bhaswati Mukherjee: India's Intangible Cultural Heritage: A Civilisational Legacy to the World. https://mea.gov.in/in-focus-article.htm?24717/Indias+Intangible+Cultural+Heritage+A+Civilisational+Legacy+To+The+World. Accessed on 05 Feb 2021

16. UNESCO: Convention For The Safeguarding Of The Intangible Cultural Heritage. https://unesdoc.unesco.org/ark:/48223/pf0000132540. Accessed on 23 Jan 2021

17. Historic England: BIM for Heritage. Developing a Historic Building Information Model. https://historicengland.org.uk/images-books/publications/bim-for-heritage/heag-154-bim-for-heritage/. Accessed 25 Jan 2021

18. Salam, N.F.A.: HBIM-a sustainable approach for heritage buildings restoration in Egypt. In: IOP Conference Series: Earth and Environmental Science, p. 12072. IOP Publishing (2020). https://doi.org/10.1088/1755-1315/410/1/012072

19. Tobiáš, P.: BIM, GIS and semantic models of cultural heritage buildings. Geoinform. FCE CTU. **15**, 27 (2016). https://doi.org/10.14311/gi.15.2.3

20. Fai, S., Graham, K., Duckworth, T., Wood, N., Attar, R.: Building information modelling and heritage documentation. Proc. 23rd Int. Symp. Int. Sci. Comm. Doc. Cult. Herit. **2011** 12–16 (2011)

21. Simeone, D., Cursi, S., Toldo, I., Carrara, G.: BIM and knowledge management for building heritage. In: Gerber, D., Huang, A., Sanchez, J. (eds.) ACADIA 2014: Design Agency, pp. 681–690. Riverside Architectural Press, University of Waterloo School Architecture Cambridge, C/O 213 Sterling Rd, Suite 200, Toronto, Ontario M6r 2b2, Canada (2014)

22. Heesom, D., Boden, P., Hatfield, A., Rooble, S., Andrews, K., Berwari, H.: Developing a collaborative HBIM to integrate tangible and intangible cultural heritage. Int. J. Build. Pathol. Adapt. (2020). https://doi.org/10.1108/IJBPA-04-2019-0036

23. Baradi, M., Malhotra, M.: At the Core: Understanding the built heritage of Surat and Rander. UCD New Ranip, India (2011)

24. Udeaja, C., et al.: Urban Heritage Conservation and Rapid Urbanization: Insights from Surat. India. Sustainability **12**, 2172 (2020). https://doi.org/10.3390/su12062172

25. Fusco Girard, L.: Toward a smart sustainable development of port cities/areas: the role of the "Historic Urban Landscape" approach. Sustainability **5**, 4329–4348 (2013). https://doi.org/10.3390/su5104329

26. Bandarin, F., Van Oers, R.: Reconnecting the City: The Historic Urban Landscape Approach and the Future of Urban Heritage. Wiley (2014)

27. Meera, P.: Heritage Route Optimization for Walled City Surat using GIS. Sarvajanik Education Society (2017)

28. Hosagrahar, J., Soule, J., Girard, L.F., Potts, A.: Cultural heritage, the UN sustainable development goals, and the new urban agenda. BDC. Boll. Del Cent. Calza Bini. **16**, 37–54 (2016)

29. Bhat, G.K., Karanth, A., Dashora, L., Rajasekar, U.: Addressing flooding in the city of Surat beyond its boundaries. Environ. Urban. **25**, 429–441 (2013)

30. Waissi, G.R., Demir, M., Humble, J.E., Lev, B.: Automation of strategy using IDEF0—A proof of concept. Oper. Res. Perspect. **2**, 106–113 (2015). https://doi.org/10.1016/j.orp.2015.05.001

Technology and Art

A Sonification of the zCOSMOS Galaxy Dataset

Sandro Bardelli[1] (ID), Claudia Ferretti[3], Luca Andrea Ludovico[2](✉) (ID),
Giorgio Presti[2] (ID), and Maurizio Rinaldi[3]

[1] Osservatorio di Astrofisica e Scienza dello Spazio, INAF – National Institute
for Astrophysics, Bologna, Italy
[2] LIM – Laboratory of Music Informatics, Department of Computer Science
"Giovanni Degli Antoni", University of Milan, Milan, Italy
luca.ludovico@unimi.it
[3] Brescia, Italy

Abstract. This paper proposes a sonification for *zCOSMOS*, an astronomical dataset that contains information about 20,000 galaxies. The goals of such an initiative are multiple: providing a sound-based description of the dataset in order to make hidden features emerge, hybridizing science with art in a cross-domain framework, and treating scientific data as cultural heritage to be preserved and enhanced, thus breaking down the barriers between scientists and the general audience. In the paper, both technical and artistic aspects of the sonification will be addressed. Finally, some relevant excerpts from the resulting sonification will be presented and discussed.

Keywords: Sonification · Galaxies · Astronomical data

1 Introduction

Sonification is the transformation of data into acoustic signals, namely a way to represent data values and relations as perceivable non-verbal sounds, with the aim to facilitate their communication and interpretation [23]. Like data visualization provides meaning via images, sonification conveys meaning via sound.

As discussed in [8], non-verbal sounds can represent numerical data and provide support for information processing activities of many different kinds.

A first scenario is the possibility to receive information while keeping other sensory channels unoccupied, as required in medical environments, process monitoring, driving, etc. Common experiences in everyday life range from the sounds naturally produced by physical phenomena and automatically associated with specific events (e.g., a whistling kettle) to sound-augmented objects (e.g., a Geiger counter). This approach is explicitly used in sensory-substitution systems, like orientation and navigation applications for blind or visually impaired (BVI) people [1].

C. Ferretti and M. Rinaldi—Independent artist

© Springer Nature Switzerland AG 2021
M. Rauterberg (Ed.): HCII 2021, LNCS 12794, pp. 171–188, 2021.
https://doi.org/10.1007/978-3-030-77411-0_12

Sonification techniques prove to be useful also when the data to represent are complex and have multiple dimensions to track [9]. In fact, music and sound present multidimensional features (e.g., pitch, intensity, timbre, spatialization, etc.), and these dimensions can be simultaneously employed to provide understandable representations of complex phenomena. An effective design of sonification can draw, e.g., on musicality, musical acoustics, sound synthesis and human perceptual capacities [10]. Listening to data can open new scientific frontiers, thanks to the human ability to parse sound for patterns and meaning. This approach can make non-trivial structures emerge and help to unveil hidden patterns [14]. Social processes [25], natural events [2], and physical observations [17] are only a few examples of applicability fields.

Finally, sonification can be applied to those scenarios where a set of data is only the base to build an experience with artistic goals. In this context, it is worth mentioning also the concept of *musification*, namely the representation of data through music. The resulting musical structures can take advantage of higher-level features, such as polyphony or harmony, in order to engage the listener. The relationships of sonification to music and sound art have been explored in [20]. After providing these definitions, we can affirm that data can be visualized by means of graphics, sonified by means of sound, and musified by means of music.

Sonifications can be enjoyed as scientific inquiries, aesthetic experiences, or both. The idea of bridging the gap between art and science in the context of scientific dissemination and "edutainment" initiatives has been explored in a number of works. An interesting point of view is reported in [6]: according to the author, sonification, as opposed to visualisation, is still an under-utilised element of the "wow" factor of science.

Proposing a sonification initiative during an exhibition or another public event can also add value to the dataset itself. First, a sound-based multimedia installation can be an engaging way to make a non-expert audience enjoy scientific subjects; in this sense, the experience can be enhanced through suitable support materials (e.g., wall-mounted panels), the stimulation of other sensory channels (e.g., a video installation), and real-time interaction with the audience (e.g., through motion detectors and ambient-light sensors). Moreover, such an initiative can play a cultural role by raising scientific data and achievements to the rank of cultural heritage to be preserved and exploited. Examples are reported in [4, 18, 34].

In the context of sensory substitution techniques, sonification can make scientific data accessible to specific categories of users, e.g. BVI people, with an important impact on their education, too [24, 32, 35].

For the sake of completeness, it is worth underlining that the legitimacy of sonification as a scientific method of data display is being debated by scholars and experts, as discussed in [37]. According to [31], widespread adoption of sonification to display complex data has largely failed to materialize, and many of the challenges to successful sonification identified in the past are still persisting. Nevertheless, since the goal of the initiative described below is dissemination, even if scientifically accurate, our proposal does not fall within the scope of problematic applications.

The rest of the paper is structured as follows: in Sect. 2 we will review some background work about astronomical data sonification, in Sect. 3 we will present the *zCOSMOS* galaxy dataset, in Sect. 4 we will describe our sonification strategy, in Sect. 5 we will discuss the achieved results, and, finally, in Sect. 6 we will draw some conclusions.

2 Sonification of Astronomical Data

The idea of sonifying astronomical data is not original at all. A forerunner of such an approach is the *photophone*, a device invented by Alexander Graham Bell that used light modulation, caught by means of photosensors, in order to transmit audio signals to a distant station [38]. In a letter written in 1880, the inventor showed excitement about the possibility to "hear a ray of the sun laugh and cough and sing". He was intrigued by the idea of applying such a technology to study the spectra of stars and sunspots by listening to the sounds produced by the *photophone* receiver [11].

Many years later, space agencies promoted sonification as a mean to explore astronomical data. For example, NASA created a Java-based software tool called *xSonify* [13,15] aiming to encourage investigation in the field of space physics through sonification. Another initiative by NASA, dating back to 2020, is a project aiming to sonify the center of the Milky Way. Users can listen to data from this region captured by Chandra X-ray Observatory, Hubble Space Telescope, and Spitzer Space Telescope. Such data can be enjoyed either as solos or together, as an ensemble in which each telescope plays a different instrument.

Lunn and Hunt [29] described case studies of astronomy-based sonification, specifically addressing the sonification of radio-astronomy data as part of the Search for Extra-Terrestrial Intelligence (SETI).

Hadhazy [21] mentioned and exemplified some interesting musical compositions based on astronomical data. Among them, "Deep-Space Sonata" converted the gamma-ray burst GRB 080916C, one of the most powerful explosions recorded in the Universe, to audible sound. In this sonification, the number of notes played represents the gamma rays received by the Fermi Gamma-ray Space Telescope, while the accompanying sounds correspond to the probability of the rays emanating from the burst itself (lowest-likelihood rays are played as a harp, medium by a cello and highest-probability by a piano).

Another experience reported in [21] is "Sunny Anthem", based on the data of charged atoms within the solar wind from 1998 to 2010 recorded by a spectrometer onboard NASA's Advanced Composition Explorer spacecraft.

Many other sonification experiments starting from astronomical data could be mentioned. For instance, "Jovian Notes" is a sonification captured by Voyager 1's plasma wave instrument as the spacecraft crossed the bow shock at the edge of Jupiter's magnetosphere. Another initiative was based on the data gathered by a scientific device onboard the Lunar Reconnaissance Orbiter concerning radiation spewed by the sun as it floods the vicinity of the moon; the radiation intensity, converted into musical sounds, can be considered as a sort of live lunar music. Other relevant experiences are discussed in [33].

This kind of initiatives is also a way for stimulating interest when teaching astronomy. An example of auditory model of the solar system integrated within a planetarium show is described in [39]. Moreover, Ballesteros and Luque [5] reported a successful application to the educational field, originally conceived for a science-dissemination radio program called "The sounds of science", heard on Radio Nacional de Espana (RNE), but easily reproducible also in a classroom environment. Finally, it is worth underlining that a sound-based approach can be particularly effective for BVI students [19].

Concerning accessibility and inclusion for people who cannot fully enjoy experiences where visual media is the primary communication mechanism, it is worth mentioning also initiatives dealing with astronomic data but relying on senses other than hearing. An example is the creation of three-dimensional printed data sets, as in the case of tactile 3D models from NASA's Chandra X-ray Observatory [3]. Also the sense of smell can be used to design astronomy-oriented programs, as reported in [41]. Finally, the multi-sensorial project called "The Hands-On Universe Project" employs edible models and common food to convey complex concepts in cosmology and astrophysics [40].

Going back to sonification of astronomical data, there are also initiatives coupling dissemination purposes with artistic goals. For example, Ballora [7] applied sonification techniques for astronomical data in the framework of a film-making process, so as to create the soundtrack for a short movie titled "Rhythms of the Universe". In [7] he described how the sonifications had been obtained from datasets describing pulsars, the planetary orbits, gravitational waves, nodal patterns in the sun's surface, solar winds, extragalactic background light, and cosmic microwave background radiation.

3   The zCOSMOS Dataset

The zCOSMOS dataset [22,26,27] is the spectroscopic follow-up of the wider Cosmic Evolution Survey (COSMOS) [36], a coordinated international effort to study the galaxy evolution in various wavelength. zCOSMOS obtained spectra for 18,143 galaxies at the apparent magnitude $I_{AB} < 22.5$ at the VLT-ESO telescope (Chile). Such a dataset describes the evolution of a relatively small portion of the Universe in the last 10 million years.

With the use of these high-quality spectra, it was possible to derive a number of physical quantities of the galaxies. Among the variables provided in the dataset, we selected:

- Stellar Mass $M_\odot$, a value describing how many stars are formed in a galaxy and, therefore, a proxy for the galaxy history. It is the sum of all the star masses;
- Star Formation Rate SFR, i.e. the total mass of stars formed per year, which reflects how active a galaxy is at the moment of the observation;
- Redshift z, namely the measure of the recession velocity of the galaxy as a consequence of the expansion of the Universe. Due to the Hubble's law, the

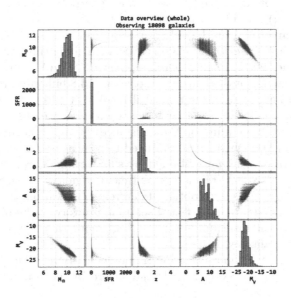

Fig. 1. Overview of the original variables. Variables distribution histograms are shown on the main diagonal; other positions display a dispersion graph of each pair of variables.

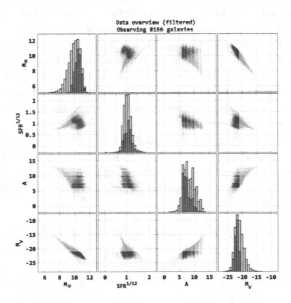

Fig. 2. Overview of the re-scaled and filtered variables. Galaxies considered for sonification are shown in dark color, while discarded galaxies are shown in light gray.

higher the redshift (measured as the shift of spectral lines toward the red part of the spectrum), the higher the galaxy distance;

- Age of the Universe A at the galaxy position, measured in billions of years. Objects that are close to us are observed with little time delay due to the finiteness of the speed of light; therefore, the value of A for this galaxy is similar to the actual age of the Universe (i.e. about 13.8 billion years). Conversely, distant objects are seen with a remarkable delay, thus, in our observations, A at that distance is lower. In other terms, even if we are observing objects at a given moment, depending on their distance we are observing a younger or a later stage of the Universe. A is linked to a measure called *lookback time*, hereafter referred to as t_L, obtained by subtracting A from the age of the Universe: $t_L = 13.8 - A$. The lookback time of a galaxy represents how much time we are looking back to obtain its current observation;
- Absolute magnitude M_V, i.e. the absolute luminosity of the observed galaxy (related to the intrinsic luminosity). Please note that lower values of M_V imply brighter galaxies;
- Position, in terms of right ascension α and declination δ. These are the coordinates of the galaxy over the celestial sphere in the equatorial coordinate system.

The number of galaxies under exam has been reduced to 18,098, since the ones presenting $M_V < -26$ or $M_\odot \leq 6$ could come from measurement errors or insufficient quality of data.

Prior to the choice of a sonification strategy, we conducted a simple statistical inspection of the dataset. In fact, a sonification is expressive when changes in sound significantly reflect those in data. For this to happen, it is important that such data take values with a sufficient resolution and within a perceptible range. Furthermore, in case of a strong correlation between some variables, we had to understand if the reason was trivial, e.g. the calculation of one datum from another, or rather it was an unexpected feature of the phenomenon. In the former scenario, the sonification should avoid redundancy, while, in the latter, it should remark these characteristics.

The top-left to bottom-right diagonal of Fig. 1 shows the statistical distribution of variables. Its analysis allows to infer the range of variation of each variable. The other areas of Fig. 1 depict the dispersion graphs of each pair of variables, so as to remark their mutual dependence. Three problematic issues mainly emerge:

1. Almost all values for SFR are condensed in the leftmost area;
2. Variables z and A are, not surprisingly, one function of the other, since z is a proxy for t_L in standard cosmological models;
3. Due to an observational bias known as Malmquist bias [30], at large distances the sample loses faint galaxies;

In Sect. 4.2 we will describe the design choices we implemented in order to solve these problems.

4   Sonification Strategy

Sonification can be seen as the junction point between the artistic use of science and the scientific use of art, thus combining the separate viewpoints of the artist and the scientist. Coherently, the project described in this paper has been designed and implemented by a working group made of scientists, technicians, and artists.

The software tools used in the whole process include: MATLAB for data inspection and preprocessing, Supercollider to parse the CSV exported by MATLAB and perform real-time sound synthesis, Ableton Live to record the distinct audio tracks generated by Supercollider, and, finally, Steinberg Cubase for post-production.

As better detailed below, the proposed sonification is based upon three main layers:

– Galaxies, sonified through a dense stream of events, each modulated independently, thus generating a synthetic sound texture (Sect. 4.3);
– Statistics, producing a very simple, continuously modulated, synthetic drone sound (Sect. 4.4);
– Outliers, causing a rare occurrence of events, each modulated independently, thus generating complex sound icons (Sect. 4.5).

Sonification examples of the listed items and portions of the final outcome can be found at the following URL: https://www.lim.di.unimi.it/demo/zcosmos.php.

4.1   Data Pre-processing

In Sect. 3 we listed three issues emerging from an *a-priori* statistical inspection of the dataset. These problems have been addressed in a pre-processing phase.

In order to solve the first issue, namely an excessive clustering of SFR values in the leftmost range, an early idea was to consider $\log(SFR)$ instead of SFR, but this would have involved an excessive flattening of the values to the right. We therefore decided to transform the data in a monotonic way by extracting the twelfth root of SFR, namely $SFR^{1/12}$, which showed a more balanced distribution (see Fig. 2).

The second issue, namely the correlation between z and A, was solved by ignoring z, whose flattening to the left was higher than the one of A. This is the reason why z is not present in Fig. 2.

The $zCOSMOS$ survey is limited in apparent luminosity and therefore at higher distances it observed only the brightest galaxies. In order to avoid this observational bias and to have an homogeneous sample, we decided to limit the time span and the brightness range: galaxies with $A < 6$ million years and $M_V > -21$ have been excluded. In this way, the number of sonified galaxies has been drastically cut, from $18,098$ to $8,156$. Even if the sonification of the full set of galaxies could have been desirable from multiple points of view, we chose not

Table 1. Lower and upper thresholds and number of outliers. Dim galaxies, presenting high M_V, have not been marked.

Variable	Lower threshold	No. of lower outliers	Upper threshold	No. of upper outliers
$M_\odot$	9.25	7	11.58	1
SFR	0.1	138	76	102
M_V	−24.19	9	-	-

to represent misleading data, such as the false correlation between magnitude and age. The remaining galaxies are visible in dark color in Fig. 2.

The reduction in the number of represented galaxies pushed us to reflect on the opportunity to provide an acoustic feedback to uncertainty in observations. The mechanism employed to achieve this goal will be described in Sect. 4.4.

Concerning A, as mentioned before, such a parameter has been converted into t_L, since the latter will better suit the design described in Sect. 4.3.

Another adjustment has involved M_V, that has been inverted in order to handle values in a more intuitive way. This parameter, indicated as $-M_V$ from now on, takes low values for dim objects and high values for bright ones.

Features have been normalized in the interval $[0, 1]$ so as to provide a simple interface to the modular sonification engine. In order to avoid very small and very big outliers that would shrink most values into a middle range, some clipping has been introduced. Clipped values have been marked, so as to be properly treated in the sonification. Please refer to Table 1 and Fig. 3 for further details.

As the final step, a moving average has been calculated for normalized $M_\odot$, $SFR^{1/12}$, and $-M_V$ to provide explicit information about the trend of these variables along the temporal axis. The results thus obtained are visible in Fig. 4.

4.2   Design Choices

The sonification is completely procedural and parametric, so it can be easily modified to respond to different requirements and use cases. In particular, modularity has been exploited to explore the space of sound-synthesis parameters, overall duration, and feature associations, with the aim of matching the sonification goals with the desired aesthetics.

In all design phases we followed the principle of *ecological metaphors*, thus trying to make the sonification coherent with users' real-world sensory and cognitive experience [12]. This approach implies that variations of auditory dimensions are consistent with those of physical parameters; for example, position values may be mapped onto left/right sound panning. The use of ecological metaphors should improve intuitiveness and learnability.

One of the goals was to keep the technical setup required to play the sonification as simple as possible, so as to make it easily reproducible in a wide

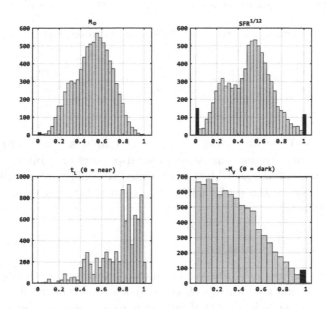

Fig. 3. Distributions of the normalized variables that are actually sonified. The uniformly distributed variable α is not shown. Outliers assigned to auditory icons are highlighted through dark histogram bars.

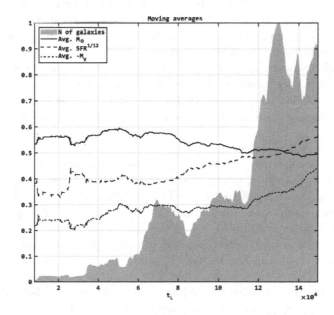

Fig. 4. Moving average of principal features against lookback time.

Table 2. Relationship between the parameters of the oscillators.

Oscillator	Pitch	Level	Release	Position	FM
O_1	f_0	a	r	p	None
O_2	$2f_0$	$0.25a$	$0.5r$	p	None
O_3	$0.75f_0$	$0.6a$	$0.6r$	p	Yes

range of contests. For this reason, the final outcome was a standard stereo file. Sound spatialization through an array of loudspeakers or a binaural approach would have extended the possibilities connected to ecological metaphors, but it would have prevented the performance in a great number of environments not adequately equipped.

4.3   Sonification of Galaxies

Each galaxy is sonified as a single and short sound event, occurring at a time which is proportional to its lookback time. When the event density is very low, single galaxies can be easily spotted and compared, while, in case of very dense and crowded sections, the overlapping of many events generates a complex texture which is more informative about the overall trend.

Each sound event is generated by 3 distinct sinusoidal oscillators, called O_{1-3}, presenting an exponential-decay envelope. Each oscillator can be controlled in terms of pitch, level, decay time, stereophonic position, and frequency modulation. O_1, O_2, and O_3 are the master, the harmonic, the sub-harmonic oscillator respectively. After computing the parameters for O_1, those for the other oscillators follow according to the schema shown in Table 2. The rationale is to have a fundamental frequency generated by O_1 which is louder and lasts longer than the harmonic and sub-harmonic sounds generated by $O_{2,3}$.

As it regards O_1, its parameters are modulated according to the following data bindings (a detailed description of modulation ranges is presented in Table 3).

The volume is determined by the absolute magnitude $-M_V$ of the galaxy under exam by exploiting an analogy with vision: brighter galaxies are represented with louder sounds, while dim galaxies (harder to see) are represented with softer sounds (harder to hear). The resulting dynamic range is about -24 dB, which is sufficient to discriminate between bright and dim galaxies without making the latter inaudible.

Since the sonification has been conceived to be reproduced through a stereophonic speakers layout, it was natural to bind galaxy right ascension with the sound position in the stereophonic space. The resulting representation of spatial information is magnified, since original right ascension of the galaxies is included in about $1°$ of the sky, while the stereophonic field can reach $180°$, depending on the installation conditions. Declination δ could have been treated in a similar

Table 3. Sonification parameters for a single galaxy.

Variable	Parameter	0	1	Unit	Type
t_L	Time	0	1500	s	Linear
$-M_V$	Level	-34	-10	dB_{fs}	Linear
α	Position	Left	Right	Pan	Linear
$M_\odot$	f_0	7000	400	Hz	Exponential
$SFR^{1/12}$	f_m	2.88	252	Hz	Exponential
$SFR^{1/12}$	d	12	1050	Hz	Exponential
$SFR^{1/12}$	Release	0.3	9.6	s	Linear

way, thanks to quadraphonic listening environments, but we decided to privilege a simpler setup, as explained in Sect. 4.2.

The frequency of O_1, namely f_0, is inversely proportional to $M_\odot$. This binding has been chosen since lower pitches are generally associated with heavier and bigger sources, while high-pitched sounds easily recall smaller sources. In order to produce well-sounding events, many sonifications (including the ones mentioned in Sect. 2) usually map values onto notes of the equal-tempered scale or consonant frequencies. Conversely, we decided to let the frequency binding be continuous; in this way, the presence of beatings as opposed to the perception of distinct sounds lets the listener clearly perceive when two galaxies are similar (beatings) or different (distinct sounds) in terms of $M_\odot$. As an aesthetic consideration, the adoption of a musical scale would have produce a sonification more pleasant in the short term, but more boring on the long run. Another potential problem was the possibility to introduce a phenomenon of data misinterpretation in case of peculiar musical structures (e.g., consonant chords, cadences, etc.), which are strongly rooted in the tonal-harmony perception of music, but have no particular meaning in the sonification.

Star formation rate SFR is linked to the parameters of the frequency modulation of O_3. In order to give the idea of very active galaxies for high values of $SFR^{1/12}$ and more relaxed galaxies for low values of $SFR^{1/12}$, we carefully tuned the sinusoidal modulator frequency f_m. This parameter runs below the audio rate (i.e. $f_m < 20$ Hz) for low star formation rate, thus producing a tremolo-like effect, while high values for $SFR^{1/12}$ produce a more distinctive and frantic modulation. For the same reason, the frequency deviation d, a measure of the frequency modulation amount [16], is modified proportionally to $SFR^{1/12}$, too.

Finally, the amplitude envelope exponentially decays with a factor proportional to $SFR^{1/12}$, so that galaxies with high $SFR^{1/12}$ present a longer tail, while low values of $SFR^{1/12}$ cause a quicker decay.

Table 3 provides a detailed view of the parameters.

4.4   Sonification of Statistics

Statistics include the average of $M_\odot$, $SFR^{1/12}$, and $-M_V$ computed within a moving window across lookback time. These are continuous signals controlling the frequency f_{1-3} of 3 distinct resonant bandpass filters, each one filtering white noise, with different pan values. Filters frequency are set by multiplying $M_\odot$, $SFR^{1/12}$, and $-M_V$ by 200, 1000, and 2000 respectively. The result is a drone sound, a non-tempered chord which is consonant only under favorable circumstances.

The quality Q of the filters is very high at the beginning of the sonification, thus producing well defined pitches; it linearly decreases in time, so as to produce band-limited noise at the end of the sonification. The idea is to suggest an increase in data variability and uncertainty of the observations as long as more distant time and space is under exam. Please note that the reciprocal of Q is the actual modulated parameter.

Table 4. Statistics sonification parameters.

Variable	Parameter	Min	Max	Unit	Pan
Avg. $M_\odot$	f_1	97	120	Hz	Center
Avg. $-M_V$	f_2	327	562	Hz	Left
Avg.$SFR^{1/12}$	f_3	401	887	Hz	Right
t_L	Q_{1-3}	0.0001	0.2	Q^{-1}	-

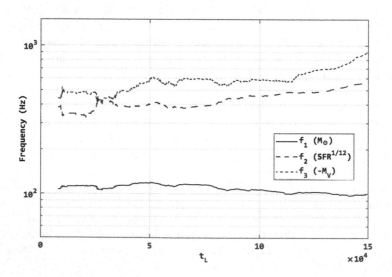

Fig. 5. Actual frequencies played by statistics-controlled filters.

Exact ranges are shown in Table 4, and the actual frequencies over time are visible in Fig. 5.

4.5   Sonification of Outliers

Outliers are galaxies whose values are out of range for at least one variable[1] and are sonified by means of auditory icons, modulated (when possible) with the same principles of single-galaxies modulations.

The icons have been carefully crafted using sound design principles coherent with other sonification-design choices. The goal is to make outliers emerge from the overall sonification, but linking their perceptibility to the frequency of their occurrence: uncommon events have to stand out with respect to more common outliers. Please refer to Table 1 for the number of outliers of each kind.

The icon for the biggest galaxy is a low-pitched percussive sound, while smaller galaxies are associated with high-pitched bells; both approaches rely on the original binding, but provide more emphasis on their outlier nature. Such sounds are modulated in position and intensity, according to α and $-M_V$.

Similarly, high and low $SFR^{1/12}$ are represented by fast and slow pulsing rumbles, respectively. These are generated through filtered noise, and modulated in pitch, level, and position according to the original bindings, and release and non-linear distortion according to $M_\odot$ and $SFR^{1/12}$ respectively.

Finally, very bright galaxies are represented through sound glitches, so as to suggest a saturation effect for the sensors, modulated in pitch and position only.

4.6   Post-Production and Final Outcome

The post-production phase consisted in fine-tuning the level balance between galaxies, outliers, and statistics. Some reverberation and equalization was added in order to improve the aesthetic result.

In particular, more reverberation has been added to background drones respect to foreground sounds in order to create a sense of depth.

Since background drone sounds are modulated quite slowly, they were slightly processed with granular synthesis based effects, so to avoid adaptation effects and to render them more appealing, by providing a more ruffled texture without compromising the intelligibility of the played frequencies.

The final outcome was a 25 min long sonification, whose musical meaning will be discussed in the next section.

5   Discussion

The proposed sonification can be formally framed according to the taxonomy outlined in [28] and called the *sonification space*. In that framework, any sonification is described as a set of *data bindings* (i.e. the single mappings between data and sound features) and one *main feature* (i.e. the overall sonic outcome). Both data bindings and the main feature can be placed over a two-dimensional plane characterized by the following axes: time granularity (continuous/regular/asynchronous), and level of abstraction (direct representation of data vs. symbolic representation). The areas that can be found are:

---

[1] Actually, no galaxies were marked as outliers for more than one variable.

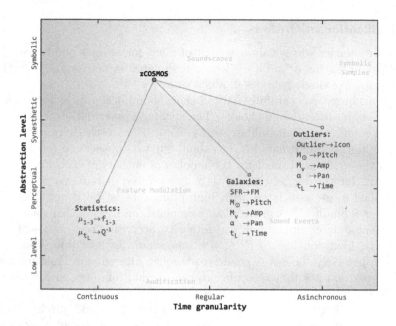

Fig. 6. Representation in the sonification space. Three groups of data bindings with different levels of temporal granularity combine into one main feature which provides a comprehensive description of the dataset.

- *Soundscapes,* i.e. holistic descriptions of a system by means of continuously modulated symbolic sounds;
- *Symbolic samples,* i.e. asynchronous symbolic signaling such as auditory icons;
- *Feature modulations,* i.e. continuous or regular sonic plotting;
- *Sound events,* i.e. asynchronous and interactive sonic plotting.

As qualitatively depicted in Fig. 6, galaxies, statistics, and outliers lay in three different areas of the sonification space. Sounds of galaxies are the constitutive atomic particles of the sonification, very small sounds which are meant to be mostly heard in swarms. The sound driven by statistics represents the scene, the space where all takes place, bent by the cumulative properties of the galaxies. Finally, outliers events are infrequent distinctive sounds, counterpointing the swarm movements.

The outcome, marked as *zCOSMOS* in Fig. 6, can be perceived as both an artificial soundscape and a contemporary music composition.

This sonification is like a journey back in time, which starts from the present, close to the Earth, and proceeds away, revealing a more and more distant past.

From a musical point of view, an overall crescendo can be clearly perceived, with a number of intermediate full-orchestra moments. Such a crescendo effect is due to both the increasing in average dynamics linked to each event (see the dotted line in Fig. 4) and to the increasing density of events (see the shape of the gray area in Fig. 4). In this sense, a 25-min.-long listening session is a good compromise to make the general dynamic trend emerge without having an excessive density of sound events. Moreover, the dashed line in Fig. 4 shows that also the average frequency-modulation amount increases with time, thus producing a darker sound at the beginning and a brighter and richer sound at the end of the piece.

The trend shown by the three lines in Fig. 5, that correspond to the frequencies of drone sounds, creates a contrary-motion effect between the bass line and the leading voices of the background layer.

In order to make the listening experience more interesting, the role played by the sonification of outliers is fundamental. In fact, in musical terms, the function of outliers can be compared to sudden variations in the orchestration, impulsive percussive events, and articulation signs. In particular, the outlier related to the biggest galaxy, rendered as a low frequency percussion, happens to be played only once, and very close to the end of the sonification: this sound event recalls the musical function of a final cadence.

6   Conclusions

In this work we have described the multiple stages bringing from the design to the realization of a sonification driven by astronomical data.

The whole process is articulated and requires heterogeneous competences. The working group embraced domain experts in different fields (physicists and astronomers, music composers, performers, sound and music computing experts, etc.) able to share ideas and cooperate.

The main activities conducted to realize the sonification (and the key actors involved) have been:

- the acquisition of the dataset (physicists and astronomers);
- its transformation in a suitable computer format (computer scientists);
- its filtering according to the scientific and aesthetic goals of the sonification (artists and sound-and-music computing experts);
- design choices concerning data bindings (the whole working group);
- data pre-processing (physicists, astronomers and computer scientists);
- technical production of single sounds (sound designers);
- mixing and post-production (sound-and-music computing experts).

This project has been mainly conceived for scientific dissemination. The goal of a sonification activity in general, and of the *zCOSMOS* initiative in particular, is to make scientific data, originally hard to retrieve and understand, easily accessible and enjoyable even by a non-expert audience. Public presentations are planned to take place in cultural institutions, together with explanatory wall-mounted panels (for museum-like installations) or support videos (for planetariums).

Thanks to the choice to diverge from tonal-harmony rules, rather focusing on the best possible rendering of the original data, this sonification challenges the listener by proposing uncommon musical structures typical of contemporary music. Such a listening activity is expected to raise users' awareness about their own perception, and highlight the importance of sound as a carrier of meaning.

References

1. Ahmetovic, D., et al.: Sonification of pathways for people with visual impairments. In: Flatla, D., Hwang, F., McGrenere, J. (eds.) Proceedings of the 20th International ACM SIGACCESS Conference on Computers and Accessibility (ASSETS 2018), pp. 379–381. ACM, New York (2018)
2. Arai, K.: Sonification method for representation of multi-dimensional meteorological data derived from Earth observation satellites. Int. J. Res. Rev. Comput. Sci. 3(2), 1538–1542 (2012)
3. Arcand, K.K., Jubett, A., Watzke, M., Price, S., Williamson, K.T., Edmonds, P.: Touching the stars: improving NASA 3D printed data sets with blind and visually impaired audiences. J. Sci. Commun. 18(4), A01 (2019)
4. Avanzo, S., Barbera, R., De Mattia, F., La Rocca, G., Sorrentino, M., Vicinanza, D.: Data sonification of volcano seismograms and sound/timbre reconstruction of ancient musical instruments with grid infrastructures. Procedia Comput. Sci. 1(1), 397–406 (2010)
5. Ballesteros, F.J., Luque, B.: Using sounds and sonifications for astronomy outreach (2008)
6. Ballora, M.: Sonification, science and popular music: In search of the 'wow'. Organ. Sound 19(1), 30–40 (2014)
7. Ballora, M.: Sonification strategies for the film Rhythms of the Universe. In: The 20th International Conference on Auditory Display (ICAD-2014) (2014)
8. Barrass, S., Kramer, G.: Using sonification. Multimed. Syst. 7(1), 23–31 (1999)
9. Ben-Tal, O., Daniels, M., Berger, J.: De natura sonoris: sonification of complex data. Math. Simul. Biol. Econ. Musicoacoust. Appl. p. 330 (2001)
10. Bregman, A.S.: Auditory Scene Analysis: The Perceptual Organization of Sound. MIT Press, Cambridge (1994)
11. Brown, E., Bearman, N.: Listening to uncertainty: information that sings. Significance 9(5), 14–17 (2012)
12. Brunswik, E., Kamiya, J.: Ecological cue-validity of 'proximity' and of other gestalt factors. Am. J. Psych. 66(1), 20–32 (1953)
13. Candey, R.M., Schertenleib, A.M., Diaz Merced, W.L.: xSonify sonification tool for space physics. In: Proceedings of the 12th International Conference on Auditory Display, London, UK, 20–23 June 2006, pp. 289–290 (2006)
14. Cooke, J., Díaz-Merced, W., Foran, G., Hannam, J., Garcia, B.: Exploring data sonification to enable, enhance, and accelerate the analysis of big, noisy, and multi-dimensional data. In: International Astronomical Union. Proceedings of the International Astronomical Union, vol. 14(S339), pp. 251–256 (2017)
15. Díaz-Merced, W.L., et al.: Sonification of astronomical data. Proc. Int. Astron. Union 7(S285), 133–136 (2011)
16. Dodge, C., Jerse, T.A.: Computer music: synthesis, composition, and performance. Macmillan Library Reference (1985)

17. Dubus, G., Bresin, R.: A systematic review of mapping strategies for the sonification of physical quantities. PloS One **8**(12), e82491 (2013)
18. Dunn, J., Clark, M.A.: Life music: the sonification of proteins. Leonardo **32**(1), 25–32 (1999)
19. Ferguson, J.: Bell3d: an audio-based astronomy education system for visually-impaired students. Ripples Everyone's Lips **1**, 35 (2016)
20. Gresham-Lancaster, S.: Relationships of sonification to music and sound art. AI Soc. **27**(2), 207–212 (2012)
21. Hadhazy, A.: Heavenly sounds: hearing astronomical data can lead to scientifi insights. Sci. Am. (2014)
22. Knobel, C., et al.: The zCOSMOS 20k group catalog. Astrophys. J. **753**(2), 121 (2012)
23. Kramer, G., et al.: The sonification report: status of the field and research agenda. report prepared for the national science foundation by members of the international community for auditory display. In: International Community for Auditory Display (ICAD), Santa Fe, NM (1999)
24. Laconsay, C.J., Wedler, H.B., Tantillo, D.J.: Visualization without vision-how blind and visually impaired students and researchers engage with molecular structures. J. Sci. Educ. Stud. Disab. **23**(1), 1–21 (2020)
25. Lenzi, S., Ciuccarelli, P.: Intentionality and design in the data sonification of social issues. Big Data & Society **7**(2), 2053951720944603 (2020)
26. Lilly, S.J., et al.: The zCOSMOS 10k-bright spectroscopic sample. Astrophys. J. Suppl. Ser. **184**(2), 218 (2009)
27. Lilly, S.J., et al.: zCOSMOS: a large VLT/VIMOS redshift survey covering $0 < z < 3$ in the COSMOS field. Astrophys. J. Suppl. Ser. **172**(1), 70 (2007). https://iopscience.iop.org/article/10.1086/516589
28. Ludovico, L.A., Presti, G.: The sonification space: a reference system for sonification tasks. Int. J. Hum. Comput. Stud. **85**, 72–77 (2016)
29. Lunn, P., Hunt., A.: Listening to the invisible: sonification as a tool for astronomical discovery. In: Making Visible the Invisible: Art, Design and Science in Data Visualisation, March 2011
30. Malmquist, K.G.: On some relations in stellar statistics. Meddelanden fran Lunds Astronomiska Observatorium Serie I **100**, 1–52 (1922)
31. Neuhoff, J.G.: Is sonification doomed to fail? In: International Conference on Auditory Display, pp. 327–330. Georgia Institute of Technology (2019)
32. Pereira, F., et al.: Sonified infrared spectra and their interpretation by blind and visually impaired students. J. Chem. Educ. **90**(8), 1028–1031 (2013)
33. Perkins, D.K.: Sonifying the universe: electroacoustic ensembles with Life 2.0. Am. Astron. Soc. Meet. Abstracts #233 **233**, 417.07 (2019)
34. Polli, A.: Soundscape, sonification, and sound activism. AI Soc. **27**(2), 257–268 (2012)
35. Reynaga-Peña, C.G., del Carmen López-Suero, C.: Strategies and technology aids for teaching science to blind and visually impaired students. In: User-Centered Software Development for the Blind and Visually Impaired: Emerging Research and Opportunities, pp. 26–37. IGI Global (2020)
36. Scoville, N., et al.: The cosmic evolution survey (cosmos): overview. Astrophys. J. Suppl. Ser. **172**(1), 1–8 (2007)
37. Supper, A.: The search for the "killer application": Ddrawing the boundaries around the sonification of scientific data. In: The Oxford Handbook of Sound Studies, Oxford Handbooks (2012)

38. Thompson, S.P.: The photophone. Science **1**(11), 130–134 (1880)
39. Tomlinson, B.J., Winters, R.M., Latina, C., Bhat, S., Rane, M., Walker, B.N.: Solar system sonification: exploring Earth and its neighbors through sound. In: The 23rd International Conference on Auditory Display (ICAD 2017), pp. 128–134 (2017)
40. Trotta, R.: The hands-on universe: making sense of the universe with all your senses. Commun. Astron. Pub. Jo. **1**(23), 20–25 (2018)
41. Wenz, J.: Making Scents of Outer Space. Astronomy Magazine (2018)

Films as Technological Artefacts

Jose Cañas-Bajo(⊠)

Aalto University, Espoo, Finland

Abstract. Since the birth of cinema and the creation of the film industry, techno-logical developments have driven changes in audio-visual language. More recently, the digital revolution and the expansion of the internet have had a major impact on the production of audio-visual content. The rapid evolution of media technologies has introduced new ways of communication and the possibility to represent more complex aspects of reality in different media, but such technologies still need to produce the desired experiences among audiences. In this context, the argument in this paper is that films should be understood as technological artefacts that can be studied with the tools offered by the human-computer interaction (HCI) field and the user-experience approach. User-centred designs, when applied to film, can provide useful methodologies to study the viewer experience of different audio-visual contents. In this paper, we present several studies in which the user approach has been taken. First, we describe a methodological tool to study emotional experiences from watching fully scripted films online and in natural contexts. Second, we describe three studies that focus on the emotional reactions to films of people with different cultural orientations. The results of these studies indicate that the integration of ideas and methods from film theory, and from the user-experience and cognitive psychological approaches to emotions, can provide a useful theoretical and methodological framework in which many aspects of films, and audience reactions to them, can be addressed.

Keywords: Films · Artefacts · Viewer experiences

1 Introduction

The worldwide scale of film consumption makes film an enormously powerful way to showcase local stories, export cultural values and share universal emotion around the world [1]. All of these factors have promoted national strategies to enhance local film industries and have also boosted studies aiming to understand audience behaviours [2]. An important barrier for researchers who study the film and television industry is the fact that films have 'artistic' characteristics that give them an 'art for art's sake' profile that it is elusive empirical scientific inquiry beyond the sociometric and managerial factors relevant for film production and distribution. In recent years, however, new theoretical and empirical approaches have spurred growing interest in film research [3, 4] that has placed films as scientifically relevant subjects for research. In the present paper, we aim to provide a new perspective in which we consider films as technological devices and identify existing challenges and questions that the scientific community should address.

M. Rauterberg (Ed.): HCII 2021, LNCS 12794, pp. 189–200, 2021.
https://doi.org/10.1007/978-3-030-77411-0_13

1.1 Early Technological Developments

Since the birth of films and the very first camera models developed by Edison and the Lumière brothers, the audio-visual language has experienced many changes and is still evolving in the present. In that sense, artists constantly experiment with new tools and techniques to enhance their contents and to play with these factors' emotional effects on audiences. This evolution has been enabled by technological developments such as camera movements and angles, cuts and shots, new lenses and lighting techniques, and video editing, among others, that together have enriched the language and created new forms of transmitting stories, ideas and messages and ways to represent reality and its complex aspects.

The appearance of sound, music and voices represented a whole new paradigm in the industry, but still more recently the move from analogue to digital technology has completely changed the industry and the way in which new audio-visual contents can be transmitted. The expansion of audio-visual technologies has also enabled the production of contents for diverse purposes. Historically, the main intention of moving images was to entertain audiences, with various cultural and aesthetic aims. In this sense, films were generally considered to be a new form of art and were understood as an artistic product created with communicative and aesthetic purposes to be expressed and transferred to other ideas and emotions.

Soon, however, audio-visual contents were discovered to be a powerful tool for propaganda and idea transmission. With the advancement of new media and the later introduction of the internet in society, audio-visual contents began to be used for many different purposes. For instance, companies now post videos to be used as marketing tools to sell products, services and ideas, to train customers to use their products and services (such as in video tutorials), to attract new investors, or as tools for internal communication [5, 6]. Entrepreneurs know that, through videos, they can influence costumers' emotions attached to their products, change their perception towards the brand or consolidate a solid virtual community.

1.2 Films in the Digital Era

During the last few decades, due to the digital revolution, the reduction in the price of cameras and the fast development of social network platforms (such as Snapchat or TikTok), the use of video for communication has become democratized. People at a very young age now learn to produce their own contents to be shared online with their followers, immediately reaching large audiences all over the world. New uses of video have introduced new agents into the industry, moved by marketing and economic interests more than the artistic aspect of the movie-going experience itself. Belton [7] has argued that software and hardware companies are the leading agents in moving forward new technologies and services that explore the possibilities of audio-visual contents, thus economically affecting the audio-visual industry.

In the last few years, hardware companies, film studios and cable companies have developed new synergies and have created companies dedicated to integrating different forms of audio-visual entertainment, including video, cable, television and video games. The integration of video, audio and data communication into a single source has enabled the delivery of the same content in different platforms and on different technological devices [8]. This integrated digital signal has produced convergence among devices as varied as video cameras, computers, televisions, phones and tablets in which the same content can be delivered in forms that increasingly resemble each other. More importantly, digital technology has transformed the audio-visual language by allowing one to represent and model the real world in many possible ways to meet the desires of the moviemaker. Imagined scenarios and special effects have flooded today's films and videos and have increased the possibilities for new expression.

Despite the general excitement for these technological advancements and developments, many theorists and practitioners see a threat in every new developmental technology that has arisen in the industry [7]. Digital technologies have enabled studios to increase their profits, but many still see these developments as a threat to the artistic and cultural function of films [7] and have raised doubts that digital projections offer audiences new experiences, improve narratives or have a better ability to reflect the real world [9]. For instance, Arnheim [10] considered technological advances in sound and colour to be the end of an art form based on images and visual expression. In the present day, the same perception of threat is taking place with the arrival of digital images in which the real world is converted into numeric information for a digital processor to read. In addition, some argue that the disruption of digital platforms and technological devices reduces the audio-visual impact of large screens and the immersive experience of a completely focussed audience in a silent and dark theatre [9].

While these fears might still be present, digital technologies introduce completely new ways to experience and interpret films [11]. The interaction between new technological advancements and novel ways of using audio-visual material that has many different purposes has led to new expressive forms that can be considered art (as aesthetic ways of communicating and transferring emotions) and artefacts, since their expressive capacity depends on technological advances and on the technological medium for expression.

Digital technologies also represent interesting challenges for film theorists and open new paths for empirical research. Technology leaves traces on the screen through the use of special effects, imaginary scenarios and characters that affect viewers' attention, and their interpretation of complex audio-visual elements, that may affect the emotional experience of the films [12]. Thus, the use of digital technology in films has led to new lines of research and inquiries into viewers' attentional strategies and their interpretation of digital elements.

1.3 Films As Art and Technological Artefacts.

The argument in this paper is that by considering films as both a *form of art* and as *technological artefacts*, they can be studied with the tools offered by the human-computer interaction (HCI) field and the user- experience approach. The user-experience approach attempts to understand people's emotional reactions towards different features of artefacts in an attempt to create products that are pleasant and easy to use by users. In the case of films and audio-visual products, the user-experience (or viewer) approach can be used in two different senses: First, it can be applied to the devices used to display audio-visual products and the quality of the image; second, it can be directed to various narrative structures and to the technical and aesthetic aspects of the audio-visual language.

Interestingly, this technological approach allows for empirically assessing many of the same elements that make films one of the more complex forms of art, involving narratives, photography, drawing, painting, visual effects, music, acting and a whole host of elements and details that are combined and integrated to compose the final feature. User-centred designs, when applied to film, provide useful methodologies to study viewers' experience of different audio-visual contents.

In my work, I have assumed that audio-visual experiences will be marked by the emotional impact that a product's concrete elements provoke in the audience, with the long-term goal of understanding the relation between textual elements of the video product and the way those elements are experienced by the viewer. The following sections describe several studies in which the users' approach has been taken in an attempt to study viewers' emotional experiences to fully scripted films online and while watching films in natural theatrical contexts.

These studies have tried to capture different features that make films a form of art. First, because aesthetic elements are used to convey and transfer emotions, empirical studies should be directed to identify which combinations of film-related features produce emotional reactions. Second, reactions to films depend not only on the intention of the creative team and on the aesthetic and narrative elements that make up the film, but also on the interaction of these elements with the personal and social backgrounds of viewers. Hence, understanding and capturing individual differences in the emotional reaction to films is also critical. Third, films, much like other forms of art, mirror culture in a complex and dynamic way. Films reflect the attitudes, concerns and beliefs of the culture that has produced them, but films also have an important influence in shaping cultural values and beliefs.

In the first section, we describe studies that have aimed to capture viewers' emotions; we focus on a specific study from my laboratory that aims to capture groups' emotional profiles to different sequences in full-length films. In the second section, we address individual differences in the reaction to films, with a focus on viewers' differences in their cultural orientation. The third section focusses on cultural differences and describes a study that looks at viewers' reactions from two different European countries to various nationally produced films. The results of these studies indicate that the integration of ideas and methods from film theory, as well as the user-experience and cognitive psychological approaches to emotions, can provide a useful theoretical and methodological framework in which many aspects of films, and audience reactions to films, can be addressed.

1.4 Capturing Viewers' Interest Profiles in Feature Films in Theatrical Contexts

As with any other artistic expression, all the elements of a film are called into play to transfer emotions to viewers, and if successful, the viewers' experiences involve emotions. As Tan has noted 'We go to the cinema to experience mirth, compassion, sadness, bittersweet emotions, thrill[s], horror, and soon in response to what we see and hear happening to characters and ourselves' [4]. What is the source and nature of the emotions that viewers experience while watching a film?

According to the appraisal theories of emotions, as Frijda notes, 'Emotions arise in response to the meaning structures of certain situations, [and] different emotions arise in response to the different structures of meaning' [13]. According to this approach, people unconsciously assess the consequences of the events happening around them, but they only experience emotions when they interpret the meanings of these phenomena. Film researchers have focused on a number of emotions elicited by films that involve this interaction between the perception and interpretation of events. Engagement, empathy and interest are core emotions in films that have been approached from this perspective [14].

The experience of being 'engaged' has been identified with the experience of *been transported* away from reality into the world depicted in a film [15, 16]. In this sense, engagement entails processes such as attention, memory, emotion and imagination becoming focused on the content of the film [17]. This mental simulation makes engagement close to empathic emotions: engaged viewers are able to take the role and simulate how the characters feel; they can mentally simulate not only the context of the narrative but also the characters' internal feelings and emotions [4, 18, 19]. A number of empirical studies have tried to capture these viewers' experiences and to identify which features of a film enhance viewers' engaged and emphatic experiences. For example, Raz and Hendler [20] recorded the brain activity of viewers of two short film excerpts and identified two type of factors driving empathic emotions in the viewers. Some features, such as dialogues or a viewer's gaze travelling from the characters to other objects of the gaze, induced parasympathetic brain responses that the authors attributed to cognitive inferences, whereas eso-dramatic features such as gestures and body movements induced increments in arousal. Guo and Stadler [21] describe the results of a pilot using a reverse camera to record the emotional responses of spectators to an emotional scene in the film *American History X*. These recorded audience responses showed strong mimicry of the characters' emotional facial expressions, indicating that people experienced empathic emotions by imitating the body reactions of the characters. In general, these studies suggest that the more closely the camera movements resemble the movement of the body (as in hand-camera shooting), the stronger the empathic responses in the viewer. The important point here is that, using this viewer-experience approach, the authors were able to identify features that induced among the viewers' emphatic inferences of the intentions, feelings and motives of the characters.

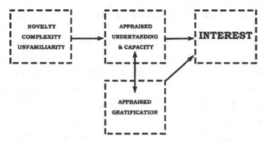

Fig. 1. Interest as perceived gain from appraisal of understanding complex and novel information.

Besides empathy and engagement, filmmakers and scriptwriters consider *interest* to be among the most important emotions in films. Interest keeps viewers' attention on the film and provides the motivation to watch the rest of the film with expectations for future sequences [22]. Although emotions such as engagement and empathy might be more intense, interest is continuous emotion that holds for a longer time. For a film to be successful, viewers must be able to maintain their interest for the entire duration of the film. Silvia [23] suggests that for interest to be experienced, people need to appraise the elements of the film as being novel and complex but still comprehensible. Such appraisals come from stylistics, aesthetics and affective features of the film that are based on combinations of multiple elements, including the types of shots, cuts, music or script elements. Some studies [24, 25] have collected viewers' judgements of novelty, complexity, interest and other emotions after watching short clips. Their results have indicated that diverse combinations of novelty, complexity and comprehensibility seem to predict interest.

A recent study from my laboratory [26] also explored viewers' interest by using a mixture of qualitative and quantitative methods, with the aim of capturing changes in the degree of interest as the film unfolded over time and the features of the film that produced these fluctuations in interest. A critical feature of this study was that participants watched full-length films in a theatrical context. This feature is important because interest is a continuous emotion that fluctuates over time. The viewer might experience interest at a specific time, which generates an increase in the expectations for the resolution of the plot, which in turn will later be perceived as being more rewarding if the resolution meets the viewer's expectations [4]. Thus, the interest generated in a specific moment increases the attention and cognitive effort necessary for the next sequence, which then will enhance the interest generated in the return on the experienced effort. This continuous loop involving interest, attention and perceived gain unfolds over the whole film, which raises the methodological point that empirical attempts to capture interest in films should continuously assess this emotion. In our study, interest was assessed online by asking participants to press a key whenever they thought their interest was raised by a particular scene while they were watching a film. They were also asked to provide the emotional valence of the interest they experienced (the system uses two different buttons to signal positive and negative emotions). The number of button presses provided online indexes of interest and emotional valence. In addition, viewers' experiences were qualified by asking participants offline to rate their experience of certain movie components (including narrative, visuals, music and characters) and by providing ratings to reflect the extent to which they felt specific emotions (such as happy, sad, angry or surprised). Analyses of the qualitative and quantitative responses allowed us to identify which sequences produced more interest among viewers and to describe the sequences' features. Overall, the analyses indicated that complex sequences that elicited different and conflicting emotions were associated with higher levels of interest.

Figure 1 represents in theoretical terms the structure of interest and the interplay between the complexity and novelty of the information in the film, the appraisal of understanding, and the rewards that led to increases or decreases of interest. Figure 2 (in the next section) represents the emotional profile of two groups of participants while watching the film.

In sum, the main argument in this section is that if we understand films as devices that produce emotional experiences among viewers, then we can use methodological approaches of user design to capture which elements of films elicit emotions such as engagement, empathy and interest that may underlie the success of a film.

2   Viewers' Individual Differences: Cosmopolitan Orientation

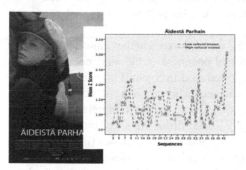

Fig. 2. Interest profiles of high and low cultural interest groups form a sample of Spanish viewers of a Finnish film (Adapted from Cañas-Bajo et al., 2019).

From a viewer-experience approach, research should be targeted not only to film features but also to features of the audience, since individual differences in personality traits, culture and education may influence aesthetic emotions and the appreciation of cultural products. Thus, a few studies have focussed on the role that individual differences in psychological traits such as sensation-seeking and empathy have in influencing the capability of being emotionally regulated by the narrative, the music and the visual content of a film [27]. For example, in a recent study, Thompson et al. [28] asked their participants, after watching two short clips from different films, to rate their degree of absorption (e.g. 'When I was watching the film it sometimes seemed as if I were in the world of the film too') and empathic feeling (e.g. 'I felt how the main character was feeling' or 'I felt sympathy for the main character'). The participants also responded to standardized sensation-seeking and empathy scales. The study's results showed that empathy and sensation-seeking predicted the participants' degree of absorption across both clips, indicating that the feeling of being transported into the narrative depicted in the film depended on individual differences in certain personality traits.

Other studies have focussed on the educational or cultural background of viewers and their 'cosmopolitan orientation'. Because films and other audio-visual products (series, clips, short films and the like) are cultural items, they might be influenced by individual factors that are not so much related to personality but to one's knowledge and orientation towards cultural products. Some studies have shown that knowledge and interest in cultural products, as well as the cultural habits of individuals, play a major role in the consumption of foreign products [29]. Cosmopolitan-oriented people are identifiable by their interest in other cultures and geographically distant places and activities, as well as by their preference for consuming products with different cultural combinations. A cosmopolitan orientation is usually associated with openness and compromise in social matters [30, 31] and is characterized by an openness to cultural products from other cultures. For example, a recent study by Savage et al. [31] analysed the geographic range of cultural and aesthetic tastes for films, books and music among Dutch participants and found different dimensions that determined people's preferences. One dimension ranged from people who were very interested in all cultures (national and transnational) and had very culturally engaged habits, to people with local tastes and very disengaged cultural habits. Another dimension ranged from preferences for American popular culture to preferences for European culture. Finally, the third dimension ranged from people who preferred exclusively Dutch cultural products to people who preferred any other combination of cultures. Some of these dimensions are related to education and age (e.g. for American products), but they also seem to reflect forms of relating to culture that vary in terms of engagement and openness. Hence the cosmopolitan orientation seems to influence the type of elements that people find interesting; from this perspective, it also makes sense to study individual differences in film preferences as they relate to people's cultural orientation.

In another study from my laboratory [26], we explored whether emotional experiences of films change depending on the cultural openness of the audience. To do so, we presented three culturally different films (produced in Spain, Finland and the US) matched in both genre and topic to a Spanish audience who varied in cultural orientation. Our aim was to investigate if cultural cosmopolitanism – people's interest in other cultures – influences their experience of culturally loaded films. We asked our participants to answer a questionnaire that included questions about demographics (including age, level of education and nationality), their interest in cultural manifestations from other countries, their frequency of travelling to foreign locations, and their knowledge of other languages, among others. Factor analysis of these items yielded two factors: *intended cultural interest* (including items related to subjective enjoyment of foreign cultures) and *objective cultural interest* (including their number of visits to other countries and their knowledge of other languages). In addition, we captured viewers' experiences by using the online response system described in the previous section, where viewers indicated what they thought were the more interesting scenes by pressing the response key. Interest scores for each sequence were obtained by calculating z scores for the number of presses for each individual and film sequence. Figure 2 represents the interest profile of our Spanish participants while they were watching the Finnish film *Mother of Mine (Aidestä Parhain)*. As the figure shows, the interest profiles of the HCO (high cultural orientation) and LCI (low cultural orientation) groups fluctuated during the film in a similar manner, indicating that their overall reactions to the film were similar. Although the groups differed in some sequences, the regression analyses indicated that cosmopolitan orientation did not predict overall interest in the film, which suggests that some emotions might have been universally triggered by certain aspects of the films. Two aspects might have produced this result: first, the overall interest scores were low for both groups, suggesting that viewers were not particularly engaged in the film; second, that the topic (a child away from his mother) included very archetypical characters and situations that might have been the source of universal emotion. These two factors require further investigation. In any case, as noted in the previous section, the main argument is that using the viewers' approach to films offers methods and tools to study people's experiences of films, including possible factors that might contribute to individual differences in these experiences.

3   Cultural Influences in Viewers' Experiences

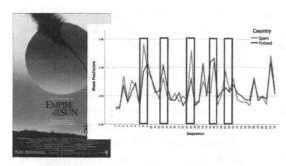

Fig. 3. Interest profiles of Finnish and Spanish viewers while watching Empire of the Sun, a US-produced film (adapted from Cañas-Bajo et al., under review).

Viewers' experiences of a film may depend not only on the quality of the film, or on the personal features and dispositions of the viewers, but also on the particular cultural context in which viewers are embedded. Audience-reception studies have shown that, after market-dominant American films, audiences prefer films produced in their own country. Thus, people select films, series and TV programmes that are culturally close to them in terms of geographical proximity, culture and language. Because films combine perceptual, memory and emotional processing, all of which are influenced by the social context in which people live, it is not a surprise that the impact of a film might be influenced by the cultural proximity of the film [32]. Perception studies have revealed that people tend to adopt a holistic/global or a local/detailed point of view, depending on their cultural background and orientation [33, 34]. Common culture and history also shape our memories to conform to collective memories that contain schematic narratives of people from a particular country or ethnic group, which guide the inferences and emotions of the people sharing them [35].

More importantly, researchers who have proposed recent models on emotion recognition have stressed that, because emotions occur in social interactions, some emotions are more frequently experienced than others within a given culture [36, 37]. For example, studies on cultural models of the self [38, 39] have shown that people in North America tend to hold an independent and individualistic model of the self, whereas people in East Asia tend to maintain a model of the self where inter-dependent and collective features are stressed. Thus, several studies [e.g. 39] have indicated that people's preferences for recreational activities (such as readings, music and sports) are congruent with their cultural models of the self (such as people from the US preferring arousing activities and people from East Asia preferring tranquil activities). This finding may come into place because national culture differs along a number of dimensions, such as individualism versus collectivism, uncertainty avoidance versus the embracing of uncertainty, masculinity versus femininity, long-term orientation versus short-term orientation, and indulgence versus restraint [40]. The effect of these cultural dimensions may influence how people experience and react to films and other audio-visual products.

In an additional study [41], we investigated the role of culture by presenting to a sample of Spanish and Finnish viewers films produced in Finland, Spain or the US. In this new study we also assessed emotional reactions online while watching a film (through the response system described above) and offline through questionnaires. We selected Finnish and Spanish viewers since their national cultures differ in some of the dimensions proposed by Hofstede [40], such as individualism, masculinity and indulgence (typically stronger among Finnish people) or power distance, uncertainty avoidance and long-term orientation (typically stronger among Spanish people).

The results indicated that the emotional reactions of the two audiences reflected both universality and cultural diversity. Thus, as shown in Fig. 3 for the US film, the emotional profiles for the two audiences were very similar, suggesting some degree of universality. But we also found differences in the way the two audiences reacted to some of the specific sequences within the films (see the marked sequences in the figure). Qualitative analyses suggested that these differences were related to certain cultural dimensions (e.g. collectivism), with Spanish viewers making more references to collective and family experiences – anguish for the child losing his parents, comments on the historical background and the like – and Finnish viewers verbalizing the individual experiences and emotions of the characters. We interpreted the data as supporting both universality and cultural mediation in the way in which the two national audiences experienced the films, and we advanced the idea that cultural variation might be more evident among audiences with stronger differences in cultural background, but also in films that vary in their narrative structure, genre or cultural origin. Further research is planned to address these questions.

In our view, a film produced in one country and in one cultural context may not have the same impact on viewers from another country or culture, and although there might be some degree of universality in the way people approach films, further studies are needed to dissociate the contribution of universal and culturally specific emotion in how viewers experience films.

4 Summary and Conclusions

The argument in this paper is that films should be understood as technological artefacts that can be studied with the tools offered by the HCI field and the user-experience approach. User-centred designs, when applied to film, provide useful methodologies to study viewers' experience of different audio-visual contents, or the visual contents in different platforms. In this paper, we have mainly focussed on viewers' experiences to different elements of the films; we have described studies that have tried to capture which film elements raised interest, engagement and empathy among viewers. We wish to draw attention to the fact that films are complex, multi-faceted audio-visual stimuli that convey complex meaning and emotion, and to the difficulties of studying the emotional reactions of an audience to the entire sequence of events that occur in the fictional narrative of a film. We also want to stress that this complexity increases when we consider that emotional reactions depend not only on the features and elements in the film, but also on viewers' personal features, such as introversion-extraversion, openness to experiences (see [42]) and cultural background [3]. Although empirical studies of viewers' experiences from many theoretical backgrounds [4] are now increasing in number, and film analysis is now a blooming field of research, researchers need to further study how emotional reactions fluctuate and change across the sequences that make up a film, and how the emotional experience of a film may vary for individuals with different personal features or cultural backgrounds. Although this enterprise might encounter many difficulties, addressing these challenges will enrich film theories and may eventually affect the industry. The results of the studies in this paper indicate that the integration of ideas and methods from film theory, and the user-experience and psychological approaches to emotions, all provide a useful theoretical and methodological framework in which many aspects of films, and audience reactions to films, can be addressed.

References

1. Dan, L.: Reflections on the cross cultural communication of Chinese films. J. Shandong Inst. Commer. Technol. **9**, 92–94 (2009)
2. Eliashberg, J., Elberse, A., Leenders, M.A.A.M.: The motion picture industry: critical issues in practice, current research, and new research directions. Mark. Sci. **25**, 638–661 (2006). https://doi.org/10.1287/mksc.1050.0177
3. Grodal, T.: How film genres are a product of biology, evolution and culture – an embodied approach. Hum. & Soc. Sci. Comm. **3**, 17079 (2017)
4. Tan, E.S.: A psychology of the film. Palgrave Commun. **4**, 82 (2018). https://doi.org/10.1057/s41599-018-0111-y
5. Prelinger, R.: The field guide to sponsored films. National Film Preservation Foundation, San Francisco (2006)
6. Wilson, H.J., Guinan, P.J., Parise, S., Weinberg, B.D.: What's your social media strategy? Harv. Bus. Rev. **89**, 23–25 (2011)
7. Belton, J.: If film is dead, what is cinema? Screen **55**, 460–470 (2014). https://doi.org/10.1093/screen/hju037
8. Forman, P., Saint John, R.W.: Creating convergence. Sci. Am. **283**, 50–56 (2000)
9. Belton, J.: Digital cinema: a false revolution, October, pp. 98–114 (2002)
10. Arnheim, R.: Film as Art: 50th Anniversary Printing. University of California Press, Oakland (1957)
11. Wood, A.: Cinema As Technology: Encounters with An Interface. Palgrave Press, London (2008)
12. Wood, A.: Encounters at the interface: distributed attention and digital embodiments. Q. Rev. Film Video. **25**, 219–229 (2008). https://doi.org/10.1080/10509200601091490
13. Frijda, N.H.: The laws of emotion. Am. Psychol. **43**, 349 (1998)
14. Cañas-Bajo J (2020) Emotional film experience. Emot. Technol. Des. Exp. Ethics 105–123
15. Gerrig, R.J.: Experiencing narrative worlds: on the psychological activities of reading. Yale University Press (1993)
16. Green, M.C., Brock, T.C.: The role of transportation in the persuasiveness of public narratives. J. Pers. Soc. Psychol. **79**, 701 (2000)
17. Busselle, R., Bilandzic, H.: Fictionality and perceived realism in experiencing stories: a model of narrative comprehension and engagement. Commun. Theory **18**, 255–280 (2008)
18. Bálint, K., Tan, E.S.: 'It feels like there are hooks inside my chest': the construction of narrative absorption experiences using image schemata. Projections **9**, 1–26 (2015). https://doi.org/10.3167/proj.2015.090205
19. Worth, S.E.: Narrative understanding and understanding narrative. Contemp. Aesthet. J. **2**, 9 (2004)
20. Raz, G., Hendler, T.: Forking cinematic paths to the self: neurocinematically informed model of empathy in motion pictures. Projections **8**(2), 1–26 (2014). https://doi.org/10.3167/proj.2014.080206
21. Stadler, J.: Empathy in film. In: Maibom, H. (ed.) The Routledge handbook of philosophy of empathy, 1–20. Routledge, New York (2017)

22. Tan, E.S.: Emotion and The Structure of Narrative Film: Film As An Emotion Machine. Erlbaum, Mahwah, NJ (1996)
23. Silvia, P.J.: Interest – the curious emotion. Curr. Dir. Psychol. Sci. **17**, 57–60 (2008)
24. Silvia, P.J., Berg, C.: Finding movies interesting: how appraisals and expertise influence the aesthetic experience of film. Empir. Stud. Arts. **29**, 73–88 (2011). https://doi.org/10.2190/EM.29.1.e
25. Tarvainen, J., Sjoberg, M., Westman, S., Laaksonen, J., Oittinen, P.: Content-based prediction of movie style, aesthetics, and affect: data set and baseline experiments. IEEE Trans. Multimed. **16**, 2085–2098 (2014). https://doi.org/10.1109/TMM.2014.2357688
26. Cañas-Bajo, J., Cañas-Bajo, T., Berki, E., Valtanen, J.-P., Saariluoma, P.: Designing a new method of studying feature-length films: an empirical study and its critical analysis. Projections **13**, 53–78 (2019)
27. Oliver, M.B.: Individual differences in media effects. Media Eff. Adv. Theory Res. **2**, 507–524 (2002)
28. Thompson, J.M., et al.: Individual differences in transportation into narrative drama. Rev. Gen. Psychol. **22**, 210–219 (2018)
29. Cleveland, M., Laroche, M., Papadopoulos, N.: Cosmopolitanism, consumer ethnocentrism, and materialism: an eight-country study of antecedents and outcomes. J. Int. Mark. **17**, 116–146 (2009)
30. Rössel, J., Schroedter, J.H.: Cosmopolitan cultural consumption: preferences and practices in a heterogenous, urban population in Switzerland. Poetics **50**, 80–95 (2015). https://doi.org/10.1016/j.poetic.2015.02.009
31. Savage, M., Silva, E.B., Meuleman, R., Savage, M.: A field analysis of cosmopolitan taste: lessons from the Netherlands. Cult. Sociol. **7**, 230–256 (2013)
32. Straubhaar, J.D.: Beyond media imperialism: asymmetrical interdependence and cultural proximity. Crit. Stud. Mass Commun. **8**, 39–59 (1991). https://doi.org/10.1080/15295039109366779
33. Colzato, L.S., van den Wildenberg, W.P.M., Hommel, B.: Losing the big picture: how religion may control visual attention. PLoS ONE **3**, e3679 (2008). https://doi.org/10.1371/journal.pone.0003679
34. Masuda, T., Nisbett, R.E.: Attending holistically versus analytically: comparing the context sensitivity of Japanese and Americans. J. Pers. Soc. Psychol. **81**, 922 (2001)
35. Hirst, W., Yamashiro, J.K., Coman, A.: Collective memory from a psychological perspective. Trends Cogn. Sci. **22**, 438–451 (2018)
36. Boiger, M., Mesquita, B.: The construction of emotion in interactions, relationships, and cultures. Emot. Rev. **4**, 221–229 (2012)
37. Gendron, M., Crivelli, C., Barrett, L.F.: Universality reconsidered: diversity in making meaning of facial expressions. Curr. Dir. Psychol. Sci. **27**, 211–219 (2018). https://doi.org/10.1177/0963721417746794
38. Markus, H.R., Kitayama, S.: Culture and the self: implications for cognition, emotion, and motivation. Psychol. Rev. **98**, 224 (1991)
39. Tsai, J.L.: Ideal affect: cultural causes and behavioral consequences. Perspect. Psychol. Sci. **2**, 242–259 (2007). https://doi.org/10.1111/j.1745-6916.2007.00043.x
40. Hofstede, G.: The GLOBE debate: back to relevance. J. Int. Bus. Stud. **41**, 1339–1346 (2010). https://doi.org/10.1057/jibs.2010.31
41. Cañas-Bajo, J., Silvennoinen, J., Saariluoma, P.: Emotional responses to culturally loaded films by Finnish and Spanish audiences. (under review)
42. Cañas-Bajo, J., Cañas-Bajo, T., Berki, E., Valtanen, J.-P., Saariluoma, P.: Emotional experiences of films: are they universal or culturally mediated? J. Audience Recept. Stud. **16**, 1–20 (2019)

Symbolic Representation and Processing of Musical Structure: Stream Segments, Pitch Interval Patterns, General Chord Types

Emilios Cambouropoulos[✉]

Aristotle University of Thessaloniki, Thessaloniki, Greece
emilios@mus.auth.gr

Abstract. The difficulty of modelling musical structure in a general and cognitively plausible manner is due primarily to music's inter-dependent multi-parametric and multi-level nature that allows multiple structural interpretations to emerge. Traditional AI symbolic processing methods, however, can be used effectively for modelling particular analytic and creative aspects of musical structure. In this paper three specific problems of music structure, namely, segmentation and streaming, pattern extraction, harmonic abstraction and generation, will be addressed with a view to highlighting the importance of problem definitions, music representation and multi-parametric hierarchical cognitively-inspired processing methodologies. Existing proof-of-concept models are used as a basis for a theoretical discussion.

Keywords: Symbolic AI · Segmentation · Streaming · Pattern matching · Harmony · Chord representation

1 Introduction

Understanding music means being able to make sense of musical structure. Musical structure does not simply contribute to musical meaning but is at the heart of musical meaning as basic musical concepts are in essence concepts relating to musical structure. Listeners are capable of discerning, encoding and remembering diverse aspects of musical structure when exposed to musical stimuli, such as scales, keys, tonal centers, motives, themes, metre, rhythmic patterns, harmonic progressions, cadences.

Through the centuries, music theorists, analysts, philosophers have attempted to describe and formalise, core musical concepts and processes. More recently, computational methodology (assisted by research in music cognition, linguistics, logic reasoning, neuroscience and so on), has offered new means of precision and formalisation, enabling the development of sophisticated representations and models of musical structure. Progress in this domain, however, has been much slower than expected and researchers are still striving for general powerful theories that can describe the complex and multifaceted nature of musical structure.

In this paper, first, we will briefly discuss why it is more difficult, than one initially believes, to model musical structure in a general and comprehensive manner. Current

© Springer Nature Switzerland AG 2021
M. Rauterberg (Ed.): HCII 2021, LNCS 12794, pp. 201–212, 2021.
https://doi.org/10.1007/978-3-030-77411-0_14

computational methodologies will be mentioned, and it will be maintained that traditional AI symbolic processing methods are still relevant and advantageous in certain respects, especially when drawing on general cognitive principles of human perception.

Then, three specific problems of music structural modelling, namely, segmentation and streaming, pattern extraction, harmonic representation, learning and generation, will be addressed. The aim is to present rather 'unconventional' definitions of the problems themselves, as well as the proposed representations and methodologies. Emphasis is given to common underlying fundamental mechanisms and interconnections that apply to seemingly disparate domains. All these suggestions draw on previous proof-of-concept models by the author that require further development and investigation.

2   Symbolic Processing and General Cognitive Principles

Perhaps, the main reason musical structure is difficult to model is its inter-dependent multi-parametric and multi-level nature that allows multiple structural features to emerge. Moreover, there exist diverse musical styles and idioms each with their own representational and processing schemes. For instance, in a musical surface for western music (in this paper we assume a piano-roll-like encoding), pitch, rhythm and harmony are basic structural features that shape the music and interact with each other on multiple levels of abstraction. Studying, for instance, patterns solely in the pitch domain, one soon discovers that absolute pitch is probably too elementary (not transposition invariant), but, then, to deal with relative pitch, a tonal center is required and emergent tonal hierarchies play a significant role depending on the structure of keys, which emerge within specific metrical and grouping structures influenced by hierarchic structures of harmony. And, soon one realizes that a fully-fleshed theory of musical structure is required to deal with 'mere' pitch patterns.

Let us briefly examine another example, namely the extraction of the musical surface itself from audio (transcription) which in the minds of many is essentially a bottom-up process. It is now accepted that higher-level aspects of musical hierarchical organisation are necessary to transcribe music in some form of symbolic notation [3, 29]; a purely bottom-up approach to score extraction has been shown to be untenable. Apart from multipitch analysis and instrument recognition, broader information is necessary such as beat tracking, rhythmic organisation, chord recognition and harmonic analysis, along with notational conventions, and, even, high-level musical structure analysis and knowledge of expressive performance. For instance, a human transcriber can fill in gaps in the audio signal (due to recording defects or noise) based on knowledge of structure (e.g., even though one or more tones may be absent from the audio input, they can be recovered due to knowledge of key or motivic structure or harmonic expectation, and so on). In essence, a comprehensive computational theory of musical structure is required for full blown score transcription. Abstraction, categorisation, hierarchic organisation and prior knowledge are all at full play in the task of music transcription. A seemingly 'simple' task is complex and significant progress in this domain will occur when high-level music analysis models mature.

The complex multi-parametric and multi-level nature of the structure of diverse musical styles renders efforts to built hand-crafted rule-based models impractical and often unworkable. For this reason, deep learning techniques have drawn the attention of researchers in recent years (e.g., [5, 13]). Often such methods are considered as the obvious, if not the only, way to deal effectively with modelling musical tasks. Deep neural networks present the important ability to abstract knowledge on higher-levels of representation, based on sample data; they are flexible, adaptive, easy to build as they do not require fully fleshed-out models, and they are resilient to noise or incomplete information. So, why bother follow a symbolic rule-based approach that requires manual coding, does not allow dynamic change and it cannot capture the complexity of the real world?

Traditional symbolic AI modelling enables the development of music models that may have both theoretical and practical advantages. In terms of theory, our understanding of music *per se* is enriched, traditional assumptions are tested, empirically-derived cognitive principles evaluated and new musical knowledge is acquired. As knowledge is explicit in such AI models, sophisticated practical systems can be created that allow intelligent interaction with musicians/users though the manipulation of meaningful symbolic representations (e.g., educational systems, compositional assistants, interactive performers, content-based music search engines, and so on). Such systems make use of prior knowledge acquired through years (or even centuries) of experience and introspection, and, also, capitalize on findings resulting from empirical work in music cognition. This way sophisticated models can be built relatively quickly combining diverse components on different hierarchical levels of organisation. Additionally, symbolic systems reinforced with simple statistical learning capacities, can adapt to different contexts based on relatively small training datasets allowing this way a certain degree of flexibility. Furthermore, such models can bridge different conceptual spaces enabling the invention of novel concepts not present in the initial input spaces.

A debate on the pros and cons of traditional symbolic AI methods vs deep neural network learning techniques can be found in studies such as [21, 24], (see also [6] for a defense of the symbolic AI approach in music modelling). Recently, attempts are made to combine the strengths of both approaches reconciling symbolic systems, that are strong in abstraction and inference, with deep learning techniques that excel in perceptual classification [10].

Our mind continuously groups sounds together based on their similarity and by trying to find simple ecological patterns that can describe them [2, 4]. The fundamental principles of perception, first studied by the Gestalt psychologists [19], give an account of the basic rules that account for such grouping. A common notion underlying many of these principles is similarity (which is directly linked to change). For instance, in music, many models that attempt to break the musical continuum into smaller constituent parts (e.g., segments, voices) have relied on principles such as pitch similarity, temporal proximity, parallel motion, i.e., similarity in the pitch, time and pitch interval domains respectively. Similarity is also at work on higher levels of cognition whereby learnt patterns (e.g. a fugue theme) can be recognised in a rather complex musical continuum. More generally, learning techniques are based on finding regular patterns in data, and commonly a distance function (similarity measure) is used somewhere in the learning process (training or classification or clustering stage).

Symbolic models in computational musicology that strive for generality (i.e., applicability in a broad spectrum of musics) often rely on general cognitive principles such as similarity/change. Additionally, specific acoustic or auditory principles are employed as constraints that help narrow down the usually large search spaces. Such auditory-specific constraints rely on aspects of sound perception that have to do with properties of sound sources, the auditory system and typical sound environments listeners are exposed to (e.g., harmonicity, octave equivalence, dissonance, masking, onset simultaneity thresholds). The use of such perceptual principles, accompanied by probabilities of features and patterns (learned from data) that reflect regularities and tendencies of specific musical environments, can give rise to rather sophisticated musical systems.

In the next three sections, three different musical problems will be presented examined from relatively unusual angles, redefining the problems themselves or suggesting novel solutions so as to be more general and idiom independent. The presentation below is mostly theoretical; it is, however, grounded on earlier proof-of-concept implementations by the author. It is suggested that further research in the proposed line of inquiry may produce new more flexible and adaptive models of musical structure.

3 Stream Segments

Voice or stream separation algorithms attempt to model computationally the segregation of polyphonic music into separate voices [12, 23]; music segmentation algorithms on the other hand, segment music voices/streams into smaller coherent groups [27]. Both segmentation and streaming rely on fundamental Gestalt principles such as temporal and pitch proximity. In principle, firstly, voices/streams are determined and then voices/streams are segmented into smaller groups. Is it possible to develop a model that separates notes vertically into streams and, at the same time, locates segment boundaries? In other words, is it possible to parse a general two dimensional pitch-time space into *stream segments*? The main advantage of adopting the concept of stream segments is that they are meaningful in any type of music, not only when music has a rather 'fixed' number of independent voices (e.g., fugues) - see stream segment illustration in Fig. 1.

An algorithm that makes use of a single set of auditory principles for the concurrent horizontal and vertical segregation of a musical texture into stream segments has been proposed by [26]. This algorithm groups together in the same stream segment notes that have proximal onsets (synchronous onsets for quantised data), similar durations (same for symbolic data) and similar pitch interval direction (parallel/similar motion), and, additionally, successive (non-overlapping) notes that are temporally proximal and similar in pitch; non-synchronous overlapping notes belong to different stream segments along with successive (non-overlapping notes) that are temporally distant and dissimilar in pitch. This prototype algorithm was tested against a small manually-annotated dataset of musical excerpts, and preliminary results were encouraging. An example of stream segmentation parsing (coherent groups of notes such as melodic segments, harmonic accompanimental fragments, homophonic passages) is presented in Fig. 1 – problems and shortcomings of the algorithm are discussed in [26].

Models that can detect stream segments can be very useful as they enable the organisation of the low-level musical surface into coherent groups that are musically meaningful; such organisation facilitates more efficient and higher-level analytic processing.

For instance, in searching for instances of the pitch pattern descending-perfect-fifth - followed-by-unison [-P5, unison] in the example of Fig. 1, a general polyphonic pattern identification algorithm would correctly detect the melodic instances in mm. 10, 11, & 18 but would also (incorrectly in perceptual terms) detect this pattern in (at least) the homophonic textures of mm. 12 and 14; being able to separate melodic from homo-phonic/accompanimental textures may contribute to more accurate and efficient search. This line of research into stream segments does not seem to have been taken on by the MIR research community (a possible problem is the lack of annotated ground truth data against which to test algorithms). However, it is herein maintained that it is a worthwhile research project in the direction of building a more general model for breaking down the musical surface into perceptually meaningful subgroups.

Fig. 1. Stream segments detected by algorithm in the opening of Beethoven's Sonata Op. 31, No. 3 (Fig. 4, [26])

4 Pitch Interval Patterns

The capacity of listeners to 'match' varied musical materials is essential to the process of identifying meaningful musical entities such as interesting motifs, themes, melodic and rhythmic patterns, characteristic harmonic progressions, and other memorable musi-cal entities. In recent years, a number of computational systems have been developed that describe symbolic melodic similarity (see overviews in [7, 30]). Such algorithms address different perspectives of this multi-faceted similarity task, such as representa-tion, scope, similarity function, polyphony and so on. For instance, most algorithms are applied on monophonic strings of symbols, whereas few employ geometric models on two-dimensional point-set representations. The latter are more powerful in the sense that they can identify melodic patterns directly in unprocessed polyphonic music, at the expense, however, of retrieving higher numbers of false positives. It is known that listeners cannot identify patterns across auditory streams [4]; in this sense, it is more practical to segregate a musical surface into distinct voices/streams, and then to apply string matching algorithms (that are computationally simpler and more efficient) on (melodic) strings of symbols identifying patterns that are more likely to be musically interesting and cognitively plausible.

Dynamic programming techniques, often based on various types of edit distance, are commonly used to find approximate matches in melodic strings. Edit distance is a very useful technique commonly applied to strings of pitches [22]. Techniques, however, using standard edit distance operations (replacement, insertion, deletion, along with con-solidation and fragmentation) applied on strings of notes have limitations and inherent shortcomings such as defining a similarity threshold (any sequence can match with any sequence if enough edit operations are applied) and lack of transposition invariance. If edit distance is applied to strings of pitch intervals, problems occur, such as the fact that the insertion or deletion or replacement of a single interval changes drastically the rest of the pitch sequence – see, however, proposal by [20].

In [1] the problem of matching is redefined in a way that is appropriate for strings of melodic intervals (not notes). Matching can be applied directly to strings of intervals (in semitones) without any preprocessing (as is required in [20]). To this aim, the replacement, insertion and deletion operations are abolished, and only consolidation and fragmentation operations are retained, adapted to the interval domain. Two or more intervals of one string may be matched to an interval from a second string through consolidation (i.e., the sum of one or more intervals of the first string should be equal to an interval of the second string) – this is the many-to-one matching problem; in a similar fashion, fragmentation is defined, i.e., one-to-many interval matching. The general case is many-to-many interval matching (the sum of two or more consecutive intervals from the first string is equal to the sum of two or more intervals of the second string) – see example in Fig. 2. Working with intervals means melodic matching is transposition-invariant. Additionally, matching is confined by equality in the consolidation and fragmentation operations (the only threshold necessary in the pitch domain is the maximum number of intervals allowed in consolidation/fragmentation).

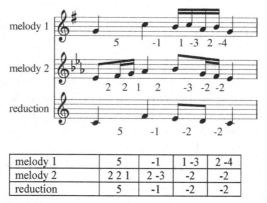

melody 1	5	-1	1 -3	2 -4
melody 2	2 2 1	2 -3	-2	-2
reduction	5	-1	-2	-2

Fig. 2. The two melodic segments can be matched via the proposed pitch interval consolidation-fragmentation operations as seen in the first two rows of the table where the sum of the intervals in corresponding cells is equal. The melodic reduction pattern can be matched to each of the melodies via fragmentation (each cell in the last row of the table is equal to the sum of two or more intervals in each corresponding cell of the two melodies).

The implementation of interval matching via fragmentation/consolidation presented in [1], allows only one-to-many and many-to-one matches; the algorithm was tested only on one piece by W. A. Mozart (Sonata in A major KV331) searching for reduced versions of the theme (one-to-many problem); preliminary results were very encouraging.

Listeners are capable of discerning common elements between varied musical material primarily through hierarchic reduction, i.e., identifying 'essential' common characteristics, such as interval patterns between disjunct salient notes. The one-to-many implementation of the proposed algorithm allows such patterns to be retrieved. An example (handmade) is presented in Fig. 3 to illustrate the kinds of themes that may be retrieved by such an algorithm from a theme database (such as the database in themefinder.org) given a reduced pitch sequence query. A variant of this algorithm that additionally takes into account rhythmic durations is presented in [11], tested on four classical theme-and-variation pieces.

Fig. 3. Example of incipits of themes that may be matched to a given pitch interval query (top) employing the proposed melodic matching via interval fragmentation methodology. Each interval of the query can be fragmented up to (this this case) four intervals; the intervals matched to the query are designated by horizontal brackets.

It is suggested that this new definition of the problem of melodic matching, requires no preprocessing and is reliable in capturing hierarchically related pitch patterns (i.e., underlying salient pitches) that are transpositionally invariant. Rethinking representation and hierarchic structure issues is sometimes useful to overcome problems and shortcomings of more standard approaches.

5 Chords and Harmony

Representing chords and harmony is the last area to be discussed in this paper. Multiple notes occurring simultaneously are grouped by listeners into a 'chord', which is an entity in its own right, carrying functions, expectations, meaning, even emotions. Note simultaneities are often perceived as 'wholes' prior to establishing finer elaborations such as individual constituent pitches, octave information, note doubling, note omission, chord inversion, roots, and so on (for instance, chords in different positions are essentially equivalent as shown by [14]). The notion of the root of a chord is attributed to a note (often missing from the simultaneity that constitutes the chord) depending on psychoacoustic phenomena and tonality hierarchies (see perceptual root calculation model by [25]).

How can the infinite variety of possible simultaneities (in terms of octave position, note doubling, note omissions, note extensions, inversions) be reduced to a cognitively manageable number of abstract chord types/families? How can note verticalities be represented? Additionally, can we represent chords in different ways (using a common cognitively-inspired mechanism) depending on different qualities of diverse harmonic systems? The standard encoding of chords for tonal music is appropriate for tonal music, but not for other non-tonal idioms; pc-set encodings, on the other hand, are useful for atonal music but have weaker explicatory power for tonal music. Is an adaptive representation possible?

The General Chord Type (GCT) representation [8, 9], allows the re-arrangement of the notes of a harmonic verticality such that abstract idiom-specific types of chords may be derived. Given a consonance-dissonance classification of intervals (that reflects sensory and/or culturally-dependent notions of consonance/dissonance), the GCT algorithm finds the maximal subset of notes of a given note simultaneity that contains only consonant intervals; this maximal subset forms the base upon which the chord type is built and the lowest note of the base is the root of the chord. This encoding is inspired by the standard roman numeral chord type labeling, but is more general and flexible (it can encode, for instance atonal normal order pc-set types). Currently the GCT is revised to account for a multi-valued ranking of dissonance that enables the disambiguation of certain ambiguities that appear in the original version that is based on a binary dissonance vector.

In the example of Fig. 4, a standard roman numeral analysis is presented along with the GCT encoding for a tonal context. The GCT analysis is given for every vertical slice of the excerpt. For instance, [0, [0,4,7]] represents a tonic major chord in the C major key, whereas [7, [0,4,7]] a dominant chord. The second beat of the second measure comprises of two vertical slices, both of which have the same chord type base [2, [0, 4, 7]]; the two chords can be merged into a single more abstract chord type (in this case a secondary dominant to the dominant). The last beat of the second measure and the first beat of the third measure correspond to two vertical slices each; choosing one of the two (following the underlying harmonic rhythm) is possible if prior knowledge regarding the Bach chorale idiom is employed (e.g., acquired via corpus-based learning), such as chord typicality (e.g., a minor dominant chord [7,[0,3,7]] is very rare) or chord progression typicality (e.g., IV → vii° more common than vi^7 → vii°). The GCT representation can be used, not only to encode any note simultaneity (in tonal or atonal or other contexts) but additionally to determine broader more abstract families of chords based on similarity and/or functionality (see [17]). It is suggested that such chord relations can be employed in the context of automated harmonic analysis, enabling not only the encoding of chords but the reduction of musical surfaces to underlying harmonic progressions; this can be done in both tonal and non-tonal musics, as the GCT can be adapted to different harmonic idioms.

Fig. 4. Roman numeral analysis and GCT encoding of the opening of J. S. Bach's, Chorale 40 (Ach Gott und Herr) BWV255.

Representing and processing harmonic structure involves developing sophisticated hierarchical representations (e.g., [28]). A simple approach for composing melodic harmonisations in relation to the GCT scheme was presented by [18], where chords are labelled employing the GCT representation, and corpus-based learning (from annotated harmonic reductions) involves learning chord transitions at the lowest chord-to-chord level and at the level of phrase boundaries (cadences). In the context of a generation (harmonisation) framework, constraints are inserted at phrase boundaries ensuring appropriate cadential schemata at structurally important positions, and, then, intermediate chord progressions are filled in according to the learned chord transition matrices. This method is incorporated in the *Chameleon* melodic harmonisation assistant [16, 17] that is adaptive (learns from data), general (can cope with any tonal or non-tonal harmonic idiom) and modular (learns and encodes explicitly different components of harmonic structure: chord types, chord transitions, cadences, bass line voice-leading).

The harmonic knowledge acquired by this system, can be used creatively in a cognitively-inspired conceptual blending model that allows the creation of combinational components between disjoint spaces, with very little (if any) training and with transparent access to what concepts are combined. The *Chameleon* melodic harmonisation assistant is essentially a proof-of-concept creative model that demonstrates that new harmonic concepts can be invented that transcend the initial harmonic input spaces. It is argued that such original creativity is more naturally accommodated in the world of symbolic reasoning that allows links and inferences between diverse concepts at high abstract levels [6, 15]. Moreover, symbolic representation and processing facilitates interpretability and explanation that are key components of musical knowledge advancement. Overall, a symbolic hierarchical modular representation coupled with basic statistical learning of harmony, not only, gives rise to a rather sophisticated description of harmonic structure but, additionally, allows generation of new harmonisations in certain styles and, even, production of more adventurous creative cross-idiom harmonisations.

6 Conclusions

In this paper, three areas of music modelling, namely, segmentation and streaming, pattern extraction, harmonic abstraction, learning and generation have been examined in terms of fundamental principles of perceptual hierarchic organisation that can form the basis for general computational systems of musical structure. Emphasis has been given to approaching these problems from somewhat 'unconventional' viewpoints that give rise to relatively new definitions, representations and methods. Common underlying fundamental mechanisms and interdependencies that apply to seemingly irreconcilable areas have been highlighted. It is maintained that cognitively-inspired computational models of musical structure should take into account psychoacoustic/perceptual constraints, fundamental cognitive principles, logical principles, and should strive for generality and parsimony. Traditional AI symbolic representations and methodologies (despite a number of drawbacks discussed above) allow building sophisticated models relatively quickly, combining diverse components on different hierarchical levels of organisation. As knowledge is explicit in such AI models, sophisticated practical systems can be created that allow intelligent interaction with musicians/users though the manipulation of meaningful symbolic representations. At the same time, such systems can be used for testing various hypotheses and acquiring new insights into our understanding of music.

References

1. Barton, C., Cambouropoulos, E., Iliopoulos, C.S., Lipták, Z.: Melodic string matching via interval consolidation and fragmentation. In: Iliadis, L., Maglogiannis, I., Papadopoulos, H., Karatzas, K., Sioutas, S. (eds.) AIAI 2012. IAICT, vol. 382, pp. 460–469. Springer, Heidelberg (2012). https://doi.org/10.1007/978-3-642-33412-2_47
2. Bendixen, A., Bőhm, T.M., Szalárdy, O., Mill, R., Denham, S.L., Winkler, I.: Different roles of similarity and predictability in auditory stream segregation. Learn. Percept. 5(Supp. 2), 37–54 (2013)
3. Benetos, E., Dixon, S., Giannoulis, D., Kirchhoff, H., Klapuri, A.: Automatic music transcription: challenges and future directions. J. Intell. Inf. Syst. 41(3), 407–434 (2013). https://doi.org/10.1007/s10844-013-0258-3
4. Bregman, A.S.: Auditory Scene Analysis: The Perceptual Organization of Sound. MIT Press, Cambridge (1994)
5. Briot, J.P., Hadjeres, G., Pachet, F.: Deep learning techniques for music generation. Springer, Heidelberg (2020)
6. Cambouropoulos, E., Kaliakatsos-Papakostas, M.: Cognitive musicology and artificial intelligence: harmonic analysis, learning and generation. In: Miranda, E.R., (ed.) Handbook for Artificial Intelligence in Music. Springer (forthcoming)
7. Cambouropoulos, E., Kaliakatsos-Papakostas, M.: Symbolic approaches and methods for analyzing similarity. In: Shanahan, D., Burgoyne, J.A., Quinn, I., (eds.) The Oxford Handbook of Music and Corpus Studies. Oxford University Press (forthcoming)

8. Cambouropoulos, E.: The harmonic musical surface and two novel chord representation schemes. In: Meredith, D. (eds.) Computational Music Analysis, pp. 31-56. Springer, Cham (2016). https://doi.org/10.1007/978-3-319-25931-4_2
9. Cambouropoulos, E., Kaliakatsos-Papakostas, M., Tsougras, C.: An idiom-independent representation of chords for computational music analysis and generation. In: Proceedings of the Joint 11th Sound and Music Computing Conference (SMC) and 40th International Computer Music Conference (ICMC), Athens, Greece (2014)
10. Garnelo, M., Shanahan, M.: Reconciling deep learning with symbolic artificial intelligence: representing objects and relations. Curr. Opin. Behav. Sci. **29**, 17–23 (2019)
11. Giraud, M., Déguernel, K., Cambouropoulos, E.: Fragmentations with pitch, rhythm and parallelism constraints for variation matching. In: Aramaki, M., Derrien, O., Kronland-Martinet, R., Ystad, S. (eds.) CMMR 2013. LNCS, vol. 8905, pp. 298–312. Springer, Cham (2014). https://doi.org/10.1007/978-3-319-12976-1_19
12. Gray, P., Bunescu, R.: From note-level to chord-level neural network models for voice separation in symbolic music (2020). arXiv preprint: arXiv:2011.03028
13. Herremans, D., Chuan, C.-H.: The emergence of deep learning: new opportunities for music and audio technologies. Neural Comput. Appl. **32**(4), 913–914 (2019). https://doi.org/10.1007/s00521-019-04166-0
14. Hubbard, T.L., Datteri, D.L.: Recognizing the Component tones of a major chord. Am. J. Psychol. **114**(4), 569–589 (2001)
15. Kaliakatsos-Papakostas, M., Cambouropoulos, E.: Conceptual blending of high-level features and data-driven salience computation in melodic generation. Cogn. Syst. Res. **58**, 55–70 (2019)
16. Kaliakatsos-Papakostas, M., Queiroz, M., Tsougras, C., Cambouropoulos, E.: Conceptual blending of harmonic spaces for creating melodic harmonisation. J. New Music Res. **46**(4), 305–328 (2017)
17. Kaliakatsos-Papakostas, M., Zacharakis, A., Tsougras, C., Cambouropoulos, E.: Evaluating the general chord type representation in tonal music and organising GCT chord labels in functional chord categories. In: Proceedings of the 16th International Society for Music Information Retrieval (ISMIR) Conference, Malaga, Spain (2015)
18. Kaliakatsos-Papakostas, M., Cambouropoulos, E.: Probabilistic harmonisation with fixed intermediate chord constraints. In: Proceeding of the Joint 11th Sound and Music Computing Conference (SMC) and 40th International Computer Music Conference (ICMC), Athens, Greece (2014)
19. Köhler, W.: Gestalt Psychology. Liveright, New York (1947)
20. Lemström, K., Ukkonen, E.: Including interval encoding into edit distance based music comparison and retrieval. In: Proceedings of the AISB 2000 Convention (Artificial Intelligence and Simulation of Behaviour) (2000)
21. Marcus, G.: Deep learning: a critical appraisal (2018). arXiv preprint: arXiv:1801.00631
22. Mongeau, M., Sankoff, D.: Comparison of musical sequences. Comput. Humanit. **24**(3), 161–175 (1990)
23. Mill, R.W., Böhm, T.M., Bendixen, A., Winkler, I., Denham, S.L.: Modelling the emergence and dynamics of perceptual organisation in auditory streaming. PLoS Comput. Biol. **9**(3), e1002925 (2013)
24. Nilsson, N.J.: The physical symbol system hypothesis: status and prospects. In: Lungarella, M., Iida, F., Bongard, J., Pfeifer, R. (eds.) 50 Years of Artificial Intelligence. LNCS (LNAI), vol. 4850, pp. 9–17. Springer, Heidelberg (2007). https://doi.org/10.1007/978-3-540-77296-5_2
25. Parncutt, R.: A model of the perceptual root(s) of a chord accounting for voicing and prevailing tonality. In: Leman, M. (ed.) JIC 1996. LNCS, vol. 1317, pp. 181–199. Springer, Heidelberg (1997). https://doi.org/10.1007/BFb0034114

26. Rafailidis, D., Nanopoulos, A., Cambouropoulos, E., Manolopoulos, Y.: Detection of stream segments in symbolic musical data. In: Proceedings of the International Conference on Music Information Retrieval (ISMIR 2008), Philadelfia, Pennsylvania (2008)
27. Rodríguez-López, M., Volk, A.: Symbolic segmentation: a corpus-based analysis of melodic phrases. In: Aramaki, M., Derrien, O., Kronland-Martinet, R., Ystad, S. (eds.) CMMR 2013. LNCS, vol. 8905, pp. 548–557. Springer, Cham (2014). https://doi.org/10.1007/978-3-319-12976-1_33
28. Rohrmeier, M.: Towards a generative syntax of tonal harmony. J. Math. Music 5(1), 35–53 (2011)
29. Ryynänen, M.P., Klapuri, A.P.: Automatic transcription of melody, bass line, and chords in polyphonic music. Comput. Music. J. 32(3), 72–86 (2008)
30. Velardo, V., Vallati, M., Jan, S.: Symbolic melodic similarity: state of the art and future challenges. Comput. Music. J. 40(2), 70–83 (2016)

Towards AI Aesthetics: Human-AI Collaboration in Creating Chinese Landscape Painting

Rong Chang and Yiyuan Huang$^{(\boxtimes)}$

Beijing Institute of Graphic Communication, No. 1 (band -2) Xinghua Street,
Daxing District, Beijing, China
{changrong-bj,yiyuan.huang}@bigc.edu.cn

Abstract. Based on the analysis of human-AI (artificial intelligence) collaboration in creating Chinese landscape painting, this article aims to develop the relationship between AI aesthetics and HCI in the context of Chinese aesthetics. We construct a multi-level analysis framework and propose three unique AI Aesthetics models under the framework—the dynamic brushwork (bi-mo) model, the imaged mind (xin-yin) model, and the embodied narrative (shi-jing) model. We believe that the most promising AI aesthetics approach is to promote the collaboration between human and AI. The primary research task at present is to develop interactive creation platforms. In the long run, brain-AI interactive communication will help realize mutual inspiration between human and AI, thereby stimulating more creativity.

Keywords: AI aesthetics · Human-AI collaboration · AI aesthetic models · Chinese aesthetics · Chinese landscape painting

1 Introduction

The research of AI aesthetics can be traced back to information aesthetics that mainly developed in Europe during the 1960s. Since then, researchers have presented a series of concepts including generative aesthetics, algorithm aesthetics, and computational aesthetics. In general, the above studies expect that algorithms would generate artworks based on automatic aesthetic decisions [1]. The rapid development of artificial intelligence technology gave birth to the new concept of AI aesthetics [2]. The well-known AI aesthetics available online are, for example, drawing system AutoDraw, music composition system Magenta and dance choreographing system Living Archive.

Chinese landscape painting is a hallmark of Chinese aesthetic thought and practice. From the 1970s to the 1990s, the formal analysis of Chinese painting had made significant progress [3, 4] that provided the epistemological foundation for computer simulation [5]. At the beginning of the 21st century, some computer researchers began to develop HCI systems for simulating Chinese painting. Recently, inspired by the power

© Springer Nature Switzerland AG 2021
M. Rauterberg (Ed.): HCII 2021, LNCS 12794, pp. 213–224, 2021.
https://doi.org/10.1007/978-3-030-77411-0_15

of Convolutional Neural Networks (CNNs), researchers turned to use AI to generate Chinese painting. However, there is no comprehensive study discussing recent advances as well as challenges within this field from the perspective of HCI.

In this article, we aim to review the progress made in applying AI technology to Chinese landscape painting creation. Our contributions are threefold. First, we define the term "AI Aesthetics" within the HCI discipline. Second, we extract main AI aesthetics research topics and outline the approaches based on the methodology of human-AI collaboration. Third, we propose three AI aesthetics models in Chinese aesthetics. The three models, which differ in the aesthetic levels and accordingly the collaboration architecture, are referred to as the dynamic brushwork (bi-mo) model, the imaged mind (xin-yin) model, and the embodied narrative (shi-jing) model.

The organization of this article is as follows. We start our discussion with the definition of "AI Aesthetics" in Sect. 2. Then Sect. 3 explores the scattered AI aesthetics studies. We find that the frameworks of previous research are algorithm-centered and designed in the context of Western aesthetics. Therefore, we propose to build a framework for strengthening human-AI collaboration in a non-Western aesthetic context. In Sect. 4, we derive an analysis framework from the practice of human-AI collaboration in creating Chinese landscape painting, and further propose three AI aesthetics models under this framework. Finally, we analyze the challenges in integrating AI into Chinese aesthetics in Sect. 5 and point out the potential of brain-AI interactive communication.

2 Definition of AI Aesthetics

It is necessary to focus since AI aesthetics studies are scatted in numerous directions. As we do so, we must be aware that there is little agreement on what does and does not constitute AI aesthetics. Nevertheless, all definitions about AI aesthetics have common notions related to aesthetic decisions and artworks generation. This forms the starting point of our investigation. We define the term "AI aesthetics" within the HCI discipline, which is expressed as follows:

> "AI aesthetics is a system of human-AI collaboration that can make aesthetic decisions in a similar taste as human can and generate artworks simulating and extending creativity of human."

While this definition is very general, it emphasizes two major aspects. One is the methodology of human-AI collaboration, and the other is the aim of creativity enhancement.

3 Main Topics and Approaches of AI Aesthetics Research

Despite the wide disagreement on the issue of what constitutes AI aesthetics, we try to extract the common topics underlying all the varying studies. We divide related research into three topics: the extraction of art symbols; the generation of art styles; the coupling of art experience. We also outline the major approaches that have been suggested in the literature.

3.1 The Extraction of Art Symbols

Researchers dedicated to this topic think that beauty comes from symbolic representation. Researchers often decompose an aesthetic object into strokes or other composition elements. Based on user survey, such as questionnaires and eye tracking, the symbols and combination rules representing beauty are selected and incorporated into the algorithms for generating artworks.

AI technology has accelerated the development of this field. Strokes automatic extraction and generation have been initially realized. For example, algorithm LPaintB can quickly produce strokes with hand-painted features. The generation process is guided by parameters describing the size, color, and position of the strokes. All the parameters are results of self-supervision learning from the classic paintings [6].

Larger composition units can also be automatically extracted and visualized. For instance, algorithm Deepdream can extract elements from the latent space of deep learning systems [7]. Since Deepdream is mainly used in combination with datasets, the algorithm can extract different symbols based on different painting datasets.

3.2 The Generation of Art Styles

Researchers focusing on this topic regard beauty as a specific stylized sequence. Researchers usually analyze styles using pairs of visual concepts, such as linear versus painterly, plane versus recession, closed form versus open form, multiplicity versus unity, absolute clarity versus relative clarity.

The iteration of AI frameworks has led to the progress of style research. The CNNs framework is widely used in style transfer, and texture pattern has been proven to be a good expression of styles [8]. The GAN framework is mainly used for style synthetic and human knowledge has been introduced into the computation by semantic labeling.

The latest studies explore the deeper cooperation method between human and AI in style generation. Take stick figure generation for example, drawing system AutoDraw can map a user's graffiti sketch with a finished drawing. When the user draws a sketch, the system will calculate the picture categories and recommend the corresponding standard design drawing [9]. Another example is semantic image synthesizing. Synthetic system GauGAN allows users control over both semantics and styles as synthesizing images. The user only needs to scribble a semantic segmentation mask, and the system will synthesize the photorealistic image [10].

3.3 The Coupling of Art Experience

Researchers in this field agreed that beauty emerges in the interaction between agents and their environment. They think that AI aesthetics always manifests itself in behavior and that we must understand complex actions in real world.

Through action mapping between human and robot, robot painting has been realized. Researchers collect brushstrokes and hand motion samples from a human artist to build the dataset for model training. During the painting process, the trained model drives the robot arm to reproduce the trajectory of the human artist, including brush replacement, dipping paint, deep strokes, deep and shallow handwriting [11].

At present, the communication between robot and its environment is mainly through the visual channel mediated by the high-speed camera. Related frameworks include visual manipulation framework GraspNet [12], Embodied Visual Navigation framework SplitNet [13], disentangled representation framework Latent Canonicalization [14], and so on.

Researchers have also realized motion mapping between people [15] through steps such as skeleton extraction, motion retargeting, and skeleton-to-video rendering. There is no public literature showing that motion mapping between people has been used in painting.

3.4 Further Discussion

There are two apparent limitations of the above studies. Firstly, the algorithm is placed in the most critical agent position in the research framework, while human is placed in the secondary position. This algorithm-centered paradigm has undesirable implications that cannot be resolved within the framework it sets up. Secondly, the studies are mainly based on Western aesthetic theories. Discussions in other cultural and aesthetic contexts have not yet attracted enough researchers, which may constitute the cultural bias in AI aesthetics.

Beauty does not come from the closed one-way representation but the interactive coupling in real world. During the creative process, human artists make countless micro aesthetic decisions and continuously adjust their expression. After completing one artwork, human artists will bring the experience and thought into the next work, whereas the algorithms cannot reflect and generalize like human artists. When AI enters the real world, data is generated in time by the in-the-moment AI behavior. The continuous, substantial, and unstructured input makes the limitation of the algorithm itself more apparent. If AI could not become an independent subject of art creation, there is an essential question must be solved: how to integrate human aesthetic judgment and creativity with AI?

From the above analysis, the AI aesthetics based on human-AI collaboration may be more feasible. Because human prior knowledge and cognitive abilities are more introduced into computing, AI aesthetics requires less data, explores curiously, and expands knowledge by analogy. More importantly, it can build relationship to real world in physical interaction. We will discuss this kind of AI aesthetics in Chinese aesthetics to broaden the culture horizons of AI aesthetics research and enrich its methodology.

4 AI Aesthetics Framework and Models

The famous 11th-century painter Guo Xi's method, as introduced in *Lin Quan Gao Zhi*, is consisted of the following steps: first, a rough space is outlined using different thickness lines; second, six or seven layers of light water ink are added; third, textures are applied. In the drawing process, the painter waits for each water ink layer to completely dry before adding another layer. This method can produce various water ink changes. Although not colored, the water ink rendering is lighter and lighter from top to bottom and very vivid.

As explained by Guo Xi, the main elements of Chinese landscape painting include lines, ink wash, and textures. Besides, one of the distinct features of Chinese landscape painting is the flowing spatial narrative. After discussing concepts, topics, and approaches, in this section, we analyze AI aesthetics using a framework including three levels: the brushwork level, the texture pattern level, and the spatial narrative level.

4.1 Symbols Simulation at the Brushwork Level

The brushwork in Chinese landscape painting refers to the speed, weight, and thick-ness of the brush, as well as the wetness, intensity, astringency, and gradation of the ink. During the Tang and North Song Dynasties, the primary function of brushwork was depicting specific shapes. Artists were able to accurately shape the three-dimensional objects using different thickness lines. However, the abstract brushwork also sprouted early. It originated in literati painting of the Song Dynasty, developed to the end of the Ming Dynasty, and finally formed a peak could be called "Brushwork centrism". Abstract brushwork got rid of the shackles of depicting shapes and had self-sufficient ornamental value. Sometimes, artists just used brushwork to express their emotions and pursue the beauty of vivid charm. artists called this kind of drawing "Brush Game" (see Fig. 1).

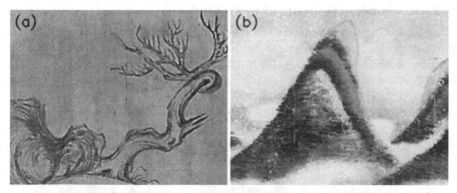

Fig. 1. Examples of human artists "Brush Game": (a) *Wood and Rock (detail)* created by Su Shi, Song Dynasty. (b) *Mountains and Pines in Spring (detail)* created by Mi Fu, Song Dynasty. Photo credit: Taipei Palace Museum.

The characteristics of brushwork come from the special Chinese painting tools. A mature Chinese artist can create effects by varying factors such as the type and size of brushes, the amount of moisture, the angle at which a brush is held, the speed and pressure applied to a brush, and the type of paper and silk. Therefore, AI aesthetics needs to simulate not only the attributes and movements of the brush itself, but its physical interaction with the environment.

To achieve natural-looking brush movement, 3D interaction based on force feedback technology is used for brush simulation [16]. Cellular automata algorithm combined with fluid dynamics is used to realize the real-time ink rending effect. With such a system, a human artist can create a "Brush Game", capture the trajectory of brushstroke, and imitate the dry or flying white stroke [17]. App "Expresii", which focusing on the simulation of brushwork, was launched in 2016 (see Fig. 2). The figure below shows the "Brush Game" based on human- "Expresii" collaboration.

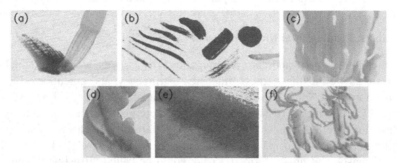

Fig. 2. "Brush Game" based on human- "Expresii" collaboration (a) different angles of the brush, (b) different strokes produced by dry or wet brush, thick or thin brush, (c) ink flow, (d) coloring, (e) rendering on paper, (f) and an abstracted horse. Photos credit: expresii.com

4.2   Pattern Mimic at the Texture Pattern Level

Texture strokes are used to express the veins and textures of mountains, rocks, peaks, and tree skins. Each famous Chinese painter uses specific pattern to draw texture (see Fig. 3). In the Five Dynasties, Jing Hao invented texture strokes, and Dong Yuan created "Hemp-fiber" on this basis. In the Song Dynasty, Fan Kuan made excellent use of "Rain dot", Guo Xi made fair use of "Cloud-head", and Li Tang made proper use of "Axe-cut". During the Yuan Dynasty, Ni Zan liked using "break-belt", and Wang Meng used "ox-hair". Texture pattern reflects the painter's aesthetic orientation, so it occupies the first place in the study of Chinese painting style.

Fig. 3. Examples of texture pattern: (a) "Cloud-head", *Early Spring (detail)* created by Guo Xi, Song Dynasty. (b) "Axe-cut", *Wind in Pines Among a Myriad Valleys (detail)* created by Li Tang, Song Dynasty. (c) "Ox-hair", *High Peaks Rising in Emerald Verdure(detail)* created by Wang Meng, Yuan Dynasty. Photos credit: Taipei Palace Museum.

The diversity of texture pattern makes the simulation result based on the general models unsatisfactory. Researchers usually try the following methods to improve the result: The first is to finetune parameters of the transfer model based on human decisions [18]. The second is to strengthen local area transfer effects based on object detection. The Chinese landscape painting's composition units can be divided into categories including trees, peaks, alum heads, pavilions, etc. [19]. Through manual annotation and training, the trained model can enhance the texture pattern according to the categories [20]. The third is to divide the generation process into two steps to mimic the painting steps of human artists. For instance, the SAPGAN consists of two models: the sketch model is used to generate the edge, and the painting model is used for the subsequent pix-to-pix conversion [21] (see Fig. 4).

Fig. 4. The generation results of SAPGAN. [21]

Style transfer or generation can replicate the painting style statically. However, other elements of style, such as the dynamics in texture pattern, have not been thoroughly analyzed. As far as this issue is concerned, human-robot painting proposes an intuitive method for generating style dynamically.

For example, Huang Gongwang's *Dwelling in the Fuchun Mountains* shows the idea of orienting brushwork to harmonize with the creation of nature (see Fig. 5): the overlap of the structure, the consistency of the texture, and the endless extension give the landscape a sense of generating. This abstract and changeable texture pattern adds a rare sense of movement to the calm picture and simple shape. To capture such dynamics, artist Victor Wong and robot Gemini have collaborated to create a series of paintings with Huang Gongwang's style. During the drawing process, Victor Wong input geological landscape data and learning program into the robot. The robot with learning ability converts the data to images and guides the robot arm to draw on real paper. Thus, the dynamics of human painting style is replicated and not only the geometry.

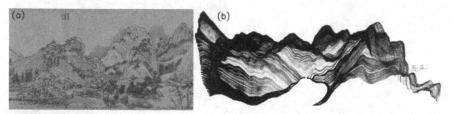

Fig. 5. The texture pattern drawn by human and human-robot collaboration: (a) *Dwelling in the Fuchun Mountains (detail)* created by Huang Gongwang, Yuan Dynasty. Photo credit: Taipei Palace Museum. (b) *Escapism 0003* created by Victor Wong and robot Gemini, 2018. Photo credit: 3812 Gallery.

4.3   Experience Creation at the Spatial Narrative Level

Confucius said, "The benevolent enjoys the mountain, the wise enjoy the water." Lao-Zhuang regarded human and nature as one. Influenced by Confucianism and Taoism, Chinese artists formed an approach of using the human body as a scale or sensor to depict nature. This approach is embodied in Guo Xi's aesthetic discourse of "The body is the mountain and the river". It also results in the unique spatial narrative of Chinese landscape painting.

Chinese landscape painting enables the viewer to reconstruct the spatial narrative. The painting elements, such as canyons, trees, roads, pavilions, and waterfalls form a three-dimensional space (see Fig. 6). The artist often fills in the space with figures engaged in various activities, such as a fisherman throwing a cast net on the boat, two or three farmers walking through the bridge, a scholar reading in the water pavilion, and a maid preparing food in the kitchen. All the above details together form a flow spatial narrative in an embodied way. However, this kind of painting is not a reproduction of a real scene somewhere, but a constructive scene that the artist wants to walk into. The figures in the painting are often portraits of the artist himself, his family, and friends. When gazing at such a painting, the viewer will feel that he is situated in the space and playing a role in the scene.

To reproduce the spatial narrative of Chinese landscape painting needs the three-dimensional illusion. Moreover, the visual perception should be modeled from an entirely

Fig. 6. Examples of spatial narrative: (a) *Pure and Remote View of Streams and Mountains (detail)* created by Xia Gui, Song Dynasty. (b) *Thatched Cottage in Autumn Mountains (detail)* created by Wang Meng, Yuan Dynasty. Photo credit: Taipei Palace Museum.

situated perspective. Take "Orchid Pavilion Gathering" for example, "Orchid Pavilion" is a symbolic site for ancient literary gatherings. Paintings of this theme usually include the following paragraphs (see Fig. 7): watching the goose in the pavilion, preparing wine, floating wine cups on a winding stream, drinking, and writing poems. Intelligent interactive artwork *Orchid Pavilion Gathering* constructs a smart interactive 3D space that the users can take their bodies into it. A meandering stream produced by interactive projection flows through the ground. The users can sit by the shore, stretch out their hands to grab the wine cups flowing by. The interactions between users and the environment will trigger more interactive narratives. For example, when the user picks up a wine cup from the stream, a poem will appear on the shore's corresponding position.

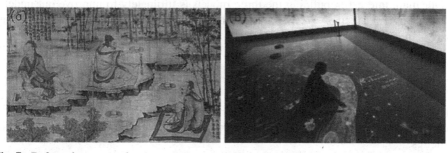

Fig. 7. Refer to human works to construct a spatial narrative based on human-AI cooperation. (a) *Orchid Pavilion Gathering(detail)* created by Guo Zhongshu, Song Dynasty. Photo credit: Taipei Palace Museum. (b) *Orchid Pavilion Gathering* in Capital Museum in Beijing created by Tencent, 2020. Photos credit: tencent.com

Chinese depiction of nature does not emphasize objective imitation but the artist's response to external world. This tradition brings imagination to human-AI collaboration.

It also poses a considerable challenge. Judging from the current experimental results, it is still thorny to ultimately present the essence of Chinese aesthetics. The gaps between artistic representation, high-level semantics, and aesthetic context needs to be bridged.

4.4 AI Aesthetics Models in Chinese Aesthetics

Chinese artists uphold the philosophy of Confucianism, Taoism, and Buddhism, and praise the inner connection between Tao and art. Tao is the way of nature – effortless, free, and of itself so. Artists pursue Tao through innocent and straightforward style and reintegrate themselves with nature. Therefore, in Chinese aesthetics, AI aesthetics is more a framework for creating the ideal world than a tool for drawing. Under the framework, we propose three AI aesthetics models:

The dynamic brushwork (bi-mo) model—This model pursuits brushwork freedom, whose core is to simulate brushworks containing natural beauty. The model requires users to provide brushstroke's elements as inputs, including attributes, styles, order, and mathematical formulas, etc. Users can try various brushes, explore the infinite changes of brushstrokes, and experience the vivid charm of dynamic generating. The model focuses on short-term interaction and cannot be personified.

The imaged mind (xin-yin) model—This model encourages users to adopt the principle of recreating nature rather than realistic representation, that leaves room for beauty emerge. The model requires the users to provide texture pattern, classification framework and semantic annotation. Therefore, both the brushstrokes and styles generated by this model are meaningful. The model focuses on high-level ontology and may learn from the specification and interaction.

The embodied narrative (shi-jing) model—This model is situated in real world and acquires information about its environment in interaction. Not only the momentum of the brush but also the dynamics of the spatial narrative can be interactively constructed. The model focuses on behavior resulting from the agent-environment interaction, that made it evolute continuously. It has the potential to generate highly creative artwork.

Our main interest in building the three models is ultimately to improve our understanding of AI aesthetics. We will systematically elaborate on these three models in subsequent articles.

5   Discussion and Conclusion

This article constructs a framework from the human-AI collaboration practice of Chinese landscape painting creation, and further proposes three AI aesthetics models in Chinese aesthetics.

Regarding the relationship between human and AI, various disputes have always existed. Chinese aesthetics penetrates the "three talents of heaven, earth and man". Artists pursue the ultimate satisfaction of living in harmony with themselves, others, and world. And at the same time, they experience the state of "I create, therefore I am". For HCI system design, Chinese aesthetics can always be used as an essential reference.

The reflection on the essence of art combined with Chinese aesthetics, make us believe that the most promising AI Aesthetics approach is to promote the integration of human and AI. The primary research task at present is to develop interactive creation platforms. In the field of painting, self-adaptive algorithms suiting the user's style, intelligent generation of 3D images, intelligent generation of dynamic images are key technologies to be solved. In the long run, brain-AI interactive communication will complement existing interaction channels and realize mutual inspiration between human and AI, thereby stimulating more artistic creativity.

Standing at the intersection of Chinese aesthetics and artificial intelligence, we can reflect on and surpass existing HCI concepts and practices. The spirit of aesthetics and the human experience in the AI age should communicate with each other. The contradictions and tensions generated in this process will broaden the horizons, which is fascinating and thought-provoking.

References

1. Galanter, P.: Computational aesthetic evaluation: past and future. In: McCormack, J., Inverno, M. (eds.) Computers and Creativity, pp. 255–293. Springer, Berlin. (2012)
2. Manovich, L.: AI Aesthetics. Strelka Press, Moskva (2018)
3. Fong, C.W.: Images of the Mind: Selections from the Edward L. Elliott Family and John B. Elliott Collections of Chinese Painting and Calligraphy at the Art Museum, Princeton University. Princeton University Press, New Jersey (1984)
4. Fong, C.W.: Beyond Representation: Chinese Painting and Calligraphy, 8th 14th Century. Yale University Press, New Haven (1992)
5. Fan, Z., Li, Y., Yu, J., Zhang, K.: Visual complexity of Chinese ink paintings. In: Stephen, N.S. (Eds) ACM Symposium on Applied Perception 2017, Vol. 9, pp. 1–8. Association for Computing Machinery, New York (2017). https://doi.org/10.1145/3119881.3119883
6. Jia, B., Brandt, J., Mech, R., Kim, B., Manocha, D.: LPaintB: Learning to Paint from Self-supervision (2019). arXiv preprint: arXiv:1906.06841
7. Mordvintsev, A.: Inceptionism: Going Deeper into Neural Networks (2015). https://ai.google blog.com/2015/06/inceptionism-going-deeper-into-neural.html. Accessed 8 Jan 2021.
8. Gatys, L.A., Ecker, A.S., Bethge, M.: A Neural Algorithm of Artistic Style (2015). arXiv preprint: arXiv:1508.06576
9. Ha, D., Eck, D.: A Neural Representation of Sketch Drawings (2017). arXiv preprint: arXiv:1704.03477
10. Park, T., Liu, M.Y., Wang, T.C., Zhu, J.Y.: Semantic Image Synthesis with Spatially Adaptive Normalization (2019). arXiv preprint: arXiv:1903.07291
11. Bidgoli, A., Guevara, M.D.L., Hsiung, C., Oh, J., Kang, E.: Artistic style in robotic painting; a machine learning approach to learning brushstroke from human artists. In: 29th IEEE International Conference on Robot and Human Interactive Communication (RO-MAN), pp. 412–418. IEEE Press, New York (2020)
12. Mousavian, A., Eppner, C., Fox, D.: 6-DOF GraspNet: variational grasp generation for object manipulation. In: 2019 IEEE/CVF International Conference on Computer Vision (ICCV), pp. 2901–2910. IEEE Press, New York (2019)
13. Gordon, D., Kadian, A., Parikh, D., Hoffman, J., Batra, D.: SplitNet: Sim2Sim and Task2Task transfer for embodied visual navigation. In: 2019 IEEE/CVF International Conference on Computer Vision (ICCV), pp. 1022–1031. IEEE Press, New York (2019)
14. Litany, O., Morcos, A., Sridhar, S., Guibas, L., Hoffman, J.: Representation learning through latent canonicalizations. In: 2021 IEEE/CVF Winter Conference on Applications of Computer Vision (WACV), pp. 645–654. IEEE Press, New York (2021)

15. Chan, C., Ginosar, S., Zhou, T., Efros, A.A.: Everybody dance now. In: 2019 IEEE/CVF International Conference on Computer Vision (ICCV), pp. 5933–5942. IEEE Press, New York (2019).
16. Guo, C., Hou, Z.X., Shi, Y.Z., Xu, J., Yu, D.D.: A virtual 3D interactive painting method for chinese calligraphy and painting based on real-time force feedback technology. Front. Inf. Technol. Electron. Eng. **18**(11), 184–195 (2017)
17. Zheng, S.Z., Hou, Z.X., Guo, C., Yang, G.Q.: The simulation of the half-dry stroke based on the force feedback technology. J. Comput. Aid. Des. Comput. Graph. **28**(6), 1016–1024 (2016)
18. Zhang, G., Cheng, J.L., Song, J., Guo, J.Q., Zhou, C.R.: Chinese landscape painting automated generation model based on generative adversarial networks. Comput. Telecommun. **280**(03), 5–9 (2020)
19. Sheng, J.C., Li, Y.Z.: Learning artistic objects for improved classification of chinese paintings. J. Image Graph. **23**(8), 1193–1206 (2018)
20. Tong, Y.: Research on the style transfer model of Chinese paintings based on deep network. Chin. Mus. **142**(3), 139–145 (2020)
21. Alice, X.: End-to-End Chinese Landscape Painting Creation Using Generative Adversarial Networks(2020). arXiv preprint: arXiv:2011.05552

Kindergarten Interactive Lighting Design Based on Cognitive Development Theory

Yansong Chen[1], Cai Wang[2], Ruxue Yang[2], Yiyuan Huang[3]([✉]), Fei Gao[4], Zhigang Wang[1], and Lin Zhang[2]

[1] Tsinghua University, Beijing, China
[2] Communication University of China, Beijing, China
[3] Beijing Institute of Graphic Communication, Beijing, China
yiyuan.huang@bigc.edu.cn
[4] Beijing Normal University, Beijing, China

Abstract. Our study focuses on the preschool education stage, taking kindergartens as the main body to explore the dynamic relationship between children's behavior and the lit environment. And then, we propose interactive lighting design strategies based on children's cognitive development. Light is closely related to children's cognitive development, but most of the existing studies on light visual cognition focus on adults. Children's visual physiological mechanisms and non-visual psychological mechanisms have yet to be fully developed, so current theories on visual and non-visual lighting effects are not applicable directly. We introduce the Swiss psychologist Piaget's theory of children's cognitive development to discover the characteristics and preferences of children's behaviors and activities in different cognitive stages. Then, to tease out the relationship between light and shadow design elements and children's cognitive development. This paper proposes a phototherapic environment's construction strategy in kindergarten. This strategy is based on equilibration in the cognitive development theory and includes physiology, intelligence, society, and emotion. This research aims to promote early child development and explore the relationship between children's growth and environment.

Keywords: Interactive lighting design · Interactive art and design · Kindergarten space · Cognitive development · Preschool children

1 Introduction

Kindergarten is such an educational space built based on children's behaviors like resting, studying, interacting, etc. There is a kind of interactive relationship between children's behavior and the environment. The Father of Kindergarten, Friedrich Frobel, had a great insight into the importance of children's learning activities [1]. The purpose of preschool education is a comprehensive education of skills or knowledge and recognizing and perceiving nature through games and activities [2]. According to that, kindergartens' space construction and activity organization should be different from other places and meet children's needs as the design goal. One of the useful methods in the space for

© Springer Nature Switzerland AG 2021
M. Rauterberg (Ed.): HCII 2021, LNCS 12794, pp. 225–243, 2021.
https://doi.org/10.1007/978-3-030-77411-0_16

kids to get multiple experiences is light. Thus, environmental light and illumination are closely related to children's cognitive development.

Many previous studies have confirmed that light and illumination are near related to children's cognitive development. On the positive side, light and shadow can be used as a cognitive tool to help children develop scientific thinking. Children gain experience of the world from light and illumination [2, 3]. For example, they can use a flashlight to explore accessible opportunities to see the world [4]. Or use their knowledge of the elements of light to understand physical phenomena such as pinhole phenomenon, image formation by mirrors and lenses [5]. On the other hand, light and shadow will also produce some deviations in cognition from constraints. For example, misconceptions result from children's ideas about light and shadows, which have been studied by Piaget [6], DeVries [7], and Feher and Rice [8]. Young children think of a shadow as an object or substance, and that light is the agent that causes the item to form or allows people to see the shadow, even when it is dark.

However, light and illumination design in kindergarten now still pays more attention to the space scale, space flow, interior, and exterior decoration, but rarely the game, the activities, and other interactive parts. At present, almost no light and illumination design start from children's physiological and psychological characteristics and cognitive ability. Weinstein's paper, books, and articles on early childhood education mainly stress the importance of careful spatial organization and provide suggestions for creating learning centers, partitioning space, and arranging materials [9]. Similarly, Mark Dudek points out that research studies relating the quality of early childhood education to the physical environment tend to concentrate on most practical aspects such as space standards or functional layouts. He believes children can understand color, texture, light, space, and functionality by architectural design. Dudek also thought that texture, sound, light, and color would challenge and inspire children and that exciting outdoor spaces allow for freedom of movement and physical daring [10].

Some studies that inspire us have noted the importance of light and illumination design from children's views. The survey from Istanbul Kultur University has demonstrated that kindergarten design can base on preschoolers' experience [11]. It has been observed that the designer can obtain instructive outcomes not only for space requirement and the importance of light but also hints for security, comfort, and general psychology of children. For Mohidin's study, it is essential to address four fundamental aspects of architectural elements that constitute a better environment for kindergarten children. They are spaces, scale and proportion, color and lighting. It is essential for a kindergarten to offer four environmental stimuli to further enhance the quality of early-age education through effective design [12].

Therefore, kindergartens' space design needs to explore lighting design methods that exert positive characteristics under local conditions. In addition to traditional lighting design strategies, we will focus on designing interactive effects of light environments in kindergartens. In our research, we will follow the theoretical path of cognitive development, focus on the goals and requirements of light and illumination design in children's mental experience, and explore the strategies to meet preschool children's cognitive development needs.

Besides, it is worth emphasizing that the interaction defined in this article is applied to network and interface fields and the real space and scene. Michael Erlhoff and Tim Marshall have interpreted hundreds of design industries' characteristics to explain interaction design as a design about the spatial experience rather than technology. And put time, feedback, control, productivity, creativity, communication, learning, and resilience at the core of interaction [13]. To be more precise, this article is more inclined to come Terry Winograd's definition. That is the interaction design is the design of human communication and interaction space [14].

2 Relationship Between Light and Children's Cognition

Light or visible light is electromagnetic radiation within the electromagnetic spectrum that can be perceived by the human eye [15]. In the complex process of human cognitive development, changes in light have become important factors that directly affect visual perception and cognition. Many scientists have proposed the cognitive elements of light and illumination in terms of image forming function and non-image-forming function (NIF function) through experiments and research [16, 17].

On the one hand, visual performance is the optical cognitive element of light and illumination. Multiple factors related to light and shadow, such as illuminance, color, spectrum, light source direction, and the timing of light exposure, will cause changes in human visual perception. On the other hand, non-visual effects are the non-visual cognitive elements of illumination. Research in the past 30 years has shown that light can also affect people's psychology and behavior to some extent [16] and impact people's rhythm, physical condition, work efficiency, mental state and other factors [17]. For example, it can affect work efficiency, improve biological alertness, regulate melatonin production, affect natural rhythm, promote cognitive processing and regulate Seasonal Affective Disorder (SAD) caused by seasonal changes.

However, most of the narratives mentioned above about visual effects and non-visual effects are derived from adults' cognitive experience and obtained through experiments. If it is merely for children, the physiological mechanism and the mental mechanism need to be matured. Therefore, it is not reasonable to talk about children's light cognition from the two aspects of visual function and non-visual function.

In Swiss psychologist Jane Piaget's theory, he used four stages to describe children's cognitive ability development. They're sensorimotor stage (from birth to age two), pre-operational stage (from two to seven), concrete operational stage (from seven to eleven), and formal operational stage (after eleven) [18]. Take the *"Regulations on Kindergarten Work"* issued by the Ministry of Education of the People's Republic of China as an example [19]. Children in kindergartens are generally 3 to 6 years old. The school system of Kindergartens is usually three years. Children in the nursery are from 3 to 4 years old, children in the lower kindergarten are from 4 to 5 years old, and children in the upper kindergarten are from 5 to 6 years old. Therefore, most preschool children are in the preoperational stage. In this stage, though they do not understand concrete logic and mentally manipulate information, they use symbols to represent physical models of the world around them (see Table 1).

From the perspective of light and shadow, children's perception is still in its infancy due to the preoperational stage's influence. They usually believe that light and shadow

Table 1. Four stages of children's cognitive development (Drawn by the Piaget's cognitive development theory).

Age	Stage	Cognitive characteristics
0–2 years	The sensorimotor stage	Infants start to build an understanding of the world through their senses by touching, grasping, watching, and listening; Differentiation between sensory and motor; Relation with the movement
2–7 years	The preoperational stage	Children develop language and abstract thought; Internalization of sensory and motor; The use of signs or language to replace or reproduce external things; Egocentric thought, or imaginal thought was formed
7–11 years	The concrete operational stage	Children learn logical concrete (physical) rules about objects, such as height, weight, and volume; Logicalization of the operation stage; Using concepts to make things outside logical; Conservation, classification, and self-centered thinking were formed
11+ years	The formal operational stage	Children learn logical rules to understand abstract concepts and solve problems; Complications in the operational stage; Free from the constraints of concrete things; Formed Self perspective and abstract thinking

result from two objects interacting or intervening, and it is difficult for them to make a correct interpretation of the shadow [6]. So, cognitive development theory will help us discover the characteristics and preferences of children's behavior and activities and provide a theoretical basis for the following research.

To sum up, we can't design just according to adults' cognitive characteristics for the light and illumination design of kindergarten. Instead, we should combine the cognitive development degree of children in the preoperational stage. It is necessary to integrate the relationship between light and shadow and children's cognitive development and intervene in children's space with multidimensional methods such as space, emotion, and activity.

3 Lighting Elements that Affect Cognitive Development

3.1 Cognitive Development Theory from Piaget

As an important place for children's cognition, kindergartens need to achieve cognitive development through multidimensional purposes such as living, dining, learning, and other activities. From visual perception, kindergartens' light and illumination design is not a simple optical design. Still, it includes all factors of electro-optical media that are related to space construction and activity organization.

According to Piaget, four interrelated factors allow movement from stage to stage. These factors include maturation, physical environment, social interaction, and equilibration [6]. Maturation is the physical and psychological growth that occurs in the child at a specific stage. The physical environment is when the child thinks and interacts with real or concrete objects in the external environment. Social interaction involves the child socializing with others, especially children. The stage movement factor is equilibration occurring when the child brings together maturation, physical environment, and social interaction to build mental schema. Equilibration is considered to be the tendency for children to seek cognitive coherence and stability.

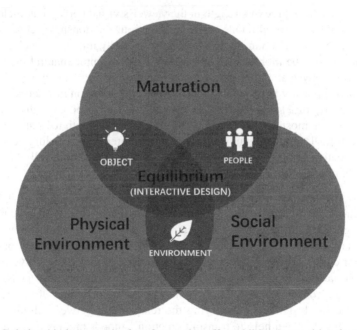

Fig. 1. Relationship between the four factors that affect children's cognitive development

Therefore, introducing the cognitive development theoretical relationship into interactive lighting design is very important. According to the previous kindergarten space design, the kindergarten is just a spatial entity through which children can implement maturation, the physical environment, and social interaction, but not equilibration. Therefore, in the kindergarten design, we must introduce interactivity to make the design achieve equilibration. On the outer layer of Fig. 1, equilibration is located in the center of the maturation, physical environment, and social interaction, which is the core for implementing cognitive development for young children. In the inner layer of Fig. 1, the interactive design contains people, objects, environment, and other elements (see Fig. 1).

3.2 Lighting Elements

We can promote children's cognitive development by changing light elements and properties for interactive lighting design. The maturation, physical environment, and social interaction are three classical aspects corresponding to the static conception of light, like light color, intensity, quality, etc. As the fourth factor to balance and coordinate the other three classical aspects, equilibration corresponds to the dynamic light design. Through the interaction and movement of light, it is to enhance children's cognition from the primary stage of light and shadow and lay an environmental foundation for them to enter the concrete and formal operational stages. Based on practical experience and case analysis, the lighting elements affecting children's cognitive development include light intensity, color, position, shadow, quality, and movement from the overall dynamic lighting design perspective.

Light Intensity. The degree of strength in the viewer's visual perception, including the entire range from dark to bright. One of the most obvious relationships between humans and light is that of the circadian rhythm, and it is especially important in children since their systems seem to be more sensitive to change. For example, natural lighting has a positive effect on physical and emotional state such as attention and mood. Sunlight is a relatively high-intensity light, which makes children's attention instinctively focus on features. In a study of 21,000 students in America, it was discovered that students in classrooms with the most daylight performed 20% faster on math tests and 26% better on reading tests [20]. But other studies show that light intensity exceeding a certain limit can have a negative impact on learning [21]. Therefore, we should fully consider the balance of illuminance when designing the kindergarten.

Light Color. It is evoked in a typical human by a single wavelength of light in the visible spectrum. The color is one of the most noticeable defining elements of any lighting design. Unlike the color of objects, light color is a function of two factors: Hue and Saturation. Hue is described as red, orange, yellow, green, blue, purple, etc. Especially for children, warm colors are best in school as they have a diverting effect that "draws visual and emotional interest outward", and cool colors have a passive effect that elicits better concentration [22]. Saturation is the colorfulness of an area judged in proportion to its brightness. Observing the relationship between children's visual perception with colors can help to transmit emotions, moods and provides the space a base atmosphere. One study of child-care centers suggests that rooms with varied colors increase cooperative behavior as opposed to single color rooms [23].

Light Position. The direction of light refers to the specific position of the lamp in the three-dimensional space. For the characters, different light positions shape various characters and portray their body, mood, and personality; for the environment, the light position determines the shape, volume, and structure of the objects, thus representing the environment's atmosphere. In the kindergarten design, light position is mainly related to the direction of the child. For example, when a child is doing homework, we tend to place lamps on the left side of the table rather than on the right so that the paper is more precise and more visually comfortable. But when the light source is on the right, the shadows on the children's hand can have a negative effect. Therefore, we should pay attention to the effect of light position on children's physiological health.

Light Shadow. A shadow is a dark (real image) area where an opaque object blocks light from a light source. The effect of shadow on cognition is mainly in two aspects, physiological and psychological. Physically, our eye has only vague recognition of shadow forms. People perceive shadows through the contrast of the luminance ladder. Thus, in comparison to real objects, shadows are virtual. Psychologically, the shadow causes a significant psychological change through visual suggestion. Until six years old, the children begin to comprehend how light travels and understand correlations between objects' shape and their shadows. Therefore, when designing for children, we should make good use of the shadow elements, which have a positive impact on children's cognitive development.

Light Quality. It also means light property, represents the soft and hard degree of illumination. For nature, sunlight is sharp, cloudy light is soft light; for artificial lights, such as spotlight, direct light, chase light, and floodlight, are smooth. Generally speaking, soft light is diffusely scattered light without clear direction. Its characteristics include no noticeable shadow on the illuminated object, uniform intensity, low contrast, weak sense of the subject, and texture; Hard light is the opposite, like butterfly lights and Rembrandt lights in photography. Children prefer the outdoor daylight, which is the union of sunlight and skylight. Direct sunlight can provide the space with a high light level and creates dramatic effects with sharp shadows. And skylight designs a uniform space with much softer shades and forms.

Light Movement. The movement of light refers to the transformation and flow of light elements. The movement of light refers to the transformation and flow of light elements. This paper specifically refers to the dynamic projection formed by the change of light, including the visual image of LED screens and the dynamic role of light projection. The movement of light is the most active and expressive element. It makes the lighting design change from static to dynamic, makes the light and shadow more energetic and vitality, and expand light's narrative function. As emerging learners, children's benefits from digital narration are often based on technical tools such as LED screen, light projection, and other light movement elements [24]. For instance, dominant colors on Walt Disney heroes and princesses like Elsa are mostly in brighter colors. Villains such as the Queen in *Snow White* tend to be represented by darker colors.

4 Interactive Lighting Design Based on the Theory of Cognitive Development

According to the equilibration of cognitive development theory, we try to establish the interactive lighting design path based on physiological, intellectual, social, and emotional development. And we illustrate how the elements of light and illumination design affect these four aspects through case studies and then propose our design strategy. As shown in Fig. 2, the previous paper comprehensively analyzed Piaget's cognitive development theory's relationship with maturation, physical environment, social interaction, and equilibration. We suggest that equilibration is related to interactive lighting design.

Children's development is realized through light intensity, color, position, shadow, quality, and movement. Also, the combination of different light elements will cause changes in children's development effect (see Fig. 2).

In terms of physiological development, light and illumination can promote children's physiological effect to achieve the dynamic equilibrium of light and health. For the intellectual, the elements are the physical contents of learning and tools to assist children's education. As to social development, the details encourage children to interact with others and enhance their social environment cognition. Finally, emotional, interactive light and illumination enhance children's psychological sense of belonging, closely related to their memories, emotions, and experiences.

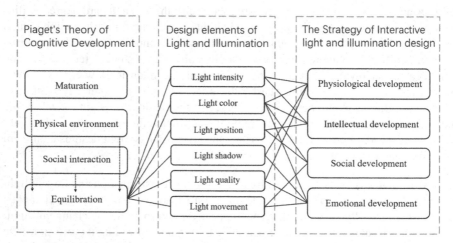

Fig. 2. The design strategy for kindergartens based on cognitive development

4.1 Physiological Development

Physiological development refers to promoting children's physiological development through light elements to achieve a dynamic balance between light and health. On the one hand, compared with structural design (such as architecture design and environment design), light and shadow are attached. So, there is no hit risk of physical damage for children. However, light and shadow will affect the physiological development of children. Therefore, when we design in kindergarten, it is necessary to fully consider children's physiological condition and promote their physiological development to a certain extent.

First of all, we should propose multiple modes of dynamic lighting, including natural light mode, behavior mode, emotion mode, medical mode, etc. They are designed to meet the indirect impact of children's daily needs on the human body clock, sleep, mood, etc. The Researchers at the University of Twente evaluate the effect of lighting conditions (with vertical illuminances between 350 lx and 1000 lx, correlated color temperatures between 3000K and 12000K) on children's concentration in three experiments [25].

They provided a flexible and dynamic lighting system to support the classroom's rhythm with four different lighting settings. At the beginning of the day or after lunch, they provide a blue-rich cold white light to activate the child and give them more energy. During challenging tasks, bright white light helps children focus more. White light with a warm red color tone makes children feel more relaxed and comfortable when they need independent and collaborative learning. And for regular classroom activities, standard white light is used. The results showed that by providing appropriate lighting models, the children could easily concentrate during different activities, read faster, and reduce restlessness and aggressive behavior.

This study shows that children's physiological development has different needs for light in various daily activities. First, high-illumination white light, which mimics outdoor natural light, can prevent myopia. When the illumination is higher than 3000lx, the axial growth of children is delayed. Therefore, we need to provide a bright environment that mimics natural light in children's general activities. Secondly, the blue radiation in the spectrum has an inhibitory effect on the secretion of melatonin. So, high temperature, high illumination environments can improve children's concentration and help them have a better performance on challenging tasks. A low temperature, low illumination environment reduces blue light release, allowing the child to relax and do what he wants to do. We need to provide a dynamic environment for children, changing the lighting environment according to their activities in the space to promote their physiological development (see Fig. 3).

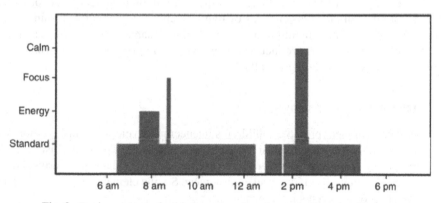

Fig. 3. Design strategy for kindergartens based on cognitive development

Secondly, we should pay attention to the importance of lighting in children's health. It is necessary to use artificial light to achieve physiological health intervention on children, including moderate ultraviolet radiation to improve children's immunity; alleviate autism spectrum disorder (ASD) in children by increasing moderate light intensity. The team from South Korea developed a smart sleep-lighting system to improve the sleep environment of children. The proposed system is composed of a sleep-lighting device and a smartphone dongle. The system was composed of a sleep-lighting device and smartphone dongle [26]. The manufactured sleep-lighting device has a high-precision temperature and humidity sensor and a luminance sensor that can accurately monitor the

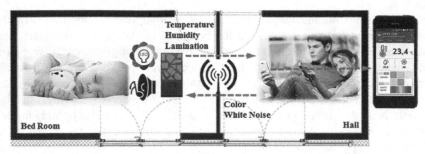

Fig. 4. Proposed smart-lighting system concept for improving the sleep environment of children, © Qun Wei, 2019

sleeping environment. The color and brightness of the sleep-lighting device are adjusted to improve the sleeping atmosphere based on the analyzed sleeping environment data (see Fig. 4).

It's worth noting that using Electronic Products just before sleep causes harmful effects on children's physical health. Continuous exposure to blue light emitted from smartphones or tablets may not only cause damages to the vision of children but also restrain the secretion of sleep-inducing hormones (e.g., melatonin), leading to sleep disturbances. This exposure will result in additional problems such as deterioration of learning abilities and growth of children. The smart lamp is a device that can adjust the environment and provide feedback in time. It reminds the users to adapt to the environment through the color changes of lights. Such as red lights for warning and a warm yellow glow to help them fall asleep at ease, we enable users to realize that it is time to stop using electronic products for no purpose. Children come to be aware of the importance of physical health gradually.

4.2   Intellectual Development

Intellectual development promotes children's intellectual development in cognition and efficiency through light elements. According to Piaget, in addition to intrinsic genetic factors and physiological basis, children's intellectual development is more critical from the influence of acquired activities and environment. So, the elements of light are crucial to the formation of children's intelligence.

Firstly, as a learning tool for children, light and shadow can effectively improve children's attention. It has been reported that digital form literacy programs are more motivating than those in print [27]. Taking the *Light Table* as an example, the focused light on the transparent table can attract children's attention to enhance children's learning interest and efficiency through psychological stimulation. Through light and shadow learning tools, children can improve their cognitive ability. For example, they can realize that light touches are solid, and the place away from light is virtual. Through light and shadow learning tools, children can improve their cognitive ability. For example, they can realize that light touches are solid, and the place away from light is virtual. Improve their academic competence, including mathematics, writing, patterns, and colors; improve their imagination, including the advanced processing of existing mental images, to create new images and art (see Fig. 5). Optical devices, projectors, scanners, lamps, mirrors, etc., can also be tools of scene teaching methods.

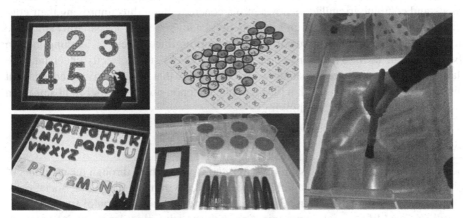

Fig. 5. Different kinds of light tables (sorting from network).

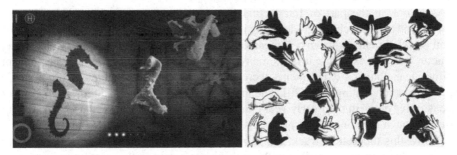

Fig. 6. A mobile game called *Shadowmatic*, © TRIADA Studio, 2015

Secondly, light and shadow, as physical content, is an essential reference for exploring and understanding the world. In America, exploring the properties of light is an important physical science part of *National Science Education Content Standard* (NRC 1996). It means where light comes from, how light travels, and how the color of light changes the appearance of objects should become a basic science knowledge for children, even adults [28]. Among them, light and shadow as physics learning content include the basic concepts, like the source of light, the eye as a receptor of light, light travels in straight lines, etc. Physical phenomena such as reflection, refraction, and scattering of light; Even scientific knowledge, the relationship between light and shadow, the color of light, and so on.

TRIADA Studio has developed a mobile game called *Shadowmatic*. Players need to rotate abstract objects in a spotlight to find recognizable silhouettes in projected shadows relevant to the surrounding environment. Some levels feature two or three floating things, adding more dimensions to the solution. The player attempts to rotate them correctly and position them relative to each other within 3D space (see Fig. 6). Although it is just a virtual video game, the inspiration comes from the familiar hand shadow game for children. In the shadow of the interactive games, light and shadow were used as learning content. When combining abstract objects, children recognize abstract objects' shadow shapes and combine irregular shadows into a concrete thing, thus improving their cognitive ability. In the process of combination, the shadows' conditions can fully stimulate children's imagination and associative ability, turning the process of learning into an adventure game of thinking. This game can also help children correctly understand the relationship between light and shadow, no longer think that a shadow is an independent object different from light. Still, a physical phenomenon produced after light shines on the item to establish scientific thinking.

4.3 Social Development

Social development encourages children to interact with others through the elements of light and enhance their understanding of social and environmental factors. Social environment refers to the interaction between people and the transmission of social culture, including social life, social communication, cultural education, language information, etc. As a structured process, social consciousness is based on the individual's cognitive system and is learned through social interaction.

As a tool, in the part of Intellectual Development, light can improve children's attention and enhance children's learning interest and efficiency. In contrast, in the part of Social Development, light can be a means to learn social concepts, including time, space, character, etc. For example, it takes many years for the children to master the concept of time. Jean Piaget's experiments were the first to provide insights into children's development concerning time [29]. The investigation proposed that children tend to feel there is only "now" in their early years, but we can strengthen children's understanding of time through the concept of space.

Follow this theoretical track, the team from the University of Oldenburg aims to support children in learning time with intuitive interaction with a prototype presenting periods unobtrusively. The light device *Timelight* keeps children updated on the duration of time in various contexts of their daily life [30]. It's a device designed to display multiple periods with RGB-LED lighting. The abstraction of periods with bricks of various lengths worked well. It also provided a tangible dimension to the ambient light display. The use of LEDs allowed for the design of suitable patterns for the presentation of temporal information. When the illumination gradually starts to fade, the kids know that time is up. Most of the children in this kindergarten group were five years old, and to keep track of the remaining time, they frequently recounted the illuminated bricks. Through different color space blocks, children expressed different lengths of time, such as 7 min, 12 min, etc. Because of light and color, children can better understand the concept of time, especially that of duration (see Fig. 7).

Secondly, the interactive light elements show social concepts and use digital narratives based on light and illumination. This method can promote children's cooperative behavior, enable children to construct meaning in light and shadow narratives, encourage them to improve communication strategies and increase the sense of cooperation with others. For instance, the project *Lands of fog* was developed in the CMTech research group. They present the design of a light and shadow interaction experience, in which a child with ASD plays together with a typically developed child. The system is aimed towards fostering social interaction behaviors and collaboration [31]. Besides, the Micropia museum is located in Amsterdam, which aims to achieve the purpose of balancing interactive experience and knowledge learning by means of interactive lighting design [32].

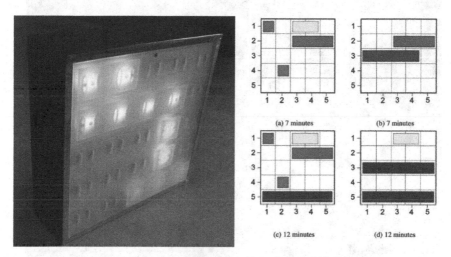

Fig. 7. The light device called *Timelight*, © Heiko Müller, 2016

Another case is the permanent exhibition *Futurepark* launched by Teamlab, a new media art group based in Japan. They focus on creating interactive works for children's education and teaching children-related social concepts through the interaction of light and shadow and objects. Among them, the work "*A Table where Little People Live*" deepens children's understanding of the concept of characters and sports. Children are encouraged to interact with the little people by placing objects on the table. As each new item is introduced, the little people's movements change; they interact with the things by jumping, climbing, and sliding onto them. The work "*Giant Connecting Block Town*" strengthens children's understanding of transportation, architecture, and cities. Children can place giant building blocks of houses, stations, and buildings to create a town. The town has a river running through it. When it rains, the river floods and flows into the city. Place a water block on top of the river and link it to the sea using more water blocks. This action enables children to stop the river from flooding (see Fig. 8).

4.4 Emotional Development

Emotional development aims to enhance children's sense of belonging through interactive light, closely related to their memories, emotions, and experiences. In addition to the socialized space such as rest, study, and communication, kindergartens should also have an independent psychological space. In terms of emotional expression of space, light, and shadow play a role in reconstruction, using its narrative nature to generate and

Fig. 8. *"A Table where Little People Live"* and *"Giant Connecting Block Town"*, © Teamlab, 2016

organize the existing scene, creating a new space-time texture, and echoing the genius loci of the original space.

First of all, the changes in light and shadow are related to children's memories, emotions, and experiences, which is more suitable for creating a sense of belonging. *Kaleidoscope* is a nonprofit kindergarten located in Tianshui City, Gansu Province, China. The kindergarten's openings are arched, and the traditional cave-like form of dwelling in the Loess Plateau, where Tianshui City is located, inspires the arch's idea.

Another fascinating feature uses ten different colors that apply to 438 pieces of colored glass as the main design element. The team adopts the color elements on the places above the glass doors and windows, including the handrails of corridors and stairs. It is supposed to be the kindergarten that applies the most significant numbers of colored glass in the current world. Since the sun's rays change at different angles, the light and shadow move between the vertical wall surface and the horizontal ground, forming long and short colored lights and shadows. This phenomenon makes the atrium a vibrant and exciting change with the external environment every minute during the daytime. The entire space is like a giant rotating kaleidoscope with constantly changing colors and patterns. Especially for children living in Loess Plateau for a long time, where has been called the "most highly erodible soil on earth" [33]. The environment without color

Fig. 9. The interaction of light and glass in *Kaleidoscope*, © SAKO Architects, 2020

often makes children feel that life is hopeless. Light and glass interaction has formed the cognition of bright sunshine in their early education, making them full of attachment to their hometown and full of longing for the future. In the day-time, the sunlight sheds into the classroom through the colored glass, forming colorful lights and shadows that evoke children's imagination and creativity. At night, in contrast, the glowing lights from the interior emit out of the windows that create an impressive and beautiful night scene (see Fig. 9).

Secondly, light and shadow images provide unique occasions for developing oral and written language by serving as an emotional memory link to a lived experience enabling young children to recall details. A researcher from the Royal Institute of Technology designed a stimulating outdoor installation for children, named *The Light-Play-Ground*. At the base of the installation are concentric circles like a labyrinth. Between the beginning and end of the maze, "3 + 1" different levels appear by creating four basic circles. Each level is made of a combination of transparent, translucent, and concrete materials according to the light level desired. It aims to evoke emotions of different nature, beginning with positive ones and ending with the most negative ones: the fear of darkness, creating an incentive change in light levels, the heart of the elements, cast shadows, and colors (see Fig. 10).

The spaces designed around a common metaphor provide a varied environment and exciting visual stimuli for preschool-aged children. The circular labyrinth aims to enable children to step out of the safety offered by the vicinity of their parents and explore the space on their own, finally reaching the center. The shapes, materials, and colors continuously transition from a warm and safe outer ring towards the more enclosed and

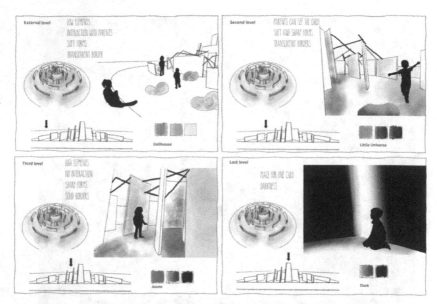

Fig. 10. *The Light-Play-Ground*, © Petra Koza, 2020

Fig. 11. Dark space design, © itD studio, 2020

darker inner world. The developing tension and fear are dissolved by familiar colors and shapes that help get used to new and foreign spaces. In the innermost part of the labyrinth, the bravest can meet darkness. Through this design, we can find that specific colors have different influences on emotion and emotional transmission. For example, red represents aggressive, fast, and anger. The green represents pleasant and safe. Therefore, we can use this as the basis for space atmosphere design.

In particular, the design uses the darkness as the endpoint of the children's emotional experience. In childhood, nighttime fear is a shared experience; darkness is often associated with anxiety. We can't just make children understand light without darkness. Negative experiences such as fear, injury, and fighting in a relatively safe and friendly environment induce children's confidence, and they no longer will consider these so scary. They will learn how to react in dangerous situations later and how to face their fears. It plays a vital role in preventing the development of phobias and anxiety. The initially scary experience of darkness and being alone in time become familiar, and the fear dissipates. This dark space design has also been applied to another design case in China, where the dark no longer inspires fear but allows children to explore as if they were in the universe (see Fig. 11).

5 Conclusion

Distinct from traditional lighting design strategies, we focus more on designing interactive effects of light environments in kindergartens. In our research, we integrate the relationship between Piaget's theory of children's cognitive development and the interactive lighting design. And we illustrate how the light and illumination design could affect the four aspects of physiology, intelligence, society, and emotion through case studies and then emphasize the importance of lighting and illumination elements. But at present, there are few designs of interactive effects of light environments in kindergartens, so we only select representative cases for analysis. And due to geographical and environmental constraints, children are subject to different early childhood education. Our study is challenging to make a more comprehensive summary to carry out more in-depth and accurate research. Next, we will focus on early childhood education in a particular area and then put forward a more precise strategy. It is also hoped that our study can give early childhood educators and light and illumination designers some inspiration to explore the design to meet preschool children's cognitive development needs.

In conclusion, light and shadow are closely related to children's cognition. The space creation of a light environment and the organization of interactive light games affect children's cognitive development. We try to put forward interactive lighting design oriented to meet preschool children's development needs and pay attention to the relationship between children's growth and environment. We hope preschool children can get physiological, intellectual, social, and emotional development through interactive lighting design.

Acknowledgements. This work was funded by Program for Postgraduate Capability Promotion of Science communication Sponsored by China Association for Science and Technology, Grant kxyjs202001.

References

1. Fröbel, F.: Mutter-und kose-lieder. A. Pichlers Witwe & Sohn, Vienna (1906)
2. Eshach, H., Fried, M.N.: Should science be taught in early childhood? J. Sci. Educ. Technol. **14**(3), 315–336 (2005)
3. Ashbrook, P.: Shining light on misconceptions. Sci. Child. **50**(2), 30 (2012)
4. Magnusson, S.J., Palincsar, A.S.: Teaching to promote the development of scientific knowledge and reasoning about light at the elementary school level. In: How Students Learn: History, Mathematics, and Science in the Classroom, pp. 421–474 (2005)
5. Rice, K., Feher, E.: Pinholes and images: Children's conceptions of light and vision. I. Sci. Educ. **71**(4), 629–639 (1987)

6. Piaget, J.: The Child's Conception of Physical Causality. Lund Humphries, London (1930)
7. DeVries, R., Kohlberg, L.: Constructivist early education: overview and comparison with other programs. National Association for the Education (1987)
8. Feher, E., Rice, K.: Shadows and anti-images: children's conceptions of light and vision. II. Sci. Educ. 72(5), 637–649 (1988)
9. Weinstein, C.S.: Designing preschool classrooms to support development. In: Weinstein, C.S., David, T.G. (eds.) Spaces for Children, pp 159–185. Springer, Boston (1987). https://doi.org/10.1007/978-1-4684-5227-3_8
10. Dudek, M.: Kindergarten Architecture: Space for the Imagination. Taylor & Francis, London (2000)
11. Şahin, B.E., Dostoğlu, N.T.: The importance of preschoolers' experience in kindergarten design. METU JFA 1(29), 1 (2012)
12. Mohidin, H.H.B., Ismail, A.S., Ramli, H.B.: Effectiveness of kindergarten design in Malaysia. Procedia Soc. Behav. Sci. 202, 47–57 (2015)
13. Erlhoff, M., Marshall, T.: Design Dictionary: Perspectives on Design Terminology. Walter de Gruyter, Berlin (2007)
14. Denning, P.J., Metcalfe, R.M.: Beyond Calculation: The Next Fifty Years of Computing. Springer, Berlin (1998)
15. CIE: International lighting vocabulary. CIE 17.4 (1987)
16. Wetterberg, L.: Light and Biological Rhythms in Man. Pergamon Press, New York (1993)
17. Haidarimoghadam, R., Kazemi, R., Motamedzadeh, M., Golmohamadi, R., Soltanian, A., Zoghipaydar, M.R.: The effects of consecutive night shifts and shift length on cognitive performance and sleepiness: a field study. Int. J. Occup. Saf. Ergon. 23(2), 251–258 (2017)
18. Stassen Berger, K.: The Developing Person Through the Life Span. Worth Publishers, New York (1983)
19. MOE of China Homepage. http://www.moe.gov.cn/srcsite/. Accessed 6 Feb 2021
20. Dudek, M.: Schools and Kindergartens: A Design Manual. Walter de Gruyter, Berlin (2007)
21. White, J.R.: Didactic daylight design for education. State University of New York at Buffalo (2009)
22. Brubaker, C.W.: Planning and Designing Schools. McGraw-Hill, New York (1998)
23. Gifford, R.: Environmental Psychology: Principles and Practice. Optimal Books, Colville (2007)
24. Gee, J.P.: What video games have to teach us about learning and literacy. Comput. Entertain. 1(1), 20 (2003)
25. Sleegers, P.J., Moolenaar, N.M., Galetzka, M., Pruyn, A., Sarroukh, B.E., Van der Zande, B.: Lighting affects students' concentration positively: findings from three Dutch studies. Light. Res. Technol. 45(2), 159–175 (2013)
26. Wei, Q., Lee, J.H., Park, H.J.: Novel design of smart sleep-lighting system for improving the sleep environment of children. Technol. Health Care 27(S1), 3–13 (2019)
27. Kinzer, C.K.: Considering literacy and policy in the context of digital environments. Lang. Arts 88(1), 51 (2010)
28. National Research Council: Inquiry and the National Science Education Standards: A Guide for Teaching and Learning. National Academies Press, Washington, DC (1996)
29. Kasten, H.: Wie die Zeit vergeht: unser Zeitbewusstsein in Alltag und Lebenslauf. Wissenschaft Buchgesellschaft, Darmstadt (2001)
30. Müller, H., Pieper, C., Heuten, W., Boll, S.: It's not that long! helping children to understand time with an ambient light display. In: 15th International Conference on Interaction Design and Children, pp. 356–366 (2016)
31. Mora-Guiard, J., Crowell, C., Pares, N., Heaton, P.: Lands of fog: helping children with autism in social interaction through a full-body interactive experience. In: the 15th International Conference on Interaction Design and Children, pp. 262–274 (2016)

32. Yansong, C., Zhigang, W., Hantian, X., Xiaoxi, L., Luhan, W., Fei, G.: Exhibition design of the thematic science popularization space based on scientific visualization. In: 2020 International Conference on Culture-oriented Science & Technology, pp. 269–273 (2020)
33. Tian, J., Huang, C.H.: Soil Erosion and Dryland Farming. CRC Press, Boca Raton (2000)

Research on "The Cinema Development Mode of Digital Art Exhibition" from the Perspective of Cultural Computing

Jieming Hu[1,2] and Xin Zhang[1](✉)

[1] Donghua University, Shanghai West Yan-an Road 1882, Shanghai 200051,
People's Republic of China
hjm@dhu.edu.cn
[2] Shanghai Normal University, Shanghai 200030, People's Republic of China

Abstract. Cultural Computing is closely related to the of Digital Art Interactive Exhibition. Based on Cultural Computing and by means of the dynamic display of digital art, culture can be recognized, inherited and innovated. This article explores the new concept of "Cinema Chain Mode of Digital Art Exhibition". Based on the development of Cultural Computing, it is proposed that Digital Art Exhibitions will become a new distributed structure of Cinema Chain with networked, dynamic and chain development, and has a flat, Interactive, entertaining, commercial and other characteristics, through distributed data sharing, form a deeper cultural computing function. Super subjective space art intervention can open the exhibition's cinema development in the future. The cultural computing information spread of "Cinema Chain Mode of Digital Art Exhibition" needs to transform from the single "transmitters" and "recipients" in traditional exhibitions to "information spread stakeholders" in the context of information space. In this spread process It is necessary to strengthen the relevance of the theme and content, pay attention to the participation of stakeholders, improve the dissemination of information, and strengthen the infection of the venue and the influence of the exhibition. Based on cultural computing, the innovation model of "Cinema Chain Mode of Digital Art Exhibition" can be divided into four layers: cultural resource layer, information integration and processing layer, information media combination layer, and exhibition and communication space layer. In this paper, digital art exhibitions such as "TeamLab: The World of Water Partitions in Oil Tank" and "2020 HUELEAD Show" are taken as main research cases to analyze the artistic characteristics, cultural connotation and immersive experience of cultural computing behind them, so as to provide experience reference for relevant practice.

Keywords: Cultural computing · Digital Art Exhibition · Cinema chain · Interactive exhibition

This article belongs to Donghua University's "Special Fund for Basic Research Business of Central Universities": 2232015B3-02; Shanghai Design Category IV Peak Discipline Funding Project: Research on Intelligent Configuration and Design of Museum Exhibition Space: DB18404; supported by the Exhibition Research Fund of Donghua University & the Shanghai University Knowledge Service Platform Shanghai Fashion Design and Value Creation Collaborative Innovation Center.

© Springer Nature Switzerland AG 2021
M. Rauterberg (Ed.): HCII 2021, LNCS 12794, pp. 244–258, 2021.
https://doi.org/10.1007/978-3-030-77411-0_17

1 The New Concept of "The Cinema Chain Mode of Digital Art Exhibition"

1.1 Cultural Computing and Digital Art Interactive Exhibition

The proposal and development of cultural computing cannot be separated from the support of big data, computer technology, interactive technology and artificial intelligence technology. The use of these emerging technologies can help the exploration, re-understanding, inheritance and innovation of culture. The protection of culture is not a simple preservation, and the revival of culture is not a copy of the original. The inheritance of culture needs persistent activation and more diversified interaction, but also needs spontaneous display and dissemination. Naoko Tosa, the early proponent of the concept of cultural computing, also believes that the combination of computer technology and cultural studies can better interpret and promote cultural exchanges. (Naoko Tosa 2004), and shows the use of technology to the public by ZENetic interpretation method of ink painting and Zen culture [1], to promote with the computer technology and the integration of art exhibition of new media played an important role in the development process. The definition of "cultural computing" (Rauterberg and Hu 2010; Tosa 2006) combines these research topics with a storytelling method that reflects differences in emotion, consciousness and memory. The process of presentation is no longer a linear single mode, but can be achieved through the technical support and principles of cultural computing Real-time interaction with visitors, enriching cultural forms, and creating an ideal state for visitors, cultural computing can realize the dynamic, continuous, and circular revival and activation, dissemination and inheritance of culture. The development of cultural computing provides a new and broad space for the deep exchange of cultural arts, especially the digital art exhibition based on the perspective of cultural computing, which not only has an immersive art and technology exhibition experience, but also integrates into new social focus topics. The universal value given to cultural exchanges has given birth to the formation of new exhibition business models. The collision of information revolution and display design has brought display design into a brand new stage. Bit stream and information flow have become an indispensable part of the display space. The future exhibition will definitely be a dynamic display space constructed by digital information. The display design has shifted from shaping the physical space to the overall display environment, and the collection, processing, and performance of display design materials has changed from the integration of objects to the integration of information.

The application and popularization of emerging technologies in exhibitions in the information age has nurtured brand-new media and transmission forms for display design. Digital art exhibitions with interactive display as the main feature have become a common display method in cultural communication exhibitions. It provides a new construction model and disseminating ideas for the exhibition space in the process of cultural inheritance and revival. Digital art exhibition under the perspective of cultural computing is a multi-dimensional dynamic process. The subject of movement can be both objects, people, and even intangible spirits and emotions. Innovative interactive display brings more diversified information dissemination carriers and richer spatial forms to the originally dull and monotonous cultural exhibitions, and at the same time allows space to mediate and virtualize, and space itself becomes a carrier of information. With the help of the digital equipment in the dynamic display, a virtual space that is attached to the physical space but exists independently is created. The cultural information carried by the exhibits replaces the exhibits as the main body of the exhibition, and the exhibition space becomes a collection of physical space and information space. The expression of information in the exhibition has shifted from static to dynamic and static coexistence, the existence of information has shifted from material to material digital coexistence, and the acquisition of information has shifted from a specific space within a specific time to a coexistence of online and offline without time and space constraints.

1.2   The Cinema Development Mode of Exhibition and the Intervention of Super Subjective Space Art

The concept of "cinema chain" refers to the brand management mechanism and management mode established by relying on cinemas, capital, film supply and other major links in the industry chain of the film industry. It refers to the network and "channel" that must be established for the purpose of controlling and monopolizing the film as a form of public entertainment when it reaches a certain amount and scale. The interactive exhibition mode of digital art based on cultural computing can lead to the new development of cinema chain exhibition. The cinema chain digital art interactive exhibition is an exhibition under the cultural computing mode of immersive multimedia participation, and it is a network, dynamic and chain exhibition mode. The cinema chain mode of digital art exhibition will be integrated into People's Daily life and urban space just like watching movies. The chain development trend of urban exhibition space also provides carrier support for the cinema chain digital art exhibition. Cultural computing can quickly generate diversified exhibition content and experience forms, and quickly generate specific exhibitions for specific people to enter the circulation of theaters. This new exhibition distribution structure, whether it is the theme content of the exhibition or the spatial form, is It revolves around the purpose of "effective dissemination" rather than a single goal of marketing.

Hyper-Subjective Space is to construct a space in the exhibition that allows visitors to change in real time according to individual behavioral experience and psychological changes in the exhibition. Visitors can explore personalized display logic and make it have unlimited possibilities. Cinema Chain Exhibitions need to analyze the real-time psychological changes and consumer demands of visitors. The material and physical needs of visitors serve as the origin of the exhibition, which is pre-judged around the emotions of the visitors, and constantly adjusts the relationship between other elements and the exhibition content. In order to ensure the effective dissemination of information, when the exhibition is generated, it is necessary to focus on the interface between humans and the material, find the triggering point from the contact point, and continuously iteratively generate the exhibition to achieve the purpose of effective communication and reception. The linkage relationship between the tangible people, objects, environment and the corresponding intangible emotions, information, and context in the exhibition breaks the single and linear rules in the traditional construction model, and forms a flat, nonlinear visiting logic. This allows visitors to feel and calculate the "Hyper subjective" of digital art exhibitions based on changes in actions in the space. Through the process and results of the accumulation of materials, the entire exhibition can be processed in a timely manner when a certain element changes. The system conducts macro-control.

The exhibition is no longer just a process of showing beauty, but an immersive experience process through cultural computing. The formal beauty, behavioral beauty, content beauty and technical beauty are integrated into it. The boundary between content space and physical space of the work is blurred and unified in the Hyper-subjective space.

2   The Structure and Operation Characteristics of "Cinema Chain Digital Art Exhibition"

2.1   The Basic Structure of "Cinema Chain Digital Art Exhibition"

With the development of The Times, exhibitions continue to expand their design connotation and scope. Nowadays, it is no longer possible to analyze and construct future exhibitions only through the thinking and strategies of traditional space design (Fig. 1). Introduce the new concept of "The Cinema Chain Mode of Digital Art Exhibition", starting from the relevance of information and information in the display and dissemination, by building a display space construction model (Fig. 2) to generate an interactive display space with a specific cultural theme. It completes the fit of display information and spatial form. This provides a new construction model and dissemination ideas for the exhibition space. According to several major elements of the exhibition, in the process of establishing the existing exhibition structure, the same exhibition is often divided into several parts according to the timeline, that is, the mining of resources—shown as the content of the exhibition, and the planning of the plan—shown as the theme of the exhibition, the implementation of the plan-manifested as the presentation of the exhibition [2]. These are controlled by independent systems, and then converge into one. Due to the lack of an overall system capable of real-time control and management of various subsystems, it often makes time-consuming and costly exhibitions inadequate in the presentation of results and unable to achieve good economic and social benefits.

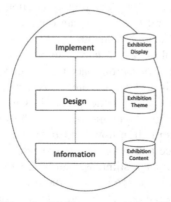

Fig. 1. Strategies of traditional exhibition space design (Illustrated by HU Jieming)

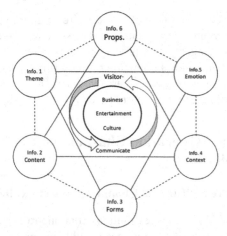

Fig. 2. The cinema chain mode of digital art exhibition's construction model (Illustrated by HU Jieming)

The Cinema Chain Digital Art Exhibition space under the perspective of cultural computing makes the information in the space more orderly and regular, and makes the transmission of information more logical. From the perspective of people and communication, establish the relationship between people, or between different circles and different circles, firstly which can allow influential individuals or people with certain characteristics to drive other "information stakeholders" spreading together, which expands the breadth of spread. Secondly, the interactive behavior of people is used, that is, the second creation content itself touches more people's creation and communication behavior, and expands the richness of content. This process needs to build a relevant system from several aspects: the relevance of the exhibition theme and content, the fit of the exhibition purpose and form, the participation of stakeholders, the dissemination of information, the appeal of the venue, and the influence of the exhibition [3].

The basic structure of "The Cinema Chain Digital Art Exhibition" is a networked, dynamic, and chain-based new distributed structure for the cinema chain. Through distributed data sharing, a deeper cultural computing function is formed. Using the technology and concepts of cultural computing can compress the process of traditional information display, make it flat and "foldable", and form more diverse display carriers and richer spatial forms. The physical space in the exhibition has a complete, orderly and harmonious structure, but the information space formed by the display content attached to the physical space exists in a flowing state. Different from the traditional display design that focuses on the "final state" of the space, The Cinema Chain Digital Art Exhibitions pay more attention to the "dynamics flow" of the space. This "dynamic flow" is actually the process of information flow carried by the media in the display space. From the perspective of space and information, the relevance and order between the displayed information firstly guides, stimulates, and triggers the interaction of people in the space, and secondly makes the knowledge structure of the displayed content more systematic. The interactive behavior of stimulus means more contact between people and space, which allows people to obtain more information. The knowledge structure of the system means that the distribution of information is more logical and regular, which allows people to obtain information more efficiently.

2.2 Operation Characteristics of the "The Cinema Chain Digital Art Exhibition"

The primary operating feature of "The Cinema Chain Digital Art Exhibition" is systematic. It is a reproducible exhibition system based on cultural calculations, networking, dynamics, and flattening. It is not a two-dimensional or multi-dimensional physical environment according to established rules. The figure or image displayed in front of the subject in form is an exhibition system that can reflect the various elements in the exhibition and the relationship between them. It needs to clearly reflect the various subsystems and their relationships involved in the exhibition, and make real-time and macro adjustments. The types and quantities of subsystems involved in exhibitions of different natures are often different. Therefore, when building an exhibition system, it is necessary to appropriately integrate, increase and decrease the elements according to the actual situation, especially for the real-time experience of the visitors in the system. Psychological changes and behavioral responses make rapid system responses. The system uses more interactive media to mobilize the audience's vision, touch and feeling, and emphasizes the interactive and participation characteristics in the process of information dissemination, so it can not only present the display results, but also receive the audience's feedback to the greatest extent, and quickly mobilize more through calculations. Relevant factors to enhance the efficiency of this spread. This cultural computing capability is based on an open and autonomous computer system that uses artificial intelligence and big data to quickly process display data and audience feedback data.

It is the real-time calculation and timely adjustment of this kind of digital art interactive exhibition that can bring the social focus and hot spots that are easy to form "topics" to the visitors present, thereby giving the exhibition a certain cultural exchange value. This digital art exhibition, which integrates audience behavior, emotion, topic, cognition and other dimensional information, also has its own entertainment, commercial functions and fashion sharpness. The exhibition consumer group cultivated based on such exhibitions also makes it possible to operate the exhibition industry as cinema chain.

As a planned, purposeful, and targeted social behavior, the exhibition system is also the result of two-way exchange of material and information with people as the core. The exchange of material and information requires people to act as "transmitters" and "recipients", and form an energy exchange between digital art exhibitions and human-related elements, namely: the exchange of energy among venue (environment) and organizers, exhibitors, service providers and visitors. As the initiator of the exhibition, the organizer serves as the issuer, which is a bridge to maintain close contact and in-depth interaction between multiple parties; the exhibitor, as the most important and direct consumer of the exhibition, acts as the operator, and is the sender of materials and information in the exhibition; As the receiver of material and information, the audience is the actual or potential consumer of the products and services provided by the exhibitor. It is also a key element for the exhibition to achieve good economic and social benefits; the service party is the implementer of the exhibition. The cooperative operator is the lubricant to maintain the smooth operation of the exhibition. The energy interaction between the relevant elements is also a characteristic of the linear operation of digital art exhibitions.

2.3 Cultural Computing Information Dissemination Process of "The Cinema Chain Digital Art Exhibition"

From the perspective of information dissemination, when the information source evolves from a linear single source to an interactive multi-point source [3], any individual or group can become the disseminator of exhibition information. The structure of the traditional media environment has been reorganized, and the role of the media has changed from a single "transmitter" and "recipient" to "information dissemination stakeholders" in the context of information space. According to the influence of information dissemination stakeholders, they are divided into Key Opinion Leader[1], Key Opinion Consumer[2] and the general public. As the core source of information, Key Opinion Leader delivers the "core content" to the recipients (Key Opinion Consumer or the general public) of this communication behavior through various channels. Create "trigger content" that includes self-consciousness, thereby driving a wide range of communication behaviors.

The process of cultural computing information dissemination needs to strengthen the relevance of the theme and content [4]. When positioning the exhibition theme and selecting participating organizations, it is necessary to constantly weigh the relationship between the two, and make overall and appropriate adjustments in time. During the implementation of the project, time, culture, and some force majeure factors or individual differences in exhibitors should not cause a low correlation between the content and content, content and themes of the exhibition, which will not cause visits. The sympathy of the audience did not meet their psychological expectations before the exhibition, and thus could not guarantee a high-quality exhibition.

The process of cultural computing information dissemination needs to pay attention to the participation of stakeholders. The organizer should select appropriate suppliers from various service providers related to the exhibition to provide services for the exhibition [5]. According to different types, numbers, scales of service providers and differences in stakeholder participation, their proportions in the exhibition are different. The specific roles played by all parties and their degree of importance require the organizer to make overall planning.

The process of cultural computing information dissemination needs to improve the dissemination of information. The organizer needs to reasonably locate the target audience based on the theme of the exhibition, and adjust the content and form of the message in a timely manner according to the audience. Information starts to flow in both directions only when visitors arrive at the exhibition site to communicate with exhibitors.

The process of cultural computing information dissemination needs to strengthen the infection of the venue and the influence of the exhibition. The infection of the venue refers to the degree of infection of the visitors by the overall atmosphere of the exhibition site produced by the service provided by the service. Surrounding the relatively stable exhibition element of the venue, the sub-systems under the main system exist in an

---

[1] Key Opinion Leader (KOL) marketing is defined as a person who has more and more accurate product information, is accepted or trusted by related groups, and has a greater influence on the purchase behavior of the group.

[2] Key Opinion Consumer (KOC) corresponds to KOL. Generally refers to consumers who can influence their friends and fans and produce consumer behavior. Compared with KOL, KOC has less influence.

intricately intertwined relationship, rather than a single linear relationship. The service needs to shape and maintain the atmosphere of the exhibition venue in accordance with the requirements of the organizer. The impact of the exhibition is to measure whether the exhibition meets the established target after the exhibition is over. As the main recipient of exhibition information, the impact of visitors after viewing the exhibition largely determines whether the exhibition has achieved good results in the promotion of social economy, the transmission of cultural context, and the promotion of group image. Income. For each unique visitor, the viewing period is not the same as the exhibition time. When the visitors are over, they are already "post-show" on the timeline. At this time, due to time inequality, visitors need to get feedback in a timely manner, and it is expected that more visitors can maintain continuous attention to the follow-up information of the exhibition after the end of the exhibition, which will help improve the influence of the exhibition.

2.4 Innovative Model of "Cinema Chain Digital Art Exhibition"

The "Cinema Chain Digital Art Exhibition" innovation model based on cultural computing can be divided into four levels: cultural resource layer, information integration processing layer, information media integration layer, and display and communication space layer (see Fig. 3). From the investigation and sorting of cultural resources to the complete arrangement of data resources, the information factors are grouped and reorganized, and the exhibition information levels are divided into primary and secondary categories, and suitable media carriers are selected for the information factors in the exhibition system, to generate a display and communication space [6], and complete the fit of display information and spatial form.

The cultural resource layer is the process of investigating, collecting and sorting out relevant information. This process enables the information to be used in the display after artistic processing. The collection of resources follows the principle of continuity. Organizing is also a continuous dynamic cycle process. On the one hand, massive information has promoted and promoted the creation of new cultural content; on the other hand, people's aesthetic and cultural thoughts continue to be collected, connected, and integrated, and continue to recognize, inherit and innovate culture.

The information integration processing layer includes two parts: the establishment of the information data resource database and the integration processing of cultural information. The establishment of the information data resource database is to organize the related objects and data that carry cultural elements after analysis and research, and arrange them into an information data resource database according to certain outward characteristics; the integration of cultural information is to screen out the information from the resource database. It needs resources, and reorganizes and aggregates them into the most basic communication ontology in the display space—information factors according to their relevance. Objects or data resources in the database are the most primitive and fundamental cultural information, including pictures, text, audio, video, symbols, books, texture, materials, colors, models, actions, events, etc.

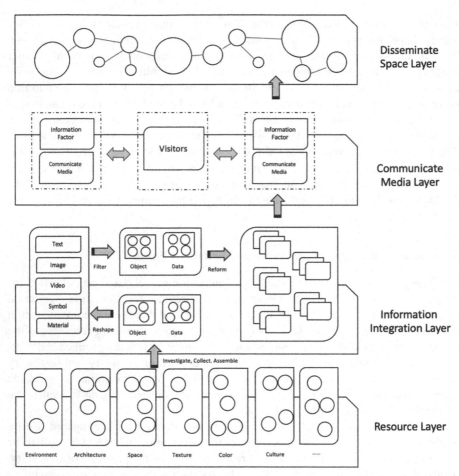

Fig. 3. Model of cinema chain digital art exhibition (Illustrated by HU Jieming and her research group)

The establishment of information data resource base follows the principle of integrity. Just as the accurate transmission of semantics needs the linguistic background, the accurate transmission of culture also needs to be based on a certain cultural background. The information conveyed in the exhibition and communication does not exist independently in isolation from the cultural environment. The integrity of data resources refers not only to the comprehensiveness of content, but also to the integrity of cultural communication background. In order to avoid the homogenization of content and space caused by neglecting its essential features, we should not stick to the obvious forms such as symbols, colors and textures of cultural resources, but pay attention to the original cultural context, regional order and cultural structure behind objects and data [7].

The integration and processing of information follows the principle of linkage. The process of information agglomeration and recombination is the process of combing and regulating the fragmented information, which needs to emphasize the linkage between the internal resources of information factors and between information factors. In this way, the disordered information space in the exhibition space can become orderly, so that the transmission of information is more logical and regular, and the efficiency of obtaining information can be improved. On the other hand, it allows information to play a detonating role in the system by activating other relevant elements to create a virtuous chain reaction.

Massive information factors bring excessive sensory stimulation to the audience and reduce their attention to a single information. Only by dividing the hierarchical relationship of information factor structure in a primary and secondary way can the core information in the display and communication play an active role in rapidly driving the surrounding elements. Then each element forms a larger scale, deeper level of display and dissemination, and finally forms a series of linkage chain reaction, forming a virtuous cycle.

The combination layer of information media is to select the appropriate dynamic display media for the information factor as the main body of communication and generate the media contact point that directly contacts with people in the display communication. The exhibition and communication space layer optimizes the details of media contact points according to the arrangement relationship of information factors in the information catalyst system [8], combined with the environmental characteristics and other elements of the exhibition and communication, so as to generate a diversified exhibition and communication space combining online and offline, and complete the combination of exhibition information and spatial form.

Under the model construction of cultural resource layer, information integration processing layer and information media combination layer, all cultural information content is transmitted through media in the exhibition space. For digital art exhibitions, through information transmission and real-time computation, computational culture is constantly triggered in the exhibition space.

3   The Practice Case of "The Cinema Chain Digital Art Exhibition"

3.1   Case Study in "TeamLab: Water Particle World in Oil Tanks"

In 2019 "TeamLab: Water Particle World in Oil Tank" exhibited in Shanghai, has a strong reference significance for the exploration of Cinema Chain Digital Art Exhibition based on cultural computing. First, the whole exhibition to create digital art immersive experience, the content of the exhibition by the "the world of water particles in oil tank", "flowers and people", "Black Waves" and "circle" and so on the series of works, the exhibition content considered in the process of land, use the tank space of Shanghai art center tank characteristic has carried on the particular display restructuring, the industrial style space will be built into the immersive experience flow space. The interactive waterfall is presented in the form of water particles. Waterfall particles and visitors together constitute the content of the exhibition, and the visitors are immersed in it and become part of the exhibition (see Fig. 4). Secondly, based on cultural computing, the whole

Fig. 4. A planar waterfall in a hyper-subjective space (Photo by HU Jieming)

exhibition has instant interactive experience, and generates different exhibition contents according to the different behaviors of different visitors, breaking the linear bondage of traditional exhibition contents. Exhibition is behind by computing the mutual influence between particles to realize build a waterfall in the tank, flowers and the visual interest of the waves, countless particles move through constantly form linear and continuous visual trace, countless such traces together to form the intention of the falls, it is also an exhibition planners calculated by the culture of subjective space art in the way of super a reflection, in this process, the visitors are seen as block falls down the river rocks, when the particle line meet visitors stop, would be a change in the direction of flow illusion (see Fig. 4). In the same way, changing the trajectories of particles can produce other images of waves and flowers. The images of flowers in the space show different states of birth and growth, and the number of growth behaviors varies with the gaze of the viewer. If touched or trampled, the flowers will wither together. Third, the content of a digital art display information through flat and systematic processing, compression showed the complex information content, and presents the content of the randomly generated, in the interaction of flat images may contain infinite random, the sound, light, electricity system is systematically constructed according to the behavior of visitors. TeamLab uses physical space design to eliminate the boundaries of works. When visitors enter the exhibition, they will completely immerse themselves in the world of works and blur the boundaries between themselves and works. Due to the use of technology to make the space of the narrative is no longer just the content of narrative, and towards digital-ization and virtualization, expanded the works of the original physical limitations, the exhibition works can present the huge volume, and achieve maximum freedom of space, in the process of the exhibition, all is random, all also is reasonable. Fourthly, the whole exhibition has produced an attempt to develop theatrically. Part of this exhibition is not the first time to show, some works such as "Black Waves" and so on had done in Spain and other parts of the exhibition, from content to the exhibition planned operation shows that this kind of exhibition can realize chaining and theatrical development potential, this kind of "web celebrity" exhibition can be a way of entertainment and leisure, and films in the spread of the Internet economy era public willing to take photos as a souvenir life demands, meet the psychological needs of the public pursuit of visual impact exhibition is no longer only have the effect of preaching propaganda or knowledge transfer, It can be integrated into the whole chain process of tourism consumption, fashion life and cultural entertainment. These provide the feasibility exploration of content, experience, business model and technical support for the theatrical development of digital art exhibition.

3.2 Practical Reference in "2020 HUELEAD SHOW"

In December 2019, "2020 HUELEAD SHOW 7.0" large-scale integrated new media Show held in Shanghai SHOW 709 media park, the display is based on the cultural computing of the digital art. Unlike "teamlab: The World of Water Particles in Oil Tanks", which focuses on visual image media exhibitions, this exhibition is a composite of image media display and live performance activities, and is based on the cultural theme of "Four Seasons Concerto" and immersive interaction. The performance of computer technology is deeply integrated.

"Four Seasons Concerto" is the theme of the exhibition, through digital image field condition change of the seasons to create four different styles of immersive interactive performance area, the four seasons of Spring, Summer, Autumn and Winter scene progressive change constantly, through the elements such as lighting, video, audio and installation performing out the change of the seasons. The layout of the space is around the type of visitors as the core (see Fig. 5), the visitor just began to enter the exhibition hall, can experience the interactive experience different seasons at random. At the beginning, viewers can randomly experience the interactive experience of different seasons. The time when the viewer enters, the different interactive behaviors, and the different routes of travel will produce very different interactive experience results. This difference in experience results The content generation, digital catalyst and "stream dynamics" proposed in the previous article are highly consistent. There are also regular concentrated experiences during the exhibition. This is called the "fifth season" immersion, that is, the experience of jumping out of the four seasons and experiencing the rapid change of the four seasons from the fifth dimension.

This is the part of the exhibition where there is a concentrated display every hour or so. The audience is located in the center of the entire exhibition hall. With the interaction of images and explanations, they watch the storytelling of the "Four Seasons" exhibition area in turn. Watching in the center of the exhibition area is beneficial to Places "read" the full picture of the exhibition content in turn. On the other hand, it also helps to enhance the immersive experience process, surrounded by four exhibition areas to form a full range of audiovisual experience. The content of the entire exhibition is developed based on a systematic construction. As mentioned above, the model architecture of the cultural resource layer, the information integration processing layer, the information media integration layer, and the display and communication space layer are all concentrated in this exhibition., The content of the entire display is also a flat and high-intensity concentration of the visual and interactive experiences of the four seasons of the Jiangnan in China, forming an immersive experience of "unbounded" space. A large number of cultural computing technology supports are used in the space, including computer programming algorithms, LED folding screens, up-and-down flow

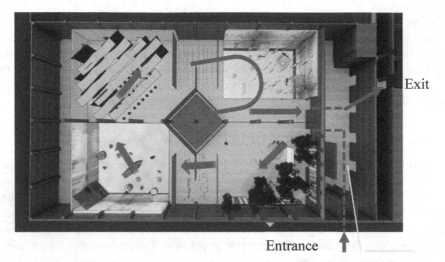

Exit

Entrance ↑

Fig. 5. 2020 HUELEAD SHOW Exhibition Floor Plan (Image source: Provided by HUELEAD Technology)

2020 HUELEAD SHOW

Fig. 6. 2020 HUELEAD SHOW The Scene of the exhibition "Summer" (Image source: Provided by HUELEAD Technology)

planets, laser phosphor projectors, and interactive sensing devices. A large number of cultural visual and auditory symbols are set up in the exhibition area, such as bamboo forests, apricot blossom rain, pipa sound, wind bells, etc. in the "spring" environment, reflecting the poetic and quiet sense of Jiangnan culture. The "Summer" scene includes lotus flowers, boats, streams, frogs, etc. (see Fig. 6), which reflects the vitality and comfort of Jiangnan culture in summer. The "Autumn" scene includes mantle tents, lanterns, zithers and flames. Out of the sorrow of autumn and the beauty of the harvest in Jiangnan culture, the "winter" scene has glass, light bars, and sound of depression, reflecting the cold weather in Jiangnan winter, and contains new vitality. In addition, the exhibition also incorporates some art works and design works of young artists, such as paintings, jewelry, clothing, luggage, installation works, etc. (see Fig. 7), carrying the dialogue environment of traditional inheritance and future innovation, integrating entertainment, Interactivity and commerciality, just like a theater-based movie, it has a multi-dimensional composite of culture and commerce, art and technology, overall and partial, visual and auditory, entertainment and education (see Fig. 8).

Fig. 7. 2020 HUELEAD SHOW Live performance and real-time presentation of music visuals in the exhibition (photo source: Photo by HU Jieming)

Fig. 8. 2020 HUELEAD SHOW Live performance and real-time presentation of music visuals in the exhibition (photo source: Photo by HU Jieming)

4   Conclusion

The development of The Cinema Chain Digital Art Exhibition based on cultural calculation needs to be based on the interpretation of local culture and the deep integration of digital technology. The specific method of cultural calculation is determined according to the specific display content. In this process, the traditional linear fixed exhibition needs to be changed. The model is transformed into a content-generating exhibition mode based on the immersive interactive experience of the visitors, which dissolves the boundaries of the exhibition and completes the realization of the ideal space for the individual visitors. The extension of the concept of cultural calculation to beauty blurs the boundaries of art and exhibitions, thus triggering viewers' ways of viewing exhibitions under the concept of Hyper-Subjective Space. Visitors are also an important part of exhibition creators, giving birth to new digital narratives in a cross-cultural context. Logic, these deep new logic discussions will play a key role in the development of "The Cinema Chain Digital Art Exhibition". In the future, The Cinema Chain Digital Art Exhibition can expand the dotted layout into a cultural computing application network with extensive social influence and cultural regeneration value, and will directly affect the new lifestyle of people in the future.

Acknowledgments. Thanks to those who provided academic help in the writing process of this paper, thanks to Chen Yingxin in the research team.

References

1. Tosa, N.: Cross-Cultural Computing: An Artist's Journey. Springer, London (2016). https://doi.org/10.1007/978-1-4471-6512-5
2. Hu, J.: Logical characteristics of museum display design. Art Des. (Theory) (11), 51–53 (2016)
3. Zuo, Y., Hu, J.: On the challenges faced by museums in the new media environment. Art Des. (4), 50–52 (2019)
4. Hu, J., Zuo, Y.: Reflections on digital art exhibitions: TeamLab: world of water particles in oil tanks. Sci. Educ. Mus. (5), 360–363 (2019)
5. Zhang, F.: IoT, IoT and Intelligentization: building a new model of government governance – based on the analytical perspective of information space. J. Huaqiao Univ. (Philos. Soc. Sci. Ed.) (06), 121–128 (2017)
6. Liu, H.: Mass communication control and research from the perspective of information space theory. China Xinjie (12), 76–79 (2011)
7. Tan, G., Sun, C.: Digital protection and communication of intangible cultural heritage under the theory of information space. J. Southwest Univ. Nationalities (Humanities Soc. Sci. Ed.) **34**(06), 179–184 (2013)
8. Hao, C., Zhang, J.: Research on the renewal strategy of historical district under the guide of cultural facilitator: a case study of the design of Ying·Xiang film museum in Qingdao. Famous Cities China **10**, 77–82 (2018)
9. Naoko Tosa, Seigo Matsuoka, and Henry Thomas. 2004. Inter-culture computing: ZENetic computer. In ACM SIGGRAPH 2004 Emerging technologies (SIGGRAPH 2004), p.11. Association for Computing Machinery, New York (2004)
10. Rauterberg, M., Hu, J., Langereis, G.: Cultural computing – how to investigate a form of unconscious user experiences in mixed realities. In: IFIP advances in information and communication technologies, pp. 190–197, vol 333. Springer, Berlin (2010)
11. Tosa, N.: Unconscious fl ow. Leonardo. 33(5), 442 (2006)

Implementation of Fast-Building Interactive Scene with Chinese Paper Cutting Style

Xingguang Mi[✉] and Wenjuan Chen[✉]

Communication University of China, Beijing, China
wjchen@cuc.edu.cn

Abstract. As one of the precious intangible cultural heritages, traditional Chinese paper cutting has a long history and profound cultural connotation. In the digital age, traditional paper cutting is gradually moving towards digital paper cutting in order for better inherit and development. In the research of paper cutting digitalization, computer has been normally adopted to make two-dimensional paper cutting, to focus on the restoration of paper cutting process. There is still a little difficult for users who are not familiar with paper cutting; three-dimensional model has also been used to improve the picture effect, but it is not easy to show the characteristics of paper cutting with three-dimensional models. In order to address such an issue, this paper innovates the artistic style of digital paper cutting by combining paper cutting with common visual effects in modern 2D games, improves the efficiency of scene construction by writing automatic generation algorithms, and perfects the interactive mode of digital paper cutting by introducing natural interaction. In this way, users can participate in the process of creating paper cutting works, and creation of paper cutting works becomes simple and efficient benefiting from the automatic generation algorithm and natural interaction. Finally, by comparing to works of other paper cutting style, the works achieved by the solution proposed in this paper illustrates the advantages of digitalization in three aspects: artistic style, fast generation, and natural interaction.

Keywords: Digitalization · Parallax scrolling technology · Effect of 2D depth of field · Automatic generation algorithm · Natural interaction

1 Introduction

Being widely spread, Chinese paper cutting is a kind of folk traditional art with a long history in China, which is to cut out various kinds of visual images and design patterns on the paper with tools such as scissors or nicking tools, and to add decorative design as embellishments in order to create image symbols with implications of blessing, good luck and prayer. Its extensive mass character, unique regional character and strong design features make it a well-known traditional art form in China as well as a cultural symbol that can represent China's distinctive characteristics [1].

However, due to the limitation of tools and materials, traditional paper cutting is made with "paper" as the carrier, which is more difficult and takes a long time. Therefore,

© Springer Nature Switzerland AG 2021
M. Rauterberg (Ed.): HCII 2021, LNCS 12794, pp. 259–277, 2021.
https://doi.org/10.1007/978-3-030-77411-0_18

people began to try to change the form of traditional paper cutting, so that the paper cutting art can be better inherited and developed. For example, *Kung Fu Panda 3* is a movie released in 2016. When doing localized promotion in China, it used paper cutting posters to attract the attention of many Chinese people (see Fig. 1), which contribute to the new vitality of Chinese paper cutting.

Fig. 1. *Kung Fu Panda 3* Chinese paper cutting style poster. Source: Li Zhao

In addition, the research on paper cutting digitalization has attracted more and more attention in recent years. Some have established a digital "paper cutting museum" by analyzing the characteristics of traditional paper cutting: for example, using web pages as a platform and the form of interactive animation, paper cutting culture is displayed with a novel interactive interface from production process to product display [2]; or built a computer-based digital protection framework of paper cutting art by developing computer-aided paper cutting design software and computer-aided paper cutting multimedia display system [3]. Some have studied how to better make paper cutting graphics with diversified shapes on computers: for example, by developing functions such as drawing patterns and editing patterns, and writing cutting algorithms of models, an editing tool capable of generating paper cuttings with good hollowing-out effects has been produced [4]; or used the idea of symmetrical origami to create different patterns after unfolding by editing the shape of folded paper cuts [5]. Some others have studied how to combine paper cutting with digital games so that players can experience the charm of paper cutting art in the process of playing games: for example, using mobile phones as the platform, players can create different shapes by touching and swiping on screens according to the given paper cutting templates [6]; the *Nishan Shaman* is a commercial work with paper cutting art style (see Fig. 2). Since releasing in 2018, its design combining shaman culture with music rhythm has been widely praised by players.

However, the form of "paper cutting museum" focuses on the accurate reproduction of paper cutting culture, and its target audience is closer to those who have a strong interest in paper cutting art; making paper cutting with computer pays more attention to

Fig. 2. Paper cutting style game *Nishan Shaman* released in 2018

the restoration of paper cutting process, and it is still a bit difficult for users who are not familiar with paper cutting; in the production of paper cutting games, a large amount of picture materials need to be provided to enrich the content of the scene. Some games try to improve the picture effect in the form of three-dimensional models, but it is not easy to express the characteristics of paper cutting by three-dimensional models and it will need better-performance hardware. Therefore, there is a demand for a method that can efficiently generate paper cutting style scenes.

This paper is to make a work which is able to generate a scene fast with the traditional Chinese paper cutting style, to present the Chinese paper cutting style art in a digitalized form. Digitalization of traditional Chinese paper cutting art is not simply copying and transplanting Chinese paper cutting from physical form into digital form, but to innovate the traditional Chinese paper cutting to a certain extent according to its features and advantages, and to improve the technique needed for a better presentation of Chinese paper cutting style, so as to find the agreement between traditional Chinese paper cutting and modern technology. At the same time, interactive content is added and paper cutting elements are generated efficiently by writing automatic generation algorithms so that users can quickly create paper cutting style scenes.

2 Analysis and Research of Digital Paper Cutting

2.1 Art Style of Digital Paper Cutting

As a kind of hollowed-out art, the presentation form of Chinese traditional paper cutting is often static, and the modeling is rather generalized. If the original artistic style of traditional paper cutting has to be completely kept, it will be difficult to give full play to the advantages of digital dynamics, and it is not easy for users to quickly distinguish various elements in the scene in the process of interaction. Therefore, by referring to the visual effects commonly used in modern 2D games, this paper makes appropriate innovations on the artistic style of digital paper cutting.

Modern 2D game screen design can often simulate 3D environmental effects while maintaining its own artistic style. More importantly, compared to 3D game scenes, it can simulate some visual effects previously available only in 3D environment with lower hardware resource occupation and more efficient algorithms. The realization of exquisite visual effects is usually inseparable from the following technologies: 2D depth of field, screen post-processing and parallax scrolling. These technologies enable developers to create a magnificent game world in two-dimensional space.

Paper cutting, as a hollowed-out art based on two-dimensional plane, pays great attention to line composition and exaggerated modeling, as well as aestheticism of outline. The planarity of paper cutting makes it easy to adapt to parallax scrolling technology. However, because paper cutting itself often appears in a single layer and there will be no other elements underneath, we need to make appropriate innovations on the hollowing-out characteristics of paper cutting art. This paper gets inspiration from "color-lined paper cutting", and replaces the hollowing-out effect of paper cutting by lining color paper under monochrome paper cutting; at the same time, as an activity that players can participate in and interact with, the elements in the scene need to be able to be distinguished quickly and clearly, so it is also necessary to make a certain degree of trade-off between exaggerated shapes and abstract outlines of paper cutting.

Therefore, based on "color-lined paper cutting" and combined with the technology used to improve visual effects in modern 2D games, this paper explores the brand-new expression pattern that digital paper cutting can bring.

2.2 Automatic Generation Algorithm

Both the traditional paper cutting and the existing digital paper cutting are difficult to make, which is not friendly to people who have just come into contact with paper cutting culture. And if you want to have more people pay attention to and interest in paper cutting art, it is very necessary to reduce the threshold of creating paper cutting works.

Therefore, this paper first puts forward the following requirements: a large number of elements in the scene need to be generated automatically, rather than being added and produced by users one by one; because of this, unlike the automatic generation algorithm often used by developers in the production of scenes, the automatic generation algorithm in this paper is processed in real-time during the operation of the work, so it requires a certain amount of low performance. Because users will participate in the generation of the whole paper cutting scene, to enable different users to get different generated results, it is necessary to have the randomness of the automatic generation algorithm, but complete randomness will make the generated results uncontrollable, so the construction of the automatic generation algorithm needs to find a balance between randomness and certainty.

Based on the above requirements, this paper refers to some commercial works in the implementation of automatic generation algorithm. For example, Ubisoft shared the automatic generation algorithm used in the development of *Far Cry 5* at the 2017 Game Developers Conference. In essence, points, curves, and surfaces are artificially arranged in the scene first and then generated by the algorithm according to these Artificial Marks [7]. And made the developer of the "*Horizon Zero Dawn*" Guerrilla Games on its website is to share the way they quickly generate scene: first to establish a complete set of brush system, the system can not only within the scope of the brush to generate the game objects, such as plants and gravel, and also consider when drawing draw area of terrain (such as too steep slopes to generate the growth of the straight tree), and the generated near the game relationship between objects, such as two trees should not be too close, the tree should have a reasonable number of bushes, grass, etc.) covering [8].In this way, the creators can quickly generate objects using the brushes, and the algorithm helps with planning in the process. It can be seen that in these two different automatic generation algorithms, the idea of automatic generation of Artificial Marks matching algorithm is adopted.

In this paper, Artificial Marks and random parameter algorithm are also adopted to generate objects in the scene, which can not only make multiple objects relatively evenly distributed in space, but also reduce the sense of repetition of the picture through random factors.

2.3 Interaction of Digital Paper Cutting

To enrich the content of the work and give full play to the digital advantages of paper cutting, users need to be able to further interact with these generated paper cutting elements. In this paper, after the user creates the desired paper cutting object, you can also configure the weather (wind volume, rainfall), time (daytime, dusk, night), and other elements in the current scene according to your own creative will. In this way, with the help of the power of digital technology, the traditional paper cutting art is no longer limited to a single, static, low transmission efficiency mode, but vividly displayed in front of the user through animation. The introduction of interaction also allows users not only to appreciate paper cutting works but also to participate in the creation process of paper cutting.

Besides, this paper also discusses the way of interaction to a certain extent. The interaction of traditional input devices is limited, which is different from the activities in the real world and is limited to some extent in the breadth and dimension of experience. For example, in traditional ball games, athletes need to pay attention to many factors such as body posture, force Angle, and force size; in digital games, players generally only need to move, click and press buttons through the mouse, keyboard, and so on. Therefore, such a limitation can have an impact on the player's immersion [9]. However, natural interaction can overcome this limitation to some extent and increase the dimension of interaction. Furthermore, natural interaction allows the user to focus on the task itself with little need to think [10]. Therefore, creating paper cutting style scenes through natural interaction not only strengthens the user experience but also leaves a deeper impression on users. At the same time, it also reduces the learning threshold, so that users can better enter the environment of paper cutting creation.

Therefore, in the process of realizing the work, this paper introduces Leap Motion as the input interface in user interaction and uses Leap Motion to identify gesture, hand position, speed, and other information to construct user interaction mode, to improve the breadth and dimension of user experience.

In conclusion, thanks to the modern 2D games perfect visual effect of the use of technology, and automatic generation algorithm and natural interaction, each user can interact through a few simple movements, using different types of trees, such as weather, time-limited control options, you can generate many different styles of paper cutting. That is to say, each user can create their unique paper cutting works, and the entire creation process is fast and efficient. This way of creation is more suitable for today's fast-paced lifestyle, and users will be more willing to participate in the process of understanding and making paper cuts.

3 Application

Through the analysis and research on digital paper cutting, this paper develops a work that can quickly generate interactive paper cutting style scenes. Thanks to the gradual maturity of the game engine, the author can spend more time on differentiated development work without investing too much in basic game functions such as graphics rendering, animation functions and physical engines. Among them, the game engine Unity has become one of the most applicable tools for developing 2D games. Therefore, according to the characteristics of Chinese paper cutting, this paper selects Unity as the implementation tool, and makes full use of the functions integrated in Unity to better achieve the research objectives of this paper.

3.1 Realization of the Automatic Generation Algorithm

As each user is expected to get different generated results, the automatic generation algorithm needs to have the participation of random functions. At the same time, it is necessary to ensure that the randomly generated results conform to certain rules of composition, so it is necessary to limit the processing of randomness. In this paper, only three Layer Objects are used to illustrate the realization of the automatic generation algorithm, and more Layer Objects can be inferred according to the same algorithm idea. In the actual work in this article, 40 Layer Objects can be configured.

The steps to implement the automatic generation algorithm in this paper are as follows:

1. Generate Layer Objects and configure the properties of these Layer Objects according to a specific pattern (see Fig. 3).

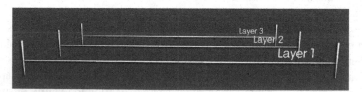

Fig. 3. Layer object generation

2. Generate a different number of Artificial Marks under each Layer Object according to a specific pattern (see Fig. 4).

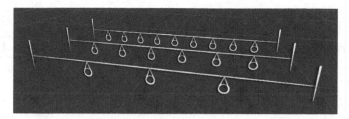

Fig. 4. Generation of artificial marks

3. Generate a paper cutting object within a certain range of each Artificial Mark. The generated paper cutting object can read the properties of its layer level, and decide some properties of itself according to the reading results (see Fig. 5).

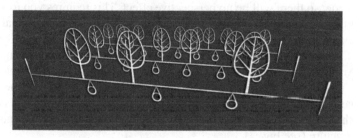

Fig. 5. Generation of paper cutting objects

Thus, the generated result is shown below (see Fig. 6):

Fig. 6. The results obtained using the automatic generation algorithm proposed in this paper

In Step 1, the properties of the Layer Object are shown below (see Table 1):

Table 1. Properties of the layer object

Layer object hierarchy	Number of artificial tags	Layer scaling factor
Layer 1	3	1
Layer 2	6	0.8
Layer 3	9	0.64

"Layer Object Hierarchy" refers to the order of layers. It can be understood that the smaller the layer hierarchy is, the closer it is to the camera. However, it should be noted that this work is built in a two-dimensional space, mainly because of the ability to use some of the functions integrated into a two-dimensional space by Unity, as well as for optimization considerations. As a result, almost all game objects in the scene have no depth information. Also, the projection of the camera in two-dimensional space is the orthogonal mode, so there will be no perspective effect. This requires you to artificially make the farther away objects look smaller, which is where the "Layer Scale Factor" attribute comes from.

In step 2, the positions of the Artificial Marks are always evenly distributed. The purpose of Artificial Marks is to limit random factors. Each Artificial Mark will generate a corresponding paper cutting object, and this paper cutting object is generated in a random range and must be near its corresponding Artificial Mark. A picture is used here to illustrate the Artificial Mark and its corresponding generation range through different colors in the picture (see Fig. 7).

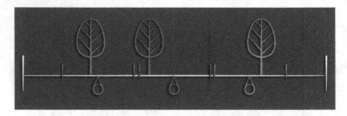

Fig. 7. Generation range corresponding to artificial mark

The following figures respectively show the generated results of different generation quantities when the automatic generation algorithm proposed in this paper is used (see Fig. 8, Fig. 9 and Fig. 10):

It can be seen that the automatic generation algorithm proposed in this paper can not only guarantee certain randomness under the condition of different generation quantities but also make each paper cutting object a relatively uniform distribution to a certain extent.

Fig. 8. Generates 11 objects

Fig. 9. Generates 20 objects

3.2   Implementation of the Automatic Generation Algorithm

By referring to the visual effects commonly used in modern 2D games, such as parallax movement technology and 2D depth of field technology, this paper creates a scene that combines the visual effects of traditional paper cutting and modern 2D games.

Parallax Scrolling Technology. Parallax scrolling technology is to create a scene with an illusion of depth in a two-dimensional space, and it has been used in traditional animation as early as the 1930s through multi-plane imaging technology [11]. Parallax scrolling is a technique that adjusts the moving speed of each Layer Object according to the camera's moving speed when the camera is moving. The layers closer to the camera move faster, while the layers farther away from the camera move slower. The main algorithms to implement the parallax movement effect is as follows:

Fig. 10. Generates 46 objects

```
void ParallaxMovementFunction()
{
  The distance the camera moves within a frame = the co-
  ordinate value of the position of the previous frame –
  the coordinate value of the position of the current
  frame of the camera;

  The position the Layer Object should reach in this
  frame = the original position of the Layer Object + the
  distance the camera moves in one frame * the parallax
  scaling factor;
}
```

The "parallax scaling factor" can control the speed attenuation between different Layer Objects. Thus, by setting different values for this variable, different degrees of parallax movement can be achieved, thus simulating the depth needed for the current scene.

2D Depth of Field Effect. The so-called depth of field effect refers to a camera that can only focus on a single object's distance at one time. Such a camera has a relatively clear imaging range before and after the focus, while the scene outside this range is blurred [12]. The depth of field effect is supposed to be a kind of screen post-processing technology, but the depth of field effect realized in a 2D environment is often different from the depth of field effect realized in 3D space by screen post-processing, so it is especially emphasized here that it is implemented in 2D space.

The fundamental reason why depth of field can't be achieved directly through on-screen post-processing is that this method requires depth information for elements in the scene. However, the Unity platform does not attach depth information to the processing of two-dimensional objects. In other words, the depth information of these objects in two-dimensional space is 0. This causes these objects to be treated as the same depth through on-screen post-processing, and therefore to be "all clear" or "all blur" for all objects. Therefore, to achieve the effect of depth of field in two-dimensional space, a completely different implementation method is needed from that in three-dimensional space.

In past games, 2D images were blurred directly by some image processing software. The advantage of this is that when rendering a two-dimensional image in a game engine, the shading process is still just sampling the texture of the original image, which puts less pressure on the GPU. But there are more obvious disadvantages. First, you need to blur each different image, which greatly increases the amount of work. Second, each image has an extra blurry version compared to the previous one. If the image is required to appear on multiple layers requiring parallax scrolling, multiple corresponding versions need to be created by setting different blurry parameters. This not only increases the memory footprint but also doubles the game's capacity. Third, if you need to change the shape of these images at a later date, you can go back to the original image and change it, but then you need to blur it again. Drawing details directly on an image that has already been blurred is a disaster.

For the above reasons, this paper attempts to use shaders that can be blurred to achieve the depth of field effect in two-dimensional space. Different from using image processing software for blur operation, blur shading is usually realized by averaging the color value of each pixel sampled from the original texture and the color value of its surrounding pixel to a given degree before the two-dimensional image is rendered on the screen, to achieve a blur visual effect. In this way, varying degrees of blurriness can be generated based on the original image simply by adjusting the blurriness intensity parameters in the program (see Fig. 11), which greatly reduces the workload, saves the game space, and facilitates the subsequent adjustment of the original details.

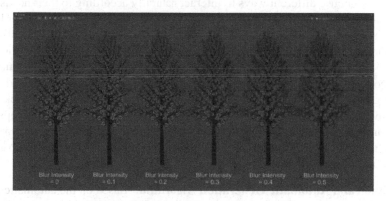

Fig. 11. Results of different blur intensities

Because of a paper cutting object blur strength is determined by its layer level, the function of configuring blur intensity can combine with the above automatic generation algorithm. When the paper cutting object is generated, read the current Layer Object information, and get the current generated paper cutting object corresponding blur strength. This can be done by adding one more property to the Layer Object. The changed properties of the Layer Object are shown in Table 2:

Table 2. The changed properties of the Layer Object

Layer object hierarchy	Number of artificial tags	Layer scaling factor	The intensity of the blur
Layer 1	3	1	0
Layer 2	6	0.8	0.25
Layer 3	9	0.64	0.5

3.3 Realization of Natural Interaction

In the process of exploring digital paper cutting, using mouse, keyboard, and mobile phone screen as interactive devices is still the mainstream operation mode. However, such a traditional interaction model is relatively simple, resulting in the actual interaction behavior of users and the behavior they act in the virtual world is always different, and this difference will bring learning costs to users. Natural interaction can overcome this limitation to a certain extent, so this paper hopes to introduce natural interaction to reduce the threshold of learning and improve the interest of the work. This paper uses Leap Motion as an attempt at natural interaction, which allows users to construct elements in the scene, control the time and weather in the scene, etc. When setting up paper cutting scenes, users can use different ways to interact naturally according to their needs.

Leap Motion is an optical sensor that can locate and collect information for human hands in human-computer interaction. Its small size, high accuracy of data collection, strong stability, good recognition, in line with the human engineering law, should be applied to a variety of fields. When human-computer interaction is carried out, Leap Motion collects the data information of human hands through the camera, identifies different gestures according to the information obtained, and can be fed back to the virtual environment to obtain the model of human hands. Leap Motion encapsulates a large number of internal APIs, which can facilitate access to relevant data, and Leap Motion officially has good support for Unity. Therefore, this paper chooses Leap Motion as the input device for the work.

Leap Motion and Automatic Generation Algorithm. Based on the automatic generation algorithm, the interactive part is added to implement the function of controlling the generation process of paper cutting objects. The position of the hand in 3D space can be easily obtained through the API provided by Leap Motion. Therefore, considering the animation effect of the paper cutting object, this paper implements the generation of the paper cutting object when the hand moves from the bottom to the top. When the hand moves from top to bottom, the paper cutting object is destroyed (see Fig. 12).

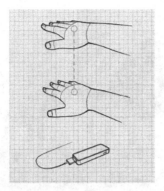

Fig. 12. The generation and destruction of paper cutting objects controlled by hand movement up and down

In the process of moving the hand from low to high, the program will detect the vertical coordinate of the hand in real-time. Based on the coordinates obtained, calculate the distance the hand has moved during this time. If the distance is greater than the set threshold, the function that generates the paper cutting object is called once. The specific execution process can be seen in the following code:

```
void HandControlGenerationFunction()
{
  The distance the hand moves in a frame = the position
  of the hand in a frame - the position of the hand in
  the current frame;

  Accumulated distance of hand movement += distance of
  hand movement within one frame;

  If (the cumulative distance of hand movement >= thresh-
  old)
  {
    Generate paper cutting object function ();
    Accumulated distance of hand movement = 0;
  }

}
```

Thus, the animation effect generated by the paper cutting object in the scene can be implemented when the hand is raised (see Fig. 13):

Fig. 13. Hand lifting control paper cutting object generation

The function of destroying the paper cutting object is the same, that is, when the hand moves from high to low, it detects its coordinates in the vertical direction.

Leap Motion and Weather Control. "Weather control" means that the user can control the intensity of the stroke and the amount of rain in the current scene, and the changes of these parameters will be reflected in real-time through the paper cutting objects in the scene. For example, the stronger the wind, the more the paper objects will shake. This is achieved mainly by writing shaders that are applied to paper cutting objects.

In this shader, a gradient noise image is sampled by a variable varying with time, and the vertex position of the paper cutting object is changed according to the result of sampling. In this way, as long as the scaling ratio of the variable that changes with time and the scaling coefficient of the gradient noise image itself is changed, the shaking degree of the paper cutting object can be changed, correspond to different wind intensities.

These variables in this shader are modified by the speed of the hand movement (see Fig. 14). When it is detected through the Leap Motion API that the current moving speed of the hand is greater than a set threshold, the value of the relevant variable will be increased. When the current speed of hand movement is detected to be less than a set threshold, the value of the relevant variable is decreased.

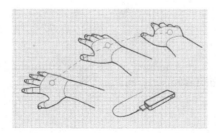

Fig. 14. Variables related to hand movement speed control shader

Rain is achieved through particle effects. So to change the size of the rain is to change the number of particles emitted in the particle system. After that, the intensity of the wind and the size of the rain are correlated to achieve the effect that the stronger the wind is, the greater the rain will be (see Fig. 15).

Fig. 15. The intensity of the wind is related to the amount of rain

Leap Motion and Time Control. "Time control" means that the user can change the time of day, dusk, or night of the current scene. This is achieved through screen post-processing technology. The screen post-processing technology refers to a series of operations on the screen image after rendering a complete scene and obtaining the screen image to achieve various screen effects. This technology can add more artistic effects to the game screen [13]. This paper uses the post-processing effect of color adjustment to map the color value of each pixel in the screen image to other colors according to specific rules, to achieve the effect of changing the scene time.

This paper changes scene time by detecting hand orientation (see Fig. 16). When the hands were down, it was daytime. Hands to the left, time is dusk; when the hands are up, time is night (see Fig. 17).

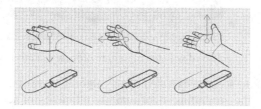

Fig. 16. Orientation control time of hand

Fig. 17. Orientation control time of hand

4   Results and Evaluation

At the present, the generated results achieved by using the algorithm in this paper are shown in the following figures (see Fig. 18, Fig. 19, Fig. 20, Fig. 21, and Fig. 22). At the same time, the implementation effects in other papers are selected for comparison (see Fig. 23).

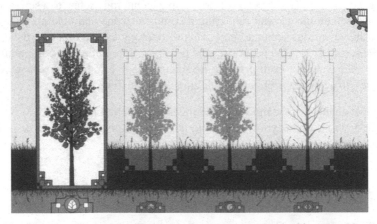

Fig. 18. The effect achieved with the algorithm proposed in this paper (No. 1)

It can be seen that the scenes generated by this algorithm are of the following advantages: with the automatic generating algorithm, the efficiency of scene construction is greatly improved, and rich scene content can be generated by a small number of paper cutting images; the unique sense of depth in 3D space is simulated in 2D space by using parallax scrolling and 2D depth of field; compared to the static paper cutting images in other works, users can also add animation effects to these paper cutting images after the paper cutting images are generated; in addition, previous works are often operated by

Fig. 19. The effect achieved with the algorithm proposed in this paper (No. 2)

Fig. 20. The effect achieved with the algorithm proposed in this paper (No. 3)

Fig. 21. The effect achieved with the algorithm proposed in this paper (No. 4)

Fig. 22. The effect achieved with the algorithm proposed in this paper (No. 5)

Fig. 23. Effects for comparison. Source: Image from [4] (right) and [6] (left)

mouse, keyboard or touch screen. This paper introduces the way of natural interaction to improve the breadth and dimension of user experience.

5 Conclusion

In view of the issues existing in traditional Chinese paper cutting and digital paper cutting, this paper starts from three aspects of artistic style of digital paper cutting, fast scenes construction of paper cutting style, and interaction of paper cutting elements, to put forward respectively the solutions of combining paper cutting with the visual effects commonly used in modern 2D games, writing automatic generation algorithm, and introducing natural interaction. From the comparative analysis of the achieved results with other works, it can be concluded that the solution in this paper shows the advantages of digital paper cutting in three aspects: artistic style, fast generation, and natural interaction. However, the current automatic generation algorithm is only adaptive to flat terrain conditions, and the obtained scenes are relatively simple and repeated. In the future, we will continue to study the design of automatic generation algorithm to achieve better varied paper cutting style scenes.

Acknowledgements. This study was supported by the National Key Research and Development Program of China (No. 2020AAA0105200).

References

1. Wang, B.: The history of Chinese folk paper cutting arts. China Academy of Art Press, Zhejiang (2006)
2. Yang, Y., Deng, H.: Interactive website "paper cutting museum" layout design and Flash interactive practice exploration (in Chinese). Art Educ. Res. **14**, 79 (2013)
3. Peng, D.: Research on digital-protection technology of non-material cultural heritage based on Chinese-paper-cut. Ph.D. thesis, Zhejiang University (2008)
4. Cui, N.: Research and implementation of computer-generated paper cutting stylization key technology (in Chinese). Master's thesis, University of Electronic Science and Technology of China (2009)
5. Huang, X.: Research and application of core algorithm in folding Paper-cut. Master's thesis, Beijing University of Technology (2012)
6. Duan, L.: The design of Shanxi Paper cutting Gaming as well as the artistic communication basing on mobile platform. Master's thesis, Harbin Institute of Technology (2015)
7. Guillaume, W., Benoit, M.: 'Ghost Recon Wildlands': Terrain tools and technology. In: Game Developers Conference, March 2017
8. van Muijden, J.: GPU-based procedural placement in Horizon Zero Dawn (2017). https://www.guerrilla-games.com/read/gpu-based-procedural-placement-in-horizon-zero-dawn. Accessed 15 Jan 2021
9. Huang, S., Ding, Z., Chen, Y.: Fundamentals of Digital Game Design. Tsinghua University Press, Beijing (2008)
10. Song, Y., Demirdjian, D., Davis, R.: Continuous body and hand gesture recognition for natural human-computer interaction. ACM Trans. Interact. Intell. Syst. **2**(1), 1–28 (2012). https://doi.org/10.1145/2133366.2133371
11. Wyatt, P.: The art of parallax scrolling. Net, vol. 165, pp. 74–76 (2007)
12. Salvaggio, N.: Basic photographic materials and processes, p 110. Taylor & Francis, England (2009)
13. Feng, L.: Getting Started with Unity Shader (in Chinese). Posts & Telecom Press, Beijing (2016)

Empathy in Technology Design and Graffiti

Mari Myllylä[✉] (iD)

Faculty of Information Technology, University of Jyväskylä, P.O. Box 35 (Agora),
40014 Jyväskylä, Finland
mari.t.myllyla@student.jyu.fi

Abstract. This paper discusses empathic understanding, what it means, and how it can be acquired. After an overview of some theories and models from the existing literature, two experiments are presented, where participants were assessing graffiti works. From the results of these experiments, it can be concluded that empathic understanding involves both embodied processes and abstract inferences. Furthermore, understanding can be based on perceived, mechanistic bodily similarities and movements or on folk-psychological inferences mentalized between the observer/empathizer and an object/empathized. Empathic understanding it can also be gained by recognizing and implementing learned bodily skills and conceptual knowledge in mental simulations and theorizations. Furthermore, people have existing schemas and stereotypes that may affect their empathic understanding. In the context of technology design, this implies that the designer as an empathizer needs to consider their own and their users' perspectives and interactions in different sociocultural contexts; their background knowledge; their future intentions; and the ways empathy can be gained through both embodied processes and mental inferences.

Keywords: Empathic understanding · Technology design · Graffiti

1 Introduction

Designers who create and develop products, services, and systems for other people must have some understanding of the potential end users' thoughts, beliefs, intentions, feelings, needs, and desires, and of how the users' unique mentally representational information content may affect their behavior. It is also important to understand if and how the users would be willing and able to use designed artifacts [1]. This makes understanding the end user an essential design issue [1, 2]. Designed interactive products, services, and systems that are pleasant to use, and that fulfill some universal psychological need, may be defined as having a good user experience (UX) [3]. However, the quality of the user experience and what is judged to be good at a particular moment in the interaction may depend on, for example, the individual and the culture, as well as the specific characteristics, purpose, timing, and the context of the thing being used [4]. Interaction is an ambiguous term [5, 6], but in the context of human-computer interaction (HCI), it can be defined as involving "two entities," that is, computers and humans, "that determine each other's behavior over time" [5, p. 10]. What constitutes good interaction depends on how

© Springer Nature Switzerland AG 2021
M. Rauterberg (Ed.): HCII 2021, LNCS 12794, pp. 278–295, 2021.
https://doi.org/10.1007/978-3-030-77411-0_19

one defines interaction, and therefore it ranges from being understandable, simple, and controllable to being psychologically satisfying or motivating, or to enabling the user to fluently participate in the world [5].

A designer's job is to "read the minds" of the potential end users or agents, and to predict and understand the relationships between the users' mental states, attitudes (e.g., beliefs or knowledge), and actions. This requires the cognitive ability to "mentalize" or create theories of others' minds [7]. One way to attain at least some level of this intersubjective understanding is through empathy, or "empathy building" [2, p. 1]. It can be argued that empathy, defined as the ability to understand others, has been an essential part of design thinking ever since things have been designed and created, especially for other people [1]. The term "empathy" was initially discussed in the context of philosophical aesthetics as a psychological phenomenon of experiencing beauty and emotions when viewing art, first by Vischer in 1873, and in the early 1900s, by both Lipps and Titchener. This idea then spread to other fields, such as psychology and neuroscience [8]. In the field of human-computer interaction (HCI), empathic design emerged in the early 1970s [2], and it was widely applied in the human-centered design (HCD) field in the late 1990s [8]. Because the study of empathy in human-centered technology design is a rather young line of research, it is useful to investigate the role of empathy in technology design by considering theories, models, and findings from other, more established fields, such as aesthetics, neuroscience, behavioral and social sciences, etc.

1.1 Definitions of Empathy and Empathic Understanding

Different scholars define the concept of empathy in different, partly conflicting ways. For example, empathy can be defined as a form of intentionality, where one individual is attuned and emotionally responding to the situated experiences, feelings, and states of mind of another [9–11]. Empathy also can be thought of as any kind of goal-oriented activity that is rich in content and that enables the recognition of subjectivity of the other individual (the empathized) from the standpoint of the observing individual (the empathizer) [2, 9]. Empathy can be understood as a passive mental association between the living bodies of oneself and of the other, based on the embodied presence of the other's personality and on the direct perception of their bodily expressions [9, 12], reflected in the observer's own imagined experience of those circumstances [10–12]. Empathy can also be understood as an ethical responsibility that an individual experiences for another individual [12]; this definition connects the phenomenon of empathy to moral theories [13].

The empathized other can also be an object, such as a work of art [8, 14–17]. For example, the empathic experience of art comes from the emotions that an artwork itself displays and from the way the perceiver relates to those emotions, rather than from the artist's mood or attitude [14]. This can even happen when an observer is viewing nonrepresentational, abstract art [18].

Empathy can be further subdivided into cognitive and emotional empathy. Cognitive empathy usually refers to an individual's cognitive ability that requires developed self-awareness and thinking to recognize and understand the thoughts, feelings, experiences, and states of mind of another person from that other's own perspective, also enabling the feelings of sympathy and compassion [10, 12, 19]. Emotional empathy may refer to feelings such as "sympathy, empathic anger and contagious joy" [10, p. 22], which make us feel concerned about and care for others [20]. In sympathy and caring, the emphasis is mostly on negative feelings and on helping and alleviating another's suffering [11, 14]. Empathy and sympathy can also exist simultaneously [14, 20]. We can also direct empathic emotions to ourselves; for example, in moments of anxiety or in tense interactions with other people [8]. According to Zahavi [20], empathy and sympathy are phenomena where the emotional content of an experience is perceived as separate from the observing individual's own emotions. This distinguishes them from emotional contagion, where one individual begins to feel the way the other does [20].

Empathy does not mean that we perceive or experience others' experiences the same way they do, nor that we can access another's consciousness in the similar fashion as into our own [9]. We can experience the mental content and mental states of others in many different ways. I can experience the personality of another individual, but I can also be misled, or simply wrong. I am experiencing another individual as another mind, whose mental content may be partly accessible and partly hidden from me [9].

1.2 Ways to Gain Empathic Understanding

One way to gain an empathic understanding of another's experiences, from the stand-point of the other positioned in a spatiotemporal "there" in relation to our own "here," is through the dynamic process based on the perceived similarities of our bodies, and on our idea of how we ourselves would feel and act, emotionally and physically, in a similar situation in order to achieve the same goals [12, 21, 22]. Newborn children already seem to have some sort of dynamic body models and prereflexive empathic abilities to understand and react to psychological phenomena of other individuals as goal-directed agents [9, 12]. The ability to interact with others automatically and unconsciously via body-mediated, embodied experiences might be the primary way for intersubjective understanding throughout our lives from birth [9, 20]. Viewers of visual art often experience empathic, bodily participation and motor simulation when they view an artwork, through, for example, seeing the direction of the brushstrokes and imagining the artist's body movements [16, 23].

According to Fuchs [21], we tend to utilize more demanding thinking mechanisms only in circumstances where we observe an event from a distance or when the object of our thought is complex and ambiguous. The concept of theory of mind (TOM) refers to an individual's mentalizing ability to attach different mental states to themselves and others and to make inferences, anticipating and explaining the behavior of oneself or others in terms of different mental states (such as intentions, desires, and beliefs) [7, 9]. This ability has often been explained using the theory-theory (TT) and simulation theory (ST) of the mind [7, 13].

Theory-theory claims that our understanding of others and their mental states and behaviors is based on an innate ability to make inferences and models based on folk-psychological information, which enables us to read others' thoughts and create common-sense explanations and predictions of behavior [9, 12, 13, 19]. We understand other people as "naïve attributors" via a cognitive process where the understanding is based on a "mentally stored set of functional laws" [13, p. 174] that we use, along with our observations, to make theoretical interpretations about the observed agent's internal mental states and behavior [13, 24]. According to the simulation theory, on the other hand, in order to understand others, we use not theories but analogies based on our own experiences of how we would think, feel, and behave in a corresponding situation. We do this by mentally putting ourselves in the place of the other, and incorporating their beliefs and desires into imagined simulations that we then project onto that person [9, 12, 19, 24]. Furthermore, instead of just TT or ST, we might have sort of hybrid mechanism, where one or the other strategy is used depending on the situation [7, 9, 19].

Simulation theory has gained support from the discovery of mirror cells and their automatic and unconscious activity in, for example, premotor, frontal, and parietal brain areas when we meet other living creatures like us. They are activated when we act or when we observe, anticipate, or imitate the goal-directed bodily actions, communicative gestures, verbal communication, and facial expressions of others [9, 12, 22, 24]. Mirror cells and their resonating may also be part of our perceptual processes that enable fast direct perceptions of others and fast reflex-like reactions through the autonomic nervous system, such as emotion-filled mental states and bodily expressions and gestures [9, 14]. Mirror cells may be essential for the brain's mechanisms that give the empathizer clues about the other's feelings, intentions, and actions, so as to enable intersubjective experiences and communication [9, 12, 14, 22, 24].

Perceiving two objects that touch one another may activate our somatosensory cortex and simulation-related processes, as if our own bodies were touched [15, 16]. Simulation processes might create a feeling of the observer's own body being in a similar geometric shape and position in relation to other objects as what is perceived in an artwork. Seeing a pole supporting a heavy object might generate the feeling of a heavy weight on the observer's own body and create empathy toward the inanimate object itself [15]. Imagining how an artist's body had moved while creating an artwork might activate the observer's own motor brain areas and mirror cells [15, 16, 25].

Some of our behavioral patterns, such as gestures or bodily expressions, are socio-culturally learned. This may affect how we perceive and interact in different situations [26]. We also learn to perform certain motor functions and behaviors in order to, for example, use devices or tools or other technological artifacts [1]. In this case, the learned bodily movements may transform into automatically activated, sensorimotor behavioral patterns and acquired skills [27, 28]. We can learn high-level information about bodily movements and action sequences from observing the actions of others, and our own learned skills may also affect how we interpret and judge the movements and outcomes of the actions of others [28]. For example, an art critic may learn to perceive and understand the skillful movements and mannerisms of an artist by immersing themselves in the artworld's social and linguistic discourse, even if the art critic does not create art [29, 30].

With the help of language and stories, we can share and understand complicated and abstract mental content, perspectives, experienced events, and learning of other people [9, 31]. When we create, share, and listen to or read stories, we also develop rational explanation models and narrative scripts and schemas for others' general behavior in relevant practical situations, whether consciously or not. We learn what has happened before, why the person in the story does what she does, what the results of her actions are; this information is reflected in our learned sociocultural categorizations, norms, practices, and contexts [7, 9, 32]. The story can be, for example, in the name or in the background narrative of an artwork and its artist [17]. These descriptions provide semantic information that directly guides the observer's attention and offers a wider cultural and cognitive context in which the artwork is evaluated [17]. Stories can also be shared through other modalities, such as pictures or bodily gestures [31]. In empathic understanding, emotions are transferred from their original context to realistically felt events in an imagined story, where emotions are created and molded by events and scenarios, and by characters and their unique histories, thoughts, goals, and emotionally filled memories [17, 33].

There are significant differences between individuals in terms of their ability to feel empathy in different situations [10]. Simulation is most successful when the observer and the object are quite similar [7, 19]. We often feel and verbally express stronger empathy toward people we already care about or people whom we consider similar to our individual or group identities [7, 11, 19, 20, 34]. Emotions are often related to our own selves, and experiencing empathy may involve things that affect and possibly benefit the empathizer, in addition to the object of empathy [11]. In social interactions, we may use mental strategies that are based on our pre-existing opinions, beliefs, and knowledge, which benefit us and help us to fulfill our self-related goals and needs. This may skew our empathic understanding of another's experiences [19]. For example, art experts may distance themselves from the direct and automatic empathic bodily and emotional reactions that the work generates in order to focus on other aspects that they consider more important [17, 35].

Kesner and Horacek [17] propose that an individual's empathic response to an artwork depends on the interaction of five things: 1) the observer's ability to respond to the perceived experiences of others; 2) the observer's cultural-cognitive ability and the observer's experiences, skills, and knowledge that help understand art and cultural artifacts; 3) the observer's individual characteristics such as age, gender, and prior life experiences; 4) how closely and in what way the observer relates to the people represented in the artwork; and 5) the observer's psychosomatic state in the moment of perceiving. The character of the empathy experienced toward art can also significantly depend on how the observer moves around and physically perceives the artwork [17].

The phenomena of empathy and empathic understanding are complex and multidimensional concepts. Implementing theories of empathy in the practical work of designers is easier said than done. Designers face several challenges when using empathic understanding in their everyday working practices. In addition to the possible biases that may affect how empathy is felt, designers may, for example, be using too-superficial or too-narrow research methods, techniques, or tools, which may yield only surface-level snapshots or stereotypes of users [2, 8, 33, 36]. As many scholars have noted [see, e.g., 2, 8, 33, 36], it is not enough to put oneself, the designer, in the user's shoes and imagine how the designer would feel there, or to describe the user in a simple, non-dialogical story that can easily be misinterpreted. Designers are not all-knowing observers who stand apart from the user. It is insufficient for designers to define what is normal based on their own perspectives and lived experiences, so that the user's experience is not appreciated, or, in the worst-case scenario, is considered a spectacle. This makes empathy an ethical design issue [2, 33, 37]. Designers are human too. Like all humans, designers experience empathic understanding in different ways and forms, involving different processes, which can be influenced by many things, such as individual and situational factors.

2   Empathic Understanding in the Experience of Graffiti

Graffiti can be described as communicative cultural artifacts, and in some cases also as works of art, that are designed by their "writers" using special techniques and tools, such as spray paint, and that are experienced and judged by their perceivers [38–40]. Graffiti writers are like designers; graffiti are like technology designs; and the people who experience graffiti are like the people who interact with and experience any other designed thing. Thus, the empathic understanding of how people experience technology design can be investigated using other domains of design, including graffiti, as reference.

Two experiments were conducted to study what kind of perceptions, emotions, and thoughts people experience when they view graffiti. Both experiments took place during the Demolition Art Project [41] in late summer of 2016, where several graffiti and mural works were painted in the research location called the Petteri building in Kerava, Finland. All the graffiti assessed were large writings or interpretations of letters painted on walls. Some of the works also included a character or a figure. The participants were volunteers. Some were random passersby, and some were asked to participate by their friends (snowballing). All participants gave oral consent for participation before the experiment. Participants were rewarded for their participation with a movie ticket. The protocols from experiment 1 contain interesting unpublished data related to empathic understanding, which is the focus of this paper. In both experiments, the data were analyzed using applied thematic analysis [42] with Microsoft Excel version 16.41 software.

2.1   Experiment 1

Method *Subjects.* 19 people participated in the experiment (8 females, 11 males; age range: 13–63; mean age: 36.6 years), divided into two skill groups. The two groups consisted of ten laypeople (people who said that they knew little or nothing about graffiti) and nine experts (people who said that they knew a lot about graffiti, and of whom most, though not all, also created graffiti themselves).

Stimuli and Procedure. Participants individually assessed four graffiti and one mural painting, selected by the researcher. An example of an assessed graffiti work is shown in Fig. 1. A semi-structured interview was done with participants as they were thinking out loud looking at each graffito. Protocols were recorded with a hand-held recorder. The interview had nine questions:

- Questions 1–4: what kinds of thoughts, emotions, meanings, or stories does the work evoke in you?
- Question 5: is the work beautiful, ugly, or something else?
- Question 6: what about the work's style and colors?
- Question 7: what draws your attention in the work?

- Question 8: where could you imagine seeing it?
- Question 9: is it art?

Fig. 1. An example of an assessed graffiti work. Photo: Jouni Väänänen

Results. The thinking-aloud protocols were transcribed into text. Data were first classified into codes based on semantic units, which were then combined into larger categories. This analysis focused only on the type of content that relates to empathy manifested as understanding the mental content and actions of others, where the other could be either a person or an object such as the graffiti work itself. Some participants produced rich and lengthy descriptions, whereas some protocols were much shorter and shallower in their content. After analysis, several types of semantic content related to empathic understanding were found in the participant protocols. These were grouped into three themes: meaning for oneself and for others; evaluation of skills, techniques, and practices of the other and of oneself; and analogies, stories, and bodily feelings.

Meaning for Oneself and for Others. All 10 laypeople and 8 out of the 9 experts discussed the graffiti work's meaning for the self and how the work fits into the participant's subjective taste and preferences in art. However, 9 laypeople and 8 experts also reflected on what the graffiti could mean for and how it could be experienced by other people, such as the artist, members of the graffiti subculture, and laypeople such as "the granny next door".

The following excerpts from both a layperson and a graffiti expert are examples of how the graffiti were thought to be interpreted and experienced by other people.

"Interest, first of all in how these have been made, where these started from, and it would also be quite nice to hear what idea [the graffiti artist] had here, because there is some thought behind these for sure, but what is it? For me this is just something nice to look at." (Layperson)

"I have to say, I appreciate that this is a complex style, which to a layperson might look like there were only arrows there, here and there, but then again it is difficult to execute this in such a way that it seems logical even to the kind of person who has more experience with these things." (Graffiti expert)

Experts mentioned how the work may have been experienced by laypeople slightly more often than laypeople did (44 mentions by 8 experts versus 29 mentions by 6 laypeople). In general, many of the participants said that the work may be appreciated and experienced differently by other people because they have, for example, different interests, different past personal experiences, and theoretical graffiti-specific cultural and technical knowledge, as well as practical skills.

Evaluation of Skills, Techniques, and Practices of the Other and of Oneself. 7 out of the 10 laypeople and all the expert participants discussed the type and level of skills that may be required to make graffiti and that the artist may possess. Whether the artist was understood to have mastered or to lack special knowledge about graffiti aesthetics and practices was determined based on the work's visual details that the observers could perceive in the work. Skills were also evaluated based on the perception of the technical level of the work and by imagining or thinking what techniques and actions its execution may have required from the artist.

Technique and how the work was made were discussed by all participants by noting visual aspects of the work, such as its level of technical details or size, and then imagining how the work may have actually been done by the artist. These discussions were often supported by detailed descriptions of what kind of bodily movements and technical tools and practices would be required specifically to create graffiti, as the following extract illustrates:

"I'm looking at this technical execution, here the mastery of the jug [i.e., spray can] is so phenomenal, from thinner to thicker line, and the color gradations where three shades are mixed together. And this looks easy. I could imagine the guy dancing in front of this, making it in half an hour, when in reality it has taken hours. It looks easy even though it is anything but easy, even those shapes of the letters. [Text extracted by researcher] What I most notice as a letter painter is those letters, and can I read it and can I grasp the rhythm? And if there was music my other leg would begin to tap a beat, this just takes you away." (Graffiti expert)

The artists' techniques and methods were often compared to observers' own techniques and methods, especially (not surprisingly) in the case of experts. Subjective technique and doing were mentioned 47 times by 7 experts, compared to only 5 mentions by 2 laypeople. These participants discussed how they would themselves feel and experience the work if they were the artist. Some participants wondered how the work had been planned or how the idea for the work had been developed by the artist. Only 2 laypeople, but 7 out of the 9 experts, discussed how they would have come up with or planned the work themselves, basing their ideas on their own style and skills and on various possible scenarios and situations.

Analogies, Stories, and Bodily Feelings. All participants used different types of analogies, where they associated their perceptions of the empathized work or artist with other familiar or imagined characters, scripts, or situations in order to describe, explain, and understand the meanings, emotions, interests, motives, and possible actions of the empathized. Some participants elaborated on how the character or events displayed in the work reminded them of some movie or cartoon characters or sequence of events that the empathizer had experienced or had learned from, for example, reading graffiti magazines. In many cases, works or artists were associated with formats of analogous stories that described the past, the present, and the implications and intentions for the future. The stories also had emotional tones or moods associated with them. For example, a layperson participant described a graffiti character as an intentional agent with plans of its own: "This does not have any meaning for me, but I bet that guy there would like to do something with all these letters and these brown balls. Maybe he is moving them somewhere."

All participants described the visual properties of the works by drawing different kinds of visual analogies to how the work feels or is physically sensed in an analogous way to the observers' own bodily sensations. For example, a large graffito was described by a graffiti expert as being "cramped" in its place. The expert added that "fortunately there is some white in the borders, so that it gets space to breathe." Some participants explained that the work seemed to create a sense of movement or a sense of heaviness or lightness through the shape or the orientation of the work's visual elements. Perceivable properties such as shapes and colors were often compared to certain moods and emotional themes. For example, light and bright "candy colors" were said to make the work or its characters seem "happy or joyous." Many participants also paid attention to the facial expressions of the graffiti characters, where the expression made the character look, for example, "surprised" or "frightened," causing the observer to feel compassion for that character.

2.2 Experiment 2

Method. *Subjects.* 30 people participated in the experiment. One form was omitted from the results because the participant returned it empty, so the analysis focused on responses from 29 participants (19 females, 10 males; age range: 11–68; mean age: 39.2 years). There were 9 people who knew nothing about graffiti, 11 people who knew very little about graffiti, 6 who knew a fair bit about graffiti, and 3 who were graffiti experts (people who knew a lot about graffiti and some of whom also created graffiti themselves).

Stimuli and Procedure. Participants were asked to assess individually two graffiti works selected by the researcher (Figs. 2 and 3). They were asked to fill out a paper questionnaire with a pen regarding how they felt and thought about the graffiti while viewing them. One question asked, "Do you know who made this work? (Yes/No). Tell us something about the maker of this work. If you do not know the maker, describe what you think they could be like." There were two sets of 12 open-ended questions, 34 semantic scale questions, and 20 Likert scale questions in the questionnaire. However, only the question mentioned above was relevant for this paper about empathic understanding, and it is the one analyzed here. While assessing work #1, 22 participants wrote about how they imagined the artist. One of them knew who the artist was. While assessing work #2, 20 participants wrote about how they imagined the artist. One of them knew who the artist was. In general, the texts were quite short, ranging from one word to a couple of short sentences. This was probably because the questionnaires were quite long and the participants had to fill out the questionnaire with pen and paper, which took quite a lot of time (on average about 30–45 min) and effort.

Fig. 2. Graffiti work #1 assessed in experiment 2. Photo: Jouni Väänänen

Results. The paper questionnaires were transcribed into a digital format. Data were classified according to codes of semantic units, which were then grouped into larger categories. The ways the participants described the imagined other can be divided into four categories: age, gender, characteristics, and background.

Age. The assumed age of the artist varied from young to middle-aged. For work #1, 14 out of 29 participants mentioned age. 9 participants thought the artist was young or in their 20s; 2 people thought the artist was about 30; and 3 thought the artist was in their 40s or older. For work #2, only 6 people mentioned age. Of them, 3 participants thought the maker was 30–40 years old, and 3 people thought the maker was young or 20–30 years old.

Fig. 3. Graffiti work #2 assessed in experiment 2. Photo: Jouni Väänänen

Gender. Most of the participants who mentioned gender assumed that the artists of both works were male. For work #1, 11 participants mentioned gender. Of them, 8 people assumed the artist was male, and 2 people thought the artist could be either male or female. For work #2, only 7 people mentioned gender, and all assumed the artist was male.

Characteristics and Background. Participants described not only the artist's mental characteristics such as personality and behavior, but also external attributes, such as what the artist may look like or where they may live in. Participants also thought about background details regarding the artist's possible expertise and professional interests, such as possibly working in a visual arts field, being a skilled graffiti writer, or having an interest in sci-fi, cartoons, or graphic novels.

For work #1, 7 participants mentioned mental characteristics of the artist: being easy-going; being chill and funny and/or sensitive; thinking and being thought-provoking. Only 4 participants commented on the artist's external attributes like body shape or brown hair. 9 out of 10 participants thought the artist had a lot of experience with graffiti.

For work #2, 12 participants described 8 mental and 4 external attributes of the artist. The artist was described as someone who thinks a lot; brave and open to new experiences; having a sense of humor; and very imaginative. 4 participants commented on external attributes, such as the artist's looks or graffiti name. 7 participants thought the artist worked in a visual arts field or was interested in visual arts and graphic forms, and 2 participants mentioned that the artist was interested in sci-fi.

Stereotypical Descriptions of a Graffiti Artist. The participants' assumptions may be summarized as the following stereotypical descriptions of the artists.

For work #1, the artist may have been something between a young and unexperienced hip-hopper man or woman who grew up on the streets to a middle-class, middle-size, middle-aged but youthful man. The artist is highly proficient in graffiti and likes graphic novels or cartoons.

For work #2, the artist may have been something along the spectrum from a young man to a middle-aged, bearded, male graffiti artist. He works in a visual arts field and likes sci-fi.

There was more variation in the assumptions about the artist for work #1 than for work #2.

3 Discussion

In order to research empathic understanding in technology design, I studied in what ways and through what kind of content empathic understanding can emerge among different people when they view graffiti. To answer these questions, I conducted two experiments. In the first experiment, 19 participants were thinking aloud in a semi-structured interview while they were assessing five graffiti works. The interview included several questions asking the participants about how they thought and felt about the works. In the analysis phase, the participants were divided into two groups, laypeople and experts, based on their knowledge of and involvement in graffiti. In the second experiment, 30 participants evaluated two graffiti by filling out a paper questionnaire. Participants were asked what they thought the person who did the graffiti was like. Two-thirds of the participants knew little or nothing about graffiti, while the rest were graffiti experts.

The literature on empathy suggests that there are two ways that people understand and empathize with the other or the empathized, whether that other is another person or an object. One is via inference-based processes or mentalizing unobservable mental states and content, and the other is via embodied processes or identifying observable or imagined behavior (or "mechanizing") [43]. The results from the first experiment in this paper suggest that both processes of empathic understanding may be involved when people assess graffiti. The results from the second experiment suggest that people have stereotypical assumptions of others.

Based on the results from the first experiment, people have several ways or use several processes to gain empathic understanding of a graffiti work, the graffiti artist, and other viewers. These ways are compared to the observer's own bodily and mental states, characteristics, and preferences. The participants explained not only what the graffiti meant to them, but also what it may mean to someone else, such as the graffiti artist, a person who was part of the graffiti culture, or a layperson without much knowledge of graffiti. Thus, empathic understanding is related to how we understand ourselves, what we know or assume about others, and how we compare our own tastes and preferences, emotions, values, knowledge, and skills to those of others. Empathic understanding requires the understanding of mental states, mental information content, and behavior to be directed to a first-person view in the form of introspection, as well as to others. Both self-oriented and other-oriented mentalizing are necessary [8, 13].

The results suggest that participants as empathizers used both simulation and theorizing to gain empathic understanding of the other as the empathized. Simulation was expressed as imagining how they would themselves feel, think, and act in the place of the other. Theorizing was expressed by making inferences based either on folk-psychological information or on learned abstract concepts and sensorimotor, bodily practices to model what other people may think, feel and do in various situations.

Based on protocol analysis from the first experiment, the ways of understanding others include understanding the similarities and differences between the perceived or imagined bodies of the empathizer and the empathized, based on embodied processes. These can be described as imagining the felt emotions, sensations, and movements of the other. People perceive them either directly in the graffiti work as simulated bodily actions of the artist, as if the work or some character in it could itself sense or act, or by imagining one's own movements as if one were in the artist's place.

We can imagine how we would experience the physical dimensions and sensations that we perceive in the graffiti, thus feeling empathy toward the graffiti painting itself. We may also imagine from the visible traces left by spray cans what and how the artist might have thought and felt when they were creating the graffiti. In the first experiment, participants also evaluated how skilled the artist was by pondering what kind of physical actions and knowledge might be necessary to execute graffiti. In particular, the people who did graffiti themselves (graffiti experts) compared the artist's skills and technical mastery to their own skills and preferences.

In order to recognize the skillful actions and evaluate the skill level, the observer needs to have learned knowledge and theories regarding what skills are required in that specific domain. Thus, this kind of empathizing that is based on an embodied process. It requires more than just understanding the bodily movements in some prereflexive manner. The results from the first experiment suggest that there is another level to embodied processes, which is the observer's knowledge of learned sensory-motor patterns and practices, and which the observer uses to infer the bodily behavior and sensations of the other. To understand the goal-oriented actions of the other, the observer or empathizer must have a sense of what those goals might be. That requires not only imagining what kinds of goals the empathizer would themselves have in that situation, but also understanding the empathized and their individual and collective sociocultural settings, backgrounds, practices, norms, values, incentives, and other abstract concepts that relate to the empathized's specific domain of expertise. In other words, the mental information content that is stored in and retrieved from the declarative memory components seems to interact with the procedural memory components in the same system that also affects empathic understanding [28].

Protocol analysis for the first experiment also suggests that people create stories in order to explain and empathically understand events and individuals when assessing graffiti. These stories have themes and plots where different events are unfolding. They have characters and involve the observer's reasoning as to why those events or characters are the way they are. They also include speculations about where those characters came from and what they were about to do next. The characters in the graffiti assessed and the other perceived content were often understood as analogous to some familiar characters or learned narratives from, for example, popular culture. However, analogies were also drawn between, for example, a work's color scheme and certain sensations, emotional themes, or moods.

Stories bind something that is already known with new information, and in this way they create coherent narratives that help the storytellers to make sense of the world with its objects and situations and of the storytellers' own life events and experiences. This allows storytellers to share their own knowledge, values, and experiences with others [31, 32]. Stories may also display the existing knowledge and beliefs of the storyteller and of the social milieu that the storyteller participates in [7]. When in the second experiment the participants were asked to imagine what the graffiti artist would be like, four distinct themes emerged in the answers. These themes were age; gender; characteristics such as personality, lifestyle, or physical appearance; and background aspects such as the level of professionalism and interests. The responses presented some fairly consistent characteristics of "a graffiti artist" (e.g., either a young or a middle-aged man; a professional in graffiti or in a visual arts field). However, it is noteworthy that not all participants imagined the artist quite the same way. There was variation in, for example, whether the artist was as assumed to be young or old; whether they could be "either a man or a woman"; whether they were from a "middle-class" background or "grew up on the streets".

Not surprisingly, some people commented on the artists' interest in cartoons or sci-fi, as there was a Mickey-Mouse-like character in the first graffito, and visual elements that could easily be associated with popular science-fiction catalogues in the second graffito. However, most of the participants did not know who the artist actually was, so either there was something in the works suggesting that the artist was some specific kind of person, or the participants were drawing conclusions based on their own pre-existing knowledge and schemas. In the latter case, the evaluations may be based on the observer's own learned cultural stereotypes regarding who makes graffiti and what kind of graffiti they make. Most of the participants were laypeople and presumably did not have much personal experience of graffiti artists, and were less capable of picking out visual nuances and information cues from the graffiti than actual graffiti artists. They may have had to rely on their own assumptions of the typical artist, not on what they could decipher from the graffito, its style, and the artist's "handwriting." However, at least in experiment 2, there was little variation in the content of the participants' replies regarding how they imagined the artist. This suggests that laypeople and experts rely at least partly on the same general stereotypes, possibly because they lacked information from firsthand interactions and experiences with those particular artists, which would have helped them construct "individuated schemas" [44, p. 76] in their mental representations of those people. The participants could not base their evaluations on individuated schemas, but instead had to rely on "social scripts, narratives and social norms" [7, p. 132], which were constructed into certain stereotypes. These stereotypes are associated with membership in the specific social category of graffiti artists. This was necessary to improve the accuracy of empathic understanding and judgement of the other [44].

Overall, the following summary can be made based on the two experiments. There are four different ways of gaining empathic understanding:

1. Through embodied processes that simulate mechanistic or prereflexive motor movements and bodily similarities;

2. Through theorizing based on folk-psychological information applied to naïve interpretations of others' mental states, mental content, and intentions;
3. Through embodied processes, which include both procedural and declarative information and help recognize learned bodily skills and practices; and
4. Through theorizing based on learned knowledge and concepts applied in the form of stories or verbal descriptions.

These ways are similar to what has been suggested in the existing literature on empathic understanding [see, e.g., 7, 9, 12, 13]. They are also relevant in empathic understanding of works of art and graffiti [14, 16–18]. Furthermore, the analysis of the first experiment suggests that participants used both mental simulation and theorizing together, rather than individually, when they directed their attention to others. This supports the idea that people use hybrid mechanisms when mentalizing about others' mental states and behaviors [7, 9, 19]. An individual's assumptions about the other may follow some learned social scripts or schemas or stereotypes [7, 44].

Even though the two experiments presented in this paper support existing models and theories of mental content and empathic understanding processes, several concerns should be mentioned, which may affect the results. First of all, the number of participants was quite small. In the second experiment, the questionnaire was very long and tedious, and in addition, participants had to fill out the questionnaire by hand with pen and paper. As a result, the answers were very few and short. Thus, in the second experiment, the analysis is based on a very small sample size and a very small amount of data. In the first experiment, by contrast, people could talk out loud, and produced much more data in their protocols. Therefore, I recommend using thinking-aloud protocols rather than written forms as the research method when investigating people's empathic understanding. As a final concern, graffiti themselves may be quite a controversial, value-laden, or emotionally charged topic to some, which can skew what and how people feel, think, and say, both about the graffiti works and about the people involved in the graffiti culture.

4   Conclusions

In this paper I have discussed empathy in technology design, why it is important, and how ways of empathic understanding can be researched using graffiti to produce knowledge that supports technology designers' work. Empathic understanding is the ability to understand and predict the thoughts, feelings, mental states, and intentions of others. In this process, the observer or empathizer tries to perceive, recognize, and make sense of the past, present, and future mental states and experiences, feelings, thoughts, intentions, and actions of the other or empathized. Empathy is understanding what the other thinks and feels, but it is different from emotional contagion, which means actually feeling the same emotions as the other. For example, designers should be able to recognize and separate their own personal experiences and emotions from those of others. The emotions evoked by graffiti from experiment 1 are discussed elsewhere [40].

As Bennett and Rosner [2] suggest, designers need to be attuned to the differences in other people's bodies and social relationships, and to connect, share experiences with, and learn from those people. To do this, designers could investigate and use at least four ways of gaining empathic understanding, which I have presented in this paper. They are understanding others (whether people or objects) via embodied processes through bodily similarities and simulations; via folk-psychological inferences; via recognizing learned skills and bodily practices; and via inferences based on learned information such as knowledge and concepts. An empathizer needs to recognize and understand not only what kind of bodily sensations the empathized other may have, but also what kind of meanings different objects and contexts may have to the empathized. Thus, the empathizer needs to have some idea of the knowledge, beliefs, interests, characteristics, past life, future goals, and the social setting of the person they are observing and trying to understand, and of which things are important to that person [1, 2].

Technology designers also need to consider whose perspective they are embracing—their own or that of others—when they are developing their user understanding. Designers also need to be aware of their own and other people's thinking biases, such as what kind of stereotypes the observer or the observed might have. This could affect whether and how people feel empathy, and how this may affect the observer's understanding of the observed.

Acknowledgements. I would like to thank Jouni Väänänen, the project manager for the Demolition Art Project, where this study was conducted and my supervisors Pertti Saariluoma, Professor of Cognitive Science in University of Jyväskylä, Annika Waenerberg, Professor of Art History in University of Jyväskylä, and Johanna Silvennoinen, Postdoctoral Researcher. This research was supported by grants from the Finnish Cultural Foundation [grant number 00180743] and the University of Jyväskylä, Faculty of Information Technology. I have no conflicts of interest to disclose.

References

1. Saariluoma, P., Cañas, J., Leikas, J.: Designing for Life: A Human Perspective on Technology Development. Palgrave Macmillan, London (2016)
2. Bennett, C.L., Rosner, D.K.: The promise of empathy: design, disability, and knowing the "other." In: CHI 2019: Proceedings of the 2019 CHI Conference on Human Factors in Computing Systems, Paper no.: 298, pp. 1–13 (2019). https://doi.org/10.1145/3290605.330 0528
3. Hassenzahl, M.: User experience and experience design. In: The Encyclopedia of Human-Computer Interaction. Second edition. Interaction Design Foundation. https://www.intera ction-design.org/literature/book/the-encyclopedia-of-human-computer-interaction-2nd-ed. Accessed 26 Feb 2021
4. Hassenzahl, M., Tractinsky, N.: User experience—a research agenda. Behav. Inf. Technol. **25**(2), 91–97 (2006). https://doi.org/10.1080/01449290500330331
5. Hornbæk, K., Oulasvirta, A.: What is interaction? In: Proceedings of the 2017 CHI Conference on Human Factors in Computing Systems, pp. 5040–5052 (2017)
6. Lilienfeld, S.O., Sauvigné, K.C., Lynn, S.J., Cautin, R.L., Latzman, R.D., Waldman, I.D.: Fifty psychological and psychiatric terms to avoid: a list of inaccurate, misleading, misused, ambiguous, and logically confused words and phrases. Front. Psychol. **6**(1100), 1–15 (2015). https://doi.org/10.3389/fpsyg.2015.01100

7. Apperly, I.: Mindreaders: The Cognitive Basis of "Theory of Mind." Psychology Press, Taylor & Francis Group, Hove and New York (2011)
8. Dong, Y., Dong, H., Yuan, S.: Empathy in design: a historical and cross-disciplinary perspective. In: Baldwin, C. (ed.) AHFE 2017. AISC, vol. 586, pp. 295–304. Springer, Cham (2018). https://doi.org/10.1007/978-3-319-60642-2_28
9. Gallagher, S., Zahavi, D.: The Phenomenological Mind, 2nd edn. Routledge, London (2012)
10. Maibom, H.L.: Affective empathy. In: Maibom, H. (ed.) The Routledge Handbook of Philosophy of Empathy, pp. 22–32. Routledge, London and New York (2017)
11. May, J.: Empathy and intersubjectivity. In: Maibom, H. (ed.) The Routledge Handbook of Philosophy of Empathy, pp. 169–179. Routledge, London and New York (2017)
12. Thompson, E.: Empathy and consciousness. J. Conscious. Stud. 18(7–8), 196–221 (2011)
13. Goldman, A.I.: Joint Ventures: Mindreading, Mirroring, and Embodied Cognition. Oxford University Press, New York (2013)
14. Carroll, N.: Empathy and painting. In: Maibom, H. (ed.) The Routledge Handbook of Philosophy of Empathy, pp. 285–292. Routledge, London and New York (2017)
15. Currie, G.: Empathy for objects. In: Coplan, A., Goldie, P. (eds.) Empathy: Philosophical and Psychological Perspectives, pp. 82–98. Oxford University Press, Oxford (2011)
16. Freedberg, D., Gallese, V.: Motion, emotion and empathy in esthetic experience. Trends Cogn. Sci. 11(5), 197–203 (2007). https://doi.org/10.1016/j.tics.2007.02.003
17. Kesner, L., Horáček, J.: Empathy-related responses to depicted people in art works. Front. Psychol. 8(228), 1–16 (2017). https://doi.org/10.3389/fpsyg.2017.00228
18. Gernot, G., Pelowski, M., Leder, H.: Empathy, Einfühlung, and aesthetic experience: the effect of emotion contagion on appreciation of representational and abstract art using fEMG and SCR. Cogn. Process. 19(2), 147–165 (2017). https://doi.org/10.1007/s10339-017-0800-2
19. Spaulding, S.: Cognitive empathy. In: Maibom, H. (ed.) The Routledge Handbook of Philosophy of Empathy, pp. 13–21. Routledge, London and New York (2017)
20. Zahavi, D.: Simulation, projection and empathy. Conscious. Cogn. 17, 514–522 (2008). https://doi.org/10.1016/j.concog.2008.03.010
21. Fuchs, T.: The brain—a mediating organ. J. Conscious. Stud. 18(7–8), 196–221 (2011)
22. Ratcliffe, M.: Phenomenology, neuroscience and intersubjectivity. In: Dreyfus, H., Wrathall, M.A. (eds.) A Companion to Phenomenology and Existentialism, pp. 329–345. Blackwell Publishing, Maiden (2006)
23. Taylor, J.E.T., Witt, J.K., Grimaldi, P.J.: Uncovering the connection between artist and audience: viewing painted brushstrokes evokes corresponding action representations in the observer. Cognition 125(1), 26–36 (2012). https://doi.org/10.1016/j.cognition.2012.06.012
24. Lohmar, D.: Mirror neurons and the phenomenology of intersubjectivity. Phenomenol. Cogn. Sci. 5, 5–16 (2006). https://doi.org/10.1007/s11097-005-9011-x
25. Leder, H., Nadal, M.: Ten years of a model of aesthetic appreciation and aesthetic judgments: the aesthetic episode—developments and challenges in empirical aesthetics. Br. J. Psychol. 105(4), 443–464 (2014). https://doi.org/10.1111/bjop.12084
26. Hofstede, G., Hofstede, G.J., Minkov, M.: Cultures and Organizations: Software for the Mind, 3rd edn. McGraw-Hill Education, New York (2010)
27. Bassett, D.S., Yang, M., Wymbs, N.F., Grafton, S.T.: Learning-induced autonomy of sensorimotor systems. Nat. Neurosci. 18(5), 744–751 (2015). https://doi.org/10.1038/nn.3993
28. Wolpert, D.M., Diedrichsen, J., Flanagan, J.R.: Principles of sensorimotor learning. Nat. Rev. Neurosci. 12(12), 739–751 (2011). https://doi.org/10.1038/nrn3112
29. Collins, H.M., Evans, R.: Rethinking Expertise. University of Chicago Press, Chicago (2007)
30. O'Connor, F.V.: Authenticating the attribution of art: connoisseurship and the law in the judging of forgeries, copies, and false attributions. In: Spencer, R.D. (ed.) The Expert Versus the Object: Judging Fakes and False Attributions in the Visual, pp. 3–27. Oxford University Press, New York (2004)

31. Shialos, M.: Human storytelling. In: Shackelford, T.K., Weekes-Shackelford, V.A. (eds.) Encyclopedia of Evolutionary Psychological Science, pp. 1–4. Springer, Cham (2017). https://doi.org/10.1007/978-3-319-16999-6_1074-1

32. McAdams, D.P.: How stories found a home in human personality. In: Goodson, I., Antikainen, A., Sikes, P., Andrews, M. (eds.) The Routledge International Handbook on Narrative and Life History, pp. 34–48. Routledge, Oxon and New York (2017)

33. Wright, P., McCarthy, J.: Empathy and experience in HCI. In Proceedings of the SIGCHI Conference on Human Factors in Computing Systems, April 2008, pp. 637–646 (2008)

34. Feyaerts, K., Oben, B., Lackner, H.K., Papousek, I.: Alignment and empathy as viewpoint phenomena: the case of amplifiers and comical hypotheticals. Cogn. Linguist. **28**(3), 485–509 (2017). https://doi.org/10.1515/cog-2016-0109

35. Leder, H., Gerger, G., Brieber, D., Schwarz, N.: What makes an art expert? Emotion and evaluation in art appreciation. Cogn. Emot. **28**(6), 1137–1147 (2014). https://doi.org/10.1080/02699931.2013.870132

36. Siegel, D., Dray, S.: The map is not the territory: empathy in design. Interactions **26**(2), 82–85 (2019). https://doi.org/10.1145/3308647

37. Heylighen, A., Dong, A.: To empathise or not to empathise? Empathy and its limits in design. Des. Stud. **65**, 107–124 (2019). https://doi.org/10.1016/j.destud.2019.10.007

38. Myllylä, M.: Graffiti as a palimpsest. SAUC—Street Art Urban Creat. Sci. J. **4**(2), 25–35 (2018). https://doi.org/10.25765/sauc.v4i2.141

39. Myllylä, M.: From experiencing sites of past to the future of the Demolition Man, and how graffiti fits to all. UXUC—User Exp. Urban Creat. Sci. J. **1**(1), 26–37 (2019)

40. Myllylä, M.: The good, the bad and the ugly graffiti. In: Rousi, R., Leikas, J., Saariluoma, P. (eds.) Emotions in Technology Design: From Experience to Ethics. HIS, pp. 87–104. Springer, Cham (2020). https://doi.org/10.1007/978-3-030-53483-7_6

41. Demolition Art Project: Taiteen kotitalo sijaitsee Keravalla. http://www.purkutaide.com. Accessed 2 Dec 2020

42. Guest, G., MacQueen, K.M., Namey, E.E.: Applied Thematic Analysis. SAGE Publications, Thousand Oaks (2012)

43. Spunt, R.P., Satpute, A.B., Lieberman, M.D.: Identifying the what, why, and how of an observed action: an fMRI study of mentalizing and mechanizing during action observation. J. Cogn. Neurosci. **23**(1), 63–74 (2011). https://doi.org/10.1162/jocn.2010.21446

44. Lewis, K.L., Hodges, S.D.: Empathy is not always as personal as you may think: the use of stereotypes in empathic accuracy. In: Decety, J. (ed.) Empathy: From Bench to Bedside, pp. 73–84. MIT Press, Cambridge, MA (2012)

Voyages Along the Star Paths: Capturing Calendrical Cycles from Kauai to Bali

Vibeke Sørensen[1], J. Stephen Lansing[2,3]([✉]), and Nagaraju Thummanapalli[1]

[1] School of Art, Design and Media, Nanyang Technological University,
Singapore, Singapore
vsorensen@ntu.edu.sg
[2] Santa Fe Institute, Hyde Park Road, Santa Fe New Mexico Complexity Science
Hub Vienna, Josefstädter Street 39, 1080 Wien, Austria
[3] School of Anthropology, University of Arizona, Tucson, AZ, USA

Abstract. Systems for the representation of temporal cycles play a vital role in all cultures, but they seldom figure prominently in studies of heritage. Anthropologists are often frustrated by he lumping together and dismissal of nonwestern concepts of time as merely "cyclical time", interpreted as changelessness or the absence of progress. Here we compare two of the most complex and sophisticated calendrical systems known to anthropology, from the islands of Bali and Hawaii. The sheer complexity of these concepts and their intimate relationship to astronomical phenomena make them very difficult to compare using the scholar's traditional toolkit of text and images. But they are admirably suited to immersive digital media. As well as facilitating descriptive exposition, real-time computer animation, music programming and other digital technology opens new avenues for research on the relationship of the abstract structure of calendrical systems to polyrhythms in music and other aspects of the phenomenology of time consciousness.

Keywords: Immersive digital media · Cyclical time · Gamelan music · Polynesian navigation · Kauai and bali

1 Introduction: Digital Media in the Service of Anthropology

Anthropologists struggle to convey the sophistication of nonwestern concepts of time to Western audiences. The idea that Western calendars express a concept of time as linear is readily acknowledged, along with the idea of progress. The association of progress with Western calendars is often contrasted with cyclical time in nonwestern cultures, implying that they remained mired in an endless unchanging present. We find this view of nonwestern cultures as "peoples without history" in the writings of Hegel and Marx, and it remains influential today among social scientists. Glossing "cyclical time" as changelessness or the absence

© Springer Nature Switzerland AG 2021
M. Rauterberg (Ed.): HCII 2021, LNCS 12794, pp. 296–317, 2021.
https://doi.org/10.1007/978-3-030-77411-0_20

of progress creates a superficial binary contrast with linear (historical, progressive) time as a key difference between the West and the Rest, in which cyclical time means merely the absence of change.

Anthropologists are often frustrated by this lumping together and dismissal of nonwestern concepts of time. Broadly speaking there are two responses. One is the analysis of the actual workings of nonwestern calendars, often in conjunction with archaeoastronomy. The second is phenomenological: how do different conceptions of time affect people's understandings of themselves and the world? A powerful example is archaeologist Vernon Scarborough's analysis of the role of time in the ancient cities of the Near East, contrasted with the "civilizations without cities" in the tropics. As Scarborough shows, the ancient Khmer and Maya could dispense with cities by creating monumental ceremonial centers where social life was scheduled by calendrical cycles. [2] Cities concentrate people in space to enable complex institutions to emerge. Tropical civilizations without cities are organized by temporal cycles, enabling them to sustain complex institutions without concentrating their populations into ecologically unsustainable urban centers. For civilizations like the Maya and the Khmer, "cyclical time" involved the application of astronomical observations to situate human activities within comprehensive models of the cosmos.

Our goal in this project is to use digital technology to convey the analytical power and functional significance of models of cyclical time on two island cultures, Kauai and Bali. The two islands share a distant historical connection: they were settled by Austronesian-speaking peoples thousands of years ago and consequently share both genetic and linguistic ancestry. That this connection exists is remarkable: the two islands are separated in space by 10,000 km of ocean. The reason for pairing them here is that despite this attenuation of cultural contact, the Hawaiians and the Balinese used many of the same ideas to create strikingly different yet astonishingly powerful models of time that were of fundamental importance to their cultures. Our intention is to explore the capacities of digital technology to bring these models to life. To do so we relate the workings of the calendars to their expression in the phenomenology of time consciousness, their relationship to other technologies and the ways they bring order to experience.

Thus our target is only incidentally the abstract mathematical beauty of the calenders; the deeper goal is to explore their relationship to music and other cultural phenomena. Part of this project has already been realized in an animation of the Balinese calendar, translated into music and film, which was the centerpiece of a multimedia installation by ETH Zurich at the Sharjah Triennale in 2020. In this paper we will explore how this piece of the story can be fitted into a more comprehensive exploration of the phenomenology of cyclical time in traditional Bali and Kauai, using digital technology.

Fig. 1. The Pleiades star cluster, observed from the Hubble telescope. NASA and the Space Telescope Science Institute (STScI). https://hubblesite.org/contents/news-releases/2004/news-2004-20.

2 Beginnings: The Luni-Solar Calendars

The representation of astronomical ideas such as luni-solar and planetary cycles in the ancient monuments of Asia such as the Khmer civilization of Angkor are well known. They still play a vital role in the living culture of Bali. Whereas the months of the European Gregorian and Julian calendars only approximate the

Fig. 2. Appearance of the Pleiades at due north just after sunset (7:15 pm), observed above a temple at Sembiran on the north coast of Bali on Feb 20, one month before the vernal equinox. This precise observation enables the priests to calculate the passage of a sidereal year (a month later, the Pleiades have moved to the west). Priests of the temple send messengers to the supreme water temple, Pura Ulun Danu Batur on the crater rim of Mount Batur, to announce this observation. The temple priests then send messages across Bali that the next new moon will mark the end of the year, and the harvest rites at the temple on the crater rim will culminate on the next full moon. Credit: Star map created by V. Sorensen with Stellarium.

lunar cycle, the Balinese reduce their 30 day lunar calendar (pangelong) by one day each 63rd solar day, and thereby keep it closely aligned with the lunar cycle of 29 days 12 h 44 min. The European calenders do not make this correction and consequently the named months are not synchronized with the actual phases of the moon. The Balinese also keep accurate track of the solar year, by observing the rising of the Pleiades from a temple on the north coast of Bali. This method of calculating the passage of years was used by many ancient cultures, including the Polynesians. The Balinese use the Pleiades to count years, and add an extra month every 2–3 years to keep their lunar months from drifting out of alignment with the seasons and the passage of solar years.

The volcanoes that dominate the landscapes of Bali and Kauai block the view to the north except from the north coast. On both islands, in precolonial times observations of the Pleiades were made from temples on the north coast to time the arrival of the new year.[1] In Bali one such temple continues to perform

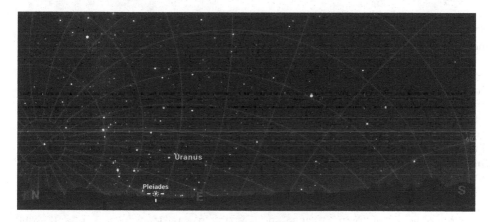

Fig. 3. Rising of the Pleiades observed from the heiau (temple) Ka-Ulu-o-Pa'oa on the North Coast of Kauai just after sunset on November 18 2020. The acronychal rising of the Pleiades constellation (Hawaiian Makali'i or "Little Eyes"), in which it becomes visible in the ENE immediately after sunset, heralded the beginning of the Makahiki season of four lunar months. The Makahiki was a season of rituals in honor of the god Lono, taking place at the time of the winter rains around the December solstice, with presentations of harvest offerings in the temples (Clive Ruggles.2009. Astronomy, Oral Literature and Landscape in Ancient Hawai'i. Archaeoastronomy; Fall 1999; 14, 2; ProQuest pg. 33. NASA and the Space Telescope Science Institute (STScI) Created using @Stellarium.)

---

[1] Archaeologist Patrick Kirch surveyed 23 heiau in Maui and found that "The east north east cluster of orientations may be related to either the summer solstice sunrise or the rising of the Pleiades. In fact the acronychal rising of this asterism determined the onset of the Makahiki season and the new year, this group of temples may be dedicated to the god Lono, who was linked to the annual rising of the Pleiades." César Esteban, "Astronomical Monuments in Polynesia and Micronesia", in Helaine Selin, ed., Encyclopedia of the History of Science, Technology and Medicine in Non-Western Cultures. Springer 2008, 287.

Fig. 4. Heiau (temple) Ka-Ulu-o-Pa'oa on the North Coast of Kauai. Orientation is north-south and east-west. Traditions recorded from early in the twentieth century identify it as associated with the goddess Laka, patroness of dance and younger sister of Pele. The alignment of the temple with respect to astronomical observation was investigated by Clive Ruggles, who concluded "Concentrating on what can actually be seen from the ground, it is still possible to accept as significant that the southwesterly aliginment from Ka-Ulu-o-Pa'oa was solsticial, although to a much lower precision: the two clear, distant landmarkls of the Makua-iki cliffs and Lehua framing the setting Sun at and around the December solstice were, and still are, a spectacular sight from this platform." Astronomy, Oral Literature, and Landscape in Ancient Hawai'i. Ruggles, Clive Archaeoastronomy; Fall 1999; 14, 2:page 63. ProQuest pg. 33

this function in the village of Sembiran (Fig. 2). In Kauai there is a temple (heiau) called Ka-Ulu-o-Pa'oa on the north coast where similar observations of the Pleiades were probably made (Figs. 4, 5 and 6).

Intriguingly, both the physical layout of the temples and their cultural functions are very similar on the two islands (Fig. 5). On both islands, these temples consist of rectangular platforms with stone walls, enclosing upright stones to which the gods are invited to alight to receive offerings timed to thc lunar calendar. From an architectural perspective, the Balinese temples to the Hindu gods are very different from the Hindu temples of South Asia, which have varied architectural styles and are usually thought to be permanent abodes of individual gods. In the South Asian temples there is no comparable lunar cycle of annual harvest rituals.

However, the Balinese temples are very similar in form and function to the rectangular marae of Oceania and the heiau of Hawaii. Harvest offerings are placed on temporary wooden altars facing the stone thrones of the visiting gods. After the rituals of the full moon are concluded, the gods are invited to depart. The key function of the sea temples used for observing the stars is to send

Fig. 5. Close-up view of the Ka-Ulu-o-Pa'oa heiau on the North Coast of Kauai. The shorter rock wall pointing out from the cliff is oriented due north and measures 5.57 m. The longer wall perpendicular to it is oriented east-west where they join, and measures 16.08 m.

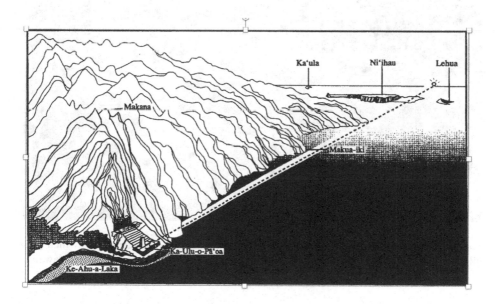

Fig. 6. Three dimensional plan of the Ka-Ulu-o-Pa'oa heiau on the Na Pali coast of north Kauai, showing the alignment to the islands of Ni'ihau and Lehua. After Meech and Warther (1996: Fig. 1).

Fig. 7. A Balinese temple. The open rectangular plan enclosing shrines on which gods will be invited to alight during the temple rites at the full moon, is similar to Hawaiian heiau temples.

messages to other major temples announcing the end of the year, which triggers the harvest festivals at the next full moon. These similarities in the form and function of the temples and luni-solar calendars are remarkable, in light of the vast distances of space and time that separate Bali from Kauai.

Archaeologists have documented the precise alignment of Polynesian temples to express this cosmological knowledge. Vivid realizations of this re-invention of time are found in the heiau of Kauai, the most distant Hawaiian island. The key alignment is observable at the winter solstice on the northern Na Pali coast. Recent ethnohistorical research on oral histories and chants surviving to the nineteenth century, such as the "Western Islands Chant", provides a context for analyzing the heiau orientations and alignments on Kauai. Heiau ceremonies including hula may have been timed with respect to the circuit of Venus. The alignment of the summit of Wai'ale'ale on Kauai to the nearby chain of islands on the June solstice sunset and the December solstice sunrise is perhaps the most visual and historical realization of this ancient Hawaiian vision by which they succeeded in "retaining the harmony of their gods, the earth, the sea and the sky" (Fig. 6).

3   Star Paths and Navigation

The astronomical observations of the Balinese were confined to the cycles of the sun, moon and the Pleiades. Their interest in calendars and time took a different turn, towards abstract models of cyclical time, as we will see below. But the seasonal alignment of the stars took on enormous importance for the ancestors of the Hawaiians, who used their knowledge of the sky to enable voyages across the Pacific lasting for weeks. The first phase of these journeys took place in what is called "Near Oceania", defined as the region east of the Malay archipelago where one is never entirely out of sight of land, at least on a clear day. These conditions ended in Micronesia, where the colonizing voyages halted for something like a thousand years. Subsequent voyages into "Far Oceania" were made possible by the invention of "star path" compasses by the Micronesians as their primary navigational tool (Fig. 9).

Each star has a specific declination, and can give a bearing for navigation as it rises or sets. Polynesian voyagers would set a heading by a star near the horizon, switching to a new one once the first rose too high. Each sequence of rising stars formed a star path, which would be memorized for each route (Figs. 8, 9, 10, 11 and 12). The latitude of islands could also be determined by the position of known stars at their zenith above the canoe at midnight[2] The latitudes of specific islands were known, and the technique of "sailing down the latitude" was used: "Point out a star to him and he would tell you the islands to which that star would lead you, if you steered your canoe toward the point where it rose or set at the horizon. He could also point out the other stars which followed it along the same diurnal path across the sky, and which could be used as bow star after it had set. He could likewise tell you what stars stood in the zenith over a given island, so that if you sailed directly south until those stars passed nightly across your zenith, you would know that you had reached

---

[2] Charles Nainoa Thompson, Hawaiian Star Compass. http://archive.hokulea.com/ ike/hookele/star_compasses.html. For a clear explanation see http://archive. hokulea.com/ike/hookele/celestial_sphere.html.

the same latitude as that of your destination." For example, the zenith star above Hawaii is Arcturus, enabling navigators to search for it along latitude 20° N.[3] Mastery of these astronomical cycles enabled colonizing canoes to reach the Hawaiian islands from the Society Islands (circa 1025–1120 C.E.) and the Marquesas (circa 1100–1200 C.E.), a distance of about 4000 km.[4]

4   The Three Calendars of the Balinese

As noted above, the Balinese keep accurate track of the lunar month with their pangelong calendar, which numbers 15 days of the waxing moon, 15 days of the waning moon, and subtracts every 63rd day, called ngunalatri (Sanskrit for "minus one night"). To calculate the solar year, the priests of a temple on the north coast in the village of Sembiran observe the appearance of the Pleiades at sunset (7 pm) one month before the vernal equinox. Priests of the temple send messengers to the supreme water temple, Pura Ulun Danu Batur on the crater rim of Mount Batur, to announce this observation. The temple priests then send messages across Bali that the next new moon will mark the end of the year, and the harvest rites will culminate on the next full moon.[5]

In addition to these two calendars, the Balinese also make extensive use of an unusual calendar called *tika*, the most mathematically complex of all traditional calenders. It has many functions in Balinese life. For example, the *tika* calendar is the principal instrument used by the farmers to manage staggered irrigation flows into their terraced rice fields [3]. The *tika* consists of a permutational calendar of 10 concurrent weeks, which vary in duration from 1 to 10 days. It is depicted in wooden or painted grids resembling matrices, that show 210 days arranged in 30 seven-day weeks depicted as columns. The reason for the otherwise arbitrary choice of 210 days may be related to the duration of the primary crop of native rice, which is also 210 days. Each of the 30 weeks has a name, and most Balinese can easily recall the names of the weeks from memory. But this is only the first and simplest classification of time portrayed on the *tika*. In addition to these 30 seven-day weeks, the tika also keeps track of nine other weeks, each of different lengths. Thus there is a three day week, consisting of the days Pasah, Beteng and Kajeng, which repeat without pause. The three day week is concurrent with the seven day week, so that if today is Sunday on the 7 day week, it will also be one of the days of the 3 day week. Symbolic notations (lines, dots, crosses etc.) are used to superimpose the days of the three day week on the grid of 30 seven day weeks displayed on the tika. Eight more weeks are also included in the tika, which range in duration from one to ten days. The 8 day week or *Astawara*, for

---

[3]   Maud Makemson. 1938. Hawaiian Astronomical Concepts. American Anthropologist New Series, Vol. 40, No. 3 (Jul. - Sep., 1938), pp. 370–383.

[4]   Janet M. Wilmshurst, Terry L. Hunt, Carl P. Lipo, and Atholl J. Anderson. "High-precision radiocarbon dating shows recent and rapid initial human colonization of East Polynesia", PNAS, vol. 108 no. 5, doi: 10.1073/pnas.1015876108.

[5]   Lansing, J. S. 2006 Perfect order: recognizing complexity in Bali. Princeton, NJ: Princeton University Press.

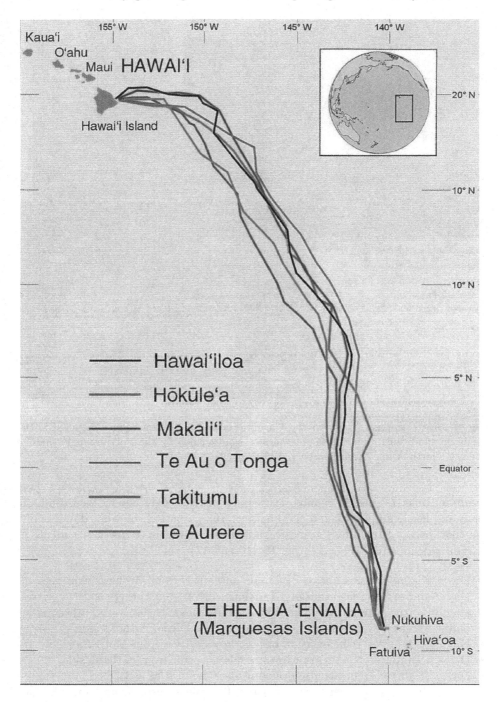

Fig. 8. Compass orientations for voyages from Marquesas to Hawaii shpwing stars used for navigation. Hokule'a (Arcturus) is at the zenith above Hawaii, enabling navigators to search for it along latitude 20° N. http://www.hokulea.com/education-at-sea/polynesian-navigation/polynesian-non-instrument-wayfinding/estimating-position/

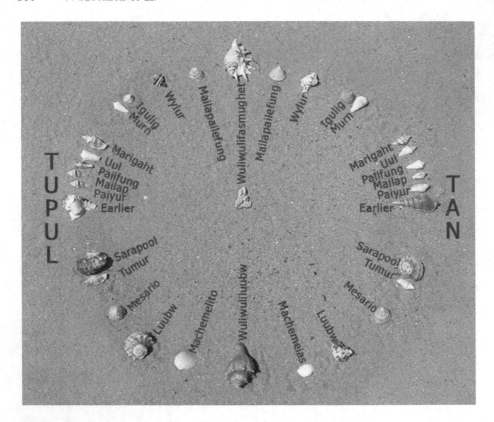

Fig. 9. Star Compass taught in the Caroline Islands with star names depicted with shells on sand, with Satawalese star names, as described by the Polynesian Voyaging Society. North is up. Original archived by Webcite.

example, consists of eight named days. Each of these days has its own use and meaning. For example, when a child is born, the parents check what day it is on the tika, because the infant's Astawara birthday is a clue to his or her identity in their previous life: (Figs. 13, 14, 15, 16 and 17)

- Day 1 (Sri) -> reincarnation of female ancestress from Mother's side
- Day 2 (Indra) -> reincarnation of male ancestor from Father's side
- Day 3 (Guru) -> reincarnation of brother of male ancestor from Father's side
- Day 4 (Yama) -> reincarnation of male ancestor from Father's side
- Day 5 (Ludra) -> reincarnation of female ancestress from Mother's side
- Day 6 (Brahma) -> reincarnation of male ancestor from Father's side
- Day 7 (Kala) -> reincarnation of someone who died as a child
- Day 8 (Indra) -> reincarnation of sister of female ancestor from Mother's side

5   Structure of the Tika Calendar

Each of the 210 cells in the tika calendar represents a day on each of the ten concurrent weeks. The idea is not unlike "Friday the 13th", a day that is special in the Anglo-American calendar marked by the intersection of two cycles, the week and the month. On the tika, there is a one-day week that consists of a single day, Luang. In principal, every day is Luang, but there are exceptions where the one day slot is empty. As we will explain below, we suggest that the reason for such exceptions has to do with the harmonies created by the concurrent cycles of days, which resemble the cyclical (polyrhythmic) musical patterns of Balinese gamelan music (Fig. 10).

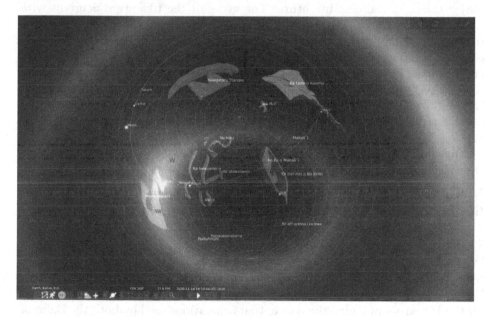

Fig. 10. Stars and constellations used by Polynesian navigators, showing the paths they travel in the night sky from dusk until morning, seen from Kailua on the east coast of Kauai on November 18, 2020.

There is also a two day week, consisting of two days, Menge and Pepet, which follow in an endless progression. The first day of the tika calendar is Day One (Menge) of the two day week, Day One (Pasah) of the three day week, and so forth. However, weeks 4 and 10 begin later in their respective cycles. When the days of the weeks are played as musical notes, this offset transforms the calendar from a monotonous sequence of notes to one that has a compelling complex structure.

The tika calendar enables groups of farmers who share a common water source to organize complex interlocking irrigation schedules, composed of varying combinations of water turns and planting schedules, and is the main instrument for irrigation management. Over the centuries, the uses of this calendar have expanded to encompass many other phenomena besides irrigation, including musical notation and cosmology. In Bali, the concept of nested cycles was extended to personal identity through the adoption of teknonyms (in which a person's name changes at each step in the life cycle, as they become parents, grandparents and great-grandparents) and birth order names, which cycle from first to fourth born and then repeat (thus the same birth order name is used for the first and fifth born child in a family). Similarly, Balinese literature is full of references to temporal cycles, and the regularity of cyclical progressions is a major theme in Balinese literature. The cycles of the tika are concurrent with the lunar months and solar years in the luni-solar Icaka calendar. The consistent application of this abstract notion to so many aspects of the Balinese world contributed to a mental and physical landscape of compelling perceptible coherence. Human lives, social life and the cosmos are all experienced as composed of interlocking cyclical patterns. These are realized not only in the movements of the moon and stars, but in the intricate patterns formed by the cycles of water flows and flooding in the irrigation systems that descend the slopes of the volcanoes. These uses of cyclical time, connecting the Balinese with the terrestrial world, offer a vivid contrast with the Polynesian navigator's focus on the night sky (Fig. 21).

6   Discussion: Cycles, Polyrhythms and the Phenomenology of Time

We have just begun to investigate whether the cycles of time that comprise the Star Paths are related to structures in Hawaiian music or other polyrhythms. We have seen that the same astronomical cycles - the moon, the sun and most of all the Pleiades - provided the conceptual foundations used by both the Balinese and the Hawaiians to build abstract models of cyclical time. We have also seen that these models became practical tools, vital adaptations to challenges such as navigating Oceania, or managing complex irrigation schedules on which dozens of neighboring villages on the slopes of Balinese volcanoes depended for their livelihood. We further saw that in the Balinese case, cyclical patterns became objectified ideas embedded in their experience of music and social life. These would have become familiar to all Balinese from childhood, as part of their experience of their kinship system, calendrical rituals, irrigation scheduling and gamelan music. Did something similar occur in Hawaiian culture? Or was the knowledge of star paths and their uses confined to priests and navigators? And might music have played a role in both cultures, by giving perceptible expression to the underlying concepts of time cycles?

Fig. 11. On November 18 at dawn, the Pleiades (Makali'i) rise in the east at dawn, signalling the beginning of the Makahiki season of four lunar months.

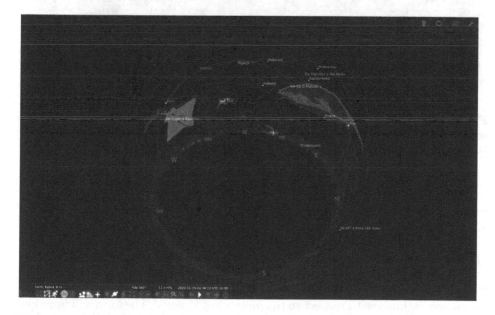

Fig. 12. On November 18, the Pleiades (Makali'i) are due north at midnight, signalling the beginning of the Makahiki season of four lunar months

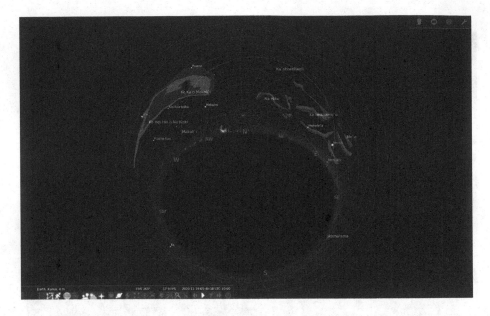

Fig. 13. On November 18 at dusk, the Pleiades (Makali'i) set in the west.

Fig. 14. A section of the days of the (tika) calendar colored as notes on the pentatonic scale. The first day of the first week is at the top left corner. Immediately below it is the second day of the first week. Credit: Guy S. Jacobs

We offer the hypothesis that the answer may lie in the role of temples in Bali and Kauai. Consider the Ka-Ulu-o-Pa'oa and Ke- Ahu-a-Laka heiau complex on Kauai's north coast (Figs. 4, 5 and 6). This temple complex was famous as a school for dance and music. Performers trained in these arts brought them to the festivals at the temples located in each chiefdom around the island, like the Poliahu temple in eastern Kauai (Fig. 18). Archaeoastronomers speculate that "the historical evidence from Ke- Ahu-a-Laka may even suggest that hula ceremonies were timed with respect to the motions of Venus".[6] The form and function of these calendrical harvest rites may be compared to the rituals performed in

---

[6] Ruggles op.cit. 2007:78.

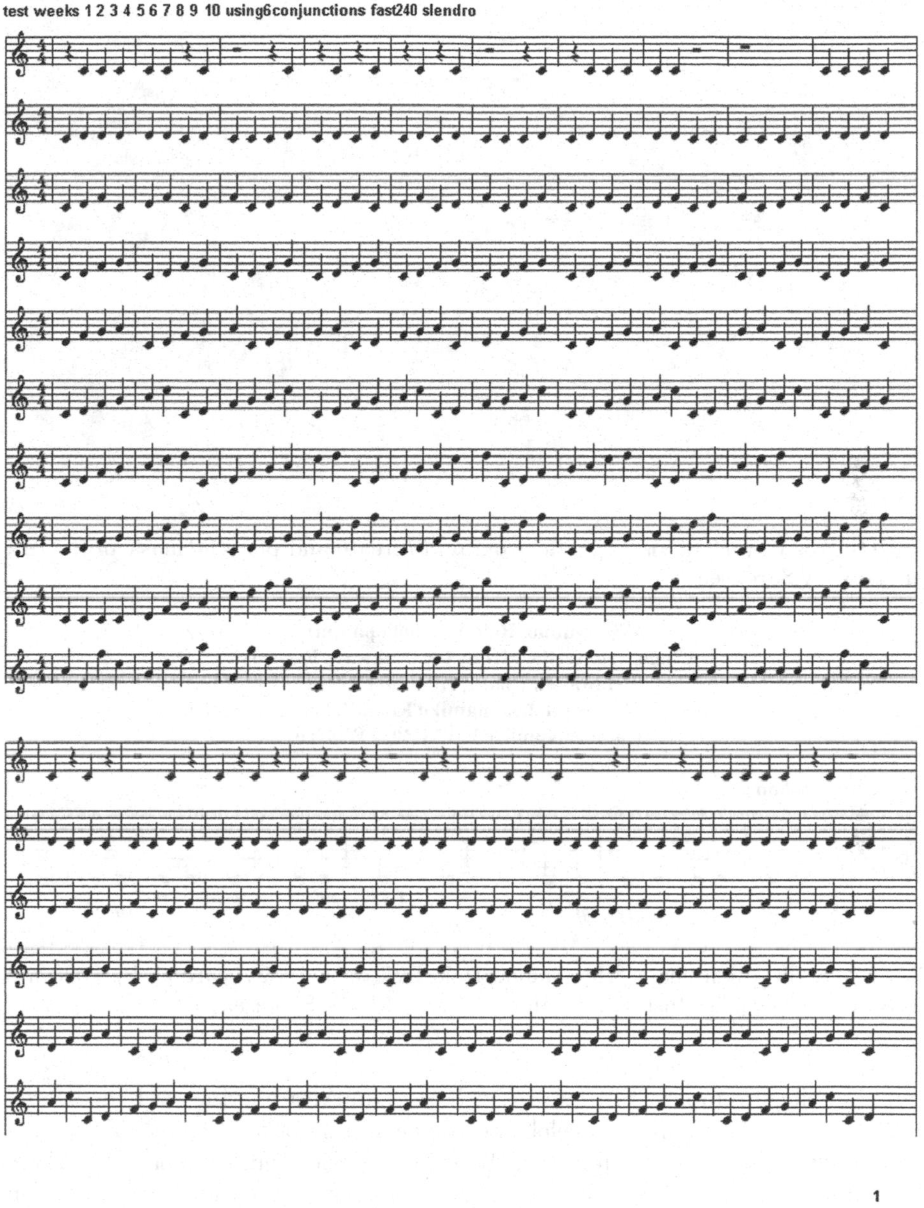

test weeks 1 2 3 4 5 6 7 8 9 10 using6conjunctions fast240 slendro

Fig. 15. First part of a musical score for the *tika* calendar, by Guy S. Jacobs

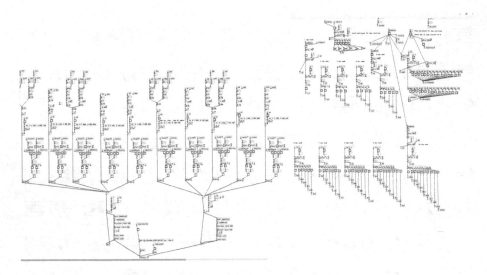

Fig. 16. The PureData visual music program to create and play the music of the tika calendar, by Sorensen.

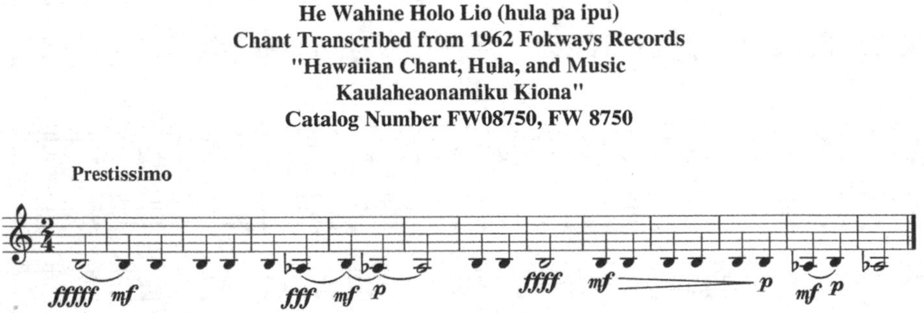

He Wahine Holo Lio (hula pa ipu)
Chant Transcribed from 1962 Fokways Records
"Hawaiian Chant, Hula, and Music
Kaulaheaonamiku Kiona"
Catalog Number FW08750, FW 8750

Prestissimo

Fig. 17. A Hawaiian chant "He Wahine Holo Lio" on a 1962 recording by Folkways Records (Smithsonian Institution) and transcribed by V.Sorensen

Balinese village temples (Fig. 19). In both cases, harvest offerings were dedicated to the gods in the temples to celebrate the beginning of a new year. They were accompanied by dances, recitations, chants and music. Temples were sites where the order of cyclical time was dramatized and experienced as polyrhythms in various forms, from the timing of the rites themselves to the dances and music performed by the people. Perhaps then, as in Bali, the polyrhythms encoded in Hawaiian star paths and calendrical systems found expression in music.

Fig. 18. The temple (heiau) of Poliahu in east Kauai, where offerings were made accompanied by dance and chants during the Makahiki season, named for the Pleiades.

Fig. 19. Baskets of offerings at a Balinese village temple, during rituals timed to the luni-solar calendar. The colors and shapes form cyclical mandalic patterns that correspond to the musical cycles of the gamelan orchestra played during the temple festival

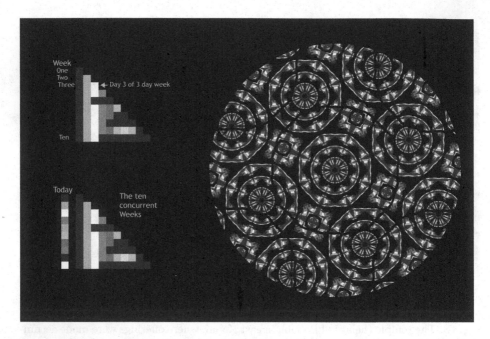

Fig. 20. Frames from the Prakempa Dome Film exhibition at Experimenta in Heilbronn. Left: explaining the logic of the calendar. Right: an image from the colour music.

7   Immersive Media: Capturing Calendrical Ideas as Polyrhythms

The Balinese calendar and ancient Balinese manuscripts such as Prakempa, describe a pervasive order that permeates their world. It took centuries to create, as both the macrocosm of the island and the human microcosm gradually came to embody the interlocking cyclical patterns of time. Balinese children hear gamelan music from infancy and many learn to play in the gamelan orchestra, which normally occupies a place of honor in the great temple of each village. Much, perhaps most of this is simply invisible to foreign visitors to Bali, despite their attraction to Balinese culture. The Balinese are clearly immersed in their world, but how are foreign visitors to discern what lies beneath the surfaces of Balinese culture, so easily mistaken for mere decoration? An answer may be discoverable in immersive media, which also aspires to enhance our ability to explore ideas and experiences that connect in unexpected and aesthetic ways.

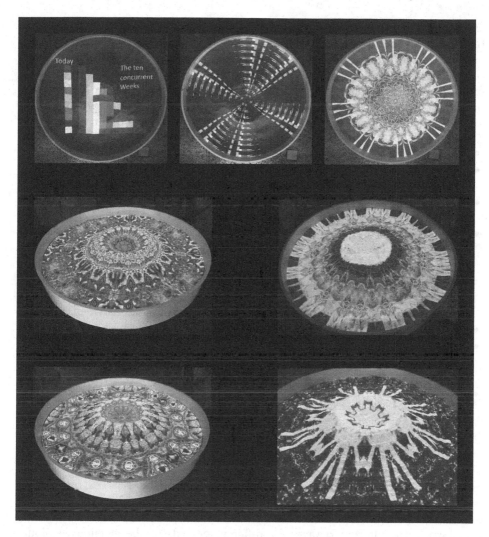

Fig. 21. Photo of the real-time sand table installation of the colour music of the Balinese calendar at "The First Sharjah Architecture Triennial: Can Art Be an Applied Science?".

It will not have escaped the reader's notice that this story - the conceptualization of time in traditional Bali and Kauai - is difficult to follow as it is laid out in this paper, despite our best efforts using text and two dimensional images. Immersive digital media offers an alternative, which can be used for both exposition and exploration. At the beginning of this project, we created an immersive sonification and visualization of the Balinese tika calendar, exhibited at the planetarium dome of the 2019 Beyond Festival in Heilbronn (see Appendix 2 below). The apparent success of that project led us to develop the expanded concept described in this paper. We are combining and synthesizing technologies such as the astronomical program Stellarium and the open source object oriented programming language PureData (PD), which offers real-time computer animation and music programming, and was used in the Bali calender music project (Prakempa 8k), and shown at the Beyond Festival in 2019 in Heilbronn. To create the next phase of the project as described in this paper, we aim to create an immersive digital environment with these components:

- For inputting star path data: Stellarium
- For input of star data and midi/data sonification: PureData; http:// musicalgorithms.org/4.1/app/
- For input of midi and output of AfterEffects opacity timing (audio envelopes > brightness envelopes) factorysettings.net MPFTLE
- Music: For transcription of traditional recorded chants to Western notation and output of .mp3 sound with Western instruments and midi data: Musescore 3.5
- For Music and computer animation: PureData/GEM programming language PureData for sound and music synthesis, synchronization with GEM animation GEM for real-time computer animation, and time-based synchronization
- For Additional music: Ableton Live, Midi with instrument and sound samples
- For immersive experience combining star paths, data sonification, music, visualization, accurate geographic location mapping, and digital film: Stellarium, Google Earth
- For animation production to be shown in Planetarium: AfterEffects

8   Appendix 1: First Phase: Dome Presentation at Heilbronn Beyond Festival 2019

Sørensen analyzed the musical aspects of the tika calendar by extracting the musical cycles, paying special to the offsets of several weeks, which yielded mathematical structure. Notes from the Balinese pentatonic scale were assigned to the days, with different octaves for different periods of the calendar. Colours were assigned to the notes as prescribed by the Prakempa manuscript, which emphasizes this association of musical notes with the colors of flowers used in offerings. For visualization, a grid-like structure was created with the PureData and GEM software, which uses OpenGL, to create real-time animation precisely synchronized with the underlying mathematics, which linked the audio synthesis and the computer-generated moving colour imagery. When the program runs, the progression of lines of colours and days appear to be visually similar to traditional Balinese ikat weaving, suggesting possibilities for further research on weaving and the calender. An 8K dome film entitled Prakempa was created and premiered at the Future Design Symposium at the Beyond Festival 2019 in Heilbronn, Germany (Figs. 21 and 22).

9   Appendix 2: First Phase: Sand Table Exhibition at Sharjah Architecture Triennale 2019

Following the Heilbronn dome premiere, Søorensen created a sand table installation "Prakempa: the colour music of the Balinese calendar" for the inaugural Sharjah Architecture Triennale, in the United Arab Emirates. The theme of the Triennial was the "Rights of Future Generations". The Architecture School of ETH Zurich organized a series of installations "ranging from films, archival documents, music, models and interactive displays that trace the history of Bali's Subak rice farming heritage".[7] These installations were named "Priests and Programmers", after Lansing's 2007 book (see Footnote 6).

References

1. Hegel, G.W.F.: Lectures on the Philosophy of World History: Introduction, Reason in History (translated from the German edition of Johannes Hoffmeister from Hegel papers assembled by H. B. Nisbet), p. 440. Cambridge University Press, New York (1975)
2. Scarborough, V., Isendahl, C.: Distributed urban network systems in the tropical archaeological record: toward a model for urban sustainability in the era of climate change. Anthrop. Rev. **7**(3) 208–230 (2020). https://doi.org/10.1177/2053019620919242
3. Lansing, J.S.: Perfect Order: Recognizing Complexity in Bali. Princeton University Press, Princeton (2006)
4. Guermonprez, F.: La religion balinaise dans le miroir de l'hindouisme. Bulletin de l'Ecole francaise d'Extreme-Orient **88**, 271–293 (2001). https://doi.org/10.3406/befeo.2001.3517
5. Cicero, M.T.: 45 B.C.E. De Natura Deorum. 2.61
6. Lansing, J.S.: Priests and Programmers: Technologies of Power in the Engineered Landscape of Bali. Princeton University Press, Princeton (2007)

---

[7] Adam Kleinman, "The First Sharjah Architecture Triennial: Can Art Be an Applied Science?". FRIEZE, 26 November 2019.

Urban Interactive Installation Art as Pseudo-Environment Based on the Frame of the Shannon–Weaver Model

Hantian Xu[✉] and Lin Zhang

Communication University of China, Beijing, China

Abstract. This paper is aiming to combine the Pseudo-Environment theory to analyze urban interactive installation. According to the Shannon-Weaver Model, the primary analysis is divided into five different elements: information source, information destination encoding, decoding, channel. Based on the analysis of the structure of installation art. Through the analysis of the communication elements, the basic elements and structure of the communication of interactive installations are combed in the paper. Moreover, the different presentation dimensions and methods of interactive installations in the Pseudo-Environment are explored on the basis of the Shannon-Weaver Model. The design methods and concepts of interactive installations in the field of communication and cultural research are studied and summarized.

Keywords: Pseudo-Environment · Shannon-Weaver model · Urban interactive installation

1 Introduction

In recent years, in line with the evolution of urbanization and digital technology, there has been an increasing proliferation of interactive installation art for the public and the general public in urban areas. Urban interactive installation art was derived from the public art that emerged in the United States in the 1960s. Rather than being exhibited in museums or galleries, these public arts are being featured in public areas such as plazas, stations, parks and other open spaces of the city. Nonetheless, in comparison to the American public art in the 1960s, the variations and disparities in today's interactive installations lie not only in the iterations of technology, but also in the evolving interpretations of urban publicness by contemporary artists. Owing to the rising availability of public and private areas and semi-public spaces today, the public realm has transformed into a freely accessible place for the public [1] (Geographer Neil Smith encompasses media, the Internet and shopping malls into this mix). Moreover, interactive installation art nowadays has been widely incorporated with digital media technologies such as motion capture, big data processing and network technology. On the one hand, the interactions presented by interactive installations are grounded in urban space. On the other hand, they transcend the temporal and spatial constraints to create digital "heterotopias". In parallel, the evolution of public space and the advancement of digital technology have ushered in an aesthetic revolution for interactive installation art per se.

© Springer Nature Switzerland AG 2021
M. Rauterberg (Ed.): HCII 2021, LNCS 12794, pp. 318–336, 2021.
https://doi.org/10.1007/978-3-030-77411-0_21

2   City and Interactive Installation

In Manovich's perspective, graphic art has adopted two formats of presentation since the Renaissance, "representation" and "stimulation". The former comprises easel painting, television and film. The latter embraces murals and mosaic art [2]. Martin Jay, in Scopic Regimes of Modernity, also introduced two visual regimes, "Cartesian Perspectivalism" and "Art of Describing". The former represents the single-view hallucinatory painting that strictly adheres to perspective. In contrast, the latter features the scattered-view painting influenced by the Dutch Southern School by describing the world in the painting rather than explaining it [3]. The installation art in public space is significantly influenced by site-specific art. The element of representation is diminished and the element of simulation is intensified. In the "whitebox" exhibition galleries, the interactive installations both suffer from a lack of simulated context and motivation with the simulation, as well as from the dual limitations of the technology and equipment available indoors. In *Command Performance* (1974) [4], Vito Acconci set up a video displaying his own behavior. An additional monitor was utilized to reveal the expressions and behaviors of the viewers watching the video (see Fig. 1). Likewise, in Chris Milk's interactive installation *The Treachery of Sanctuary* (2012) [5], cameras and motion capture devices were employed to record and project the participants' silhouettes on a projection screen (see Fig. 2). Furthermore, the participants' waving arms were reshaped into wings and angels through algorithmic design. Both of these devices impose certain restrictions on the viewers' range of activities and behaviors. It is only by being trapped in a specific place that the viewers can experience the interactive content, which both presents some limitations and facilitates the interactive design. However, ever since the Renaissance, artworks presented in such a mode have been decoupled from the exhibition space, be it in palaces, cabinets of curiosities or art museums. Upon the relocation of the interactive installation from the art galleries to the public spaces, as the public spaces represent the venues of our daily practice. "The Other" constructed by the interactive installation is enclosed by the larger scenario of daily life, namely "the Other of the Other" [6]. Consequently, interactive installations sometimes surrender a part of their symbolic significance system, or establish their symbolic system entirely on the basis of a place, in exchange for the likelihood of being understood. As Richard Serra reacted with what can be considered a definition of site-specific art: "To move the work is to destroy the work." [7]. This environmental simulation feature developed by the interactive installations can be interpreted as a "Pseudo-Environment".

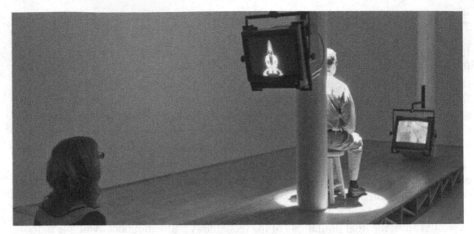

Fig. 1. Command performance ©Vito Acconci [4]

Fig. 2. The Treachery of Sanctuary ©Chris Milk [5]

3 Pseudo-Environment and Interactive Installation in Shannon–Weaver Model

Pseudo-Environment has been developed by Walter Lippmann, an American scholar, in his book *Public Opinion*. In Chapter One of *Public Opinion*, Walter Lippmann presented a narration of the Pseudo-Environment. It is by no means a real environment, but rather an image generated by the reconstruction of the real environment by people reacting to it. It incorporates real constituents, rather than being the entirely fictitious environment; however, people act as if it were the real environment [8]. There are three tiers of the Pseudo-Environment: its external, middle and inner layers are Physical Environment, Media Environment and Mental Environment, respectively. Thereinto, Media

Environment mirrors Physical Environment, whereas Mental Environment integrates Media Environment (see Fig. 3).

In 1948, Claude Elwood Shannon put forward the Information Theory and published it in *Bell System Technology Journal*. Shannon's original intention was to improve the transmission of information by telegraph or telephone affected by electronic interference or noise. It was held that the best solution was not to improve transmission lines, but to package information more effectively. At the beginning, it was declared by Shannon that his model was not suitable for human communication. The latter was a type whereby an individual explained the meaning of a message. Shannon had a mathematical tendency. His model was limited to engineering communication or technology communication. The significance of human communication was limited beyond his concept. However, the value of the Shannon-Weaver Model lies in that all the elements with subjective value judgment are abandoned, such as the meaning, authenticity and value of information and the characteristics of the audience. As a result, as a kind of purely subjective concept, information seems to be objective. Some basic methods and principles of information generation and dissemination are interpreted. Among them, noise, coding, decoding and other concepts are taken as the core to provide a basic paradigm for the field of modern media communication. Originally, there was only a kind of one-dimension linear concept. Later, a model to describe about the information flow and the information transmission method clearly is formed (see Fig. 4).

In contrast, the pseudo-stimulation of an interactive installation constitutes more than just a reflection of the medium's reality and the perception of the participants. Judging from the communication structure of the medium, the generation of the Pseudo-Environment involves more than just an enclosed unidirectional structure. It should also be holistically analyzed in conjunction with elements such as noise, feedback and extraneous conditions of the entire communication system. The information dissemination of the interactive installations through the Shannon-Weaver Model is further disassembled and analyzed. As a result, it is feasible to further elaborate the communication structure in the Pseudo-Environment of the interactive installations into several segments: source, host, channel, encoding, decoding and noise. In this regard, the source (artists or participants) encodes the information and conveys it to the host (participants or the installation per se) through the channel (interactive installations and places). Throughout this course, the information is lost or misinterpreted by the interference of noise. Upon information acquisition by the host, following the processing and exploitation of the information, the reverse dissemination is undertaken through this process. It fulfills the reprocessing and secondary or multiple dissemination of information. In particular, the channel serves as the construction of the material space in the Pseudo-Environment within the holistic dissemination structure. In turn, the whole interference procedure of encoding, decoding and noise echoes the generation of the mimetic environment. The source and host eventually contribute to the subject-object composition of the dissemination system (see Fig. 5).

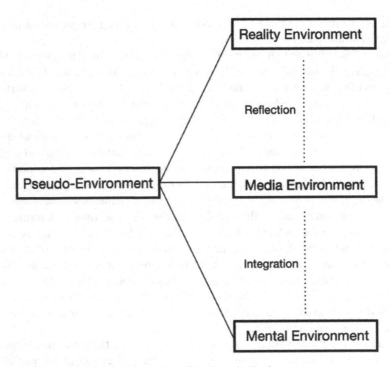

Fig. 3. Three tiers of the Pseudo-Environment

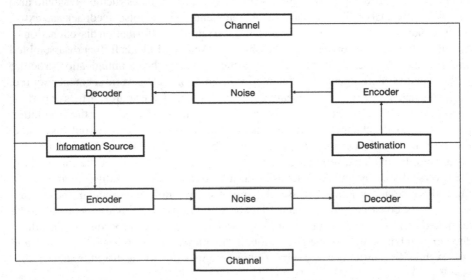

Fig. 4. Shannon–Weaver Model

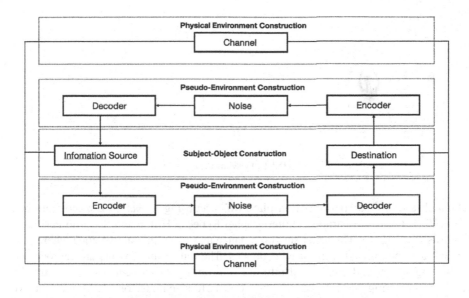

Fig. 5. Pseudo-Environment in Shannon-Weaver Model

3.1 Sources and Hosts: Subject-Object Construction in the Dissemination of Interactive Installations

The classic aesthetic model of the subject-object relationship represents a hierarchical order grounded in a power structure. Danny Cavallaro argued that "when we are gazing at particular objects, the intention is to control them." [9]. The essence of the gaze lies in the existence of a power mechanism in vision, where aesthetics per se manifests as an act of power and constitutes a sort of socialized viewing. However, the aesthetic logic of interactive installation art has shattered such a visual order. As discussed in the foregoing, within the communication structure of the interactive installations, the subject-object construction evolves constantly. In the constant transformation, the source and the host act as the object of the "gaze", whereby the human being achieves "anti-materialization". As Andy Warhol's words "In the future, everyone will be world-famous for 15 min". The audience is the actor, all of whom present themselves with a "public face" at all times [10]. Furthermore, this subject-object transformation occurs not only among participants (humans), but also in some interactive installations. The subject-object transformation of interaction takes place among humans and objects. As a result, in some interactive installations, objects also achieve socialization and acquire an equal identity of interaction through the communication system.

Concerning the compilation of existing urban interactive installations, the subject-object composition of the communication system can be roughly categorized into the following groups: individual-individual, individual-collective, and individual-object. Within the individual-individual model of interactive installation, the artist is often absent, or rather the artist cedes some of his or her creative authority to the participants. In this context, the interactive installation per se frequently functions only as

Fig. 6. HELLO ©Matt Park (2011)

a channel, a so-called "participation platform" according to Rafael Lozano-Hemmer. *Hello* (2011) [11] by Australian choreographer Rebecca Hilton and Soon-ho Park uses no words (see Fig. 6). The artist sets up a dance tent as an interactive zone where participants are encouraged to improvise dances. The dance movements are reprocessed by choreographers and condensed into a 2-min library of movements. Subsequently, participants entering the tent will be exposed to a life-size image on a led screen for live dance instruction. Afterwards, the teaching party leaves, while the new participant will learn from the previous participant's dance images. The relationships between teaching and learning, source and host, are reversed and repeated consistently. From a micro perspective in this project, each dance teaching in the tent presents an individual-individual act of dissemination. In contrast, from a macro perspective, each teaching constitutes a collective act, as each individual learns dance moves that are versions of movements recreated by countless others. The collective perspective also contributes to individuals conquering the fear and embarrassment of public performance. There is no actor if everyone involved is an actor, while the spectacle of performance dissipates when everyone is performing. In the case of interactive installations, the subject-object construction of communication is the individual-collective model. As the source, the collective tends to express itself as certain specific data through the processing of big data. Conveying information to individuals through the installation has emerged as a trendy expression of "information visualization" in public space nowadays. *Symulakra* (2019) [12] is a live data sculpture on a large street-facing LED display on a mall in Warsaw, Poland. Its visualized content is directly influenced by things like car traffic on the nearby street and data from cell phones of people gathered around the screen, such as the general intensity of mobile internet usage, and computer vision pattern detection for the age ranges of people nearby. In this project, each and every neighboring passerby unconsciously serves as a source of information, co-shaping the images on the screen and constituting a collective symbol of the digital era (see Fig. 7).

In another project of *Voice Tunnel* (2013) [13], Rafael Lozano-Hemmer has designed 300 powerful theatrical spotlights that produce columns of light along the walls and cladding of the tunnel (see Fig. 8). All fixtures have shined past the spring line, fading along the internal curved surface of the tunnel, just reaching its crown. There was a microphone recording visitors' voice and turned it into a morse-like code of flashes. The voices can be heard through an array of 150 loud-speakers placed along the tunnel, in perfect synchronicity to the blinking lights that are near-by. Via the editing and collage of audio, personal characteristics are concealed in the changing light and sound clips, which also encourages interactive participation of the general public. Considering the individual-medium dimension, the phenomenon of human-medium interaction can be observed everywhere in the present day. Paper-making, printing and photographing have rendered media as an integral part of people's daily lives and have heightened their significance. However, the advent of the Internet and computing has formatted and consolidated all previous media of human history [14]. A wide variety of media and screens can be observed almost everywhere in day-to-day life. Windows have enlarged, and counters have been substituted by self-service facilities. The medium constitutes almost the vast majority of the world beyond the body, thereby giving rise to the digital urban, the digital idol, and the digital nature. In the Teamlab's project *Resonating of Life in the Acorn Forest* (2020) [15], the acorn forest in Musashino will be converted into an interactive art space, one that evolves in response to the presence of humans. Knee-high artificial acorns are designed by artists to be positioned in the forest, which resemble the characteristics of a roly-poly toy (see Fig. 9). While these acorns are being pushed down, or blown down by the wind, they will emit a special tone and resume upright. Meanwhile, the surrounding acorns will also progressively echo, issuing the same tone and diffusing out. At night, all the acorns will glow with interior transmission light, which is echoed by the lighting system of the entire forest, yielding a rhythmic change of light. Simulation of nature remains a universal theme in almost all Teamlab projects. Teamlab has been a determined enforcer of Pseudo-Environment construction. In their projects, they deliberately conceal all interactive mediums in the viewers' visual blind angles, or wrap them up through images or screens. They allow this human-medium interaction to operate with a supernatural logic of sympathetic sorcery, despite being constructed upon natural logic. In other words, "things are reciprocally interlinked through a certain unrecognized sympathetic interconnectivity, crossing distances and creating interactions nowadays." [16].

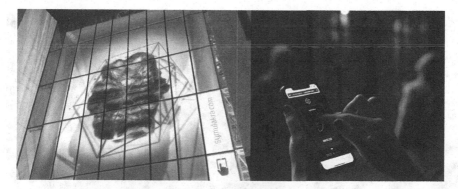

Fig. 7. Symulakra ©panGenerator [12]

On the other hand, following the further advancement of digital media, the integration of media has emerged as a trend. It involves not only the consolidation of other media, but also the technical penetration and data infiltration of the human bodies, namely the "cyborgs". The proliferation of mobile phone functionalities appears to announce an inevitable dawn of such an era. From an "extension of the body" to a "digital organ", mobile phones have been increasingly challenging to disassociate from humans. The subject-object construction of the interactive medium has commenced to be ambiguous, with the subject of communication having evolved from the natural person who masters the tools to the cyborgs whose technology is embedded in bodies. The AR mobile game *Pokémon Go*, which was launched in 2016, is one such game that requires a combination of physical activity and media interaction. Players are required to arrive at a real geographic location with a hand-held smartphone device to capture a specific Pokémon on the phone screen. The players' real spatial coordinates will be fed back to the virtual character in the game through GPS information, fulfilling the medium and body interaction and convergence.

Fig. 8. Voice Tunnel ©Rafael Lozano-Hemmer [13]

Fig. 9. Life in the Acorn Forest ©Teamlab [15]

3.2   Channels: Material Construction of Information Dissemination

As a means and tool for bearing and transmitting messages, the channel also serves as a tie that interconnects various factors in the communication process. In the interactive installation, when interacting with the external world, the human subject invariably utilizes various sensory organs to facilitate the interaction. Consequently, the construction of information dissemination is oriented to simulate various forms of human senses and is classified into the visual channel, auditory channel, tactile channel, and associative channel.

There are diverse processing methods in the construction of visual channels in accordance with the interaction installations, such as visual detection, visual recognition and visual tracking. Visual detection involves the reception of visual information from the external world via an image or video capture device such as a camera, whereas visual recognition can be more sophisticated. In the interactive process, the computer captures the live image through the camera, and further determines the detected target upon identifying the target in the image. Different corresponding feedback is offered in accordance with the specific judgment results, such as gesture recognition interaction, expression recognition interaction, and pose recognition interaction, etc. Visual tracking consists of tracking the movement of a specific target in the image by a computer. In interactive artworks, the movement of such a particular target often falls under the real-time control of the viewers or participants. In a similar way, the construction of auditory channels can be primarily divided into two categories, acoustic detection and acoustic recognition. Acoustic detection entails recognizing the presence or absence of sound and the pitch of the sound, while acoustic recognition involves identifying the content of the sound on this basis. Acoustic recognition technology has been further refined and intellectualized. The computer is capable of acknowledging the precise content of the participants' speech and providing varied feedback in response to the specific content of the participants' speech.

Mainstream audio-visual channel construction devices contain hardware such as Kinect and Leap Motion. As a three-dimensional somatic interactive device, Kinect comprises three cameras with different functions. The BGB VGA color camera in the middle which acquires color images, and the infrared transmitter and CMOS infrared camera on the left and right sides constitute the three-dimensional depth sensor. Beyond that, the device also features hardware components such as microphone arrays, motors, and logic circuits designed to acquire voice information. Its primary functionalities cover motion capture, posture analysis, voice recognition, target recognition, and community interaction. The Leap Motion somatic interaction device focuses on the sensing of hand movements and gestures. Although the device is not envisioned to substitute for interactive devices such as a mouse, keyboard, or tablet, it is capable of functioning in tandem with these devices. With a superior accuracy and a frame rate of 200 frames per second, Leap Motion not only tracks the hands, but also the position and gestures of each finger, thereby allowing for almost latency-free interaction. Of course, similar to the Kinect somatic sensing device, its sensing scope is limited, and the existence of the target will not be detectable beyond its sensing range.

The Wall of Sound (2019) [17] is a street-based interactive installation that incorporates acoustic recognition and acoustic detection. Inspired by a graffiti wall, the exterior of the installation resembles a nebula, or a neural net, with 47 hexagonal node modules (see Fig. 10). Each node module is equipped with a sampler and sequencer. They are respectively dedicated to recording and playing audio, while also controlling the direction of sound signal dissemination. The designer connects each node module through the led light belt. As participants control the flow direction of recorded audio by rotating the buttons on the node module, the led light belt will demonstrate the transmission trajectory of sound flow. When several audiences vocalize simultaneously, the trajectory of sound dissemination will continuously collide and interact. Just like the emotional communication among individuals, it will ultimately present a unique "music".

Tactile channel construction involves the entire interaction process through authentic contact between a part of a person's body and the work per se. From a general sense, it is the sensation of pressure triggered by the deformation of the deeper tissues in the human body induced by a relatively intense mechanical stimulus. In a narrower sense, tactile sensation typically refers to the skin sensation evoked by the superficial receptors of human skin by a weak mechanical stimulus. The construction of tactile channels primarily has undergone several evolutionary courses such as remote-control devices, electronic sensing devices and tactile interface interaction. For instances, remote control devices, such as mechanical arms and robotic manipulators, connect operators and feedback providers by means of sensing devices, electronic sensing devices that communicate the operator's hand signals with feedback providers through electronic signals. Also, touch-screen interfaces are responsible for electronic devices such as touch-screen mobile phones and iPads.

The Light Waves (2020) [18] is an interactive light sculpture for the "MęskieGranie" festival in Poland. It consists of three principal components - the central red sphere, a cluster of supports in the middle as a path, and an interactive zone (see Fig. 11). The installation incorporates 200 m of addressable RGB LEDs and occupies an area of approximately 300 m^2, probably the largest such installation ever built to date. Each drum is equipped with a custom PCB that features an Arduino Nano and a microphone, and utilizes an MCP2515-based CAN setup for signaling. Visitors are allowed to transmit tactile signals to the red sphere by drumming to stimulate varying lighting effects. By means of tactile and behavioral design, the artist has delivered a highly participatory experience and an extraordinary creation of the atmosphere in the place by the installation. Through the creation of a space that emulates a primitive tribe, it enables the emotional bonding among strangers by drawing people together, with the emotional liberalization constituting its essence.

Other than modern digital media technologies, urban space constitutes another material element of the channel. It is imperative for any urban interactive installation to be situated in a specific space, which is not, per se, an Aristotelian coordinate space. "It is not only the empirical setting of a physical object in a certain locational scene, rather an attitude and habitual practice that can be appreciated as the spatialisation of social order." [19]. The convergence of interactive installations and urban space has created a new communication channel - the interactive medium has deconstructed the original material deconstruction of urban space and diminished the material boundaries of urban space. In many cases, supermaterial scenarios can be exhibited through screens or images, in which even the subject and object of interaction are not necessarily in the urban material space [20]. On the other hand, the interactive installation actually assumes the role of "Place-Maker" through the simulation of the environment or the reenactment of culture, reinforcing the cultural image of the place through the information dissemination.

During the COVID-19, NBA announced the official cooperation with Microsoft, which will adopt "Together Mode" system to establish a virtual auditorium in the NBA (see Fig. 12). As a multiplayer video mode introduced by Microsoft earlier this month, "Together Mode's" greatest feature is to extract the image of each user independently and to integrate them into the same virtual scenario. It is designed for participants to observe others' positions and expressions on the screen, while also engaging in actions such as "waving" and "high-fiving" with the people in the vicinity. These "cloud viewers" will enjoy a live view of the game in real time, and will be empowered to "virtually cheer" through a specific APP whenever players score. Such feedbacks will selectively be presented on the main screen of the stadium during the tournament. All other audiences watching the game via the live Internet broadcast could visualize the virtual image of the 300 spectators on the big screen. By means of cloud technology, the screen and the tournament field are being constructed to constitute a geographically mediated channel.

In the 2017 Moment Factory's project *Illuminations: Human/Nature* (2017) [21], the design team arranged audiences to group and carry multi-media devices such as injected speakers, projectors, spotlights, etc. to embark on a night tour in Banff National Park (see Fig. 13). During the exploration of the park, audiences are encouraged to utilize multi-media devices to acquaint themselves with the park's history, culture, flora and fauna, with the interactive devices functioning as an annotation and extension of the space.

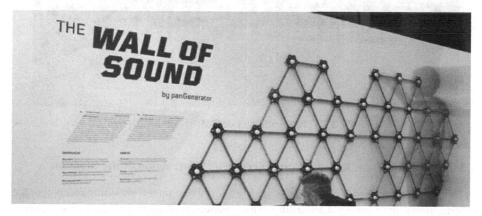

Fig. 10. The wall of sound ©panGenerator [17]

Fig. 11. Light waves ©panGenerator [17]

Fig. 12. The together mode ©Microsoft (2020)

3.3 Encoding, Decoding and Noise: Scenario Construction of the Medium

In terms of interactive installations in the Pseudo-Environment, encoding refers that the information source encoded according to its experience, feelings and ideas acts on others actively in the form of appropriate information. There are different purposes and means of coding among different coding subjects. However, the purpose of interactive installation coding is scene simulation and illusion creation in the Pseudo-Environment. Artistic creation was first carried out by Plato around the concept of "realistic imitation". In Plato's philosophical system, ideas originated from the creator and occupied the highest level. Real life was the projection and imitation of ideas. Art originated from real life and it could be regarded as the imitation of ideas, which was the lowest level [22].

Fig. 13. Illuminations: human/nature ©Moment Factory [21]

The simulation of Western paintings gradually reached its peak from the Renaissance Period. With the development of perspective and anatomy, artists could understand and imitate the reality more scientifically. Louis Daguerre founded a diorama theatre in Paris in 1821. Daguerre displayed a large realistic landscape painting about 70 feet. wide and 45 feet. high in the theatre. The real scene of mottled tree shadows and flying clouds was simulated in combination with light and shadow. It became a popular artistic form (see Fig. 14).

Since the 20th Century, the artistic creation of paintings and sculptures has been transformed into abstract creation. The analog coding has been transferred to the image art represented by films. In the field of architecture, it is reflected in the post-modernism architecture of New Historicism and Simulated Reality. In terms of the Pseudo-Environment, it was held by Andre Bazin that this kind of media illusion was endowed with different "features" in different periods. For the audience, it reflected the improvement of the coding technology. The more "real" environment of the media technology at the latter stage was always presented [23]. For example, the film development history is divided into four stages, including silent films, sound films, color films and 3D films. When the coding method was not limited to vision, some media like smell and touch was involved in the construction on the Pseudo-Environment and the coding method of interactive installations was expanded. As John Naisbitt said: "Whenever a kind of new technology is introduced into the society, there will inevitably appear to be a balanced response (a high emotion) in the human society. The higher the technology is, the stronger the emotional response is." [24]. In this dimension, the Pseudo-Environment for interactive installations surpasses any artistic form in the human history.

Corresponding to the encoding is the decoding of the audience in the Pseudo-Environment. Decoding is a process of interpretation and elaboration of information. In the process, information must be disturbed by noise or obstacles so that everyone has a unique understanding of art. It was held by Shannon that noise referred to "something beyond the intention of all information sources in the signal". The meaning of communication is to eliminate the noise in the process of decoding [25]. However, "noise elimination" is very difficult and even unrealistic in the actual operation process. For the design of interactive installations, it is not achieved by artists but in the continuous interaction between installations and the audience. Not only is the modern interactive installation art a kind of artwork, but it is also a text to be interpreted and experienced. There is an important difference between texts and works in the understanding of noise. The purpose of works in communication is to achieve effective communication through reasonable coding and noise reduction. Texts are aimed to reflect the meaning continuously. The audience's attitude towards noise (ambiguity) in the process of decoding is a kind of positive "anti communication" [26]. In a project of William Forsythe called *Nowhere and Everywhere at the Same Time* (2015–2017) [27], Forsythe sets sixty pendulums hanging on strings and moving in the space of the room (see Fig. 15). Every pendulums can be controlled and choreographed by Forsythe. The movement of the weights is programmed in such a way as to produce a kinetic and acoustic counterpoint that divides the room into many unpredictable, changing parts. Filled with unpredictable complexity, the space addresses the state of the visitors' perceptions and reflexes and leads them into a light and surprising choreography of perpetual avoidance. For Forsythe, this project was not a piece of artwork, but a text. Forsythe's goal was not to design a room with sixty pendulums, but a group of audience who could dance with pendulums, even though the artist did not know how the audience would deal with the project in the end. Therefore, for the contemporary audience, an interactive installation always means the diverse decoding. There are double meanings. On the one hand, interactive means is diverse. The interaction between the audience and installations is not only based on the assistance of electronic devices. In a broad sense, it even includes the temperature of installations. Taste brings the sense of stimulation as well as information to the audience. There is no any digital device in Olafur Eliasson's artwork *Ice Watch* (2014) [28]. The artist only transports 30 blocks of glacial ice from the waters of Greenland and placed them in front of Tate Modern in London. The ice was left here to melt. Participants can observe and touch ice cubes (see Fig. 16). Environmentalists can pay attention to the melting of ice cubes in cities and associate it with the theme of environmental protection. However, it does not prevent others from taking ice cubes as urban furniture or local temperature regulators by sitting and climbing on them. Artists construct the Pseudo-Environment based on glaciers and nature, but it does not prevent different audience from trying and interpreting it diversely.

Shannon's coding decoding logic forms a set of communication rules which are similar to game rules. In terms of the interpretation of noise, readers are more like "spoil-sport". Dutch scholar Johan Huizinga has argued that there is an absolute and unique order that dominates within any game. Games create the order and games are the order [29]. In an interactive installation, the rules of interaction feature similarly to the order of so-called games by Huizinga. To engage in interaction, it is imperative that the participants first understand the manner or means of interaction, specifically "how the designer encodes through the medium" and "what form I (the participant) can utilize to decode". In the event of inappropriate encoding and decoding formats, participants may not be engaged in the interaction at all. It is due to the differences between the interactive rules of the interactive installations and the traditional order of games. Huizinga has considered the existence of a population in the game known as spoil-sport, who are distinguished from the cheaters in the game. While cheaters actually still pretend to obey the rules, spoil-sport simply disowns the rules and shatters the illusion created by the game. In interactive installations, in contrast, such spoil-sport rarely occurs because the rules of interaction are often embedded in the computation by programmers. Participants' feedback merely disseminates within the framework of the interaction, leaving it hardly possible to modify and violate the coding and decoding patterns set by designers. Despite the presence of daily simulations, the coding and decoding patterns of interactive installations can be differentiated from people's daily behavioral norms and behaviors. Such discrepancies sometimes convert the interactive installations into agents of social activities, into extensions of social rituals. In Rafael Lozano-Hemmer's interactive installation called *Under Scan* (2005) [30], the artist has designed a very intriguing coding and decoding model, with the installation being set in a square installed with a large searchlight. Participants can hang out under the lights and will randomly discover some portraits in their own shadows recorded in advance by the designer, including male, female, youth and children, who will recount their own stories. In this installation, the yearning for communication and interaction amongst strangers is stimulated, albeit only being image-based. Nevertheless, the artist purposeizes the act of chance encounter, which turns chance encounter with strangers into a purposeful act of exploration, shattering the wariness and defensiveness people have towards strangers in their daily lives. Therefore, in the square, instead of only the communication between human beings and images being activated, the communication among strangers also intensifies, resulting in a distinctive social space.

Fig. 14. Daguerre's Diorama ©Gillian Young (2020)

Fig. 15. Nowhere and everywhere at the same time ©William Forsythe [27]

Fig. 16. Ice watch ©Olafur Eliasson [28]

4   Conclusion

Upon the evolution of the interactive installations from museums to urban public spaces, their geographic characteristics have been more prominent, with the installations revealing a spatial orientation. In this process, the aesthetic logic of interactive installations has evolved from presentation to simulation. The reenactment of the real environment and people's daily behavioral activities, known as the Pseudo-Environment, has emerged as a significant attribute of artistic expression. While the interactive installations are studied and investigated as a kind of media communication, the entire communication process of the interactive installations is subdivided and researched through the Shannon-Weaver Model. Each communication link and each element essentially shape the interactive installations. Through the research and analysis of interactive installations in recent years, it is easy to find that with the emergence of 5G technology, cloud computing and a variety of somatosensory interactive installations, interactive installations have become increasingly mature and realistic for the presentation of the Pseudo-Environment. On the other hand, with the diversity of technical means, interactive installations have been on a more diverse development trend. The richness, interest, concept and audience participation of interactive installation works will become the key to the success or failure of works in the future. It is held that with the passage of time as well as the constant development of technology, the artistic forms of image installation works will become increasingly novel and diverse in the future.

References

1. Tonnelat, S.: The sociology of urban public spaces. In: Wang, H., Savy, M., Zhai, G. (eds.) Territorial Evolution and Planning Solution: Experiences from China and France, pp. 40–45. Atlantis Press, Paris (2010)
2. Manovich, L.: The Language of New Media, p. 111. The MIT Press, Cambridge (2002)
3. Jay Martin, J.: On Scopic Regimes Visual Cultures. Routledge, London (1987)
4. VitoAcconci: Command Performance: Collection SFMOMA (1974). https://www.sfmoma.org/artwork/90.325/. Accessed 25 Feb 2021
5. Milk, C.: The Treachery of Sanctuary. Fort Mason Center (2012). http://milk.co/treachery. Accessed 25 Feb 2021
6. Žižek, S.: Looking Awry: An Introduction to Jacques Lacan through Popular Culture, p. 31. The MIT Press, Cambridge (1992)
7. Kaye, N.: Embodying site: Dennis Oppenheim and Vito Acconci. In: Site-Specific Art: Performance, Place and Documentation, p. 2. Routledge, New York (2000)
8. Lippmann, W.: Public Opinion, p. 12. Free Press, New York (1997)
9. Cavallaro, D.: Critical and Cultural Theory, p. 127. The Athlone Press, London (2001)
10. McQuire, S.: Geomedia: Networked Cities and the Future of Public Space, p. 126. John Wiley & Sons, Hoboken (2017)
11. Hilton, R., Hello, S.P.: https://espace.library.uq.edu.au/view/UQ:336291 (2011). Accessed 25 Feb 2021
12. panGenerator: Symulakra.: Puławska Street (2019). https://pangenerator.com/projects/symulakra/. Accessed 25 Feb 2021
13. Rafael Lozano-Hemmer, Voice Tunnel: New York City, USA (2013). https://www.lozano-hemmer.com/voice.tunnel-php. Accessed 25 Feb 2021
14. Manovich, L.: The Language of New Media, p. 89. The MIT Press, Cambridge (2002)
15. Teamlab: Life in the Acorn Forest: Musashino Woods Park in Higashi-Tokorozawa Park (2020). https://www.teamlab.art/e/acornforest/. Accessed 25 Feb 2021
16. Frazer, J.G.: The Golden Bough - A Study in Magic and Religion - Adonis Attis Osiris - Studies in the History of Oriental Religion, p. 21. Oxford University Press, Oxford (2008)
17. panGenerator: The Wall of Sound. Katowice Street Art (2019). https://pangenerator.com/projects/the-wall-of-sound. Accessed 25 Feb 2021
18. panGenerator: Light Waves (2019). Meskie Granie. https://pangenerator.com/projects/the-lightwaves/. Accessed 25 Feb 2021
19. Shields, R.: Lefebvre, Love and Struggle: Spatial dialectics, p. 53. Routledge, London and New York (1999)
20. Fang, L.: Media Space, the Imagination of Media Space and Urban Landscape, p. 122. Communication University of China Press, Beijing (2011)
21. Moment Factory: Illuminations: Human/Nature: Banff Centre for Arts and Creativity (2017). https://momentfactory.com/work/all/all/illuminations-human-nature. Accessed 25 Feb 2021

22. Plato.: Republic Oxford Paperbacks, Oxford (2008)
23. Bazin, A.: What is Cinema?, p. 71. University of California Press, Berkeley (1967)
24. Naisbit, J.: Megatrends-Ten New Directions Transforming Our Lives, p. 53. Warner Books, New York (1985)
25. Shannon, C.E., Weaver, W.: The Mathematical Theory of Communication, p. 7. University Illinois Press, Chicago (1963)
26. Barthes, R.: S/Z, p. 200. Hill and Wang, New York (1975)
27. Forsythe, W.: Nowhere and Everywhere at the Same Time, 2015–2017, MMK Museum für Moderne Kunst. https://www.williamforsythe.com/installations.html?&no_.cache=1&detail=1&uid=65. Accessed 25 Feb 2021
28. Eliasson, O.: Ice Watch.: Bankside, Outside Tate Modern, London (2014). https://olafureliasson.net/archive/artwork/WEK109190/ice-watch. Accessed 25 Feb 2021
29. Huizinga, J.: Homo Ludens, p. 9. Editora Perspectiva, Amazonas (2020)
30. Lozano-Hemmer, R., Under Scan: East Midlands Development Agency, Brayford University Campus, Lincoln, United Kingdom (2005). https://www.lozano-hemmer.com/under_scan.phphttps://www.lozano-hemmer.com/under_scan.php. Accessed 25 Feb 2021

The Multileveled Rhythmic Structure
of Ragtime

Jason Yust[1]([✉]) and Phillip B. Kirlin[2]

[1] Boston University, Boston, MA 02215, USA
jyust@bu.edu
[2] Rhodes College, Memphis, TN 38112, USA
kirlinp@rhodes.edu

Abstract. Syncopation in ragtime music has been defined in multiple ways. In this study we propose a method using the Hadamard transform. We extract four-measure phrases from a corpus of ragtime pieces by Scott Joplin, James Scott, and Joseph Lamb, and convert them to 32-element binary onset vectors. The Hadamard transform converts this to another 32-element vector that can be interpreted as representing syncopation at various metrical levels. This method is closely related to a similar application of the discrete Fourier transform. Using the Hadamard representation, we show that syncopation is strongest at the quarter-note level, and that tresillo-like rhythms are especially characteristic of the genre. We identify a number of significant differences based on the position of a phrase in a sixteen-measure strain, the position of the strain in the rag, and the composer. The Hadamard representation also facilitates discovery of relationship between different levels of rhythmic organization.

Keywords: Ragtime · Syncopation · Rhythm · Hadamard transform · Discrete fourier transform

1 Introduction and Methodology

1.1 Introduction

When Scott Joplin's "Maple Leaf Rag" was published in 1899, it and other ragtime pieces created a decades-long sensation in American music publishing. Contemporaneous critics consistently described the new and distinctive element of ragtime as syncopation (Blesh and Janis 1971). But syncopation is not a precisely defined term, as is evidenced by the numerous and divergent ways that it has been defined for empirical purposes (Temperley 2010; Longuet-Higgins and Lee 1984). Nevertheless, a number of recent studies have been performed with the intention to uncover patterns in the way syncopation has been used in ragtime music. Volk and de Haas (2013), for instance, were able to confirm a musicological hypothesis originally put forth by Berlin (1980) that *untied* syncopations (those occurring completely in the first or second half of a measure) dominated in the early era of ragtime before 1900, whereas *tied* syncopations (those

M. Rauterberg (Ed.): HCII 2021, LNCS 12794, pp. 337–354, 2021.
https://doi.org/10.1007/978-3-030-77411-0_22

occurring across the midpoint of a measure or across a measure boundary) only became prevalent in the later ragtime period starting in roughly 1902. Koops et al. (2015) were able to precisely identify the most prevalent syncopated rhythmic patterns used in the ragtime era and also showed that the overall amount of syncopation in ragtime music tended to increase over time. Kirlin (2020) showed that certain ragtime composers in general used more syncopations than their contemporaries, and also that syncopation is typically not equally distributed throughout a composition: highly syncopated measures tend to immediately follow other highly syncopated measures.

In this paper, we propose a new way of parsing a rhythm using the Hadamard transform, and an interpretation of this transform as a measure of different kinds of syncopation. The Hadamard transform requires periodic rhythms in cycles that multiply a basic pulse by powers of two. Ragtime is well-suited for this type of analysis, since it is consistently written in multi-leveled pure-duple meters. A typical ragtime piece is made up of about four sixteen-measure strains, which divide symmetrically into four-measure phrases of 2/4. With a basic rhythmic unit of a sixteenth note, these can be treated as 32-element rhythmic cycles, with five potential duple metrical levels.

An important theoretical advantage of the Hadamard transform is that it is a reversible transformation, so it translates the rhythm into an organized metrically interpretable form without any loss of information. In this respect it is similar to the discrete Fourier transform (DFT), which has been used to give metrical interpretations of periodic rhythms by Amiot (2016) and Yust (2021a–b). The DFT and Hadamard transformations are, in fact, closely related; we will explore this connection further below.

1.2 Methodology

Musicologists who study ragtime often refer to Scott Joplin (1867/8–1917), James Scott (1885–1938), and Joseph Lamb (1887–1960) as the "big three" ragtime composers, due to their prolific output and the adherence of their compositions to what would become known later as the "classic ragtime" musical form, namely a composition having a sequence of sixteen-measure strains made up of four-measure phrases. The music of these three composers, while not always acknowledged as such during their lifetimes, is now seen as best exemplifying the ragtime genre.

Due the big three's adherence to the classic ragtime form, specifically the conformance to sixteen-measure strains, we chose to focus our study solely on their music. We collected 71 compositions in total, 31 by Joplin, 28 by Scott, and 12 by Lamb. We restricted ourselves to compositions known to follow the "classic ragtime" form, which in this case meant pieces for solo piano, in duple meters (mostly 2/4, some in 4/4), with clearly defined sixteen measure strains. We specifically excluded songs and ragtime waltzes from our corpus. We used the sheet music on the International Music Score Library Project website (www.imslp.org) and located computer-readable scores of each composition (Blesh and Janis 1971; Magee 1998; McNally 2015).

For each composition, we manually identified the starting and ending measures of each sixteen-measure strain, labeling them "*a*," "*b*," "*c*," and so forth, in the order in which they first appear in the music. Because most strains are repeated, sometimes with slight variations, we identified repetitions and used only the first version in our analyses. We then isolated the right-hand part of each strain and converted each one into a representation called a *binary onset pattern* (Sethares 2007). These patterns illustrate the rhythmic content of a musical passage by using ones and zeroes to represent a note onset and the absence of a note onset, respectively. Binary onset patterns are produced by examining a musical phrase at a specific level of rhythmic granularity; here, at the sixteenth-note level for music in 2/4, and at the eighth-note level for music in 4/4. For every each possible "beat" of the music at that metrical level, if there is a note onset on that beat, a "1" is placed into the binary onset pattern, and a "0" otherwise. For instance, the binary onset pattern 10101010 represents the rhythm of a 2/4 measure of four eighth notes or a 4/4 measure of four quarter notes. The different metrical granularities for 2/4 and 4/4 compositions reflect the notational conventions of the genre, where the 4/4 notation simply doubles the notational values of the more common 2/4 notation. This is clearly evident in the conventional oom-pah patterns of the left hand, which proceed in eighth-notes in 2/4 and quarter-notes in 4/4. Discussions below will ignore the 2/4 versus 4/4 notational distinction and describe note values with reference to the 2/4 convention, which are implicitly doubled to apply to the 4/4 convention.

The end result of this conversion was a dataset consisting of, for each composition, a set of sixteen-measure strains with accompanying binary onset patterns, each pattern having 128 bits (8 bits per measure times 16 measures). We then took each strain and corresponding binary onset pattern and divided it into four four-measure phrases. We then ran the DFT and Hadamard transformation on each of the phrase-level binary onset patterns, resulting in a series of vectors which we analyzed.

1.3 Defining Syncopation with the Hadamard Transform

The Hadamard transform converts a vector of length 2^n into another vector of the same length, such that one can recover the original vector by multiplying by the Hadamard

$$\begin{pmatrix} + & + \\ + & - \end{pmatrix} \tag{1}$$

$$\begin{pmatrix} + & + & + & + \\ + & - & + & - \\ + & + & - & - \\ + & - & - & + \end{pmatrix} \tag{2}$$

$$\begin{pmatrix} + & + & + & + & + & + & + & + \\ + & - & + & - & + & - & + & - \\ + & + & - & - & + & + & - & - \\ + & - & - & + & + & - & - & + \\ + & + & + & + & - & - & - & - \\ + & - & + & - & - & + & - & + \\ + & + & - & - & - & - & + & + \\ + & - & - & + & - & + & + & - \end{pmatrix} \tag{3}$$

Fig. 1. Hadamard matrices for $n = 1, 2,$ and 3.

matrix. Figure 1 shows Hadamard matrices for $n = 1, 2$, and 3, where "+" stands for 1 and "−" stands for −1. The matrix can be constructed by a recursive rule: make four copies of the 2^{n-1} Hadamard matrix arranged in a 2×2 grid, and multiply the last one, in the lower righthand corner, by −1.

In our interpretation, each row of the Hadamard matrix is a rhythm in a metrical cycle of length 2^n, with an onset present wherever a "+" appears. The number n corresponds to the number of metrical levels. At $n = 1$, there is only one level. The zeroth row of the matrix, ++, is a trivial rhythm, and the second, +−, is a basic rhythm distinguishing on-beat from off-beat. The Hadamard transform of a rhythm will decompose it into these two elements: how many onsets does it have in total (level 0) and what is the difference between on-beat and off-beat (level 1). A positive value for coefficient 1 indicates an *unsyncopated* rhythm, while a negative value indicates a *syncopated* rhythm, one that favors off-beats over beats.

At $n = 2$, we reproduce the trivial rhythm and the level-1 rhythm by repetition of the ++ and +− rhythms in rows 0 and 1. The new rows give two basic rhythms for level 2 by taking these two patterns and negating them in the second half of the rhythm, giving ++−− and +−−+. This process can be understood as contrasting the two halves of the rhythm using the patterns of coefficients 0 and 1. So coefficient 2 (++−−) contrasts the two halves according to total number of onsets, and coefficient 3 (+−−+) by the difference in syncopation at level 1. These give a complete account of metrical level 2, with positive values again associated with unsyncopated and negative values with syncopated rhythms. In our interpretation of ragtime, level 1 is the eighth-note level and level 2 is the quarter-note level, with the sixteenth note as the basic unit. Together, coefficients 2 and 3 amount to a description of quarter-note level syncopation that contrasts on-beat onsets with those that occur on the second eighth.

We can extend this logic recursively as we increase the number of levels. A 2/4 measure is described by the 8×8 matrix, where coefficient 0 counts the number of onsets, coefficient 1 measures eighth-note syncopation, coefficients 2 and 3 measure quarter-note-level syncopation, and coefficients 4–7 represent four basic types of half-note level syncopation, defined by contrasting the two halves of the measure according to coefficients 0–3 of the 4×4 matrix. So coefficient 4 weights the first half of the measure against the second, coefficient 5 weights the eighth-note-level syncopation of the first half against that of the second half, and coefficients 6 and 7 weight the two kinds of quarter-note level syncopation between the two halves of the measure.

According to this logic, the Hadamard matrix losslessly converts the 2^n-cycle rhythm into a cardinality plus $2^n - 1$ measures of syncopation of different kinds. These break up into 1 type of eighth-note-level syncopation, 2 kinds of quarter-note-level syncopation, 4 kinds of half-note-level syncopation, etc. A given coefficient may be directly interpreted by converting it into a binary number. Each place in the binary number is a metrical level, and if a 1 appears in a place, it means we make a contrast based on that level. For instance, for $n = 3$, coefficient 1 is 001, meaning it makes simple eighth-note level contrasts. Coefficient 5 is 101, meaning it contrasts eighth-note level syncopation at the quarter-note level. Coefficient 7 is 111, meaning it contrasts type-11 syncopation at the half-note level, where type-11 syncopation is the contrast of eighth-note level syncopation at the quarter-note level.

Each coefficient of the Hadamard transformation has an associated coefficient of the DFT on the 2^n-place rhythmic vectors. The DFT converts a rhythm of length 2^n into 2^n complex numbers (coefficients) where coefficients 0 and 2^{n-1} are real (1-dimensional) and coefficients of index greater than 2^{n-1} are conjugates of those less than 2^{n-1}. The zeroth coefficients of each transform are equivalent, and the first Hadamard coefficient is equivalent to the 2^{n-1}-th DFT coefficient. Each of the other DFT coefficients, from 1 to $2^{n-1} - 1$, has two oblique axes in complex space such that each corresponds to one Hadamard coefficient. Rhythms with a high value on that Hadamard coefficient will also have a large value on the DFT coefficient. The two Hadamard rhythms that relate to the same DFT coefficients are rotations of one another, such that they have oblique phase values in the complex space of the DFT coefficient. Since each DFT coefficient k corresponds to a sinusoidal function with a periodicity of c/k for cycle length c ($=2^n$), the DFT suggests an alternate interpretation of the Hadamard coefficient.

For example, consider the Hadamard transform for $n = 3$ ($2^n = 8$). The matrix rows for coefficients 5 and 7 are +−+− −+−+ and +−−+ −++− respectively. The second is a rotation of the first back two places (an eighth note). If we rotate it back another eighth note we get the opposite (complementary) rhythm −+−+ +−++−+ , another such rotation gives the opposite of the second rhythm, −++− +−−+, and one more such rotation returns us to the first rhythm. These are all prototypes of coefficient 3 of the DFT for an 8-cycle, and the eighth-note rotation is a 90° rotation in the complex plane for coefficient 3. The best approximation to an even rhythm dividing the 8-cycle into 3 is the *tresillo* rhythm, 10010010. Its complement, rotated to align with the downbeat, is known as the *cinquillo* rhythm, 10110110. Both rhythms are common in a variety of popular and traditional musics, especially African diasporic traditions of the Americas. Both are also *maximally even* rhythms, which are prototypes of the corresponding DFT coefficient (Amiot 2007). While maximally even rhythms give a maximum value on the corresponding DFT coefficient for their cardinality (the definition of a prototype), the absolute maximum for any cardinality occurs instead at half the cycle length, for a rhythm exactly halfway between the two complementary maximally even collections, in the sense that it is a subset of one and a superset of the other. For coefficient 3 of an 8-cycle, this is the rhythm of Hadamard matrix rows 5 and 7, 10010110.

Cohn (2016) has pointed out that the *tresillo* and *cinquillo* are typical ragtime rhythms. We verify this assertion empirically below, and in fact can go somewhat farther to assert that these are defining rhythms for the style.

2 Results and Discussion

2.1 ANOVAs

We conducted two sets of ANOVAs to help identify significant trends in the data according to a few available factors in our dataset. For the first set of ANOVAs, we used the raw Hadamard transform results (Table 1), and for the second we used the absolute values of these (Table 2). The absolute values indicate the presence of a certain rhythmic type, regardless of its orientation with respect to the downbeat. The raw values indicate whether rhythms of that type tend to be syncopated or not. For instance, higher absolute values of coefficient 1 in some condition would indicate greater presence of eighth-note-based

Table 1. ANOVA results on raw Hadamard data. F-values are given for significant results only. *$p < .01$, **$p < .001$, ***$p < .0001$

	eighth	quarter	half	2-meas.	4-meas.	Betw.
Coefficient	—		57***	42***	8.6*	310***
Position	34***					
Composer		40***	33***			
Strain		5.7***	5.6**	9.2***		4.4*
Coefficient × Position	—					33***
Coefficient × Composer	—			7.2**		7.2**
Coefficient × Strain	—			4.9*		7.0**
Composer × Strain		6.9***				
Coeff. × Comp. × Strain			3.4*	3.8**		3.4*

Table 2. ANOVA results on absolute values of Hadamard data.

	eighth	quarter	half	2-meas.	4-meas.	Betw.
Coefficient	—		83***	115***	209*	2456***
Position		8.5*			451***	119***
Composer			19***	13***	47***	13***
Strain			4.1*	3.9*	18***	
Coefficient × Position	—					128***
Coefficient × Composer	—	5.9*			4.9*	34***
Coefficient × Strain	—	8.5***	10***			13**
Position × Strain					5.2*	
Position × Composer				7.0**	8.4**	
Composer × Strain		4.7**		4.4**	5.4***	
Coeff. × Pos. × Comp						6.8*
Coeff. × Comp. × Strain			4.4*	3.4*		3.5*
Pos. × Comp. × Strain					3.3*	

rhythms, without distinguishing on-beat eighth notes from syncopated eighth notes. A trend in raw values of coefficient 1 would indicate a tendency for eighth-note-based rhythms to be more or less syncopated in one condition or another.

In each set of ANOVAs, we treated coefficient number as a factor, in order to compare different coefficients. Since the number of coefficients was large, to narrow down the sources of significant results, we split the analysis into six separate ANOVAs, by dividing the coefficients into the five different levels (eighth, quarter, half, two-measure, four-measure), and then averaging across each level for a sixth between-level ANOVA. Because these ANOVAs have high statistical power, and to avoid false positives due to multiple tests, we set a relatively conservative α of $p < .01$, and focus on highly significant ($p < .001$) results in our analysis and discussion.

The factors included in all the ANOVAs were • coefficient, • composer, • position in strain, • strain position in piece, and all possible interactions. The great majority of the pieces in the corpus consist of four strains of sixteen measures each. There are four possible positions in each strain for the four-measure phrases (1–4). The position of the strain in the piece is indicated by the letters *a, b, c,* and *d.* Isolated introductions and interludes between the strains were excluded to better target possible effects of the strain position factor.

The results of greatest interest are those involving the coefficient factor. There are highly significant simple effects of coefficient on both dependent variables at all levels except eighth-note (which has only one coefficient and therefore no possible contrasts of coefficient), and quarter-note, which has only two coefficients (numbers 2 and 3). The between-level coefficient factor also interacts with all of the other factors (position, composer, and strain) significantly on both dependent variables. Interactions of coefficient number and strain are significant on both dependent variables within all the high levels (half-note, two-measure, and four-measure). We also found a number of three-way interactions of coefficient, composer, and strain at the higher levels, and between levels.

Clearly all factors were significant in a number of respects. To investigate these further we consider two different descriptive statistics for different combinations of factors below: (1) The mean absolute values of coefficients, and (2) what we will call the *bias*, the mean raw value divided by the mean absolute value of a coefficient. The bias varies from -1 to 1, where -1 indicates that all instances of a given coefficient are negative, 1 means they are all positive, and 0 means they are perfectly balanced between positive and negative. The bias is a measure of the tendency towards syncopation for each rhythmic type.

In all the analyses that follow, when averaging across the three composers, we weight each composer equally, so as not to privilege Joplin and Scott, who are represented by a larger number of pieces than Lamb.

2.2 Effects of Position and Coefficient

The position factor varies from 1 to 4 and indicates the position of each four-measure phrase within the sixteen-measure strains. We can see very clearly in the data that differences relating to position are largely due to position 4, the concluding phrase. Figure 2 shows the mean absolute values of all coefficients for the different positions. Positions 1 and 3 are nearly identical, and show a clear between-level trend, with high values at the eighth and half-note levels, smaller values at the two-measure level, and still smaller at the four-measure level. Final phrases are different in two salient ways: they have larger values across the board at the four-measure level (coefficients 16 through 31), especially the simple measure-by-measure contrasts of coefficients 16 and 24. The reason for this is obvious: since cadences typically occur in these measures, there is less overall rhythmic activity in the last two measures, leading to high values for all contrasts at the four-measure level. The other difference of position 4 is at the half-note level, with lower values for all coefficients at this level except for number 7. This indicates less overall contrast between the two halves of each measure.

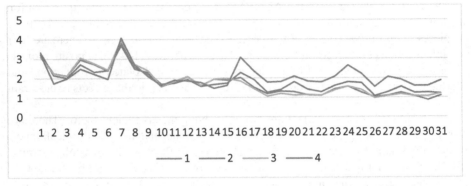

Fig. 2. Absolute value by coefficient number, averaged over the position in the strain

Position number 2 shows similar tendencies to position 4, but to a lesser extent. The reason for this is also evident: since this phrase occurs at the midpoint of the strain, it can sometimes also have cadential rhythms, similar to those in the final phrases. The cadential rhythms in that position are either less frequently occurring, or less extreme, leading to a smaller difference.

We can also use Fig. 2 to make some observations about the main effects of coefficient. One coefficient stands out distinctly: number 7. This coefficient identifies tresillo-type rhythms, and its prominence is quite striking. As noted above, Cohn (2016) and others have pointed out that this rhythm is distinctive of ragtime, and our data, as it turns out, bears out this observation quite clearly. Not only is coefficient 7 by far the largest one across the corpus, it is also consistently so, across all phrase positions, and, as we will see below, all strain positions and composers. In particular, position 4, even though it generally gets lower values at the half-note level, still has about the same values on coefficient 7.

We found highly significant main effects of coefficient number at all levels from the half note up, and between levels, for both absolute values and raw values. The primary between-levels effect on absolute values is a gradual reduction in coefficient size at higher levels. At the 2-measure level, coefficients 8 and 9, and to a lesser extent 12, are more heavily weighted, while numbers 10 and 13 less so. Numbers 14 and 15 appear to be more important in first and third phrases (coefficient × position effects at the half-note and 2-measure level only barely fell short of our significance criterion, at $p = .01$ and $p = .02$ respectively). At the four-measure level, we see consistently higher values for coefficients 16, 17, 23, 24, and 25. The general pattern at higher levels is that multiples of 8 and 4, which make contrasts of density between measures or half-measures, are typically important, as are coefficients one higher than a multiple of eight, which contrast the eighth-note syncopation from one measure to the next. This means that eighth-note syncopation is an important element of the rhythmic style, and tends to be maintained within measures, and contrasted, as opposed to sustained, from one measure to the next.

Other higher-level coefficients of possible interest other than these are 14, 15, and 23. These all share a relationship with the tresillo-like rhythm of coefficient 7. Coefficient 15 contrasts this rhythm from one measure to the next: +−−+ −++− −++− +−−+. We can also interpret it as *extending* the dotted-sixteenth-generated pattern of the tresillo through two measures (with the basic framework 10010010 01001001), a possibility discussed by Cohn (2016). Coefficient 23 indicates a similar kind of contrast of coefficient-7-type rhythms at the four-measure level (from the first two to the second two). Finally, coefficient 14 may be understood as an augmentation of the coefficient-7 pattern: ++−−−−++ −−++++−−.

Figure 3 compares biases of coefficients between the positions. Again, position 4 behaves very differently than the others. Of particular interest are coefficients 1–3. Coefficient 1, the eighth-note level, gets amongst the highest absolute values (Fig. 2). However, its bias is relatively low for positions 1, 2, and 3 (Fig. 3), meaning that, while rhythms are more often unsyncopated at the eighth-note level (the bias is positive), syncopated rhythms at this level are fairly common (high absolute magnitude despite low bias). The quarter-note level (coefficients 2 and 3) is negative-biased for positions 1, 2, and 3, meaning that this form of syncopation (favoring the weak eighths) is prevalent. Both of these trends are weak or absent for position 4: these phrases have a high positive bias for coefficient 1, and zero bias for coefficients 2 and 3, meaning that eighth-note-level syncopation is largely absent in final phrases, and quarter-note level syncopation is not so prevalent.

The bias pattern for cadential rhythms includes high positives for coefficient 16 and high negatives for coefficient 24, which together indicate a lower density of attacks in the fourth measure. At the same time, we see the opposite trend in coefficients 17–19 (negative bias) and 25–27 (positive bias). These coefficients all involve contrasts of eighth- and quarter-note-level syncopation, and indicate that fourth measures, in addition to being lower density, have less of these kinds of syncopation.

In Sect. 1 we noted the relationship of the Hadamard transform to the DFT. We briefly illustrate the correspondence in Fig. 4 by displaying the average magnitudes of DFT coefficients. Along the x-axis are DFT coefficient numbers, which refer to a possible division of the 32-beat cycle. The corresponding Hadamard coefficients are labeled above each point. The lines connect points at three levels, multiples of 4, 2, and 1, which correspond to the first three levels up to the measure, the two-measure, and the four-measure levels respectively. This illustrates the general tendency for lower magnitudes at higher levels, already observed in the Hadamard-transformed data. The high value at DFT coefficient 12 matches the high value at Hadamard coefficient 7. At the two- and four-measure levels, we see a tendency for higher values on the lower, density-based coefficients (1 and 2), lower values just above this, and a slight increase approaching 16. We could continue to use DFT phase values to detect syncopations, but since an analysis of DFT transforms would essentially duplicate our analysis using the Hadamard transform, we will take it no further at present and continue the analysis of Hadamard-transformed data below.

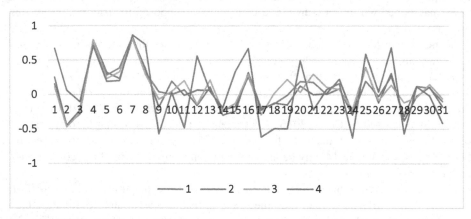

Fig. 3. Bias by coefficient number, averaged over the position in the strain

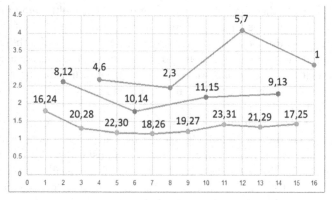

Fig. 4. Average DFT magnitudes across the corpus. The corresponding Hadamard coefficients are listed above each point.

2.3 Differences Between the Three Composers

In light of the evident special status of final phrases, we will largely focus our analysis of differences between the three composers on positions 1 and 3. Before putting final phrases aside, however, consider the pattern of results, separated by phrase, for Lamb alone, in Fig. 5. While Joplin and Scott (not shown) tend to look a lot like the overall trends in Fig. 3, with Joplin having slightly greater tendency to use cadential rhythms in position 2, Lamb seems to treat position 2 very differently. The higher values at the four-measure level overall suggest that he uses cadential rhythms frequently in this position, but the pattern of four-measure-level coefficient values is very different from that for final phrases, which means that his mid-strain cadential rhythms are distinct from the usual final-phrase cadential endings. In particular, the mid-strain cadential rhythms for Lamb seem to have more to do with contrasts of syncopation (coefficients 17, 23, 25) than overall density of the measures (coefficients 16 and 24).

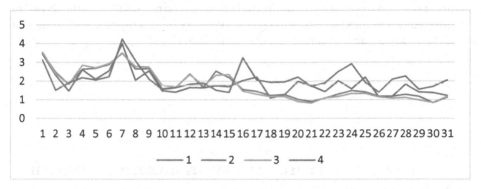

Fig. 5. Absolute values by Hadamard coefficient for Lamb, separated by position in the strain

The ANOVAs in Tables 1 and 2 found significant interactions of composer and coefficient between levels and at the quarter-note level. Figure 6 breaks the data up by composer for phrase positions 1 and 3 only. An evident between-levels difference is that the half-note level (coefficients 4–7) is stronger for Scott overall, indicating a tendency to use more measure-to-measure rhythmic repetition, especially with the tresillo-type rhythms (coefficient 7). At the quarter-note level, we find that Lamb has a preference for simple quarter-note syncopations (of the form $--++$, coefficient 2) while Joplin prefers those compounded with eighth-note level contrasts (of the form $-++-$, coefficient 3).

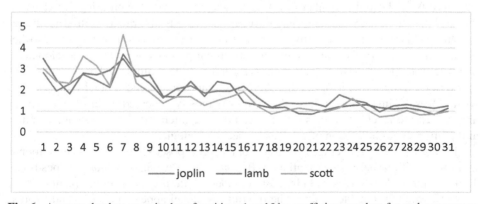

Fig. 6. Average absolute magnitudes of positions 1 and 3 by coefficient number, for each composer

Figure 7 shows the biases for positions 1 and 3 separated by composer. Overall, Joplin has a noticeably less predictable rhythmic palette, resulting in a flatter bias curve.

Lamb stands out for his large biases. The ANOVA for raw values found a significant composer × coefficient interaction at the two-measure level (coefficients 8–15). There is a large difference between Lamb and the others on coefficient 9 where Lamb strongly prefers eighth-note syncopations in the second and fourth measures of the phrase, while the others prefer it in the first and third measures. There is also a divergence between Lamb and Scott on coefficient 15, with Scott tending to start two-measure units with downbeat oriented tresillo-type rhythms, and Lamb instead putting these in the second of a two-measure unit. In salsa terminology, we might say Scott's rhythms tend to suggest a 3–2 clave, while Lamb's more of a 2–3 (Peñalosa 2012).

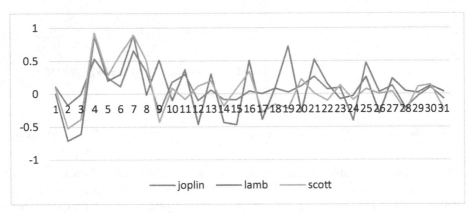

Fig. 7. Biases for positions 1 and 3 by coefficient number, for each composer

2.4 Effects of Strain Order

The ANOVAs showed a number of effects having to do with the ordering of strains in the rag. Although there is a tendency to regard the strains of a rag as arbitrarily strung together, in fact the variation of rhythm from strain to strain creates an overall shape to the typical rag. Our data shows that there are consistent patterns of rhythmic development over the strains that lead to reliable identifying traits of the strains based on their position in the rag. Furthermore, it shows that there are composer-specific strategies to how this works. Results involving strain in the ANOVAs mostly appeared within the half-note and 2-measure levels, and the strongest results were interactions of coefficient, strain, and composer, an indication of composer-specific strategies.

Figure 8 shows the averages by strain for each composer separately. Since we found that final positions behave substantially differently, these averages include only positions 1 and 3, although averages including all positions would present a similar picture.

An especially notable trend at the quarter-note level appears in Lamb and Scott's data, involving coefficients 5 and 7. Though coefficient 7 is high overall, for these composers it is especially high in *c* strains. On the other hand, coefficient 5 stands out in *d* strains. This coefficient detects rotated versions of the tresillo pattern, with the basic rhythm 10100110, and eighth-note rotation of the coefficient-7 rhythm 10010110. This suggests an importance of the tresillo-type rhythms to larger formal narratives for these composers, where the eighth-note rotation of these rhythms is distinctive of the transition from *c* strains to final *d* strains. Considering biases however, shown in Fig. 9, we see an important difference between Lamb and Scott: Lamb has a positive bias for coefficient 5 in *d* strains where Scott's is negative. This means that, for Lamb, the transition into the final strain is characterized by a rotation of the tresillo that remains unsyncopated, where for Scott is a rotation to a syncopated tresillo, the former typified by the rhythm 10100101 and the latter by 01011010.

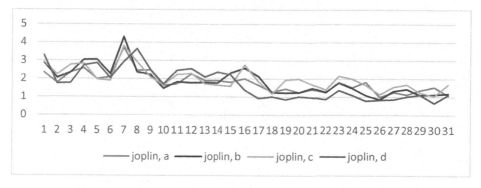

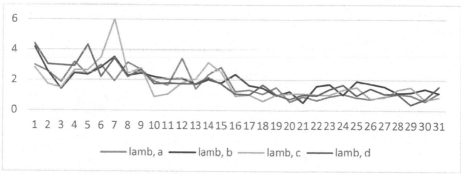

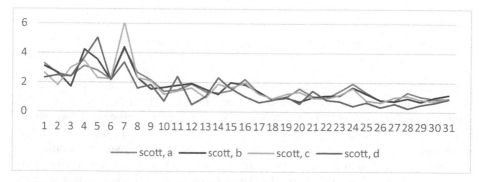

Fig. 8. Absolute values by Hadamard coefficient number and strain, for each composer

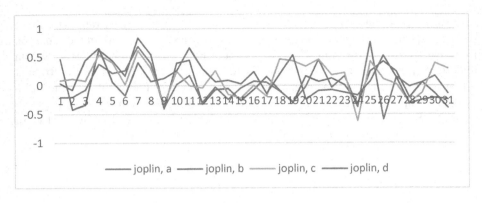

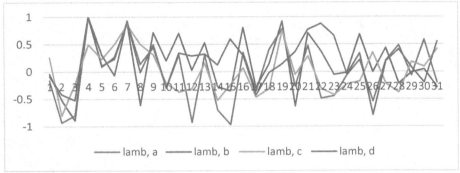

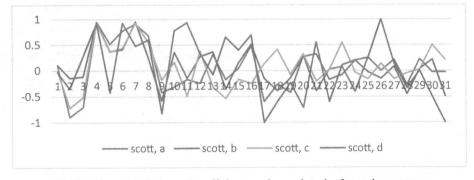

Fig. 9. Biases by Hadamard coefficient number and strain, for each composer

Coefficients 5 and 7 also appear to be important to distinguishing strains for Joplin. Like Lamb and Scott, Joplin's strain *d* rhythms show a sharp reduction in coefficient 7 and increase in coefficient 5. We do not see the increase in coefficient 7 for *c* strains in Joplin's data, however. Instead, we see similar values across all the earlier strains, and coefficient 5 has a similar prominence is *b* strains as well as *d* strains. A difference between these appears in the bias data in Fig. 9, which is about zero for coefficient 5 in *d* strains, and strongly positive in *b* strains. Thus, Joplin tends to use both syncopated and unsyncopated versions of the coefficient-5 rhythm in *d* strains, while strongly favoring the unsyncopated type in *b* strains.

A general between-level trend, evident most strongly in Joplin's data but also consistent with Scott's, is smaller values at the four-measure level for strain d, meaning these tend to have more rhythmic repetition between the two-measure units. For Joplin specifically, c strains show higher values across the four-measure level, indicating greater contrasts between the two measure units.

The 2-measure level (coefficients 8–15) seems to be a particularly important locus on different treatments of the strains between composers. For Lamb, coefficient 12, with a strong negative bias ($----++++ ++++----$), is especially distinctive of a strains, while for Scott, coefficient 11 ($+-- ++--+ -++--++-$) with a strong positive bias is especially distinctive of d strains.

Coefficient 9, which contrasts eighth-note syncopation from measure to measure, is one of the most important at the two-measure level. Relatively high absolute values of this coefficient are consistent across composers and strains, but we see distinct differences in bias. For Scott, coefficient 9 is negative-biased in all strain positions, though weakly so in c strains. A negative bias indicates a tendency to put eighth-note syncopation in the first measure of a pair. Lamb is the opposite, with positive biases in all strain positions, especially b strains. Joplin, like Scott, usually has a negative-biased coefficient 9, except in d strains, where he puts more eighth-note syncopation in second measures, like Lamb.

Each composer appears to have a distinctive method of syncopation for a strains. Scott and Lamb stand out with almost perfect negative bias for coefficient 2, an extremely consistent use of quarter-note syncopation. Lamb also has near perfect negative bias in coefficients 12 and 15, indicating syncopation at the two-measure level that favors the second beat of an initial measure and the downbeat of a second measure. The prominence of these coefficients in a strains is also visible in the absolute value data. Coefficient 15 may also indicate the presence of tresillo-type rhythms oriented around the downbeats of second or fourth measures of phrases.

3   Concepts of Syncopation and Multi-leveled Structure

Concepts of syncopation based on the Hadamard transform or DFT are not equivalent to ordinary common-sense usage of the term, but there is a definite relationship between the two. Two special properties of the definition proposed here are its balance and completeness. It is balanced in the sense that there are exactly as many theoretically possible unsyncopated rhythms as syncopated ones on every dimension. It is complete in the sense that every possible difference between two rhythms can be characterized as more or less syncopation on some set of individual dimensions. Ordinary concepts of syncopation have neither of these properties: they are unbalanced, since there are more ways to be syncopated than unsyncopated, and incomplete, since certain differences between rhythms may not affect how it is classified. More specifically, ordinary concepts of syncopation primarily focus on the ones with simpler Hadamard representations, especially low-level coefficients that are powers of 2 (1, 2, 4) or sums of two powers of two (3 and 6). A rhythm might be syncopated, in conventional terms, not only by having a negative value on these coefficients, but also by having a zero or small positive value. Rhythms that concentrate their energy in other coefficients, especially 5 and 7, may be regarded as syncopated even if they have high positive values on those coefficients. For instance, a version of the tresillo rhythm like 10100100 has positive values on coefficients 1, 2, and 4, but still be understood as syncopated because it has a much larger coefficient 5, even though it is a positive value.

Therefore, we propose that the Hadamard representation can be calibrated fairly well to common-sense notions of syncopation by focusing on certain parameters and adjusting thresholds. With that in mind, consider the question: in what sense is ragtime, the "syncopated idiom," syncopated? Our analysis identifies three relevant features:

1. Eighth-note-based rhythms (large absolute values on coefficient 1) are common, but they have a bias typically close to zero, meaning that they are often highly syncopated (negative).
2. At the quarter-note level, levels of syncopation are very high, such that coefficients 2 and 3 have negative biases in most conditions.
3. The most prominent type of rhythm is represented by coefficient 7. This has a high positive bias, but rhythms with large positive values on coefficient 7 count as "syncopated" in conventional terms, because they concentrate energy in a more complex coefficient. The same can be said of coefficient 5, which, though not nearly as prominent as coefficient 7, has a substantial presence and seems to be important in certain circumstances, such as in concluding (d) strains.

All of these points focus on lower-level rhythmic organization, from the measure level down. At higher levels, concepts of syncopation become more diffuse and less salient as such. Our results at the two- and four-measure levels are more readily understood by thinking of them as patterns of distribution of onset density and lower-level forms of syncopation across the four measures of a phrase.

The Hadamard transform helps us relate forms of syncopation at different levels in this way. As an illustration, let us consider a specific case, comparing Joplin and Scott's practice in c and d strains, using raw Hadamard values rather than splitting them into absolute values and biases. Figure 10 averages the four conditions across levels, using just first and third phrases. The basic strategy is the same, only more extreme for Scott: the eighth-note level is balanced, quarter-note syncopated, and half-note unsyncopated, more strongly in c strains and less so in d strains. At the two-measure level, contrastingly, we see balance in c strains and positive values in d strains. Since the two-measure level contrasts pairs of measures, this means that c strains usually have similar rhythms from measure to measure, while in d strains they are more varied. In other words, d strains trade low-level rhythmic contrast for between-measure contrast, shaping rhythmic ideas over somewhat longer spans.

We can get a closer look at this by comparing the first three levels directly to the two-measure level. Figure 11 overlays them, separately for Joplin and Scott. The solid lines show coefficients 1–7, and the dotted lines show 8–15, such that coefficients differing by 8 are aligned. An outward movement going from solid to dashed (away from zero) indicates that a balance in some low-level parameter becomes differentiated when split into paired measures. An inward movement shows that some prominent low-level rhythm type is simply repeated measure to measure. For both composers, c strains have purely inward motion: the low-level rhythms tell the whole story. In d strains, there is outward motion at coefficients 1 and 3. The comparison of coefficients 1 and 9 for Scott show that what appears to be a balance between notes on and off the eighth-note metrical positions, when viewed at the two-measure level, turns out to be? a tendency to alternate from eighth-note syncopation in odd-numbered measures to straight eighths in even-numbered measures. The similar comparison of coefficient 3 to 11 (and 2 to 10 for Joplin) shows something similar at the quarter-note level. A balance between on-beat and weak eighth is actually an alternation of straight quarter-note and syncopated quarter-note rhythms.

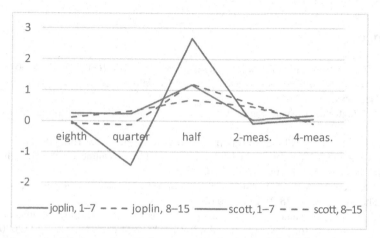

Fig. 10. Average of Hadamard coefficients over levels, for Joplin and Scott in *c* and *d* strains

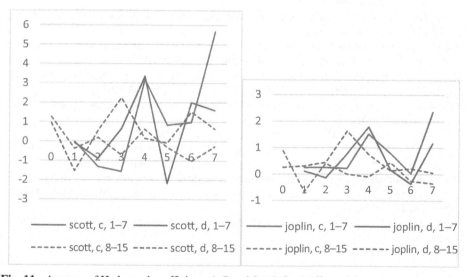

Fig. 11. Average of Hadamard coefficients 1–7 and 8–15, for Joplin and Scott in *c* and *d* strains. These are overlaid such that coefficient numbers 8–15 appear at the same x-positions as those less by eight.

This specific case is illustrative. The structure of the Hadamard transform is well suited to detecting these sorts of interactions between levels. It also provides a way of characterizing syncopation that, unlike other definitions, has the character of a lossless transform, making it particularly flexible and useful for the kind of data analysis research represented here. This allows us to answer a question like, "in what sense are ragtime rhythms syncopated?", very precisely. It also has the potential to reveal many stylistic features with great detail, of which we have only highlighted a select few here.

References

Amiot, E.: David Lewin and maximally even sets. J. Math. Music **1**(3), 157–172 (2007)

Amiot, E.: Music through Fourier Space. Springer: Heidelberg (2016). https://doi.org/10.1007/978-3-319-45581-5

Berlin, E.A.: Ragtime, A Musical and Cultural History. University of California Press, Berkley (1980)

Blesh, R., Janis, H.: They All Played Ragtime, 4th edn. Oak Pub, New York (1971)

Cohn, R.: A Platonic Model for Funky Rhythms. Music Theory Online **22**(2) (2016). http://mto smt.org/issues/mto.16.22.2/mto.16.22.2.cohn.html

Huron, D., Ommen, A.: An empirical study of syncopation in American popular music, 1890–1939. Music Theory Spectrum **28**(2), 211–230 (2006)

Kirlin, P.: A corpus-based analysis of syncopated patterns in ragtime. In: Proceedings of the 21st International Society for Music Information Retrieval Conference, pp. 647–653 (2020)

Koops, H.V., Volk, A., de Haas, W.B.: Corpus-based rhythmic pattern analysis of ragtime syncopation. In: Proceedings of the 16th International Society for Music Information Retrieval Conference, pp. 483–489 (2015)

Longuet-Higgins, H.C., Lee, C.S.: The rhythmic interpretation of monophonic music. Music Perception **1**(4), 424–441 (1984)

Magee, J.: Ragtime and Early Jazz. In: Nicholls, D. (ed.) The Cambridge History of American Music, pp. 388–417. Cambridge University Press, Cambridge (1998)

McNally, W.M.: Ragtime then and now: composers and audiences from the ragtime era to the ragtime revival. Ph.D. dissertation, The City University of New York (2015)

Peñalosa, D.: The Clave Matrix: Afro-Cuban Rhythm: Its Principles and African Origins. Bembe Books, Redway (2012)

Sethares, W.A.: Rhythm and Transforms. Springer, London (2007)

Temperley, D.: Modelling common practice rhythm. Music Perception **27**(5), 355–376 (2010)

Volk, A., de Haas, W.B.: A corpus-based study of ragtime syncopation. In: Proceedings of the 14th International Society for Music Information Retrieval Conference, pp. 163–168 (2013)

Yust, J.: Steve Reich's signature rhythm, and an introduction to rhythmic qualities. Music Theory Spectrum **43**(1) (2021a)

Yust, J.: Periodicity-based descriptions of rhythms and Steve Reich's rhythmic style. J. Music Theory **65**(1) (2021b)

Visitors' Experiences in Digital Culture

Redefining the Digital Paradigm for Virtual Museums
Towards Interactive and Engaging Experiences in the Post-pandemic Era

Archi Dasgupta[1]([⊠]) [iD], Samuel Williams[1] [iD], Gunnar Nelson[1] [iD],
Mark Manuel[1] [iD], Shaoli Dasgupta[2] [iD], and Denis Gračanin[1] [iD]

[1] Virginia Tech, Blacksburg, VA, USA
{archidg,shwilliams,ngunn,mmark95,gracanin}@vt.edu
[2] Liberation War Museum, Dhaka, Bangladesh

Abstract. The COVID-19 pandemic has greatly accelerated the digitization of services. As physical spaces become harder to access, there is a growing shift towards the use of virtual spaces for remote work, education and entertainment. In 2020, brick-and-mortar spaces like museums, art exhibits and galleries were especially affected by a lack of visitors. Shifting to a virtual medium would allow these entities to reach out and retain visitors more effectively. However, the use of virtual spaces to support these kinds of services is still quite under-explored. Presence, engagement and a real connection are difficult to establish through virtual exhibits. To explore these challenges, we partnered with the Liberation War Museum in Bangladesh and created a web-based 3D virtual museum to represent three of their historical galleries. Each virtual gallery has a different presentation modality - "self-guided", "avatar-guided" and "game-based". We sought to explain which of these artifact presentation modes led to the best performance in learnability, usability and engagement by conducting a user study. Our findings and user feedback are presented in this paper. We hope that these findings will be useful for designing virtual experiences that can allow users to learn and engage with virtual artifacts as effectively as they would with real-world ones.

Keywords: Virtual museum · Web-based museum · 3-D Virtual Museum · Post-pandemic · Digital paradigm · Digital age · Learning · Engagement · COVID-19 · Avatar-guided museum · Game-based museum

1 Introduction

Museums are an essential part of preserving and defining the history, culture, technology and identity of people. They offer an immersive and well-curated learning experience that helps visitors develop a better understanding of their

M. Rauterberg (Ed.): HCII 2021, LNCS 12794, pp. 357–373, 2021.
https://doi.org/10.1007/978-3-030-77411-0_23

history through the exhibition of artifacts. Museums are a predominantly 'brick-and-mortar' presence that preserve, create and disperse knowledge. However, the COVID-19 pandemic has created an unforeseen barrier for in-person interactions. Physical distancing measures have led to an unprecedented downturn in tourism and hospitality [3]. As a result, museums have been getting fewer visitors. If this trend continues, some museums might have to close permanently. This should be a wake-up call to the need for having a well-defined digital paradigm for museums [13]:

> *"The transformation won't mean that museums lose what they have to offer as physical sites conveying knowledge through the medium of material objects. It means that the museum will get another dimension, a digital one."*

Digitizing museums democratizes access and education for people regardless of location, resources, and age. The digital medium can be a powerful agent for learning, but it is significantly underutilized by museums. Some popular museums, such as the Smithsonian National Museum of History, offer a virtual self-guided experience but lack in interactive experiences. Whereas, Swartout et al. [23] specifically emphasize on designing interactive methods for facilitating engagement and learning in museum visitors who sometimes ignore the exhibits. Current practices of developing virtual museums can be categorized as brochure museums and content museums [22]. They are mostly limited to a digital collection of images, A/V files and text documents which scarcely inspire learning. However, the development and analysis of interactive methods for facilitating engagement and learning in museum visitors is a novel paradigm to explore. Our study focuses on the unique potential of the digital medium in developing interactive and engaging learning experiences. We aim to examine and evaluate three modes of virtual education through museums - a free roam self-paced experience, a guided experience led by an instructor (authority) and a puzzle-based experience, all to assess the users' engagement, motivation and knowledge retention in the virtual experience.

To explore these three modalities, we partnered with the Liberation War Museum (LWM) of Bangladesh and created a web-based virtual museum for them. The LWM has a strong presence and a rich history of research into museology. Therefore they were an ideal group for us to collaborate with. We conducted multiple rounds of focus group meetings with the members of the board of trustees of the LWM to better understand their requirements. We compared three methods—"self-guided", "avatar-guided", and "game-based" experiences using this virtual museum. The "self-guided" experience facilitates visualization of virtual exhibitions in the form of 3D galleries and lets the virtual visitor walk around at their own pace and explore the artifacts. The "avatar-guided" experience is created by developing a virtual museum guide that uses narrations to explain the 3D virtual artifacts [9]. The "game-based" experience utilizes the gamification technique for making the artifacts interactive and part of a puzzle game/scavenger hunt for conveying a story. We use learning, engagement and usability as metrics for evaluating and comparing the three methods by conducting a user study.

Overall, the aim of this research is to reexamine the digital paradigm for museums and identify best practices for curating virtual museums in the post-pandemic world. Hopefully our findings will be useful for designing similar virtual experiences that inspire curiosity and the desire to learn more in museum visitors.

2   Related Work

Virtual museums have been researched for decades but the current digital approaches still do not offer a quality of experience comparable to their physical counterparts [15]. The COVID-19 pandemic has expedited the need for people to embrace virtual environments. There are different methods of engagement that museums can adopt to shift over to the virtual paradigm which include free-roam, guide-based, and game-based museums [8]. Museums in different countries have been implementing 3D virtual web-based museums using VR technology. A virtual environment can also be setup in a stereoscopic view. It gives the visitors illusion of being in the real place instead of visiting an exhibit [21]. Such museums include the Smithsonian Natural Museum of History and the British Museum. These museums also provide information about specific artifacts through different mediums like image and audio transcripts [11].

Another method of learning is through gamification techniques. Some video games provide historical simulations giving players the opportunity to learn, such as "The Civil War – a Nation Divided" [17]. Gamers can interact with each other synchronously within the simulated historical era. There are vast amounts of virtual exhibits and museums, such as the Mayan recreation made through "Second Life";

Embracing virtual reality environments can help improve learning and education. Such works include a "Hidden Waterfall City", an underwater archaeology virtual reality (VR) experience, and a digital Malaysian cultural heritage compendium. The "Hidden Waterfall City", presented a mystical place in the virtual environment [8]. Meanwhile, the underwater VR experience, introduced people to underwater archaeological overview of Iceland and the country's underwater life [18]. The Malaysian compendium aims to preserve the Malaysian culture [24]. Mixed-Reality is also seeing increased application as a digital medium for educational experiences [10]. However, the exact contribution of these mediums to enhancing engagement and learning needs to be further explored.

When focusing on curated experiences in museums in a virtual setting, there are factors to consider in terms of information being conveyed. For instance, acceptance of the use of a tour guide versus a self-guided experience. In terms of learning, the guide serves as a medium to fully convey information, preventing information from being overlooked. The appearance of avatars as guides in virtual museums need to be relevant to the information that they present. Their assumed specialization affects the way that they are perceived, since people tend to ignore elements that are diverging from their perceived experience [20]. In a virtual game-like setting, interacting with digital avatars enhance user's engagement and presence [7].

Our idea of incorporating new technology with learning derives from the technology-mediated learning (TML) approach introduced by Alavi and Leidner [2]. The technologies described in their work have advanced and have become more accessible to the average user in web browsers, allowing new levels and modes of education to be implemented in online educational services.

Hou et al. investigated and compared three approaches to museum learning for university students—a traditional museum experience, a paper-based supplement, and a mobile device supplement [12]. Results from their pre and post-test examinations found that participants in the mobile device learning group received the highest average scores and had the largest overall increase in their post-test scores. Collected data also showed that the mobile device group paid more attention to exhibits than the other two groups. Klopfer et al. found game-based learning in museums to be an effective mode of learning for both children and their parents [14]. Feedback from their study indicates increased user engagement, with several participants claiming to have learned materials they had not learned before, whereas in some cases the user had visited the museum before on multiple occasions. We hope to find similar results and compare user feedback between modes of learning in our museum. Yiannoutsou et al. examined the incorporation of mobile devices with educational games used in a museum education for junior-high school children [25]. They noted that participants developed a task oriented approach of searching for clues and answers in the games, and results indicated that this approach helped students develop a clear understanding of each exhibit's main ideas. Their study also found that some exhibits were better suited for game-based education than others.

3   Problem Definition

The current era is termed as the "digital age". The widespread use of the internet and personal computers have dramatically established the digital world as being almost as important as the physical world. Hence digitization has become an inevitable trend for any service, be it education, museums, galleries, retail etc. Because of COVID-19, museums around the world were forced to close off for the general public. This event has intensified the need for a virtual presence.

Museums are an agent for learning and the preservation of history and culture. The trend of digitization has already begun in the museum sector. But one persistent problem in this domain is that until now, the primary focus of research in this space has been in digitization of the artifacts [15] rather than focusing on users' virtual experience for enhancing learning, engagement and presence. The term "brochure museums" is used for most virtual museums, because of their brochure-like approach for developing a website. The problem with this approach is that flat, 2D images of artifacts cannot fully capture users' attention and encourage learning. More recently researchers have started exploring informal learning through museums using web-based stereoscopic views, virtual museum guides in physical museums, and virtual reality (VR) experiences. But a lot of these approaches are not readily available for the average user, for example, VR solutions are not remotely accessible to the general population. On the other hand, the stereoscopic view-based approach lacks the interactive component. Moreover this approach focuses more on creating an illusion of being in the real-life museum using images rather than focusing on the artifacts themselves.

However, we focus on creating an interactive experience that will enhance learning through an user-centered perspective. We examine different approaches to retain visitor's attention through providing 3D interactable artifacts, audio-visual media and game-like 3D walkable space design. Web-based services are also more accessible to the underprivileged population and can bridge the gap in resource availability for students. We feel that the current pandemic makes this a timely and relevant topic to explore. As mentioned by Pallud, the primary two components of a visitor's experience are education and entertainment [19]. Designing a museum requires both aspects to be implemented appropriately. Hence we examine and report our findings of using three approaches—a self-guided experience, a guided experience using virtual avatar and a puzzle-type game based approach. We hope that our exploration of the three modalities will help redefine the digital paradigm for museums.

4 Approach

In this section, we describe our approach for comparing the three modalities and reasons for choosing them to create an engaging, interactive and immersive virtual experience. The three modalities are "self-guided", "avatar-guided" and "game-based" experiences. The "self-guided" 3D walk through experience is currently the most prevalent format in web-based virtual museums. For example, the web-based Smithsonian National Museum of History provides one type of free-roam experience to the visitors.

Current avatar-guided museum experiences, such as the Ada and Grace experience [23], dictate to visitors virtually, but are in a physical museum. We aim to integrate this into the virtual museum experience using a digital animated avatar narrating descriptions to the visitors.

Finally, game experience for virtual museums is a growing body of research, which integrates content into game-based learning due to the proven positive effects of games on learning [5]. However, learning by gaming is not presently recognized by formal educational systems, primarily in low and middle-income countries, and games for museums are a relatively new concept. They require mechanics in the design where the experience is not only stimulating, by presenting a challenge, but also provide an educational experience for the user.

To compare the learnability, engagement and usability aspects of these three approaches, we developed a web-based 3D virtual museum [6] and conducted a user study. The website was created in collaboration with the LWM to present the journey of Bangladesh towards becoming a sovereign nation.

The LWM collaborators conducted the survey-based user study to evaluate the museum. The survey responses (without identifiers, such as email address,

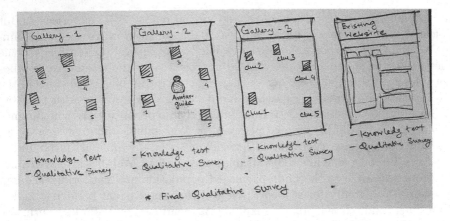

Fig. 1. User study: concept sketch of three galleries. Gallery 1: self-guided. Gallery 2: avatar-guided. Gallery 3: game-based.

IP address, name, phone number, etc.) were shared with Virginia Tech students for evaluation and analysis. The study was conducted with 22 participants. We used Mozilla Hub, Unity Game Engine, Web3D, and Google Tour Creator for developing the three experiences of the museum.

The virtual museum consists of three galleries, with five different artifacts in each gallery (Fig. 1). The three galleries are designed using the three approaches for an one-hour study. Participants explore each gallery for 10 min and then complete a knowledge-based test and a qualitative survey. First, in the self-guided experience, participants walk around exploring the different artifacts. The second gallery has a avatar-guide that leads the visitor to artifacts and conveys information about them. Finally, the third gallery has participants solve a puzzle by investigating artifacts to find information.

After participants finish experiencing the three galleries, they take an overall qualitative survey to determine which experience was the most educational and enjoyable. We analyze the knowledge-based tests, qualitative surveys, and the final survey to compare the learnability, usability and engagement of each approach.

4.1 Focus Group Discussions

The board of trustees of the LWM is the focus group for the purposes of this study. We chose them as a focus group because of their decades-long experience and expertise in the domain of museology.

The museum was established in 1996 by this board of trustees with the vision to commemorate the heroic struggle of the Bengali nation for their democratic and national rights. Prior to the pandemic, school students (high school) from all over Bangladesh, would participate in extra-curricular activities organized by the LWM. However, due to lockdowns and safety measures, the museum had to close

Fig. 2. Top left: Gallery 1 (self-guided). Top right: Gallery 2 (avatar-guided). Bottom: Gallery 3 (game-based).

its galleries for visitation, requiring the museum to adapt to the transitions of the digital age and the new normal. One of the members of the board of trustees said, *"...it is the responsibility of the current generation to preserve history for their future generations."*.

We curated the virtual museum based on the focus group discussions with the board members of the LWM. The meetings were conducted virtually and the goal was to create an interactive virtual museum experience to enhance learning. We discussed the other museums, like the Topography of Terror museum in Berlin, Germany, that provide different types of choices (text, audio and video narration) in addition to the physical artifacts to engage visitors. Therefore, our virtual museum has been developed with each gallery highlighting a different method of engagement to understand its effect on learning.

4.2   Design Development

The galleries are designed as hexagonal rooms where five walls are used as a backdrop for five sets of artifacts. The first gallery is self-guided, second gallery is avatar-guided and third one is game-based (Fig. 2).

We designed the artifacts for each gallery in the following manner:

1. Image-based artifacts: A combination of 2D images and 3D models. Textual description appears once the visitor interacts with the artifacts.
2. Video artifacts: A combination of 2D images/3D models and a video clip. The video clip appears once the visitor interacts with the artifact.

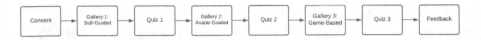

Fig. 3. User study flow diagram: data collection process.

3. Text with narration: A combination of 2D images/3D models/video clip and narration from the avatar-guide.

For the second gallery, we chose an avatar-guide which was a symbolic reference to the nation of Bangladesh, the Royal Bengal Tiger. For the third gallery, we chose a puzzle-type game where hints are provided to the visitors that leads to different artifacts.

4.3 Application Development

The virtual museum is developed using Unity3D, a 3D game development engine with C# back-end. Artifacts are mostly provided by the LWM, while some of them are collected from publicly available sources [1,16]. Utilizing open source software and servers, we host the work on GitHub pages with "000Webhost" to contain diagnostic user interaction data. WebGL, a JavaScript API that supports rendering 3D objects and environments, is used to provide intuitive interaction.

Gallery 2 contains an avatar-guide, a 3D tiger model with nine animations of walking, conversing, and referring to artifacts. Standard artifacts allow the visitor to rotate the artifact by holding and moving the left mouse button, a brief description is shown on the bottom of the screen while interacting. An exit button is enabled only after a period of five seconds to ensure that the participants engage with the artifacts.

Diagnostic data is collected internally to be cross-examined with the qualitative feedback and knowledge-test scores of each user. We use Unity RayCast to determine whether an user is looking at an artifact from within a certain distance. Once the user completes visiting a gallery, the color of an "exit door" changes from black to green prompting the user to leave through the door. Once the user collides with the door, a post request with diagnostic data is sent to the database hosting site.

5 User Study Description

In this section, we describe the user study as a step by step process (Fig. 3). The following brief instructions are communicated virtually and through e-mail.

1. The participants are provided a consent form and information sheet to explain that their personal identifiable information (email address, name, IP Address, contact number) will be kept confidential and solely accessible by the principal investigator from the LWM. The consent form also includes sections for collecting demographic information.

2. The User is then provided with the URL [6] of the virtual museum through which they generate their unique identification number (user ID).
3. From the home page, they are prompted to enter the first gallery by clicking a link. They are redirected to the web page of the first gallery. This page remains open for the entire duration of the experience.
4. Upon completing each gallery, a new tab opens with a link to the survey for the corresponding gallery. The participants are instructed to disable their pop-up blocker to have an uninterrupted participation. The surveys include knowledge tests and qualitative questions.
5. After the completion of the survey of the third gallery, the user is provided with a URL of the overall survey by the principal investigator. This final survey seeks feedback based on the overall experience of the museum in terms of user friendly interface, comfort in using the interface, impact on learning through the curated instructiveness etc.

Demographic Information

We conducted the user study with 22 participants. The selected participants were chosen on the basis of their age. All participants were at least 18 years old. Table 1 depicts the demographic information of the participants. Seven of the participants are private service holders, four students, three interns, three lawyers, two engineers, one entrepreneur, one homemaker and one volunteer at the LWM. All of the participants are Bangladeshi citizens.

Table 1. Demographic information: 22 participants.

Gender	Age (median)	Education	Visited the LWM In-person Before (%)	Visited Any Virtual Museum Before (%)	Experience with Digital Systems (%)
Male: 6	27	PhD: 2	Yes: 68.18	Yes: 36.16	Beginner: 36.36
Female: 16		Masters: 11	No: 31.82	No: 63.64	Intermediate: 45.45
		Undergrad: 9			Advanced: 18.18

6 Results

In this section, we analyze the usability, engagement and the effectiveness of the three approaches as learning media. We also explore the engagement aspects of the artifacts. The avatar guide, an animated 3D model of the Royal Bengal Tiger, is the unique feature of the second gallery. The game-based puzzle-solving approach is the unique characteristic of the third gallery.

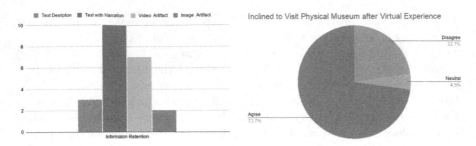

Fig. 4. Left: artifact type vs. number of participants—most effective artifact for information retention. Right: inclination to visit physical museum after virtual museum experience.

6.1 Learnability

Qualitative Results: Artifacts in each gallery are designed as either video artifacts, image-based artifacts, textual description with narration or only textual description focused artifacts. Based on the responses from the final survey, the artifacts consisting of textual description with narration were the most effective for information retention (Fig. 4(Left)). Participants were enthusiastic about the avatar-guide, as it was fun and interactive: *"Of course the guide itself! Brilliant idea and execution."* The second most preferred artifacts were the video artifacts. One of the participants mentioned, *"The Concert for Bangladesh was engaging, as it was informative and music always helps."*

72.7% of the participants expressed interest in visiting the physical museum after the virtual museum experience (Fig. 4(Right)). Which means the virtual experience was able to encourage learning within the visitors.

Quantitative Results: Participants took a knowledge test after completing each gallery. These scores might reflect a possible bias arising from the varying level of difficulty for the questions in each gallery. Moreover, the participants are Bangladeshi nationals, so there can be a possible bias arising from pre-existing knowledge. However, these scores help us understand the effectiveness of the three design approaches as learning media. For gallery 1 (self-guided), participants scored an average of 98.4% in the knowledge-based test. In case of gallery 2 (avatar-guided), the score was 93.91% on avergae. For gallery 3 (game-based), the average score was 91.44%. We conclude that all three galleries performed well on the learnability aspect as the average scores were above 90%. As a future work, we are curious to explore the results by conducting an user study with non-Bangladeshi participants to see how these scores vary.

While discussing the gallery 3, one user said, *"(I found) the scavenger hunt (engaging) as it helped me remember the learnings. However, I think it should end with some reward, for example, a badge that can be shared on Social Media."* Another user responded, *"The quiz made me look through the gallery with more details."*

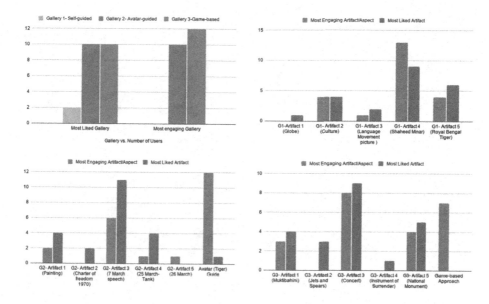

Fig. 5. Gallery/artifacts vs number of participants—most liked and most engaging. Top left: most liked/engaging gallery. Top right: Gallery 1. Bottom left: Gallery 2. Bottom right: Gallery 3.

6.2 Engagement

Qualitative Results: Most liked gallery and most engaging gallery: As evident from Fig. 5, Gallery 2 and 3 were the most liked galleries because of the avatar-guide and game based approach. On the other hand, the third gallery was found to be the most engaging because of its puzzle-solving, game-based approach. This gallery was well-liked also because of its interactive nature—*"...the game based version. The clues were nice and interactive."*

Most Engaging and Liked Artifact/Aspect: The most engaging artifact in gallery 1 was the "Shaheed Minar" replica and the audio and visual display that was associated with it. This was also the most liked artifact in this gallery. Followed closely by the 3D model of the tiger.

One of the participants mentioned, *"Shaheed Minar model was engaging and pretty, the 3d nature allowed me to walk around and see it from multiple angles."*

For gallery 2, the most engaging aspect was the animated, 3D avatar-guide. The participants really enjoyed the avatar and its narrations as a unique mode of learning.

To quote a participant, *"The guide, audio visual aspect gives an immersing story telling which is beautiful."* Another participant had some suggestions about the text description and the narration, *"(The most engaging aspect was) the talking tiger as he acted as a guide. However, the mismatch between the voice and the writing was a bit distracting for me as I was not being able to concentrate on either of them."*

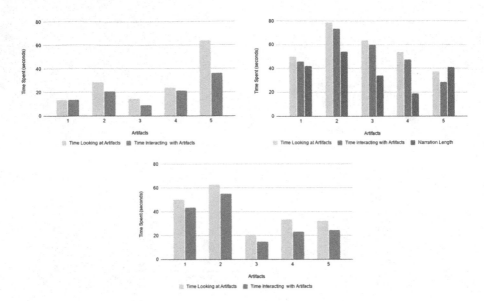

Fig. 6. Artifacts vs time looking and time interacting. Top left: Gallery 1. Top right: Gallery 2. Bottom: Gallery 3.

The second most engaging aspect/artifact was the video artifact (7 March speech). It was also the most liked artifact. To quote a user, *"The 7th March speech. Visually more stimulating than still artifacts."* The second most liked artifact was the 3D model of a tank. To quote a user, *"The 3-D model of the tank, as it felt alive."*

For gallery 3, the most engaging aspect was the video artifact depicting the concert. One user said, *"The Concert for Bangladesh (was the most engaging), due to it being audiovisual."* The approach of puzzle solving scored a close second place as a unique mode of learning. To quote a participant: *"Game based Gallery is very interactive, fun and gives a different experience to museum visits."* The most liked artifact in this gallery was the video artifact. The 3D model of the freedom fighters was also appreciated because of its details. One user mentioned that, *"(I liked) the weapons of the freedom fighters. That the freedom fighters started engaging the war by traditional weapons, it gives the visitors a proper idea of the level of dedication and love of the martyrs."*

Overall, we can see that participants overwhelmingly preferred the video artifacts. They also thoroughly enjoyed an animated guide who would walk them through history in a chronological order. The game-based approach was also very engaging for the participants as they were working toward a goal and the reward of completing the tasks. participants said that, *"...this would be amazing for children"* and *"The experience is not monotonous"*. So, a combination of these approaches could be considered while designing a virtual museum.

Quantitative Results: We collected three data points from each user—the total time they spent in each gallery, the total time they spent looking at each artifact, the total time they spent interacting with each artifact (Fig. 6). The "time looking" at an artifact was the amount of time the user spent looking at the artifact from a certain distance. "Time interacting" with an artifact was the amount of time the user spent after clicking the artifact until the time they exited. It is important to note that the user interacts and looks at an artifact simultaneously.

In the first gallery, the artifact that was both looked at and interacted with for the longest amount of time was artifact 5, the model of the Royal Bengal Tiger. Artifact 5 was likely examined for a longer period of time due to the complexity of the 3D model compared to other artifacts in the first gallery. The qualitative data (Fig. 5) also suggests that artifact 5 was the second most liked/engaging artifact.

For the second gallery, it is worth noting that the participants were required to interact with the artifact throughout the length of the narration given by the avatar-guide. Participants could exit only after the narration ended. The qualitative data (Fig. 5) suggest that the avatar-guide was the most engaging aspect of this gallery. It also appears that participants spent additional time examining and interacting with artifacts before or after the narration (Fig. 6). According to the collected diagnostic data, approximately 86% of the participants appeared to follow the guide's directed order for visiting the artifacts.

In the third gallery, the riddles provide hints to lead towards a specific artifact and the answer to the riddle can be found by exploring the artifact's description or video. Participants appeared to be the most engaged with the first two artifacts. However, qualitative data (Fig. 5) suggest that artifacts 3 and 5 were the most liked/engaging. One probable explanation could be that, after the first two riddles, participants got the hang of the game, hence required less time for the later ones. In this gallery, solving the puzzle was likely a bigger motivation for participants rather than visiting the artifacts which is also supported by qualitative data.

6.3   Usability

At the end of the study, participants were asked to fill out a survey which contained a modified version of the System Usability Scale (SUS) [4]. The SUS is a simple tool for measuring the usability of an application. It consists of a 10-item questionnaire with five response choices ranging from "strongly disagree" to "strongly agree". Each of these responses are given a numeric value on a scale of 1–5 (strongly agree (5), strongly disagree (1)). These scores are summed up and scaled to 100 to get a representative measure of each user's usability score for their experience with the museum. The questions used for the SUS questionnaire are provided below.

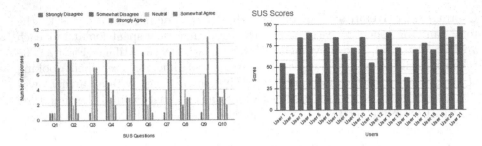

Fig. 7. Usability evaluation. Left: SUS responses per question. Right: SUS scores per user.

1. I think that I would like to revisit the virtual museum.
2. I found this virtual museum experience unnecessarily complex.
3. I thought this museum was easy to navigate.
4. I think I would need assistance to be able to use this virtual museum.
5. I found the various functions in this virtual museum were well-integrated.
6. I thought there was too much inconsistency in this virtual museum.
7. I would imagine that most people would learn to use this virtual museum very quickly.
8. I found this virtual museum very cumbersome/awkward to use.
9. I felt very confident using this virtual museum.
10. I needed to learn a lot of things before I could get going with this virtual museum.

A total of 22 participants provided their responses to these SUS prompts. However, one user's data contained missing entries and had to be discarded. The responses of these participants can be seen in Fig. 7(Left). The prompts that received the highest scores from the participants were numbers 5, 7, and 9. Figure 7(Right) depicts the final SUS scores per user, scored out of 100 points. The average score per user was 72.5 and the median score was also 72.5. According to [4], a score of above 68 classifies as above average. This finding suggests that the majority of our participants considered the virtual museum to be usable as a more accessible online extension of the LWT.

7   Discussion and Conclusion

In this research, we provide a comparative analysis between three different modalities for developing web-based 3D virtual museums towards achieving interactive and engaging learning experiences. Whereas other related efforts have mostly focused on mimicking the physical museums in the virtual world, we have focused on enhancing the visitor's experience by utilizing the unique capabilities of the digital medium. As evident from our user study, the novelty of the application was received with enthusiasm by the participants.

Fig. 8. Word-cloud from participants' final comments.

While testing the three modalities for virtual museums—self-guided, avatar-guided and game-based experiences, we received useful feedback from the participants. A word-cloud (Fig. 8) generated from the qualitative feedback represents overall user enthusiasm about the novel approaches like 3D walkable environment, learning through narration and interactive artifact design, engaging game-experience.

Our collected diagnostic data and qualitative feedback align closely. To summarize, our user study results show that the avatar-guided and game-based galleries received the highest scores from the participants based on interest and engagement.

Participants were the most enthusiastic, and spent the most amount of time while interacting with video artifacts and 3D models. Collected data also suggest that the narration from the animated avatar-guide increased the participants' attention towards the artifacts.

We also find that game-based learning is an effective mode of learning as it offers a reward-model which increases engagement and satisfaction. 72% of the participants expressed interest in visiting the physical museum after visiting the web-based version which represents the effectiveness in encouraging learning. The SUS score also suggests that the 3D virtual experience was usable and an welcome experience for the visitors.

One user commented, *"The overall experience was very good. I liked both the avatar-guided and the game-based versions and I think they can be mixed to keep both the flavours alive."* We conclude that a multi-modal approach is best suited for encouraging learning and engagement in visitors.

For designing the individual artifacts, participants suggest that providing all three options of audio-visual, narration and text-description for each artifact will engage people more with the topics. Having the galleries designed with bright colors will also make it visually attractive to children. Also having an artifact list in each gallery can be an useful reference for visitors. One participant mentioned that, *"However, I wish that I could see the actual artifacts, articles and pictures from the museum better and more clearly instead of just having a text that describes it."* That means, providing the functionality to select and read/look at the artifacts closely as a digital asset will prove useful.

Some of the participants suggested that the narration by the avatar-guide could be clearer and if the text descriptions matched the narration, it would have been a better experience. This comment provides us with an interesting future study topic. We are curious to explore the effect of having the narration in user's native language or having the voice-over done by a speaker of the same nationality as the user.

Few of the participants complained about the cumbersome navigation and implementation flaws where the program becomes unresponsive. We presume that participants without previous gaming or 3D virtual environment navigating experience have a learning curve to use this sort of experience. But overall majority of the participants who experienced a virtual museum for the first time were excited and enthusiastic about the unique experience.

Extensive research in the domain of web-based virtual museums is required as the creation and demonstration of virtual architectural, cultural and historical reconstructions make it possible to transfer the cultural heritage to the newer generation. This digitization will help facilitate remote learning and democratize access to information and education. Another important aspect is providing continued accessibility in case of pandemic-like emergencies or other natural disasters. We hope educators and researchers of museuology will find our results valuable to identify best practices and develop effective educational strategies through virtual museums.

References

1. 7th March Foundation: 7th March, 1971 speech of Bangabandhu sheikh Mujibur Rahman. https://www.7thmarch.com/7th-march-video/. Accessed 02 May 2021
2. Alavi, M., Leidner, D.E.: Research commentary: technology-mediated learning-a call for greater depth and breadth of research. Inf. Syst. Res. **12**(1), 1–10 (2001)
3. Becker, E.: How hard will the coronavirus hit the travel industry. National Geographic, April 2020
4. Brooke, J., et al.: SUS–a quick and dirty usability scale. Usability Eval. Ind. **189**(194), 4–7 (1996)
5. Ćosović, M., Brkić, B.R.: Game-based learning in museums-cultural heritage applications. Information **11**(1), 22 (2020)
6. Dasgupta, A.: Video: 3D, web-based virtual museum: the Liberation War Museum, Bangladesh. https://youtu.be/go1LsJa0pxI. Accessed 02 Oct 2021
7. Dasgupta, A., Buckingham, N., Gračanin, D., Handosa, M., Tasooji, R.: A mixed reality based social interactions testbed: a game theory approach. In: Chen, J.Y.C., Fragomeni, G. (eds.) VAMR 2018. LNCS, vol. 10910, pp. 40–56. Springer, Cham (2018). https://doi.org/10.1007/978-3-319-91584-5_4
8. Esmaeili, H., Thwaites, H., Woods, P.C.: A conceptual human-centered approach to immersive digital heritage site/museum experiences: The hidden waterfall city. In: Proceedings of the 3rd Digital Heritage International Congress (DigitalHERITAGE) Held Jointly with 24th International Conference on Virtual Systems & Multimedia (VSMM 2018), pp. 1–4. IEEE (2018)

9. Gilbert, R.L., Forney, A.: Can avatars pass the turing test? Intelligent agent perception in a 3D virtual environment. Int. J. Hum. Comput. Stud. **73**, 30–36 (2015)

10. Handosa, M., Schulze, H., Gračanin, D., Tucker, M., Manuel, M.: Extending embodied interactions in mixed reality environments. In: Chen, J.Y.C., Fragomeni, G. (eds.) VAMR 2018. LNCS, vol. 10909, pp. 314–327. Springer, Cham (2018). https://doi.org/10.1007/978-3-319-91581-4_23

11. Hill, V., Mystakidis, S.: Maya island virtual museum: a virtual learning environment, museum, and library exhibit. In: Proceedings of the 18th International Conference on Virtual Systems and Multimedia, pp. 565–568. IEEE (2012)

12. Hou, H.T., Wu, S.Y., Lin, P.C., Sung, Y.T., Lin, J.W., Chang, K.E.: A blended mobile learning environment for museum learning. J. Educ. Technol. Soc. **17**(2), 207–218 (2014)

13. Jones-Garmil, K. (ed.): The Wired Museum: Emerging Technology and Changing Paradigms. American Association of Museums, Arlington (1997)

14. Klopfer, E., Perry, J., Squire, K., Jan, M.F., Steinkuehler, C.: Mystery at the museum: a collaborative game for museum education. In: Proceedings of the 2005 Conference on Computer Support for Collaborative Learning: Learning 2005: The next 10 Years! pp. 316–320. International Society of the Learning Sciences (ISLS) (2005)

15. Li, P.P., Chang, P.L.: A study of virtual reality experience value and learning efficiency of museum-using shihsanhang museum as an example. In: Proceedings of the 2017 International Conference on Applied System Innovation (ICASI), pp. 1158–1161. IEEE (2017)

16. Liberation War Museum: LWM. https://www.liberationwarmuseumbd.org/. Accessed 02 May 2021

17. Mastel, K., Huston, D.: Using video games to teach game design: a gaming collection for libraries. Comput. Libr. **29**(3), 41–44 (2009)

18. McCarthy, J., Martin, K.: Virtual reality for maritime archaeology in 2.5D: a virtual dive on a flute wreck of 1659 in Iceland. In: Proceedings of the 23rd International Conference in Information Visualization – Part II, pp. 104–109 (2019)

19. Pallud, J.: Impact of interactive technologies on stimulating learning experiences in a museum. Inf. Manage. **54**(4), 465–478 (2017)

20. Podzharaya, N.S., Sochenkova, A.S.: The virtual museum development with the use of intelligent and 3D technologies on the basis of the maritime museum in Kotor. In: Proceedings of the 23rd International Scientific-Professional Conference on Information Technology (IT), pp. 1–4. IEEE (2018)

21. Sooai, A.G., Nugroho, A., Al Azam, M.N., Sumpeno, S., Purnomo, M.H.: Virtual artifact: enhancing museum exhibit using 3D virtual reality. In: Proceedings of the 2017 TRON Symposium (TRONSHOW), pp. 1–5. IEEE (2017)

22. Styliani, S., Fotis, L., Kostas, K., Petros, P.: Virtual museums, a survey and some issues for consideration. J. Cult. Herit. **10**(4), 520–528 (2009)

23. Swartout, W., et al.: Ada and Grace: toward realistic and engaging virtual museum guides. In: Allbeck, J., Badler, N., Bickmore, T., Pelachaud, C., Safonova, A. (eds.) IVA 2010. LNCS (LNAI), vol. 6356, pp. 286–300. Springer, Heidelberg (2010). https://doi.org/10.1007/978-3-642-15892-6_30

24. Thwaites, H., Santano, D., Esmaeili, H., See, Z.: A Malaysian cultural heritage digital compendium. Dig. Appl. Archaeol. Cult. Heritage **15**, e00116 (2019)

25. Yiannoutsou, N., Papadimitriou, I., Komis, V., Avouris, N.: "Playing with" museum exhibits: designing educational games mediated by mobile technology. In: Proceedings of the 8th International Conference on Interaction Design and Children, pp. 230–233 (2009)

Research on Factors Influencing Users' Technology Acceptance of Virtual Museums

Wenxuan Gong and Bing Xiao[✉]

Department of Design, Shanghai Jiao Tong University, Shanghai, China

Abstract. With the development of information technology and experience economy, virtual museums has become the digital development and extension of traditional museums. At the beginning of this year (2020), virtual museums have been rapidly popularized in the form of "cloud exhibition" in the epidemic situation, and have shown great market development potential. This study aims to analyze the factors influencing users' technology acceptance on virtual museums. 15 related factors have been defined through desktop research, among which the key elements and their internal association have been summarized through the method of DEMATEL. The results show that "Improving the quality of the tour", "Having a multi-sensory experience" and "Accessing to rich information" are the key influencing factors, while "Positive media comment" and "Assurance of the brand" are the main influenced ones. In the internal mechanism of users' technology acceptance of virtual museums, the perceived ease of use encompasses the main cause factors and has a strong impact on the dimensions of perceived pleasure, perceived usefulness and perceived safety. Based on the above findings, several suggestions have been proposed to help practitioners further enhance the use experience of virtual museums.

Keywords: Interactive digital museums · Visitors experiences in digital culture · Technology acceptance model · The method of DEMATEL

1 Introduction

Virtual Museum, also known as the Digital Museum, Electronic Museum or Hypermedia Museum, refers to the various types of services or experiences which the cultural institutions provide based on the use of Internet technology and digital media [1]. As a digital extension of physical museum as a whole or in part, the emergence of the virtual museum has benefited from the rapid development of information technology and the strong support of cultural tourism policies. The advent of the new media age gives every user the right to link to works that span generations, geographies and genres, thus allowing the virtual museum to show the more distinct characteristics of preservation and openness when compared to the traditional physical museum. Therefore, the virtual museum is the product of a good combination of "culture and technology" as well as the inevitable result of the digital transformation of museums.

This paper uses the method of DEMANTEL to quantitatively analyze the internal mechanisms of the factors that influence users' technology acceptance of virtual

© Springer Nature Switzerland AG 2021
M. Rauterberg (Ed.): HCII 2021, LNCS 12794, pp. 374–388, 2021.
https://doi.org/10.1007/978-3-030-77411-0_24

museums. The key influencing and influenced factors can be extracted from the data to help stakeholders such as museum staff, designers and government decision makers to rethink the direction of museum digitization in the context of the information age and the experience economy.

1.1 Background

At present, the number of physical museums in China has reached 5354, which is an important part of public cultural service system [2]. However, the functions of museums have shifted from the collection and research to public education and cultural services under the transformation of social needs, market directions as well as consumer perception, and have begun to further expand the function of leisure, recreation and life enrichment in recent years [3]. The display experience design of museums have been gradually from the "exhibit-centric" to "people-centric".

The epidemic earlier this year (2020) has hit the offline physical display industry. On the other hand, it drives the explosive growth of virtual museum projects so that the "cloud exhibition" has become a new fashion of public cultural life during the epidemic. At present, the typical virtual museum in China is no longer limited to the museum's official website, but is an Internet product that relies on multiple media platforms and integrates storage, display, education and interactive services. For example, the Palace Museum has launched the "Daily Palace App" to help visitors break through the restrictions of time and location. Every visitor could have a daily up-close and comprehensive tour of an exhibit on their mobile device. the WeChat widget of "Cloud Travel to Dunhuang", which was jointly launched by the Dunhuang Research Institute and Tencent in April this year (2020), distinguishes the display content based on interest tags such as art form, dynasty, color, etc. to fully meet the personalized tour needs of users. Story dubbing and other mini-games are also adds to make the online tour more interesting. "Online Graduation Design Exhibition of Academy of Arts & Design, Tsinghua University" has built the 2.5D Cloud Gallery to present the exhibition space of nearly 100 square meters, creating an immersive exhibition experience and exploring a variety of ways to present information.

The reports by the Center for the Future of Museums stated that, it is an important trend for future museums to "creating a multisensory immersive environment in a personalized way" by combining its intellectual resources, digital technologies, and new sensory reproduction technologies [4]. In the face of a future full of variables, museums and other physical exhibition institutions have gradually realized that, it is far from being able to meet the diverse cultural needs of the public by offering a short-term and emergency-style online exhibitions in the form of simply copying the offline ones. The urgent consideration for them is how to taking advantage of the digital platform and find effective ways to adjust the curatorial direction, as well as to enhance the virtual museum experience, in order to improve the revisit rate.

1.2 Related Work

Research on museums in recent years has undergone a conceptual shift from objects to people. The new shift in how museums adopt new technologies to enhance the public reception of their own exhibits, as emphasized by Hooper Greenhill, focuses on the contexts in which collections are encoded and their interactions with the viewers.

Around 2010, the museum studies community enhanced its research on the viewers in virtual museums. For example, Nina Simon et al. (2010) studied audience participation and contribution mechanisms [5]. John H. Falk (2009) expanded the social attributes of virtual museums [6], while Kikuo Asi (2010) highlighted the fun and collaborative study of the touring process [7], and so on. At present, however, most domestic and foreign researches on virtual museums are limited to the evaluation of existing projects, or the discussion of production and technical implementations of new ones; little research has been conducted on the audience in virtual museums, especially on the influencing factors of audiences' reception of them. The article therefore complements this aspect.

1.3 Technology Acceptance Model

The acceptance of information technology by users is a gradual process that involves psychological and cognitive changes. Davis (1989) first proposed the Technology Acceptance Model to explain and predict this phenomenon [8], which has been generally accepted by the academic community (see Fig. 1). According to Davis (1989), it is a gradual process for users to accept new information technology, and factors that hinder this process often cause the promotion of information technology to lag behind the hardware development.

As the emerging forms in the process of upgrading museum display design, virtual museums combines multiple new technologies such as the Internet, social media, virtual reality and big data technologies, thus it is also applicable to the Technology Acceptance Model that the process for users from "learn about the virtual museum" to "accept it in attitude", and finally to "be willing to use it". Therefore, it is Meaningful to study users' acceptance of technology as a key element in the development and promotion of virtual museums.

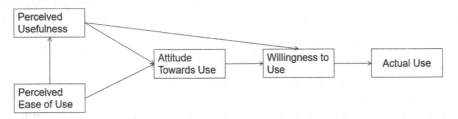

Fig. 1. Technology acceptance model

2 Research Design

2.1 Research Methods

The study began with background analysis and problem definition through the literature research. Next, the researcher adopted a questionnaire to collect user data, and analyzed these data quantitatively by the method of DEMATEL.

DEMATEL, which was presented by the Batttelle Association of the Geneva Research Centre in 1973, is a data research method that helps to effectively understand complex question by observing the two-two influence relationship and its extent between the constituent elements of the question [9]. The introduction of the DEMATEL method in this paper allows for a clearer analysis of the degree of influence and causality among the factors, which helps researcher to understand the nature of virtual museum experience design based on users' technology acceptance, and to optimize the experience design approach.

The specific steps of the DEMATEL method include: (1) defining the elements; (2) determining the relationship, i.e., questionnaire research; (3) forming a direct relationship matrix; (4) calculating the direct/indirect matrix and using it to calculate the degree of centrality (D+R) and the degree of cause (D-R); (5) drawing a cause-effect diagram to form visual findings.

In order to ensure the accuracy and validity of the questionnaire results, as well as taking the difficulties of offline questionnaire distribution in the current epidemic situation into account, the questionnaire was completed by using an online one-to-one approach.

2.2 Analysis of Influencing Factors

The factors influencing user's technology acceptance of virtual museums in this study firstly are based on the key elements of the Technology Acceptance Model. The study by Furong Gao et al. (2011) have pointed out that, according to TAM, the process of users' technology acceptance is mainly based on the perception of "usefulness" and "ease of use", which combined with other subjective factors to determine attitudes towards use and ultimately influence the propensity of their behaviors [10].

Considering that there are few systematic studies in the field of technology acceptance of virtual museums, as well as taking the characteristics of convergence, non-linearity, personalization and interactivity that virtual museums present when being used into account, the researcher here refers to the findings of studies on new media that has overturned traditional mass communication models. Yoonhyuk Jung (2008) summarized the relationship between perceived attention and intention to use in a study of mobile TV usage based on TAM, and proposed the idea that immersive experience is equivalent to perceived attention [11]. Dong Hee Shin (2009) studied the internal and external motivations for the use of IPTV based on the Theory of Rational Behavior. The key influencing factors he suggested include perceived usefulness, perceived entertainment and perceived security [12]. Fang (2008) further added specific subjective factors including perceived entertainment, subjective norms, trade-off needs and perceived risks based on TAM, TRA and new media Trade-off Demand Theory. The mind-flow experience in this case is defined as the psychological and physiological satisfaction obtained in the state of human-computer interaction, which can be specifically split into perceptual control, mental concentration and pleasure. Additionally, based on the conclusion, the willingness of consumers to purchase goods based on VR technology and the willingness of users to continue using mobile games were explored [13].

To conclude, based on the above findings, the researcher here added the dimensions of "perceived pleasure" and "perceived safety" to the factors influencing users' technology acceptance of virtual museums. Among them, "perceived pleasure" is derived from the theory of heart-flow experience in the process of experience design, which is to realize the psychological and physiological satisfaction of users in the immersive experience through "using anytime and anywhere", "feeling in control" and "feeling motivated".

Ultimately, taking into account several practical examples of virtual museum applications, 15 primary influencing factors (PIFs) under four dimensions are proposed for the factors that influence users' technology acceptance of virtual museums as shown in Table 1.

Table 1. 15 PIFs under 4 dimensions influencing users' technology acceptance of virtual museums (source: authors' own illustration).

Number	Dimension	PIFs
1	Perceived Ease of Use	**Convenient and Quick Operation** (The system has low threshold for learning, the system has friendly interactive, the system is accessible regardless of time and place, etc.)
2		**Operation in Line With Physiological Habits** (The speed at which characters walk and switch between screens is reasonable, the viewing distance from the exhibit is comfortable, etc.)
3	Perceived Usefulness	**Reducing Travel Costs** (Including saving money and avoiding the risk of epidemics during offline tours, etc.)
4		**Accessing to Rich Information** (Users could get detailed information and background of the exhibits on all aspects or in various interesting formats, etc.)
5		**Improving the Quality of the Tour** (A clearer and more comprehensive view than on offline tours, which may help in making decisions on offline tours.)
6	Perceived Pleasure	**Having a Multi-sensory Experience** (The system can provide a wide range of simulation experiences including visual, olfactory, tactile, and auditory.)
7		**Touring with a Non-daily Perspective** (Such as users could view the entire museum from above, or the exhibits become huge and users could move between them to see the details, etc.)
8		**Effective Interaction with Display Content** (Such as users could participate in changing the display content and receive timely feedback, etc.)

(*continued*)

Table 1. (*continued*)

Number	Dimension	PIFs
9	Perceived Pleasure	**Effective Interaction with Virtual Characters** (AI guides, virtual characters, etc. could provide timely guidance or gamified interactions based on user needs.)
10		**Effective Interaction with Other Users** (Such as the system offers a group mode that allows users to communicate with peers, or one user's operation may affect the experience of others on the tour, etc.)
11		**Sense of Inspiration** (Users effective interaction could be encouraged by the system or other users in the form of coins, gifts or leaderboards)
12		**Follow-up Personalized Service** (Such as users could learning about the latest exhibition information based on interest, or recording the journey in various ways as a souvenir, etc.)
13	Perceived Security	**Assurance of the Brand** (Greater public acceptance of virtual museums brought by well-known physical museum brands, such as the Palace Museum, etc.)
14		**Influence of Acquaintances** (such as receiving recommendations through online and offline social channels, or using for reasons of having common social topics with peers)
15		**Positive Media Comment** (Effective advertising in official channels)

Perceived Ease of Use. This dimension reflects the degree to which individuals find it easy to use a specific system, in the context of this paper, including that users believe it is quick and easy to operating the virtual museum (the system has low threshold for learning, the system has friendly interactive, the system is accessible regardless of time and place, etc.) and the operation is physiological(the speed at which characters walk and switch between screens is reasonable, the viewing distance from the exhibit is comfortable, etc.).

Perceived Usefulness. This dimension reflects the extent to which an individual perceives that the use of a specific system has improved his performance, in the context of this paper, including that users believe that if they use the virtual museum, they could reduce travel costs (including saving money and avoiding the risk of epidemics during offline tours, etc.), access to rich information (including getting detailed information and background of the exhibits on all aspects or in various interesting formats, etc.), and improve the quality of the tour (referring to a clearer and more comprehensive view than on offline tours, which may help in making decisions on offline tours.).

Perceived Pleasure. This dimension reflects that virtual museums could leverage advanced technology to provide users with a delightful, surprising and immersive experience, which specifically includes a multi-sensory experience (the system could provide a wide range of simulation experiences including visual, olfactory, tactile, and auditory.), a non-routine perspective touring (such as users could view the entire museum from above, or the exhibits become huge and users could move between them to see the details, etc.), effective interaction with display content (such as users could participate in changing the display content and receive timely feedback, etc.), effective interaction with virtual characters (such as AI guides, virtual characters, etc. could provide timely guidance or gamified interactions based on user needs.), effective interaction with other users (such as the system offers a group mode that allows users to communicate with peers, or one user's operation may affect the experience of others on the tour, etc.), sense of inspiration (user's effective interaction could be encouraged by the system or other users in the form of coins, gifts or leaderboards) and follow-up personalized service (such as users could learning about the latest exhibition information based on interest, or recording the journey in various ways as a souvenir, ect.).

Perceived Security. This dimension reflects an individual's perception that a system is safe and trustworthy. The specific reasons that affect this dimension include assurance of the brand (refers to that greater public acceptance of virtual museums brought by well-known physical museum brands, such as the Palace Museum, etc.), influence of acquaintances (such as receiving recommendations of a certain virtual museum through online and offline social channels, or using for reasons of having common social topics with peers) and positive media comment (refers to the effective advertising in official channels).

2.3 Experiment and Data Analysis

Based on the 15 PIFs presented in the above section, the researcher first asked the subjects to experience three typical virtual museums prepared in advance (Including the APP of "Daily Palace", the WeChat widget of "Cloud Travel to DunHuang", and "Online Graduation Design Exhibition of Academy of Arts & Design, Tsinghua University"). Then a questionnaire was designed for the subjects to make a two-by-two comparison of the 15 PIFs after the tour, in which there are 4 measures were set: no impact (0 points), mild impact (1 points), moderate impact (2 points) and high impact (3 points). 224 valid data are obtained after filtering by the length of time the questionnaire was filled out.

The direct relationship matrix of 15 PIFs could be obtained by calculating the average of the 224 data (see Table 2).

The direct relationship matrix was formalized by using the Excel formula calculations to obtain the direct/indirect matrix (see Table 3). The threshold value of 0.313 was calculated by quartile method. Thus the two PIFs: "3 Reducing travel costs" and "14 Influence of acquaintances", which did not reach the threshold value, were deleted from the table.

Next, the degree of centrality (D+R) and the degree of cause (D-R) were calculated. The results are ranked from highest to lowest, and the final results are shown in the Table 4.

Table 2. Direct Relationship Matrix of influences on users' technology acceptance of virtual museums (source: authors' own illustration)

PIFS	1	2	3	4	5	6	7	8	9	10	11	12	13	14	15
1	0.00	1.71	1.79	2.07	2.04	1.57	1.64	1.93	1.39	1.64	1.29	1.29	1.04	1.14	1.39
2	1.89	0.00	1.29	1.46	2.04	1.93	1.50	1.93	1.29	1.57	1.14	1.00	0.89	0.96	1.25
3	0.82	0.89	0.00	0.86	1.14	0.82	0.82	0.68	0.64	0.64	0.79	1.07	1.11	1.00	1.29
4	1.21	0.96	0.96	0.00	2.39	1.82	1.71	2.04	1.21	1.21	1.04	1.43	1.36	0.86	1.71
5	1.32	1.32	1.43	1.96	0.00	2.11	1.71	1.75	1.29	1.25	1.29	1.86	1.68	1.21	1.75
6	1.25	1.79	1.07	2.21	2.29	0.00	1.71	2.14	1.36	1.57	1.46	1.61	1.57	1.11	1.46
7	1.21	1.07	0.93	1.96	2.07	1.96	0.00	1.79	1.04	1.29	0.93	1.21	1.18	0.82	1.54
8	1.46	1.18	0.79	2.04	2.14	2.21	1.18	0.00	1.14	1.36	1.29	1.54	1.32	1.04	1.46
9	1.11	0.96	1.04	1.54	1.89	1.68	0.86	1.32	0.00	1.32	1.64	1.50	1.11	1.79	1.32
10	1.21	0.96	0.75	1.82	1.86	1.75	1.25	1.75	0.89	0.00	1.50	1.50	1.07	1.00	1.39
11	0.57	0.68	1.00	1.11	1.79	1.04	0.75	1.43	1.11	0.93	0.00	1.36	1.29	1.43	1.29
12	1.00	0.82	1.07	1.96	1.89	1.29	0.96	1.36	1.21	1.00	1.61	0.00	1.57	1.25	1.50
13	0.61	0.71	0.82	1.39	1.57	1.00	0.79	1.04	0.93	0.89	1.00	1.25	0.00	1.86	2.11
14	0.43	0.46	0.64	1.04	0.75	0.50	0.46	0.46	1.46	0.61	0.96	0.89	1.32	0.00	1.29
15	0.54	0.68	0.79	1.43	1.04	0.68	0.54	0.64	0.71	0.50	0.71	0.93	1.79	1.46	0.00

Table 3. Direct/Indirect Matrix of influences on users' technology acceptance of virtual museums (source: authors' own illustration)

PI-FS	1	2	3	4	5	6	7	8	9	10	11	12	13	14	15
1	0.219	0.284		0.420*	0.445*	0.367*	0.308	0.379*	0.290	0.302	0.299	0.329*	0.318*		0.363*
2	0.284	0.201		0.376*	0.423*	0.363*	0.288	0.361*	0.272	0.285	0.278	0.301	0.295		0.338*
3	0.158	0.158		0.227	0.252	0.205	0.170	0.198	0.160	0.160	0.173	0.201	0.204		0.229
4	0.252	0.237		0.310	0.429*	0.353*	0.291	0.358*	0.265	0.266	0.270	0.313	0.310		0.352*
5	0.271	0.266		0.413*	0.358*	0.384*	0.308	0.368*	0.284	0.283	0.297	0.349*	0.342*		0.376*
6	0.279	0.294		0.437*	0.467*	0.313	0.319*	0.397*	0.297	0.307	0.315*	0.351*	0.349*		0.377*
7	0.244	0.234		0.378*	0.405*	0.348*	0.213	0.339*	0.250	0.261	0.257	0.295	0.293		0.335*
8	0.265	0.249		0.398*	0.425*	0.372*	0.275	0.281	0.266	0.275	0.284	0.321	0.312		0.347*
9	0.233	0.223		0.352*	0.388*	0.327*	0.242	0.312	0.201	0.256	0.280	0.299	0.284		0.319*
10	0.239	0.225		0.366*	0.390*	0.333*	0.260	0.332*	0.240	0.202	0.275	0.301	0.283		0.323*
11	0.179	0.180		0.285	0.329*	0.257	0.201	0.270	0.213	0.204	0.175	0.253	0.251		0.273
12	0.223	0.212		0.360*	0.379*	0.304	0.240	0.305	0.245	0.236	0.272	0.230	0.296		0.319*
13	0.178	0.179		0.293	0.317*	0.252	0.200	0.251	0.204	0.200	0.215	0.246	0.196		0.303
14	0.127	0.126		0.212	0.213	0.172	0.139	0.169	0.178	0.143	0.165	0.176	0.195		0.209
15	0.143	0.146		0.244	0.243	0.194	0.155	0.192	0.160	0.150	0.167	0.192	0.228		0.172

Note: * represents a value greater than the threshold value of 0.313, while a blank indicates that neither the row nor column values are greater than the threshold value, so that the factor has been deleted

Table 4. The degree of centrality (D+R) and the degree of cause (D-R) (source: authors' own illustration)

The Degree of Centrality (D+R)			The Degree of Cause (D-R)		
5	Improving the Quality of the Tour	**10.329**	1	Convenient and Quick Operation	1.611
6	Having a Multi-sensory Experience	**9.617**	2	Operation in Line With Physiological Habits	1.378
4	Accessing to Rich Information	**9.580**	7	Touring with a Non-daily Perspective	0.723
8	Effective Interaction with Display Content	**9.090**	10	Effective Interaction with Other Users	0.713
12	Follow-up Personalized Service	**8.262**	9	Effective Interaction with Virtual Characters	0.708
1	Convenient and Quick Operation	**8.201**	6	Having a Multi-sensory Experience	0.527
7	Touring with a Non-daily Perspective	7.945	8	Effective Interaction with Display Content	0.068
2	Operation in Line With Physiological Habits	7.807	12	Follow-up Personalized Service	−0.050
10	Effective Interaction with Other Users	7.773	11	Sense of Inspiration	−0.221
9	Effective Interaction with Virtual Characters	7.761	4	Accessing to Rich Information	−0.565
13	Assurance of the Brand	7.626	5	Improving the Quality of the Tour	−0.595

(*continued*)

Table 4. (*continued*)

The Degree of Centrality (D+R)			The Degree of Cause (D-R)		
15	Positive Media Comment	7.376	13	Assurance of the Brand	−0.684
11	Sense of Inspiration	7.220	15	Positive Media Comment	−1.895
Average value		**8.059**			

Note: bolded values are greater than D + R's overall average value of 8.059

In the method of DEMATEL, centrality indicates the degree to which this element influences and is influenced. Thus, according to the Table 4, the three key influencing factors (KIFs) for users' technology acceptance of virtual museums are, in order of importance, "5 Improving the quality of the tour", "6 Having a multi-sensory experience" and "4 Access to rich information".

While the degree of cause is bounded by zero, with a positive value indicating that the element is biased toward the cause category, and a larger value indicating that the element has a greater influence on other factors. On the contrary, a negative value indicating that the element is biased toward the effected category, and a larger absolute value indicating that the element is more influenced by other factors. Therefore, according to Table 4, among the 15 PIFs, "1 Quick and easy to operating" mainly influences other factors, while "15 Positive media comment" is most influenced by other factors.

The following table extracts the first and the last three items of the degree of centrality and causality respectively (see Table 5 and Table 6), since the rows of "3 Reducing travel costs" and "14 Influence of acquaintances" are below the threshold value, they are not considered here.

Table 5. The first and last three items of the degree of centrality (D+R) (source: authors' own illustration)

The First 3 Items of (D+R)	The Last 3 Items of (D+R)
5 Improving the Quality of the Tour	13 Assurance of the Brand
6 Having a Multi-sensory Experience	15 Positive Media Comment
4 Accessing to Rich Information	11 Sense of Inspiration

Ultimately, a cause-and-effect diagram was drawn by using centrality as the horizontal axis and causality as the vertical axis, with each PIFs (centrality, cause) as a set of coordinates, which is shown in Fig. 2.

In the above cause-and-effect diagram, the influencing factors of different dimensions are distinguished by different colors, where blue indicates the factors of perceived ease of use, yellow indicates the factors of perceived usefulness, red indicates factors of perceived pleasure, and green indicates the factors of perceived safet. The arrows show

Table 6. The first and last three items of the degree of cause (D-R) (source: authors' own illustration)

The First 3 Items of (D-R)	The Last 3 Items of (D-R)
1 Convenient and Quick Operation	5 Improving the Quality of the Tour
2 Operation in Line With Physiological Habits	13 Assurance of the Brand
7 Touring with a Non-daily Perspective	15 Positive Media Comment

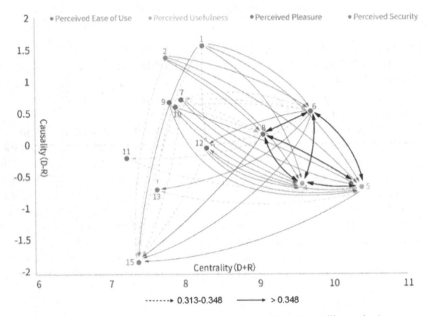

Fig. 2. Cause-and-effect diagram (source: authors' own illustration)

the direction of influence of one factor on the other. Additionally, taking two-thirds of all values in the direct/indirect matrix greater than the threshold of 0.313 could obtain the value of 0.348, which is used as a distinction between arrows with dashed lines and solid lines. The following conclusions can be clearly drawn from the cause-and-effect diagram:

Firstly, the impact relationships exist among the four dimensions is shown as the Fig. 3. In the internal mechanism of users' technology acceptance of virtual museums, the perceived ease of use encompasses the major causal factors and has a strong impact on the dimensions of perceived pleasure, perceived usefulness and perceived safety, while is not affected by other dimensions. On the other hand, the perceived security covers the main influenced factors, which are mainly affected by the other three dimensions. Perceived pleasure has a great influence on perceived usefulness, while some factors of perceived usefulness affect perceived pleasure in turn.

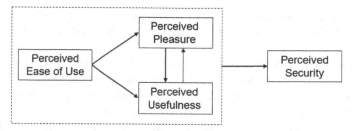

Fig. 3. Internal mechanisms of influence for each dimension (source: authors' own illustration)

Therefore, for exhibition planners and designers, improving the perceived ease of use for virtual museums by lowering the entry barrier and simplifying the operation could effectively achieve a change in users' perception of content and attitude towards virtual museums. It is also beneficial for users to receive brand new information and knowledge about the exhibition by providing them with a pleasant and satisfying tour experience.

Secondly, there is a strong inter-relationship between the four main influencing factors of "Accessing to rich information" "Improving the quality of the tour" "Having a multi-sensory experience" and "Effective interaction with display content", which means that improving one of these factors could correspondingly enhance the user's experience of the other ones, as well as promote users' acceptance of virtual museums. At the same time, this shows that the important concerns for users during the virtual museum tour are still the exhibits, display content, as well as the sense of presence.

Thirdly, "Positive media comment" and "Assurance of the brand" are the main influenced factors. Thus, by providing a virtual museum platform with a good experience, it could in turn help promote social media communication, which is beneficial to the brand building and marketing of physical museums.

3   Analysis and Discussion

3.1   Discussion

By using questionnaire survey and DEMATEL method, a clear understanding of the cause-and-effect relationship among 15 factors in four dimensions that influence users' technology acceptance of virtual museums has been achieved. Based on these findings, the following recommendations could be made to exhibition planners and designers, with a view to making the new technology of virtual museums more accessible to viewers.

Ensuring the Ease of Use of the Virtual Museums. Ease of use is the basis for user acceptance of new technologies. A virtual museum that is easy to operate, is friendly to interact with, has the physiological habitual field of view, as well as could be accessed anytime and anywhere is more likely to enhance the user's enjoyment of the exhibition and acceptance of the content on display. Based on the characteristics of Internet, it is the basis for building an easy-to-use virtual museum experience by improving the construction of digital platforms to minimize the occurrence of accidents such as lagging and flashing back. For designers, it has to be considered that different exhibits need to be displayed in a distinctive way that in conjunction with the interactive features of the mobile platform.

At the same time, more targeted design on the interface of virtual museums including timely text prompts, concise and clear information levels as well as fewer superfluous and redundant decorative effects could help the users to reduce the frustration and to focus more on the tour. Some virtual museums are currently experimenting with technologies such as gesture interaction to simplify operations and help users focus on the act of visiting itself, which is also an effective attempt to enhance the ease of use of virtual museums. But likewise, the consistency of new interaction rules with daily life habits should be considered to avoid increased learning costs.

Actively Integrating Cultural Resources to Realize Inter-museums Linkage From the findings in the above section, it is clear that the important focus of users during the virtual museum tour is still the exhibits and content. The rich and high-quality information and excellent experience is what the virtual museum should eventually present to its users. The virtual museum, with the help of the Internet and social media, has the advantage of breaking spatial boundaries, helping physical museums to realize inter-museums linkage, which is an important platform for cultural resource integration. The integration of cultural resources facilitates the screening and presentation of fine resources, helping to provide users with higher quality exhibitions, as well as to promote the common development of small local museums.

Expand the Functions of the Digital Platform and Build a Sense of Presence
The importance of interactivity and realism in virtual museums could be seen in the fact that "Multi-sensory experience" and "Effective interaction with the content" are the main influencing factors in users' technology acceptance of virtual museums. It is critical in the design of a virtual museum experience to create a sense of presence for the audience. Considering the different ways in which different works need to be presented, many curators have found that it is monotonous to have exhibits just shown in a virtual wall or booth. In such situation, users have difficulty to get a three-dimensional realistic viewing experience simply by zooming in and out on the screen. At present gamification is an effective way to enhance the fun interaction between users and exhibits, which could help users to form deeper and unique memories. Besides, the change of seasons, weather, light or other elements in the virtual environment could be realized with the help of auditory and olfactory sensors, which could improve the simulation experience under multi-sensory.

Meanwhile, with the transformation of user needs, the relationship between users and cultural knowledge begins to shift from passive acceptance to active acquisition. The subjective initiative of users should also be fully considered in the design of virtual museums, providing them with a choice and allowing for a more accurate personalized service experience based on big data analysis.

In the post-epidemic era, the linkage between virtual museums and offline venues could also be promoted to distinguish the focus of experience design based on their respective spatial characteristics, allowing users to feel the extension of museum tour experience, while making focused tour choices out of individual needs. At the same time, for the museum side, breaking the boundaries of virtual museums and physical museums facilitates the sharing of online and offline user resources, providing more scientific service guidance, which may bring the common development.

3.2 Further Deepened Directions

The study utilizes the DEMATEL method for data analysis and derives suggestions for optimization of the virtual museum experience design. Through the review of the research methodology, the researcher believes that there exists some discussable and deepening directions as follows.

Firstly, the originally predicted factor of "Avoiding the risk of offline visitation" is not strongly influencing nor influenced by other factors in users' technology acceptance of virtual museums. Thus, although the number of virtual museums has exploded in the context of the epidemic, users choose to use virtual museums, to a large extent, not because they "have to do it"; rather, they believe that virtual museums could provide a more complete and high-quality touring experience compared to offline tours. It is foreseeable that the use of virtual museums is an inevitable direction of development under the pursuit of high quality display experience by users even without the requirements of epidemic prevention in the future.

Secondly, due to the time and environment constraint, the sample size of the user study could be further expanded to obtain more accurate conclusions. Meanwhile, due to the complexity of the questionnaire, the subjects easily lost their patience when fill in it, which probably reduce the accuracy of the data. The questionnaire could be further simplified in the later deepening.

4 Conclusion

The study takes the exploding virtual museum in the context of the epidemic as the main research object. 15 primary factors influencing users' technology acceptance of virtual museums have been proposed based on Technology Acceptance Model and the findings of the research fields of experience design and museum display design. Then the method of DEMATEL has been introduced to analyze the influence relationship among the PIFs, concluding that "Improving the quality of the tour", "Having a multi-sensory experience", and "Accessing rich information" were the key factors influencing users' acceptance and enjoyment of virtual museums. Then, the inter mechanisms between the four dimensions of perceived ease of use, perceived usefulness, perceived pleasure and perceived safety have been analyzed through a cause-and-effect diagram. Relevant suggestions have been proposed in the discussion section to improve the virtual museum experience, which would provide reference for the digital construction of museums in China in the post-epidemic era.

Acknowledgments. We thank the course instructor, Chunrong Liu, who provided useful suggestions and ideas for the study. We are grateful to the subjects who participated in the questionnaire study and provided strong support for the conduct of this experiment.

References

1. Sun, D.: A brief review of virtual museum theory and museum construction in Europe and America. Fine Arts. **06**, 20–26 (2020). https://doi.org/10.13864/j.cnki.cn11-1311/j.005975
2. Liu, J., Jialing, L.: Finding opportunities in danger: response and optimization of digital cultural services in public museums under the new crown pneumonia epidemic. Hum. World. **07**, 35–40 (2020). https://doi.org/10.16737/j.cnki.rwtx81281190.2020.07.007
3. Huang, K., Li, W.: From the analysis of limitations to targeted practice - Reflections on breakthrough the predicaments of theme exhibition in science and technology museum. J. Nat. Sci. Museum Res. **3**(02), 47–54 (2018). https://doi.org/10.19628/j.cnki.jnsmr.2018.02.007
4. Merritt, E., Xie, Y.: U.S. Museum Trends Watch (2017). https://am-us.org/docs/default-source/center-for-the-future-of-museums/trendswatch-2017.pdfsfvrsn=2
5. Simon, N.: Where's the mobile museums project for intact social groups (2010). http://museumtwo.blogspot.com/search?q=mobile+media+intact
6. John, H.: Falk: Identity and the Museum Visitor Experience, 1st edn. Routledge, New York (2009)
7. Asai, K., Sugimoto, Y., Billinghurst, M.: Exhibition of lunar surface navigation system facilitating collaboration between children and parents in science museum. In: Proceedings of the 9th ACM SIGGRAPH Conference on Virtual-Reality Continuum and its Applications in Industry, pp. 119–124. ACM, New York (2010). https://doi.org/10.1145/1900179.1900203
8. Davis, F.D.: Perceived usefulness, perceived ease of use, and user acceptance of information technology. MIS Quart. **13**(3), 319–340 (1989)
9. Li, Y., Yin, B.: Research on influencing factors of corporate environmental behavior based on DEMATEL. J. Guangxi Cadres College Econ. Manage. **31**(1), 26–33 (2019). https://doi.org/10.3969/j.issn.1008-8806.2019.01.005
10. Gao, F., Gao, X.: A review on foreign Information technology acceptance models. Res. Dev. Manage. **23**(2), 95–105 (2011). https://doi.org/10.13581/j.cnki.rdm.2011.02.014.
11. Jung, Y., Perez-Mira, B., Wiley-Patton, S.: Consumer adoption of mobile TV: examining psychological flow and media content. Comput. Hum. Behav. **25**(1), 123–129 (2009). https://doi.org/10.1016/j.chb.2008.07.011
12. Shin, D.H.: The evaluation of user experience of the virtual world in relation to extrinsic and intrinsic motivation. Int. J. Hum.-Comput. Interact. **25**(6), 530–553 (2009). https://doi.org/10.1080/10447310902963951
13. Fang, X.: Research on the consuming behavior of IPTV audience. Huazhong Science and Technology University. Ph.D. dissertation (2008). https://kns.cnki.net/KCMS/detail/detail.aspx?dbname=CDFD0911&filename=2009141740.nh

Unlocking Learning: Promoting Cultural Brand Through Interactions with Ancient Locks in an SL Virtual Space

Pei-Hsuan Hsieh[✉]

National Chengchi University, Taipei 116, Taiwan
hsiehph@nccu.edu.tw

Abstract. This study started with designing a virtual museum to exhibit the ancient Chinese locks that are in the collection of the National Cheng Kung University Museum in Taiwan (NCKUM). The exhibition is marketed with a cultural brand, Ancient Locks, in a virtual space in Second Life (SL). The purposes of this study are thus threefold: 1) to explore the museum visitors' perspectives and their information technology (IT) needs, 2) to determine their different visiting styles when interacting with the museum docents, exhibition objects (i.e., ancient Chinese locks), and other visitors, and 3) to establish a model for marketing the cultural brand through the exhibition of ancient Chinese locks in both the real and the virtual museums. All visitors were invited to respond to a questionnaire after visiting either the real or the virtual exhibition sites to collect their feedback and suggestions. In total, 766 valid responses were received from visitors from different educational levels. The average level of satisfaction with their visits was above the midpoint, but they gave a below-midpoint score for their visiting needs, specifically, IT demands. In addition, visitors from different education levels gave significantly different responses regarding the satisfaction level and IT demands for their visit to the real and SL exhibitions. At the end of this study, a four-construct model containing different services for future visitors to select from is established for marketing the cultural brand internationally, especially through SL.

Keywords: Second life · Visitor satisfaction · Information technology demands · NCKU museum · Ancient locks

1 Research Motivation and Background

Ancient locks are valuable collector's items and worthy of digital archives. The vivid history of this brilliant technology deserves appreciation, imitation, and passing on as it is highly charged with cultural import [25]. Locks and keys are practical objects used since antiquity, and they are full of significance in historical, social, and economic respects [6, 24]. Ancient locks need the attention of collectors to be preserved and kept from being neglected and discarded. Dr. Yan Hong-Sen, a collector and professor in the Department of Mechanical Engineering, National Cheng Kung University (NCKU),

© Springer Nature Switzerland AG 2021
M. Rauterberg (Ed.): HCII 2021, LNCS 12794, pp. 389–405, 2021.
https://doi.org/10.1007/978-3-030-77411-0_25

discovered this collectible item after he picked up the hobby of collecting from his two advisors after becoming a graduate student in the United States in 1986. To date, Dr. Yan has collected more than 900 items. Recently, he has donated more than a hundred items to the National Science and Technology Museum (NSTM). A digital archive for the items has also been completed. The website maintained by the NSTM offers the digital version of the Ancient Chinese Locks exhibition [1]. Visitors do not need to travel a long distance to the designated place to see these ancient Chinese locks [23]. However, the way visitors and collectors interact with website-based exhibits is different from interactions in physical museums or virtual spaces. In the latter, global visitors can obtain rich experiential interactions with the exhibited items.

The NCKU Museum (NCKUM) borrowed from Dr. Yan some items with special mechanical designs and launched the exhibition at the NCKUM local site [14]. Soon after, the researcher began to extend this digital archive into a cultural brand in Second Life (SL), with the intent to promote the brand in a multiplayer/multiuser three-dimensional (3D) space [3]. Similar to its real counterpart, the virtual museum in SL lets visitors from all over the world see the locks and understand the wisdom of the people in ancient times. With regard to the ancient lock's cultural heritage, the researcher hoped to present the cultural implication that people should cherish those practical items in daily life that may be worth collecting as artifacts and that we should humbly learn the intricate mechanisms inside the locks to know more about these objects. The virtual Ancient Chinese Locks exhibition is always open at the address of its SL landmark: http://maps. secondlife.com/secondlife/HITHOP/218/253/22.

In this study, several research questions were raised: What are the visitors' perspectives and their information technology (IT) demands when visiting the virtual Ancient Chinese Locks exhibition in SL? What is their overall satisfaction level after the visits? How do SL virtual museum visitors' evaluations compare with on-site visitors' responses? As visitors came from different educational levels, their visiting styles may be different when interacting with the museum docents, exhibition objects (i.e., the ancient Chinese locks), and other visitors. Those differences might be some of the reasons behind their perspectives and IT demands. Their satisfaction level might also supply the researcher with a more comprehensive understanding of their perspectives of this kind of museum visiting experience. Finally, ways to effectively manage this cultural brand in the SL virtual space are worthy of discussion. For example, how can the museum establish and then revise a promotion model that contains different service options for future visitors and to carry out marketing activities to promote internationally the spirit of ancient lock as a cultural brand? And how can this cultural brand promotion model be applied to other historical objects with cultural heritage which have been digitally archived in a museum collection database?

Overall, the researcher intended to conduct a study of the visitors to the digital archive "Ancient Chinese Locks" and to provide an innovative idea for cultural expansion. This means using the 3D virtual environment SL in combination with modern Internet network to stage the ancient locks with abundant historical significance and practical values. The virtual site is accessible at all times so that visitors around the world can visit the virtual museum directly or through Internet links. The mechanical structures of ancient locks that demonstrate the cumulative wisdom throughout history can also work as teaching materials and become an international cultural brand. The purpose of this research is to explore the visitor types, attitudes, and demands with regard to the acceptance of this cultural brand under this innovative marketing strategy. A discussion on the visitors' information technology needs for the real and virtual exhibitions is necessary for the management of this international cultural brand. The main clientele can also be identified for better management. And most important of all, the study aims to establish a model of promotion for this cultural brand, further pushing it toward internationalization.

2   Literature Review

2.1   Cultural Brand

From the perspective of management studies, a brand is an intangible asset of a corporation that signifies a competitive advantage for sustainable operation. On the one hand, it can be taken as a trade secret [12, 20], which is concerned with the production process, post-sale service, social image, and enterprise culture. On the other hand, it is related to such psychological factors as leading styles, reward systems, staff performance, and consumer demands [4, 7, 22]. Kotler [13] has pointed out that a brand exists primarily in the intangible overall service and quality after the business is established and that it works through a graphic symbol (i.e., the trademark) to expand its market domain.

The rich cultural implication that ancient locks represent is a cultural brand that incorporates both practical and informational values [23]. This cultural brand emphasizes that modern people should cherish these practical and collectible objects used in people's daily life and even emulate and learn about their previous social and economic status and class identity as well as the different dynasties, periods, and customs [1]. A lock, with its appearance, mechanism, and paired key integrated as a complete locking unit, offers information to be learned and value for collecting. Through the lock, a culture can be creatively sculpted into a brand, which not only explains the invention and benefits of ancient technology but also generates creative thinking from an international angle for the cultural brand in terms of the cross-cultural, multi-lingual, diversified expansion, sustainable operation, and absence of time and space constraints [8, 17, 21, 26].

2.2   Virtual Museum in Second Life

Effective innovation is in favor of the technology user (or brand consumer) [18]. With the virtualization of the historical artifacts in 3D virtual space instead of physical locations, people can visit the space anytime from anywhere, much like attending an on-site museum tour for ancient artifacts, learning about their historical changes and cultural heritage [11, 16]. Second Life (SL), established by Linden Lab in 2003, offers multiple users (called residents or avatars) to interact with each other in a 3D virtual environment. Its mature transaction structure allows users to exchange SL virtual currency, called Linden Dollars (LD), with real ones (1 LD = 0.00313 USD). SL users can establish a virtual museum by purchasing a virtual island or an acre or a larger size of virtual land to obtain ownership of the land. Various activities can be hosted on the land, such as carrying out a marketing campaign and offering learning opportunities [9]. Case studies or action research can also offer traditional classes in the virtual world to propose potential teaching designs and methods [5, 10]. For non-profit organizations, especially schools, Linden Lab offers viewer codes to website developers so that learners of various age levels can learn freely on the platform in specific areas assigned by the teachers. Third parties complying with the SL Policy on Third-Party Viewers and the SL Terms of Service are also authorized to directly authenticate SL users' accounts upon users' agreements on their developed SL web-based version, e.g., SpeedLight [19]. In sum, the effectiveness of teaching in SL environments is quite obvious. Learners with an introverted personality or hobby of gaming and Internet learning are provided with opportunities to communicate and interact with other people [1, 3]. They are given more chances to improve teamwork, increase sharing among members, and solve problems, which may stimulate interests in learning, probing, and creating more interactive methods to raise participation rate and learning incentives [3, 5, 9, 10].

3   Methodologies

This study adopted both quantitative and qualitative approaches to achieve the aforementioned purposes. The quantitative approach consisted of developing a survey for visitors to complete after their visits. The qualitative approach was an action research involving observing visitors' behaviors and interactions during their visits to the museum. Thus, as the visitors' needs for information technology were confirmed upon their requests, adjustment for the exhibition was made shortly after. The special exhibition of the Ancient Chinese Locks in the real museum (Fig. 1) was open to the public first. The visitors could see the beauty of the ancient locks through the display cases with clear covers under dim lighting. They could also obtain the history of each lock by reading the wall posters and the descriptions on the labels in the exhibition room, which were all bilingual.

The development project for the SL virtual exhibition of "Ancient Chinese Locks" was initiated right after the real one was open (Fig. 2). In the SL virtual exhibition, a video clip replayed automatically to demonstrate the key-lock interaction of three selected ancient locks in a larger size with 3D animated effects. When it was first open to the online visitors, most were not satisfied with the video clips and requested to further enlarge the locks so that they can better see the inside of the key-lock interactive mechanism. Thus, a large-size "pullback lock" was then created to allow the visitors to "fly" inside the internal part of the lock (Fig. 3). They can explore the key-lock interactive mechanism from the perspective of the key.

To be noted, the real and the virtual exhibitions were somewhat different to prevent visitors from replacing the real exhibition with the virtual one. The layout of the virtual exhibition room, including the posters and the labels, mimics the real one. The way the virtual exhibited objects are placed in the display cases is similar to the real one as well, except the middle cylinder display case was not created in the virtual room. The visitors, i.e., SL avatars, can easily look around the room. Besides, the virtual ancient Chinese locks are shinier than the real ones. The visitors, no matter where they are from, would realize that the real locks are made of different metal materials, such as aluminum, copper, iron, nickel, silver, and steel. As the real locks have somewhat corroded over time, it was not the study's intention to realistically imitate the textures and designs of the real locks.

Fig. 1. (Left) Real NCKU Museum; (right) real Ancient Chinese Locks Exhibition.

Fig. 2. (Left) SL virtual NCKU Museum; (right) SL virtual Ancient Chinese Locks exhibition.

Fig. 3. A large-size pullback lock and the corresponding key.

3.1 Participants

Once the special exhibition of the Ancient Chinese Locks in the real museum and the SL virtual one were both ready, this study started to invite museum visitors of different age levels from different parts of the world to either visit the real exhibition or the virtual one. The real-site visitors' age range was broad, including little and older kids, teenagers, adults, and elders. Some visitor groups, such as elementary and middle or high school students' field trips, requested the museum's guided tour service. SL visitors were all adults and included a few elders. All the visitors were asked to complete a survey after the visit, in either paper or online format.

3.2 Questionnaire Development

The survey contains three parts (Table 1) in addition to the questions regarding the visitors' demographic background, i.e., the previous visiting experience [real/virtual], gender [female/male], age [fill in the blank], academic level [elementary/middle school/ senior high school/college-university/master's program/doctoral program], and subject matter expert [liberal arts/social science/natural science/others]. The first part asks the visitors to rate their degree of satisfaction with their museum experience (A2–A6). The second part asks for a rating of the importance of different IT demands (A7–A9). The third part asks visitors to evaluate their understanding of the exhibition's contents and determine the degree of difference between the real exhibit and the SL exhibit (A13–A18).

A 10-point Likert-type scale, ranging from 0 to 9, was used. In the survey, four open questions (A10, A11, A12, A19) were also given to obtain specific feedback from the visitors. The initial draft of the survey was reviewed for clarity and completeness by 14 college students who majored in multimedia design and had abundant experience with using and designing multimedia. Only two questions (A9 and A13) needed revision. Table 1 contains the final version of the survey questions. Both the paper-based and the online survey were provided in bilingual versions in the real site and the virtual one.

Table 1. Questions of the survey.

Part	Question number and item description
	A1 - Previous visiting experience and demographics
First	A2 - How satisfied are you with the overall planning of this exhibition in the virtual museum? A3 - How satisfied are you with the descriptions of the items in this exhibition? A4 - How satisfied are you with the information provided by the docent in this exhibition? A5- How willing are you to visit this exhibition again? A6 - How willing are you to recommend that others should visit this exhibition?

(continued)

Table 1. (*continued*)

Part	Question number and item description
Second	A7 - How could the hardware be improved in this exhibition? (e.g., computer monitor size, download speed, and mouse) A8 - How could the software improve in this exhibition? (e.g., video, audio content, and database content) A9 - How could the multimedia effects be improved in this exhibition? (e.g., animation)
Third	A13 - How well do you now understand the <u>historical value</u> of the ancient locks? A14 - How well do you now understand the <u>history</u> of the ancient locks? A15 - How well do you now understand the <u>appearance</u> of the ancient <u>fish</u> locks? A16 - How well do you now understand the <u>appearance</u> of the ancient <u>implement</u> locks? A17 - How well do you now understand the <u>appearance</u> of the ancient <u>letter</u> locks? A18 - How well do you now understand the <u>carving</u> of the ancient locks?
Other: Open-ended questions	A10 - What are your suggestions to improve the software and hardware used in this exhibition? A11 - Please give any other suggestions you have for this exhibition A12 - What are you most impressed by in this exhibition? A19 - If there was something you were very interested in or did not understand, did you talk to someone about it in this exhibition? How?

3.3 Data Collection and Analyses

The statistical software SPSS 17.0 was used to analyze the visitors' responses to the surveys. In addition to carrying out the descriptive analyses of visitors' demographics, the satisfaction level, IT needs, and comprehension level data were also statistically analyzed as a whole and by visitor type (real and virtual). The next step was to conduct a one-way ANOVA analysis on the visitors of these two exhibition modes, specifically, their satisfaction level (A2–A6), IT demands (A7–A9), and comprehension level (A13–A18) to see if there were significant differences between them. If there were, subsequent comparisons were made and incorporated into the analyses on open-ended feedback (A10, A11, A12, and A19) to draw the conclusions. The key point of the qualitative written feedbacks is not merely to locate the keywords in the same answers from different visitors, but also to adapt the promotion model of the cultural brand of the ancient locks with clarification on why and how to make the adaptations.

In addition, the elementary school students were given a short version of the survey that contains ten questions with ping-yin attached to each Chinese character (see the Attachment). These responses were analyzed separately from the other educational level groups. The responses were also helpful to continuously carry out the action research for this study.

4   Results

This research received 766 valid surveys in total, among which 112 (14.62%) were the short version. Table 2 displays the demographics of the survey respondents from the middle school level and above. Generally, there were more males than females; there were more adults ages 19 to 22 than youth; there were more college or university students than the other educational levels; the background of the real museum's visitors tend to be liberal arts while more of the virtual museum's visitors had an engineering background.

Table 2. Demographics of real and virtual museum visitors in numbers and percentages.

	Real	Virtual
Total	278 (36.29%)	376 (49.09%)
Gender[a]: male	149 (55.81%)	203 (56.23%)
female	118 (44.19%)	158 (43.77%)
Age[b]: 15–18	68 (26.46%)	121 (34.57%)
19–22	100 (38.91%)	166 (47.43%)
23 and above	87 (33.85%)	61 (17.43%)
Education level[c]: middle and high school	56 (21.05%)	101 (27.90%)
College or university	165 (62.03%)	204 (56.35%)
Master's or doctoral program	45 (16.92%)	57 (15.75%)
Subject matter expert[d]: literacy and arts	64 (29.36%)	45 (13.64%)
Social science	66 (30.28%)	47 (14.24%)
Natural science	62 (28.44%)	183 (55.45%)
Others	26 (11.93%)	55 (16.67%)

4.1   Analysis Results of Elementary School Students' Survey Responses

Sixty-one students felt happy to have visited the exhibition (57.1%), 47 who felt a little bit happy (42%), and 3 who did not feel happy (2.7%). One did not respond to the question. As for the fun level, 53 thought it was fun (47.3%), 52 thought it was a little bit fun (46.4%), and 6 thought it was not fun (5.4%). One (the same person) did not respond to the question. When asked if they understood the docent's explanations, 59 said that they understood (52.7%), 50 said that they understood somewhat (44.6%), and 3 (2.7%) said that they did not understand. As to whether they would want to visit again, 82 would visit again (73.2%) and 26 would not (23.2%). Four did not give a firm response to the question (three unanswered, and one said not sure). As to whether they would bring their friends or parents to the exhibition, 76 said they would (67.9%), and 35 would not (31.3%). Again, one person did not respond to the question. Overall, the elementary students' visits were enjoyable, and they would visit again and would bring friends and parents to visit.

In the open-ended responses, the elementary school visitors wrote that the locks in the exhibit were the most attractive, such as the Chinese zodiac locks, the figurine locks, the letter locks, etc. Some young visitors sketched the locks that they liked. However, because parental permissions have not been obtained, these drawings could not be presented in this paper. They also felt that if the exhibition room could add music, interactive models, and stamps. The more active children wished there was computer equipment that provides interactive games. Additionally, because the visiting time was short, some children suggested a longer visiting time so they can look at the exhibits longer. Most children asked their questions (if any) to their teachers and the docents. Some had discussions with their peers.

4.2 Analysis Results of Other Visitors' Survey Responses

Excluding the surveys taken by the elementary school students, the overall reliability of the surveys taken by the rest of the visitors is 0.922, 0.706, and 0.910 for A2–A6, A7–A9, and A13-A18, respectively. This shows the earnest attitude of the respondents in filling in their answers, proving that the survey scales have high consistency and stability. Table 3 shows the descriptive analysis results of their survey responses regarding the satisfaction level, the IT demands, and the comprehension level. Table 3 shows that the real museum's visitors had higher satisfaction, better learning, and lower IT demand than the virtual museum's visitors. Overall, the real museum was able to provide a learning environment that helped the visitors better understand what they were looking at. However, the virtual world allowed the visitors more interactivity, and the visitors had a closer experience with the interactive designs. As for the facility requirements, the real museum should improve in providing interactive devices to let the visitors learn in a more interesting and fun environment. The real locks had a greater affective impact on the visitors such that they would be more supportive in promoting the culture of ancient locks. Although technology was used to simulate the real exhibits, it was not able to present the artifacts a hundred percent. However, it was able to publicize the beauty of the ancient locks so that more people can see them, thereby fulfilling the purpose of cultural brand promotion.

Table 3. Mean values (standard deviation) of visitors' survey responses.

	Satisfaction level	IT demands	Comprehension level
All visitors	6.04 (1.67)	4.63 (1.87)	5.23 (1.62)
Real	6.65 (1.40)	3.21 (1.22)	5.69 (1.54)
Virtual	5.59 (1.71)	5.68 (1.55)	4.88 (1.60

Next, a Chi-square analysis was conducted and found that there was a significant difference between the responses of the real museum's visitors and those of the virtual museum (A2–A6 satisfaction level: 110.557, $p < 0.001$; A7–A9 IT demands: 399.120, $p < 0.001$; A13–19 comprehension level: 448.918, $p < 0.001$). This indicates that the real museum differs from the virtual museum in its presentation. If visitors do not experience an authentic presence in the virtual world, their satisfaction level decreases. Also, the virtual museum shows eight representative ancient locks. It needs to increase the number of artifacts to improve the visitors' satisfaction and comprehension. It is foreseeable that as the number of virtual locks increases, the IT demand is likely to increase also.

4.3 Differences in Responses from Visitors from Different Educational Levels

The current study employed one-way ANOVA to detect significant differences between the real museum's visitors and the virtual museum's visitors in their responses to questions A2–A6, A7–A9, and A13–A18. Any F value that was less than the criteria ($p < 0.05$) indicated a significant difference between these two groups (Tables 4 and 5). To further understand how different types of visitors may have different demands in terms of the promotion of the ancient locks cultural brand, the study divided the visitors into three groups: middle/high school students, college students, graduate school students. The differences between the different educational levels were investigated in their satisfaction level, IT demands, and comprehension level at different sites (real vs. virtual). The results showed that for middle/high school students, there was no significant difference between the real and the virtual museums in terms of satisfaction level, IT needs, and comprehension level (p-values = 0.265, 0.188, 0.051; F-values = 1.252, 1.749, 3.859, respectively). Significant differences were found in the satisfaction level and comprehension level of college students ($p = 0.000^*$, 0.000^*; $F = 49.125, 26.367$, respectively) and graduate students ($p = 0.000^*$, 0.000^*; $F = 19.488, 9.905$, respectively), but not in IT demands ($p = 0.703$, $F = 0.145$). The tables show that both college and graduate students had higher satisfaction and comprehension levels for the real museum than the virtual museum. Thus, it can be concluded that different types of visitors have different needs and comprehension levels associated with each museum format (real vs. virtual).

In summary, middle and high school students' demand for the ancient locks exhibition is primarily in the entertainment aspects. Their wish list included more gaming and computer equipment. Visitors in higher education have a higher demand in the cultural aspects and wish to understand more meaningful information at a deeper level. They do not expect the virtual museum to be a replica of the real museum. Rather, they understand that using technological advantages can diversify the visiting format to allow those who have not been to the real museum to comprehend the beauty and historical-cultural value of the ancient artifacts that the real museum is meant to convey.

Table 4. One-way ANOVA (F, p-value) of real vs. virtual visitors' survey responses.

	Satisfaction level	IT demands	Comprehension level
All visitors	67.595, <0.001	501.929, <0.001	43.020, <0.001
Middle and high school	1.252, 0.265	1.749, 0.188	3.859, 0.051
College and university	49.125, <0.001	0.145, 0.703	26.367, <0.001
Master's and doctoral program	19.488, <0.001	1.856, 0.176	9.905, 0.002

Table 5. Mean values (standard deviation) of different visitor groups' survey responses.

		Satisfaction level	IT demands	Comprehension level
Middle and high school:	Real	6.09 (1.58)	5.21 (1.98)	5.23 (1.30)
	Virtual	5.79 (1.60)	5.61 (1.70)	4.73 (1.58)
College and university:	Real	6.68 (1.34)	5.74 (1.69)	5.80 (1.43)
	Virtual	5.56 (1.62)	5.67 (1.44)	4.96 (1.62)
Master's and doctoral program:	Real	6.92 (1.15)	5.66 (1.72)	6.02 (1.60)
	Virtual	5.51 (1.81)	6.08 (1.34)	4.90 (1.83)

4.4 Open-Ended Responses from Visitors

The real museum's visitors from middle schools or above wished to see lock samples and interactive installations that would allow them to physically experience the unlocking of the locks and understand the mechanisms. Furthermore, they wanted to understand the historical and cultural background of the artifacts and believed that the exhibition should be better publicized so more people could know about it. This group was most impressed by the beautiful appearance of the locks (mentioned by 176 people), followed by the internal structures of the locks (155 people), and the relevant history (127 people). When they had a question or curiosity, they discussed it with their friends (134 people) instead of the docent (47 people).

The virtual museum's visitors from middle schools or above thought that the exhibition should have more 3D models of the ancient locks, that the models could be zoomed in, and that they should be presented in more diverse ways to enable better observation. Also, interactivity, sound effects, and voice-overs were suggested as facilitators of willingness to visit and comprehension of the meaningfulness of the locks. They were most impressed by the museum's visiting format (mentioned by 169 people), followed by the design of the exhibition room (135 people), and the beautiful appearance of the ancient locks (105 peopled). When having questions or curiosity, they either discussed them with friends or teachers. As the virtual museum did not provide docent service, the visitors could only ask questions to their friends, teachers, or peers.

Table 6 shows the key ideas in the responses of these two visitor groups (A10–A12). The real museum's visitors expected more abundant exhibits and historical information, 3D interaction, and particularly on-site imitation locks for people to play with the interesting unlocking movements. On the other hand, the virtual museum's visitors wanted a magnified version of the intricate ancient locks. With more opportunities and more people online, they would like to chat with other visitors or online docents. Note that both groups felt that the docent played an important role and that the infrastructure of the Internet was important to both the real and virtual museums.

Table 6. Key ideas from the two visitor groups' feedback.

	Real exhibition	SL virtual exhibition
A10	• Adding 3D multimedia interactive elements • Adding elements of fun to the traditional exhibition	• More multimedia animations • Faster Internet connection speed • Better graphic card for computers
A11	• More hand-on operations on imitation locks • More historical information	• Increasing the number of exhibition items • Enlarging the exhibition space • Adding more details to the wallpaper and exhibition items • Offering interactive designs for authentic experiences
A12	• Only three respondents proposed animation to attract the audience.	• Only two respondents proposed to enrich the contents.

In summary, the visitors' feedback on the exhibition space design consists of more locks being exhibited, providing physical manipulation of locks, images, or 3D models that help explain the internal structures of the locks; they tend to discuss questions with friends and were impressed with the beauty of the ancient locks. Furthermore, the analyses found that, regarding the internationalization of the cultural brand, visitors from different backgrounds (middle/high school, college, and graduate students) were all deeply impressed by the beauty of the ancient locks and their internal mechanisms (middle/high school: 176 and 155 people, respectively; college: 133 and 144; graduate school: 23 and 29). In the virtual museum, the most memorable were the exhibition room design and the visiting format of the museum (middle/high school: 135 and 169 people, respectively; college: 69 and 88; graduate school: 19 and 32). In conclusion, visitors from different backgrounds have mostly the same visiting needs. The differences lie in the different presentation modes and how much of the exhibits' meaning the visitors are able to grasp. Each museum format has its advantages. If these advantages can be combined, then not only can the visitors reap the benefits, but it would also mean a great advance in exhibition planning and research.

5 Conclusion and Discussions

This research is conducted by designing and administering a survey for the two different kinds of museums, the real museum and the virtual one, and aimed at finding the proper way of modifying "the promotion model of the cultural brand of ancient locks" based on the results of the quantitative and qualitative data analyses. From the results, we learned that the audiences of the different exhibition formats have different satisfaction levels, and this difference further affects their learning. In addition, the virtual museum audiences have higher IT demands for entering and visiting the virtual museum.

The real museum featured more thorough designs and planning, more ancient locks, and explanations from docents, while the virtual museum was planned and designed following the overall concept of the museum but fell short of the concrete representation of the historical traces left by the ancient artifacts. Therefore, the way the virtual museum is presented needs a very innovative IT design to reinforce the sense of realness for the historical artifacts. In addition, most visitors expected better lighting and audio effects in the physical exhibition room, while more real experiences such as seeing the working of large locks were anticipated in the virtual exhibition. Finally, this research makes some adaptations to the virtual looks of the ancient locks. The "promotion model of the cultural brand of ancient locks" has been developed according to the research results and audience suggestions.

As shown in Fig. 4 and Table 7, the management strategy for the cultural brand includes two parts (learning-oriented services and fundamental facility-related services). Further suggestions are offered based on the characteristics of the environments of the special SL exhibition and the physical exhibition of ancient locks. Regarding the fundamental facility-related services, there was a strong demand for guided tours in both environments. The multimedia interactive function should also be reinforced. As for the learning-oriented services, since the audiences place much emphasis on the rich content of the historical information, multi-lingual audio-video information is also indispensable.

Table 7. International cooperation in research and techniques.

Learning-oriented services Real (R) & SL Virtual (V)	Fundamental facility-related services Real (R) & SL Virtual (V)

• To display more 3D models of the lock mechanism.
  o V: larger size for the locks
• To offer historical and cultural information about the locks
  o R: (1) information in Chinese and English, (2) animated instruction
  o V: (1) multilingual communication in text, (2) multilingual communication in speech
	• To provide interactivity: audio-video effects (1) background sound and music, (2) oral introduction to the locks.
	  o R: webpages
	  o V: (1) Internet URL link, (2) fly tour
	• To run promotional ads and event announcements on billboards with explanations and illustrations of the exhibited objects.
	  o V: (1) flyers, (2) posters
	• V: To provide docents

Consumers of the cultural brand of ancient locks have different feelings, recognition, and demands towards different exhibition modes. While the virtual museum was constructed by referencing the real museum, its exhibition could neither fully represent nor replace the real one. Only the real exhibition can express the real charms of the ancient locks. While the virtual world simulates real objects, the historical traces of ancient

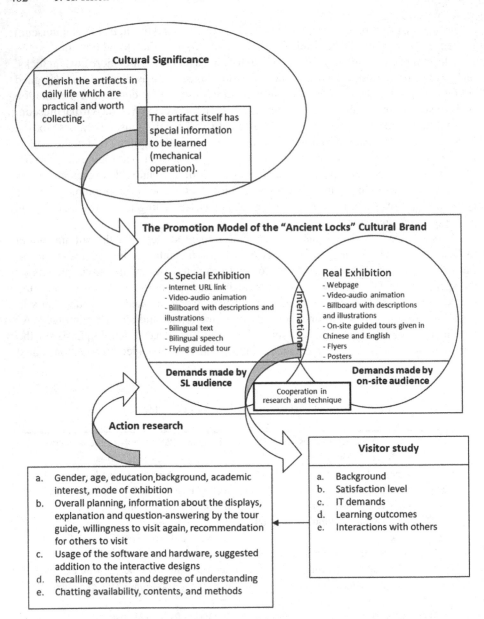

Fig. 4. The promotion model of the "Ancient Locks" cultural brand.

artifacts cannot be replicated. For example, the angle, as well as the way the items are displayed, may transfer existing values from the real museum to the virtual one. The virtual museum is not meant to replace the real museum but to push the cultural brand onto the international stage through the advertising of the virtual museum so that more people can have access to the beauty of the ancient locks and their cultural value can be elevated. The virtual museum focuses on the ancient lock exhibition as a primary cultural promotional tool. Over 50% of the surveyed visitors had positive feedback on the overall satisfaction and IT demands, which supports this cultural brand promotion model. Therefore, to internationalize the cultural brand, different strategies are necessary. Designing different modes of visits and exhibitions by targeting different visitor types can ensure that all visitors reap the maximum benefit from their visits. To represent the real museum, the virtual museum should not just mimic the appearance of the real museum, but more importantly, convey the meaning and charm of the exhibits to the audience. The value and significance of the real museum are not to be replaced by the virtual museum. However, the real museum can gain additional support through the virtual museum's promotion and endorsement. Learning and growth are never-ending and without borders. Virtual museums' value in promoting cultural brands is especially meaningful in that regard.

Attachement

1. 我的名字是 ＿＿＿＿＿＿＿＿ ，今年 ＿＿＿ 歲。

2. 今天的參觀開不開心？（圈一圈）

　　☺開心　　☺還可以　　☹不開心

3. 今天的參觀好不好玩？（圈一圈）

　　好玩　　還可以　　不好玩

4. 大哥哥、大姊姊跟你說話聽不聽的懂？（圈一圈）

　　懂　　還可以　　不懂

5. 會不會想再來一次？（圈一圈）

　　會　　不會

6. 會不會帶其他小朋友和爸爸媽媽來？（圈一圈）

　　會　　不會

7. 在參觀中哪些東西最好玩？（可以畫圖）

8. 在參觀中還要加上什麼東西會比較好？（可以畫圖）

9. 在參觀中哪些東西最喜歡？（可以畫圖）

10. 在參觀中看不懂什麼？怎麼辦？（可以畫圖）

Name and age: item 1; satisfaction level: items 2, 3, 5, 6, 7, and 9; comprehension level: items 4 and 10; visiting needs: item 8; open-ended questions by drawing: items 7-10.

Acknowledgment. This study was funded for more than four years by the Ministry of Science and Technology for different sub-projects of varying scales. Associate Prof. Ya-Hsien Wu (SL: Nomilly Valeska) and Ms. Syuan-Yu Chen (SL: Pacino1225) were my technical advisors and friends whose help is very much appreciated. Special thanks go to Prof. Hon-Sen Yan, the collector of the ancient Chinese locks. He offered his vast knowledge and digital resources to the researcher so that this study could be conducted smoothly. Many thanks also go to this study's co-chairs, Prof. Ching-Hui Chue and Prof. Ing-Chao Lin, and all personnel at the NCKUM.

References

1. Ahmad, N., Abdulkarim, H.: The Impact of flow experience and personality type on the intention to use virtual world. Int. J. Hum. Comput. Interact. **35**(12), 1074–1085 (2018)
2. Ancient Chinese Locks Museum - Digital Exhibition website. https://lock.nstm.gov.tw/intro. aspx. Accessed 07 Jan 2021
3. Atkinson, T.: Second life for educators: inside linden lab. TechTrends **52**(3), 16–18 (2008)
4. Chang, H.P., Ma, C.C.: Managing the service brand value of the hotel industry in an emerging market. Int. J. Hosp. Manag. **47**, 1–13 (2015)
5. Chen, C.C.: The crossroads of English language learners, task-based instruction, and 3D multi-user virtual learning in Second Life. Comput. Educ. **102**, 152–171 (2016)
6. Chenchi College website. https://college.nccu.edu.tw/tw/publication/news-letters/2016-01-07-07-08-53?start=30. Accessed 07 Jan 2021
7. Dhiman, P., Arora, S.: A conceptual framework for identifying key employee branding dimensions: a study of hospitality industry. J. Innov. Knowl. **5**(3), 200–209 (2020)
8. Hajdas, M.: Cultural codes and brand equity relations – exploratory study and research implications. Manag. Sci. **24**(1), 19–27 (2019)
9. Hsieh, P.H., Chen, S.Y.: Imagine the future smart school from the virtual world. In: The Annual Yearbook of Chinese School Building Research Association, The Chinese School Building Research Association, Taipei, Taiwan, pp. 153–174 (2020)
10. Kawulich, B.B., D'Alba, A.: Teaching qualitative research methods with Second Life, a 3-dimensional online virtual environment. Virtual Real. **23**(4), 375–384 (2018). https://doi.org/10.1007/s10055-018-0353-4
11. Kersten, T.P., Tschirschwitz, F., Deggim, S.: Development of a virtual museum including a 4d presentation of building history in virtual reality. In: The International Archives of the Photogrammetry, Remote Sensing and Spatial Information Sciences, Volume: XLII-2, International Society for Photogrammetry and Remote Sensing, Hannover, Germany, pp. 361–367 (2017)
12. Kim, M.Y., Moon, S., Lacobucci, D.: The influence of global brand distribution on brand popularity on social media. J. Int. Mark. **27**(4), 1069031X19863307 (2019)
13. Kotler, P.: Marketing Management: Analysis, Planning, Implementation, and Control. Prentice Hall, Singapore (1992)
14. NCKUM website. http://museum.ncku.edu.tw/p/406-1008-183596,r2482.php?Lang=zh-tw. Accessed 07 Jan 2021
15. Peng, G., Li, F., Chen, P., Cheng, Y.: Chinese ancient locks: Shapes, forms and cultural connotations. In: Proceedings of the 2nd International Conference on Education, Sports, Arts and Management Engineering, pp. 1477–1482. Atlantis Press, Amsterdam, The Netherlands (2017)
16. Perry, S., Roussou, R., Economou, M., Young, H., Pujol, L.: Moving beyond the virtual museum: engaging visitors emotionally. In: The 23rd International Conference on Virtual System & Multimedia, pp. 1–8, IEEE (2017)

17. Schroeder, J., Borgerson, J., Wu, Z.: A brand culture approach to Chinese cultural heritage brands. J. Brand Manag. **22**(3), 261–279 (2015)
18. Shams, R., Alpert, F., Brown, M.: Consumer perceived brand innovativeness: conceptualization and operationalization. Eur. J. Mark. **49**(9/10), 1589–1615 (2015)
19. SpeedLight website. https://speedlight.io/. Accessed 12 Jan 2021
20. Thomas, V.L., Jewell, R.D.: I can't get you out of my head: the influence of secrecy on consumers' self-brand connections. J. Consum. Psychol. **29**(3), 463–471 (2019)
21. Vredeveld, A.J., Coulter, R.A.: Cultural experiential goal pursuit, cultural brand engagement, and culturally authentic experiences: sojourners in America. J. Acad. Mark. Sci. **47**(2), 274–290 (2018). https://doi.org/10.1007/s11747-018-0620-7
22. Wirtz, J., Jerger, C.: Managing service employees: literature review, expert opinions, and research directions. Serv. Ind. J. **36**(15–16), 757–788 (2017)
23. Wu, Z., Wu, Z.: A study on the quality factors of brand culture and its transmission path-taking Eral group corporation as an example. In: Proceedings of the 2nd International Conference on Management, Education and Social Science, Amsterdam, The Netherlands, pp. 161–164. Atlantis Press (2018)
24. Yan, H.S.: Reconstruction Designs of Lost Ancient Chinese Machinery. Springer, Netherlands (2007).ISBN 978-4020-6459-3
25. Yan, H.S.: The beauty of ancient Chinese locks, 2nd edn. Culture and Education Foundation of Chinese Ancient Machinery, Tainan City, Taiwan (2003). ISBN 957–28707-0-X
26. Zhang, K., Wang, Z., Zhang, J.: The research content, characteristics and future trend of Chinese cultural brand-from the perspective of literature analysis. In: IOP Conference Series: Materials Science and Engineering, **688**(5), 055025 (2019)

Breaking Boundaries, Creating Connectivities: Enabling Access to Digitized Museum Collections

Cassandra Kist[1] and Quoc-Tan Tran[2]($\boxtimes$)

[1] University of Glasgow, Glasgow, UK
cassandra.kist@glasgow.ac.uk
[2] University of Hamburg, Hamburg, Germany
quoc-tan.tran@uni-hamburg.de

Abstract. Museum staff as gatekeepers to cultural heritage are central to enabling or constraining user interaction with museum objects. However, organizational barriers frequently hinder staff's ability to invest in expanding user access to digitized collections. In this chapter, we analyze staff practices that help create online opportunities for user engagement, which we argue is a process of actively expanding and negotiating infrastructural boundaries of connective capacities. These boundaries constitute and expose an "installed base", which refers to the backbone of infrastructure, and the existing practices and norms from which work takes place. Drawing on two case studies, our analysis suggests that changes to the infrastructure, including the expansion of digitized collections and tools, builds on and is shaped by the installed base. By centering user needs and leveraging their place in diverse heritage networks, staff are able to overcome infrastructural boundaries that shape and hinder practices of designing for access. This study illustrates, in particular, the ways in which staff are compelled to negotiate perceptions of what constitutes both an "authentic" museum object and a professional museum role in order to enable user access to digitized collections.

Keywords: Digital cultural heritage · Digitized collections · Infrastructure studies · Accessibility · Museum staff · Installed base

1 Introduction

In an increasingly pervasive digital media ecology, museums have been restructuring and shifting their work practice including how they create access to cultural heritage. Forms of digital media, such as online collections and social networking tools, are typically associated with increased access. Adopting an infrastructure studies perspective, we aim to explore in this paper, technologically mediated forms of enabling user access to digitized collections, through which museum staff actively negotiate the institution's connective potential. By paying attention to the insider practices of staff working to overcome new complexities of the museum's infrastructure, we claim that the adoption of digital tools and practices might challenge socio-technical bases upon which infrastructures are built and growing. This base or foundation we refer to as "installed base",

© Springer Nature Switzerland AG 2021
M. Rauterberg (Ed.): HCII 2021, LNCS 12794, pp. 406–422, 2021.
https://doi.org/10.1007/978-3-030-77411-0_26

an insightful conceptual device being used in infrastructure studies [1, 32, 34]. Through close analysis of two case studies—the Open Museum within the context of Glasgow Museums, and Swedish National History Museums—it is evident that designing for user access becomes visible as a process in which staff bump up against and negotiate the boundaries of the museum's connective capacities. Our analysis exposes how staff in both cases are actively engaged in negotiating these boundaries and crafting the activities that determine what kind of access the digital can help manifest. In particular, we find that staff in our case studies are compelled to negotiate perceptions of what constitutes an "authentic" museum object and a professional museum role.

The paper is organized as follows: First, we reflect upon multiple ways of positioning access in cultural heritage, acknowledging the complexity and interconnectedness of the sector. We highlight how access, through different digital means, could pose tensions for museums and how these tensions, and potentially their resolution, can be practically understood through an ethnography of infrastructure framework. We then discuss the methodologies used for our two case studies to delve into staff's experience, contradictions and tensions. Our research data was collected through a year-long social media ethnography, together with semi-structured interviews with museum staff. Three important themes emerge from our results: (i) expanding boundaries that define professional museum roles; (ii) what constitutes a museum object as "authentic" and valuable for engagement; and (iii) enhancing the institution's connectivities. These findings suggest that the expansions of the installed base and associated boundaries are continually negotiated by museum staff. Lastly, stemming from staff's negotiations, we conclude that enabling user access to digitized collections is intertwined with how the institutions are prepared for user's emerging needs and changing behavior.

2 Professional Roles and Access to Museum Collections

Designing for access to cultural heritage through digital means is considered essential for today's museums to maintain relevance. Museum and media studies' scholars describe access in cultural heritage work to refer to different practices that open up the institution and the collections to potential visitor interaction and participation. Access in the museum field is frequently associated with "audience building" and "social inclusion" [28]. According to Carpentier [6], from a media studies perspective, access entails a user presence to both technology and content, which is a requirement for participation. He further suggests that access encompasses both a social and cognitive component, which aligns with its use in the museum field. On the one hand, access in museology is correlated with cognition, where concerns are centred around legibility and readability of text, the inclusion of alternative text and subtitles and further design considerations for people with disabilities [24]. On the other hand, access to cultural heritage is also considered to be not only cognitive and physical, but also social and emotional, encompassing sensory and affective qualities of cultural heritage objects and display [22, 24]. This is what Witcomb refers to as the "affective possibilities" of objects which "engage emotions and in the process produce a different kind of knowledge—one that embodies in a very material way, shared experiences, empathy, and memory" [37, p. 36]. Access in our two case studies is the process of bringing together users and digitized objects which is fraught with ideas regarding the objects' affective potential and associated information.

Expanding access to digitized collections can bump up against pre-existing conceptions specific to institutional contexts and histories, regarding social and cognitive accessibility. Specifically, the materiality of objects and their ability to be "touched" is regularly idealized for their associated affective powers which can enable new forms of understanding, empathy and shared social connections [19, 30, 37]. The Open Museum (OM) for instance, is intended to fulfill a vision of an accessible museum by bringing museum objects out to communities to be safely handled, enabling "true" access. This access according to the Open Museum has to do with emotional and social affect that material objects can enable. O'Neill explains, "[t]he OM is based on the belief that opportunities to handle objects and host community-led exhibits reveal the human dimension of objects in ways that significantly enrich people's lives" [25, p. 34]. Initiatives such as the ones at the OM, forefront accessibility by taking material objects to users and communities which raises critical questions regarding the affective potential of digitized museum objects.

Digitized objects can also call into question professional roles, as they are constituted by existing values and insider knowledge, including perceptions of 'access'. For instance, questions regarding affect and authenticity have often led to the de-prioritization of the digitized object and artwork, compared to its authentic and material counterpart. As a result, Meecham [20] calls for a reconsideration of museum staff's conception of authenticity and their relationships with material culture. On the other hand, digitized collections can create further tensions with professional roles due to the decentralized nature and interconnectivities between digitized collections and the web. Specifically, with various kinds of non-hierarchical and decentralized practices, institutions can no longer control definitively how their users reuse the material which has been published online. Individuals and commercial actors alike can easily manipulate the uses of objects, transforming them beyond the intent of the institution. Virtual environments can even reshape people's understanding of the object's cultural value and transcend it into other contexts to incite new experiences—from a social and participatory to a culturally immersive experience [8]. As a result, some might say that online anyone can be a curator, critically calling into question the form of professional cultural heritage roles.

The move toward museum digitization and decentralization are tearing down barriers that define the responsibilities of museum's personnel. Calling it "a changing profession", Boylan [4] claims that the traditional profession of "museologist" or "scholar-curators", i.e. those who care for and maintain the collections, is put under threat as professional training fails to keep up with the ever-increasing specialization and complexity of museum work. The shift provides a greater need to fill gaps in the specialized staffing, such as those who undertake exhibition work, education, and documentation, either by contracting out to private-sector services [4] or developing the digital literacies of the museum workforce [26]. The digital transformation and pervasive social media engagement also influence the changing profession, demanding new roles that encompass crafting access to digitized forms of cultural heritage. Geismar [11] reminds us of how digital practices in contemporary museums are shaped by institutional context, infrastructure and a legacy of practice. While digital cultural heritage is often idealized as a radical alternative to the historical form of museum artefacts, there are persisting tensions in using digital tools to make cultural heritage accessible. That is because, Geismar argues, digital components of today's museum practices provoke "a new kind of materiality, a digital poetics that can be used to unpack the politics of museum collections" [11, p. xviii]. This digital poetics highlights fundamental questions about new forms of infrastructure, accessibility requirements and skill, which can challenge existing forms of museum professional roles. In the following section, we discuss how the concept of an installed base in infrastructure studies can shed light on an institution's compatibility with online engagement practices.

3 Infrastructure and the Installed Base

Due to the connective turn, which has increased pervasiveness of digital technologies, GLAMs are called to change their practices and expand access to fit within new media infrastructures [16]. Many GLAMs are breaking from the old forms of social, collective memory-making, and relying more on digital infrastructures for enabling modes of support, instantaneous communication, and global interconnectivity [3, 5]. It is common to address the connective capacities of GLAM institutions not necessarily as static, but as intertwined with institutional and social contexts. There is a vibrant literature in museum studies that employs the assemblage approach to analyze how organizational settings and techniques of museum practice are intertwined. Macdonald [18] and Witcomb [36] look at how routine practices shape knowledge presentation and determine relationships between museums and audiences. Morse [23] pays attention to an expanded set of museum practices and asks how they "make up museum work-worlds". The complexity and interconnectedness of the sector indicate that the museum's infrastructure ought not to be studied as a merely isolated object; rather, it is a lively assemblage of internal institutional and, in a lesser extent, cross-institutional practices such as displaying collections, preservation, or community engagement programmes [10, 15, 17, 28].

From an infrastructure perspective, the intertwined museum work-worlds do not grow from scratch; rather, they are built upon a common set of practices and conventions. Infrastructure scholars often take the case of optical fibres that run along old railroad lines, or information systems that are designed for backward compatibility, as examples of how new developments inherit both strength and limitations from the installed base and struggle continually with the inertia of that base [21, 33]. Monteiro and Hanseth [21], discussing the relationship between information infrastructures and organizational issues, observe that when the installed base grows, it becomes more and more irreversible. The museum work-worlds can become a resistant assemblage, as their pre-existing arrangements create compatibility issues and cause organizational resistance towards change [29]. Our discussion in Sect. 5 will illustrate how, while introducing digital infrastructures to accommodate a broad range of users, museum staff might encounter contradictions and tensions that expose and call into question museum boundaries which shape and hinder a practice of assembling "access".

Under Susan Leigh Star's infrastructural lens [32], re-making boundaries is part of the infrastructure's ability to reach beyond one-site practice, i.e. the backbone construction or an existing installed base [32–34]. Infrastructures tend to be considered as invisible and relational, the substrate in which substance takes place [31]. Star proposes bringing an ethnographic sensibility to the hidden fabric of technical work in order to get into inner depths of the built infrastructures [32]. An ethnographic sensibility enables the researcher to observe how infrastructures are expanded, shifted and changed which is related to the concept of infrastructuring [14, 32]—a process of design in embedding new technologies into practice and existing socio-technical arrangements. However, the initiation of change or the embedding of new technologies can create tensions with the existing infrastructure, commonly referred to as the installed base. According to Edwards et al., an installed base "includes not only artifacts but human habits, norms, and roles that may prove its most intractable elements" [9, p. 366]. Research on information infrastructures points out that the evolution of infrastructures happens gradually and requires negotiation [31]. To comprehend the compatibility of systems innovation and existing socio-technical arrangements, or their congeniality, it is essential to examine "the merged parts' ability and willingness to mutually adjust and co-evolve" [29, p. 235].

In the two case studies that follow, we explore how elements of the installed base merge with and bump up against the incorporation of new tools and protocols for enabling user access; how staff negotiate the boundaries of an installed base to expand access to digitized collections; and how access is shaped by the merging of parts, impacts the end-user experience. Aanestad et al. [1] outline four areas that institutions must confront to reach the stage where the use of the new infrastructure achieves momentum, or what they call an "installed base-friendly" approach: coordination across multiple actors, addressing heterogeneity, responsiveness to evolving needs, and strategies towards transformation [1]. This approach implies that infrastructural development must align with existing work practices and require minimal changes to the technological base. The following analysis, building off this perspective, identifies an additional area that staff must devote energy to in order to catalyze the momentum of new infrastructure for expanding user access to digitized collections in today's pervasive digital media ecology. We aim to trace how emerging digital initiatives are grown organically on an installed base of established structures, professional roles and practices of the organization, contributing to infrastructural development.

4   The Two Cases

The analysis of this paper is based on the data obtained from qualitative interviews and ethnographic fieldwork conducted at two GLAM institutions: Glasgow Museum's Open Museum (OM) and Swedish National History Museums (SHM). Through these two cases, we investigate how everyday staff negotiate user accessibility for engagement with digital cultural heritage, in the former through a year-long social media ethnography, and the latter through semi-structured interviews with SHM staff working in digital data management. The merging of these two cases is due to observed overlaps between the emergent categories stemming from our datasets and a mutual interest in infrastructure. Over the course of our fieldwork, we frequently discussed our research trajectories and even collaborated on pilot interviews with experts in digital cultural heritage during August 2019, which provided essential background on our shared field.

From its conception, the Open Museum (OM) was intended to fulfil a vision of access that would provide pathways to cultural value for individuals and groups who normally cannot or would not engage with the museum. The Open Museum is the outreach branch of Glasgow Museums, and is an institution without walls meaning it has no physical venue. Instead, it pops-up in local communities and non-profit/partner organizations bringing participants and collections together to create engagement in dynamic ways. As a result, the OM is virtual in nature, making the use of social and digital media seem complimentary to their access initiatives. Nevertheless, from a series of pilot interviews in 2019 with Glasgow Museum staff, it became evident that the OM rarely used digital and social media in everyday outreach initiatives. Thus, the OM was perceived as a pivotal case in understanding the relation between museum infrastructure from which social inclusion work takes place and social media practices.

A year-long social media ethnography [27] was undertaken to understand how infrastructure shapes staff's use of social media and lack thereof in relation to inclusion and access initiatives. Social media ethnography traverses online and offline contexts and thus, could be considered an internet-based ethnography rather than an internet ethnography. As such, it aligns with the central research question due to its emphasis on the interconnections between social media and local histories, political structures, or in this case, institutional infrastructures. During this placement, Covid-19 motivated staff to enable additional forms of user access to objects through social and digital platforms.

Comparatively, the Swedish National History Museums (SHM) is a central museums agency whose tasks are promoting knowledge of Sweden's history and preserving the cultural heritage that the agency administers. As a result of the Cultural Heritage Bill that the Swedish parliament adopted in 2017, the new central agency of SHM was created in January 2018 which aims to create access and pathways to cultural heritage engagement through its expansive collective digital offerings. All six museum members jointly developed a focus plan outlining starting points and development areas for the new agency to achieve this vision: "History should inspire people to be active in the present in order to shape the future" [35, p. 8, our own translation]. As people's historical awareness increases, so do their opportunities to see the connection between the past, the present and the future. The data is obtained from qualitative interviews with a specific group of staff working on a daily basis with the museums' digital infrastructure and involved in the development of the agency's digital strategies.

5 Staff as Catalysts of Connectivities: Critical Factors for Enabling Access

In the following sections, we analyze staff practices that attempt to expand user access to digitized collections in different ways. In the process of expansion and the resulting tensions that arise, we identify elements of infrastructure or an "installed base" that causes uncertainty in staff practices. Specifically, two shared aspects of existing infrastructure in our case studies caused tensions in expanding digital access for users, which are here referred to as boundaries. These two boundaries include staff's perceptions of their professional role and associated responsibilities, and what constitutes a museum object as authentic and valuable for engagement. Expanding boundaries must build off of existing practices and norms that constitute the installed base allowing the infrastructures of which they are a part of, to be expanded [2, 29]. Staff in the following analysis, build and catalyze connectivities, leveraging existing relationships across their respective networks to expand and negotiate infrastructural limits. Through these connectivities staff expose the importance of an installed base friendly approach to infrastructuring, which includes support from relevant actors and embracing the vulnerability and risk brought by digital transformation [1].

5.1 Expanding Boundaries of Professional Roles

For outreach staff at the Open Museum, their professional role is based on working with local under-served and hard-to-reach communities and participants, often enabling access to objects in diverse ways, such as through handling kits. Handling kits are large boxes constructed in-house which contain a small collection of "real" (accessioned and not reproductions) museum objects based on a social or cultural theme. These kits are referred to by staff as the "bread and butter" of OM's outreach work, which are frequently used when meeting participants in the city and are also borrowed by partner organizations. OM's participants are groups and individuals in Glasgow often connected to by networking with other organizations. For example, the OM has collaborated with several different non-profits related to mental health, Alzheimer's, migration, and poverty. Staff's outreach role focuses on local participants, as is defined by and emphasized in contrast to that of the larger institution, Glasgow Museums.

The role of the OM's curators is unique in being based on different social portfolios with associated strategies to fill these remits, including mental health and incarceration, poverty and homelessness and ageing populations. As part of their role, Open Museum staff describe their work as going out into communities rather than relying on participants to come into the venues like other Glasgow Museums. As OM staff suggest, "[it is] our local geographic location we are engaging with", which enables staff to cater for the interests and needs of specific communities and participants. In comparison, staff occasionally critique the dual priorities of Glasgow Museums, citing a potential contradiction between its role as an international museum service and in serving locals. For instance, staff question Glasgow Museum's understanding of its communities: "I think sometimes there is a lack of reality of what is happening on the street and in the communities, we are intended to serve". This critique emphasizes and defines in contrast, OM's outreach role and responsibilities.

However, in investing in digital and social media platforms during Covid-19, OM staff suggest that their audience priority and associated outreach role was to some extent critically questioned, causing initial inertia in adopting these tools into regular outreach practices. Staff sometimes expressed a critical view of social media suggesting associated practices as potentially outside of or even contradictory to a focus on local participants and hard-to-reach audiences. For instance, it can be impossible to engage with hard-to-reach audiences through social and digital media when participants are faced by homelessness or are confined to spaces without technological access and may lack digital literacies: "Yes, thank god for social media and online resources but what about the people in hospital and prisons, and care homes and stuff who don't access the internet." One OM staff member reflecting on the digital changes from pre to mid pandemic suggested, "I suppose before you feel quite strongly what Open Museum and Learning and Access team values are and goals are, but during this [pandemic] I felt like they melted away a bit…".

When discussing the increased investment of Glasgow Museums broadly in social media work during the pandemic, an OM staff member reflected, "[w]hat I've been doing is sticking to I think local, [which] is the most important thing for me. We're outreach right, so our target is vulnerable communities and so on…" Conversely, one staff member, discussing the use of video chats in their outreach sessions in relation to a local focus reflected, "[o]f course we are still trying to keep this very sort of local, which is quite interesting in terms of, I don't know if that's a contradiction or not". During this period, a local focus for those participants who had technological access was somewhat maintained in several of the OM's online engagement projects through the privacy functions of video chats, the use of email and private Youtube video links. Such commentary and resulting digital practices suggest that in attempts to broaden access to digitized collections and engagement during the pandemic, a focus on local audiences resulted in initial uncertainty regarding staff's professional role and shaped how engagement with digitized collections was enabled.

In a similar way, staff's perception of their professional role at SHM impacted how and by whom objects are made accessible through digitization. The merging of six museum bodies has been extensive, resulting in the overconsumption of resources which strained the work environment. Due to the complexity of the change, the work of adapting systems, internal control documents, routines, working methods and IT environment will continue for several years to come. From the point of view of a staff member who is responsible for the museum documentation system, the merging work has created confusion and uncertainty related to the specific roles and responsibilities that a group of staff needs to perform: "They [the curators and conservators] have a lot to do. There is a lot of exhibitions and things that they need to be involved in and maybe also do kind of leadership, but their boss doesn't encourage them to… they're not telling them that one of the most important things to do is register and keep the information about the collections up to date in our systems. And it's hard for us, who are working with the structure of the data and the system, to go and tell their bosses, 'you have to prioritize this.'".

Due to the complexity of the change, the problem of not keeping information about the objects completed, correct and up to date in the system becomes more acute. It seems that the only one who cares about keeping information about the objects complete, correct and up to date in the system are those who work on a daily basis with the museum documentation system. Even though these tasks seem insignificant to top management, they are very important because the whole agency is dealing with millions of objects. The staff acknowledge that but they can't transfer that knowledge to their colleagues in the collection department. The disconnect between upper management's goals and staff's everyday practices become apparent when the digital plays a definitive role. How about multimedia and digital-born objects? What shall we do with nested authorship? These issues are tackled by re-inscribing or breaking the boundaries of museum objects.

During attempts to expand user access to digitized collections, staff's roles were destabilized due to questions arising about responsibilities. At the Open Museum there was uncertainty about how digital tools maintained or broke staff's professional outreach role due to the association of digital/social media with a different audience priority. The merging work at SHM and its complexity, on the other hand, created uncertainty regarding staff's resulting responsibilities and priorities. In these two cases, existing perceptions of their roles and responsibilities hinder and shape the ability of staff to invest in expanding user access to digitized objects from the collection. Yet, as will be further discussed in Sect. 5.3, these instances also provide insights on how boundaries can be expanded through an installed base friendly approach.

5.2   Negotiating Boundaries of Authentic Museum Objects

The analysis above regarding professional roles in association to audience priorities and digitization responsibilities, created some hesitancy in using digital tools to enable user access to cultural heritage. However, in this section we describe how the authenticity of objects also hindered and shaped how staff enabled user access to digitized objects. The prevailing strand of discussions on what makes an object valuable for engagement has been strongly framed by the object-centered museum discourse. Within this token, the value and meaning of a digital object are bound by the established conventions derived from the material/immaterial binary and "subsequently judged from the standpoint of the 'superior' physical counterpart" [5, p. 49]. However, another viewpoint suggests that "the experience and negotiation of authenticity also relate to networks of relationships between objects, people, and places" [13, p. 183]. Staff at both OM and SHM expand the boundaries of what traditionally constitutes a valuable museum object by decentralizing museum practices. That is, staff in both case studies, open-up object selection to participant input, in terms of both outreach sessions and digitization, allowing the relation between people, objects and context to shape authenticity.

At the Open Museum, staff highly value the use of object handling kits for outreach sessions due to the ability to take out, hold and pass around the objects. As one OM staff member stated, they work closely with the conservation team to make this happen: "That is the point of these kits – the museum objects can be handled". The tactile nature of objects is often seen as central for participants to engage with the material and in turn, connect socially and emotionally with other participants and staff. This was reflected in a conversation amongst staff regarding the differences between an "Enigma handling kit" and "Reminiscence handling kits" in how they enable emotional and social connections in different ways. The Enigma kit for example, which is filled with strange looking objects is valued for how it can jump start conversations between participants while the Reminiscence kits enable participants to share and connect over memories. Passing around objects from each box provides not only sensory entry points such as "touch and smell" but also sets the group dynamic, as the participant who is holding an object is frequently empowered as speaker.

However, during the pandemic, staff were forced to rely more on social and digital media to create access for participants to engage with objects and each other. It is perhaps, therefore, no surprise that staff invested in creative ways to enhance sensory elements of digitized objects through social and digital media. As one OM staff reflected: "So, I suppose in some ways you can actually do a wider variety of different things because you can draw on a variety of collections but having to do it in a very different way and being very reliant, I suppose on the visual rather than more tactile elements of what we do." One example during this period included a video chat session in which a painting of a seascape was shared, and participants were encouraged to imagine how it would sound and feel to be in the scenery. During this session, participants longed for past vacations, with some sharing memories of previous visits to water landscapes, including surfing on Scotland's cold shores. In another outreach project, poetry was used in conjunction with objects as a form of interpretation, potentially engaging participants with the artist's work and emotions.

In the process of creating online engagement sessions, participants and non-profit partners were involved in iterative feedback, influencing which digitized objects were chosen for sessions and the structure of different activities. The resulting interactions and engagement of users, for some staff resulted in a new value attributed to digitized objects. Notably, objects were perceived by staff as similarly enacting emotional and social connections: "It's that idea that these objects are catalysts of discussion and conversation and you know us being there gives people something to talk about..." Another staff member reflecting on the use of digitized art suggested, "If you can engage with other people through that art, it's like an infection it makes you feel something, and it makes other people feel the same things and you're sharing in that feeling". On the other hand, despite catering to participants' interests and needs, digitized collections were still sometimes expressed as not as good as the real thing. For the OM's particular audiences, this was often related to restrictions of social and digital media that hinder the level of sociality and the ability according to one staff to "share emotions" around museum objects.

As in the case of the SHM, their digital strategies endorse the view that digital objects can exist in their own right and perform roles that might go beyond reproduction and interpretation. This view is complemented by a decentralized approach on who performs the process of selection, who decides what is significant, and, to some extent, who has the authority to dictate what should be remembered and forgotten. The SHM's architecture allows the community to be involved in this process and these decisions. The publication of 3D models to promote the value of the collection is one successful example. Let us examine the case of the Royal Armoury in Stockholm, one SHM member that holds many artefacts of Swedish military history and Swedish royalty.

Among the Royal Armoury's valuable collections, there is a set of armour that was made in the 16th century and may have been worn by King Erik XIV when he returned to Stockholm from a campaign. The museum made 3D models of different objects in the collection and put them online on Sketchfab, a platform where users can upload digital scans, and the others can download, use and reuse them for free. One staff member working in the communication and digitization department describes the ecosystem where this museum puts the digital copies of its objects online: the 3D models are uploaded to Sketchfab, other versions of the images on Imgur, audios and videos on Youtube and SoundCloud, and articles about the objects on Wikipedia. There is still much work to be done to encourage more sustainable research practices, if the museum aims to communicate the need for long-term preservation of physical artefacts and intangible heritage [7]; yet, these above-mentioned practices are simple mechanisms to increase public access to 3D digital models.

Museum professionals have begun to notice that accessibility aimed at social inclusion might fail to serve marginal users or under-served social groups, if the idea of "accessible spaces" focuses more on objects than people. These above decentralized practices show that there are different ways of giving access to the collection, and that instead of developing a standalone platform on their own and giving access through one family of platforms, museums can promote connections to objects through diverse platforms and media. As one SHM staff said, "we place our digital resources on suitable platforms that are already well established among the public and that have many users," so the institution can choose different platforms for different types of digital resources to reach as many users as possible. Making their 3D models available for reuse, the SHM invites their users to enhance the use via other platforms. The Swedish case highlights the strength of the agency's information architecture, which allows each member institution to facilitate the engagement of external actors with its ongoing extended installed base.

5.3 Enhancing Internal and External Connectivities

Expanding access is a continual form of craftwork which builds off of and expands the installed base, including as previously discussed, the boundaries of authentic objects and professional roles. As further outlined below, staff at SHM and OM negotiate the limits of infrastructure by facilitating internal connectivities and enhancing the connective capacities of digital infrastructures outwards. Enhancing connectivities outwards entailed shifting how staff accommodate or focus on users, on one hand at SHM, through staff's digitization efforts and on the other hand, at the OM, through iterative feedback and communication with its stakeholders.

The SHM's services have changed from creating, personalizing and navigating cultural heritage to curating their collections in digital formats and accommodating users in co-knowledge production. A SHM's documentation staff member recalls the process of organizing information in their day-to-day work situations: "The four of us that work with this have good knowledge about the museum. We have worked for these museums for a long time, so we could understand that this information in this field is going here, but still, it's not perfect. And we are discovering things. Now, when we have worked with the system for a few years, we [realize that we] didn't do it correctly. Sometimes we have to do it again, the [data] migration task."

The above reflection underlines the importance of non-engineered activities, which is unplanned and emergent, in generating effects and structuring social relations [12]. The documentalist refers to the task of making information consistent in every field as a crucial problem derived from the struggle of the new infrastructure to support and align with existing work practices. In terms of engineered activities that are purposefully crafted, digitalization efforts at the SHM provide a useful account. Pressure of crafting access to as many objects as possible from multiple internal actors thrust the digitalization team into nearly a point of digitizing everything. The infrastructure in this case can fail not because of internal disruption but of "a breakdown in the relations between the infrastructure and the domain of activity it is expected to sustain" [12, p. 5]. One staff's response sheds light on why an extended installed base might make an already existed engineered activity, that is digitization of digital resources, fail to deliver as intended:

"I get a steady stream [of demands] from our colleagues they want to digitize this, they want to have this archived, maybe digitized so they can read it on their computers, instead of going to the place where all the books are. They want to digitize everything in this specific storage and make a nice digital exhibition and we are struggling with the infrastructure. We are telling them that, 'we can't do this, we need somewhere to keep all their digital resources.' So, we need a process for how to manage all the data that we are producing in such a project, and we are not there yet in this new government agency."

Similarly, at the Open Museum, the importance of not only internal but also external connectivities in enabling access to digital cultural heritage became apparent. While the use of digital and social media may seem at points contradictory to the OM's professional role and the role of tangible objects in outreach sessions, they overcame these boundaries to meet participant needs. Staff were highly motivated to adopt new platforms and digital tools in the midst of the pandemic to sustain relationships with community groups and continue to fulfill emotional and social needs. Staff reflecting on their activities suggested, "So you know, the role that museum engagement played for those people in their lives was maybe more around fulfilling basic emotional, mental, physical needs in terms of museum wellbeing type things. I think that Covid has heightened that". In keeping up connections and access to digitized collections, there was increasing recognition that these tools could be used to focus on specific local communities and non-profit partners—enabling their joint access to digital cultural heritage. As discussed in the previous sections, staff used the affordances of social and digital media to create private spaces, focusing on local groups and leveraged the social and emotional connective capacities of digitized objects by emphasizing different sensory elements.

Integral to this expansion was the feedback of participants and non-profit partners which emphasizes the importance of external connectivities but also the emergent digital practices of staff in expanding the installed base. Through back-and-forth discussion with non-profits and participants on their experiences and what could be improved in online engagement sessions, staff were able to continuously tweak their approach to the content used, the sensory elements leveraged and even the type of platform. For instance, staff explain that for digital outreach sessions, "[i]t's a collaborative, co-creation or whatever you want to call it or co-participation whatever terminology you want to use. It's not us developing stuff and putting it out there and hoping people will engage it is about talking to people asking what do you want from us, what can we do for you?" As a result of positive participant responses, some staff are accepting that online and social media tools can be used to continue their outreach work.

For example, an OM curator reflected that from the online projects: "… actually I suppose one of the things out of this, is that you can work with groups and respond to their needs and then put things out digitally working with groups in the same way you develop a face-to-face community engagement session". Consequently, the OM curator acknowledged, "I think I always separated out digital engagement with community engagement and always had them as two separate things in my head. I guess one thing I've learned from doing all this is that they can be one and the same". This suggests that while authenticity and credibility can hinder digital adoption, they can also be reconfigured in online spaces to expand user access. Central to this process as indicated in the above quote is through partnering and discussions with other organizations and community groups, their feedback and the ability of staff to respond through emergent or crafted practices.

6 Designing for User Access

In attempting to expand access to digital cultural heritage, it became evident that museum staff in both cases are actively engaged in designing and crafting the activities that determine what kind of access the digital can help manifest. However, our central question does not directly interrogate the value of this extended access. Instead, we focus on the role of museum staff in opening-up infrastructures by increasing access to digitized forms of the collection. Here it is useful to understand infrastructures as "doubly relational" [12, p. 5], which recognizes not only their internal connectivities but also their capacities to reach outwards. Our ethnographic focus on staff practices interrogates the ways in which breaking boundaries and creating connectivities become a process of negotiations that is legitimized, and somewhat routinized, through user interaction and through the institution's respective networks. The case studies reveal the importance of listening and centering the viewpoint of users and being part of cross-institutional networks, which emerge around specific concerns and interests about enabling access to digital cultural heritage.

SHM's and OM's strategies of designing for user access show a kind of infrastructural development that starts from what was already there. Their engagement in ongoing processes of extension—breaking boundaries and creating connectivities—is a clear illustration of considering the installed base as a facilitator for user-driven innovation [1, 2]. The coordination across multiple actors and responsiveness to evolving needs is evident in SHM's efforts to develop a digital teaching resource called *Sveriges historia* (Sweden's history), in collaboration with 17 other museums around Sweden and the National Heritage Board's archives. With the goal of providing an immersive and more inclusive learning environment, the project illustrates how museums can acknowledge the position of underrepresented groups of users—in this case, children and students who need support with reading and understanding the historical information on the website. This new development reveals that staff are able to both align infrastructures with existing work practices as well as the potential to expand them to a nation-wide scale. As shared by a project leader at the SHM,

> "I believe that what we are best at is to be a reliable source, 'a friend to talk to'. We need to add on content, interesting content. So right now, we have a tight dialogue with schools. All lessons that are created around Sweden and different museums must be tested with teachers and students before it's published. We also test the entire web structure and the functions with schools. We will have 'ambassadors' who will be telling us what we miss and what we should develop, of course, but right now, we will not make it interactive for co-creation. Maybe that could be next step."

The discussion above also exemplifies that in order to design for digital access and reach out to communities, GLAM institutions need to be part of a cross-disciplinary and cross-institutional digital heritage network that shares a set of central activities and collective action. The OM, despite being fairly analogue prior to the pandemic, has always been "networked" [19]. They are integrated into several local communities in Glasgow and connected to a number of diverse partner organizations. As a result, this ecosystem of organizations and people has allowed the OM to collaborate and co-create projects that suit participants' interests and needs. This was also enacted in online spaces during Covid-19 which enabled staff to overcome some hesitancy in adopting digital tools that initially brought into question their outreach role and the value of museum objects.

Our cases also challenge the self-image of the museum profession primarily as traditional scholar-curators and outreach staff and emphasize their ability to catalyze new connectivities. Museums in some European countries, such as the Netherlands and the UK, have experienced new types of governance and staff structure in the face of increased technical work related to curatorial and collections management duties which impacts user accessibility [4]. In relation to the digital transformation within the two institutions, the SHM and OM show that to be present and relevant in the digital age means opening up oneself to the vulnerability of digital infrastructures and the risks of failure. In creating connectivities staff build on an existing base by centering user perspectives and leveraging existing networks for support which help legitimize and routinize new forms of user access to digitized collections.

7 Conclusion

Digital aspects of today's museum practices imply a digital poetics that not only foretells the changing paradigms of collecting, sharing and digitizing, but also indicates the challenges museum professionals must face. In this contribution, we call for a greater internal reflection on factors that shape how staff design and enable access to cultural heritage through digital means. Through case studies of two GLAM institutions—Glasgow's Open Museum in the United Kingdom and National History Museums in Sweden, we discuss staff's efforts to overcome organizational resistance towards change. Adopting an infrastructure studies perspective, we use the concept of "installed base" as an analytical lens for studying incremental innovation of infrastructures. Our analysis reveals how, in the two cases, the installed base shapes the practices of museum staff and gives rise to emergent effects at the junction of creating and designing for user access to digitized forms of cultural heritage.

While continuing with efforts of "opening up" themselves to the new connective potentials, different museum bodies within the SHM engage with the existing elements of their infrastructure in an informed and conscious manner. That approach allows them to enhance responsiveness to evolving user needs and ensure the institution's compatibility with online engagement practices. At the OM, staff are beginning to recognize and embrace with a critical eye the use of social and digital media to widen user access and leverage their position as networked with local communities to incorporate their feedback and input on staff's digital practices. In expanding pre-conceptions of their professional roles and authentic museum objects, staff expose the importance of an institution's networks and centering user perspectives in order to not only craft new forms of access but also legitimize and routinize associated practices.

Throughout this chapter, we have analyzed how attempting to expand access to digital cultural heritage becomes a continual form of museum craftwork. Indeed, the ongoing process of expansion requires negotiating a pre-existing set of expectations specific to institutional contexts and histories, including perceptions of staff's role and responsibilities, and what constitutes an authentic museums object which is valuable for engagement. Actively creating spaces for user engagement, staff in both cases are expanding the institutional boundaries of what user engagement could mean and expose hierarchies of value in relation to their professional role in the era of participation and openness. It is evident in the two cases that the prioritization of user's needs and changing behavior has directed the organization's efforts towards effective coordination across multiple actors within the large agencies (Glasgow Museums and Swedish National History Museums) and better integration with other segments of the cultural heritage sector. Without broad support from relevant actors and agreement concerning what should be offered to each group of stakeholders, the engineered activities might break down and cease to work.

Acknowledgements. . This work is part of the POEM (Participatory Memory Practices) project and has received funding from the European Union's Horizon 2020 research and innovation program under the Marie Skłodowska-Curie grant agreement No. 764859. The authors would like to thank Prof. Dr. Gertraud Koch, Susanne Boersma and Inge Zwart for their comments and suggestions on different drafts of this chapter.

References

1. Aanestad, M., Grisot, M., Hanseth, O., Vassilakopoulou, P. (eds.): Information infrastructures within European health care. HI, Springer, Cham (2017). https://doi.org/10.1007/978-3-319-51020-0
2. Andersen, S.T., Jansen, A.: Installed base as a facilitator for user-driven innovation: how can user innovation challenge existing institutional barriers? Int. J. Telemed. Appl. **2012**, 673731 (2012). https://doi.org/10.1155/2012/673731
3. Benardou, A., Champion, E.M., Dallas, C., Hughes, L. (eds.): Cultural Heritage Infrastructures in Digital Humanities. Routledge, London (2018)
4. Boylan, P.J.: The Museum Profession. In: Macdonald, S. (ed.) A companion to museum studies, pp. 415–430. Blackwell, Oxford (2006)
5. Cameron, F.R., Kenderdine, S. (eds.): Theorizing Digital Cultural Heritage A Critical Discourse. . MIT Press, Cambridge (2007)
6. Carpentier, N.: Beyond the ladder of participation: an analytical toolkit for the critical analysis of participatory media processes. Javnost - Public **23**(1), 70–88 (2016). https://doi.org/10.1080/13183222.2016.1149760
7. Champion, E., Rahaman, H.: 3D digital heritage models as sustainable scholarly resources. Sustainability **11**(8), 2425 (2019). https://doi.org/10.3390/su11082425
8. Champion, E.M., Dave, B.: Dialing up the past. In: Cameron, F.R., Kenderdine, S. (eds.) Theorizing Digital Cultural Heritage. A Critical Discourse, pp. 333–347. MIT Press, Cambridge, Massachusetts (2007)
9. Edwards, P.N., Bowker, G.C., Jackson, S.J., Williams, R.: Introduction: an agenda for infrastructure studies. J. Assoc. Inf. Syst. **10**(5), 364–374 (2009)

10. Fouseki, K.: 'Community voices, curatorial choices': community consultation for the 1807 exhibitions. Museum Soc. **8**(3), 180–192 (2010)
11. Geismar, H.: Museum Object Lessons for the Digital Age. UCL Press, London (2018)
12. Harvey, P., Jensen, C.B., Morita, A. (eds.): Infrastructures and social complexity. A companion. Taylor & Francis, Abingdon (2017)
13. Jones, S.: Negotiating authentic objects and authentic selves. J. Mater. Cult. **15**(2), 181–203 (2010). https://doi.org/10.1177/1359183510364074
14. Karasti, H., Blomberg, J.: Studying infrastructuring ethnographically. Comput. Support. Cooper. Work (CSCW) **27**(2), 233–265 (2017). https://doi.org/10.1007/s10606-017-9296-7
15. Karp, I., Lavine, S.D. (eds.): Exhibiting Cultures The Poetics and Politics of Museum Display. Smithsonian Inst. Press, Washington (1991)
16. Lievrouw, L.A., Livingstone, S. (eds.): Handbook of New Media Social Shaping and Consequences of ICTs. SAGE, London (2006)
17. Lynch, B.T.: Custom-made reflective practice: can museums realise their capabilities in helping others realise theirs? Museum Manag. Curator. **26**(5), 441–458 (2011). https://doi.org/10.1080/09647775.2011.621731
18. Macdonald, S.: Behind the Scenes at the Science Museum. Berg, Oxford & New York (2002)
19. MacLeod, F. (ed.): Out there. The Open Museum: Pushing the boundaries of museums' potential. Glasgow Museums, Glasgow (2010)
20. Meecham, P.: Social Work. Museums, Technology, and Material Culture. In: Drotner, K., Schrøder, K.C. (eds.) Museum Communication and Social Media. The Connected Museum, pp. 43–63. Routledge, New York (2013)
21. Monteiro, E., Hanseth, O.: Social shaping of information infrastructure: on being specific about the technology. In: Orlikowski, W.J., Walsham, G., Jones, M.R., Degross, J.I. (eds.) Information Technology and Changes in Organizational Work, pp. 325–343. Springer, Cham (1996). https://doi.org/10.1007/978-0-387-34872-8_20
22. Morgan, J.: The multisensory museum. Glasnik Etnografskog instituta **60**(1), 65–77 (2012). https://doi.org/10.2298/GEI1201065M
23. Morse, N.: Patterns of accountability: an organizational approach to community engagement in museums. Museum Soc. **16**(2), 171–186 (2018)
24. O'Neill, M.: The good enough visitor. In: Sandell, R. (ed.) Museums, Society, Inequality, pp. 24–40. Routledge, London (2002)
25. O'Neill, M.: The open museum, objects and wellbeing. In: MacLeod, F. (ed.) Out there. The Open Museum: Pushing the boundaries of museums' potential. Glasgow Museums, Glasgow (2010)
26. Parry, R., Eikhof, D.R., Barnes, S.-A., Kispeter, E.: Development, supply, deployment, demand. Balancing the museum digital skills ecosystem. First findings of the 'One by One' national digital literacy project. MW18: Museum and the Web (2018)
27. Postill, J., Pink, S.: Social media ethnography: the digital researcher in a messy web. Media Int. Australia **145**(1), 123–134 (2012)
28. Sandell, R. (ed.): Museums, Society Inequality. Routledge, London (2002)
29. Sanner, T.A., Manda, T.D., Nielsen, P.: Grafting: balancing control and cultivation in information infrastructure innovation. J. Assoc. Inf. Syst. **15**(4), 220–243 (2014)
30. Silverman, L.H.: The Social Work of Museums. Routledge, London (2010)
31. Simonsen, J., Karasti, H., Hertzum, M.: Infrastructuring and participatory design: exploring infrastructural inversion as analytic, empirical and generative. Comput. Support. Cooper. Work (CSCW) **29**(1–2), 115–151 (2019). https://doi.org/10.1007/s10606-019-09365-w
32. Star, S.L.: The ethnography of infrastructure. Am. Behav. Sci. **43**(3), 377–391 (1999)
33. Star, S.L., Bowker, G.C.: How to infrastructure. In: Lievrouw, L.A., Livingstone, S. (eds.) Handbook of new media. Social shaping and Consequences of ICTs, pp. 230–245. SAGE, London (2006)

34. Star, S.L., Ruhleder, K.: Steps toward an ecology of infrastructure. Design and access for large information spaces. Inf. Syst. Res. **7**(1), 111–134 (1996)
35. Statens Historiska Museer (SHM): Årsredovisning [Annual Report], Stockholm (2019)
36. Witcomb, A.: Re-imagining the Museum. Beyond the Mausoleum. Routledge, London (2003)
37. Witcomb, A.: The materiality of virtual technologies. A new approach to thinking about the impact of multimedia in museums. In: Cameron, F.R., Kenderdine, S. (eds.) Theorizing Digital Cultural Heritage. A Critical Discourse, pp. 35–48. MIT Press, Cambridge (2007)

Toward Extended Sensory Interface
for Impaired Person

Kanghoon Lee and Jong-Il Park[✉]

Hanyang University, Seoul, Korea
jipark@hanyang.ac.kr

Abstract. Interfaces are needed for humans and machines to interact with each other. Recently, various interface methods have been used in real life. Especially for those who cannot use the hand, it is not possible to use the hand movement or finger contact-based interface. Therefore, research is needed for user-friendly interfaces for users who are difficult to use by hand.

The extended sensory interface described in this paper is an interface that utilizes the heat generated by the convection generated by the user in the exhaled breath.

The exhaled breath can be a new invisible hand. And, in this paper, this is expressed as an extended sensation. The exhaled breath towards the surface of things convection causes the surface temperature to rise above the surroundings. By analyzing these temperature differences with a thermal image camera, it is possible to detect traces of conduction heat points due to the extended sensation. Since the traces of conduction heat point is directly generated by the user, it can be utilized for the interface.

In this study, we explain the results derived through various experiments and discuss how the extended sensory interface can be utilized by impaired per-son who have difficulty using their hands.

Keywords: Interface for impaired person · Exhaled breath · Thermal image · Heat from convection

1 Introduction

Interfaces have been studied for the purpose of human interaction with computers or mechanical devices. Among these interfaces, methods for recognizing hand movements and finger touches are widely used, and many methods using cameras are being studied in the Human computer interface field. RGB cameras, depth cameras, and near-infrared cameras that are mainly used are often unusable de-pending on the usage environment, or cause a result of an operation not intended by the user.

To complement these shortcomings, research has been conducted on the use of Traces of conduction heat generated by the user's direct action as a medium. Traces of conduction heat are generated directly by the user's finger contact, reducing unintended malfunctions. And these interface methods have the advantage that they can be used

© Springer Nature Switzerland AG 2021
M. Rauterberg (Ed.): HCII 2021, LNCS 12794, pp. 423–435, 2021.
https://doi.org/10.1007/978-3-030-77411-0_27

in places where the touch screen cannot be used without being affected by changes in lighting.

The interfaces mentioned above and most interfaces are not available to every-one. Especially for those who cannot use the hand, it is not possible to use the hand movement or finger contact-based interface. Research on new interfaces that are easy to handle for the general public is important, but research on interfaces for impaired person is also necessary from the viewpoint of public interest. Therefore, research is needed for user-friendly interfaces for users who are difficult to use by hand.

The interface is closely related to the five human sensory organs. Interfaces that use hands and fingers are based on tactile properties in the human senses. For those who have difficulty using these hands, there is a need for an auxiliary sensation that can replace the sense of touch.

Nowadays, Artificial devices such as artificial hands and arms have been developed with auxiliary senses, but they are not available to everyone in need. In addition, it cannot be used in people with spinal nerve problems. And for those who have injured their arms or hands and are not using them temporarily, there is no need for artificial ones.

Therefore, in this study, we use the exhaled breath of a person without using an artificial device to describe this as an extended sensation. In other words, the ex-haled breath can be a new invisible hand. The extended sensory interface proposed in this paper is an interface that utilizes the heat generated by the convection generated by the user in the exhaled breath. The extended sensory interface described in this paper is an interface that utilizes the heat generated by the convection generated by the user in the exhaled breath.

The breath that a person exhales is warmed by body heat, and its temperature is basically higher than the average temperature. The exhaled breath towards the surface of things convection causes the surface temperature to rise above the surroundings. By analyzing these temperature differences with a thermal image camera, it is possible to detect traces of conduction heat points due to the extended sensation. However, in general, since breath spreads widely in the air, the detection range is large and the temperature distribution is irregular. To solve these problems, straws were used as a tool to allow warm breath to be concentrated in the surface without spreading in the air. Straws is lightweight and allows the user to know where to generate traces of conduction heat. This made it possible to detect stable traces of conduction heat points.

In this study, we explain the results derived through various experiments and dis-cuss how the extended sensory interface can be utilized by impaired per-son who have difficulty using their hands. In the future, if an extended sensory interface is applied to a system intended for the general public, an environment that can be used by people with disabilities will be created. In order to apply such an interface, consideration of the general public is also required, so a questionnaire survey was conducted for the general public.

This paper is organized as follows. Section 2 is a related study, and Sect. 3 describes the breath-extended sensory interface scheme and experimental results. Section 4 is the evaluation of the survey, and finally Sect. 5 bears conclusions.

2 Related Work

There are various types of interfaces, and the finger touch method is the most widely used. A touch screen is a typical method for recognizing a finger touch. However, a large-scale touch screen is not technically easy, and its installation location is limited due to its weight and volume. There is also a method based on a difference in electrical signal by touch instead of a touch screen, but it has a drawback that the hardware configuration is complicated and is not widely used [1, 2]. Vision-based finger touch has been extensively researched for ease of use and high accessibility.

RGB cameras are the most used cameras, but they are very vulnerable to strong light and dark lighting. Especially when the intensity of the illumination is high or low, it is very difficult to compare the skin color or detect the contour of the hand. For these reasons, there is a drawback that the recognition performance of hand movement and finger contact is unstable [3].

An infrared camera is a camera that is often used together with an RGB camera. Infrared cameras have the advantages of low illumination and being able to distinguish things even in dark environments. In particular, the skin reflects near infrared rays after penetrating up to about 5 mm, so you can see your hands and fingers more clearly than with an RGB camera. In the study of table top interaction, when using a projector or LED display, it is easy to use the projector or LED display because it is less affected by the brightness of visible light [4, 5]. However, in order to take advantage of the characteristics of near infrared cameras, infrared LEDs in the proper wavelength band are necessary.

Thermal imaging cameras measure the amount of thermal energy and show it in a visual image. The thermal image camera is less affected by sunlight and can see invisible visual cues because it looks at the scene in the field of view of the camera even at night or in a dark room. Due to these characteristics, thermal imaging cameras were so expensive that they were mainly used in the military and security fields. Recently, the price has become lower due to technological progress, and the fields of application have diversified. Recently, it has been developed for mobile phones and can be easily used by the general public.

Research was conducted to utilize these thermal imaging cameras for pose recognition and finger touch interfaces. Since the shape of a person is clearly included in the thermal image due to the temperature difference with surrounding objects, it is used in various fields. Generally, fingers are warmer than room temperature, so when they come into contact with the surface of something, heat transfer occurs. The heat energy conducted on the surface now creates hotspots based on conductivity, where the conduction heat point is usually higher than the temperature of things, but not recognizable by humans. The conduction heat generated by this method is recognized as a visual clue and is used as an interaction medium.

A representative study is the Enhanced Desk, which attempts to interact by combining a projection system with a thermal imaging camera on a table [6]. In addition to these studies, TurboTablet with a projector projected on a transparent screen [7], HeatWave with further development of surface interaction [8], Dante vision combining Kinect's depth image and thermal image [9], an Interactive curtain applied to bathroom curtains [10], and a Swipe Pressure classification for natural surface interactions [11].

The above-mentioned research is valuable as a research on interface methods. However, these are for the general public, and there are very few studies on interfaces that consider people with disabilities. In this study, we are studying the interface for people with cervical spine injury who have difficulty in behavior among the interfaces that can be used by people with disabilities. These people may also use special mouthpiece sticks to operate the device [12]. Or you can fix the pen to your mouth and write or draw. However, it is very difficult to hold a stick in your mouth for a long time. Therefore, there is a need for an easy method.

Therefore, in this study, we focused on the breath that a person exhaled breath. Very little research has been done on user exhaled breath interfaces. There is an idea to sense the heat of the breath and guess the direction, but it is very difficult to measure because the temperature of the exhaled breath drops sharply in the air. There is a study that analyzes the behavior of exhaling with something similar [13]. This is an interface that analyzes the difference between breath and electromyogram and classifies it into four types. However, it is not easy to breathe differently each time.

In this study, the exhaled breath is expressed as an expanded sensation. In other words, the exhaled breath can be a new invisible hand. The extended sensory interface is an interface that utilizes the heat generated by the convection generated by the user in the exhaled breath. This paper is an extension of previous research [14].

3   Interface for Impaired Person

Interfaces for persons with disabilities vary in the methods that can be used depending on the degree and type of disability, and the number is very small. This chapter describes an interface method that can be used by people who have difficulty moving due to cervical spine injury. This method has the advantage that the interface can be used even when the arms and hands cannot be used or are temporarily not used.

3.1   Extended Sensory Interface

The extended sensory interface described in this paper is an interface that utilizes the heat generated by the convection generated by the user in the exhaled breath. People unknowingly exhale warm breaths to warm their cold hands on cold weather. Or people may exhale warmly to draw letters or pictures on the windows. The breath that a person exhales is warmed by body heat, and its temperature is basically higher than the average temperature. These properties can be an advantage that they can be used anytime, anywhere. The interface for the disabled utilizes the heat of warm exhalation.

The exhaled breath towards the surface of things convection causes the surface temperature to rise above the surroundings. By analyzing these temperature differences with a thermal image camera, it is possible to detect traces of conduction heat points due to the extended sensation. Figure 1 is a thermal image when breathing on the surface of the wall surface.

In the case of a disabled person who has no problem breathing, the degree of breathing can be adjusted at his/her own will. Therefore, it is possible to exhale warmly and perform simple operations. Leaving traces of conduction heat on the surface of things with breath

Fig. 1. Generation of conduction heat points by exhaled breath.

is unfamiliar to most people. In the early stages of the experiment, participants in the experiment often could not generate heat well. Figure 2 shows the basic difference in breath between people. Traces of conduction heat are not constant and are different. Looking at Fig. 2, it can be seen that the trace of conduction heat is much larger than when the residual heat is generated by the finger. In addition, since it is very close to the target location to generate a conduction heat point, a lot of errors occur.

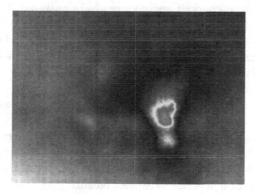

Fig. 2. Traces of irregular exhaled breath conduction heat

The reason for these is that we do not usually think about conduction heat while exhaling. Therefore, it is important that the user must be able to use it easily. A straw was used to solve these problems. The straws focus your breath and show a hotspot size that is about the same as your fingertip contact. And since it is about 25 cm to 30 cm away from the surface, it is easy for the user to generate residual heat anywhere. Figure 3 shows a thermal image of fingertip contact and breathing with a straw. Difficult to use hands in this way People with disabilities can generate hotspots and interact in much the same way as using fingers.

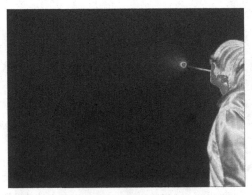

Fig. 3. Exhaled breathing through a straw produces a circular, high conduction heat point. (Thermal image)

3.2   Compare Conduction Heat Point

Basic research on conduction heat generation is necessary to efficiently generate trace of conduction heat at the position intended by the user. In addition, it must be carried out in order to utilize it for applied research using a thermal image camera and trace of conduction heat. In the experiment, the center position of the trace of conduction heat and the temperature were checked and comparatively analyzed. The experiment was conducted indoors and the room temperature was between 20 and 24 °C. The thermal imaging camera used for the experiment uses a VarioCAM hr head 420, the resolution of the camera is 384 × 288 pixels. A laser pointer was attached to each vertex on the outside of the thermal imaging camera, and was used as a tool by which the experimenter could be notified of the residual heat generation point.

The method of generating residual heat used in the experiment was divided into three. The experiment is to guide and generate residual heat on the prepared material mounted on the wall. Figure 4 shows the temperature of the conduction heat point due to fingertip contact and breath. The surface material is coated paper and the surface temperature is between 22.5 and 24.8°. Figure 4 (a) shows the case of fingertip contact, and Fig. 4 (b) shows traces of conduction heat due to exhaled breath.

In the case of fingertip contact, the temperature distribution differs depending on the participants. These causes occur due to the difference in skin temperature and the difference in pressing force of each person. Basic exhalation breathing is slightly different for each participant. The cause is that the direction, intensity, and duration of exhalation are slightly different for each participant in the experiment. And participants 1 and 2 have different exhaled breaths each time they perform an experiment. As a result, it shows a large temperature difference. As a result, in the case of fingertip touch, the temperature distribution is constant, but some participants are affected by low temperature fingers. In the case of breath, the temperature distribution of all participants is irregular and wide.

When exhaled using a straw, it can be seen that the conduction heat point temperature of all participants has increased. In particular, the conduction heat point temperature of participant 2 was increased to a similar level to that of other participants. Hold the Hollow rod in your mouth, breath your breath, warm air will not be spread to the air outside the

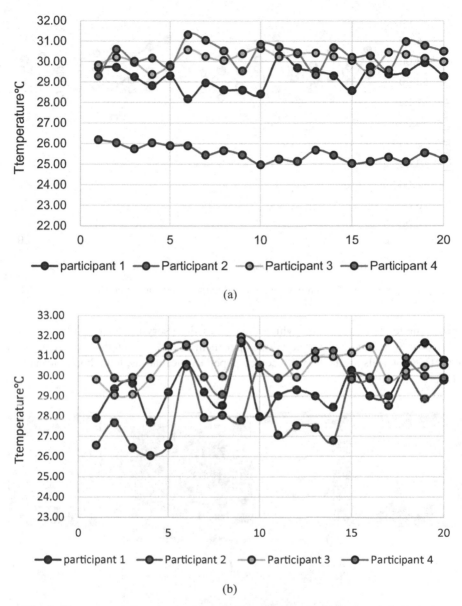

Fig. 4. Temperature of conduction heat. (a) Fingertip Touch, (b) Basic exhaled breath

mouth and will be concentrated, so the temperature of the residual heat on the surface will rise (see Fig. 5). This confirms that breathing using a straw is very easy to generate conduction heat points and the temperature is also high.

The conduction heat generated by a person has different thermal conductivity depending on things, so that the temperature of the conduction heat point also differs. The purpose of the conduction heat generation experiment for each material is to establish

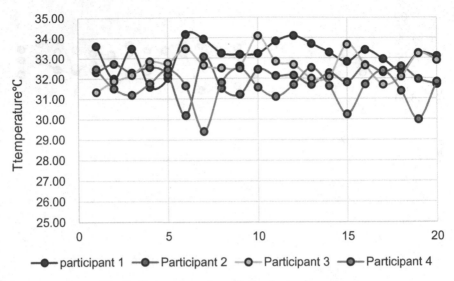

Fig. 5. Temperature of conduction heat using a straw

a guideline to the materials for which the extended sensory interface can be used. For this reason, conduction heat generation experiments were conducted on frequently used ones. The materials used here were coated paper acrylic, canvas, foam board, iron plate, MDF, etc. (see Fig. 6).

Fig. 6. Types of materials used in the experiment (a) coated paper, (b) acrylic, (c) canvas oil painting paper, (d) foam board, (e) iron plate and (f) MDF

For the conduction heat point temperature data generated for each material, the highest temperature in the range in which the traces of conduction heat was generated was selected. The data were classified by material, participant, fingertip contact, and breath through a. hollow rod. The data were classified by material, participant, fingertip contact, and breath through a straw.

Figure 7 is a temperature graph of the conduction heat of breath using a straw for each material. By looking at the graph, it is possible to confirm materials that are difficult to generate traces of conduction heat and materials that easily generate traces of conduction heat depending on the materials.

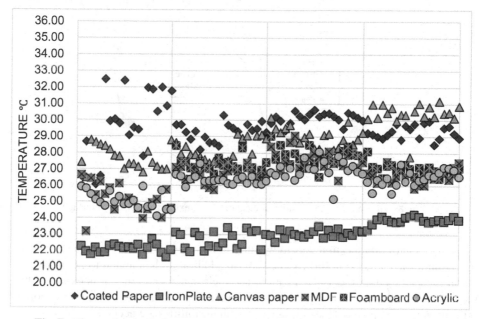

Fig. 7. The conduction heat temperature by material: breath exhaled using the straw

As a result of the analysis, in the case of coated paper and oil painting paper, it can be confirmed that the temperature of the contact of the fingertip and the heat of breath conduction using the straw is relatively high. Especially in the case of paper, it can be said that stable conduction heat generation is possible because most of the conduction heat temperature of the participants is 30° or more. In contrast, iron plates show very low temperatures.

4 Usage Evaluation Survey

In this chapter, we conduct a user evaluation of the general public to evaluate the need and usefulness of extended sensory interfaces for people with disabilities. Each assessment was explained and the results were analyzed.

The evaluation participants were 33 males (68%) and 17 females (33%) between the ages of 20 and 27. Evaluation participants expect the evaluation to be useful because they are good at mobile phones and tablet devices and are sensitive to the latest technology torrents. Question 1 is a question about the usefulness of the extended sensory interface when it is difficult to use the hand, and the result is shown in Fig. 8. The extended sensory interfaces described in this work were positively evaluated by 90% of participants in that they are novel methods.

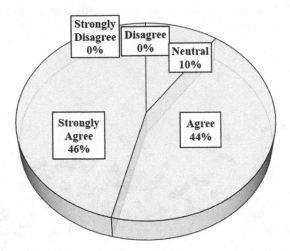

Fig. 8. Graph of survey results of ease of use of extended sensory interface

The result of the question.2 as to whether or not to use the provided interface when one cannot use the hand is shown in Fig. 9. In addition to the method to be introduced when the participants themselves cannot use their hands and arms, it is expected that they gave a good evaluation in that they do not know other methods. From these points, interfaces with various devices for persons with disabilities are needed.

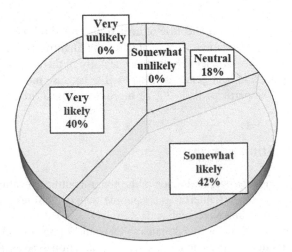

Fig. 9. Self-use Survey Results Graph

The result of the question.3 as to whether or not to recommend to others is Fig. 10. Question 3 Asks the intention to use that it is related to Question 2. It is positive that most of the evaluators recommend it to others, but it is presumed that this is the result because there are very few related interfaces.

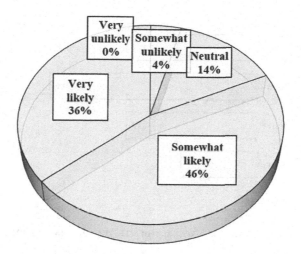

Fig. 10. Graph of the result of the investigation whether to recommend others

The contents of Question 4 regarding public nature are as follows. Is the enhanced sensory interface introduced suitable for use in public facilities such as schools and hospitals? (see Fig. 10) Due to the lack of devices for the disabled in public facilities, 78% responded positively to the installation of devices for the disabled.

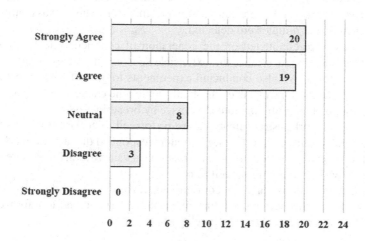

Fig. 11. Graph of the result of suitability survey for use in public places

Figure 11 shows the result. Question 5 asks the possibility of utilizing the possibility of use for persons with disabilities who are physically handicapped. Figure 12 shows the result. The participants responded positively to the possibility of 60% of participants being utilized as an expanded sensory interface because there are very few tools used by disabled people who are uncomfortable with physical movement.

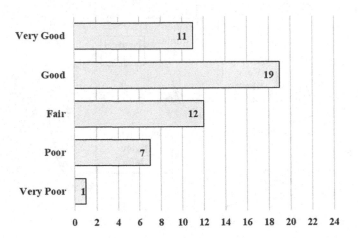

Fig. 12. Graph of the result of the possibility survey of utilization of persons with disabilities

5   Conclusion

In this paper, we have described an extended sensory interface for those who cannot use their hands. The extended sensory interface is an interface that utilizes the heat generated by the convection generated by the user in the exhaled breath. Since the basic breath is not useful, a straw was used to concentrate the breath. As a result, it was confirmed that stable conduction heat points were detected.

Experiments were conducted on the generation of conductive heat points on the surfaces of various objects so that the extensible sensory interfaces could be used in various environments. We also conducted experiments to guide how to use and verify usability. Experiments show that even disabled people who cannot use their hands in the general environment can fully operate the device by breathing out.

Finally, in this work, user evaluations are performed to confirm the need and usefulness of extended sensory interfaces. Evaluators responded that an "extended sensory interface" for those who could not use their hands was valuable, and that more than half said they were willing to recommend it to others.

Although the system is currently configured in a fixed form on the wall, it plans to improve it to the kiosk form in the future to enable movement and to improve it to an interface that is also available in private wheelchairs.

Acknowledgements. This work was supported by the National Research Foundation of Korea (NRF) grant funded by the Korea government (MSIT) (No.2019R1A4A 1029800).

References

1. Dietz, P., Leigh, D.: DiamondTouch: a multi-user touch technology. In: Proceedings of the 14th Annual ACM Symposium on User Interface Software and Technology, pp. 219–226 (2001)
2. Rekimoto, J.: SmartSkin: an infrastructure for freehand manipulation on interactive surfaces. In: Proceedings of the SIGCHI Conference on Human Factors in Computing Systems, pp. 113–120 (2002)
3. Kane, S.K., et al.: Bonfire: a nomadic system for hybrid laptop-tabletop interaction. In: Proceedings of the 22nd Annual ACM Symposium on User Interface Software and Technology, pp. 129–138 (2009)
4. Oka, K., Sato, Y., Koike, H.: Real-time tracking of multiple fingertips and gesture recognition for augmented desk interface systems. In: Proceedings of Fifth IEEE International Conference on Automatic Face Gesture Recognition, pp. 429–434 (2002)
5. Wilson, A.D.: PlayAnywhere: a compact interactive tabletop projection-vision system. In: Proceedings of the 18th Annual ACM Symposium on User Interface Software and Technology, pp. 83–92 (2005)
6. Grudin, J.: Integrating paper and digital information on EnhancedDesk: a method for realtime finger tracking on an augmented desk system. ACM Trans. Comput.-Hum. Interact. (TOCHI), 8(4), 307–322 (2001)
7. Iwai, D., Sato, K.: Heat sensation in image creation with thermal vision. In: Proceedings of the 2005 ACM SIGCHI International Conference on Advances in Computer Entertainment Technology, pp. 213–216 (2005)
8. Larson, E., et al.: Heatwave: thermal imaging for surface user interaction. In: Proceedings of the SIGCHI Conference on Human Factors in Computing Systems, pp. 2565–2574 (2011)
9. Saba, E.N., Larson, E.C., Patel, S.N.: Dante vision: in air and touch gesture sensing for natural surface interaction with combined depth and thermal cameras. In: 2012 IEEE International Conference on Emerging Signal Processing Applications, pp. 167–170 (2012)
10. Funk, M., Schneegass, S., Behringer, M., Henze, N., Schmidt, A.: An interactive curtain for media usage in the shower. In: Proceedings of the 4th International Symposium on Pervasive Displays, pp. 225–231 (2015)
11. Dunn, T., Banerjee, S., Banerjee, N.K.: User-independent detection of swipe pressure using a thermal camera for natural surface interaction. In: 2018 IEEE 20th International Workshop on Multimedia Signal Processing (MMSP), pp. 1–6 (2018)
12. Cook, A.M., Polgar, J.M.: Cook and Hussey's Assistive Technologies-E-Book: Principles and Practice. Elsevier Health Sciences (2013)
13. Sra, M., Xu, X., Maes, P.: BreathVR: leveraging breathing as a directly controlled interface for virtual reality games. In: Proceedings of the 2018 CHI Conference on Human Factors in Computing Systems, pp. 1–12 (2018)
14. Lee, K., Lee, S.H., Park, J.-I.: Hands-free interface using breath residual heat. In: Yamamoto, S., Mori, H. (eds.) HIMI 2018. LNCS, vol. 10904, pp. 204–217. Springer, Cham (2018). https://doi.org/10.1007/978-3-319-92043-6_18

User Experience in Digital Museums: A Case Study of the Palace Museum in Beijing

Wenhua Li[1](✉) and Jia Xin Xiao[2]

[1] Guangzhou Academy of Fine Arts, No. 257, Changgang East Road, Haizhu District, Guangzhou 510000, China
[2] Guangdong University of Technology, No. 257, Changgang East Road, Haizhu District, Guangzhou 510000, China

Abstract. Digital technologies have enhanced the user experiences of museum visiting, both on-site visiting and online visiting. With smart mobile devices, people can visit digital museums and acquire information, service and learning materials anytime that they want. During virtual tours, the visitors have the right to design their own paths and interact with the collections in their own ways without barriers and glass walls. Augmented reality technologies allow museums to bring collections to life and change the perspectives of the viewers. The interactions between museums, visitors and artifacts raises new requirements for exhibition designs. How to design valuable and enjoyable virtual experiences for dynamic and effective communication between museums and visitors is an important issue for museum professionals and designers. This paper provides a case study of an important museum in China, the Palace Museum. This paper analyzed the user experiences of the mobile applications of the Palace Museum and examine the factors affecting the user experience in digital museums with the Interactive Experience Model [1]. The findings of this case study will be valuable for museum professional, designers and researchers in designing enjoyable experiences for digital museums.

Keywords: Digital museums · User experience · The interactive experience model

1 Introduction

One of the most important duties of museums is cultural communication and social education. As the educational level of common people rises and their leisure time increases, cultural consumption and museum visiting becomes popular. Traditionally, visiting famous museums has been difficult, expensive and seldom because the visitors need to travel to cities and encounter long queues with the crowds. With digital technologies, museums can offer virtual tours and online exhibitions for global visitors without time and space restrictions. In addition, digital museums interact with visitors with emerging technologies, such as virtual reality and mixed reality technologies, to deliver knowledge in attractive and accessible ways for new cultural experiences. Online visitors will not

© Springer Nature Switzerland AG 2021
M. Rauterberg (Ed.): HCII 2021, LNCS 12794, pp. 436–448, 2021.
https://doi.org/10.1007/978-3-030-77411-0_28

miss any collections they want to see. A lot of user research studies have examined the impacts of digital technologies on museum experiences. In the New Museology, visitors are not passive receivers, but creators who can cooperate with museums and participate in the future development of museums [2]. The visitors hope to be part of museum narratives, connecting with museums and sharing their experiences with others [3]. Digital museums make these connections and cooperation possible. With smart mobile devices, people can visit digital museums and acquire information, service and learning materials anytime that they want. During virtual tours, the visitors have the right to design their own paths and interact with the collections in their own ways without barriers and glass walls. Augmented reality technologies allow museums to bring collections to life and change the perspectives of the viewers. The interactions between museums, visitors and artifacts raises new requirements for exhibition designs. How to design valuable and enjoyable virtual experiences for dynamic and effective communication between museums and visitors is an important issue for museum professionals and designers. This study aims to analyze the user experiences of the mobile applications of the Palace Museum and examine the factors affecting the virtual experiences for users.

2 Theoretical Background

Digital technologies are reshaping our leisure life, including the way we visit museums. A lot of research studies have investigated the influence of digital technologies on the interactions between museums and visitors. Museum websites used to offer information about the museums and facilitated on-site visiting, such as ticket service, bookings, traffic information and latest exhibition news. With digital technologies, museum websites have shifted from being information deliverers to digital museum experience providers [4]. Researchers and museum professionals placed the emphasis on the usability of websites. Now, the goal of a museum website has shifted to provide enjoyable visiting experiences to appeal to more visitors [5]. Digital museums adopt virtual reality and augmented reality technologies to provide authentic experiences for online visitors, where visitors can navigate through the three-dimensional digital museum just like walking in physical space [6]. Many research findings support that digital technologies have enhanced the user experiences of museum visiting, both on-site visiting and online visiting [6, 7].

Museum visiting experiences are complex. Falk and Dierking [1] proposed the Interactive Experience Model, identifying three factors associated with museum experiences: personal, social and physical factors. The personal context of a museum experience refers to personal background, including personal experience, knowledge, belief, motivation, interest in a museum and personal choice and control over the museum experience [1, 3]. Sundar [6] pointed out that the quality of a visiting experience is maximized if a visitor has relative knowledge and makes his/her own decision(s) in their museum visiting schedule. In another words, active visitors with knowledge, independent choice and control would better enjoy their museum visiting. The social factor of museum experiences refers to social interactions with other people, including in-group collaborations and out-group assistance [1]. The quality of a museum experience relates to a visitor's degree of interactions within families and social groups [8]. Out-group refers to other visitors and museum staff. The assistance from an out-group is also important in enhancing museum experiences. The interactive experience model can be used to define what is a good museum user experience (Table 1).

Table 1. The interactive experience model

The factors of the interactive experience model	Keywords
Personal	Motivation, purpose, expectation, prior knowledge and experience, choice and control, belief, value, lifestyle, emotion
Social	Social groups, interactivity, collaboration, interact with other visitors, interact with museum staff, shareable interactive exhibits
Physical	Physical environment, atmosphere, navigation, technological factors, exhibition design, visual attractiveness

Adapted from The Interactive Experience Model [1, 3].

3 Methodology

This paper provides a case study of an important museum in China, the Palace Museum. The Palace Museum is representative in studying the topic of user experience in a digital museum. We mainly collected data from the virtual platform of the Palace Museum and from secondary sources, including books, journal papers, published materials, news and articles online. We analyzed the virtual experience offered by the Palace Museum, to find out how it has been designed to provide sound experience and satisfy its users.

Case Study: The Digital Palace Museum
Established in 1925, the Palace Museum is one of China's foremost-protected cultural heritage sites, which was first listed as a UNESCO World Heritage site in 1987. The digital Palace Museum project started from the end of the 1990s, which aims to offer a one-stop platform for visitors to acquire the digital resources of the Palace Museum. The digital Palace Museum can be accessed via the museum's official website and mobile application. There are 7 main sections in the digital Palace Museum, undertaking different duties, which are listed in the table below (Table 2 and Fig. 1).

4 Discussion and Analysis

The user experience of the digital Palace Museum application is analyzed below in terms of the Interactive Experience Model [1].

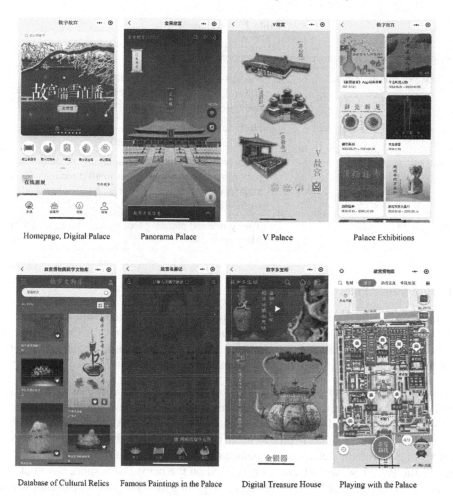

Fig. 1. The interface design of Digital Palace and seven sections. (Source: screen captured from Wechat Mini Apps of Digital Palace; the website of digital Palace www.dpm.org.cn)

Table 2. Seven sections in the digital palace museum

Sections in the digital palace museum	Functions and contents
Panoramic palace	360-degree panorama video represent the buildings of Forbidden City online
V palace	Virtual reality tour of three palaces
Palace exhibitions	360-degree panorama video, represent all the exhibitions in Palace Museum

(continued)

Table 2. (*continued*)

Sections in the digital palace museum	Functions and contents
Database of cultural relics	Visitors can search and view the details of 50,000 cultural relics collected by the Palace Museum via the database
Famous paintings in the palace	High-definition pictures of 611 ancient paintings collected in the Palace Museum
Digital treasure house	High-precision 3D models displaying the details and panorama of the cultural relics in all directions. The visitors can touch and interact with the cultural relics from 360°
Playing with the palace	Tour guide and planning tool for upcoming visit to the Museum

4.1 Panoramic Palace

The Palace Museum is the largest and most complete timber-framed building complex in the world. In order to view the spectacular building complex online, the Palace Museum launched the project "Panoramic Palace" in 2001, which used three-dimensional panorama technology to represent the architecture online.

Personal. Museum visitors are usually passive, following the routes designed by the museum staff. When visiting the panorama museum, the users become active explorers. The visitors of the digital Palace Museum can use regular displays, such as their mobile phones, laptops or computers to take a virtual tour online. The "Panoramic Palace" allows visitors to examine the details of the palace architecture without limits. All digitalized sites in the Palace Museum have been marked on the map. The visitors can click the marks of the sites to freely visit them and avoid getting lost. The visitors can choose and control their visiting routes with an easy-used navigation system.

Social. Two social interactions, "like" and "share" are designed in the Panoramic Palace. There have been more than 180 thousand likes, which will increase the sense of perceived social presence. The users can share the Panoramic Palace to two of the most popular social platforms, Weibo and WeChat, easily with system generated posters.

Physical. The navigability is related to wayfinding and spatial presence [9]. In a virtual environment, navigability is important in boosting user experience. In the Panoramic Palace, the 3D panorama of the architectures is rotating slowly, which means that a user can view the palaces with first-person perspective without any operation. The user can click on a button which is of interest to check the information and details of a certain building or sculpture. Beside 3D environmental navigation, users can easily find a flat map to check their location in the virtual environment and shift to the buildings that they want to visit (Fig. 2).

Fig. 2. The interface design of Panoramic Palace. (Source: screen captured from Wechat Mini Apps of Digital Palace; the website of digital Palace www.dpm.org.cn)

4.2 V Palace

The V Palace section has integrated the data resources of the Forbidden City since 2000, with three-dimensional data visualization and virtual reality technology, to reproduce the magnificent Forbidden City virtually. By 2021, it has released three palaces: Hall of Mental cultivation, Juan Qin Zhai, Lin Zhao Pavilion.

Personal. The V Palace provides visitors with two different VR experiences. The first level of interaction is to follow the craftsmen to learn about the traditional decoration process, and the second level of interaction is to follow the cultural relic restoration experts to appreciate ancient architecture and cultural relics. The users can choose the set route to browse, or choose free mode to browse.

Social. In the V Palace, there are two non-player characters interacting with users. One is the old craftsman, and another is a cultural relic restoration expert. They will accompany users to visit, and to avoid users getting lost in the palace. When they reach a new location, users need to explore the interactive items in the scene. Non-player characters will give users knowledge points, puzzle games and Q & A to help them acquire relevant knowledge. Their expressions will also change if the user answers the question correctly. Users will feel engaged with the companion of non-player characters.

Physical. The experts in the Palace Museum repair the palaces virtually with three-dimensional virtual reality technology. The V Palace has used 3D digital modeling techniques to generate an accurate virtual reality representation of its physical space, which allows users to navigate through the virtual palace via head-mounted displays. The virtual tour of the three palaces use a first-person perspective to increase the sense of immersion (Fig. 3).

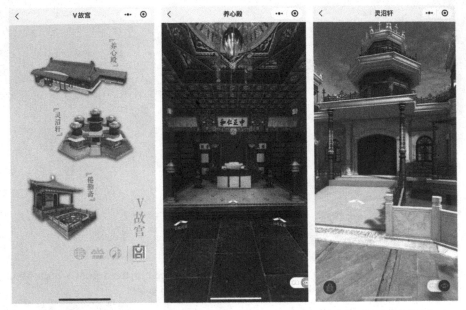

Fig. 3. The interface design of V Palace. (Source: screen captured from Wechat Mini Apps of Digital Palace; the website of digital Palace www.dpm.org.cn)

4.3 Palace Exhibitions

The Palace exhibition section in the digital Palace Museum creates a 7 × 24-h online exhibition hall for users to visit the ancient palace at their fingertips. All the exhibitions have been on-site since the year 2015 have been digitalized so that the users can have a panoramic view of the exhibitions in the Palace Museum.

Personal. From the perspective of purpose and motivation, the Palace exhibition section is designed for people who have an interest in visiting exhibitions. Online exhibitions offer the same contents and artworks as physical exhibitions, so that the visitors can experience the rich connotation of traditional art and palace culture via the online platform. Compared to on-site visiting, online exhibitions give the visitors more control on their visits. In physical exhibitions, the visitors cannot touch physical artifacts. With an online system, the users can examine the artworks in detail with the zoom-in function and conveniently check the information and stories of the artworks. With the search button, the visitors can easily find the artworks they want to visit. They can search the artworks with key words or pictures. Searching with pictures makes their experience interesting.

Social. The user system supports the third party login. The users can collect the artworks in a wish list and share with friends via social media platforms, including Weibo and WeChat Applications. The exhibition system generates fine posters for each exhibition for users to broadcast the exhibition on a social media platform. Within the system, the users can also interact with other visitors via a "Like" button and write their comments.

Physical. Panoramic virtual roaming and virtual reality experience in the exhibition hall makes the visiting experience at home just like visiting the scene in person. The navigation system is simple with "the next scene" and "the last scene" buttons. With the help of a flat guide map, the users can position their locations fast. The exhibits information is presented in multiple ways to make sure the users can easily obtain the information of each artifact (Fig. 4).

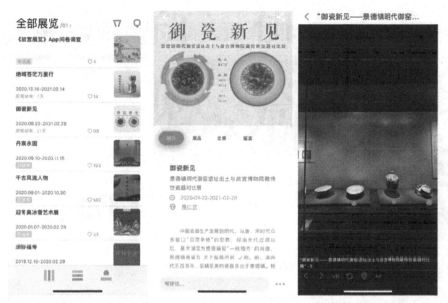

Fig. 4. The interface design of Palace Exhibitions. (Source: screen captured from Wechat Mini Apps of Digital Palace; the website of digital Palace www.dpm.org.cn)

4.4 Database of Cultural Relics

There are 1,863,404 collections in the Palace Museum, and 52,558 collections have been digitalized, to meet the needs of cultural enthusiasts, experts and scholars of the Palace Museum for appreciation and study. The database also provides support for the conservation of cultural relics.

Personal. The users are active in exploring the database of cultural relics since they can learn cultural and art knowledge from the system. They can also customize their own museum through collecting favorite cultural relics to their personal account. With the search engine, the users can find the collections they want easily. The database of cultural relics can be great value for people who need it.

Social. The users can share the collections with friends or post via social media.

Physical. The database of the cultural relics includes high-definition images of thousands of cultural relics. The users can navigate on the list of all cultural relics and click to view the collection. In the collection page, there are pictures of the collection that can be enlarged. In addition to the collection name and number, the collection content page of the website also provides the collection category, age and related collection information. The design of the system and interaction is very simple (Fig. 5).

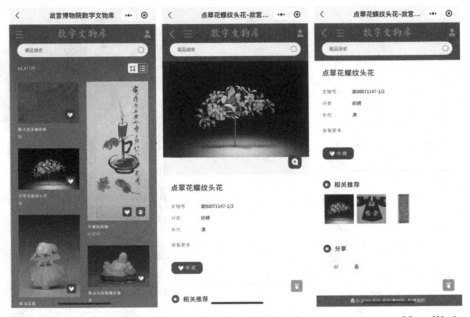

Fig. 5. The interface design of Database of Cultural Relics. (Source: screen captured from Wechat Mini Apps of Digital Palace; the website of digital Palace www.dpm.org.cn)

4.5   Famous Paintings in the Palace

This section mainly provides high-definition pictures and multimedia materials of ancient Chinese painting treasures collected in the Palace Museum.

Personal. The section of Famous Paintings in the Palace is valuable for people who need to acquire the detailed information about the famous paintings. In addition to high-definition images, the system continues to add audio and video files, related papers and other materials to enrich the research results and multimedia appreciation contents, so as to meet the needs of researchers, students and museum fans in traditional calligraphy and painting art research and appreciation. The quality of user experiences in this section is enhanced with detailed supplementary materials.

Social. This section focuses on personal collection. A user can create an account in the system and collect the paintings and related articles in the member center to construct their own private online museum. A user can collect, mark on certain parts, comment and share when browsing one painting.

Physical. The Palace Museum's famous paintings section is a two-dimensional webpage system with a simple interface. The section has the unlimited zoom function of ultra-high definition digital images, and can be adapted to various mainstream terminals and browsers. The users can browse the artworks by paintings, schools or painters. Related articles and multimedia materials are listed in the page of the painting (Fig. 6).

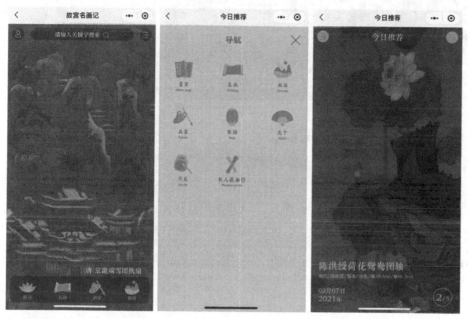

Fig. 6. The interface design of Famous Paintings in the Palace. (Source: screen captured from Wechat Mini Apps of Digital Palace; the website of digital Palace www.dpm.org.cn)

4.6 Digital Treasure House

The digital treasure house contains the digitalized collections of gold and silver ware, bronze ware, jade ware, stationery, enamel ware, carving artwork, ceramics, sculpture, religious relics, lacquerware, and other handicrafts, which adopt high-precision 3D models displaying the details and panorama of the cultural relics in all directions. The visitors can touch and interact with the cultural relics from 360°.

Personal. The digital treasure house is built for people who have strong needs in acquiring the details of certain handicraft collections. It excludes all unnecessary functions, such as the personal museum.

Social. There are no socialized functions in this section.

Physical. This section displays all the cultural relics in a waterfall information flow list with simple interface without unnecessary functions. Interesting animations are adopted to present the story behind the artworks. Rotatable 3D models enable users to view the artworks in all directions (Fig. 7).

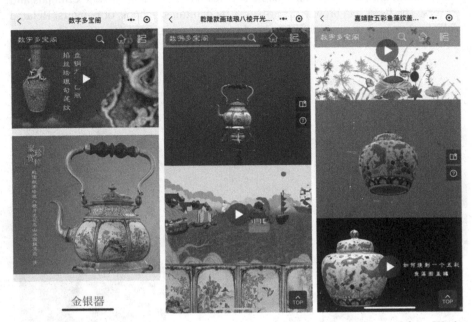

Fig. 7. The interface design of Digital Treasure House. (Source: screen captured from Wechat Mini Apps of Digital Palace; the website of digital Palace www.dpm.org.cn)

4.7 Playing with the Palace

"Playing with the Palace" provides a convenient trip planning tool for upcoming visits to the Palace Museum.

Personal. The section of Playing with the Palace provide a useful tool for potential visitors to plan their trips. An AI navigation assistant in the system can interact with users via voice and text to provide personalized, customized and intelligent services for visitors.

Social. An AI assistant can chat with the users, answer questions about travel, history, culture, art, even the location of the nearest washing room. The visiting experience will be enhanced with a smart virtual travel guide.

Physical. The main interface of the system is a flat map. All the interactions between users and the system are location-based. The navigation of the system is simple and easy to understand (Fig. 8).

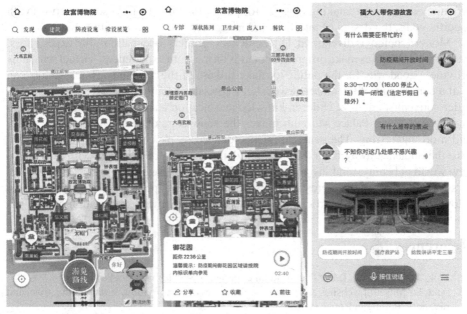

Fig. 8. The interface design of Playing with the Palace. (Source: screen captured from Wechat Mini Apps of Digital Palace, the website of digital Palace www.dpm.org.cn)

5 Conclusion

We analyzed the digital Palace Museum with the Interactive Model. From the personal level, the digital Palace Museum provides a valuable personal space for Palace Museum lovers and cultural researchers, where they can collect works of art, mark details, read research articles and multimedia materials. The personal archives can be permanently preserved and consulted at any time. At the same time, the digital Palace Museum provides an easy-to-use virtual space for ordinary people who want to visit the Palace Museum. From the social level, in order to create a virtual sense of company, each section of the digital Palace Museum has the functions of like, share and comment, so that users can see the comments of other users on the artworks, and can easily share their experiences on social media. By providing users with exquisite posters generated by the system, the digital Palace Museum can improve the quality of social communication and attract more people to click on the posters to visit the digital Palace Museum. From the physical level, in order to create a sense of presence, the panoramic Palace Museum provides visitors with snow and flower scenery appreciation. Through the climate changes of the Palace Museum, we can see the Palace Museum as an environment that changes by day and night as our living environment, rather than a virtual and unchanging illusion. Through panoramic technology and 3D virtual roaming, users can simulate their experiences of visiting the physical Palace Museum, easily locating and switching scenes. Through a variety of multimedia auxiliary materials, the historical and cultural background of the exhibits can be displayed. Some exhibits are put in a story or game environment, making it easier for people to understand. In some sections with specific goals, the design of interface and navigation is consistent with the goals.

Modern society is diversified. Different ages, genders, occupations, life experiences, interests and hobbies make different demands on museum experiences. Virtual museums provide a good way for the public to make full use of the museums. Here, visitors can visit a certain part of the museum website, a special exhibition, consult some literature, order souvenirs, and give children knowledge education games to meet their individual needs. The digital Palace Museum makes the knowledge of history and culture richer and more interesting. The peak experience defined by psychologist Maslow [10] is to take the audience away from their normal daily life and provide them with a beautiful new world of beauty, thinking and memory. The value of the digital Palace Museum lies in stimulating people's interest and desire to visit and experience physical museums, allowing more people to participate, and realize the effective dissemination of culture.

References

1. Falk, J.H., Dierking, L.D.: The museum experience. Whalesback Books (1992)
2. Ana, L.: Museum websites and social media: issues of participation, sustainability, trust, and diversity. Berghahn Books (2015)
3. Falk, J.H., Dierking, L.D.: Learning from museums: visitor experiences and the making of meaning. AltaMira (2000)
4. Macdonald, C.: Assessing the user experience (UX) of online museum collections: perspectives from design and museum professionals. MW2015: Museums and the Web 2015 (2015). https://mw2015.museumsandtheweb.com/paper/assessing-the-user-experience-ux-of-onl ine-museum-collections-perspectives-from-design-and-museum-professionals/. Accessed 30 Dec 2020
5. Hassenzahl, M., Tractinsky, N.: User experience-a research agenda. Behav. Inf. Technol. **25**(2), 91–97 (2006)
6. Sundar, S.S., Go, E., Kim, H.S., Zhang, B.: Communicating art, virtually! Psychological effects of technological affordances in a virtual museum. Int. J. Hum.-Comput. Interact. **31**(6), 385–401 (2015)
7. van Dijk, E., Lingnau, A., Kockelkorn, H.: Measuring enjoyment of an interactive museum experience. In: Proceedings of the 14th ACM International Conference on Multimodal Interaction (ICM 2012), pp. 249–256. ACM Press (2012)
8. Falk, J., Storksdieck, M.: Using the contextual model of learning to understand visitor learning from a science center exhibition. Sci. Educ. **89**(5), 744–778 (2005)
9. Balakrishnan, B., Sundar, S.S.: Where am I? How can I get there? Impact of navigability and narrative transportation on spatial presence. Hum.-Comput. Int. **26**(3), 161–204 (2011)
10. Maslow, A.H.: Religions, Values, and Peak Experiences. Penguin Books Limited (1964)

Before You Visit-: New Opportunities for the Digital Transformation of Museums

Hyungmin Park, Jeongyun Heo(⊠), and Jongkeon Kim

Kookmin University, Seoul, Republic of Korea
{dearfps,yuniheo,jkeon72}@kookmin.ac.kr

Abstract. This study aims to develop a service model for an effective museum viewing experience. It conducted a literature review and benchmarking to analyze the ongoing digital transformation (DT) of the entire process of museum visits. The study confirmed that the DT implemented by museums focuses on visitors' viewing experience. In particular, this research observed that accessing the appropriate exhibition information before viewing was challenging. In addition, the lack of DT in recording the viewing experience was confirmed. User surveys were administered to confirm visitors' viewing experience. Data on the exhibition viewing process were collected from the first round of interviews, and insights such as "information search" and "collection" were derived. Based on these insights, another survey was conducted to confirm the task during exhibition viewing. A second round of interviews was held with survey respondents to determine user needs and insights necessary for the proposed service. Based on user needs and insights, this study proposed a DT concept that can collect personalized data on visitor taste based on the display of favorite works. This is expected to provide an effective exhibition viewing experience by recommending exhibitions that suit the taste of visitors and integrate the entire viewing process.

Keywords: Museum experience · Digital transformation · Service design

1 Introduction

1.1 Background and Necessity of Research

Advancements in information and communication technologies (ICT) are driving change in many industries in terms of individuals, organizations, and social and economic activities [1]. The non-face-to-face society that has emerged because of the COVID-19 pandemic is fueling rapid digital transformation (DT). Some industries are making new efforts to digitize long-established models to fit the existing industrial environment [2]. While these attempts are not entirely new [3], they provide opportunities for value creation by digitally transforming products and services in existing industries [4].

DT is happening in many industries [5]. In the past, art museums have been recognized as cultural spaces that house physical collections and open them to the public [6]. The Museum of Contemporary Art is striving to transform into a space that provides customer-centered experience and creativity beyond social and cultural education [7].

The original version of this chapter was revised: The corresponding author has been changed. The correction to this chapter is available at https://doi.org/10.1007/978-3-030-77411-0_31

© Springer Nature Switzerland AG 2021, corrected publication 2021
M. Rauterberg (Ed.): HCII 2021, LNCS 12794, pp. 449–466, 2021.
https://doi.org/10.1007/978-3-030-77411-0_29

In this regard, the use of digital technology can be particularly useful in planning the next exhibition or creating content by collecting information from museum visitors [8]. Therefore, cultural institutions such as art galleries are making special efforts to keep up with changes in the technology industry [5]. However, as a traditional institution whose main function is to preserve [9], research, and exhibit works, art museums cannot respond swiftly to the changing digital environment [4]. Therefore, DT in art museums requires a modern direction for the following reasons.

First, DT in art museums focuses only on visiting experience. Museums adopt methods to maximize the viewing experience based on the confidence [8] that knowledge can be transmitted through physical works. However, according to Hooper-Greenhill, interactions between the museum and its visitors take place not only through functional elements such as exhibitions and programs but also through the overall experience associated with the museum [10]. Therefore, it is necessary to expand the perspective of customer experience (CX) management and evaluate experiences before, during, and after museum viewing. Second, information exchange between museums and visitors is insufficient. Museums are not meeting the expectations of individual users because their provision of unilateral information does not reflect visitors' needs [11]. Third, no system has been established with regard to viewing museum information at a glance [8]. In a modern society where one can easily access information, visiting museums and viewing items requires much time and effort. Fourth, there is a lack of media for archiving data on information collection and museum activities. Considering the increasing number of visitors who obtain information online, museums need to construct an integrated research archive [12].

1.2 Research Question

This study was developed based on the following research questions:

RQ1: Before the Exhibition. As a result of the changing times of digitalization, it has become easy for users to obtain information. Information on the purpose, direction, scale, and accessibility of exhibitions has also become diversified. How can a user easily find exhibition information that suits their taste in the large volume of data?

RQ2: After Viewing the Exhibition. After users have viewed the exhibition, can the exhibition be not just a glimpse of everyday life stored on their cell phone but also part of a documentation of their museum visit?

Through this study, the researcher analyzes the DT that occurs in the entire process before, during, and after museum visits from a CX perspective and proposes a service that can expand such an experience before and after viewing where DT is not activated.

1.3 Research Overview

Research Method. This study aims to develop a service model for an effective museum viewing experience. In addition, this research presents a DT concept that can be used to recommend exhibitions and provide additional information before and after museum visits by collecting data based on users' personal taste. It also reviews relevant studies to summarize the theoretical background as well as examples of DT and exhibition viewing experience. To confirm the level of information that users can access before viewing, this study examines a Database (DB) of national and public art museums in Seoul, Korea. To highlight the lack of DT research in existing museums, cases of museum-related DT were benchmarked. Afterward, the first round of interviews was held to collect data on the exhibition viewing process and organize insights. From the first interview sessions, the insights "information search" and "collection" were identified, based on which a questionnaire survey was administered to confirm the task during the exhibition viewing process. A second round of interviews was then conducted with the same respondents, from whom relevant users' needs and insights for the proposed service were derived. Finally, by verifying users' acceptance of the proposed service, this study confirmed the expected effect.

2 Background and Related Work

2.1 Digital Transformation (DT)

DT refers to any innovation process that links traditional business thinking to creative design approaches based on problem-solving [13]. It also includes important changes that take place in society and industry via digital technology [14]. DT aims to improve an entity through substantial changes in properties with a combination of communication connection technologies such as information and computing [13]. For this reason, creativity based on networking ideas and mindsets is a particularly important factor in DT [15]. The potential effects of creativity-based DT are diverse: innovation of industry value creation, sales growth and economic benefits, and new forms of interaction with customers or stakeholders [16]. Therefore, DT research is important to rapidly adapt to and innovate during changing situations.

2.2 DT Research Trends Related to Art Museums

Cultural institutions such as art museums are also striving to keep up with the changes in the technology industry [5] and are conducting many studies related to DT. In particular, digital technology can be used to collect information from museum visitors and may be useful in planning the next exhibition or producing content [8]; therefore, many museums are focusing on digitalization. To investigate the DT phenomenon, this study investigated ongoing art museum-related cases.

Representative examples of digital technology use in art museums include websites, virtual art museums, service platforms, and virtual reality (VR) and augmented reality (AR).

Websites are the most common example of DT in art museums, through which visitors can easily access works even if they do not exist physically [17]. Websites break down barriers between museums and their visitors and connect the two, as access to information had been previously difficult [18]. Lopatovska and the current researchers conducted a study that evaluated the factors for website development and confirmed that content manipulation functions such as image download are important in determining the possibility of website revisits [19].

Museum websites have since been expanded to virtual museums, in which physical objects can be shown digitally and relevant digital objects can also be collected [20]. However, recent research has argued that virtual collections are one of the least popular features of art museum websites because poor user experience has made it difficult to find information digitally [21]. Therefore, research has focused on the experience of viewing museums, such as the user-centered virtual museum design framework [20].

Some studies have also proposed platforms and services centering on user experience and processes. Rose, the researchers, and three others personalized users' viewing experience by providing a viewing itinerary tailored to visitors' taste at the designated museum [22]. Hsi, S proposed related services such as electronic guidebooks that use mobile web content [23].

Some examples can also be found regarding the use of advanced technologies for a three-dimensional art museum experience. Research on VR applications such as AR content development [24] is underway to provide a more interesting experience during museum visits. VR provides an opportunity to freely handle fragile works by merging the physical and virtual worlds. As such, VR provides an opportunity for DT in a way that had not been possible [25].

DT in art museums provides a considerable change in the culture of exhibitions. Our case study confirmed many attempts to digitalize the viewing method and viewpoint of displaying works. Art museums have focused on improving their exhibition viewing services in recent years, which improved the quality of interaction between museums and visitors [26]. However, art museums tend to lack interest in technological advancement before exhibition viewing [27]. The interaction between museums and users takes place not only through the latter's experience during the exhibition but also through their overall museum experience [12]. Therefore, art museums need to expand their CX perspective, which would include the entire process both before and after viewing.

2.3   Customer Experience (CX)

CX was first conceived in the mid-1980s to provide a new empirical approach involving customers as rational decision-makers [28]. It refers to the total experience resulting from the interactions between industries and customers. CX is an important factor that drives customer preferences and decision-making [29] and is a tool that differentiates CX management to gain an edge in an increasingly competitive environment [30]. Thus, industries need to monitor and investigate the entire range of customers' expectations: previous, current, and future [31].

2.4   Research Trends on Art Museum Visiting Experience

Museum visits include planning and are extended to include the period before and after visits to remember the exhibition [32]. Visitors can access a significant portion of information on an exhibition after participating in it at home or in a different context. This allows visitors to focus on discoveries while in the museum and identify the information they want to remember later [12]. Visitors are no longer satisfied with limited access to museum collections. Many people always want access to museum information no matter where the data is located or how it is organized [33]. If the audience studies the works before viewing, they can acquire more information when they actually view these works. Also, if a user reviews a museum after viewing, they can remember and revisit the place [8]. However, when visitors go to art galleries, they must search the websites of many individual museums to find the information they require, or they try to find related blogs, posts, and social media content [32]. This is why people spend time preparing before visiting an art gallery and looking for relevant information that reflects what they have seen or missed after visiting [34]. This is due to the lack of information provided by the museum system, which makes it difficult for users to obtain the information they need online [32].

Therefore, a personalized museum viewing model that uses digital technology is vital. Information retrieval using personalization is popular because it can provide a response that is appropriate to a user's taste [12]. In addition, personalization through IT is an increasingly important trend in the world of art museums [35]. A personalized system allows users to quickly and easily find data that suits their taste by prioritizing relevant information and sorting the results. Through the personalization of museum information, visitors can gain more knowledge and excitement beyond pleasure [12].

Integrating visitors' online and field experiences into a single cycle supports continuous learning experiences, retains memories over time, and enables individual interests to be pursued, allowing visitors to focus on experimentation, discovery, and aesthetic experiences during museum visits [22]. From an art museum perspective, personalized recommendations are considered not only to help cope with the threat of information overload by providing information tailored to a visitor's interests and background but also to increase their interest and stimulate physical visits [12]. This is becoming increasingly important to users who face a large amount of metadata to help them select the appropriate information or provide accidental references to relevant information [36]. Recommendation systems are becoming more popular for suggesting information to individual users and helping them search for items of interest that are not normally found using query-based searches [37].

Falk and Dierking (2012) conceptualized museum visits and included the entire process of recollection before, during, and after the visit as the museum experience [38]. All processes before, during, and after museum visits accumulate and shape other experiences. To gather and store memories after visiting the museum, users need collections and records. Museums have recognized the need for a comprehensive and elaborate process to document exhibition information [39]. The recent trend toward automation allows museums to collect information in a variety of ways [40]. Through this, records are accumulated in the entire museum visit process and influence other experiences [39].

Overall, this study confirmed the problem of the lack of DT in a user's experience before and after visiting a museum. Visitors had difficulty collecting information before and after viewing because of the absence of DT. In this study, to address the problem that viewers spend too much time collecting the information they want, this study intends to offer personalized recommendations before and after viewing.

3 Benchmarking

3.1 Technology-Oriented Art Museum DT Application

This study aims to examine the focus of DT in the art museum viewing experience. Thus, it summarizes examples of the active use of DT in domestic and international museum visits. Each category is based on AR, VR, artificial intelligence (AI), robots, and online archives, which are examples of DT in five national and public art museums in Seoul. Because museum experience can be stored in one's memory, the museums were restructured with the addition of a recorded method of viewing [41]. Through AR, artistic works can be experienced in the real world through devices such as AR glasses. VR provides a realistic experience, as if a user is in their workplace. VR can also be viewed in a non-face-to-face situation, such as the prolonged COVID-19 pandemic, which has made it impossible to enjoy cultural life. AI enables a detailed analysis of the work and provides an opportunity to examine a wide variety of related information. A robot, through autonomous driving technology, accommodates requests for guidance and provides visitors customized information.

An online art archive provides users the opportunity to access works more easily by converting volumes of information about these works into digital data. By benchmarking the above examples, this study confirmed many attempts at DT to present works. However, the area of DT, through records of exhibition experience, tends to be insufficient compared to the above applications. Therefore, more DT studies are required to integrate exhibition viewing experience records. Figure 1 provides a summary of the above cases.

3.2 Examples of Online Art Archive Platform

In recent years, mobile technology has provided different opportunities for multimedia tours to enhance visitors' museum experience [23]. Hence, this study investigated the function of online art archive platforms, reconstructing the behavioral patterns of Lopatovska, the researchers, and three others. Based on the different uses of information on the platform (e.g., content tagging, favorites, etc.), this research examined four types of online art archives: the Rijks Studio, Mu-um, Google Arts & Culture and the VART (Table 1).

This confirmed that online art archive platforms have various functions that can enhance visitors' museum experience. In addition, the present study verified the provision of a differentiated platform through such functions as high-definition enlargement/reduction of works, sharing of appreciation, and editing and sequencing of works. However, while all four platforms use personalization by selecting preferred works, they only referred to related works within their respective museums. Therefore, this study intends to expand the use of personalized records beyond works to recommend related exhibitions.

3.3 Range of Information Accessed by Real Users: Korean Cases

The main purpose of this study was to confirm the range of information that can be accessed by actual visitors. Five art museums were selected based on national and public art museums located in Seoul, Korea. From December 1, 2018 to December 31,

Classification	Case			
AR	AR contents using mobile devices 	AR-based exhibition viewing platform 	AR docent contents using AR glass 	Mobile AR Content Using AR Glass 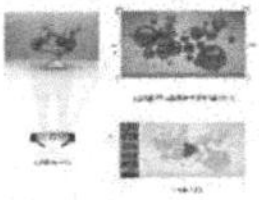
VR, MR, XR	Virtual reality museum using cloud computing platform 'AZURE' 	Contents using 'Microsoft's MR device 'Holo Lens' 	Virtual exhibition viewing tour service 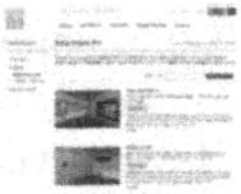	'Hakuhodo-VRAR's mixed reality cultural property experience 
AI	Exhibition of works through artificial intelligence matching 	The work of 'Xiaoice' an artificial intelligence chatbot from 'Microsoft' 	AI curator of art trading platform 	AI-powered applications, bots and plugins 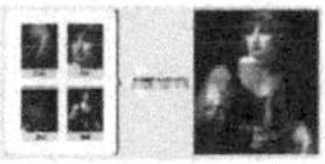
Robot	Telepresence robot 'Double' 	'Whatever's Robot Viewing system Robot 'Double 3' 	'QI', a curating bot using AI and robotics technology 	'I-RO', an autonomous driving guidance robot 
Online Art Archive Platform	'google art & culture' 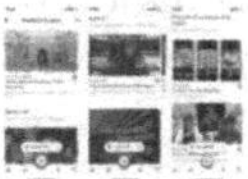	Mobile personal gallery 'VART' 	Rijks Studio, a visitor's co-creative content run by the Rijks Museum 	Artist DB archiving platform 'Mu-um' 
Records of Exhibition Experience	Social Media (Facebook, Instagram)	Memo (Notes)		

Fig. 1. Technology-oriented art museum DT applications.

Table 1. Examples and features of online art archive platform.

Platform	Function
Google arts & Culture	Provides a tour of a virtual museum using Street View technology Has a powerful zoom in/out functionality for works Enables a user to search a favorite work or an author's favorite
VART	Offers online and offline ticket purchase Collects reviews from friends and popular exhibitions Provides a 360-degree AR art museum Provides its own "art museum that listens to the ears" Has a VIP-exclusive online exhibition available through paid service Stores online exhibition works and descriptions Provides a tour of a virtual museum using Street View technology Has a powerful zoom in/out functionality for works Enables a user to search a favorite work or an author's favorite
Rijks studio	Presents works from the Rijks Museum by categorizing them Recommends images of works that suit individuals Edits work directly with the production and printing of personalized creations Stores works in its own collection Provides a "60 s Art Museum" where a curator explains the designated work When a user returns to a page without viewing a work, a pop-up appears asking for feedback
MU-UM	Displays individual works of approved artists Checks records of artists, works, and exhibitions stored in MU-UM Classifies works under Eastern Art History, Western Art History, and Contemporary Art History and provides explanations and representative works for each trend

2020, a total of 53 exhibitions were confirmed. The information that can be checked when selecting information for each exhibition on the museum website is summarized. Actual users were able to see the exhibition title, the exhibition period, exhibition location, viewing hours, admission fees, docent schedule, participating artists, images of the exhibition and information on major works. However, the information provided for each exhibition was different. In some cases, only some of the representative works of the exhibition could be viewed, or there were cases where there were no images of works and posters. Among the selected exhibitions, the information provided was different for eight exhibitions that the researcher had personally visited. If the information provided for each exhibition is different, it may be difficult for visitors to check the information (Table 2).

Table 2. Scope of research on museum information.

Exhibition period	Museum name	Exhibition
2018. 12. 01–2020. 12.31	National Museum of Modern and Contemporary Art, Seoul	18 exhibitions
	National Museum of Modern and Contemporary Art, Deoksugung	5 exhibitions
	Seoul Museum of Art Seosomun Hall	11 exhibitions
	Seoul Museum of Art Namseoul Annex	7 exhibitions
	Seoul Museum of Art, Buk Seoul Annex	12 exhibitions

4 User Research

The demographic information of the participants in the first interview, survey, and in-depth interview conducted by the user survey is summarized in Table 3 below.

Table 3. Summary of demographic information from three user surveys.

User research	Total	Gender		Age		Period
		Male	Female	20s	30s	
Interview	9 people	5	4	7	2	2020/10/24–27 (4 days)
Survey	32 people	12	20	28	4	2021/2/–5 (3 days)
In-depth interview	8 people	4	5	8		2021/2/9–12 (4 days)

4.1 First Round of Interview

The first interviews were conducted to explain the process of the entire viewing experience. A total of nine people participated in the interviews; they were selected from a group of people in their have attended exhibitions in the past year. The interview sessions did not exceed 30 min per person. Subjects with skills to find online information about museums and are proficient in using digital devices were recruited. Asked about the exhibitions they most recently visited, the respondents were reminded of which ones they had attended. Afterward, information about the exhibition before viewing was collected, in which the participants were asked about the process until the end of the viewing as well as the overall experience of using and recalling the information collected after viewing. Through the first round of interviews, this study collected data that can confirm the entire exhibition viewing process. It was confirmed that in the entire process, the spectators commonly performed "information search" and "collect and view."

4.2 Survey

Survey Objective Criteria and Questions. A survey was conducted to determine the process of performing "information search" and "collect and view," two keywords derived from the first interviews. This survey involved regular people in their 20 s and 30 s who are familiar with online platforms and consume high volumes of information. A total of 32 people responded to the survey. Each question has multiple choices.

The question of the questionnaire survey was first, whether or not visitors search for and collect information in the process of viewing. Second, we asked about the types of information collected by visitors and the media used. Third, we asked about how to use and store the collected information.

Survey Results. From the "information search" questionnaire, 30 respondents (96.8%) stated that they search for information before viewing the exhibition. The types of information include the author and the author's life, the description of the work, and related exhibitions. In addition, information was derived from search engines, social media, and homepages, in that order. Meanwhile, from the questionnaire on "collect and view," 29 respondents (90.6%) said that they take pictures to collect information. The types of information they collected include works, appearances of exhibitions, and certified photos. In addition, the collected information was used to recall the viewing experience and share it on social media (Table 4).

Table 4. Insights from survey results.

Category	Classification	Insight
Information Retrieval	Whether to perform	96.7% of respondents search for information
	Kinds	Writer and writer's life
		Description of the work
		Related Exhibitions
	Media used	Search engine
		Social media
		Homepage
Collect and View	Whether to perform	90.6% of respondents shoot for information collection
	Kinds	Art Work
		Exhibition environment
		Certification Photo
	Usage	Recollection of the viewing experience
		Social media sharing

4.3   In-Depth Interview

Target Criteria and Questions.   A total of 8 people were interviewed based on random extraction based on those who answered that they recalled memories by using and sharing the data collected from the previous survey respondents. The questions were composed based on the insights from the first interviews and the survey. This study intended to determine what exhibition information was being searched before viewing and why it was difficult to find and collect such information. It also examined the researchers' thoughts on the work guide service during viewing and the pain points and needs they felt while using it. It then investigated how the collected information was stored and used as well as what additional data users want after viewing the exhibition.

In-depth Interview Results

Before the Exhibition.   The searched information before exhibition viewing can be classified into "background information on the contents of the exhibition" and "basic information on the exhibition." Visitors felt tired in their search, as they used various platforms interchangeably because of the dispersion of exhibition information. Out of the many exhibitions, it was difficult to find one that suited one's taste. In addition, there was not enough space to collect the information, which complicated information sorting.

> Search the exhibition title through a search portal such as Naver. After that, I search again through the artist's name and main work. These things seem a little laborious. (Participant A)

> I tend to take notes with the Send to Me function of personal messengers and capture image-type information. It is inconvenient to see information at a glance due to different media. (Participant B)

> I think you should go to the exhibition knowing the time and location of the exhibition and the overall contents of the exhibition. Because I have to check whether it suits my circumstances and my tastes. (Participant C)

During the Exhibition.   Information was obtained from information services such as audio guides and docents. However, it was impossible for visitors to select only the information they want. Also, while viewing the works, they experienced difficulty collecting information.

> It takes too long to see all the information. I'd rather be able to hear only the information I need. (Participant F)

After the Exhibition.   After the users viewed the exhibition, they did not actively utilize the information on the photographs. This was because it was difficult to reconfirm the information as the pictures were mixed with others. Also, because of the lack of space to store souvenirs, the users did not check them often after they collected souvenirs. Visitors will expand their spectrum of knowledge after viewing the exhibition. Therefore, they need additional information about the work they like.

[If I watched a photo exhibition, I would be interested if you provide information about other photo exhibitions. Also, I would like to inform you of when and where this exhibition is held. (Participant E)

The picture is in the gallery, but it is difficult to find among many pictures. I took it because I wanted to record it, but it is difficult to find the photos I took. So I don't seem to see it. (Participant B)]

Table 5 summarizes the insights derived through the in-depth interview.

Table 5. Key insights derived from in-depth interviews.

Classification	Insight
Before viewing the exhibition	Classified into "background information on the exhibition contents" and "basic information on the exhibition" Difficulty searching because of information distribution Difficulty searching for an exhibition that suits a user Difficulty in collecting and storing information
While viewing the exhibition	Personalized information service required Lack of independent storage space to collect information
After viewing the exhibition	Lack of utilization of collected information Reconfirmation of collected information is not well done Limited space to store souvenirs Expansion of the audience's knowledge spectrum

5   Service Offer

5.1   Service Structure Diagram

A service structure diagram was proposed based on the insights from the in-depth interviews. In this study, the experience of viewing museums from a CX perspective is extended before, during, and after the exhibition. Before viewing, visitors receive exhibition recommendations tailored to their preferences based on their own exhibition viewing data. Also, information is provided through the exhibition information feed (post). If a user likes the recommended exhibition and goes to see it, they can view the exhibition while checking the digitized work data provided on the platform. Personalized preference data can be collected by marking works that suit a user's taste among digitized works. Then, based on the preference data, additional information desired by the user is provided. After viewing, the work marked by the user falls under "taste data," and personal exhibition viewing information is created within the service. In this study, the viewing experience does not stop when the exhibition is over; rather, other exhibitions are recommended through individual exhibition viewing data through which one's experience before viewing the exhibition is provided again. Using this circular structure, the entire process of the art museum viewing experience can be integrated (Fig. 2).

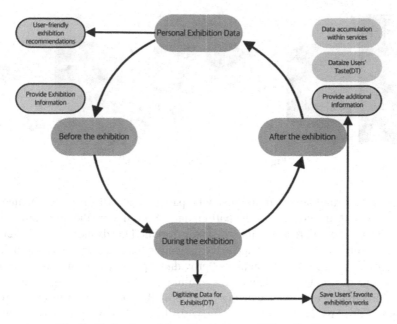

Fig. 2. Technology-oriented art museum DT applications.

5.2 "Floating Museum"

Based on the service structure diagram, this study proposed a personalized exhibition DB collection platform called "Floating Museum," whose main function is to collect personalized DBs in such a way that users' preferred works are displayed. Before viewing an exhibition, users are provided exhibition information through the information feed, including exhibitions that suit their taste. Users can collect their own "flavor data" by displaying their preferences by session and by work. Later, during the exhibition, information on the works is provided. A visitor can collect their own "flavor data" by marking it on the work. After viewing the exhibition, users can find detailed and related information about the work they have displayed. This process is integrated to populate the viewer's "personal taste DB." After that, through the accumulated "personal taste DB," it recommends suitable exhibitions for visitors. It recommends an exhibition that is more suitable for you, makes it easier to search, and provides an environment where you can more easily record information and experiences gained while viewing. The images in each service visualization were taken from "Unsplash," a free image site due to copyright. The service visualized text was also written by the researcher according to the image (Fig. 3).

5.3 Verification of the Proposed Service (FGI Focus Group Interview)

Through focus group interviews, we intend to evaluate whether the service proposed in this study reflects the insights derived from the interview. Focus group interviews were conducted to find out the opinions and improvements of the service through several participants. Interviews were conducted online due to COVID-19, and a total of 6

Fig. 3. UI of "Floating Museum."

participants were randomized from those who participated in the survey. The interview was recorded with the consent of the participants. Accordingly, the interview contents and key insights derived from the interview were notified in advance to six participants. After that, the proposed service image and explanation for each service were provided to answer questions. Each service includes "providing appropriate exhibition recommendations for the person before viewing the exhibition", "function to display and collect favorite works during exhibition viewing", and "providing additional information mainly on the works displayed by the user after viewing the exhibition." A total of 9 questions were asked by asking 3 questions about 3 concepts. First, we asked whether the function for each service could be helpful by meeting the needs of users. Second, we asked if we would like to use the function. Third, we shared free opinions and improvements for each service.

Verification Result of the Proposed Service

Before the Exhibition. Before viewing the exhibition, 5 participants answered that it would be helpful to search for information if they were recommended for the exhibition that was suitable for them, and 5 participants answered that they are willing to use it. As for free opinions and suggestions, opinions such as communication and sharing of opinions with people with similar tastes, selection of viewing area, and comparison of tastes with companions came out. However, there were concerns that a turning point would be necessary as the recommendation-oriented system would be stuck in a certain framework.

It took a long time to search among a vast amount of information, but I think it can shorten that time. (Participant 1)

There is no specific theme for the exhibition, so if only one theme is provided, it would be inconvenient. (Participant 3)

During the Exhibition. During the exhibition, all six people answered that it would be helpful to collect the experience of viewing the exhibition if they were able to collect and display works in their own minds. However, only 3 participants(50%) replied that they were willing to use additional information based on the work I displayed. They were divided into opinions that it is very good to be able to obtain information when they want, and that it is not likely to be necessary because they are viewed in the direction of the exhibition. In addition, there was an opinion that it would be better to provide information on the work I selected after viewing the exhibition. As for free opinions and suggestions, he replied that the works I marked need to go to the top or need to be classified, and that it would be nice if the works that I marked would be categorized as well.

> Since the fields of interest are different, it is good to be able to gather similar things like Netflix and Watcha, and to check the fields that suit my taste. (Participant 2)
>
> I don't think it's necessary because I watch it according to the flow of the exhibition (Participant 1)

After the Exhibition. After viewing the exhibition, four participants answered that it would be helpful if they provided relevant information mainly on the works they displayed. In addition, all six responded that they were willing to use it in terms of collecting the' personalized work viewing experience' and storing the exhibition information. As for free opinions and suggestions, he replied, 'If we can collect personal exhibition viewing experiences and produce them in the form of books or portfolios, it will be memorable for a long time.' They also answered that it would be nice if they could share my experiences with others through social networking features. However, there was an opinion that it would be necessary to set the frequency of information provision because it would be tiring to receive information continuously.

> I want to record, but there is no place to record, so I used Instagram, but it would be nice to be able to record information systematically (Participant 2)
>
> It seems to be helpful. Since it is to provide information in my preferred work, it seems to be my choice to accept the information. (Participant 6)
>
> It depends on what kind of information it is, but I think you should be able to set whether you want to receive additional information. I think I will be tired even if I keep giving information (Participant 3)

6 Discussion and Future Research

6.1 Background of the Paper

This study discussed the experiences before and after exhibition viewing in which DT was not activated. Through literature research and benchmarking, this study observed difficulties in finding appropriate information before exhibition viewing. It then confirmed the lack of DT in documenting the experience after exhibition viewing. Afterward, users' needs and insights were extracted by analyzing exhibition viewing experience through user surveys. Based on the derived insights, the study proposed a service model that provides an effective exhibition viewing experience. Personalized preference data were collected based on chosen works. In addition, based on taste data, the entire viewing process was integrated by recommending exhibitions that suit a user's preferences.

6.2 Verification Result

The findings through the verification of this study are summarized as follows. First, it is expected that the function of recommending an appropriate exhibition before viewing the exhibition can shorten the information search time. However, there was a concern that it was likely to be focused only on one's own taste. Therefore, it is necessary to expand to other categories, such as nearby exhibitions and new exhibitions, in addition to recommending exhibitions that suit your taste. Second, the function of collecting information by displaying favorite works during exhibition viewing is expected to solve the difficulty of collecting information. However, providing additional information while viewing the exhibition differs depending on the viewing method, so additional research is needed according to the viewing method. Third, after viewing the exhibition, the ability to leave personalized records centering on the works displayed by them is expected to be easy to record and store the visitors' experience viewing the exhibition.

6.3 Future Works

There is a limitation that the service proposed in this study is made only as a concept. By supplementing the improvements made through focus group interviews, future research will produce applications that can run on real screens. We will expand research on whether it contributes to the actual art museum visit decision from a service design perspective by constructing the system. In addition, we intend to conduct research on the structure of recommendations based on taste data built by users. After that, I hope that small-scale exhibitions that are difficult to develop individual services will actively participate and become active DT.

References

1. Iacono, S., Wigand, R.T.: Information technology and industry change: view from an industry level of analysis. J. Inf. Technol. **20**, 211–212 (2005). https://doi.org/10.1057/palgrave.jit.200 0052
2. Fichman, R.G., Dos Santos, B.L., Zheng, Z.: (Eric): digital innovation as a fundamental and powerful concept in the information systems curriculum. MIS Q. **38**, 329–A15 (2014)
3. Li, F.: The digital transformation of business models in the creative industries: a holistic framework and emerging trends. Technovation **92–93**, (2020). https://doi.org/10.1016/j.tec hnovation.2017.12.004
4. Tim, Y., Pan, S.L., Ouyang, T.: Museum in the age of digital transformation, p. 9 (2018)
5. Srinivasan, R., Boast, R., Furner, J., Becvar, K.M.: Digital museums and diverse cultural knowledges: moving past the traditional catalog. Inf. Soc. **25**, 265–278 (2009). https://doi. org/10.1080/01972240903028714
6. Karp, C.: Digital heritage in digital museums. Mus. Int. **56**, 45–51 (2004). https://doi.org/10. 1111/j.1350-0775.2004.00457.x
7. Axiell.   https://www.axiell.com/report/digital-transformation-in-the-museum-industry/. Accessed 22 July 2016
8. Hirose, M., Tanikawa, T.: Overview of the digital museum project. In: Proceedings of the 9th ACM SIGGRAPH Conference on Virtual-Reality Continuum and its Applications in Industry, pp. 11–16. Association for Computing Machinery, New York, NY, USA (2010). https://doi. org/10.1145/1900179.1900181

9. Harada, T., Hideyoshi, Y., Gressier-Soudan, E., Jean, C.: Museum Experience Design Based on Multi-Sensory Transformation Approach, https://www.designsociety.org/publication/40618/MUSEUM+EXPERIENCE+DESIGN+BASED+ON+MULTI-SENSORY+TRANSFORMATION+APPROACH. Accessed 24 Feb 2021. https://doi.org/10.21278/idc.2018.0150
10. Hooper-Greenhill, E.: Museums and their Visitors. Routledge, London (2013)
11. Wang, Y., Aroyo, L.M., Stash, N., Rutledge, L.: Interactive user modeling for personalized access to museum collections: the rijksmuseum case study. In: Conati, C., McCoy, K., Paliouras, G. (eds.) UM 2007. LNCS (LNAI), vol. 4511, pp. 385–389. Springer, Heidelberg (2007). https://doi.org/10.1007/978-3-540-73078-1_50
12. Bowen, J., Filippini-Fantoni, S.: Personalization and the web from a museum perspective. In: Museums and the Web (2004)
13. Vial, G.: Understanding digital transformation: a review and a research agenda. J. Strateg. Inf Syst. 28, 118–144 (2019). https://doi.org/10.1016/j.jsis.2019.01.003
14. Research Commentary—The Digital Transformation of Healthcare: Current Status and the Road Ahead| Information Systems Research. https://pubsonline.informs.org/doi/abs/10.1287/isre.1100.0327. Accessed 24 Feb 2021
15. Gurusamy, K., Srinivasaraghavan, N., Adikari, S.: An integrated framework for design thinking and agile methods for digital transformation. In: Marcus, A. (ed.) DUXU 2016. LNCS, vol. 9746, pp. 34–42. Springer, Cham (2016). https://doi.org/10.1007/978-3-319-40409-7_4
16. Matt, C., Hess, T., Benlian, A.: Digital transformation strategies. Bus. Inf. Syst. Eng. 57, 339–343 (2015). https://doi.org/10.1007/s12599-015-0401-5
17. Jonsson, A., Svingby, G.: The use of scoring rubrics: reliability, validity and educational consequences. Educ. Res. Rev. 2, 130–144 (2007). https://doi.org/10.1016/j.edurev.2007.05.002
18. Marty, P.F.: Museum websites and museum visitors: before and after the museum visit. Mus. Manage. Curatorship. 22, 337–360 (2007). https://doi.org/10.1080/09647770701757708
19. Lopatovska, I.: Museum website features, aesthetics, and visitors' impressions: a case study of four museums. Mus. Manage. Curatorship. 30, 191–207 (2015). https://doi.org/10.1080/09647775.2015.1042511
20. Perry, S., Roussou, M., Economou, M., Young, H., Pujol, L.: Moving beyond the virtual museum: engaging visitors emotionally. In: 2017 23rd International Conference on Virtual System Multimedia (VSMM), pp. 1–8 (2017). https://doi.org/10.1109/VSMM.2017.8346276
21. Assessing the user experience (UX) of online museum collections: Perspectives from design and museum professionals| MW2015: Museums and the Web 2015. https://mw2015.museumsandtheweb.com/paper/assessing-the-user-experience-ux-of-online-museum-collections-perspectives-from-design-and-museum-professionals/. Accessed 26 Feb 2021
22. Roes, I., Stash, N., Wang, Y., Aroyo, L.: A personalized walk through the museum: the CHIP interactive tour guide. In: Proceedings of the 27th international conference extended abstracts on Human factors in computing systems - CHI EA 2009, p. 3317. ACM Press, Boston, MA, USA (2009). https://doi.org/10.1145/1520340.1520479
23. Hsi, S.: The electronic guidebook: a study of user experiences using mobile web content in a museum setting. In: IEEE International Workshop on Wireless and Mobile Technologies in Education Proceedings, pp. 48–54 (2002). https://doi.org/10.1109/WMTE.2002.1039220
24. Serravalle, F., Ferraris, A., Vrontis, D., Thrassou, A., Christofi, M.: Augmented reality in the tourism industry: a multi-stakeholder analysis of museums. Tourism Manage. Perspect. 32, (2019). https://doi.org/10.1016/j.tmp.2019.07.002
25. Bimber, O., Encarnação, L.M., Schmalstieg, D.: The virtual showcase as a new platform for augmented reality digital storytelling. In: Proceedings of the workshop on Virtual environments 2003 - EGVE 2003, pp. 87–95. ACM Press, Zurich, Switzerland (2003). https://doi.org/10.1145/769953.769964

26. Rowley, J.: Measuring total customer experience in museums. Int. J. Contemp. Hospitality Manage. **11**, 303–308 (1999). https://doi.org/10.1108/09596119910281801
27. Amitrano, C.C., Gargiulo, R., Bifulco, F.: Creating value through social media: fresh evidence from cultural organizations. J. Creating Value. **4**, 243–254 (2018). https://doi.org/10.1177/2394964318805616
28. Holbrook, M.B., Hirschman, E.C.: The experiential aspects of consumption: consumer fantasies, feelings, and fun. J. Consum. Res. **9**, 132–140 (1982). https://doi.org/10.1086/208906
29. Gentile, C., Spiller, N., Noci, G.: How to sustain the customer experience: an overview of experience components that co-create value with the customer. Euro. Manage. J. **25**, 395–410 (2007). https://doi.org/10.1016/j.emj.2007.08.005
30. Dirsehan, T.: Analyzing museum visitor experiences and post experience dimensions using SEM. Bogazici J. Rev. Soc. Econ. Admin. Stud. **26**, 103–125 (2012). https://doi.org/10.21773/boun.26.1.6
31. Understanding Customer Experience
32. Goulding, C.: The museum environment and the visitor experience. Euro. J. Mark. **34**, 261–278 (2000). https://doi.org/10.1108/03090560010311849
33. Hamma, K.: The role of museums in online teaching, learning, and research. First Monday (2004). https://doi.org/10.5210/fm.v9i5.1146
34. Wang, Y., et al.: Cultivating personalized museum tours online and on-site. Interdisc. Sci. Rev. **34**, 139–153 (2009). https://doi.org/10.1179/174327909X441072
35. Ardissono, L., Kuflik, T., Petrelli, D.: Personalization in cultural heritage: the road travelled and the one ahead. User Model. User-Adap. Inter. **22**, 73–99 (2012). https://doi.org/10.1007/s11257-011-9104-x
36. Wang, Y., Stash, N., Aroyo, L., Gorgels, P., Rutledge, L., Schreiber, G.: Recommendations based on semantically enriched museum collections. J. Web Seman. **6**, 283–290 (2008). https://doi.org/10.1016/j.websem.2008.09.002
37. Adomavicius, G., Tuzhilin, A.: Toward the next generation of recommender systems: a survey of the state-of-the-art and possible extensions. IEEE Trans. Knowl. Data Eng. **17**, 734–749 (2005). https://doi.org/10.1109/TKDE.2005.99
38. Falk, J.H., Dierking, L.D.: The Museum Experience. Howells House (1992)
39. Falk, J.H., Dierking, L.D.: The Museum Experience Revisited. Routledge, London (2016)
40. Zoller, G., DeMarsh, K.: For the record: museum cataloging from a library and information science perspective. Art Documentation J. Art Lib. Soc. North Am. **32**, 54–70 (2013). https://doi.org/10.1086/669989
41. Lowenthal, D.: History and memory. Public Historian **19**, 30–39 (1997). https://doi.org/10.2307/3379138

Analysis of the Influencing Factors of User Experience in Online Art Forms During the COVID-19—Based on the DEMATEL Method

Chenqi Zhang, Ting Han[⊠], and Chunrong Liu

School of Design, Shanghai Jiao Tong University, 800 Dongchuan Road, Minhang District, Shanghai 200240, China
hanting@sjtu.edu.cn

Abstract. This research aimed to investigate the relevant factors that influence users' choice of online art forms during the Covid-19 pandemic. The research used interview, questionnaire survey and literature research combined with factor analysis to summarize 10 major influencing factors on users' choice of online art forms. The depth interviews were deployed with Decision-Making Trial and Evaluation Laboratory (DEMATEL) questionnaires to evaluate the influencing directions and the degrees of the interactions among the 10 influencing factors.

The finding showed that three key factors that affect users' choice of online art form are performance-price ratio, required equipments and technical means, and these three factors can greatly affect other influencing factors. According to the influential relation diagram, three key influencing factors were used as entry points to fully explore the role and advantages of online art. A user satisfaction optimization model of online art service was proposed, aiming at providing a feasible way to enhance the user experience of online art, and to propose suggestions on optimizing online art forms. It is hoped that in the post-pandemic era, this research can help the online art continue to flourish and complement offline art forms to enrich the art field, and improve the art cognition level of the public.

Keywords: Online art forms · Consumer decision · DEMATEL method · User research

1 Introduction

1.1 Background

In early 2020, the novel coronavirus (severe acute respiratory syndrome; SARS-CoV-2) pandemic had spread rapidly throughout the planet. China, Korea, Japan, Italy, the United States, the United Kingdom, and many other countries paid a heavy price in this sudden outbreak. In the process of raising the strength of the country and using various high-tech means to prevent and fight the pandemic, our country has paid a great price, but also achieved remarkable results.

© Springer Nature Switzerland AG 2021
M. Rauterberg (Ed.): HCII 2021, LNCS 12794, pp. 467–482, 2021.
https://doi.org/10.1007/978-3-030-77411-0_30

Due to the need to prevent and control of the Covid-19 pandemic, museums and art galleries closed one after another, and many scheduled exhibitions and lectures were temporarily cancelled, bringing modern art activities to a standstill. To meet the public's demand for exhibitions and visits, many museums, art institutions and performance venues launched 'Cloud Exhibitions' and 'Cloud Performance'. Along with the postponed opening of the national education system and the cancellation of various offline courses, the 'Cloud Classroom' has emerged with the development of online teaching and live webcasting. These 'Cloud Arts' are diverse and rich in content. 'Art is still there, just a different way to watch and participate.'

From the perspective of art history, online art is a new visual derivative of traditional 'offline art', a new visual phenomenon in the context of the Internet, a cross-border and multi-dimensional interaction marked by visual images, and a grammatical revolution of visual art innovation [4]. Online art forms include digital museums, online exhibitions, online galleries, online art healing, online art auctions, online art classes, online concerts, art live streaming and so on, which have many advantages like break of time and space restrictions, strong audience interaction, two-way information transmission, low curation costs and high participants freedom. Online art can be optimized through a variety of advanced technologies, such as virtual reality technology, computer network technology, 3D hologram technology, visual and auditory special effects technology, interactive entertainment technology, etc., to optimize offline art forms into online art. New technology can present a variety of content reasonably and bring a multi-faceted sense of 'immersion'.

As people's pursuit of spiritual life increases, online art audience is gradually expanding and can be divided into the following four categories according to their preference for art and art consumption (Fig. 1).

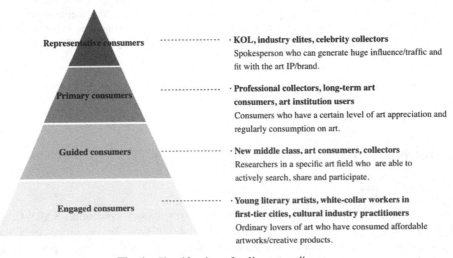

Fig. 1. Classification of online art audience

1.2 Literature Review

The literature research is carried out through databases and search engines, primarily initiated through ScienceDirect, Web of Science, CNKI and Google Scholar but includes findings from papers reference sections as well. The research started from collecting studies from database, based on 4 keywords ("online art", "art forms", "online muscum", "user experience"), for the publication year range 2019 to 2020. The authors kept the relevant literatures according to the abstracts, and extracted from the articles about the introduction of online art and the factors influencing its user experience.

Online Art Forms. The sudden COVID-19 pandemic forced many national/regional governments to forcibly close all non-essential structures and activities. Art events of all kinds that could not be opened to the public had to resort to online means of disseminating culture and knowledge, which led to an acceleration of the digital transformation process. Online art, in simple terms, is the transformation of traditional offline art forms into online through digital means and the process may involve the use of new technologies and forms. Taking the digitization of museums as an example, the first approach is cultural education, in which the museum delivers cultural materials to the user. This is a one-way relationship involving the storyline of the artwork, expert presentations, etc. The second approach involves asynchronous interaction, in which a message or material is delivered to the user but does not require a response from the user. In this case, the relationship flows in two ways between the museum and the visitor, and it requires an (asynchronous) response from the user, despite being instigated by the museum. Finally, the third method is synchronous interaction, in which the muscum and the visitor interact in real time. The relationship here is two-way, but it is simultaneous. It includes real-time interactions between the museum and the students/children, as well as educational activities organized with the museum, etc.

According to statistics from the National Cultural Heritage Administration of China, during the Spring Festival, museums nationwide conducted more than 2,000 online exhibitions, and more than 1,300 cultural and art expo venues opened online exhibitions [1].On March 5, 2020, the Art App launched the "Spring 2020-Collect + Art Week" online event, in which a total of 33 galleries, 27 art galleries and 24 auction houses participated, collaborating with many partners and brands to discuss the art industry's "Collaboration and Power" model [2]. At the same time, there are also online participatory art practices for COVID-19 in the form of drawings, posters, newspaper clippings and music releases on platforms such as Kuaishou, tiktok and WeChat, showing sincerity and support for the frontline staff of COVID-19 [3], and in so doing they produce alternative media that is more informative, conscientious, and consoling than the state media [4].

Foreign studies have shown that social media platforms have become the preferred means for museums to spread their culture during the COVID-19 lockdown in Italy. Museum-related online activities have also increased significantly due to the availability of digital tools. The data showed that online activities on all social media platforms has doubled since Italy went into embargo in March 2020. On average, museums make 25 prior posts per month on Facebook, but that increased to 40 by March. On Twitter, the first 32 posts per month increased to 60, while on Instagram they more than doubled, from 15 to 33 per month per museum [5]. Not only have museums increased their online activity, but they have also changed the content sent through these channels. From mere tools of communication, social media have evolved into tools for spreading knowledge. For example, some museums have used Facebook to share information about an artwork and to reveal certain or other unknown aspects about that artwork. Other museums have arranged for expert interviews or guided tours with the museum director. Others have opted for a more 'playful' approach, running virtual treasure hunts among the museum's collections or organizing quiz events. The Ministry for Cultural Heritage has also stimulated creativity in social initiatives, joining in with virtual culture-related flashmobs and inviting museums to take part, and these museums have, in turn, galvanised cultural participation.

The COVID-19 pandemic has also led to a decline in face-to-face art therapy and has contributed to a widespread shift to remote delivery by some art therapists. More generally, digital technology is increasingly being used to deliver health care services remotely. Studies of online art therapy in both the Arab region and the UK have shown that the COVID-19 pandemic has assisted in the development of online art therapy services, with many therapists able to respond immediately to the new demand for remote service provision to ensure continuity of treatment for their clients. More than three-quarters of respondents felt more comfortable using technology than before, suggesting that new ways of working, while challenging, can allow for greater familiarity with digital technology, and more than 90% of respondents said they would continue to practice distance therapy to some degree, providing greater coverage of art therapy in the region [6, 7].

Another new model we found was an increased opportunity for children to participate in cultural and arts-related experiences through an open-door policy of virtual museums, art galleries, and live performances for children. Parenting blogs and websites recommend free online museum tours around the world, including the Louvre in Paris, France; the Uffizi Gallery in Florence, Italy; the British Museum in London, England; and the U.S. National Gallery of Art in Washington, D.C. Online museum tours are available to everyone connected via the Internet no matter where they are, and they offer children in the United States the opportunity to interact with art. In Korea, the National Museum of Korea, as well as the Seoul Museum of Art, the SAVINA Museum and the Daz Museum of Art have also opened online exhibitions with curators in response to school closures. Another source of relief may be cinemas, with the Korean government providing over 200 million won to the Busan Film Center for an online art education program for children and teenagers [8].

Influencing Factors of Online Art Forms. Because of the differences in the extent of the pandemic and the period of severity of the pandemic at home and abroad, and the variability in ethnicity and geography, etc., and considering the selection of subsequent subjects, this study was analyzed and summarized with a focus on the literature and the current situation in China.

Regarding the influencing factors of online art, in the analysis of the characteristics of online art exhibitions under the influence of the COVID-19 pandemic, four elements of exhibition content diversification, richness, uniqueness, and popularization of publicity are mentioned [1]. An article on online art sales mentions that the online content itself and the fluidity of the experience are more important in planning the campaign, and that interactivity, freedom of time and space, transparency of information, and presentation also have an impact [2]. In a study on the application of digital technology in museum exhibitions, the authors argue that factors such as exhibit display effect, information transferability, interactivity, interestingness, personalization, experience realism, mobilization of multiple senses such as visual, auditory and tactile, and real-time share ability have a greater impact [9]. In the study of the Internet on the operation of art museums, the authors believe that low energy consumption, intelligent and share ability are the advantages of online art, and that in the process, attention needs to be paid to factors such as the user experience, the degree of content optimization and knowledge dissemination [10]. However, most studies have been conducted from a certain perspective or on a particular online art form, and do not involve the user's decision making process, which does not provide a complete and clear overview of the whole problem and its internal structure. Therefore, this study hopes to conduct a comprehensive analysis of the issue of users' choice of different online art forms during the pandemic with the help of the Decision-Making Trial and Evaluation Laboratory method.

1.3 Research Purpose

In order to fully understand the relevant factors influencing users' choice of online art forms, explore the advantages of online art during the pandemic, and then discuss the content and future enhancement directions that need to be paid attention to when holding online art. It is hoped that in the post-pandemic era, online art will continue to flourish and complement offline art forms to enrich the art field. Based on the online art process and combining literature research and user research, this study summarized the relevant factors that influence users' choice of online art forms and used the Decision-Making Trial and Evaluation Laboratory method to analyze the relationship between factors that influence users' choice of different online art forms and their degree of importance.

2 Analysis of Factors Influencing Users' Choice of Different Online Art Forms

2.1 Summary of Factors Influencing Users' Choice of Different Online Art Forms

Based on the literature search, the following 28 preliminary influencing factors (PIF) for users to choose different online art forms were summarized from four aspects: online art factors, user factors, service factors, and promotion factors as shown in Table 1.

Table 1. Preliminary summary of the preliminary influencing factors for users to choose different online art forms

Number	Dimension	Influencing factors	Description of factors
1	Online art	Online art types	Types of online art, such as exhibitions, auctions, concerts, etc.
2	Online art	Online art contents	Content of online art, such as artifacts, music, courses, etc.
3	Online art	Online art background	The cultural, historical, environmental and other contexts in which online art content is generated
4	Online art	Interactivity	The interactivity and engagement of the audience in online art
5	Online art	Uniqueness	The uniqueness of online art content
6	Online art	Immersion	The audience's level of engagement in sensory and cognitive experiences
7	Online art	Interestingness	The fun of the online art content, the fun of the audience experience process
8	Online art	Preciousness	The preciousness of online art content
9	Online art	Environmentalism	Environmental protection of online art content and display process
10	Online art	Quality-price ratio	The matching degree of price and the quality of online art
11	Online art	Multi-sensory experience	Mobilize the audience's vision, hearing, touch, smell and other senses
12	User factors	Gender	Differences of audience's gender
13	User factors	Age	Differences of audience's age
14	User factors	Monthly income	Differences of audience's monthly income
15	User factors	Career	Differences of audience's career

(continued)

Table 1. (*continued*)

Number	Dimension	Influencing factors	Description of factors
16	User factors	Education level	Differences of audience's education level
17	User factors	Artistic preference	Differences in audience's preferences for art type, content, presentation, etc.
18	User factors	Artistic awareness	Differences of audience's art cognitive level, aesthetic level, etc.
19	User factors	Experience of online art	Experience of audience's participation in the online art
20	Service factors	Technical means	Technology for demonstration and form of presentation, such as VR, AR, panorama, live streaming, etc.
21	Service factors	Presentation effect	The final presentation of the online art form
22	Service factors	Organizers	Types of organizations holding online art, popularity, etc.
23	Service factors	Duration	Duration of online art
24	Service factors	Required equipments	Equipments required for audience's participation in online art, such as cell phones, computers, VR glasses, etc.
25	Service factors	Network Status/Experience smoothness	Requirements for network conditions in online art forms
26	Promotion factors	Multimedia promotion	Diversity of promotional channels, such as physical and video advertising, etc.
27	Promotion factors	Promotion efforts	Diversity of publicity platforms, length of publicity, availability of celebrity promotion, etc.
28	Promotion factors	Audience groups	Differences in the audience for publicity

2.2 Screening of Factors Influencing Users' Choice of Different Online Art Forms

Since an excessive number of preliminary influencing factors will result in homogeneity of factors and bring about the problem of lack of accuracy of the subsequent survey data, this study used factor analysis to extract important factors from the above 28 factors that influence users' choice of different online art forms as the main influencing factors (MIF) of the research construct.

The degree of influence of each of the above 28 factors on online art forms was collected through one-on-one interviews and used to study the importance of the influencing factors and the extraction of principal components. Seventeen users, aged 20–50 years old, distributed in different professions and different occupations, were selected to ensure the objectivity of the interviews. The interview process began with a detailed description of the 28 factors, followed by asking the interviewees to select the 10–15 factors they felt had the greatest impact on the online art forms. Any doubts during the process were answered immediately. Based on the interview results, the final summary of the 10 main influencing factors (MIF) for users to choose different online art forms is shown in Table 2. Based on the external and internal factors of online art forms, the 10 main influencing factors are the three dimensions of online art, user factors and service factors.

Table 2. Main influencing factors for users to choose different online art forms

Number	Dimension	Influencing factors	Description of factors
1	Online art	Online art contents	Content of online art, such as artifacts, music, courses, etc.
2	Online art	Uniqueness	The uniqueness of online art content
3	Online art	Immersion	The audience's level of engagement in sensory and cognitive experiences
4	Online art	Quality-price ratio	The matching degree of price and the quality of online art
5	Online art	Multi-sensory experience	Mobilize the audience's vision, hearing, touch, smell and other senses
6	User factors	Artistic preference	Differences in audience's preferences for art type, content, presentation, etc.
7	User factors	Artistic awareness	Differences of audience's art cognitive level, aesthetic level, etc.
8	Service factors	Technical means	Technology for demonstration and form of presentation, such as VR, AR, panorama, live streaming, etc.
9	Service factors	Presentation effect	The final presentation of the online art form
10	Service factors	Required equipments	Equipments required for audience's participation in online art, such as cell phones, computers, VR glasses, etc.

2.3 DEMATEL Procedure

Decision-Making Trial and Evaluation Laboratory (DEMATEL) method is often used to analyze the complex relationship between management problems. It is a methodology put forward by Battelle Geneva Research Center in 1971 to solve the complex and difficult problems between science, technology and human beings in the real world and clarify the essence of the problems [11]. It is a method of system analysis using graph theory and matrix tools [12]. The DEMATEL procedure in this study is carried out in the following steps: (1)identifying the main influencing factors that impact the users' choice of online art forms; (2) collecting opinions of target users to estimate the influence of factors on each other using the DEMATEL questionnaire with one of five level values; (3) generating the direct relation matrix Z; (4) Calculating the λ value, the normalized direct relation matrix and the direct/indirect relation matrix T; (5) From the direct/indirect relation matrix, obtaining the corresponding Prominence value (D + R), and Relation value (D − R) of each influencing factor; (6) obtaining the influence relation map (IRM) with (D + R) value and (D − R) value of each influencing factor to help observe the interrelationship structure.

Questionnaire and Data Statistics. The 10 main influencing factors of users' choice of different online art forms were formed into a 10*10 matrix of rows and columns in DEMATEL questionnaire. The DEMATEL questionnaire is used to estimate the direction of interaction and the degree of relative priority of each factor listed in first column to each factor listed in first row. The relationships between the factors in the rows and columns are defined as five levels, i.e., value '0' means "no impact", value '1' means "low impact", value '2' means "distinct impact", value '3' means "big impact", and value '4' means "extreme impact".

The questionnaire survey was screened by the control of questionnaire filling time and the restrictions of age and whether wired on art experience, and 31 pieces of effective data were calculated based on the following equation to obtain the direct relation matrix Z.

$$Z = \frac{1}{n} \sum_{m=1}^{n} \left[z_{ij}^{m} \right], \quad ij = 1, 2, 3, \ldots, k. \tag{1}$$

The questionnaire data were organized and normalized to obtain the normalized direct relation matrix as shown in Table 3.

Table 3. Normalized direct relation matrix

	1	2	3	4	5	6	7	8	9	10
1	0.000	0.095	0.092	0.111	0.086	0.076	0.080	0.080	0.102	0.099
2	0.090	0.000	0.095	0.111	0.107	0.074	0.090	0.097	0.092	0.109
3	0.078	0.092	0.000	0.099	0.090	0.088	0.113	0.088	0.074	0.088
4	0.086	0.105	0.111	0.000	0.128	0.109	0.105	0.113	0.120	0.122
5	0.092	0.103	0.097	0.105	0.000	0.090	0.105	0.086	0.074	0.086
6	0.065	0.086	0.078	0.090	0.084	0.000	0.069	0.090	0.071	0.107
7	0.080	0.084	0.080	0.090	0.078	0.076	0.000	0.103	0.069	0.103
8	0.109	0.118	0.099	0.113	0.101	0.109	0.107	0.000	0.101	0.095
9	0.090	0.103	0.086	0.090	0.086	0.080	0.101	0.097	0.000	0.088
10	0.099	0.109	0.092	0.116	0.109	0.113	0.111	0.109	0.097	0.000

Users only estimated the direct influence of factors on each other. Hence, the direct/indirect relation matrix T is obtained from matrix X by applying the transition theory and summing up all direct and indirect effects. The direct/indirect relation matrix T (Table 4) was derived, by using Eqs. (2)–(4). Matrix X is the normalized direct relation matrix, and I is the identity matrix.

$$X = \left[x_{ij} \right]_{k \times k} = sZ \tag{2}$$

$$s = min \left(\frac{1}{\displaystyle \max_{1 \leq j \leq k} \sum_{i=1}^{k} z_{ij}}, \frac{1}{\displaystyle \max_{1 \leq j \leq k} \sum_{j=1}^{k} z_{ij}} \right) \tag{3}$$

$$T = \lim_{m \to \infty} \left(X + X^2 + \ldots + X^m \right) = X(1 - X)^{-1} \tag{4}$$

The upper quartile Q3 of all the elements in the total relations matrix T (keep 3 decimal places), i.e., 0.652, is taken as the threshold to measure the strength of interactions between factors. If all values in the row and the column that correspond to a factor in the matrix T are below the threshold value, this factor and the corresponding row and column will be removed. So the '1 online art content' factor was deleted.

Then, the upper third of Q3 (0.707) is taken as the boundary value of strong influence relation and general influence relation. Values higher than 0.707 are considered as strong influences, and values between 0.701 and 0.652 are considered as general influences. As shown in Table 6, the general influences are marked with bold type, and the strong influences are marked with underlines.

Value D and R are achieved by summing up the rows and columns of total relation matrix T, using Eqs. (5)–(6).

$$D_i = \sum_{j=1}^{n} t_{ij}, (i = 1, 2, 3, \ldots, n) \tag{5}$$

Table 4. The direct/indirect relation matrix T

	1	2	3	4	5	6	7	8	9	10
1	0.474	0.618	0.581	0.649	0.599	0.560	0.600	0.590	0.573	0.623
2	0.582	0.559	0.609	**0.677**	0.644	0.583	0.636	0.630	0.590	**0.659**
3	0.539	0.607	0.489	0.629	0.594	0.562	0.619	0.589	0.541	0.606
4	0.645	0.729	**0.692**	**0.654**	0.734	**0.682**	0.722	0.717	**0.679**	0.744
5	0.566	0.632	0.592	**0.652**	0.527	0.579	0.628	0.602	0.556	0.621
6	0.495	0.565	0.526	0.584	0.553	0.447	0.545	0.554	0.505	0.584
7	0.519	0.576	0.539	0.597	0.559	0.529	0.492	0.576	0.515	0.593
8	0.638	0.711	**0.655**	0.726	0.683	**0.655**	**0.695**	0.587	0.638	**0.694**
9	0.556	0.623	0.574	0.630	0.597	0.561	0.615	0.602	0.478	0.613
10	0.633	0.707	**0.653**	0.731	**0.693**	**0.662**	**0.701**	**0.689**	0.637	0.611

represents all values in the row and the column that correspond to a factor in the matrix T are below the threshold value

Bold type represents general influences

Underline represents strong influences

$$R_i = \sum\nolimits_{j=1}^{n} t_{ij}, \ (i = 1, 2, 3, \ldots, n) \tag{6}$$

Value D is called the degree of influential impact, and value C is called the degree of influenced impact. Di is the sum of the ith row of matrix T and represents all the direct and indirect effects which are dispatched from Factor i to other factors. And Rj is the sum of the jth column of matrix T and represents all the direct and indirect effects that Factor j receives from the other factors [13].

The prominence value (importance) played by the factor in a system is represented by (D + R) value, where (D − R) value stands for the net effect (i.e. the degree of importance) of the factor contributed to the system. The factors are categorized into two groups of cause (driver) and effect (receiver) factors.

When the D + R value is higher, it indicates that the factor is more important in the overall evaluation factors. Table 5 shows that the four factors with higher than average centrality are, in descending order: quality-price ratio, required equipments, technical means, and uniqueness, and the above factors are the core factors that influence users' choice of different online art forms.

If the (D − R) value of a factor is positive, this factor is grouped under the category of driver factors which has an influence on other factors; if the value of (D − R) is negative, this factor is grouped under the category of receiver factors which receives influence from other factors. technical means, quality-price ratio, required equipments, and presentation effect are driver factors, while others are receiver factors.

The value (D + R), (D − R) of factors were listed in Table 5.

Table 5. Prominence (D + R) and Net effect (D − R) values.

	Prominence (D + R)		Net effect (D − R)
4 Quality-price ratio	**13.529**	8 Technical means	0.547
10 Required equipments	**13.065**	4 Quality-price ratio	0.470
8 Technical means	**12.818**	10 Required equipments	0.370
2 Uniqueness	**12.498**	9 Presentation effect	0.136
5 Multi-sensory experience	12.139	3 Immersion	−0.136
7 Artistic awareness	11.750	2 Uniqueness	−0.158
3 Immersion	11.686	5 Multi-sensory experience	−0.230
9 Presentation effect	11.563	6 Artistic preference	−0.462
6 Artistic preference	11.179	7 Artistic awareness	−0.759
Average value of D + R	12.174		

Bold type represents exceeding the average value

The Influential Relation Diagram. The influential relation diagram can be plotted in the $(D_i + R_i, i − R_i)$ layout, using $(D_i + R_i)$ as the horizontal axis and $(D_i − R_i)$ as the vertical axis. Ten main influencing factors are marked in the coordinate axis, and the influential relation diagram is made. According to the position of each factor in the diagram, the ones which have a great effect on other factors or have a complicated relationship with other criteria can be found.

The factors under different dimensions are distinguished by different colors in the figure, orange indicates the online art own attribute dimension, blue indicates the user dimension, and green indicates the service dimension.

The relationship with the influence strength lower than 0.652 will not be marked. The relationship with the influence strength between 0.652 and 0.707 will be regarded as general influence and marked with dotted line; the relationship with the influence strength greater than or equal to 0.707 will be regarded as strong influence and marked with solid line. The direction of the arrow indicates the direction in which one factor affects the other factor. The specific location of each factor is shown in Fig. 2.

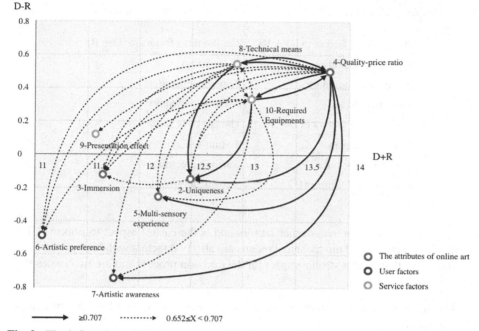

Fig. 2. The influential relation diagram of 10 influencing factors for users to choose different online art forms.

2.4   Discussion

Key Factors for Users to Choose Different Online Art Forms. Table 6 lists the top three and bottom three of prominence $(D + R)$ and net effect $(D - R)$. The top three of $D + R$ are quality-price ratio, required equipments, and technical means, which are the three factors that have the greatest impact on users' choice of different online art forms and other factors, with the quality-price ratio factor having the largest $D + R$ value and being the most important factor influencing online art decisions and requiring significant consideration. The three factors of immersion, presentation effect, and artistic preference have the smallest $D + R$ and less overall impact.

The top three D-R rankings are technical means, quality-price ratio, and required equipments, which are more likely to influence other factors and are driver factors. The bottom three D-R rankings are Multi-sensory experience, artistic preference, and artistic awareness, which are more likely to be influenced by other factors and are receiver factors. The factor of uniqueness is not listed in the table, but it has a higher prominence and lower net effect, and the influence of other factors on uniqueness can be considered to influence users' decision.

Analysis and Discussion. The influential relation diagram shows that the service factors have a stronger influence on the attributes of online art itself, while the technical means and the required equipments will have a stronger influence on the three factors of immersion, uniqueness and multi-sensory experience. The user factors, on the other hand, are vulnerable to other factors. Among them, the factor of quality-price ratio has

Table 6. Key influencing factors for users to choose different online art forms

The top three factors in (D + R)	The last three factors in (D + R)
4 quality-price ratio	3 immersion
10 required equipments	9 presentation effect
8 technical means	6 artistic preference
The top three factors in D − R>0	The last three factors in D − R<0
8 technical means	5 Multi-sensory experience
4 quality-price ratio	6 artistic preference
10 required equipments	7 artistic awareness

a strong interaction with many other factors and is the easiest aspect to improve. The required equipments and the technical means are also two factors with high prominence and net effect that have a strong impact on the decision process and are two issues that could be improved.

The following analysis and recommendations were made based on the influential relation diagram:

Enriching Online Art Presentation Forms and Enhancing Online Art Experience. From the influence relationship diagram, it is clear that the two factors of technical means and required equipments are at the core and have a strong influence on other factors, especially the decision-making process, which will directly affect the final presentation of online art and thus the user's sense of experience.

It is suggested that emerging digital technologies such as virtual reality, augmented reality, and panoramic scanning can be introduced when presenting art online content. These technologies can digitize and store offline art, break the restrictions of venues, spaces, and personnel, realize high freedom art dissemination, and effectively display art contents within a certain spatial range through the network and mobile terminal devices, which can maximize the expression effect. In this kind of presentation, users can get closer to the artwork, observe and understand the details in all aspects, and have a better sense of immersion and interactivity.

In the process of art display, the application of digital technology establishes a connection between the audience and the artwork, transforming the traditional "one-way" information transfer into a 'two-way' information transfer. The audience can interact in the process of enjoying online art, and establish the best virtual environment in multiple senses such as sight, sound and touch, and finally provide users with a real display environment, making the audience immersive, to a certain extent, to get the best real experience (Fig. 3).

Improving the Quality-Price Ratio of Online Art and Expanding the Scale of Engaged Consumers. In the influence relationship diagram, the factor of quality-price ratio has a strong influence relationship with many other factors, so it is considered to start from quality-price ratio to influence users' choice of different online art forms.

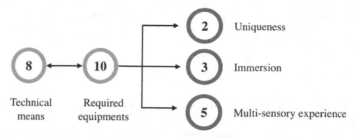

Fig. 3. Interrelationship diagram of factors 2, 3, 5, 8 and 10

First of all, quality-price ratio and technical means, the required equipments both have a strong influence relationship with each other, so it is possible to use lower cost technical means and presentation equipments to lower the price for users to participate in online art and attract more engaged consumers and guided consumers to experience online art.

Secondly, the three factors of quality-price ratio, technical means, and the required equipments all influence the user's artistic preference and artistic awareness. So appropriately lowering prices of online art, such as launching free art activities, increasing online art student discounts, and releasing online art discount tickets for seconds, can attract more art enthusiasts to experience multiple art forms, expand the scale of engaged consumers, and raise the overall art cognition level of society (Fig. 4).

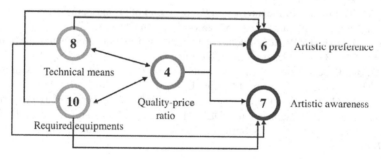

Fig. 4. Interrelationship diagram of factors 4, 6, 7, 8 and 10

3   Conclusion

This study identified the main factors influencing users' choice of online art forms during the COVID-19 pandemic, used DEMATEL method to analyze the interrelationships of 10 main influencing factors. It was clarified that the main three key factors influencing users' choice of online art forms were quality-price ratio, required equipments, and technical means. Based on the influence relationship diagram, these three key influencing factors were used as entry points to propose suggestions on optimizing online art forms. This was of great significance for developing the online art market in China in the post-pandemic era, optimizing the sense of user experience, and raising the level of art awareness in society.

References

1. Liu, Y.: Analysis of the characteristics of online art exhibitions under the influence of the pandemic. Popular Literature Arts 127–128 (2020). (in Chinese)
2. Hong, X.: Online art sales, seeking breakthrough in the pandemic. China Auction 64–67 (2020). (in Chinese)
3. Feng, X.: Curating and exhibiting for the pandemic: participatory virtual art practices during the COVID-19 outbreak in China. Soc. Media Soc. **6**, 2056305120948232 (2020)
4. Moreno Almeida, C.: Memes as snapshots of participation: the role of digital amateur activists in authoritarian (2020)
5. Agostino, D., Arnaboldi, M., Lampis, A.: Italian state museums during the COVID-19 crisis: from onsite closure to online openness. Mus. Manag. Curatorship **35**, 362–372 (2020)
6. Zubala, A., Hackett, S.: Online art therapy practice and client safety: a UK-wide survey in times of COVID-19. Int. J. Art Therapy **25**, 161–171 (2020)
7. Carlier, N.G., Powell, S., El-Halawani, M., Dixon, M., Weber, A.: COVID-19 transforms art therapy services in the Arabian Gulf. Int. J. Art Therapy **25**, 202–210 (2020)
8. Choi, M., Tessler, H., Kao, G.: Arts and crafts as an educational strategy and coping mechanism for Republic of Korea and United States parents during the COVID-19 pandemic. Int. Rev. Educ. (2020)
9. Wang, H.: Application of digital technology in museum exhibitions. Ident. Apprec. Cult. Relics 144–145 (2019). (in Chinese)
10. Wang, M.: The impact of the internet on the operation of art museums: from the 'online art museums'. Popular Literature Arts 252–253 (2020). (in Chinese)
11. Gabus, A., Fontela, E.: World problems, an invitation to further thought within the framework of DEMATEL. Battelle Geneva Research Center, Geneva, Switzerland, pp. 1–8 (1972)
12. Li, Y.Y., Bin. Research on influencing factors of corporate environmental behavior based on DEMATEL. J. Guangxi Vocational Normal Univ. 31, 26–33 (2019). (in Chinese)
13. Xie, Y., Xiao, H., Shen, T., Han, T.: Investigating the influencing factors of user experience in car-sharing services: an application of DEMATEL method. In: Krömker, H. (ed.) HCII 2020. LNCS, vol. 12213, pp. 359–375. Springer, Cham (2020). https://doi.org/10.1007/978-3-030-50537-0_26

Correction to: Before You Visit-: New Opportunities for the Digital Transformation of Museums

Hyungmin Park, Jeongyun Heo, and Jongkeon Kim

Correction to:
Chapter "Before You Visit-: New Opportunities for the Digital Transformation of Museums" in: M. Rauterberg (Ed.):
Culture and Computing, **LNCS 12794,**
https://doi.org/10.1007/978-3-030-77411-0_29

In the originally published version of chapter 29, the corresponding author was not correctly marked. This has now been corrected.

The updated version of this chapter can be found at
https://doi.org/10.1007/978-3-030-77411-0_29

© Springer Nature Switzerland AG 2021
M. Rauterberg (Ed.): HCII 2021, LNCS 12794, p. C1, 2021.
https://doi.org/10.1007/978-3-030-77411-0_31

Author Index

Printed in the United States
by Baker & Taylor Publisher Services